Computing

Second Edition

Nick Waites BSc, MSc, Cert Ed

Geoffrey Knott BA, AIB, Cert Ed

D1333515

Business Education Publishers Limited

1996

©Nick Waites and Geoffrey Knott 1996

ISBN 0-907679-87-0

First published in 1992
    Reprinted 1993
    Reprinted 1994
Second Edition 1996

Published in Great Britain by

Business Education Publishers Limited
Leighton House
10 Grange Crescent Stockton Road
Sunderland
SR2 7BN

Tel. 0191 567 4963

Fax. 0191 514 3277

British Cataloguing-in-Publications Data
A catalogue record for this book is available from the British Library

Printed in Great Britain by The Bath Press

To Carolyn and Anne, with love

Acknowledgements

We wish to thank Carolyn Knott for her meticulous proof reading of the book, which took many hours of concentration and her patience in preparing and checking the extensive index. We also wish to record thanks to the following Examination Boards for their kind permission to reproduce selected questions set from recent, past papers.

The Associated Examining Board
Joint Matriculation Board
University of Cambridge Local Examination Syndicate
University of London Examinations and Assessment Council
Welsh Joint Education Committee

Acknowledgement is made to the relevant Examination Board beside each question reproduced.

All errors and omissions remain the responsibility of the authors.

NW
GK
Durham, July 1996

The Authors

Nick Waites is a Senior Lecturer in Computing at New College Durham. He has taught Computing and Information Technology for many years and is currently responsible for staff development in Computing and IT. He is co-author of *Information Technology GNVQ Advanced, Computer Studies for BTEC, Information Processing for BTEC, Business GNVQ Advanced, Core Skills for GNVQ* and is the author of *GCSE Information Systems*. He lives in the North East of England in an old chapel which he has converted to a Martial Arts Centre.

Geoffrey Knott is a Lecturer in Computing and Information Technology at New College Durham. He has wide experience of developing and teaching Computing and IT courses. He is co-author of *Information Technology GNVQ Advanced, Computer Studies for BTEC, Information Processing for BTEC, Business GNVQ Advanced, Core Skills for GNVQ* and is the author of *Small Business Computer Systems* and *Information Technology Skills - a student guide*.

Preface

This text covers the Advanced Level Computing Syllabuses of the major examining boards, but also contains much supplementary material, which makes it suitable for students following Higher National and Degree Courses in Computing, Software Engineering and Information Technology, or studying for British Computer Society examinations.

The book is concerned with the science of computing, that is the theory which underpins the internal structure, operation and control of computers, but it also deals extensively with the methods, processes and results of their application in commerce, industry, science and society in general.

The breadth of topics covered in the book, has led us to divide it into several sections, titled as follow.

Fundamental Concepts

Hardware

Software

Data Processing

Databases

Program Design and Implementation

Applications and Social Issues

The logical grouping of related topics facilitates access to particular areas of interest, as well as providing a framework for a teaching or self-study programme. However, the sequence of the chapters is not meant to indicate the order in which topics should necessarily be introduced. Students without previous knowledge of the subject may benefit from reading the following two pages (v) and (vi), A Brief Introduction.

Many of the chapters are followed by exercises to test the reader's retention of facts or understanding of ideas developed within the text. The sections on Databases and Program Design and Implementation, in particular, are followed by extensive developmental exercises.

Examination practice is also provided through a range of actual examination questions, selected from a number of major examining boards. A tutor's manual containing suggested solutions to these questions is available for centres which adopt the book.

A disk produced by Microfile, the educational software house, containing software to supplement a number of selected topics from the text, can be purchased from Business Education Publishers Limited. The disk includes an integrated suite of programs for an assembler specifically designed for educational use, a number of programs to illustrate data structures and the source listings of a number of sorting programs described in the book.

A Brief Introduction

The computer is the central component of a number of technological systems. For example, in combination with data communications technology, computers form what is commonly referred to as the Internet (Chapter 37), which connects computer systems from all over the world, and allows their users to communicate with one another and exchange information. Combined with electro-mechanical systems, computers are used to control, for example, industrial robots, aircraft, rockets, cars and domestic appliances. Integrated with administrative systems and procedures, computers are at the centre of information processing systems, such as payroll, stock control and invoicing. Without computers the information processing requirements of large and complex organizations would be almost impossible to deal with effectively. What we normally mean when we talk about a computer is a digital computer system, a collection of complex devices, (or hardware), which, under the control of computer programs (or software), process data. Such is their remarkable usefulness, speed and versatility that computer systems now perform invaluable services in all areas of modern society.

Whatever their size or form, computers are essentially devices for performing high speed operations on data to produce some useful result. The data is usually provided by an input device such as a keyboard or some type of sensor, and the result is presented by an output device such as a printer or a digital display. Systems which involve the use of computers are called information systems, since the result, or output, from a computer system is information of some kind. A data processing computer system uses raw data, in the form of numbers or text, to produce data that we can understand more easily and use; in other words, such a system produces information.

Computer hardware

The electronic and mechanical devices comprise the *hardware* of a computer system. In general terms, the hardware of a computer system consists of a *central processing unit* (CPU) connected to a number of external devices collectively called *peripherals*. The CPU is the heart of the computer system and it contains an amount of fast memory in the form of ROM (Read Only Memory) and RAM (Random Access Memory) for storing data and programs, a *control unit* which co-ordinates the flow of data within the computer system, and an *arithmetic logic unit* (ALU) which performs calculations of various types.

Peripheral devices are often grouped according to their functions as follows: (i) *input* device such as a keyboard or a mouse; (ii) *output* device such as a monitor or a printer; (iii) data *storage* device such as a floppy disk drive. An input device, such as a keyboard, converts keystrokes representing letters or numbers into electrical signals which the CPU can 'understand'. Conversely, an output device such as a printer or a monitor converts electrical signals produced by the CPU into a form that we can readily understand. As a storage device, a floppy disk drive allows large amounts of data to be stored in a magnetic form (a bit like the way a domestic tape recorder stores music) thus; data is not lost when the computer is switched off, and the data can be read back into the computer at some later date. The CPU controls the operation of these peripheral devices according to instructions temporarily stored in its memory. Another of its main functions is to perform calculations on data also stored in its memory.

The total operation of the computer is controlled by a sequence of numeric codes called a computer *program*. The program, stored inside the computer system, and consisting of combinations of a set of very simple operations, or steps (sometimes hundreds of thousands of them), is executed at enormous speed (typically several million steps each second) so that the computer appears to be performing very complex, sophisticated operations. In fact, as we shall see, computers perform only very simple tasks, but do so without mistake (most of the time!) at great speed. Computer programs are created using *programming languages*, such as BASIC and Pascal. They allow computer programmers to express their requirements in a form closely related to the type of task being programmed. For example, COBOL is frequently used for data processing tasks, FORTRAN is used for mathematical and scientific applications, and Prolog is often used for writing knowledge-based systems.

Computer software

Computer programs are often known as software, but the term software is usually connected with sets of programs covering fairly broad application areas. Examples of terms that occur frequently in computer-related texts are: *system* software; mathematical and scientific software; computer-aided design (CAD) software; *applications* software. An information system will normally use a number of different types of software: the *operating system*, a component of system software, controls the overall operation of all the components of the computer system; applications software perform or aid commonly required tasks, such as word processing, accountancy and the calculation and production of customer bills; database managers, also a type of system software, allow databases to be created, modified and searched.

Computer processing methods

Another aspect of an information system is the manner in which the computer system is organized or used. Here are some common examples:

- batch processing - tasks are grouped and processed on the basis of some common requirement, usually at a predetermined time. For example, customer electricity bills and employee wages would usually be processed as separate batches.

- interactive - a number of users are connected to the computer via terminals consisting of a keyboard and a display screen. The computer shares its processing time between the separate users by giving each one in turn a time 'slice'.

- real-time - again this is where a number of users might require simultaneous access to the computer, but each request for the use of the computer is acted upon with as little delay as possible. A typical example of this type of information system is for airline reservations in which a number of travel agents would be connected to a central computer providing access to the airline's flight database.

- distributed systems - these are systems which rely on computer networks. With increasing frequency, companies with a number of computers will connect them together to form computer networks in order to share hardware and software resources. In other words, both the hardware and software of the information system may be distributed over some large area rather than being located in a single room. Local area networks (LANs) connect computers that are close to each other (on the same site, for example) and wide area networks (WANs) connect together computers, that are distant from each other, by means of telephone lines or satellite links.

Contents

Data Processing

Databases

Program Design and Implementation

Applications and Social Issues

Chapter 34
Business Applications

Chapter 35
Industrial and Control Applications

Chapter 36
Modelling and Simulation

Chapter 37
The Internet

Chapter 38
Organizational and Social Issues

Exam Questions

Chapter 1
Number Systems

Although the denary number system has proved to be the simplest for people to use, it is more convenient for computers to use the binary number system. The electronic components used in computers can be in either one of two physical states, permitting the representation of 0 and 1, the two symbols of the binary number system. This chapter explains the basis of this and other number systems relevant to the subject of computing.

The base of a number system

First consider the denary system. There are ten symbols, 0, 1, 2, 3, 4, 5, 6, 7, 8 and 9; the *base* or *radix* of a number system is identified by the number of different symbols it uses. Thus, the denary number system has a radix or base of 10. To identify a number, for example 123, as a denary number, it can be written as 123_{10}.

Place value

Each symbol can be given a weight or place (or positional) value, according to its position within any given number. In the denary system, each place value is a power of ten. Remember that the base of the denary number system is ten. Thus, for denary integers each place value is ten raised to a power. Starting from the least significant digit on the right, there are units (10^0), tens (10^1), hundreds (10^2), thousands (10^3) and so on. The idea of place value can be illustrated

power 10^3	10^2	10^1	10^0
thousands	hundreds	tens	units
1	2	6	3

Table 1.1. *Place values example 1263_{10}*

with examples of integer (whole) numbers. Table 1.1 shows that 1263_{10} can be expressed as one thousand, plus two hundreds, plus six tens and three units, or $1\times1000 + 2\times100 + 6\times10 + 3\times1 = 1263_{10}$.

Similarly, Table 1.2 shows that 487_{10} is the same as zero thousands, plus four hundreds, plus eight tens and seven units, or $0\times1000 + 4\times100 + 8\times10 + 7\times1 = 487_{10}$. Note that any number (*n*) raised to the power of zero (n^0) is equal to 1. This can be seen from Tables 1.1 and 1.2 and from the place value tables shown later, for each of the binary, octal and hexadecimal number systems. The *fractional* component of a number is also determined by position, except that the power is negative, as shown in Table 1.3.

power 10^3	10^2	10^1	10^0
thousands	hundreds	tens	units
0	4	8	7

Table 1.2. *Place values example 487_{10}*

		10^{-1}	10^{-2}	10^{-3}
decimal point		tenths	hundredths	thousandths
.		6	2	5

Table 1.3. *Fractional place values*

Table 1.3 shows that 0.625_{10}, can be seen as: $6 \times \dfrac{1}{10} + 2 \times \dfrac{1}{100} + 5 \times \dfrac{1}{1000} = \dfrac{5}{8}$

Binary system

The binary system uses only two symbols, 0 and 1. Each digit in a binary number is known as a binary digit or *bit*. An example binary number is 11001_2, which is equivalent to 25_{10}. The binary system has a base of 2, so each place value is a power of two. The next two tables each show a range of integer place values and an example binary number. Table 1.4 demonstrates that the binary number 11101_2 is equivalent to denary $1 \times 16 + 1 \times 8 + 1 \times 4 + 0 \times 2 + 1 \times 1$ or 29_{10}. Table 1.5 shows that denary $0 \times 128 + 1 \times 64 + 1 \times 32 + 0 \times 16 + 0 \times 8 + 1 \times 4 + 1 \times 2 + 1 \times 1 = 103_{10}$.

2^4	2^3	2^2	2^1	2^0
16	8	4	2	1
1	1	1	0	1

Table 1.4. *11101_2 or 29_{10}*

2^7	2^6	2^5	2^4	2^3	2^2	2^1	2^0
128	64	32	16	8	4	2	1
0	1	1	0	0	1	1	1

Table 1.5. *01100111_2 or 29_{10}*

Binary *fractions* can also be represented and an example is shown in Table 1.6.

	2^{-1}	2^{-2}	2^{-3}	2^{-4}
binary point	half	quarter	eighth	sixteenth
.	0	1	1	1

Table 1.6. *Fraction 0.0111_2*

We can see from this that 0.0111_2 is equivalent to $0 \times \dfrac{1}{2} + 1 \times \dfrac{1}{4} + 1 \times \dfrac{1}{8} + 1 \times \dfrac{1}{16} = \dfrac{7}{16}$

Table 1.7 shows the binary equivalents of 0 to 9 in the denary system.

base$_{10}$	base$_2$	base$_{10}$	base$_2$	base$_{10}$	base$_2$	base$_{10}$	base$_2$	base$_{10}$	base$_2$
0	0000	1	0001	2	0010	3	0011	4	0100
5	0101	6	0110	7	0111	8	1000	9	1001

Table 1.7. *Denary symbols and binary equivalents*

Using the place values for the binary system shown in Tables 1.4 and 1.5, it can be seen how each of the denary numbers in Table 1.7 equates with its binary representation.

Rules of binary arithmetic

Addition rules are given, together with example sums, in Table 1.8. The rules for binary addition are needed when studying computer arithmetic in Chapter 3.

addition rules	carry	example sum		example sum	
$0 + 0 = 0$		0 1 1 0 1 0		1 0 1 1 0 0	
$0 + 1 = 1$		1 1 0 1 0 0	+	0 0 0 0 1 0	+
$1 + 0 = 1$		1 0 0 1 1 1 0	=	1 0 1 1 1 0	=
$1 + 1 = 0$	1				

Table 1.8. *Binary addition rules and examples*

Octal and hexadecimal numbers

These number systems are often used as a shorthand method for representing binary numbers. As can be seen from the binary numbers in the earlier tables, they are very confusing to the eye and it is sometimes difficult, even with small groupings, to distinguish one pattern from another. Where it is necessary for the computer's binary codes to be written or read by programmers, for example, it is invariably more convenient to use alternative coding methods. Octal and hexadecimal (*hex*) notations are used in preference to denary because they are more readily converted to or from binary. It must be emphasized that computers can only handle binary forms of coding. Therefore octal and hexadecimal codes must be converted to binary before they can be handled by the computer.

Octal coding

The octal number system has a base of 8, using 0, 1, 2, 3, 4, 5, 6 and 7 as its symbols. Each place value is a power of eight; some of the place values are shown in Table 1.9.

8^4	8^3	8^2	8^1	8^0	8^{-1}	8^{-2}	8^{-3}
4096	512	64	8	1	$\frac{1}{8}$	$\frac{1}{64}$	$\frac{1}{512}$

Table 1.9. *Some octal place values*

Octal coding uses three bits at a time, allowing 8 or 2^3 (see Table 1.10) different patterns of bits.

Binary	0 0 0	0 0 1	0 1 0	0 1 1	1 0 0	1 0 1	1 1 0	1 1 1
Octal	0	1	2	3	4	5	6	7

Table 1.10. *Octal symbols and binary equivalents*

To represent any given value, a binary number can be split into groups of 3 bits, starting from the right-hand side, as the two 16-bit examples in Table 1.11 show. Because the 16 bits will not divide exactly into groups of 3, the left-most or *most significant bit* (MSB) can only take the values 0_8 or 1_8.

0111001101100110_2	0	1 1 1	0 0 1	1 0 1	1 0 0	1 1 0
Octal code	0	7	1	5	4	6
1101010100101011_2	1	1 0 1	0 1 0	1 0 0	1 0 1	0 1 1
Octal code	1	5	2	4	5	3

Table 1.11. *Octal coding examples*

Hexadecimal coding

The hexadecimal number system has a base of 16, and uses the following symbols: 0, 1, 2, 3, 4, 5, 6, 7, 8, 9, A, B, C, D, E and F. The six letters, A to F, are used instead of the denary numbers 10, 11, 12, 13, 14 and 15, respectively. This brings the number of

16^3	16^2	16^1	16^0	16^{-1}	16^{-2}	16^{-3}
4096	256	16	1	$^1/_{16}$	$^1/_{256}$	$^1/_{4096}$

Table 1.12. *Hexadecimal place values*

hexadecimal symbols to sixteen. Some place values, each being a power of 16, are shown in Table 1.12.

A group of 4 bits provides 16 unique binary patterns, the number required to represent all 16 symbols of the hexadecimal number system. The symbols and their binary equivalents are given in Table 1.13.

Binary	0 0 0 0	0 0 0 1	0 0 1 0	0 0 1 1	0 1 0 0	0 1 0 1	0 1 1 0	0 1 1 1
Hexadecimal	0	1	2	3	4	5	6	7
Binary	1 0 0 0	1 0 0 1	1 0 1 0	1 0 1 1	1 1 0 0	1 1 0 1	1 1 1 0	1 1 1 1
Hexadecimal	8	9	A	B	C	D	E	F

Table 1.13. *Hexadecimal symbols and binary equivalents*

Therefore, a binary number can be coded by grouping the bits into groups of four and using the appropriate hexadecimal symbol for each group, as the examples in Table 1.14 show.

11000011111101110_2	1 1 0 0	0 0 1 1	1 1 1 1	0 1 1 0
Hexadecimal code	C	3	F	6
0101011010111101_2	0 1 0 1	0 1 1 0	1 0 1 1	1 1 0 1
Hexadecimal code	5	6	B	D

Table 1.14. *Hexadecimal coding examples*

In practice, hexadecimal is used in preference to octal code because computers organize their internal memory in 8-bit groupings (*bytes*) or multiples of bytes. These groupings conveniently divide into 4-bit *nibbles* which can be coded in the shorthand of hexadecimal. A knowledge of hexadecimal is essential for the interpretation of computer manufacturers' manuals, which use the coding system extensively to specify memory and backing storage features. Programmers using low level languages (see Chapter 30), such as assembly code, also need to be familiar with this number system.

Number base conversion methods

Conversion of binary numbers into their hexadecimal and octal exquivalents is described in the preceding section. The following section provides methods and examples of conversion from:

- denary to binary;

- denary to octal;

- denary to hexadecimal.

Denary to binary

Method 1 - using conversion tables

Table 1.15 contains a range of place values for integer conversion; Table 1.16 can be used for fractions.

2^{14}	2^{13}	2^{12}	2^{11}	2^{10}	2^9	2^8	2^7	2^6	2^5	2^4	2^3	2^2	2^1	2^0
16384	8192	4096	2048	1024	512	256	128	64	32	16	8	4	2	1

Table 1.15. *Denary to binary conversion table - integers*

2^{-1}	2^{-2}	2^{-3}	2^{-4}	2^{-5}	2^{-6}	2^{-7}	2^{-8}	2^{-9}
$1/2$	$1/4$	$1/8$	$1/16$	$1/32$	$1/64$	$1/128$	$1/256$	$1/512$

Table 1.16. *Denary to binary conversion table - fractions*

To convert a denary number to binary requires the identification of those place values which, when added together, will equal the denary number. By reference to the appropriate table, a binary 1 is placed in each position, where the value is required and a binary 0 is recorded in each of those remaining. Starting with the largest value in the table, which is less than, or equal to the denary number, successive values to the right are selected and accumulated until the sum is obtained; a binary 1 is placed in each such position. Table 1.17 provides an integer example.

2^{14}	2^{13}	2^{12}	2^{11}	2^{10}	2^9	2^8	2^7	2^6	2^5	2^4	2^3	2^2	2^1	2^0
16384	8192	4096	2048	1024	512	256	128	64	32	16	8	4	2	1
		1	0	1	0	0	1	1	0	0	1	1	1	0

Table 1.17. *Integer 5326_{10} converted to 1010011001110_2*

Obviously, any value which will result in the required sum being exceeded is skipped, a binary 0 being placed in the relevant position. The place values containing a binary 1 can be summed and the result checked as follows.

$1\times4096 + 0\times2048 + 1\times1024 + 0\times512 + 0\times256 + 1\times128 + 1\times64 + 0\times32 + 0\times16 + 1\times8 + 1\times4 + 1\times2 + 0\times1 = 5326_{10}$

Similarly, Table 1.18, shows a denary fraction converted to binary.

		2^{-1}	2^{-2}	2^{-3}	2^{-4}	2^{-5}
binary point		$1/2$	$1/4$	$1/8$	$1/16$	$1/32$
	.	0	1	1	1	0

Table 1.18. *Fraction $^7/_{16}$ converted to 01110_2*

Again, the binary 1 place values can be totalled and the result confirmed, as follows.

$$0 \times \frac{1}{2} + 1 \times \frac{1}{4} + 1 \times \frac{1}{8} + 1 \times \frac{1}{16} + 1 \times \frac{1}{32} = \frac{7}{16}$$

Method 2 - successive division by the base

Integers

This technique requires that the denary number is successively *divided by 2*, the base of the binary system, until the result of a division is zero. If a division leaves a *remainder* of denary 1, a binary 1 is placed in the next available position in the binary number being formed; if there is a denary 0 remainder, a binary 0 is entered. Table 1.19 illustrates the process. Note that the binary number should be read, beginning with the most significant bit (MSB), from the bottom of the table, to the least significant bit (LSB).

The binary number is written as follows: $1273_{10} = 100111110001_2$, the last binary 1, at the bottom of Table 1.19, being the most significant bit (MSB).

denary	divided by	equals	remainder	binary	
1273	2	636	1	1	LSB
636	2	318	0	0	
318	2	159	0	0	
159	2	79	1	1	
79	2	39	1	1	
39	2	19	1	1	
19	2	9	1	1	
9	2	4	1	1	
4	2	2	0	0	
2	2	1	0	0	
1	2	0	1	1	MSB

Table 1.19. *Integer 1273_{10} to 100111110001_2*

Real number conversion

Tables 1.20 and 1.21 show how a *real* (having a fractional component) denary number is converted; the integer and fractional parts must be dealt with separately and differently. The *integer* part of 34.375_{10} is converted as shown in Table 1.20, by successive division (as in the previous example in Table 1.19). The *fractional* part is converted by a process of successive *multiplication*, as shown in Table 1.21; this table shows that, if a multiplication results in a 1 appearing before the decimal point, the 1 is placed in the next available place to the right of the binary point; otherwise, 0 is placed there. Note that the binary fraction is read from the top of the table, identified by MSB. The process is complete when a product of denary 1 is obtained (much of the time, an exact figure will not be achieved and the process is continued until the de-

denary	divided by	equals	remainder	binary	
34	2	17	0	0	LSB
17	2	8	1	1	
8	2	4	0	0	
4	2	2	0	0	
2	2	1	0	0	
1	2	0	1	1	MSB

Table 1.20. *Conversion of 34_{10} (integer part of 34.375_{10})*

denary	multiplied by	equals	binary	
0.375	2	0.75	0	MSB
0.75	2	1.5	1	
0.5	2	1.0	1	LSB

Table 1.21. *Conversion of 0.375 (fractional part of 34.375_{10})*

sired accuracy is reached). Looking at Tables 1.20 and 1.21 together, the result can be seen to be as follows: $34.375_{10} = 100010.011_2$.

Conversion with limited precision

Sometimes, a decimal fraction cannot be converted to its precise binary equivalent (as achieved in Tables 1.20 and 1.21). This topic is dealt with, in more detail, in the section on *floating point arithmetic*, in Chapter 3.

Table 1.22 shows the conversion of denary 0.425 to its binary equivalent, but with some loss of precision. The level of precision is determined by the number of place values allocated for the storage of the binary fraction; more places would allow a greater degree of precision. Table 1.22 shows that, in this example, absolute accuracy cannot be achieved (the Product column will continue with the pattern shown and denary 1 will never be reached) and that, at this stage, 0.425_{10} is approximately equal to 0.0110110011_2.

denary	multiplied by	equals	binary	
0.425	2	0.85	0	MSB
0.85	2	1.7	1	
0.7	2	1.4	1	
0.4	2	0.8	0	
0.8	2	1.6	1	
0.6	2	1.2	1	
0.2	2	0.4	0	
0.4	2	0.8	0	
0.8	2	1.6	1	
0.6	2	1.2	1	LSB

Table 1.22. *Denary to binary conversion with loss of accuracy*

Referring to the place values in Table 1.16, it can be seen that the binary fraction is, in fact, equal to the following expression.

$$0 \times \frac{1}{2} + 1 \times \frac{1}{4} + 1 \times \frac{1}{8} + 0 \times \frac{1}{16} + 1 \times \frac{1}{32} + 1 \times \frac{1}{64} + 0 \times \frac{1}{128} + 0 \times \frac{1}{256} + 1 \times \frac{1}{512} = \frac{217}{512} = 0.423828125$$

The difference is $0.425_{10} - 0.423828125_{10}$ or $0.001172187 5_{10}$. A greater degree of accuracy (although not absolute) could be obtained by continuing the process shown in Table 1.22 and using more significant digits.

Denary to octal

Method 2 (successive division by the base), described in the denary to binary section, is also used here, in each case using the relevant base of 8. Table 1.23 shows an example of denary to octal conversion. LSD and MSD stand for least significant *digit* and most significant *digit*, respectively.

denary	divided by	equals	remainder	octal	
1273	8	159	1	1	LSD
159	8	19	7	7	
19	8	2	3	3	
2	8	0	2	2	MSD

8^3	8^2	8^1	8^0
512	64	8	1
2	3	7	1

Table 1.23. *Integer 1273_{10} converted to octal 2371_8*　　**Table 1.24.** *Integer 2371_8 and place values*

That $1273_{10} = 2371_8$, is proved, with the following expression (and by reference to the place values shown in Table 1.24).

$$2371_8 = 2 \times 512 + 3 \times 64 + 7 \times 8 + 1 \times 1 = 1273_{10}.$$

Denary to hexadecimal

Method 2 (successive division by the base), described in the denary to binary and denary to octal sections, is also used here, in this case using the relevant base of 16. Table 1.25 shows an example of denary to hexadecimal conversion. Remember that the symbol 'F' is equivalent to denary 15.

denary	divided by	equals	remainder	hex	
1273	16	79	9	9	LSD
79	16	4	15	F	
4	16	0	4	4	MSD

Table 1.25. *Integer 1273_{10} to $4F9_{16}$*

That $4F9_{16} = 1273_{10}$ can be proved by the following expression (the relevant place values appear in Table 1.26).

$$4F9_{16} = 4 \times 256 + 15(F) \times 16 + 9 \times 1 = 1273_{10}.$$

16^2	16^1	16^0
256	16	1
4	F	9

Table 1.26. *Integer $4F9_{16}$ and place values*

Exercises

1. Calculate the *denary* equivalents of the following binary numbers:

    a. 11001110   d. 00000100   g. 00100000   j. 11111111
    b. 10101011   e. 00001000   h. 01000000   k. 11110000
    c. 01001100   f. 00010000   i. 10000000   l. 00001111

2. Using the conversion tables provided in the text, write down the *octal* and *hexadecimal* equivalents of the binary values in 1.

3. Using *successive division by the base*, convert 2165_{10} to binary.

4. Using the same method used in 4., convert the real number values 26.325_{10} and 0.4685_{10} to binary. Comment on the results.

5. Use hexadecimal notation to represent the denary numbers 325_{10} and 2967_{10}.

6. Why is hexadecimal notation used in preference to other number bases, to represent binary codes?

Chapter 2
Data Representation

Data, in the context of this chapter, is a general term which covers any data or information which is capable of being handled by the computer's internal circuitry, or of being stored on backing storage media such as magnetic tape or disk. To be processed by computer, data must be in a form which the computer can handle; it must be *machine-sensible*.

Forms of coding

To be machine-sensible, data has to be in *binary* format. In Chapter 1, it is explained that the binary number system uses only two digits, 0 and 1. Both main memory and external storage media, such as magnetic disk and tape, use electrical/magnetic patterns representing the binary digits 0 and 1 to record and handle data and instructions.

Why binary? - bi-stable devices

Computer storage uses two-state or bi-stable devices to indicate the presence of a binary 0 or 1. The circuits inside a computer represent these two states by being either conducting or non-conducting, that is, current is either flowing or is not flowing through the circuit. A simple example of a bi-stable device is an electric light bulb. At any one time it must be in one of two states, on or off. Magnetic storage media use magnetic fields and the two possible polarities (north and south) are used as bi-stable devices to represent 0 and 1.

To understand the benefits of using binary representation, consider the electronic requirements which would be necessary if the denary system were used. To record the ten denary symbols 0 to 9, a computer's circuitry would have to use and accommodate ten clearly defined physical electronic states. Extremely reliable components would be needed to avoid the machine confusing one physical state with another. With bi-stable devices, slight changes in performance do not prevent differentiation between the two physical states which represent 0 and 1.

Character and numeric codes

Much of the data processed by computer and stored on backing storage are represented by *character* codes. The codes used inside the computer are referred to as *internal* codes, whereas those used by various peripherals are termed *external* codes. Data transferred between peripheral devices and the processor may use a variety of binary character codes, but when processing data the processor will tend to use a particular internal code, which will vary with machines of different manufacture. Sometimes, an external character code may continue to be used for storage of data in main memory; alphabetic data remains in character code form during computer processing. On the other hand, numeric data, presented by a peripheral in character code form, is converted to one of a number of numeric codes for processing purposes. Code conversion may be executed within a peripheral, within the *interface* (see Chapter 14) device between a peripheral and the processor, or within the processor itself.

Characters may be grouped according to the following categories:

- alphabetic (upper and lower case);

- numeric (0 to 9);

- special characters (apostrophe, comma, etc.);

- control characters and codes.

Control characters are used in data transmission, perhaps to indicate the start or end of a *block* of data; *control codes* can be used to affect the display of data on a VDU screen and include those which cause, for example, carriage return, delete, highlight or blinking. Control characters and control codes do not form part of the data which are to be usefully processed, but are needed for control. The range of characters which can be represented by a computer system is known as its *character set*.

The ASCII (American Standard Code for Information Interchange) code uses seven binary digits (*bits*) to represent a full range of characters. Data passing between a peripheral and the computer is usually in character code, typically ASCII or EBCDIC (Extended Binary Coded Decimal Interchange Code). This latter 8-bit character code has a 256 character set and is generally used with IBM and IBM-compatible equipment. Extracts from both the ASCII and EBCDIC character sets are given in Tables 2.1 and 2.2, respectively.

character	ASCII code	character	ASCII code	character	ASCII code	character	ASCII code
0	0110000	9	0111001	I	1001001	R	1010010
1	0110001	A	1000001	J	1001010	S	1010011
2	0110010	B	1000010	K	1001011	T	1010100
3	0110011	C	1000011	L	1001100	U	1010101
4	0110100	D	1000100	M	1001101	V	1010110
5	0110101	E	1000101	N	1001110	W	1010111
6	0110110	F	1000110	O	1001111	X	1011000
7	0110111	G	1000111	P	1010000	Y	1011001
8	0111000	H	1001000	Q	1010001	Z	1011010

Table 2.1. *Extract from ASCII character set*

character	EBCDIC code	character	EBCDIC code	character	EBCDIC code	character	EBCDIC code
0	11110000	9	11111001	I	11001001	R	11011001
1	11110001	A	11000001	J	11010001	S	11100010
2	11110010	B	11000010	K	11010010	T	11100011
3	11110011	C	11000011	L	11010011	U	11100100
4	11110100	D	11000100	M	11010100	V	11100101
5	11110101	E	11000101	N	11010101	W	11100110
6	11110110	F	11000110	O	11010110	X	11100111
7	11110111	G	11000111	P	11010111	Y	11101000
8	11111000	H	11001000	Q	11011000	Z	11101001

Table 2.2. *Extract from EBCDIC character set*

Parity checking of codes

The ASCII code shown in Table 2.1 is a 7-bit code. An additional bit, known as the *parity bit* (in the left-most or most significant bit position), is used to detect *single bit* errors which may occur during data transfer. Such errors may result from a peripheral fault or from corruption of data on storage media.

The parity scheme used for detecting single bit errors is simple (the detection of multiple bit errors is more complex and is dealt with in the chapter on Data Communications). There are two types of parity, odd and even, though it is of little significance which is used. If odd parity is used, the parity bit is set to binary 1 or 0, such that there is an odd number of binary 1s in the group. Conversely, even parity requires that there is an even number of binary 1s in the group. Examples of these two forms of parity are provided in Table 2.3.

data with no parity	parity bit	data with odd parity	parity bit	data with even parity
1 0 0 1 0 1 0	**0**	1 0 0 1 0 1 0	**1**	1 0 0 1 0 1 0
0 1 0 1 1 0 1	**1**	0 1 0 1 1 0 1	**0**	0 1 0 1 1 0 1

Table 2.3. *Examples of data with odd and even parity*

The parity bit for each group is in bold. If even parity is being used and main memory receives the grouping 10010100 then the presence of an odd number of binary 1s indicates an error in transmission. Provided that the number of bits corrupted is odd, all transmission errors will be detected. However, an even number of bits in error will not affect the parity condition and thus will not be revealed. Additional controls can be implemented to detect multiple bit errors; these controls make use of parity checks on blocks of characters; known *as block check characters* (BCC), they are used extensively in data transmission control and are described in Chapter 11 on Data Communications.

Data storage in main memory

Character codes, such as the ASCII code (Table 2.1), are primarily of use during data transfer between a peripheral and the main memory. They are also generally used to represent non-numeric data inside the computer. Numeric data is usually converted to one of a number of *numeric codes*, including binary coded decimal (BCD) and floating point formats (Chapter 3)

Internal parity checks

Most mini and mainframe computers use parity bits to detect and sometimes correct, data transfer errors within the computer, so the actual length of codes is extended to allow for this. Parity checking, built into the circuitry of the memory chips is a feature of many microcomputer systems. Memory chips can develop faults, so it is important that a user is made aware of parity errors (which may indicate the beginnings of major memory faults), before significant data loss occurs.

Binary coded decimal (BCD)

As the name suggests, BCD uses a binary code to represent each of the decimal symbols. It is a 4-bit code, using the natural binary weightings of 8, 4, 2 and 1 and is only used for the representation of numeric values. Each of the ten symbols used in the decimal system is coded with its 4-bit binary equivalent, as shown in Table 2.4.

denary	0	1	2	3	4	5	6	7	8	9
BCD	0000	0001	0010	0011	0100	0101	0110	0111	1000	1001

Table 2.4. *BCD equivalents of denary symbols*

In this way, any decimal number can be represented by coding each digit separately. Some examples are given in Table 2.5.

denary	6	2	4
BCD	0110	0010	0100

Table 2.5. *BCD representation of 624_{10}*

BCD arithmetic

Floating point arithmetic can introduce small inaccuracies which can be a problem in financial data processing applications. For example, an amount of 120.50 stored in floating point form may return a value of 120.499999; although the application of *rounding algorithms* (see Chapter 3) can adjust the figure to the required number of significant figures, the rounding is being carried out on the binary representation, when it is the decimal form which should be rounded.

For BCD numbers, each decimal character is separately coded and their addition cannot be accomplished with the normal ADD instruction (Chapter 4); more complex electronics are needed to carry out arithmetic on data in BCD form than are necessary for pure binary numbers. BCD numbers also take more memory space than pure binary numbers. For example, with a 16-bit word the maximum BCD number is 9999_{10}, while using binary it is 65535_{10}. *BCD arithmetic* is described in Chapter 3. Numbers with a fractional element (*real* numbers) are represented with an implied decimal point which can be located between any of the 4-bit groupings.

Boolean values

Apart from characters and numeric values, binary code can also represent the *Boolean* values of *true* or *false* (Chapter 5), the former by 1 and the latter by 0. Boolean variables can be used to indicate, for example, the condition of a *flag register* (Chapter 7) used to signal the occurrence of an overflow condition after an arithmetic operation, or an *interrupt* from a peripheral indicating its need for servicing by the processor.

Bit-mapped graphics

Chapter 8 refers to bit-mapping for the pixel-level control of displayed output; thus a monochrome VDU screen with a resolution of 720 pixels by 350 rows needs 252,000 bits of memory, each bit capable of being set to 1 for white or 0 for black. Colour screens need to use more bits for each pixel, to allow the setting of a variety of colours; one *byte* (eight bits) per pixel permits 256 (2^8) separate colours to be used. By definition, bit-mapped device control is inflexible and very device-dependent, but its use is essential for graphical work, word processing and text output which uses a variety of sophisticated fonts. Since large amounts of memory are needed, particularly for high resolution colour display, graphics adapter cards provide additional VRAM (*video RAM*) for screen memory.

Gray or cyclic code

Gray code is used in mechanical systems, for example, shaft encoders, which generate a binary number according to the angle of the disk, but is of no use for arithmetic operations. Table 2.6 illustrates a 3-bit Gray code and shows how each grouping is related to its natural binary coding. A normal 3-bit binary number would, according to the place values of each bit and beginning with the most significant bit, have a 421 weighting.

To produce the Gray codes each of the natural binary weightings of 421 is multiplied by 2 and then 1 is subtracted. This can be written as an expression of the form $2n-1$, n being the normal binary weighting. Thus, the Gray code weightings become 731. The denary values in the leftmost column of Table 2.6 are obtained from each Gray code as follows. Working from the most significant to the least significant bit and ignoring zeroes, the new weighted values are alternately added and subtracted.

denary	Gray code weighting ($2n-1$)	converts to	normal binary weighting (n)
	7 3 1		4 2 1
0	0 0 0		0 0 0
1	0 0 1		0 0 1
2	0 1 1	3 – 1	0 1 0
3	0 1 0	3	0 1 1
4	1 1 0	7 – 3	1 0 0
5	1 1 1	7 – 3 +1	1 0 1
6	1 0 1	7–1	0 1 1 0
7	1 0 0	7	0 1 1 1

Table 2.6. *3-bit Gray code conversion*

An examination of the codes will reveal that if any individual code is incremented or decremented, only one bit changes, thus removing any prospect of ambiguity when, for example, an encoded disk (see later) crosses the boundary between two segments. Obviously, an increased number of bits will allow a larger number of unique codes with the consequent ability to determine the position of an increased number of segments on a shaft encoder's disk. Gray Code can also be used in disk drives for identifying sectors on magnetic disk.

Applications of Gray code

Coded plate transducers

This device uses a plate or disk, such as that shown in Figure 2.1, which contains a number of binary coded concentric tracks. The most widely used code is called *Gray code*, which is shown in Table 2.7 in 3-bit form. Gray code is used in preference to standard binary code because it has the property that each successive value in the sequence of codes changes by only a single bit. In pure binary, also shown in Table 2.7, this is not the case: you can see that, for example, going from 011 to 100, all three bits change, whereas in Gray code the transition is from 010 to 110 in which only the most significant digit changes from 0 to 1. The significance of this can be seen if we consider what might happen if the disk shown in Figure 2.1 were to be 3-bit binary coded rather than 3-bit Gray coded.

value	Gray code	binary	angle
0	000	000	0(360)
1	001	001	45
2	011	010	90
3	010	011	135
4	110	100	180
5	111	101	225
6	101	110	270
7	100	111	315

Table 2.7. *3-bit Gray code and angles represented*

The angular position of the disk is determined by the light detectors. They are able to detect the presence of light in the three positions corresponding to the disk's three concentric tracks. However, the disk can stop at any angular position, including the boundaries between two adjacent codes. For example, because of the limited sensitivity of the light detectors, if the disk is at the boundary of 001 and 010, it is possible that two adjacent transparent and opaque areas will be read incorrectly. This means that the position of the disk could be mistakenly read as 000 or 011 just as easily as one of the two correct values.

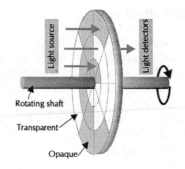

Figure 2.1. *Coded plate transducer*

However, using Gray code the equivalent codes to 001 and 010 are 011 and 010 respectively, in which only the least significant bit changes value. Thus the position of the disk cannot be misinterpreted. This is illustrated in Figure 2.2. In (a) the Gray coded disk is at the boundary of 001 and 011. The only possible ambiguity is with sensor *b*, but the three sensors will still only detect either 001 or 011 as

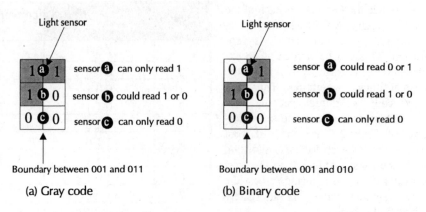

Figure 2.2. *Comparing binary code and Gray code for measuring angle of rotation*

required. However, with the binary coded disk shown in (b), sensors *a* and *b* could read a zero or a one, possibly providing an erroneous value for the angle of rotation of the disk.

In order to be able to relate the Gray code output signals from the light sensors to an angular position, the code must be converted into binary. This may be accomplished in two ways:

1. Using a logic circuit (Figure 2.3) - the outputs from the sensors are fed into a logic circuit which produces the correct binary outputs which can then be related to an angular rotation (listed in Table 2.7).

Figure 2.3. *Logic circuit to convert Gray code to binary*

2. Using a look-up table - after appropriate conditioning, the outputs from the light sensors are used to access a small amount of ROM or RAM containing a table such as that shown in Table 2.8 for a 3-bit code. The memory locations in the first column contain the appropriate binary code allowing any Gray code to be quickly looked up.

address	contents
000	000
001	001
011	010
010	011
110	100
111	101
101	110
100	111

Table 2.8. *Look-up table Gray code to binary*

Shaft encoders

This type of transducer also uses a rotating disk but this time it has a set of equally spaced radial lines on its surface. A special track on the disk has a zero reference mark on it. An optical sensor is used to detect the radial lines, incrementing a counter each time a mark is detected. This allows the angular position of a shaft to be accurately determined. A typical shaft encoder might have over a thousand radial lines giving a resolution of less than a third of a degree. Some shaft encoders also provide outputs allowing the direction of rotation of the shaft to be determined as well as its current position and rotational speed. By linking the spindle of a shaft encoder to the spindle of another rotating shaft, speed, position and directional data can be accurately obtained.

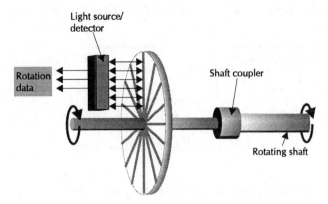

Figure 2.4. *Shaft encoder*

Figure 2.4 illustrates the operation of a shaft encoder. The rotating shaft of the spindle to be monitored is linked to the shaft of the encoder by means of a suitable shaft coupler. The rotation of the shaft thus causes the shaft of the encoder to rotate at the same rate. An optical sensor uses reflected light to detect the radial lines on the encoders disk.

The structure of main memory

Main memory is divided into a number of cells or *locations*, each of which has a unique name or *address* and is capable of holding a unit or grouping of bits which may represent data or an instruction. More is said about instructions in Chapter 4. Memory locations are normally addressed using whole numbers from zero upwards. The *size* of memory location used varies from one make of computer to another and is related to the coding methods employed and the number of bits it is designed to handle as a unit.

Memory words and bytes

A *memory word* is a given number of bits in memory, addressable as a unit. The addresses of memory locations run consecutively, starting with address 0 and running up to the largest address. Each location contains a word which can be retrieved by specification of its address. Similarly, an instruction to write to a location results in the storage of a word into the quoted address. For example, the word 01100110 may be stored in location address 15 and the word 11000110 in location address 16. A memory word may represent data or an instruction. The topic of memory addressing is dealt with in Chapter 4. The memory's *word length* equates with the number of bits which can be stored in a location. Thus, memory which handles words of 16 bits is known as 16-bit memory, whilst that which makes use of 32-bit words is known as 32-bit memory (the related topic of *processor word length* is dealt with in Chapter 7. In practice, a machine may use words of different lengths for different operations. Word length is one of the most important design characteristics of computers, in that it can be fundamental to the efficiency and speed of the computer. Generally, the larger and more powerful the computer, the greater the word length. Until recently, 32-bit and 64-bit words were largely used by mainframe and minicomputer systems exclusively. When first introduced, microcomputers were 4-bit or 8-bit machines, but advances in technology have made 32-bit and 64-bit microcomputers commonplace.

Even if a machine normally handles words of 16 or 32 or 64 bits, reference sometimes needs to be made to a smaller unit, the *byte*, which is 8 bits. Programming in a low level language (Chapter 31) requires separate identification of bytes. Table 2.9 illustrates the formation of a 16-bit word, with byte subdivisions. The leftmost bit in a word is referred to as the most significant bit (MSB) and the rightmost as the least significant bit (LSB). The most significant *byte* in a 16-bit word is identified as the *high order byte*, the least significant byte as the *low order byte*.

high order byte								low order byte							
MSB															LSB
bit-15	bit-14	bit-13	bit-12	bit-11	bit-10	bit-9	bit-8	bit-7	bit-6	bit-5	bit-4	bit-3	bit-2	bit-1	bit-0

Table 2.9. *High and low order bytes*

A 32-bit word would be divided into byte-1 (the lowest order byte), byte-2, byte-3 and byte-4 (the highest order byte). A number of different memory structures have been used, based on different word lengths, which have sufficient flexibility to accommodate the requirements of both numeric and non-numeric data.

Exercises

1.   Why do computers use binary code in preference to, for example, the denary system?

2.   (i)   Differentiate between *internal* and *external* codes.

     (ii)   When may the ASCII or EBCDIC codes be used both internally and externally?

     (iii)   What is the name of a device which converts an external code to its internal equivalent and vice versa?

     (iv)   What is the purpose of *parity checking*?

3.   Give two examples of the use of *control codes*, one relating to display screens and the other to data transmission.

4.   (i)   What is a *coded plate transducer*?

     (ii)   Why is *Gray code* used instead of standard binary code, to mark the divisions on a coded plate transducer?

     (iii)   Give an example of the kind of read error the transducer may produce if standard binary code is used and explain how Gray code avoids such errors.

5.   In the context of computer storage and processing, what does *word length* mean and why is it important?

Chapter 3

Internal Numbers and Computer Arithmetic

A number stored without indication as to whether it is positive or negative, but simply as having a given magnitude (25_{10}, 129_{10}, for example,) is known as an *unsigned number*. To be of practical use, a computer must be able to store, manipulate and differentiate between positive and negative numbers (*signed numbers*). There are a number of different ways this can be done. The most common are:

- sign and magnitude;

- complementation.

Sign and magnitude

With this method, the MSB position is occupied by an explicit *sign bit*; binary 0 and binary 1 are used to indicate, respectively, a positive and a negative number. The remainder of the binary word holds the *absolute* (independent of the sign) *magnitude* of the number.

The examples in Table 3.1 illustrate this method, using a 16-bit word.

	MSB															LSB
$+0_{10}$	0	0	0	0	0	0	0	0	0	0	0	0	0	0	0	0
$+33_{10}$	0	0	0	0	0	0	0	0	0	0	1	0	0	0	0	1
33_{10}	1	0	0	0	0	0	0	0	0	0	1	0	0	0	0	1
$+85_{10}$	0	0	0	0	0	0	0	0	0	1	0	1	0	1	0	1
85_{10}	1	0	0	0	0	0	0	0	0	1	0	1	0	1	0	1
	bit-15	bit-14	bit-13	bit-12	bit-11	bit-10	bit-9	bit-8	bit-7	bit-6	bit-5	bit-4	bit-3	bit-2	bit-1	bit-0
	sign	<							magnitude							>

Table 3.1. *Sign and magnitude format*

Note from the top row in Table 3.1, that the number zero uses a positive sign (0).

Two's complement numbers

To follow the computer arithmetic examples in this chapter, you need to know the rules for binary addition, which can be found in Chapter 1.

A computer can carry out *addition*, using *two*'s complement notation. *Subtraction* can also be effected, through addition (by first negating the number to be subtracted). A two's complement number has an *implicit sign bit*. In other words, it has a place value which contributes to the magnitude of the number, as well as indicating its sign (positive or negative). Table 3.2 shows two 8-bit

	MSB	place values						LSB
	-128_{10}	64_{10}	32_{10}	16_{10}	8_{10}	4_{10}	2_{10}	1_{10}
$+33_{10}$	0	0	0	0	0	0	0	0
-33_{10}	1	0	0	0	0	0	0	0
$+85_{10}$	0	0	0	0	0	0	0	0
-85_{10}	1	0	0	0	0	0	0	0
	bit-7	bit-6	bit-5	bit-4	bit-3	bit-2	bit-1	bit-0

Table 3.2. *Examples of two's complement positive and negative numbers*

examples. The positive number examples ($+33$ and $+85$) contain a binary 0 in the sign bit position, so the place value of -128 does not contribute to the magnitude of the numbers. The negative number examples (-33 and -85) contain a binary 1 in the sign bit position, so its place value of 128 forms part of each numbers value. The negative value is calculated by adding the negative place value of the sign bit to the positive values of the remaining bits, which contain a binary 1. These points can be illustrated with the following analysis of the numbers already shown in Table 3.2.

$$+33_{10} = 00100001_2 = 0 + 0 + 32 + 0 + 0 + 0 + 0 + 1$$
$$-33_{10} = 11011111_2 = -128 + 64 + 0 + 16 + 8 + 4 + 2 + 1$$
$$+85_{10} = 01010101_2 = 0 + 64 + 0 + 16 + 0 + 4 + 0 + 1$$
$$-85_{10} = 11010111_2 = -128 + 0 + 32 + 0 + 8 + 0 + 2 + 1$$

Subtraction, using two's complement numbers uses the following method. The second number (the *subtrahend*) is negated and is added to the first (the *minuend*). This is equivalent to expressing in denary, for example, $(+55) - (+25)$ as $(+55) + (-25)$.

Conversion of binary to two's complement

The two's complement of a binary number is obtained through the following stages:

Stage 1

The number is converted to its *one's complement* representation by inverting the values of all the bits in the number. In other words all ones are flipped to zeroes and all zeroes are flipped to ones. The examples in Table 3.3 illustrate the one's complements of some binary numbers.

	Example (i) $+13_{10}$	Example (ii) $+36_{10}$	Example (iii) $+76_{10}$
binary number	00001101	00100100	01001100
one's complement	11110010	11011011	10110011

Table 3.3. *One's complement of binary numbers*

Stage 2

The one's complement of the binary numbers in Table 3.3 can then be converted to *two's complement* by adding 1, as shown in Table 3.4.

	Example (i) $+13_{10}$	Example (ii) $+36_{10}$	Example (iii) $+76_{10}$
one's complement	1 1 1 1 0 0 1 0	1 1 0 1 1 0 1 1	0 1 0 0 1 1 0 0
+	1	1	1
two's complement	1 1 1 1 0 0 1 0	1 1 0 1 1 0 1 1	1 0 1 1 0 0 1 1

Table 3.4. *Converting from one's to two's complement*

The two's complement numbers in each example now represent the following denary values.

$$\text{two's complement of } 13_{10} \text{ is } -128 + 64 + 32 + 16 + 0 + 0 + 2 + 1 = -13_{10}$$
$$\text{two's complement of } 36_{10} \text{ is } -128 + 64 + 0 + 16 + 8 + 0 + 0 + 0 = -36_{10}$$
$$\text{two's complement of } 76_{10} \text{ is } -128 + 0 + 32 + 16 + 0 + 4 + 0 + 0 = -76_{10}$$

Integer arithmetic using two's complement

Binary subtraction

Subtraction can be carried out by negating the second number (the *subtrahend*), in this case by conversion to two's complement form and adding it to the first number (the *minuend*). The ease with which binary numbers can be switched from positive to negative and vice-versa, by complementation, makes subtraction by addition suitable for computers. Consider the examples in Tables 3.5 and 3.6, assuming a 6-bit word length.

minuend	0 1 1 1 0 1		29_{10}
subtrahend	0 0 0 1 1 1		7_{10}
one's complement of subtrahend	1 1 1 0 0 0		
	1	+	
two's complement of subtrahend	1 1 1 0 0 1	=	7_{10}
minuend	0 1 1 1 0 1	+	$+29_{10}$
result	1 0 1 0 1 1 0	=	22_{10}
ignore carry (c)	c		

Table 3.5. *Two's complement arithmetic* 29_{10} 7_{10} = 22_{10}

The result in Table 3.5 (the carry is ignored) can be proved as follows.

$$010110_2 = 0_{10} + 16_{10} + 0_{10} + 4_{10} + 2_{10} + 0_{10} = 22_{10}.$$

Now consider the example in Table 3.6, where the minuend is smaller than the subtrahend, resulting in a negative answer.

minuend	0 0 0 1 1 1		$+7_{10}$
subtrahend	0 0 1 0 0 1	–	$+9_{10}$
one's complement of subtrahend	1 1 0 1 1 0		
	1	+	
two's complement of subtrahend	1 1 0 1 1 1	=	-9_{10}
minuend	0 0 0 1 1 1	+	$+7_{10}$
result	1 1 1 1 1 0	=	-2_{10}

Table 3.6. *Two's complement arithmetic example $+7_{10}$ $(+9_{10}) = 2_{10}$*

The result in Table 3.6 can be proved as follows.

$$1 1 1 1 1 0_2 = -32_{10} + 16_{10} + 8_{10} + 4_{10} + 2_{10} + 0_{10} = -2_{10}$$

Number range and arithmetic overflow

The *number range* for any given word is determined by the number of bits in the word and the fact that the MSB is needed to indicate the sign (unless, of course, the number is unsigned). This applies whatever method is used to indicate the sign of numbers. The number range which can be stored in any given word length can be readily calculated. Thus, in an 8-bit word using *two's complement* (illustrated in Table 3.7), the maximum number which can be represented is either $+127$ ($2^{n-1} - 1$) or -128 (2^{n-1}), where n = word length.

$0 1 1 1 1 1 1 1_2 =$	$0_{10} + 64_{10} + 32_{10} + 16_{10} + 8_{10} + 4_{10} + 2_{10} + 1_{10} = +127_{10}$
$1 0 0 0 0 0 0 0_2 =$	-128_{10}
	sign bit (bit-8) implicit (–128)

Table 3.7. *Two's complement number range in an 8-bit word*

With *sign and magnitude*, the range is 127_{10} (2^{n-1} 1), as shown in Table 3.8.

$0 1 1 1 1 1 1 1_2 =$	$+(64_{10} + 32_{10} + 16_{10} + 8_{10} + 4_{10} + 2_{10} + 1_{10}) = +127_{10}$
$1 1 1 1 1 1 1 1_2 =$	$-(64_{10} + 32_{10} + 16_{10} + 8_{10} + 4_{10} + 2_{10} + 1_{10}) = +127_{10}$
	sign bit (bit-8) explicit (0 = +, 1 = –)

Table 3.8. *Sign and magnitude number range in an 8-bit word*

Detection of overflow

If the result of an operation involving two numbers exceeds the maximum permitted by the word, then overflow occurs. For example, with the use of 16-bit words and two's complement arithmetic, overflow occurs if the result is outside of the range -32768_{10} (2^{16-1}) to $+32767_{10}$ ($2^{16-1}1$). Similarly, a 24-bit word would permit a range of $+8388608_{10}$ (2^{24-1}) to 8388607_{10} ($2^{24-1}-1$).

Overflow needs to be detected by the computer so that an incorrect result is not overlooked. The hardware in the arithmetic logic unit (ALU) can detect an overflow condition by comparing the states of the *carry in* to, and the *carry out* from, the sign bit. If they are not equal, overflow has occurred and the answer is incorrect.

Consider the two's complement examples in the next two tables, assuming an 8-bit word length. The sum in Table 3.9 shows a correct result, but the example in Table 3.10 appears to result in a negative sum (−96); this incorrect result is a consequence of overflow, indicated by the conflicting *carry in* and *carry out* states. Overflow will also occur when two *negative* numbers are added to produce a sum beyond the range of the word.

	64₁₀	0 1 0 0 0 0 0 0	
+	**4₁₀**	0 0 0 0 0 1 0 0	
=	**68₁₀**	0 1 0 0 0 1 0 0	
	carry	0 0	

	96₁₀	0 1 1 0 0 0 0 0	
+	**64₁₀**	0 1 0 0 0 0 0 0	
=	**−96₁₀**	1 0 1 0 0 0 0 0	incorrect answer
	carry	0 1	carries differ - overflow

Table 3.9. *Sum with no arithmetic overflow*　　　**Table 3.10.** *Incorrect sum resulting from arithmetic overflow*

An *overflow flag* (a single bit) in the *condition codes*, *status* or *flag register* is set as soon as an overflow occurs. Thus, following the execution of an arithmetic process, a low level programmer can include a single test on the overflow flag to determine whether or not incorrect results are due to arithmetic overflow. Other machines may use the flag to implement an *interrupt* (see Chapter 13), which interrupts the CPU operation, to suspend processing and display an error message.

The problem of limited number range and the need for accuracy can be overcome by the use of two or more words of memory to store a single number.

Real numbers

The first part of this section has concentrated on the storage and handling of *integers*. Although a programmer could choose to restrict numbers to integer format, all general-purpose computers must be able to deal with *real numbers*. Real numbers include all the integers and fractions of a number system, that is, all numbers above and below zero and including zero. Many computer applications require the use of numbers with a fractional element, that is, real numbers. Clearly, this can provide for a greater level of accuracy than is permitted by integer numbers, but at the cost of increased storage requirements. There are two basic methods of representing real numbers in computer storage:

- fixed-point representation;

- floating-point representation.

Fixed-point representation

Fixed-point numbers use what can be seen as a conventional format. The binary point is *assumed* to be immediately to the right of the integer part, which is where we would locate the decimal point if we were expressing real denary values. A programmer can require the binary point to be in any position within a memory word, according to the number of bits he or she wishes to assign to the integer and fractional parts. If more bits in a memory word are assigned to the fractional part, greater precision is possible; on the other hand fewer bits are then available for the integer part and this reduces the magnitude range. Conversely, increasing the proportion of a word given to the integer part increases the magnitude range,

Table 3.11. *Fixed point format*

but reduces the possible level of precision. Table 3.11 illustrates fixed point format.

Of course, a programmer may equally assume a given memory word to be entirely integer, with no fractional part. The binary point is said to have an *assumed* position which gives meaning to a number. Using 8-bit words, the programmer may instruct that the binary points for two numbers, labelled (i) and (ii), are located as shown in Table 3.12.

	integer part		fractional part
(i) 2.75_{10}	0 1 1 1 0 0	.	1 1_2
(ii) 28.25_{10}	0 1 1 1 0 0	.	0 1_2

Table 3.12. *Fixed point numbers*

If the programmer then relocates the binary points, the same binary groupings take on different values. Using the numbers from Table 3.12, the point for number (i) is shifted one place to the left, which *halves* its value; the point in number (ii) is shifted one place to the right, which *doubles* its value (for clarification of this, refer to Chapter 4. The results of the shifts are shown in Table 3.13. Therefore, a programmer using fixed point numbers must keep track of the point position in order to know their value. This problem is of particular concern to the programmer using low level languages.

	integer part		fractional part
(i) 1.375_{10}	0 0 0 0 1	.	0 1 1_2
(ii) 56.5_{10}	0 1 1 1 0 0 0	.	1_2

Table 3.13. *Fixed point numbers after moving binary point*

If a programmer is using fixed point numbers, this simply means that the decisions on the degree of precision are made by the programmer. If no floating point facility is available, the programmer must use integer arithmetic (see earlier) and set the precision after each calculation. The practicalities of this are of concern to the low level programmer, but briefly, involve the *scaling* of numbers to remove any fractional part, carrying out integer arithmetic and then re-scaling the result to the required number of fractional places. Today, all computers provide a floating point number facility, but there was a time when a programmer had to represent all real numbers in fixed point form. As explained later, floating point numbers require a longer word length than 8 bits, which was the norm, for example, for the first generation of microcomputers.

Number range and precision of fixed point numbers

Continuing with the topic of fixed point numbers, consider a 16-bit word with the binary point assumed to be between the bit-4 and bit-5 positions; sign and magnitude format is being used, so the sign bit (shown in bold) occupies the most significant bit position, which leaves 10 bits for the integral part and 5 bits for the fractional part of the number. The number range which can be represented is limited to that given in Table 3.14.

Positive 0_{10} to $+1023.96875_{10}$	Negative 0_{10} to -1023.96875_{10}
0000000000000000 . 00000$_2$	0000000000000000 . 00000$_2$
0111111111111111 . 11111$_2$	**1**111111111111111 . 11111$_2$
sign	sign

Table 3.14. *Example sign and magnitude range*

Precision is limited by the number of bits allocated to the fractional part of the number and no matter what word length is used, some loss of precision is, occasionally inevitable.

Arithmetic overflow

Consider the multiplication of the two denary values in Table 3.15, where only 3 places are available for the fractional parts. The fractional part of the product has overflowed and by rounding, the computer stores the

| $1.363_{10} \times 1.112_{10} = 1.515656_{10} = 1.516_{10}$ | accurate to 3 decimal places |

Table 3.15. *Loss of precision by overflow*

result as 1.516, which is 0.000344 greater than the product (accurate to 6 decimal places). Given a particular word length for *fixed point* numbers, the allocation of more bits to the fractional part improves precision but at the cost of reduced number range; conversely, number range can be improved at the cost of reduced precision. However, the main drawback of fixed point form is the small range of numbers which can be represented. *Floating-point* number representation helps overcome this problem at the cost of slightly slower computation and some reduction in precision; this latter point is discussed later.

Arithmetic underflow

This condition occurs when a number (a fraction) is too small to fit into a given length word. The term

| $0.125_{10} \times 0.025_{10} = 0.003125_{10} = 0.003_{10}$ | accurate to 3 decimal places |

Table 3.16. *Loss of precision by underflow*

underflow is a little misleading, in that some significant digits are lost because they overflow into non-existent storage, but the loss is owing to the smallness of the fraction. The term underflow is used to differentiate from circumstances of arithmetic overflow, resulting from an increase in the magnitude of a number. The denary example in Table 3.16 illustrates underflow. As in the previous example in Table 3.15, provision is made for a maximum of 3 decimal places.

In Table 3.16, two decimal fractions are multiplied to give a product which underflows; some significant digits are lost and precision is reduced by 0.000125_{10}.

Floating-point representation

A *mantissa* and *exponent* (or *index*) can be used to represent a number. Denary numbers, written in *standard index* form, reveal a format similar to that used for the storage of binary floating point numbers. Examples of binary floating point and denary standard index numbers are given in Table 3.17. Note that the formats are not exactly the same.

binary	Binary floating point		denary	Denary standard index	
	mantissa m	exponent r^e		mantissa	exponent
101.0101_2	0.1010101_2	$\times 2^3$	$6,800,000_{10}$	6.8_{10}	$\times 10^7$
0.0011001_2	0.11001_2	$\times 2^2$	0.0000564_{10}	5.64_{10}	$\times 105$

Table 3.17. *Binary floating point and denary standard index examples*

In floating-point notation, the point is not fixed by the programmer. Instead it remains in a position at the left of the mantissa. Floating-point notation is based on the expression: $m \times r^e$, where m is $\pm$ and e is $\pm$, m is the mantissa, r is the radix or base and e is the exponent (power). In binary, the radix is 2 (see Chapter 1).

Fixed-point numbers can be converted to floating-point numbers by a process of *normalization*. As the first example (101.0101_2) in Table 3.17 shows, if the number is *greater than* 1_2 then the point floats to the left (actually achieved by shifting the mantissa to the right), to a position immediately before the most significant bit. This part becomes the mantissa (m). The point in Table 3.17 has moved 3 places to the left, the mantissa is now 0.1010101_2 and the exponent (e) is therefore, 3. The second example (0.0011001_2) in Table 3.17 shows that, if the number is a *fraction* and a binary 1 does not immediately follow the point, then the point floats to the right (actually achieved by shifting the mantissa to the left) of any leading zeros, until the first non-zero bit is reached; the mantissa becomes 0.11001_2. The point has moved 2

fixed point	binary floating point	
	mantissa *m*	exponent r^e
1110.001_2	0.1010101_2	$\times 2^4$

Table 3.18. *Fixed point > binary 1 converted to floating point*

fixed point	binary floating point	
	mantissa *m*	exponent r^e
0.000111_2	0.111000_2	$\times 2^{-3}$

Table 3.19. *Fixed point < binary 1 converted to floating point*

places to the right, so the exponent (e) is 2. Two more examples are given in the adjacent tables. In Table 3.18, the point moves four places to the left, so the exponent is 4; in Table 3.19, the fraction is normalized by moving the point three places to the right, so the exponent is 3.

The floating point format (there are alternatives) used in this text follows a number of rules.

- With normalized *positive* numbers the binary point must not be followed immediately by a binary 0. Only positive, floating point number examples have been provided so far.

- Conversely, normalized *negative* numbers require that the binary point is not followed immediately by a binary 1. The next section, on storage of floating point numbers, describes the format for negative numbers in more detail.

- Any normalized binary mantissa must be a fraction falling within the range $+0.5$ to less than $+1$ for positive values and 1 to greater than 0.5 for negative values. The range of possible normalized mantissas, given a 4-bit allocation, is shown in Table 3.20.

positive mantissas	denary equivalent	negative mantissas	denary equivalent
0.100_2	$+^1/_2$	1.000_2	1
0.101_2	$+^5/_8$	1.001_2	$^7/_8$
0.110_2	$+^3/_4$	1.010_2	$^3/_4$
0.111_2	$+^7/_8$	1.011_2	$^5/_8$

Table 3.20. *Range of possible normalized, 4-bit mantissas, with zero exponent*

Storage of floating-point numbers

As already indicated, floating-point numbers are stored in two parts:

- The *mantissa*, the length of which is determined by the precision to which numbers are represented. Clearly, if fewer bits are allocated to the mantissa (which is always a left-justified fraction) then less precision is possible.

- The *exponent*, which is usually allocated one-third to one-half of the number of bits used for the mantissa.

Table 3.21 assumes the use of a 16-bit word for the storage of each floating-point number, in two's complement form, 12 bits being used for the mantissa and 4 bits for the exponent.

sign	mantissa (fraction)												exponent (integer)		
bit-15	bit-14	bit-13	bit-12	bit-11	bit-10	bit-9	bit-8	bit-7	bit-6	bit-5	bit-4	bit-3	bit-2	bit-1	bit-0

Table 3.21. *Example floating point format using a 16-bit word*

The binary point in the mantissa fraction is immediately to the right of the sign bit, which is 0 for a positive and 1 for a negative floating-point number. Table 3.22 illustrates these points.

positive floating point form		negative floating point form	
12 bits	4 bits	12 bits	4 bits
0 . 1 * * * * * * * * * *	* * * *	1 . 0 * * * * * * * * * *	* * * * *
mantissa	exponent	mantissa	exponent

Table 3.22. *Positive and negative representation in floating point form*

In two's complement form, the most significant digit to the right of the binary point is 1 for a positive and 0 for a negative floating-point number. It should be noticed that the sign bit and the most significant non-sign bit differ in both cases. As explained earlier, any representation where they are the same indicates that the mantissa needs to be normalized. This may be necessary after any floating-point arithmetic operation.

Floating-point conversion

To obtain the denary equivalent of a number held in floating point form requires the mantissa to be multiplied by 2, raised to the *power* of e, which has the value stored in the exponent part of the number. For example, the floating point number in Table 3.23, which uses 8 bits for the mantissa and 4 bits for the exponent, converts to denary as follows.

8-bit mantissa		4-bit exponent
0 . 1 1 0 1 0 0 1	×	0 1 0 1 (2^5)

Table 3.23. *Floating point number*

$$\left(\frac{1}{2} + \frac{1}{4} + 0 + \frac{1}{16} + 0 + 0 + \frac{1}{128} \right) \times 2^5 = \frac{105}{128} \times 32 = 26\frac{1}{4}$$

Therefore, the floating point number $0.1101001_2 \times 2^5$ is equivalent to fixed point 11010.01_2.

If 4 bits are allocated to the exponent, e can have a value between $+7$ and 8 (assuming two's complement form). Alternatively, in a 16-bit machine, two words with a total of 32 bits may be used to store each floating-point number, the mantissa occupying 24 bits, and the exponent, 8 bits. In such a representation, the exponent e could have a value between $+127$ and 128 (assuming two's complement). The earlier section entitled Number Range and Arithmetic Overflow gives an explanation of these calculations.

Alternative floating-point forms

Different machines may use different methods for coding floating-point numbers. The mantissa may be coded in two's complement, as described previously, or it may be stored as sign and magnitude. The advantage for machine arithmetic of storing numbers in two's complement form has already been identified, but machines with the circuitry to handle floating-point numbers may also have the facility to carry out subtraction without two's complement representation. The above illustrations of floating-point numbers assume that the exponent is also stored in two's complement form. In practice, the exponent is often stored in sign and magnitude.

Floating-point arithmetic

The floating point addition and subtraction examples used in this section assume the use of a 6-bit mantissa and a 4-bit exponent. Both mantissa and exponent are expressed in two's complement form.

Addition

To add two floating-point numbers, they must both have the same value exponent. If they differ, the necessary *scaling* is achieved by *shifting*, to the right (equivalent to the binary point floating to the left), the mantissa of the number with the smaller exponent and *incrementing* the exponent at every shift until the exponents are equal. The shifting process follows the rules for arithmetic shifts, which are described in Chapter 4. The addition procedure consists of equalising the exponents by scaling, adding the mantissas and then, if necessary, normalizing the result. Tables 3.25 to 3.26 illustrate the floating-point addition procedure with the example sum in Table 3.24.

	mantissa		exponent	
6.75_{10}	0.11011_2	$\times$	0011_2	2^3
$+12.50_{10}$	0.11001_2	$\times$	0100_2	2^4

Table 3.24. *Binary floating point sum $6.75_{10} + 12.5_{10} = 19.25_{10}$*

- *Scaling.* In Table 3.25, the mantissa with the smaller exponent is shifted one place to the right and the exponent is incremented. As a result, a binary 1 is lost from the least significant bit position.

mantissa		exponent		mantissa		exponent
0.11011_2	$\times$	0011_2	**scales to**	0.01101_2	$\times$	0100_2
6.75_{10}		2^3		LSB (1) lost)		2^4

Table 3.25. *Equalize the exponents by scaling*

- *Add the mantissas.* Table 3.26 shows that this is clearly incorrect, because the sign bit is now 1, indicating a negative value, when the result should be positive. The method by which the computer detects this type of error is explained earlier in the section on Arithmetic Overflow.

	mantissa		exponent	
	0.01101_2	$\times$	0100_2	2^4
+	0.11001_2	$\times$	0100_2	2^4
=	1.00110_2	$\times$	0100_2	2^4

Table 3.26. *Mantissas added*

- *Normalize the result* (100110_2) shown in Table 3.26, which is beyond the permitted range (see Table 3.20) for a positive number. The mantissa and normalization is required. Table 3.27 shows the result of shifting the mantissa one place to the right and incrementing the exponent.

mantissa		exponent	
0.10011_2	×	0101_2	2^5

Table 3.27. *Result normalized*

The floating-point result in Table 3.27 can be expressed as follows.

$$0.10011_2 \times 32_{10}(2^5) = \left(\frac{1}{2} + 0 + 0 + \frac{1}{16} + \frac{1}{32}\right) \times 32_{10} = 19_{10}$$

Some loss of accuracy has resulted (19_{10} instead of 19.25_{10}). The loss of accuracy results from the right-shift operation required to equalize the exponents (Table 3.25); a significant bit is lost when the binary value for 675_{10}, ($0.11011_2 \times 2^3$) becomes 6.5_{10} ($0.01101_2 \times 2^4$). The decimal value of this discarded bit is its fractional value of 1/32, multiplied by the exponent (before scaling) of $2^3(8)$, giving a result of 0.25_{10}. Although a further right-shift is needed to normalize the result (Table 3.27), the discarded bit is a 0 and does not produce any additional inaccuracy.

Subtraction

The procedures for subtraction are the same as for addition except that the mantissas are subtracted. This can be achieved by negating the subtrahend and then adding it to the minuend. In denary, this is the same as saying $12.5_{10} + (-6.75_{10}) = 5.75_{10}$. Consider this example, shown in Table 3.28. The procedures for carrying out this subtraction, using floating point arithmetic are illustrated in Tables 3.29 to 3.32.

	mantissa		exponent	
12.50_{10}	0.11001_2	×	0100_2	2^4
-6.75_{10}	0.11011_2	×	0011_2	2^3

Table 3.28. $12.5_{10} - 6.75_{10} = 5.75_{10}$

- Scale the mantissa (Table 3.29) with the smaller exponent and increment the exponent, repeatedly if necessary, until the exponents of the two numbers are equalized. In this case, one right-shift is needed.

mantissa		exponent		mantissa		exponent
0.11011_2	×	0011_2	**scales to**	0.01101_2	×	0100_2
6.75_{10}		2^3		LSB (1) lost		2^4

Table 3.29. *Scale mantissas*

- Negate the subtrahend by finding the two's complement of its mantissa, as shown in Table 3.30.

	mantissa
6.75_{10}	0.01101_2
One's complement	1.10010_2
+	1_2
Two's complement	1.10011_2

Table 3.30. *Convert subtrahend to two's complement*

- Add the mantissas, as shown in Table 3.31; the carry of binary 1 (in bold) is ignored.

	mantissa		exponent	
	0.11001_2	$\times$	0100_2	2^4
+	1.10011_2	$\times$	0100_2	2^4
=	10.01100_2	$\times$	0100_2	2^4
carry ignored				

Table 3.31. *Add the mantissas*

- If necessary, normalize the result. In this case, the answer is not in normal form because the sign bit and the most significant bit to the right of the binary point, are the same. The result is normalized by carrying out a left-shift of one on the mantissa and decrementing the exponent accordingly; the result is shown in Table 3.32.

mantissa		exponent	
0.11000_2	$\times$	0011_2	2^3
zero inserted in LSB position			

Table 3.32. *Normalize result*

The result in denary $= \left(\dfrac{1}{2} + \dfrac{1}{4}\right) \times 2^3 = \dfrac{3}{4} \times 8_{10} = 6_{10}$

Note that a zero (in bold) is inserted into the least significant bit position of the mantissa. This floating point example has resulted in some significant loss of accuracy (and answer of 6_{10} instead of 5.75_{10}). In reality, inaccuracies of this order would clearly be intolerable and techniques are used to ensure that floating point arithmetic operations produce the degree of precision needed for the most demanding applications. Some aspects of these techniques are introduced in the next section.

Fixed Point versus floating point representation

Precision. As stated earlier, given a particular word length, fixed point representation allows greater precision than is possible with floating point form. Consider, for example, a word length of six bits, used to store wholly fractional numbers. In fixed point form, all the bit positions can be used by significant digits, but in floating point form, if two bits are reserved for the exponent, this leaves only four bits for the mantissa and thus a maximum of four figure precision.

Range. As is demonstrated in the previous section, a major advantage of floating point form is the facility for storing an increased number range.

Maintenance of floating point arithmetic precision

Floating-point arithmetic precision can be improved by: increasing the number of bits allocated to the mantissa; rounding; double precision numbers and arithmetic.

Mantissa length

Increasing the number of bits allocated to the *mantissa* will improve precision but inaccuracies can never be completely eliminated. In practice, memory words are much longer than those used for illustration here and where memory words are of insufficient length to ensure acceptable accuracy, two adjacent locations may be used. Machines which make use of this method are providing what is referred to as *double-precision floating-point* facilities.

Rounding

The subtraction example in Tables 3.28 to 3.32 demonstrates a loss of accuracy through *truncation*; a significant bit 1 is lost when the mantissa is shifted one place to the right, in order to equalize the exponents of the minuend and the subtrahend. If a computer process requires a series of calculations, each using the results of previous ones, repeated truncation may accrue considerable inaccuracy and this will be reflected in the final result. As can be seen from the example of floating-point addition in Tables 3.24 to 3.27, the process of normalizing the result also requires the shifting or justification of the mantissa.

	mantissa	
	0.1001_2	
+	0.1100_2	
=	1.0101_2	sign bit now 1
	0.10101_2	right shift of 1

Table 3.33. *Normalization of mantissa*

Consider the example in Table 3.33, which only shows the mantissas to illustrate the normalization process. In Table 3.33, normalization has resulted in the loss of a binary 1 from the least significant bit position (a 0 is inserted into the sign bit position) and consequent loss of accuracy. Rounding dictates that, if during an arithmetic shift the last bit to be discarded (the *most significant* of those which are lost) is a 1, then 1 is added to the *least significant* retained bit. Consider an 8-bit mantissa, rounded as in Table 3.34. The accumulated errors caused by repeated truncation of values during a lengthy arithmetic process can partially, though not entirely, be avoided by rounding. In practice, rounding can sometimes result in greater inaccuracies than would result without rounding. Many

	7 bits	1010111_2
10101101_2	6 bits	101011_2
rounded to	5 bits	10110_2
	4 bits	1011_2

Table 3.34. *Rounding*

rounding algorithms exist to try to overcome this problem and the type of inaccuracy which occasionally occurs will depend on the rounding algorithm.

Double precision numbers and arithmetic

As the term (also known as *double length numbers*) suggests, where a single memory word is of insufficient length to accommodate a number, two contiguous words are used. Double precision numbers may be used to increase accuracy or when the product of a multiplication operation will not fit into a single location. The example addition in Table 3.35 provides a basic

most significant half		least significant half		
0	1 0 1	0	0 1 0	$101010_2 = 42_{10}$
0	0 0 1	0	1 1 1	$001111_2 = 15_{10}$
0		1	0 0 1	{1}
0	0 0 1			{2}
0	0 1 0			{2}
0		0	0 0 1	{3}
0	1 0 1			{4}
0	1 1 1	0	0 0 1	{4} $111001_2 = 57_{10}$
sign		carry		

Table 3.35. *Double precision arithmetic*

idea of double precision arithmetic; in the example, each number occupies two contiguous 4-bit *nibbles*.

The procedure is also described with the pseudocode algorithm in Listing 3.1.

Listing 3.1.   Double precision arithmetic

```
{double precision}
add least significant halves of numbers {1}
if carry = 1 then
   add 1 to most significant half {2}
   set carry bit to 0 {3}
endif
add most significant halves of numbers {4}
```

Floating-point multiplication and division

To multiply two floating-point numbers, the mantissas are multiplied and their exponents are added. For the sake of simplicity, the multiplication process is best illustrated using denary numbers, but the principles are the same for binary floating point numbers. Tables 3.36 to 3.38 illustrate the process.

mantissa		exponent		mantissa		exponent
0.3	$\times$	10^3	**multiplied by**	0.2	$\times$	10^4

Table 3.36. *Floating point multiplication $300_{10} \times 2000_{10}$*

- Multiply mantissas and add exponents.

mantissa		exponent
0.06	$\times$	10^7

Table 3.37. *Result of multiplying mantissas and adding exponents*

- Normalize the result; the exponent is decremented each time the mantissa is shifted one position to the left.

mantissa		exponent
0.6	$\times$	10^6

Table 3.38. *Normalize result*

Tables 3.39 to 3.41 show a second example.

mantissa		exponent		mantissa		exponent
0.237	$\times$	10^2	**multiplied by**	0.415	$\times$	10^3

Table 3.39. *Floating point multiplication $237_{10} \times 415_{10}$*

- Multiply mantissas and add exponents.

mantissa		exponent
0.098355	×	10^5

Table 3.40. *Result of multiplying mantissas and adding exponents*

- Normalize the result; the exponent is decremented each time the mantissa is shifted one position to the left.

mantissa		exponent
0.98355	×	10^4

Table 3.41. *Normalize result*

Floating-point division is carried out by dividing the mantissas and subtracting their exponents.

Hardware and software control of computer arithmetic

The execution of computer arithmetic operations often involves a mixture of hardware and software control. Increasingly, to improve processing efficiency, many computers are equipped with additional circuitry to handle floating-point numbers directly.

Excess codes

Excess-128

An excess code involves the addition of an excess to the value to be represented. Thus, an 8-bit *excess-128* code would add 128_{10} to each byte. The excess-128 representations for $+26_{10}$ and 42_{10} are shown in Table 3.42.

$+26_{10}$	0 0 0 1 1 0 1 0		-42_{10}	1 1 0 1 0 1 1 0
$+128_{10}$	1 0 0 0 0 0 0 0		$+128_{10}$	1 0 0 0 0 0 0 0
$= 154_{excess-128}$	1 0 0 1 1 0 1 0		$= 86_{excess-128}$	0 1 0 1 0 1 1 0

Table 3.42. *Excess-128 numbers*

The number range for 8 bits, without an excess, is –128 to +127. Adding an excess of 128 means the range becomes 0 to 255; effectively, the excess makes all numbers in the range positive and unsigned. An advantage of the excess code is that no complementation is needed for arithmetic; Table 3.43 provides an example.

$+26_{10}$ becomes $154_{excess-128}$	1 0 0 1 1 0 1 0
42_{10} becomes $86_{excess-128}$	0 1 0 1 0 1 1 0
=	1 1 1 1 0 0 0 0
subtract 128_{10}, as answer is in excess-256	1 0 0 0 0 0 0 0
= 16_{10} or $112_{excess-128}$	0 1 1 1 0 0 0 0

Table 3.43. *Example $+26_{10}$ 42_{10} using excess-128 numbers*

Another advantage stems from the fact that an illegal result, that is one outside of the permitted range, is easily identified. Table 3.44 shows an example sum, with an illegal result; the binary 1 in the bit-8 position indicates a result outside of the number range.

+ 122_{10} becomes $250_{excess-128}$	1 1 1 1 1 0 1 0
112_{10} becomes $240_{excess-128}$	1 1 1 1 0 0 0 0
produces carry of 1 into bit-8 position	1 1 1 1 0 1 0 1 0
subtract 128_{10}, as answer is in excess-256	1 0 0 0 0 0 0 0
carry of 1 into bit-8 signals error	1 0 1 1 0 1 0 1 0

Table 3.44. *Excess-128 sum with result out of range*

Excess-3

Each excess-3 code is 3 greater than its binary-code decimal (BCD) equivalent. For example, denary 2 in excess-3 code is 5 (2+3) or 0101_2. The excess-3 codes for all the denary symbols, are given in Table 3.45.

n_{10}	$n_{10} + 3_{10}$	excess-3		n_{10}	$n_{10} + 3_{10}$	excess-3
0	3	0 0 1 1		5	8	1 0 0 0
1	4	0 1 0 0		6	9	1 0 0 1
2	5	0 1 0 1		7	10	1 0 1 0
3	6	0 1 1 0		8	11	1 0 1 1
4	7	0 1 1 1		9	12	1 1 0 0

Table 3.45. *Excess-3 codes*

Any of the excess-3 binary codes can now be complemented (nines complement), for the purposes of subtraction, without the production of any invalid codes. The nines complements of each the excess-3 codes in Table 3.45, are listed in Table 3.46.

n_{10}	excess-3	nines complement		n_{10}	excess-3	nines complement
0	0 0 1 1	1 1 0 0		5	1 0 0 0	0 1 1 1
1	0 1 0 0	1 0 1 1		6	1 0 0 1	0 1 1 0
2	0 1 0 1	1 0 1 0		7	1 0 1 0	0 1 0 1
3	0 1 1 0	1 0 0 1		8	1 0 1 1	0 1 0 0
4	0 1 1 1	1 0 0 0		9	1 1 0 0	0 0 1 1

Table 3.46. *Excess-3 codes and nines complements*

Before subtraction, 1 is added to the subtrahend, to form the tens complement. Subtraction can then be carried out, by addition (in the same way as two's complement numbers).

Excess-3 addition

Excess-3 addition requires that: if there is a carry, add 3; if there is no carry, subtract 3.

	carry	excess-3	carry	excess-3	carry	excess-3
746		1 0 1 0		0 1 1 1		1 0 0 1
+ 168		0 1 0 0		1 0 0 1		1 0 1 1
=		1 1 1 0	1	0 0 0 0	1	0 1 0 0
add carries		1		1		
=		1 1 1 1		0 0 0 1		0 1 0 0
add 3 if carry				+ 1 1		+ 1 1
=		1 1 1 1		0 1 0 0		0 1 1 1
subtract 3 if no carry		1 1				
= 914		1 1 0 0		0 1 0 0		0 1 1 1

Table 3.47. *Excess-3 addition*

BCD arithmetic

The valid BCD (binary-coded decimal) codes are given in Chapter 2. A problem of using BCD numbers is that, using normal integer arithmetic, an addition would sometimes produce invalid BCD numbers; 10 to 15 are illegal codes. So, for example, when 5_{10} (0101_2) is added to 7_{10} (0111_2), the result of 12_{10} (1100_2) is not a valid BCD number. The problem of invalid codes is dealt with as follows. Six is added to a BCD code if, during the addition process: an *illegal code* is produced; **or** if there is an *overflow carry* from the 4-bit BCD code.

Consider the addition examples in Tables 3.48 and 3.49

	carry	BCD	carry	BCD	carry	BCD
746		0 1 1 1		0 1 0 0		0 1 1 0
+ 168		0 0 0 1		0 1 1 0		1 0 0 0
=		1 0 0 0		1 0 1 0		1 1 1 0
add 6 if illegal code **or** if carry beyond 4 bits				1 1 0		1 1 0
=		1 0 0 0	1	0 0 0 0	1	0 1 0 0
add in carries		1		1		
= 914		1 0 0 1		0 0 0 1		0 1 0 0

Table 3.48. *BCD addition $746_{BCD} + 168_{BCD} = 914_{BCD}$*

If both circumstances occur in respect of one BCD code, 6 is only added once. Table 3.49 illustrates such a case.

	carry	BCD	carry	BCD	carry	BCD
269		0 0 1 0		0 1 1 0		1 0 0 1
+549		0 1 0 1		0 1 0 0		1 0 0 1
=		0 1 1 1		1 0 1 0	1	0 0 1 0
add 6 if illegal code or if carry beyond 4 bits						1 1 0
=		0 1 1 1	1	1 0 1 0	1	1 0 0 0
add in carries			1			
=		0 1 1 1		1 0 1 1		1 0 0 0
add 6 if illegal code or if carry beyond 4 bits				1 1 0		
=			1	0 0 0 1		
add in carries	1					
=818		1 0 0 0		0 0 0 1		1 0 0 0

Table 3.49. *BCD addition* $269_{BCD} + 549_{BCD} = 818_{BCD}$

Exercises

1. (i) If a computer uses a 16-bit word to represent integers, show how the numbers 30_{10} and 362_{10} would be represented in *binary coded decimal* (BCD).

   (ii) Show how the same computer would represent the values –30, –72 and –473 in (a) *sign and magnitude* and (b) *two's complement*.

2. Using two's complement representation and an 8-bit word, calculate the following:

   (i) 42 + 74;

   (ii) 74 – 42;

   (iii) 35 – 46.

3. Use the addition 75 + 96 to illustrate *arithmetic overflow* and explain how the computer's circuitry might detect the condition. Assume use of an 8-bit word.

4. What would be the denary, integer *number range*, for a 12-bit word, using two's complement representation?

5. Why is the number range for sign and magnitude different from that for two's complement?

6. If real numbers are to be represented in fixed point format, how does the low-level programmer determine the degree of precision?

7. How does floating point notation allow greater number range, for a given word length, than fixed point notation?

8. Given a particular word length, why does fixed point notation allow greater precision than floating point notation? Use an example to illustrate.

9. A particular computer uses a 16-bit word to store floating point numbers, allocating 10 bits to the mantissa and 6 bits to the exponent; both parts are stored in two's complement notation. Numbers are normalized when the bit immediately to the right of the binary point has a value of 1. The format is illustrated below.

sign	binary point														
					mantissa						exponent				

    (i)   Calculate the denary values of:

        a.   0110100101000011;

        b.   1010010100100101;

        c.   0001010101010011101

    (ii)   Write down the bit patterns to represent the following numbers, in normalized form:

        a.   +5.4;

        b.   −0.625.

    (iii) Add the numbers in part (ii), showing each stage, as described in the text.

    (iv) Subtract 4.25 from 10.75, showing each stage as described in the text.

10. In the context of floating point arithmetic, what is meant by *arithmetic underflow*? Give and example of this condition

11. How can the precision of floating point numbers be improved?

12. Convert the following floating point numbers to fixed point notation:

    (i)   0.1101011 × 0110;

    (ii)   0.1001111 × 1100;

    (iii) 1.010011 × 1010;

    (iv) 1.011101 × 0011.

13. Using an 8-bit word, convert the following numbers to excess-128:

    (i) 37_{10}

    (ii) 25_{10}

14. In the context of computer arithmetic, what benefit may derive from the use of excess-128 code?

15. (i)   List the valid BCD codes;

    (ii)   Use BCD arithmetic for the following sums:

        a.   347 + 216;

        b.   514 + 112.

Chapter 4
Computer Instructions

This chapter deals with activity of the Central Processing Unit (CPU) and the ways in which computer program instructions are stored, interpreted and executed in order that the computer can perform its tasks. The various methods for addressing memory are also examined. In Chapter 2 it is stated that data can take various forms when stored as a *memory word*, namely:

- pure binary;

- coded binary, for example, binary-coded decimal (BCD);

- character codes, for example, ASCII.

All the above are considered to be *data* and can be interpreted as such by the CPU, but in order to perform any tasks, it has to have access to computer *instructions*. During processing, data currently being processed and the instructions needed to process the data are stored in main memory. Thus, a memory word can also form an instruction, in which case, it is referred to as an *instruction word*; one formed from data is known as a *data word*.

The central processing unit (CPU)

The CPU has a number of *registers* which it can use to temporarily store a number of words read from memory. These registers are used to apply meaning to memory words. It should be noted that memory words cannot be determined as being data or instructions simply by examination of the code. The CPU differentiates between data and instructions by locating:

- instructions in an *instruction register*;

- data in *data registers*.

A computer program stored in main memory comprises a sequence of instructions, each of which is transferred, in turn, into the CPUs instruction register, thus identifying the next operation which the CPU is to perform. The instructions are retrieved from consecutive memory locations, unless the last instruction executed requires the next one to be fetched from a different location. Those dealing with the latter circumstance are called *branch* or *jump* instructions. The various types of instruction are described later. The process of fetching, interpreting and executing instructions is called the *fetch-execute cycle* but may also be referred to as the *instruction cycle* or *automatic sequence control*.

As indicated in Chapter 6, the *control unit* has the function of governing all hardware operation, including the activities of the CPU itself. To understand the fetch-execute cycle it is necessary to be aware of the names and functions of the various CPU *registers* used.

The program counter (PC)

The PC keeps track of the locations where instructions are stored. At any one time during a program's execution the PC holds the memory address of the next instruction to be executed. Its operation is possible because, in all computer systems, the instructions forming a program are stored in adjacent memory locations, so that the next instruction will normally (except when a branch instruction is executed) be stored in an address a single increment more than the address of the last instruction to be fetched. By incrementing the address in the PC each time an instruction is received, the PC always has the address of the next instruction to be retrieved.

The program counter is also known by a variety of other names, including the *Sequence Control Register* (SCR) and the *Instruction Address Register* (IAR).

Memory buffer register (MBR)

Whenever the contents of a memory word are to be transferred into or out of main memory, they pass through the MBR. This applies to both data and instructions.

Memory address register (MAR)

The MAR provides the location address of the specific memory word (both instructions and data) to be read from or written to memory via the MBR.

Current instruction register (CIR)

As the name suggests, the function of the CIR is to store the current instruction for decoding and execution.

Accumulators and general-purpose registers

These registers are situated within the arithmetic/logic unit (ALU) and provide a working area for data fetched from memory. Values about to be added or subtracted can be copied, via the MBR, into the accumulators. The arithmetic result can be placed in one accumulator and copied from there into a main memory location. All communications between the CPU and the memory take place through the MBR, as Figure 4.1 illustrates.

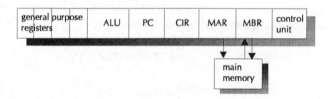

Figure 4.1. *CPU registers used in fetch-execute cycle*

In order to fetch an instruction from memory the CPU places the address of the instruction in the MAR and then carries out a memory read; the instruction is then copied into the MBR and from there, into the CIR. Similarly, an instruction which itself requires the reading of a particular data word causes the address of the data word to be placed into the MAR. The execution of the memory read then results in the copying of the addressed data word into the MBR, from where it can be accessed by the processor. The MBR acts as the point of transfer for both data and instructions passing, in either direction, between the main memory and the CPU.

Fetch-execute cycle

The instruction fetch-execute cycle can be described as follows:

Fetch phase - common to all instructions.

- the contents of the PC are copied into the MAR. The MAR now contains the location address of the next instruction and a memory read is initiated to copy the instruction word from memory into the MBR.

- the PC is incremented and now contains the address of the next instruction.

- the instruction word is then copied from the MBR into the CIR.

Execute phase - the action taken is unique to the instruction.

- the instruction in the CIR is decoded

- the instruction in the CIR is executed.

- unless the instruction is a STOP instruction, then the cycle is repeated.

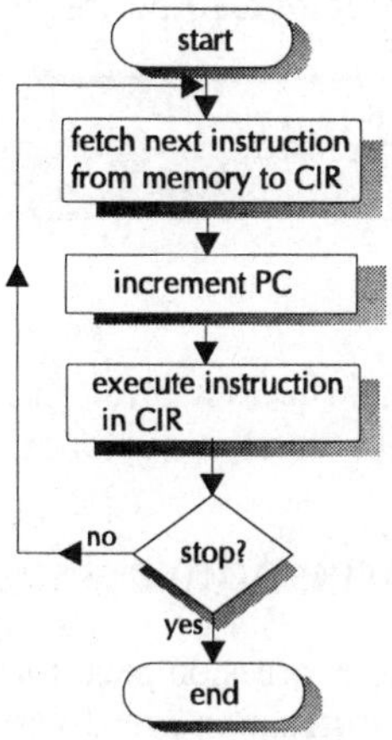

Figure 4.2. *Fetch-execute cycle*

The cycle is illustrated in the flowchart in Figure 4.2. The fetch-execute cycle is carried out automatically by the hardware and the programmer cannot control its sequence of operation. Of course, the programmer does have control over which instructions are stored in memory and the order in which they are executed.

Types of instruction

All the instructions available on a particular machine are known collectively as the *instruction set* of that machine. There are certain types of instruction commonly available in most computer systems. They can be classified according to their function as follow:

- arithmetic and logical operations on data;

- input and output of data;

- changing the sequence of program execution (branch instructions);

- transfer of data between memory and the CPU registers;

- transfer of data between registers within the CPU.

Examples of these instructions and their effects are given in Chapter 31 on Assembly Language Programming.

Instruction format

An instruction usually consists of two main components, the *function* or *operation code* (*opcode*) and the *operand*. The opcode part of the instruction defines the operation to be performed, for example to add or to move data and the operand defines the location address in memory of the data to be operated upon. The storage of a 16-bit instruction word is illustrated in Table 4.1.

bit-15															bit-0
opcode				operands											

Table 4.1 *Instruction format*

Thus, the four most significant bits determine the type of instruction and the remaining twelve bits specify the operand or operands to be used.

Three-address instruction

If an expression requiring the use of three memory variables is to be accommodated by one instruction, then the instruction word will need to contain the address of each variable, that is three operands. An addition instruction can be expressed symbolically as,

        ADD Z,X,Y

that is, add the contents of X to the contents of Y and store the result in Z. The instruction word needs to be large enough to accommodate the three addresses and the format is illustrated in Table 4.2. Because of the large number of bits required this format is not often used.

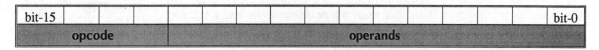

opcode	operand address	operand address	operand address

Table 4.2. *Three-address instruction format*

Two-address instruction

With this format, only two addresses are available in the instruction, so it is implicit that the result is to be stored in one of the operands (X or Y). This means that one of the original numbers is overwritten by the result. If only one instruction is used, then adding the contents of X and Y and placing the result in X is expressed symbolically as,

        ADD X,Y

The instruction word format is shown in Table 4.3. In order to place the result in Z (as in the first expression) and to preserve the original contents of X, a preceding instruction could be used to copy the contents of X to Z. Assuming that a MOVE instruction has this effect, then the following two expressions will effect the addition.

opcode	operand address	operand address

Table 4.3. *Two-address instruction format*

        MOVE Z,X
        ADD Z,Y

One-address instruction

It should be obvious that this format only allows an opcode to refer to one operand and that two assumptions regarding storage are implicit. Firstly, as with the two-address format, it must be assumed that the result is to be stored in Z. Secondly, if only one operand can be referred to, the addition process must use another storage area for the second operand. Generally, a CPU general-purpose register, called the accumulator, is used. The single-address instruction is used where there is only a single accumulator, so the instruction does not need to refer to the address of the accumulator; it is implicit. The instruction word format is shown in Table 4.4.

Table 4.4. *One-address instruction*

The processes needed to achieve the addition are described below.

- Copy the contents of one operand, X, into the accumulator. This operation uses a LOAD (accumulator) instruction.

- ADD the contents of operand Y, placing the result in the accumulator. At the time of the addition, the contents of operand Y are in the MBR, having been read from memory as part of the instruction. An ADD instruction usually has this effect.

- Copy the result from the accumulator into address Z using a STORE command.

An assembly language coding for the above process may be as follows:

```
LDA X        {copies the content of X, via the MBR into the}
             {accumulator}
ADD Y        {reads the contents of Y to the MBR, adds it to the}
             {accumulator and  leaves the result there}
STA Z        {copies the result from the accumulator into memory}
             {address Z, via the MBR}
```

One-and-a-half-address instruction

Where there is more than one accumulator, an instruction using the accumulator must indicate which one is to be used. Since the number of accumulators is generally small, the number of bits needed to refer to a single accumulator is usually less than the number needed for a memory location address. The processes for carrying out the example sum are the same as for the one-address format, except that a specified accumulator is used. Table 4.5 shows the instruction format.

Table 4.5. *One-and-a-half address format*

Zero-address instruction

This type of instruction is particularly popular with small machines because of its economy in size. Many microcomputer systems operate with a combination of one-address and zero-address instructions. A zero-address instruction does not specify any operands within it and relies on the use of a memory-based data structure called a *stack*, to provide the operands.

A stack consists of a group of adjacent memory locations, the contents of which are addressed by a *stack pointer*, a register that contains the address of the current top of stack. Values can only be added (*pushed*) to or removed (*popped*) from the top of the stack, which is indicated by the current position of the stack pointer. The value of the stack pointer is incremented or decremented when an item is pushed or popped. A value located below the top item on the stack (as indicated by the stack pointer) cannot be removed until any values above it have been removed.

Consider, for example, an ADD instruction which requires the addition of two operands, X and Y. The operands X and then Y are pushed onto the stack; Y is thus at the top of the stack and is the first one which can be removed. The ADD instruction causes the popping of Y and X from the stack; they are added and the sum is pushed onto the top of the stack.

Although this instruction format is extremely short, additional instructions are needed in order to transfer operands from memory to the stack and from the stack to memory; obviously these instructions need to be longer in order to allow specification of memory addresses. They are similar to single instruction words, except that operands are copied to and from the stack rather than to and from the accumulator.

Instruction format and memory size

Given a particular word length (the number of bit positions), single-address instructions can directly address (specify the actual memory address) a larger number of memory locations than one-and-a-half or multiple-address formats because all the address bits can be used for one address. Many computers allow a variable length instruction word so that the number of bits available for the address portion of the instruction can be increased, to allow a larger number of memory locations to be directly addressed. If, for example, there are 16 bits for the address, then the highest location which can be *directly* addressed is:

$$2^{16} - 1 = 65,535$$

Therefore, 65,536 locations can be addressed, numbered 0 to 65,535 (computer memory sizes are quoted in nK, K being 1024 and n being a variable) and this example illustrates a 64K memory, that is, 64×1024 which equals 65,536. Clearly, this is insufficient for modern computer systems and a number of approaches are used to extend addressable range.

By increasing the number of bits available for the address to, say 20, the number of locations which can be addressed is over a million, although in practice, not all memory words need to be addressed directly. For example, to enable the direct addressing of all locations in a 256K ($256 \times 1024 = 262,144$) memory requires the use of 18 bits ($2^{18} = 262,144$). There are addressing techniques to reduce the number of bits needed for a memory address and some of these are described later in the chapter. An increase in word size also allows an increase in the number of bits available for the opcode and the possibility of an increase in the size of the instruction set. It has to be said, however, that a recent development in computer architecture, namely that of the RISC (Reduced Instruction Set Computer) processor, is making this latter benefit somewhat less relevant.

Instruction set

The range of instructions available for any particular machine depends on the machines architecture, in terms of word length and the number and types of registers used. For this reason it is only possible to list some typical types of instruction (the names LOAD etc are not actual mnemonic opcodes) some of which were used in the earlier example:

- *Load* - copies the contents of a specified location into a register.

- *Add* - adds the contents of a specified memory location to the contents of a register.

- *Subtract* - subtracts the contents of a specified memory location from the contents of a register.

- *Store* - copies the contents of a register into a specified memory location.

- *Branch* - switches control to another instruction address other than the next in sequence.

- *Register-register* - moves contents from one register to another.

- *Shift* - moves bits in a memory location to the left or to the right for arithmetic purposes or for pattern manipulation.

- *Input/output* - effects data transfers between peripherals and memory.

- *Logical operations* (AND, OR, NOT, NAND and so on) which combine the contents of a register and a specified memory location or register. These operations are described in Chapter 5 on Computer Logic. The first four instruction types in this list have already been explained in the earlier addition example, so the following sections deal with those remaining.

Branch instruction

These instructions cause the program to divert from the sequence which is dictated by that of contiguous memory locations containing program instructions. A branch instruction causes the value of the Program Counter (PC) to be altered, to direct the next instruction to be fetched from a location which is not physically adjacent to the current instruction. A branch may be *conditional* (dependent on some condition) or *unconditional*. In the latter case, the branch is always made, whereas in the former, the branch only occurs if a specified condition occurs. The conditions tested usually include tests on CPU register contents for zero, non-zero, negative and positive number values. The branch or jump may be to a specified address or simply to skip the next instruction (or several instructions). In either case the program counter must be altered accordingly to change its contents to the address specified by the branch instruction. Branching can be used to repeat a sequence of instructions in a *loop*. Usually this is conditional to avoid an infinite program iteration.

Subroutine or subprogram

As explained in the previous paragraph a branch instruction is used to jump or skip to a specified instruction address, so that the program sequence may continue from that address. On the other hand if the branch is to a subroutine, the original sequence can be restored after its execution. This requires a special form of branch instruction. It may be necessary, for example, to carry out a particular sequence of calculations at different points in a program. Instead of coding the instructions

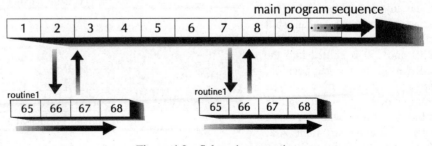

Figure 4.3. *Subroutine operation*

at each point where they are required, the coding can be written as a subroutine. Whenever a subroutine is used or *called*, there must be a mechanism for returning control to the original program sequence. One method is to save the current contents of the PC in the first location of the subroutine before the branch to the subroutine is made. Upon completion of the subroutine the contents of the first location can be loaded into the PC and control returned to the calling program. The process of branching to a subroutine and then returning to continue the instruction sequence is illustrated in Figure 4.3.

Alternatively, the return address may be placed on a *stack* (a memory facility described earlier in this chapter) and copied back into the PC to allow a resumption of the normal program sequence. The stack is particularly useful where subroutines are nested, which means that a subroutine may be called from within another subroutine. The return addresses are placed onto the stack and removed in reverse order so that the last return address is the first to be removed. The technique is described in detail in Chapter 32 on Data Structures. Subroutines called in this way are referred to as *clos*ed, but where a subroutine is inserted, as and when required, as part of the main program, it is referred to as *open*.

Register-register instruction

As the name suggests, instructions of this type are used to transfer the contents of one register to another. Its format is similar to that of the two-address instruction described in the previous section, and is illustrated in Table 4.6. Although operands to address memory are

| opcode | reg 1 | reg 2 |

Table 4.6. *Register-register instruction*

not used, the instruction allows two operands to address the registers involved. The number of registers available will tend to be small, perhaps two or three, so that a single byte may be sufficient to contain the two operands. In an 8-bit machine, such instructions may be two bytes long, one for the opcode and one for the two register addresses. Data transfers between registers within the CPU are carried out through a communications system which is a subdivision of the computer systems *architecture*.

Shift instruction

| opcode | register no | no. of shifts |

Table 4.7. *Shift instruction format*

A shift operation moves the bits in a register to new positions in the register, either to the left or to the right and may be *logical* or *arithmetic*. A shift instruction format is given in Table 4.7.

Logical shift

Logical shifts are used for pattern manipulation of data and are not concerned with arithmetic operations. Examples of left and right logical shifts are provided in the adjacent tables. Table 4.8 shows an example logical shift left where a 0 is lost from the MSB and a 0 is shifted into the LSB (to fill the vacated position, formerly occupied by a 1). The example of a logical shift right in Table 4.9 starts with the same register contents as Table 4.8. This time the right shift of 1 moves each bit, one position to

bit-	5	4	3	2	1	0
initial contents of register	0	0	1	1	0	1
shift contents 1 place to the LEFT	0	1	1	0	1	0
0 dropped from MSB			0 moved into LSB			

Table 4.8. *Logical shift left of 1*

bit-	5	4	3	2	1	0
initial contents of register	0	0	1	1	0	1
shift contents 1 place to the RIGHT	0	1	1	0	1	0
0 moved into MSB			1 dropped from LSB			

Table 4.9. *Logical shift right of 1*

the right, causing the loss of a 1 from the LSB and the insertion of a 0 to fill the vacated MSB position. Another type of logical shift, referred to as *rotational* or *cyclic*, involves rotation of bits in a register or location.

Rotational logical shift

A rotational shift can be either to the right or to the left, as shown in the next two tables. Table 4.10 shows that for a right shift the 1 in the LSB position is moved to the MSB position, as each bit moves one place to the right.

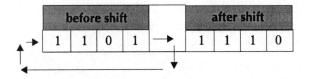

Table 4.10. *Rotational shift right of 1*

In the left shift example in Table 4.11, the 1 in the MSB position is moved to the LSB position as each bit moves one place to the left.

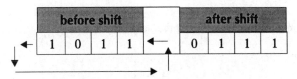

Table 4.11. *Rotational shift left of 1*

Arithmetic shift

Left and right shift operations are used for multiply and divide operations but arithmetic meaning must be maintained. A left shift of one doubles the number and a right shift of one halves the number. Computer multiplication can be carried out through a sequence of additions and shifts, and division by a sequence of subtractions and shifts. Some examples of arithmetic shifts using two's complement notation are provided in the adjacent tables. Table 4.12 illustrates an arithmetic shift left of 1 where zeros are inserted into the LSB position. Note that in the last example in Table 4.12, the sign has been changed from positive to negative by the shift left operation. In these circumstances an overflow signal would be set. Table 4.13 shows two shift right examples. In the second example, a 1 is shifted into the sign bit position to maintain the integrity of the sign.

before shift						after shift				
sign						sign				
0	0	1	1	+3		0	1	1	0	+6
1	1	0	0	4		1	0	0	0	8
1	1	1	0	2		1	1	0	0	4
0	1	1	0	+6		1	1	0	0	4
sign changed to negative, indicating overflow										

Table 4.12. *Arithmetic shift left examples*

before shift						after shift				
sign						sign				
0	1	1	0	+6		0	0	1	1	+3
1	1	0	0	4		1	1	1	0	2

Table 4.13. *Arithmetic shift right examples*

Register transfer language (RTL)

Processor architecture can be described diagrammatically, but RTL is used to define the ways in which data move within it. More particularly, RTL identifies the effects of an instruction by specifying the sequence of data transfers between registers and any arithmetic/logical operations needed for its execution.

The RTL examples used in this section assume knowledge of the fetch-execute cycle and the functions of each of the registers referred to earlier. RTL can be as simple or as complex as is necessary to describe the data transfers within any particular system, but for the purposes of understanding its general function, a number of *primitive operations* are identified.

The *fetch-execute* cycle can be described in RTL as follows:

Fetch phase

        PC ⇨ MAR

specifies that the contents of the program counter (PC) must be copied into the memory address register (MAR), thus ensuring that the next memory word to be fetched is a program instruction;

        PC ⇨ PC + 1

describes the incrementation of the PC to point to the next instruction;

        M [MAR] ⇨ MBR

indicates that the contents of the memory (M) location identified by the MAR are to be copied into the memory buffer register (MBR);

        MBR ⇨ CIR

shows that the instruction is then copied from the MBR into the current instruction register (CIR).

The fetching of any instruction follows this pattern, but the point at which the PC value is changed may vary, provided it occurs after its previous value has been copied to the MAR.

After the fetch phase an instruction must be *decoded* and *executed* and the nature of the instruction will determine the register transfers which are required. The first example which follows relates to a structure which uses *single address* instructions. Later, an example for *two address* instructions is provided.

Single Address Instructions

As is explained earlier, machines using this type of instruction must make use of an accumulator (ACC) register to perform arithmetic and logic operations and the following addition example illustrates this point; as already explained the fetch phase is common to all instructions.

fetch

```
                                comments
        PC ⇨ MAR            {instruction address to MAR}
        M [MAR] ⇨ MBR       {copy instruction to MBR}
```

```
        PC ⇨ PC + 1           {increment PC to next instruction}
        MBR ⇨ CIR             {copy instruction to CIR}
```

decode and thus identify the instruction

execute the instruction

```
                                comments
        CIR<adr> ⇨ MAR         {the <adr> indicates the operand portion of the
                               instruction word and this is copied to the MAR}
        M [MAR] ⇨ MBR          {read the operand value which is to be added to
                               the contents of the ACC}
        ACC + MBR ⇨ ACC        {add operand value to contents of ACC and store in
                               the ACC}
```

A complete addition process may involve the following operations (expressed in a hypothetical assembly code), assuming that two values are to be summed, that their respective memory addresses are A and B and that the result is to be stored in location C.

```
        LDA A                 {copy contents of location A into the ACC}
        ADD B                 {add the contents of B to those of the ACC,
                               storing the result there}
        STA C                 {copy contents of ACC to location C}
```

Remembering that each instruction executed is preceded by the fetch and decode phases detailed previously, it can be described in RTL thus:

execute LDA A

```
                                comments
        CIR<adr>A ⇨ MAR       {specifies the operand A to be read}
        M [MAR] ⇨ MBR         {operand A copied to MBR}
        MBR ⇨ ACC             {operand A copied to ACC}
```

execute ADD B

```
                                comments
        CIR<adr>B ⇨ MAR       {specifies second operand to be read}
        M [MAR] ⇨ MBR         {operand B copied to MBR}
        ACC + MBR ⇨ ACC       {add operand B to ACC giving result}
```

execute STA C

```
                                comments
        CIR<adr>C ⇨ MAR       {specifies location C as memory location to store
                               result}
        ACC ⇨ MBR             {copy contents of ACC to MBR}
        MBR ⇨ M [MAR]         {copy result from ACC to memory location C}
```

Two address instructions

As explained earlier, with two addresses available in the instruction it is implicit that the result of an operation is to be stored in one of the operands, thus overwriting its original contents. For example,

```
ADD A, B
```

would sum the contents of operand addresses A and B, and depending on the architecture, place the result in either the first or second named address.

The addition example which follows is based on the instruction set used in Chapter 31 on Assembly Language Programming. It differs from the single address addition process described earlier, not only in the number of addresses held within the instruction word, but also in the fact that the addresses refer to registers rather than memory locations. This means that the operands have to be moved from memory to their respective *registers* before the operation can be effected.

Thus,

```
LDW R1, A        {load word from memory address A into register R1}
LDW R2, B        {load word from memory address B into register R2}
ADD R1, R2       {add contents of R1 and R2, place result in R1}
STW R1, C        {store result from R1 into memory address C}
```

loads the contents of memory location with the *symbolic* address A into a register R1 and similarly, the contents of B into R2. The contents of R1 and R2 are added and the result is placed in R1, the *destination* register. The store instruction completes the process by copying the result from R1 to memory location C.

The data transfers for this operation can be specified in RTL as follows. As before, it is assumed that each instruction is preceded by the fetch and decode phases.

execute LDW R1, A

```
                               comments
    CIR <adr>A ⇨ MAR    {specifies operand A to be read}
    M [MAR] ⇨ MBR       {operand A copied to MBR}
    MBR ⇨ R1            {operand A copied to register R1}
```

execute LDW R2, B

```
                               comments
    CIR <adr>B ⇨ MAR    {specifies operand B to be read}
    M [MAR] ⇨ MBR       {operand B copied to MBR}
    MBR ⇨ R2            {operand B copied to register R2}
```

execute ADD R1, R2

```
                               comments
    R1 + R2 ⇨ R1        {contents of R1, R2 added and result placed in
                        destination register R1}
```

execute STW R1, C

```
                               comments
    CIR <adr>C ⇨ MAR    {next memory write is to address C}
    R1 ⇨ MBR            {copy contents of R1 to MBR}
    MBR ⇨ M [MAR]       (contents of MBR to memory address C, as
                         indicated by current value of MAR}
```

Input/output instructions

Input/output (I/O) instructions are concerned with the transfer of data between peripherals and memory or between peripherals and registers in the CPU. Chapter 14 on Input/Output Control deals with this topic.

Memory addressing methods

The physical memory addresses ultimately used by the hardware are the *absolute* addresses. As explained earlier, addressing memory locations directly restricts the size of usable memory and for this reason a computers instruction set will normally include facilities for addressing locations beyond those directly addressable with a given address length.

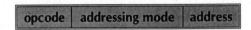

Table 4.14. *Instruction with addressing mode*

Thus, absolute addresses may be referenced in a variety of ways and the addressing mode used is indicated in the operand of an instruction word. The format of an instruction word may be as shown in Table 4.14.

The following addressing modes are common to most machines:

- *immediate*;

- *indirect*;

- *relative*;

- *indexed.*

Immediate addressing

With this method, the operand to be accessed by the instruction is stored in the instruction word or in the word immediately following it in memory. In the former case, the operand would be fetched with the instruction and no separate memory read would then be necessary. In the latter case, an ADD instruction which employed this method of addressing would indicate that the operand is to be found immediately after the opcode in memory. In a byte organized machine, the first byte would contain the opcode, the execution of which would involve the fetching of the next byte in memory which contained the required operand. Computers based on the Intel 8080 or Motorola 6800 processor series use this latter method for immediate addressing. The Intel 8080 provides the opcode ADI (add immediate) as part of its instruction set. Immediate addressing is useful when small constants or literals are required in a program, for example, a set value of 3 to be subtracted from the contents of a register at some stage in the program. It is inappropriate to use this method if there is any need for the value to be changed as this would require changing the program coding.

Direct Addressing

As the name suggests, this addressing mode specifies the actual or effective memory address containing the required operand, in the address field of the instruction word. The addressed memory location specified must be accessed to obtain the operand.

Indirect addressing

With this method, the location address in the instruction word does not contain the operand. Instead, it contains the address of another location which itself contains the address of the data item. Thus, an indirect address is, in effect, a pointer to the address containing the operand. For example, IAD 156 (indirect add) indicates that the address 156 contains the address of the required operand.

If specific indirect addressing instructions are not provided, an instruction word may contain a flag bit to indicate whether or not an operand is an indirect or direct address; the flag bit may be set to 1 if the address is indirect and to 0 if it is direct. In this way, an LDA (load accumulator) instruction is able to refer to a direct or indirect address by the appropriate setting of the flag bit. Figure 4.4 illustrates the principle of indirect addressing.

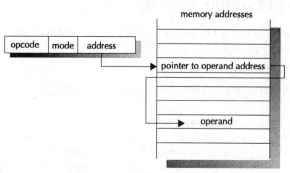

Figure 4.4. *Indirect addressing*

Indirect addressing is generally slower in execution than direct addressing as an extra *memory cycle* is needed each time the actual address is deferred. Indirect addressing is also known as *deferred* addressing and if the address is deferred more than once it is known as a *multi-level* address.

Relative addressing

With relative addressing, the instruction word contains an *offset* address which indicates the location of the operand relative to the position of the instruction in memory (sometimes known as *self-relative* addressing). Thus, if an instruction is stored in address N and the offset is 5, then the operand is in address N + 5. It is a useful technique for branching a program, in which case the offset address will indicate the relative address of the next instruction to be fetched, rather than a data item.

The program counter (PC) is used to calculate the effective address in that it contains the address of the current instruction. By adding the offset to the PC, the address is determined. The instruction set usually contains instructions which allow such program jumps to be made.

Absolute addresses may also be determined as being relative to a *base* address and as is explained in the chapter on Operating Systems, by alteration of this base address, programs can be *relocated* rather than be tied to particular absolute addresses each time they are loaded. Multi-programming or multi-tasking techniques demand that programs are relocatable.

Indexed Addressing

With this method, the effective address is calculated by the addition of an index value to the address given in the instruction. The index value is usually stored in either a general-purpose CPU register or a special *index* register.

The method can be employed by a programmer when an ordered block of data is to be accessed and each data item is to be processed in the same way. If the value of the index is N and the address in the instruction is X, then the effective address for an operand is N + X. The register is set to an initial value and incremented as the instructions step through the memory locations. A branch instruction is used to create a program loop to repeat the same set of instructions needed for each item of data in the block.

Exercises

1. How does the CPU differentiate between a *data word* and an *instruction word*?

2. (i) Which registers are identified by the initials: PC; MBR; MAR; CIR?

   (ii) Briefly explain the function of each of these registers in the *fetch-execute cycle*.

3. Use register transfer language (RTL) to describe the *fetch* and *execute* stages for the following instructions:

   LDA F

   ADD G

   STA H

4. (i) If an addition is to be expressed as ADD A, B, C and the values in A and B are to be preserved, show how the process would be completed using a:

   a. three address instruction;

   b. two address instruction;

   c. three address instruction.

   (ii) Show the instructions if the result of the addition could be placed in either A or B.

5. (i) What is meant by the term *absolute* address?

   (ii) Describe the difference between *direct* and *indirect* addressing.

   (iii) What is the main benefit of indirect addressing?

6. What is an *instruction set*?

7. Name two kinds of *branch* instruction.

8. When a *subprogram* is called, what methods may be used to return program control to the normal sequence?

9. An 8-bit word contains the binary pattern 10110010. How does the pattern alter after:

    (i)   a logical left shift of 1 bit;

    (ii)   a logical left shift of 2 bits;

    (iii)   a logical right shift of 3 bits;

    (iv)   a rotational right shift of 2 bits;

    (v)   a rotational left shift of 3 bits?

10. An 8-bit word contains the binary pattern 10110010. If the pattern is interpreted as a number in two's complement form, what would the denary value be after an arithmetic right shift of 2 bits?

Chapter 5
Computer Logic

In Chapter 2 it is explained that data and instructions in a digital computer are represented by the binary numbering system. Internal registers and locations within the memory of the computer must be able to remember data and instructions as sequences of binary digits. The ALU (Arithmetic and Logic Unit) must be able to perform arithmetic on numbers held in this form, and the decoding circuitry of the Control Unit must be able to recognize and interpret program instructions represented by binary numbers. All of these functions, and many more, are performed by logic circuits. Computer logic is based on a branch of mathematical logic called Boolean Algebra (named after the English mathematician George Boole) which allows the symbolic manipulation of logical variables in a manner very similar to the manipulation of unknowns in an ordinary algebraic expression of the form

$$x.(y+z) \text{ or } x.y + x.z$$

Just as laws are needed for ordinary algebraic expressions, fundamental laws exist for the manipulation of Boolean expressions. By means of these laws, complex logical expressions, representing logic circuits, can be analysed or designed. This chapter introduces the foundations of Boolean Algebra, its relevance to computer circuitry, and the processes by which such circuitry may be designed and analysed. The chapter concludes with a brief discussion of the evolution of integrated circuits.

Boolean variables

A Boolean variable has one of two values, normally represented by 1 and 0. In terms of computer circuitry, a Boolean variable represents a voltage on a line which may be an input to a logic circuit or an output from a logic circuit. For instance, a value of 1 might represent five volts and a value of 0, zero volts. Boolean variables are denoted by letters of the alphabet. Thus the variables X, Y, Z, P, Q, R are each able to represent a value of 1 or 0.

Gates

The term gate is used to describe the members of a set of basic electronic components which, when combined with each other, are able to perform complex logical and arithmetic operations. These are the types of operations associated with the ALU of the CPU. For present purposes, the physical construction of the gates is of no direct concern, and the discussion will be restricted to their functions only.

The OR gate

Gates have one or more inputs but only a single output. The nature of the gate determines what the output should be, given the current inputs. For example, the OR gate could be defined as in Table 5.1 which shows that

- the output is 1 if the X or Y input is 1.

X and Y are Boolean variables capable at any time of having the value 1 or 0. Thus at any instant X could have a value of 0 and Y a value of 1, or X could have a value of 1 and Y could have a value of 1; there are four such combinations of the values of X and Y as shown in Table 5.1. With an OR gate, when there is at least one 1 in the input variables, the output is 1. The third column of the table shows the output produced by each combination of the two inputs. The complete table is known as a *truth table* and completely defines the operation of the OR gate for every combination of inputs. As will be shown throughout this chapter, truth tables are extremely useful for describing logic circuits. Symbolically, the combination of X and Y using an OR gate is written

X	Y	X OR Y
0	0	0
0	1	1
1	0	1
1	1	1

Table 5.1. *Truth table for OR gate*

$$X \text{ OR } Y \text{ or } X + Y \text{ (read as X or Y)}$$

Both forms mean that X and Y are inputs to an OR gate. The second form is that required for Boolean Algebra and the + is known as the OR operator. The symbol used when drawing an OR gate in a logic circuit is shown in Figure 5.1.

Figure 5.1. *Logic circuit for OR gate.*

Gates are the physical realizations of simple Boolean expressions. The design of logic circuits is performed symbolically using Boolean Algebra. A Boolean algebraic expression can then be converted very easily into a logic circuit consisting of combinations of gates.

The OR gate is only one of several which are used to produce logic circuits. The other gates of interest are AND, NOT, XOR, NAND and NOR. The first two, in conjunction with the OR gate, are of the greatest importance since these three are directly related to the Boolean operators used in Boolean Algebra.

The AND gate

The AND gate is defined by the truth table shown in Table 5.2, which shows that

X	Y	X AND Y
0	0	0
0	1	0
1	0	0
1	1	1

Table 5.2. *Truth table for AND gate*

- the output is 1 when the X input AND the Y input are 1s.

This time, the gate only produces an output of 1 when both inputs are 1s. The Boolean operator equivalent to the AND gate is the AND operator '.', and is written

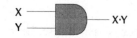

Figure 5.2. *AND gate symbol*

$$X.Y \text{ (read as X and Y)}$$

The symbol for the AND gate is shown in Figure 5.2.

The NOT gate

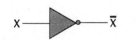

Figure 5.3. *NOT gate symbol*

X	NOT X
0	1
1	0

The third important gate is the NOT gate which has the truth table shown in Table 5.3. This gate only has a single input which is inverted at the output. A NOT gate is often called an inverter for this reason and is written $\overline{X}$ or $\sim X$ in Boolean expressions. The symbol for a NOT gate is shown in Figure 5.3.

Table 5.3. *Truth table for NOT gate*

Example of a useful logic circuit

At this point it is worth considering an example of a widely used logic circuit to illustrate the relevance of this chapter. The circuit, which is called a *half adder*, performs the addition of two binary digits to give a sum term, S and a carry term, C, both being Boolean variables. The inputs to the circuit are X and Y representing the two binary digits to be added. The rules for binary addition are shown in Table 5.4 and the equivalent truth table is shown in Table 5.5.

0 + 0 = 0 carry 0 (00)	
0 + 1 = 1 carry 0 (01)	
1 + 0 = 1 carry 0 (01)	
1 + 1 = 0 carry 1 (10)	

Table 5.4. *Rules of binary addition*

X	Y	S	C
0	0	0	0
0	1	1	0
1	0	1	0
1	1	0	1

Table 5.5. *Truth table for binary addition*

The requirement is for a combination of AND, OR and NOT gates to give two separate outputs for (S)um and (C)arry given any two binary digits represented by X and Y. The circuit is shown in Figure 5.4 and the equivalent Boolean expressions for S and C are

$$S = X.\overline{Y} + \overline{X}.Y$$
$$C = X.Y$$

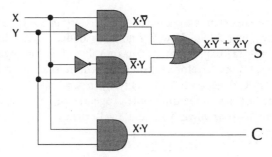

Figure 5.4. *Half adder circuit*

To prove that the circuit actually works a truth table is constructed (Table 5.6) showing the output from every component in the circuit, from stage to stage, given the inputs to that stage.

X	Y	$\overline{X}$	$\overline{Y}$	X.$\overline{Y}$	$\overline{X}$.Y	X.$\overline{Y}$+$\overline{X}$.Y	X.Y
						(S)	(C)
0	0	1	1	0	0	0	0
0	1	1	0	0	1	1	0
1	0	0	1	1	0	1	0
1	1	0	0	0	0	0	1

Table 5.6. *Truth table for half adder circuit*

Thus if X=0 and Y=0, $\overline{Y}$=1 and using the truth table for the AND gate (Table 5.2), X.$\overline{Y}$ = 0.1 = 0 and $\overline{X}$.Y = 1.0 = 0. The rightmost OR gate in Figure 5.4 has inputs X.$\overline{Y}$ and $\overline{X}$.Y, that is, 0 and 0 , and using the truth table for the OR gate (Table 5.1), it can be seen that this results in an output of 0 for S. Similarly, if X=0 and Y=0, the truth table for the AND gate shows that X.Y=0, that is C=0 for this combination of inputs.

Following this type of argument for the remaining rows in the truth table, it can be seen that the circuit produces exactly the right output for each combination of inputs to perform binary addition on the input bits. Thus a combination of a few elementary components has produced a most important circuit. A truth table allowed the operation of the circuit to be confirmed. Later it will be shown how the Boolean expressions representing the circuit can be derived directly from the first truth table defining the required operation of the circuit.

Deriving boolean expressions from truth tables

Suppose that it is required to produce a suitable logic circuit from the following circuit specification:

- A circuit has two binary inputs, X and Y. The output from the circuit is 1 when the two inputs are the same; otherwise the output is 0.

X	Y	OUTPUT
0	0	1
0	1	0
1	0	0
1	1	1

Table 5.7.

The first step is to produce a truth table to define the circuit fully and this is shown in Table 5.7. Each possible combination of X and Y has been listed. Where X and Y are the same, OUTPUT has been assigned a value of 1; where X and Y are different, OUTPUT has been assigned a value of 0.

The next step is to define, for each entry in the OUTPUT column having a value of 1, a Boolean expression involving X and Y which uniquely defines that value. So for the first row in Table 5.7, where X=0 and Y=0, the expression $\overline{X}.\overline{Y}$ has a value of 1; for any other combination of X and Y it has a value of 0. The expression therefore satisfies the requirement of uniquely defining this combination of values. The expression X.Y has a value of 1 only when X=1 and Y=1, otherwise it has a value of 0, and so it uniquely defines the last row in the truth table. Together the expressions $\overline{X}.\overline{Y}$ and X.Y will produce an output of 1 when X=0 and Y=0 or when X=1 and Y=1. Hence

$$\text{OUTPUT} = \overline{X}.\overline{Y} + X.Y$$

The truth table (Table 5.8) confirms this result and the circuit is shown in Figure 5.5.

X	Y	$\overline{X}$	$\overline{Y}$	$\overline{X}.\overline{Y}$	X.Y	$\overline{X}.\overline{Y}+X.Y$
0	0	1	1	1	0	1
0	1	1	0	0	0	0
1	0	0	1	0	0	0
1	1	0	0	0	1	1

Table 5.8.

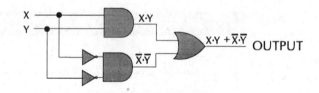

Figure 5.5.

The process of converting a truth table to a Boolean expression is summarized as follows:

(a) Consider only the rows of the truth table for which the output is to be 1.

(b) Take each of these rows in turn and write alongside the row an expression containing the input variables connected by the AND operator. If the value of an input variable is 0 then it will appear inverted in the expression.

(c) Combine these expressions using the OR operator.

To provide another illustration of the process suppose that three binary signals, A, B and C, are required to represent a number in the range 0 to 4. The variable A represents the most significant digit of the binary number ABC, B is the next significant digit, and C is the least significant digit. A circuit is required to detect an illegal combination (that is the numbers 5 to 7) by producing an output of 1. The truth table is shown in Table 5.9. Therefore, OUTPUT $=A.\bar{B}.C + A.B.\bar{C} + A.B.C$, and the required circuit is shown in Figure 5.6.

A	B	C		OUTPUT	
0	0	0	(0)	0	
0	0	1	(1)	0	
0	1	0	(2)	0	
0	1	1	(3)	0	
1	0	0	(4)	0	
1	0	1	(5)	1	A.$\bar{B}$.C
1	1	0	(6)	1	A.B.$\bar{C}$
1	1	1	(7)	1	A.B.C

Table 5.9.

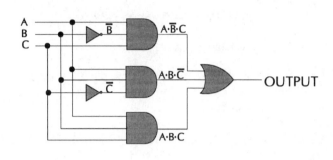

Figure 5.6.

As an exercise, use a truth table to prove that the Boolean expression above does indeed produce the required outputs.

The laws of Boolean algebra

Though the circuit above does perform as specified, it is very inefficient; it uses more gates than are absolutely necessary to produce the required outputs. In fact rather than six gates, only two are necessary because, as the truth tables in Tables 5.10 and 5.11 show,

$$A.\bar{B}.C + A.B.\bar{C} + A.B.C = A.(B + C)$$

A	B	C	$\bar{B}$	$\bar{C}$	A.$\bar{B}$.C	A.B.$\bar{C}$	A.B.C	(A.$\bar{B}$.C + A.B.$\bar{C}$ + A.B.C)
0	0	0	1	1	0	0	0	0
0	0	1	1	0	0	0	0	0
0	1	0	0	1	0	0	0	0
0	1	1	0	0	0	0	0	0
1	0	0	1	1	0	0	0	0
1	0	1	1	0	1	0	0	1
1	1	0	0	1	0	1	0	1
1	1	1	0	0	0	0	1	1
								= OUTPUT

Table 5.10.

A	B	C	A.(B + C)
0	0	0	0
0	0	1	0
0	1	0	0
0	1	1	0
1	0	0	0
1	0	1	1
1	1	0	0
1	1	1	0
			= OUTPUT

Table 5.11.

The circuit for the simplified expression is shown in Figure 5.7.

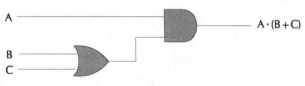

Figure 5.7.

The laws of Boolean Algebra enable Boolean expressions such as that in the example to be transformed and, where possible, simplified. The most useful of these laws are as follow:

1. Commutative laws.

   (a) $X+Y=Y+X$; (b) $X.Y=Y.X$

2. Associative laws.

   (a) $X+(Y+Z) = (X+Y)+Z$; (b) $X.(Y.Z) = (X.Y).Z$

3. Distributive laws.

   (a) $X.(Y+Z) = X.Y + X.Z$; (b) $X + Y.Z = (X+Y).(X+Z)$

4. De Morgans laws.

   (a) $\overline{(X + Y)} = \overline{X}.\overline{Y}$; (b) $\overline{(X.Y)} = \overline{X} + \overline{Y}$

5. Laws of absorption.

   (a) $X + X.Y = X$; (b) $X.(X + Y) = X$

6. Laws of tautology.

   (a) $X + X = X$; (b) $X.X = X$

7. Law of complementation.

   $\overline{\overline{X}} = X$

8. Other useful identities.

   (a) $X + \overline{X} = 1$; (b) $X.\overline{X} = 0$

   (c) $X + 1 = 1$; (d) $X.1 = X$

   (e) $X + 0 = X$; (f) $X.0 = 0$

Notice that with each of the first six laws, there is a connection between (a) and (b). Given one of these rules, the other may be derived by replacing the + operator with the . operator or vice-versa. Thus if it is known that $X + X.Y = X$, then the dual of the rule, that $X.(X+Y)$, is also true. All identities in Boolean algebra have this useful property.

To illustrate the use of these laws in the simplification of Boolean expressions, consider the expression derived earlier:

$$A.\overline{B}.C + A.B.\overline{C} + A.B.C$$

Simplification of this expression could proceed as follows:

(i) $A.\overline{B}.C + A.B.\overline{C} + A.B.C = A.\overline{B}.C + (A.B.\overline{C} + A.B.C)$

Rule 1 allows us to deal with terms in any order.

(ii)   Considering the bracketed pair of terms,

$$A.B.\overline{C} + A.B.C = A.B.(\overline{C} + C) \text{ by rule 3(a)}$$

Here A.B is treated as if it were a single variable, and the expression is therefore of the form

$$X.\overline{C} + X.C = X.(\overline{C} + C) \text{ where X represents A.B}$$

(iii)   Rule 8(a) shows that $\overline{C} + C = 1$, so that

$$A.B.(\overline{C} + C) = A.B.1$$

and by rule 8(d),

$$A.B.1 = A.B$$

(iv)   Hence,

$$A.\overline{B}.C + (A.B.\overline{C} + A.B.C) = A.\overline{B}.C + A.B$$

(v)   Again using rule 3(a),

$$A.\overline{B}.C + A.B = A.(\overline{B}.C + B)$$

This is of the form

$$X.Y + X.Z = X.(Y + Z)$$

(vi)   Now consider the term $\overline{B}.C + B$.

Using rule 1(a), this can be rewritten $B + \overline{B}.C$, and now using rule 3(b),

$$B + \overline{B}.C = (B + \overline{B}).(B + C)$$

As in step (iii), $(B + \overline{B}) = 1$ and $1.(B+C) = (B+C)$.

Hence $B + \overline{B}.C = (B + C)$ and therefore

$$A.(B + \overline{B}.C) = A.(B+C)$$

Thus the original expression has been considerably simplified and confirms the identity stated earlier.

Fortunately, the process of simplifying expressions involving AND terms separated by OR operators can be performed in a much simpler way using the Karnaugh Map method. This method, as well as being quicker and less prone to error, is also more likely to result in the best simplification possible, particularly where four variables are involved. In certain cases, however, a knowledge of the laws of Boolean algebra are required. Examples of such instances will be provided later.

Karnaugh maps

A Karnaugh map consists of a two-dimensional grid which is used to represent a Boolean expression in such a way that it can be simplified with great ease. For example, consider the expression

$$\overline{X}.Y + X.\overline{Y} + X.Y$$

This expression involves two Boolean variables, X and Y. The number of different terms possible with two variable is four, and therefore the Karnaugh map for expressions involving two variables is a 2×2 grid (Figure 5.8).

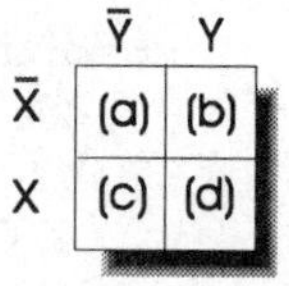

Figure 5.8.

Each cell in the grid may be regarded as having a co-ordinate formed from a combination of X and Y. Thus the cell labelled (a) has the co-ordinate $\overline{X}.\overline{Y}$, (b) has the co-ordinate $\overline{X}.Y$, (c) has the co-ordinate $X.\overline{Y}$, and (d) has the co-ordinate $X.Y$. When entered onto the map, the expression quoted above translates to the map in Figure 5.9.

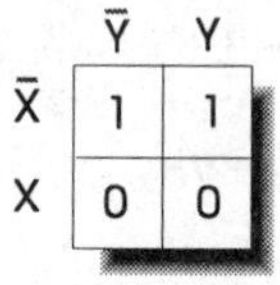

Each 1 on the map indicates the presence of the term corresponding to its cell co-ordinate in the expression, and each 0 indicates its absence. Using a further example, the expression $\overline{X}.Y + \overline{X}.\overline{Y}$ translates to the map shown in Figure 5.10.

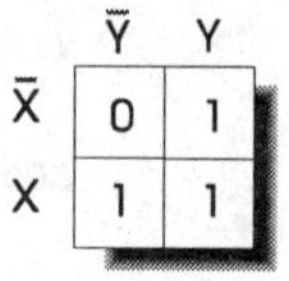

Figure 5.9   **Figure 5.10.**

Having drawn the appropriate Karnaugh map, the next stage is to attempt to identify a simplified expression. The procedure is as follows:

(i)   Identify all pairs of adjacent 1s on the map (horizontally and vertically).

(ii)   Draw loops around each pair.

(iii)   Attempt to include every 1 on the map in at least one loop; it is allowable to have the same 1 in two different loops.

(iv)   The aim is to include each 1 in at least one loop, but using as few loops as possible.

Thus the expression $\overline{X}.Y + X.\overline{Y} + X.Y$ becomes the map shown in Figure 5.11.

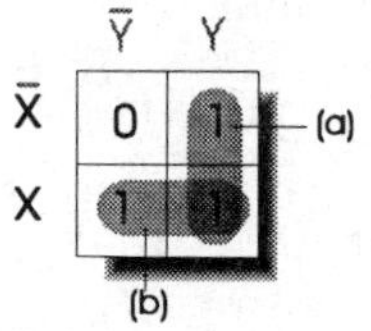

(v)   Take each loop in turn and write down the term represented: the loop labelled (a) in Figure 5.11 spans both X and $\overline{X}$, but Y remains constant. The loop is therefore given the value Y. In the loop labelled (b), both Y co-ordinates are covered but X remains constant. This loop has the value X.

Figure 5.11.

(vi)   The loop values are ORed together. In the example, the expression is therefore equivalent to $X + Y$.

Karnaugh maps take advantage of a small number of the laws of Boolean algebra. The Distributive Law allows terms with common variables to be grouped together:

$$X.\overline{Y} + X.Y = X.(\overline{Y} + Y) \text{ (see rule 3(a))}$$

Another law, 8(a), gives the identity $\overline{Y} + Y = 1$.

And finally, law 8(d) says that $X.1 = X$.

The Karnaugh map allows this sequence of applications of laws to be performed in a single step:

the loop (b) representing $X.\overline{Y} + X.Y$ becomes X.

1s may be included in more than one loop because of the Law of Tautology (Tautology is saying the same thing twice). Thus $X + X = X$, and conversely, $X = X + X$. In other words, any term in an expression may be duplicated as many times as desired without affecting the value of the expression. So, given the expression

$$\overline{X}.Y + X.\overline{Y} + X.Y,$$

the term X.Y may be duplicated to give the equivalent expression

$$\overline{X}.Y + X.Y + X.\overline{Y} + X.Y,$$

where loop (a) is $\overline{X}.Y + X.Y$, and loop (b) is $X.\overline{Y} + X.Y$.

As a further example, the expression

$$\overline{X}.\overline{Y} + \overline{X}.Y + X.Y$$

gives the map in Figure 5.12 and the equivalent expression is $\overline{X} + Y$.

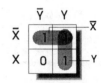

Figure 5.12.

Karnaugh maps for three variables

Expressions containing three variables can contain up to eight terms. The 3-variable map is drawn as shown in Figure 5.13.

This time a co-ordinate pair comprises an $\overline{X}$ variable and a YZ term. For example, the cell (a) represents the term $\overline{X}.\overline{Y}.Z$, and (b) represents X.Y.Z.

The map in Figure 5.14 represents the expression $X.\overline{Y}.Z + X.Y.\overline{Z} + X.Y.Z$.

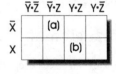

Figure 5.13.

In loop (a), X and Z are common factors, but Y changes ($\overline{Y}.Z + Y.Z$). The loop has the value X.Z. In loop (b), X and Y are constant but Z changes (Y.Z + Y.$\overline{Z}$). Thus (b) has value X.Y. The expression therefore simplifies to

$$X.Y + X.Z$$

and a further application of law 3(a) gives the final solution

$$X.\overline{Y}.Z + X.Y.\overline{Z} + X.Y.Z = X.(Y + Z)$$

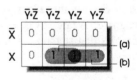

Figure 5.14.

With a 3-variable map, as well as looping pairs of 1s, it is necessary to look for groups of four 1s. For example, the map shown in Figure 5.15 could represent the expression

$$X.Y.Z + \overline{X}.\overline{Y}.Z + \overline{X}.Y.Z + X.\overline{Y}.Z$$

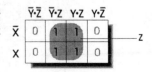

Figure 5.15.

The single loop spans the X co-ordinate completely, and so X can be removed from the simplified expression. In the YZ terms spanned, Y changes and Z is constant. The simplified expression is merely Z.

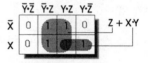

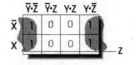

Figure 5.16.   **Figure 5.17.**

Two further examples of groups of four are shown in Figures 5.16 and 5.17.

In Figure 5.18 the group of four is formed from opposite sides of the grid.

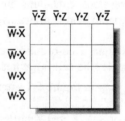

Figures 5.19 to 5.22 show some further examples with combinations of different types of loops illustrated.

Figure 5.18.   **Figure 5.19.**

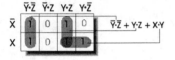   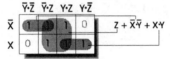   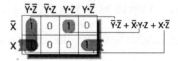

Figure 5.20.   **Figure 5.21.**   **Figure 5.22.**

Note that the largest groups are identified first, and then sufficient smaller groups so that every 1 is in at least one loop.

Karnaugh maps for four variables

With four variables there can be up to sixteen different terms involved, and the 4-variable map is a 4×4 grid as shown in Figure 5.23.

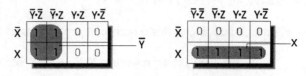

It is necessary to look for groupings of 8, 4 and 2 with the 4-variable map. Figures 5.24 to 5.27 illustrate a number of possible groupings, including some that occur on the edges of the maps and which are sometimes difficult to recognize. Again, to determine the term equivalent to the loop, look for the variables that remain common to the co-ordinates of the loop's range horizontally and vertically.

Figure 5.23.

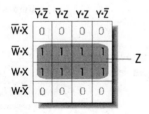   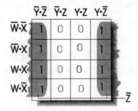

Figure 5.24.   **Figure 5.25.**

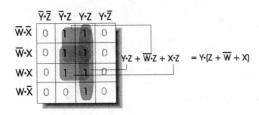

Figure 5.26.

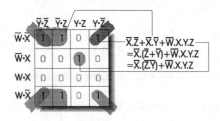

Figure 5.27.

The design of logic circuits

The complete process of designing a logic circuit may be summarized as follows:

(i)   Identify Boolean variables equivalent to the inputs to the circuit required.

(ii) Identify the outputs from the circuit.

(iii) Draw a truth table to define the output required for each possible combination of the input variables.

(iv) Derive an expression from the truth table for the output in terms of the input variables.

(v)   Simplify this expression using a Karnaugh map.

(vi) Examine the simplified expression for possible further simplifications using direct applications of the laws of Boolean algebra.

(vii) Draw the circuit using the appropriate gate symbols.

The following problem illustrates the process. Four binary signals A, B, C, D represent a single Binary Coded Decimal (BCD) digit. A logic circuit is required to output logic 1 on the occurrence of an invalid combination of the signals, that is, when they represent a number in the range 10 to 15.

(i)   The inputs to the circuit are clearly defined and it is assumed that A is the most significant digit and D the least significant digit.

(ii) The single output is to be 1 when the binary number represented by ABCD is in the range 10 to 15, that is, 1010 to 1111 in binary.

(iii) The truth table (Table 5.12) has 16 entries, representing the numbers 0 to 15.

A	B	C	D		OUTPUT	
0	0	0	0	(0)	0	
0	0	0	1	(1)	0	
0	0	1	0	(2)	0	
0	0	1	1	(3)	0	
0	1	0	0	(4)	0	
0	1	0	1	(5)	0	
0	1	1	0	(6)	0	
0	1	1	1	(7)	0	
1	0	0	0	(8)	0	
1	0	0	1	(9)	0	
1	0	1	0	(10)	1	$A.\overline{B}.C.\overline{D}$
1	0	1	1	(11)	1	$A.\overline{B}.C.D$
1	1	0	0	(12)	1	$A.B.\overline{C}.\overline{D}$
1	1	0	1	(13)	1	$A.B.\overline{C}.D$
1	1	1	0	(14)	1	$A.B.C.\overline{D}$
1	1	1	1	(15)	1	$A.B.C.D$

Table 5.12.

(iv)   The expression for the output is given by

$$\text{OUTPUT} = A.\overline{B}.C.\overline{D} + A.\overline{B}.C.D + A.B.\overline{C}.\overline{D} + A.B.\overline{C}.D + A.B.C.\overline{D} + A.B.C.D$$

(v)   The Karnaugh map is shown in Figure 5.28.

(vi)   Using the Distributive law, 3(a), the expression A.B + A.C may be written A.(B + C).

(vii)   This expression translates to the logic diagram shown in Figure 5.29.

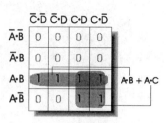

Figure 5.28.

Figure 5.29.

More logic gates

The gates that have yet to be defined are the NOR(Not OR), NAND(Not AND) and XOR (eXclusive OR) gates. The truth table for the NOR gate (Table 5.13) shows that its outputs are the inverse of those for the OR gate.

Algebraically, the NOR gate is written $\overline{(X+Y)}$. Thus the gate appears to be formed from one OR gate and one NOT gate inverting the output from the OR gate. In practice, however, the OR gate outputs are generated from a single simple circuit and not by the combination of an OR gate followed by a NOT gate.

X	Y	X NOR Y
0	0	1
0	1	0
1	0	0
1	1	0

Table 5.13.   *Truth table for NOR gate*

The symbol for the NOR gate is shown in Figure 5.30(a).

(a) NOR gate   (b) NAND gate

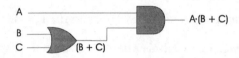

Figure 5.30.

The truth table for the NAND gate (Table 5.14) shows that its outputs are the inverse of those for the AND gate.

In Boolean algebra, the gate is written $\overline{(X.Y)}$. The comments above regarding the construction of the NOR gate similarly apply here; the NAND gate is not constructed from an AND gate followed by a NOT gate, but consists of a single circuit no more complex than the other gates.

X	Y	X NAND Y
0	0	1
0	1	1
1	0	1
1	1	0

Table 5.14.   *Truth table for NAND*

The symbol for the NAND gate is shown in Figure 5.30(b).

The importance of the NAND gate and NOR gate

The importance of these gates may be attributed to two factors:

(i)   each may be manufactured cheaply and easily;

(ii)   each can be used in the production of any circuit using AND/OR/NOT logical components. In other words, NOR gates and NAND gates can be used in the place of AND, OR or NOT gates.

These two properties mean that a logic circuit using, for instance, NOR gates only, can be produced more easily and cheaply than the same circuit using combinations of three different types of components (AND, OR and NOT gates). A unit using a number of the same component is much easier to manufacture than one using several different components.

Figures 5.31 (a), (b) and (c) show how NOR gates may be used to represent the functions of NOT, AND and OR gates.

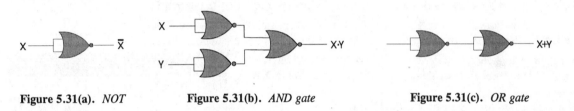

   Figure 5.31(a). *NOT*   **Figure 5.31(b).** *AND gate*   **Figure 5.31(c).** *OR gate*

Figures 5.32 (a), (b) and (c) show how NAND gates may be used to represent the functions of NOT, AND OR gates.

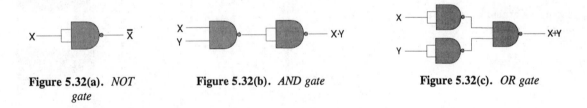

   Figure 5.32(a). *NOT*   **Figure 5.32(b).** *AND gate*   **Figure 5.32(c).** *OR gate*
       gate

(As an exercise, write down Boolean expressions equivalent to the circuits shown above and prove their validity using truth tables).

It may appear from Figures 5.31 and 5.32 that circuits using NAND or NOR gates will generally require more gates than when using AND/OR /NOT components. This may be true on occasions, but at other times fewer gates may be required. The number of gates required often may be reduced by transforming the Boolean expression into a more suitable form. For example, the following expression, when implemented directly using NOR gates, uses more gates than the expression requires using AND/OR/NOT logic:

$$X.\overline{Y} + \overline{X}.Y \; (2 \text{ AND gates, 2 NOT gates, 1 OR gate } = 5 \text{ gates})$$

However, it can be shown that the following identity is true:

$$X.\overline{Y} + \overline{X}.Y = \overline{\overline{(\overline{X} + \overline{Y})} + \overline{(X + Y)}}$$

which may not look very helpful but, in fact, shows that the original expression can be transformed into one much more suited to implementation by NOR gates. The circuit based on this transformed expression has only five NOR gates. (See Figure 5.33)

$X \cdot \overline{Y} + \overline{X} \cdot Y$

Figure 5.33.

The exclusive OR gate

This is usually abbreviated to XOR or EOR.

The truth table for the XOR gate is shown in Table 5.15. The exclusive OR gate is so named because, of its output values, the case where both inputs are logic 1 is excluded; in the OR gate these inputs produce an output of 1. In effect, the XOR gate has an output of

X ———⊃D—— $X \cdot \overline{Y} + \overline{X} \cdot Y$
Y ———

Figure 5.34. *Symbol for XOR gate*

X	Y	X XOR Y
0	0	0
0	1	1
1	0	1
1	1	0

Table 5.15.   *Truth table for XOR gate*

logic 1 when the inputs are different; when the inputs are the same, the output is logic 0. Algebraically, the XOR gate is $X \cdot \overline{Y} + \overline{X} \cdot Y$ and the symbol that is frequently used is shown in Figure 5.34. As an example of its use, suppose that it is required to generate an even parity bit for a four bit word ABCD. The truth table for this problem is shown in Table 5.16.

The expression for even parity is thus Parity bit =

$$\overline{A} \cdot \overline{B} \cdot \overline{C} \cdot D + \overline{A} \cdot \overline{B} \cdot C \cdot \overline{D} + \overline{A} \cdot B \cdot \overline{C} \cdot \overline{D} + \overline{A} \cdot B \cdot C \cdot D + A \cdot \overline{B} \cdot \overline{C} \cdot \overline{D} + A \cdot \overline{B} \cdot C \cdot D + A \cdot B \cdot \overline{C} \cdot D + A \cdot B \cdot C \cdot \overline{D}$$

and the Karnaugh map representation is shown in Figure 5.35(a).

	$\overline{C} \cdot \overline{D}$	$\overline{C} \cdot D$	$C \cdot D$	$C \cdot \overline{D}$
$\overline{A} \cdot \overline{B}$	0	1	0	1
$\overline{A} \cdot B$	1	0	1	0
$A \cdot B$	0	1	0	1
$A \cdot \overline{B}$	1	0	1	0

Figure 5.35(a).

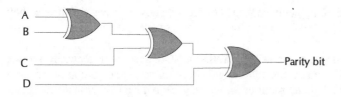

Figure 5.35(b). *Circuit using XOR gates*

A	B	C	D	parity bit	
0	0	0	0	0	
0	0	0	1	1	$\overline{A} \cdot \overline{B} \cdot \overline{C} \cdot D$
0	0	1	0	1	$\overline{A} \cdot \overline{B} \cdot C \cdot \overline{D}$
0	0	1	1	0	
0	1	0	0	1	$\overline{A} \cdot B \cdot \overline{C} \cdot \overline{D}$
0	1	0	1	0	
0	1	1	0	0	
0	1	1	1	1	$\overline{A} \cdot B \cdot C \cdot D$
1	0	0	0	1	$A \cdot \overline{B} \cdot \overline{C} \cdot \overline{D}$
1	0	0	1	0	
1	0	1	0	0	
1	0	1	1	1	$A \cdot \overline{B} \cdot C \cdot D$
1	1	0	0	0	
1	1	0	1	1	$A \cdot B \cdot \overline{C} \cdot D$
1	1	1	0	1	$A \cdot B \cdot C \cdot \overline{D}$
1	1	1	1	0	

Table 5.16.

As the map shows, there is no way of simplifying the expression. However, if the terms are grouped together as follows, a pattern begins to emerge:

Parity bit = $\overline{A} \cdot \overline{B} \cdot (\overline{C} \cdot D + C \cdot \overline{D}) + \overline{A} \cdot B \cdot (C \cdot D + \overline{C} \cdot \overline{D}) + \overline{A} \cdot B \cdot (\overline{C} \cdot \overline{D} + C \cdot D) + A \cdot B \cdot (\overline{C} \cdot D + C \cdot \overline{D})$

Rearranging the terms,

Parity bit = $\bar{A}.\bar{B}.(\bar{C}.D+C.\bar{D}) + A.B.(\bar{C}.D+C.\bar{D}) + \bar{A}.B.(C.D+\bar{C}.\bar{D}) + A.\bar{B}.(C.D+\bar{C}.\bar{D})$

Again, using the Distributive law, the first two and the last two terms can be grouped together to give

Parity bit = $(\bar{A}.\bar{B}+A.B).(\bar{C}.D+C.\bar{D}) + (\bar{A}.B+A.\bar{B}).(\bar{C}.\bar{D}+C.D)$

Notice that two of the terms in brackets are immediately recognisable as XOR functions. In addition it can be shown that

$$\overline{\bar{X}.\bar{Y} + X.\bar{Y}} = (\bar{X}.\bar{Y} + X.Y)$$

Using this identity, the expression for parity becomes

$$\text{Parity bit} = \overline{(\bar{A}.B + A.\bar{B})}.(\bar{C}.D + C.\bar{D}) + (\bar{A}.B + A.\bar{B}).\overline{(\bar{C}.D + C.\bar{D})}$$

Now each bracketed term looks like an XOR gate and, treating each bracketed term as a unit, the complete expression has the form

$$\bar{X}.Y + X.\bar{Y}, \text{ where } X = (\bar{A}.B + A.\bar{B}) \text{ and } Y = (\bar{C}.D + C.\bar{D})$$

Thus the whole expression, and every term within it, represent XOR gates. The equivalent circuit is shown in Figure 5.35(b).

Logic circuits for binary addition

The logic circuits which perform the function of addition in the Arithmetic and Logic Unit of the Central Processing Unit are called *adders*. A unit which adds two binary digits is called a *half adder* and one which adds together three binary digits is called a *full adder*. In this section each of these units will be examined in detail, and it will be shown how such units are combined to add binary numbers.

Half adders

Earlier in this chapter, the function of a half adder was explained in order to illustrate the relevance of computer logic. Remember that the function of a half adder is to add two binary digits and produce as output the Sum term and Carry term. The operation of the half adder is defined by the truth table in Table 5.17.

X	Y	Sum		Carry	
0	0	0		0	
0	1	1	$\bar{X}.Y$	0	
1	0	1	$X.\bar{Y}$	0	
1	1	0		1	$X.Y$

Table 5.17.

Thus, the expressions for the Sum and Carry terms are given by

$$\text{Sum} = \bar{X}.Y + X.\bar{Y}$$
$$\text{Carry} = X.Y$$

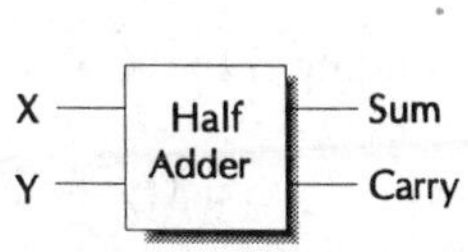

The circuit equivalent to these expressions was presented earlier in Figure 5.4.

Figure 5.36.

The symbol shown in Figure 5.36 will henceforth be used for a half adder.

Full adders

X	Y	Z	Sum		Carry	
0	0	0	0		0	
0	0	1	1	$\overline{X}.\overline{Y}.Z$	0	
0	1	0	1	$\overline{X}.Y.\overline{Z}$	0	
0	1	1	0		1	$\overline{X}.Y.Z$
1	0	0	1	$X.\overline{Y}.\overline{Z}$	0	
1	0	1	0		1	$X.\overline{Y}.Z$
1	1	0	0		1	$X.Y.\overline{Z}$
1	1	1	1	$X.Y.Z$	1	$X.Y.Z$

Table 5.18.

Table 5.18 shows the truth table for the addition of three binary digits.

Considering the Sum term first, the expression derived from the truth table is

$$Sum = \overline{X}.\overline{Y}.Z + \overline{X}.Y.\overline{Z} + X.\overline{Y}.\overline{Z} + X.Y.Z$$

Grouping together the first and fourth terms, and the middle two terms gives

$$Sum = \overline{Z}.(\overline{X}.Y + X.\overline{Y}) + Z.(\overline{X}.\overline{Y} + X.Y)$$

Using the identity

$$\overline{\overline{X}.Y + X.\overline{Y}} = (\overline{X}.\overline{Y} + X.Y) \text{ (the proof for this has been given earlier)}$$

the Sum term can be written

$$Sum = \overline{Z}.(\overline{X}.Y + X.\overline{Y}) + Z.\overline{(\overline{X}.Y + X.\overline{Y})}$$

which is of the form

$$\overline{Z}.S + Z.\overline{S} \text{ where } S = \overline{X}.Y + X.\overline{Y}$$

In other words, S is the sum term from a half adder with inputs X and Y, and Sum is one of the outputs from a half adder with inputs Z and S.

The Sum term can now be produced using two half adders, as shown in Figure 5.37.

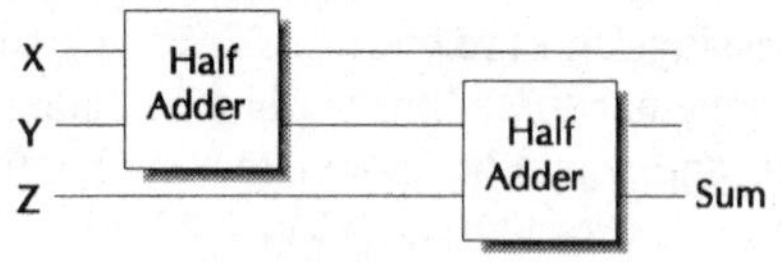

Figure 5.37.

Returning to the Carry term, the expression derived from the truth table is

$$Carry = \overline{X}.Y.Z + X.\overline{Y}.Z + X.Y.\overline{Z} + X.Y.Z$$

Again gathering terms,

$$Carry = Z.(\overline{X}.Y + X.\overline{Y}) + X.Y.(\overline{Z} + Z)$$

$$= Z.(\overline{X}.Y + X.\overline{Y}) + X.Y \text{ since } \overline{Z} + Z = 1 \text{ and } X.Y.1 = X.Y$$

Substituting S for $\overline{X}.Y + X.\overline{Y}$ as before, the expression becomes

$$Carry = Z.S + X.Y$$

Both of these terms look like the carry term from a half adder; Z.S is the carry term from a half adder with inputs Z and S (the carry term from the second half adder in the diagram above); X.Y is the carry output from the first half adder in the diagram. The two carry outputs merely need to be ORed together, to give the final circuit shown in Figure 5.38.

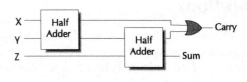

Adding binary numbers

So far, the circuits for addition have only been capable of adding two or three binary digits; more complex schemes

Figure 5.38.

are necessary in order to add two binary numbers each comprising several digits. Two approaches will be considered. The first adds numbers bit by bit, one pair of bits after another and is termed *serial addition*; the other accepts as inputs all pairs of bits in the two numbers simultaneously and is called *parallel addition*.

Serial addition

Suppose that the numbers to be added have a four-bit wordlength, and the two numbers A and B have digits $a_3\ a_2\ a_1\ a_0$ and $b_3\ b_2\ b_1\ b_0$ respectively. The circuit for a four-bit serial adder is shown in Figure 5.39.

In this particular design, a single full adder is presented with pairs of bits from the two numbers in the sequence $a_0\ b_0$, $a_1\ b_1$, $a_2\ b_2$, $a_3\ b_3$. As each pair of bits is added, the sum term is transmitted to a shift register to hold the result, and the carry term is delayed so that it is added in to the next addition operation.

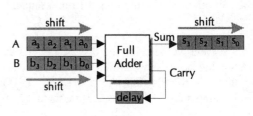

Figure 5.39.

Though this method is cheap in terms of hardware requirements, it is not often (if at all) used in modern digital computers because of its slow operation. The degree to which hardware prices have dropped in recent years has resulted in the almost universal adoption of parallel addition.

Parallel Addition

In parallel addition, a separate adder is used for the addition of each digit pair. Thus for the addition of two four-digit numbers, one half adder and three full adders would be used. In this type of circuit, all the digits are input simultaneously, with the carry term from each stage being connected directly to the input of the next stage. This is shown in Figure 5.40.

Though faster than serial addition, one fault of the type of parallel adder shown above is the successive carry out to carry in connections which cause relatively long delays; more elabo-

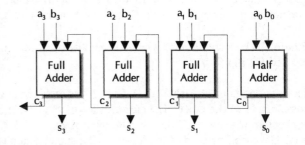

Figure 5.40.

rate schemes are capable of overcoming this problem (at the expense of added circuitry).

The efficiency of the addition circuits is of particular importance in microprocessors where the functions of multiplication and division, as well as subtraction, often use these circuits. Larger computers (and many of the more recent 16 and 32 bit microprocessors) have special purpose circuitry for multiplication and division.

Flip-flops

One of the fundamental functions performed by digital computers is the storage of data in memory. The electronic component which is usually used for this purpose is called a *flip-flop*. Other names for the same device are *bistable*, *latch* and *toggle*, but flip-flop is the most commonly used name.

A flip-flop is capable of storing, in electrical form, a single binary digit. Thus, a collection of eight flip-flops can store a byte of data. As well as being used for memory, flip-flops form the basis of other useful CPU components, such as *shift registers* and *binary counters*.

Flip-flops are frequently constructed with gates, but using *sequential logic* rather than the *combinational logic* described in the previous part of this chapter. As we have seen, a combinational logic circuit produces an output which is entirely dependent on the current inputs; with sequential logic, because of the use of feedback, the output from a sequential logic circuit depends on its current state in addition to the current inputs. In other words, the output from a sequential logic circuit is partly determined by the previous inputs it received.

In this section we describe the operational characteristics of the simplest type of flip-flop, the *SR flip-flop*, before going on to show how it may be constructed using NAND gates. We then discuss the synchronous version of the SR flip-flop, the *clocked SR flip-flop* before showing how shift registers, binary counters and memory units may be fabricated using them.

Though there are a number of different types of flip-flops in common use, including JK, Master-Slave and D-type flip-flops, essentially they are all based on the SR flip-flop, and it is beyond the scope of this book to discuss the precise differences between them and why one type is preferred over another for certain types of application.

Operation of the SR flip-flop

The term flip-flop derives from its characteristic of being in one of two stable states at any instant, and hence the alternative name, *bistable*. These two states we conveniently designate 0 and 1. In state 1, the device is said to be *set*, and in state 0, *reset*, hence SR flip-flop. If the flip-flop is in state 1, it will remain in that state until an input causes it to change to state 0, in which state it will also remain until changed. Thus it remembers its current state until some signal causes it to change state.

Figure 5.41(a) shows the symbol generally used for an un-clocked SR flip-flop.

The two outputs are labelled Q and $\overline{Q}$ because each is the complement of the other. The current state of the device is by convention that of the Q output. The input lines, S and R, are used to control the state of the flip-flop. If a signal is applied to the S line, the flip-flop is set (ie Q=1); a signal on the R line

Figure 5.41(a).
Unclocked

Figure 5.41(b).
Clocked

resets it (ie Q=0). The absence of any signal leaves the state of the flip-flop unchanged. Applying a signal to both lines simultaneously is not allowed. Table 5.19 illustrates these rules with a sequence of input signals and the resulting state of the flip-flop.

S	R	Q	Q'	effect of input
1	0	1	0	set
0	0	1	0	remains in same state
0	0	1	0	
0	1	0	1	reset
0	0	0	1	remains in same state
1	0	1	0	set
1	0	1	0	already set so no effect
0	1	0	1	reset
0	1	0	1	already set so no effect

Table 5.19.

Construction of the SR flip-flop

A simple form of an SR flip-flop may be implemented using two NAND gates connected as shown in Figure 5.42.

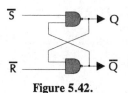

Figure 5.42.

The operation of this flip-flop is defined by Table 5.20.

The current state of the circuit is denoted by Q and the resulting state, due to the two inputs, is Q'. We can verify the operation of the circuit by tracing each pair of inputs and comparing them with the outputs shown:

(i) $\overline{S}=1$, $\overline{R}=1$ and Q=1. This corresponds to the null input, self-sustaining state. The inputs to the lower NAND gate are both 1, producing an output, Q', of 0. This means that the inputs to the upper NAND gate are 1 and 0, producing an output of 1; no change in the outputs. If the current state is Q=0, the lower gate has inputs 0 and 1, producing an output of 1, and the upper gate now has both inputs at logic-1, producing an output of 0; again no change.

S	R	Q'
0	0	Q
0	1	0
1	0	0
1	1	not defined

Table 5.20.

(ii) $\overline{S}=0$ and $\overline{R}=1$. This is the *set* condition. Because $\overline{S}=0$, the upper gate must output logic-1; the inputs to the lower gate both being 1, the output is 0.

(iii) $\overline{S}=1$ and $\overline{R}=0$. This is the *reset* condition. Because $\overline{R}=0$, the lower gate must output logic-1 this time, and the two logic-1 inputs to the top gate produce an output of 0.

(iv) $\overline{S}=1$ and $\overline{R}=1$. In this instance the output from the flip-flop cannot be determined; the resulting state will be unpredictable and will depend on such factors as temperature and component tolerances.

The clocked SR flip-flop

Figure 5.41(b) shows the symbol for a clocked SR flip-flop. It has an additional input designated *clock* or *enable*. The circuit for a clocked SR flip-flop is shown in Figure 5.43.

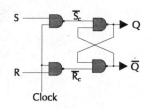

Figure 5.43.

The extra input allows the operation of the flip-flop to be controlled by a timing signal which is used to synchronize the operation of the separate components of a circuit. Circuits controlled by a clock are called *synchronous* circuits; where a clock is not used the circuit is *asynchronous*. Because of the added complexity of asynchronous circuits, most circuits are of the synchronous variety.

The effect of the additional gates in the circuit is to hold the S and R inputs at the null state ($\overline{S}=\overline{Q}=1$) until a clock pulse is applied to the first two gates, at which time set and reset signals are applied to the flip-flop. In effect, the clock pulse *enables* the flip-flop to assume a new state.

Shift registers

A four stage shift register is shown in the Figure 5.44.

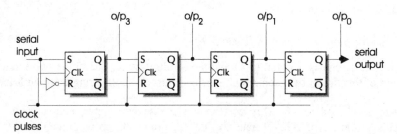

Figure 5.44.

A sequence of signals representing a binary number is applied to the input. Each input is set up while the clock is at logic-0. When the clock pulse becomes logic-1, each flip-flop is enabled and assumes the value of the signal being applied to the S input. Therefore, the complete contents of the flip-flops are shifted along by one bit at every clock pulse. The current state of each flip-flop is available on the lines labelled O/P0 to O/P3. Table 5.21 illustrates the process with the binary sequence 1101, assuming that the initial contents of the shift register is 0000.

clock pulse	input	O/P0	O/P1	O/P2	O/P3
		0	0	0	0
1	1	1	0	0	0
2	0	0	1	0	0
3	1	1	0	1	0
4	1	1	1	0	1

Table 5.21.

Binary counters

A binary counter consists of a collection of flip-flops each of which is associated with a bit position in the binary representation of a number. If there are n flip-flops in a binary counter, the number of possible states is 2^n and the counting sequence is from 0 to 2^n-1. If the maximum value is exceeded, the counting sequence starts at 0 again.

A simple form of a binary counter is based on an SR flip-flop connected to act as a *toggle circuit* shown in Figure 5.45.

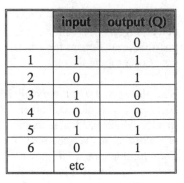

Input

Figure 5.45.

Each pulse applied to the clock input inverts the output, Q, of the circuit; in effect, this is dividing the input frequency by two by performing alternate *set* and *reset* operations. Table 5.22 shows how the output changes after each logic-1 input, assuming that the current output is logic-0.

Notice that logic-0 inputs have no effect on the output. A four-bit counter uses four toggle circuits connected in series. (See Figure 5.46)

	input	output (Q)
		0
1	1	1
2	0	1
3	1	0
4	0	0
5	1	1
6	0	1
	etc	

Table 5.22.

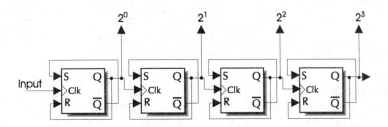

Figure 5.46.

The output from the first toggle circuit alternates between 0 and 1 as shown in the previous table. Each time a logic-1 is output from the first toggle component, the second one is enabled and its output inverts; each time the output from the second component is logic-1, the third one is enabled and its output inverts, and so on. Therefore, the first component inverts after each logic-1 input, the second one inverts after two logic-1 inputs, the third after four and the fourth after eight. Table 5.23 shows how the outputs of each of the toggle circuits, A, B, C and D change for a sequence of logic-1 inputs.

Thus, A represents the least significant bit of the 4-bit number and D the most significant bit. The counter thus counts up from 0 to 15 cyclically.

Memory circuits

One of the fundamental characteristics of the digital computer is its ability to store data and programs in random-access memory. We have seen already that sequential circuits are capable of storing binary signals and that collections of such components may be used to store bytes or larger words of data. Large arrays of such circuits constitute the

input	A	B	C	D
	0	0	0	0
1	1	0	0	0
2	0	1	0	0
3	1	1	0	0
4	0	0	1	0
5	1	0	1	0
6	0	1	1	0
7	1	1	1	0
8	0	0	0	1
9	1	0	0	1
10	0	1	0	1
11	1	1	0	1
12	0	0	1	1
13	1	0	1	1
14	0	1	1	1
15	1	1	1	1
16	0	0	0	0
17	1	0	0	0
	etc.			

Table 5.23.

internal memory of a computer. Figure 5.47 shows one possible arrangement for a random-access memory unit.

The *Address Lines*, typically 16 or 32 for a microcomputer, specify which particular memory word is to be accessed; a *Chip Enable* line (not shown) enables the chip if it is logic-1, or disables the chip if it is logic-0; when enabled, the chip may be written to, by making *Write=1* and read from, using Write=0.

Each horizontal row of memory elements represents a word of memory which may be selected by an Address Decoder.

So for an 8-bit word there will be a row of eight memory ele-

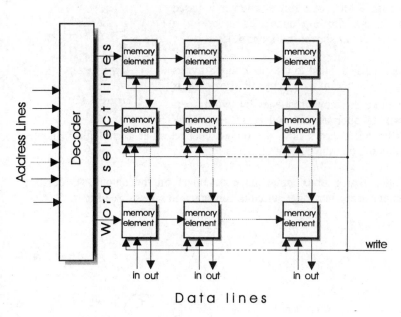

Figure 5.47.

ments. When an address is input to the address decoder, it selects the corresponding word. For a 16-bit address, the decoder will select one line from 2^{16} possibilities. If a read operation is required, the word, corresponding to the states of the eight memory elements, will appear on the *Out* lines; a write operation will cause the eight memory elements to take on the binary values on the *In* lines.

The construction of the memory elements, each storing a single bit, is shown in Figure 5.48.

Each element comprises a flip-flop and a number of other gates to control the transfer of data between the flip-flop and the common internal data lines. Notice that the AND gates are used to control the passage of signals; only when all inputs to an AND gate are 1 will the output become 1. Each *word-select* line is used to enable all elements in a row for reading or writing, and each column has two internal data lines, one for reading - data-in - and one for writing - data-out. The data-out line takes the value of the element in the currently enabled word.

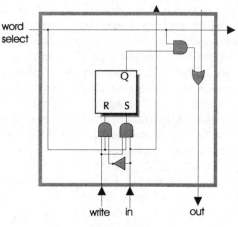

Figure 5.48.

Thus, when *Word select=1* the Q output from the memory element is ORed with the data-out line. A word is written into a memory location by presenting the appropriate address to the decoder (which enables the word memory elements), the bit pattern of the word to the data-in lines and then setting *Write=1*. Two AND gates in each memory element allow its state to be changed to the value on the data-in line providing *Write* and *Word select* are both at logic-1.

Integrated circuits

The logic elements described earlier in this chapter are fabricated using semi-conductors, transistors in particular. The speed of operation of transistors, which act as electronic switches in logic circuits, is dependent on their size; the power consumption, amount of heat generated and cost are also dependent on their size. Since size is such a critical factor, a great deal of research has been done to reduce the size of a transistor as far as possible. The result of this research has been the steady evolution of the Integrated Circuit (IC). Though invented in 1959, integrated circuits were first used in computers in the late 1960s. The PDP-11 was one of the first commercial machines to use such devices. At that time an integrated circuit contained less than one hundred transistors; today, microprocessors can contain one million transistors on a single chip, and it is predicted that by the turn of the century there will be one hundred million transistors on a single microprocessor chip. Electronic devices contain combinations of components such as resistors, capacitors and transistors. The most common material of microelectronic circuits is silicon, the same type that is found in ordinary sand. The silicon is first refined and made into thin discs which form the base material, the substrate, for a number of ICs. The manufacturing process produces several identical ICs, each perhaps only a quarter of an inch square, on one wafer of silicon. The circuit to be set into the silicon is first designed, often with the aid of a computer to minimize the number of components, before being used to prepare a series of masks. After being photographically reduced to the actual chip size, the masks are used in a photographic process which sequentially isolates each chip from its immediate neighbours, defines the position of the components, modifies the structure of the substrate to give it the required semiconducting characteristics and interconnects the components using etched metallic films. Further stages are required to test the circuits, separate them and package them into the familiar 'bug' shape. Table 5.24 is a rough guide to the five generations of ICs, in terms of chip complexity.

Since its invention in 1959, the IC has undergone rapid growth, its complexity following a progression known as Moores Law which states that the maximum number of components on a microprocessor chip doubles every one and a half years. Currently, the maximum dimension, the *feature* size, of a transistor on a one-million transistor microprocessor is about one micrometre, that is, one millionth of a metre. Such a microprocessor is capable of processing perhaps twenty million instructions per second. It has been estimated that by the year 2000 the norm will be microprocessors containing forty million transistors of feature size 0.25 micrometers processing *one billion instructions per second*. Such a processor would be capable of handling animated

generation	no. of components
Small Scale Integration (SSI)	2 - 64
Medium Scale Integration (MSI)	64 - 2000
Large Scale Integration (LSI)	2000 - 64,000
Very Large Scale Integration (VLSI)	64,000 - 2,000,000
Ultra Large Scale Integration (ULSI)	2,000,000 - 100,000,000

Table 5.24. *Generations of integrated circuits (ICs)*

graphics of photographic quality in real time. However, as the feature sizes of components approach atomic proportions, stability problems become increasingly problematic; with perhaps only a few hundred atoms separating components, their behaviour can become unusual. This behaviour is referred to as *quantum effects*. Obviously there is a limit to how small a transistor can be made, so continued micro miniaturization depends on additional innovative research, and in fact quantum effects are providing one such possible avenue of research. When electrons are constrained to move in less than three dimensions, their normal range of energy states is changed. When electrons are confined to two dimensions, in a very thin film of conducting material, certain electron energy states restrict the flow of current through the film, allowing it to act like an electronic switch. Furthermore, when constrained to move in less than two dimensions, in lines or even dots, other quantum effects occur, providing opportunities for multi-state devices and therefore multi-valued logic offering greatly enhanced speeds. Another quantum effect device is a type of transistor whose operation is based on the charge of a single electron, and yet another invention from IBM scientists is a switch which turns on and off with the motion of a single atom. These new devices are an order of magnitude smaller than those in current use and are capable of operating at much greater speeds, but at the moment there are serious problems to be overcome before they can be implemented in actual machines. The most serious problem is that quantum effect devices will only operate correctly at extremely low temperatures (around -450°F). However, experience tells us that apparently insurmountable technological problems remain so for only a short time and that we can expect that the near future will see a new breed of computers having capabilities greatly in excess of those in current use.

Exercises

1. For each of the following, simplify the expression using a Karnaugh map and draw a circuit of the simplified expression:

    (i) $X.Y.\overline{Z} + X.Y.Z + X.\overline{Y}.Z$

    (ii) $A.B.C + A.\overline{B}.C + A.B.\overline{C} + \overline{A}.\overline{B}.C + \overline{A}.B.C$

    (iii) $A.B.C.D + A.B.\overline{C}.D + A.B.C.\overline{D} + \overline{A}.B.\overline{C}.D + \overline{A}.B.C.\overline{D} + A.\overline{B}.\overline{C}.\overline{D}$

    (iv) $\overline{W}.X + X.\overline{Y} + X.\overline{Y}.Z + \overline{W}.\overline{Y}.\overline{Z} + W.X.\overline{Y}.\overline{Z}$

2. Use truth tables to prove the laws of Boolean algebra.

3. Given two binary signals, X and Y, produce a truth table to define the difference of the two digits for every combination. There will be two outputs representing the difference and a 'borrow'. Hence, draw the circuit for a 'half subtractor'.

4. Produce a truth table which defines the 4-bit product when two numbers are multiplied together (the largest number produced will be $3 \times 3 = 9$, which requires 4 bits). Simplify each of the four outputs, using Karnaugh maps and produce a circuit for hardware multiplication of 2-bit numbers.

5. The adjacent figure shows the layout of a seven segment display, commonly used in calculators. Each segment of the display can be emphasized by applying a logic-1 to the input to that segment. By simultaneously emphasizing the appropriate segments, the device can be used to display the digits 0 to 9.

    Design seven logic circuits, one for each segment, such that when four signals representing a binary coded decimal (BCD) digit are applied to each circuit, the appropriate digit is displayed. The truth table has the following form.

inputs (BCD)	digit	outputs
A B C D		a b c d e f g
0 0 0 0	0	1 1 1 1 1 1 0
0 0 0 1	1	0 1 1 0 0 0 0
etc	....	.....
1 0 0 1	9	1 1 1 1 0 1 1

Chapter 6
Computer Systems

Any system consists of a number of separate components working together to achieve a common aim. A car, for example, is a form of transport system comprising amongst other items, an engine, wheels and a gear box. Its aim is to transport people from one place to another. The system will only operate successfully if all these major components work. An essential additional element is the driver, without whom the car is simply a motionless piece of metal. The components of a system and the ways they interrelate constitute its architecture (Chapter 7). The term *hardware* describes all the physical electronic and mechanical components forming part of a computer system.

Functional components

The hardware components of a computer system can be categorized by function, as follows:

Input

To allow the computer to process data it must be in a form which the machine can handle. Before processing, data is normally in a human-readable form, for example, as it appears on an employee's time sheet or a customer's order form. Such alphabetic and numeric (decimal) data cannot be handled directly by the internal circuitry of the computer. Firstly, it has to be translated into the binary format which makes the data *machine-sensible*; this is the function of an input device.

There are a wide variety of such devices, but the most common make use of a keyboard. Data is transferred from the input device to main memory.

Main memory

This element, also commonly known as *RAM*, has two main functions:

- to temporarily store programs currently in use for processing data;

- to temporarily store data:

    - entered through an input device and awaiting processing;
    - currently being processed;
    - which results from processing and is waiting to be output.

Central processing unit (CPU)

Often referred to as the *processor*, the CPU handles program instructions and data and consists of two elements:

- *Arithmetic/logic unit (ALU)*. The ALU carries out arithmetic operations such as addition, multiplication, subtraction and division. It can also make logical comparisons between items of data, for example, it can determine whether one value is greater than another. Such logical operations can also be performed on non-numeric data.

- *Control unit*. The control unit governs the operation of all hardware, including input and output devices and the CPU. It does this by fetching, interpreting and executing each instruction in turn, in an automatically controlled cycle; this *fetch-execute cycle* is described in detail in Chapter 4.

Output

Output devices perform the opposite function of input devices by translating machine-sensible data into a human-readable form, for example, onto a printer or the screen of a visual display unit (VDU). Sometimes, the results of computer processing may be needed for further processing, in which case, they are output to a storage medium (Chapter 9) which retains it in machine-sensible form for subsequent input.

Backing storage

Backing, or auxiliary, storage performs a filing function within the computer system. In this context it is important to consider a couple of important concepts.

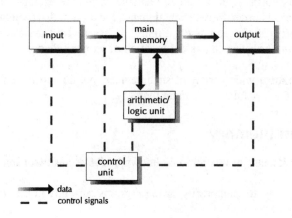

- *Memory volatility*. It is not practical to store data files and programs in main memory because of its volatility. This means that the contents of the main memory can be destroyed, either by being overwritten as new data is entered for processing and new programs used, or when the machine is switched off. Such volatile memory is termed random access memory (RAM).

Figure 6.1. *Logical structure of computer system*

- *Retrievable data*. Backing storage media provide a more permanent store for programs (which may be used many times on different occasions) and data files (which are used for future reference or processing).

Peripherals

Those hardware devices which are external to the CPU and main memory, namely those devices used for input, output and backing storage, are called peripherals. Figure 6.1 illustrates the logical structure of the computer and thereby, the relationships between various hardware elements. It shows the data flow through the system and the flow of control signals from the processor.

Computer systems classified

Computer systems can be classified according to the following characteristics: purpose; size and complexity; generation.

Purpose

There are two categories under this heading:

General-purpose computers

As the term suggests, general-purpose machines can carry out processing tasks for a wide variety of applications and most organizations will make use of this type of machine.

Dedicated or special-purpose computers

In their logical structure, these machines are fundamentally the same as the general-purpose machine except that they have been programmed for a specific application. Dedicated word processors provide one example. The advent of cheap, microprocessor-based, special-purpose systems has led to an expansion of their use in controlling machines and many household products, such as washing machines and microwave ovens, are controlled by such systems.

Size and complexity

It should be emphasized that the following categories are only broad guidelines and changes in technology are continually blurring the differences between them. For example, there are now powerful microcomputer systems (often referred to as super-micros) which far exceed the power and flexibility of earlier generation minicomputer systems. However, the generally accepted categories of computer system are as follow:

Mainframe Computers

Such computers are commonly used by large national and multi-national organizations such as banks, airlines and oil companies. They usually support a large number and variety of peripherals and can process a number of applications concurrently (*multi-programming*). The mainframe's power stems from the phenomenal speeds of the processor and the large size of the main memory.

Mainframes may also play a central role in *wide area networks*. Their huge capital cost invariably places them in centralized processing roles; for the same reason, about fifty per cent of the mainframes currently in use are rented or leased from specialist companies.

Mainframe computers are generally accommodated in special-purpose, air-conditioned rooms to ensure trouble free operation.

Supercomputers with processing speeds many times those of mainframe systems are used for scientific and statistical work, being capable of completing such work in a small fraction of the time that a mainframe would require.

Minicomputers

Minicomputers are scaled-down versions of mainframe computers. The division between the two types becomes rather blurred when referring to small mainframe and supermini systems. Costing less and being robust enough to operate without a special environment, they can be used in *real-time* applications such as controlling manufacturing processes in an engineering factory. They are also used by medium sized organizations for all their processing needs or by larger organizations as part of a network system. The mini computer is technically very similar to the mainframe, with the following differences:

- it usually only has magnetic disk storage;

- the main input/output peripherals tend to be visual display units (VDUs).

Minicomputers can support a number of applications concurrently and are often used with *time-sharing* operating systems (Chapter 13) and *intelligent terminals* to provide organizations with decentralized processing facilities. Used in this way, many applications such as word processing, invoicing and customer enquiry can be carried out by users in their own departments. Generally, the volumes of input will be relatively small. This contrasts with the multiprogramming mode of operation often used in mainframe systems where, in addition to handling on-line terminals for interactive work, large volume, batch processing jobs are processed centrally and users are not directly involved.

Medium-sized organizations may use minicomputers for their main processing applications. Larger organizations may apply them to *front end processing* (FEP). Employed in this way, a minicomputer handles a mainframe's communications traffic (Chapter 11) with remote terminals or other computers, leaving the mainframe free to handle the organization's information processing tasks.

Microcomputers

The microcomputer is the smallest in the range and was first developed when the Intel Corporation succeeded in incorporating the main functional parts of a computer on a single *chip* using *integrated circuits* (IC) on silicon. Subsequently, the technique of *large scale integration* (LSI) further increased the number of electronic circuits which could be packed onto one chip. LSI has been superseded by *very large scale integration* (VLSI) which packs even more circuitry onto a single chip thus further increasing the power and storage capacity of microcomputers and computers generally. This type of computer storage is known as *metal oxide semiconductor* (MOS) storage and has completely replaced the *core store* used in earlier mainframe computers.

Originally, microcomputers were only capable of supporting a single user and a single application at any one time. The increase in processor speed and memory capacity now permits their use for *multi-tasking* (the running of several tasks concurrently by one user). *Multi-user* operation is made possible through networking; it is now extremely popular to link microcomputers into a *local area network* (LAN), to allow resource-sharing (disk, printer, programs and data files), as well as electronic communications between users (*electronic mail*). Microcomputers can now support applications packages previously restricted to mini and mainframe systems, including, for example, those used for database and *computer aided design* (CAD) work.

The range of microcomputer software is now extremely wide and the quality generally very high. There are software packages available for most business applications. One area of recent rapid growth has been in the development of graphics-based applications and most popular applications software can now be operated via a *graphical user interface* (GUI) and a *mouse*.

The low cost of microcomputers and the increase in the range of software available, makes their use possible in almost any size and type of organization. In the small firm, a microcomputer may be used for word processing, stock control, costing, and general accounting. In the larger organization they may be used as intelligent terminals. Such systems provide the user with the processing facilities of a central mini or mainframe computer and at the same time, a degree of independent processing power through the use of the microcomputers own processor and memory store.

Multi-media systems

The term 'multi-media' is used to describe systems which allow the integration of sound, video, graphics and text in a single software product. Thus, the user of a multi-media encyclopaedia, can not only read about the life of Martin Luther King, but also see video sequences and hear his voice.

At present, much multi-media software still leaves the user relatively passive, but future developments are likely to give the user increased flexibility to alter the outputs from a package. The meaning of multi-media has to be frequently updated as advances in software and hardware enable the range of media to be increased. Thus, computer animation may be used to illustrate, for example, the movement of a horse when walking, trotting and galloping, without any interaction with the user, save for the selection of the initial type of movement; the multi-media experience can be enhanced by allowing the user to hear different sounds by selecting the type of ground on which the horse is moving, for example, on a muddy field, on gravel, sand or in shallow water, or a sequence of different surfaces, perhaps over a route planned by the user. Future developments could allow the use of more senses than just sight and hearing, perhaps touch and smell.

At present, microcomputers configured to run multi-media software include a *sound card* (to process sound files), speakers, a microphone (for voice input) and CD-ROM drive. Memory and processor requirements are higher than for routine business machines, because multi-media software has to handle complex graphics, animation and sound files in *real-time*. It should be pointed out that a CD-ROM drive is now a standard component of all microcomputer systems, partly because most software packages are now available on CD-ROM, as well as floppy disk, but also because the storage requirements of packages requires the capacity of CD-ROM.

Portable computers

The first portable computer was developed in the early 1980s, but was nicknamed a 'luggable', because of its size and considerable weight (more than 10 kilogrammes). It also used a CRT (cathode ray tube) screen, which added to its power requirements. Today's portables are worthy of the name. Apart from pen-based, personal digital assistants (PDAs - see earlier), the A4 size notebook computer is the main portable product.

Features include:

- powerful processor;

- liquid crystal display (see earlier) screen. Sometimes, the screen is backlit to improve definition. Colour displays are available, although the resolution cannot match that of conventional screens;

- memory is either static RAM (SRAM - see Main Memory) or flash memory. SRAM is volatile and its contents need battery power to be maintained. Typical capacity is 8 Mb. Flash memory is cheaper and does not require battery power. Unfortunately, flash memory is slower and wears out after, approximately, 10,000 erasures. Flash memory cards can be write protected and include a standard interface, which allows them to appear as hard disks to the rest of the system;

- integral hard disk, typically, with hundreds of megabytes capacity;

- ports for connection to external devices. These include: serial connections for use with a modem and communications network; parallel printer port; mouse port; external VGA screen connection;

- keyboard, sometimes full layout (but no numeric keypad).

Smaller notebooks, often referred to as sub-notebooks and about half the size of the A4 variety, are becoming increasingly popular. Many machines include a number of card slots for the connection of additional devices, such as a modem and network adapter. The most widely used standard for these card slots is PCMCIA (Personal Computer Memory Card International Association). The display size is between 180 mm and 235 mm, across the diagonal. A typical sub-notebook weighs about 1.5 kilogrammes.

Pen-based computers

A pen can be used as an alternative to the mouse but is most effective for handwriting, in conjunction with a digitizing tablet, which is either separate or integral to the screen. The latter option is chosen for personal digital assistants (PDAs), pocket-sized computers designed for use on the move; the inclusion of a keyboard would destroy its usefulness as a light, highly portable device. A pen is used to write directly onto the screen. Recognition software attempts to identify and then translate hand-written characters by reference to stored prototypes; some symbols may represent commands, called gestures, whilst others may be letters of the alphabet. Hand-written input can then be handled as if it had been keyed in. The system can be trained to recognise how any given user draws a particular shape, if the recognition software cannot read their writing. The pen is the only feasible technology because touch-screens and mice lack the necessary precision, and light pens only function with CRT (Chapter 8) displays.

Generations

Since the first electronic computers were built in the 1940s, a number of developments in electronics have led to computer hardware being categorized by generation, that is, its place in the history of the computer. These generations can be simply defined as follows:

First generation

During the 1940s, this first generation of computers used electronic components including vacuum tubes. The first computer to allow a program to be stored in memory (a stored-program computer) was EDSAC, developed at the University of Manchester. The vacuum tubes were fragile, subject to overheating and caused frequent breakdowns.

Second generation

The introduction of low-cost and reliable transistors allowed the computer industry to develop at a tremendous rate during the late 1950s. The cost and size of the machines were radically reduced so it became possible for large commercial organizations to make use of computers. Examples of such machines include LEO III, UNIVAC and ATLAS.

Third generation

The development of integrated circuit (IC) technology in the mid-1960s heralded the development of more powerful, reliable and compact computers, such as those of the IBM 360 series.

Fourth generation

This generation is typified by large scale integration (LSI) of circuits which allowed the development of the microprocessor, which in turn allowed the production of the microcomputer. All computers used today make use of such silicon chip technology.

Fifth generation

At present, most computers are still of the fourth generation variety. Developments are continuing towards expanding memory size, using very large scale integration (VLSI) techniques and increasing the speed of processors. This increasing power is allowing the pursuit of new lines of development in computer systems:

- more human orientated input/output devices using voice recognition and speech synthesis should allow communication between computers and humans to be more flexible and natural. In the future, the aim is to allow computers to be addressed in languages natural to the users. Current techniques on some microcomputers allow acceptance of some spoken commands. Others allow the selection of user options displayed as graphics on the screen via a hand-held mouse.

- parallel processing techniques.

Analogue computers

Whereas digital computers store numerical information in discrete form, that is, by coded sets of electrical pulses representing digits, analogue computers use physical quantities which are proportional to the numbers involved. Examples of such physical quantities, generically referred to as analogues, include electric current, voltage, temperature, length, or the angle of a shaft. Thermometers, slide rules (obsolete since the advent of the electronic calculator), barometers, pointer instruments such as voltmeters, ammeters, speedometers and the weathervane are typical examples of analogue devices. Analogue information is in continuous form, often depicted on a graph or an oscilloscope screen. Electrical analogue computers use current or voltage as analogues.

Uses. Analogue computers are used by mathematicians and engineers to solve differential equations which occur in science and engineering, for example, in fluid flow, robotics, atomic physics and in the field of simulation. Aircraft and rocket simulation, for example, is useful for training of personnel and as a design aid, particularly where experiments might be too expensive to carry out fully, or where failure may be hazardous to life.

Advantages and disadvantages. The over-riding advantage of an analogue computer, compared with a digital system, is its ability to solve differential equations extremely quickly. Therefore, it is ideally suited to real-time operation, in other words, the performance of operations in the time-scale in which they actually occur. It must be said that the speed and power of modern digital machines permits their application in areas of real-time operation formerly only suited to analogue techniques. Nevertheless, there are a number of situations in control and simulation where analogue computers provide a simpler and less expensive alternative to the digital computer.

Analogue computers have a number of disadvantages:

- relatively inaccurate, 0.1 percent accuracy being typical;

- setting up time can be lengthy and alteration to suit another problem may be difficult;

- having no memory, they cannot store problems;

- output is only possible in graphical form;

- input is only acceptable in the form of dial settings;

- extensive maintenance is needed and the user must understand electrical engineering.

Hybrid computers

These were developed to combine the speed of the analogue computer with the flexibility of its digital counterpart. Users must possess skills in both analogue and digital computing. The analogue section of the hybrid computer is used to give an approximate solution, which is then enhanced by the digital section. The latter generates, by table look-up, functions that the analogue part cannot easily simulate. Output from the analogue section is edited by the digital section and printed out in a convenient form. Methods are needed to convert analogue form to digital form and vice versa and these same methods are used to interface a digital computer to the real, physical world. Examples of such interfacing are found in, for example, furnace temperature control systems and image scanners.

Exercises

1. Draw the *logical structure* of a computer system.

2. Briefly define the function of each component identified in 1.

3. List the main types of computer, in the order of their historical development.

4. Define the term *multi-media*.

Chapter 7

Computer Architecture

This chapter looks at a number of aspects of computer systems architecture and builds on some of the basic ideas dealt with in Chapter 6. The technical specification for any particular computer system will not only refer to the types of component, but also their performance and capacity ratings, which individually and in combination with one another contribute to the overall system performance. The following sections explain the operation and function of each component within the architecture of a computer system. Typical capacity and performance ratings are also given. The components examined are: *memory*; *processor* (including CISC, RISC and parallel processing architectures); *buses* (including standards for bus architecture).

Memory

RAM

RAM constitutes the working area of the computer and is used for storage of program(s) and data currently in use. Computer memory is measured in Kb (kilobytes), where 1 Kb is 1024 bytes; for larger memory, the unit of measurement is Mb (megabyte), which is 1024 Kb. Generally, the performance of a computer system can be improved by the addition of more memory. Other upgrading measures, such as the addition of a hard disk controller (see Chapter 9) will make less impact on system performance if main memory capacity is inadequate. If there is too little memory, more frequent access to disk is required. As a hard disk drive is a relatively slow component, compared with main memory, frequent disk accesses slow down overall system performance. Large main memory enables the system to keep *resident*, all the files it needs for an application. RAM is volatile (the current contents are lost when power is removed or different programs and data are entered), so all programs and data files are held more permanently on a magnetic storage medium; invariably this is floppy or hard disk.

Technical features

RAM is directly accessible by the processor and memory/processor transfers which occur during a program's execution have to be made as quickly as possible to maximize the use of the processor's power. The section on processors describes the use of a 'clock' which generates regularly timed pulses to synchronize the activities of the processor and explains that different activities take different numbers of clock pulses. Memory/processor transfers, although extremely quick, typically 60 to 80 nanoseconds (ns) for a read from RAM, are relatively slow when compared with typical processor speeds. Thus, the quicker the transfer can be carried out, the less time that the processor spends unoccupied. One quality RAM should possess, therefore, is speed. Predictably, the higher the speed, the greater is the cost.

Types of RAM

Broadly, two types of RAM are used in computers. They are: static RAM (SRAM); dynamic RAM (DRAM). A number of comparisons can be drawn between the two types:

- DRAMs are easier to make than SRAMs;

- more DRAM can be packed onto a single integrated circuit or 'chip' than is possible with SRAM;

- DRAM consumes less power than SRAM;

- static RAM, as the term suggests, retains its contents as long as power is maintained, whereas Dynamic RAM needs to be refreshed (the contents of each location are rewritten) at intervals not exceeding 2 milliseconds (ms);

- SRAM can be written to and read from more quickly, but is more expensive than DRAM.

The most important features for comparison relate to speed of access and cost. To maximize use of a powerful processor SRAM is the obvious choice. Unfortunately, the needs of modern software for large main memory would make computer systems based wholly on SRAM very expensive. The use of *graphical user interfaces*, such as Windows95 and the increasing sophistication of software packages, calls for a minimum of 16 to 32 Mb of RAM. As software becomes more sophisticated even more memory will be needed. So, for economic reasons, main memory consists of DRAM chips grouped together on a memory board. A conflict exists between processor speed and memory cost. Doubling the clock speed of a processor from 50 MHz to 100 MHz does not necessarily double the speed of the computer's overall operation because of other factors, including *disk access* time and memory read time. To help improve the speed of memory accesses and still keep down the cost of memory, a system of *cache memory* can be used.

EDO RAM

EDO (*extended* or *enhanced data out*) RAM, is used in many of the most recent microcomputer systems because of its superior access times. Despite this performance improvement, *cache memory* is still an essential part of a computer's configuration.

Cache memory

To understand the function of cache memory it is necessary to refer to a feature identified in the section on the processor, namely *wait-state*. A wait-state is an extra clock pulse added to a processor cycle when it accesses memory. The slower the memory, the more wait-states which have to be added to processor cycles to give the memory time to respond. The greater the number of wait-states, the lower the overall computer system performance. Thus, a high performance processor is wasted if it is used with a slow memory system which requires many wait-states. A memory system which requires zero wait-states will allow the system (ignoring peripheral device performance) to function at the maximum

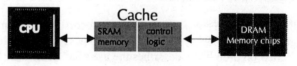

Figure 7.1. *Cache memory*

performance of the processor. It must be emphasized that overall system performance depends on all components forming a computer system and that *disk access time* also plays a major part in determining such performance. The topic of disk storage is dealt with in Chapter 9. A cache memory system aims to provide the performance of fast Static RAM (SRAM) but at the lower cost of Dynamic RAM (DRAM). A cache is a small amount of very fast SRAM located between the processor and main memory. Figure 7.1 illustrates the relationship between main memory, the processor and the cache.

The cache size is typically 256Kb to 512Kb and its purpose is to hold a copy of frequently used code and data. Instead of accessing the slower main memory (consisting of DRAM) for such data, the processor can go directly to the cache memory without incurring any wait-states. The effectiveness of cache memory is based on the principle that once a memory location has been accessed, it is likely to be accessed again soon. This means that after the initial access, subsequent accesses to the same memory location need go only to the cache. Much computer processing is repetitive, so a high hit rate in the cache can be anticipated. The cache hit rate is simply the ratio of cache hits to the total number of memory accesses required by the processor. Systems using cache memory may achieve an 85 to 90 per cent hit rate. Thus, system performance can be radically improved beyond that possible with other systems using the same processor but lacking a cache memory system.

Cache memory aims to improve memory access times and keep down memory costs. The larger the cache, the greater the hit rate but the greater the cost of the memory. For example, a cache the same size as the main memory would obviously give a 100 per cent hit rate but would defeat the object of having a cache. Modern processors have an integral cache (on the same chip) which provides even better cache performance.

ROM (read only memory)

The term *firmware* is used to describe programs and data which are hard-wired into the computer, using integrated circuit ROM chips. ROM is non-volatile, so its contents are not lost when the machine is switched off and the they cannot be overwritten by other programs or data. ROM is normally used to store an initial set of instructions which allow the booting of a computer system and the subsequent loading of the rest of the operating system. ROM (Read Only Memory) is a permanent storage area for special programs and data which have been installed during the process of computer manufacture. The contents are hard-wired and cannot be altered by software.

The software contained within ROM is fairly standard for most machines and generally includes part of the BIOS (Basic Input/Output System). As the name suggests, the BIOS handles the basic hardware operations of input and output. The aim of the BIOS is to provide an interface between the programmer and the computer. The interface relieves the programmer of concern about the physical characteristics of the hardware devices which form the system. As such, the BIOS is machine orientated and will vary from one make of machine to another.

There are two other types of ROM:

- *PROM* or programmable ROM chips, which can be purchased content-free and used to store software, such as word processors and spreadsheets, which are used regularly. Plugged into vacant slots inside a computer's system casing, the software they contain can then be accessed without reference to conventional backing storage, but simply by transfer to RAM (Random Access Memory - main memory). It has to be said that this is now less common, and most packages are stored on either a CD-ROM or hard disk drive, from where they can be loaded very quickly. Software is frequently being upgraded and the trouble of replacing ROM chips makes it an unattractive option. Once recorded upon, PROM chips cannot be re-used for any other purpose;

- *EPROM* or erasable programmable ROM chips fulfil a similar function to PROM chips, except for the fact that their contents can be erased by exposure to ultra-violet light and then replaced using a special EPROM programmer device.

Flash memory

The main memory in notebook computers is sometimes provided by flash memory, which requires no battery power to maintain its contents. Power is required to read from and write to the memory. Unfortunately, the access times are slower than those available with conventional forms of RAM and a flash memory card will wear out after approximately 10,000 erasures. Of course, they can be replaced when this happens. A flash memory card can be write-protected and because it includes a standard *interface* (see Chapter 14), it can be made to appear as a hard disk to the rest of the computer system.

Associative or content addressable memory

This type of memory allows its addressing according to the *contents* of locations rather than their physical addresses. Apart from Search (or Match) operations, associative memory also allows Reading and Writing according to the addressing principles used in RAM systems. For search operations, the contents of each memory word are compared with a given character string. Each memory word has an associated flag bit and if a match with the search string is found, the relevant flag is set. It is quite possible that the search string will not be unique to one memory location, so multiple matches are likely to be discovered in a single search operation. With the use of a *mask register*, the search string does not have to be compared with the full contents of each memory word; thus, for example, it can be compared with the contents of only the first 4 bits of each 8 bit memory word. Table 7.1 illustrates a masked search operation.

A *logical AND* operation (Chapter 5) is carried out between the search register and the mask register; this ensures that only those bits in the search register which correspond with bit 1s in the mask register will be used in the search string.

	masked bits							
search register	0	0	1	1	0	1	0	1	
mask register	1	1	1	1	0	0	0	0	logical AND with search register
	0	0	1	1	0	0	0	0	resulting search string
memory word 0	0	1	0	1	0	1	0	1	0 flag (no match)
memory word 1	0	0	1	1	0	1	1	1	1 flag (match)
memory word 2	0	0	1	1	1	1	0	1	1 flag (match)
memory word 3	0	0	0	1	1	1	1	0	0 flag (no match)

Table 7.1. *Use of a mask register on 4 bits*

Associative memory has obvious application for on-line information retrieval systems, but to be useful must make use of much longer word lengths to allow for example, search criteria involving names of people or products. To date, high cost has restricted its application.

Processor

The processor is a CPU (Central Processing Unit) on a chip and provides the central base for a machine's power. The following section examines a number of processor features and standards.

Registers

Apart from the registers used in the *fetch-execute cycle* (Chapter 4), most processors have a number which are general-purpose and as such, can be used by the low-level programmer to store intermediate results of processing. *Index* registers can be used to hold offset values to allow indexed indirect addressing methods (Chapter 4) or can be used as counters. Another register contains the *stack pointer*, which is used to store the address of the next available location in a special area of memory called the stack. The operation of the stack is described in Chapter 32 on Data Structures. A *flag* or *status* register is used for the storage of various flag bits which can be set to 1 or cleared to 0 depending on some condition, and typically include:

- *sign* flag (positive or negative) indicating the sign of the result of the last arithmetic operation; this would be copied from the sign bit of the result of this last operation;

- *carry* flag, set to 1 if the last arithmetic operation produced a carry;

- *zero* flag, set to 1 if the result of the last arithmetic operation was zero and to 0 if the result was non-zero;

- *overflow* flag to indicate the occurrence of arithmetic overflow in the last operation;

- *break* status, set to 1 if a break instruction has been executed;

- *interrupt* disable flag, set to 1 if interrupts are disabled (Chapters 13 and 14).

Clock speed

As the initiator of all the activities in a computer, the processor has a wide range of tasks to perform and to ensure that these tasks are properly synchronized, an internal clock mechanism is used. The speed of the clock is one determinant of how quickly a processor can *execute* instructions.

A *program* (a set of instructions designed to make the computer perform in a particular way) is executed by *fetching* each instruction in turn from the computer's memory, *decoding* the operation required and then performing the operation under the direction of the processor. The control of *program execution* is exercised through the processor's *automatic sequence control mechanism*. The activity it controls is known as the *fetch-execute cycle*.

Certain steps in the fetch-execute cycle must wait until the previous step is completed. For example, during the fetching of a program instruction from memory the instruction cannot be moved from the Memory Buffer Register (MBR) to the Current Instruction Register (CIR) until the transfer from memory to MBR has been completed. The time taken for the latter transfer is dependent on the speed of the memory read operation. Not all activities are dependent on the prior completion of another or others. For example, once the value of the Program Counter (PC) has been copied to the Memory Address Register (MAR), the PC can be incremented at any time during the fetch-execute cycle.

Synchronising operations

To synchronize the processor's operations, the clock generates regularly timed pulses, often in excess of a 100 million per second. A technical specification will express this rating in MHz (Megahertz or million *cycles* per second). For example a 166 MHz processor operates with a clock running at 166 million pulses or cycles per second.

Different processor activities take different times to complete. For example, it takes longer to read the contents of a memory location (a *memory read*) than to increment a value stored in one of the registers within the processor. Any such processor activity must be synchronized with a clock cycle. The number of clock cycles which the processor needs to complete an operation will depend on the type of operation. For example, one operation may be completed within a single clock cycle, whilst another may take several cycles. The most recent processors are able to execute one or more instructions for each clock pulse.

Wait state

When a processor handles data more quickly than it can be accessed from main memory, a memory read may take more than one clock cycle to complete. Each additional clock cycle is known as a wait state. The topic is referred to earlier, in the section on *cache memory*. Subject to certain limitations to be explained later, the greater the clock rate, the quicker the computer system (as a whole) will perform. For example, a 100 MHz processor will carry out processing more quickly than a 66 MHz processor.

Word length

Any given processor is designed to handle a particular number of bits as a unit. The size of this unit is known as the processor's *word length*. A processor with a word length of, for example, 32 bits, uses that unit size during the execution of arithmetic, logic, data transfer or input/output instructions. In addition, any working registers within the processor are also equal to the word length of the processor.

Processor data bus

Within the processor, data are transmitted along a set of parallel lines called an *internal data bus*. An *external data bus* acts as the interface with the system's *motherboard*. The motherboard is a circuit board into which the system components are plugged. If the board is designed for the needs of a particular processor, the data path between the processor and memory components is at least as wide as the processor's internal bus. Thus, a motherboard designed to take a 32 bit processor has a 32 bit data path to connect it to other processor or memory chips. The processor's external data bus (which connects with the motherboard) is also 32 bits wide. The motherboard is connected to a *system data bus,* which acts as the communication channel between the motherboard and the other system components. It is worth mentioning that the ISA (Industry Standard Architecture - first used in the IBM AT) design, which is still used in most PCs, has a system data bus which is only 16 bits wide. It also operates at a clock speed of 8 MHz, which is too slow for modern processors. Such imbalance affects the performance of a computer system as a whole (see Bus Architecture). Table 7.2 shows the word lengths of generations of Intel processors.

Processor	word length	internal bus	external bus
8080	8 bits	8 bits	8 bits
8088	16 bits	16 bits	8 bits
8086	16 bits	16 bits	16 bits
80286	16 bits	16 bits	16 bits
i386	32 bits	32 bits	32 bits
i486	32 bits	32 bits	32 bits
P24T	32 bits	64 bits	32 bits
Pentium	32 bits	64 bits	64 bits

Table 7.2. *Generations of Intel processors showing word lengths and bus widths*

Maths co-processors

Most processors have an associated faster processor (known as a maths co-processor) which can radically improve the performance of processor-intensive applications, such as spreadsheets and computer-aided design (CAD). For example, associated with the Intel processors mentioned earlier are the 8087, 80287, i387 and i487. The Intel i386DX, i486DX and Pentium processors, on the other hand, house a maths co-processor on the same chip; data flow is much faster than is possible with a separate co-processor (the SX versions of the i386 and i486 processors do not incorporate a co-processor, and can be upgraded with the i387 and i487, respectively). The co-processor can only improve system performance if the software recognizes and makes use of it.

Processor architecture

The internal structure of a processor is generally referred to as its *architecture*. Within the integrated circuits that form the processor, are contained a complex collection of component units, including registers, counters, arithmetic and logic circuits and memory elements. Although the details of such architecture are mainly of concern to the programmer working at machine code level, two main approaches to processor design are briefly described below. All the instructions available with a particular processor are known as its *instruction set*. CISC is an acronym for *complex instruction set computer* and RISC stands for *reduced instruction set computer*.

CISC architecture

For some time, the view was that longer word lengths should be used to create more complex instruction sets and thus, more powerful processors. This approach has given way to the RISC design, which makes more effective use of the increased word lengths available in modern processors.

RISC architecture

A RISC processor exhibits a number of particular design features:

- A reduced instruction set processor, as the name suggests, is one which provides only a small number of different instructions compared with the prevailing standards for its CISC competitors. Research into conventional CISC architecture has suggested that the average processor spends most of its time executing only a handful of simple instructions. Each instruction type in a RISC processor can be executed in only one clock pulse. More complex instructions can take several clock pulses.

- Super scalar execution. This is the ability to execute more that one instruction at once (in parallel pipelines). Thus, for example, a floating point arithmetic calculation can be executed in one pipeline, at the same time as an integer operation in the other. A separate arithmetic unit is available to deal with each. Intel's Pentium processor can, therefore, execute two instructions in one clock pulse, compared with its predecessor's (the i486) one.

- Integral cache memory. The topic of cache memory is examined earlier, but the location of this component on the processor provides faster data flow than is possible with a separate cache memory component.

- Branch prediction. The processor contains circuitry to predict the outcome of conditional branch instructions (when a certain condition is true, the program branches to an instruction out of the usual sequence) before they even enter the pipeline. Predictions are based on previous execution history. A correct prediction avoids retrieval of irrelevant instructions into the pipeline; instead, the valid instruction is fetched from the branch target address. An incorrect prediction means that the pipeline has to be cleared, but the algorithms for prediction achieve a high success rate, which makes the technique worthwhile.

A British microcomputer manufacturer, Acorn, was among the first to produce a RISC microcomputer called the ARM (Acorn RISC Machine). Now, all the world's major computer manufacturers produce their own RISC-based machines. Notable examples of modern RISC processors include the IBM RISC/6000 series, IBM/Motorola PowerPC601, DEC Alpha AXP and the Sun Microsystems/Texas Instruments SuperSparc. Such processors are designed for high performance systems, to be used as *file servers* or *workstations* in networks (see Chapter 10), rather than as stand-alone machines, where the power would be wasted. Unlike the Alpha, PowerPC and SuperSparc processors, which have been designed purely as RISC processors, the Intel i486 and Pentium processors have had to retain some CISC features, to remain compatible with the huge range of PC software designed for the i386 and its predecessors. The Alpha, PowerPC and SuperSparc processors are pure RISC processors and not compatible with software designed for the Intel range. This means that they are excluded from the lucrative PC software market. Although the Pentium still includes some complex instruction support, its design includes all the RISC features outlined earlier.

Parallel processing architectures

The potential for increasing computation speed through parallelism has long been recognized, its first real manifestation being in the change from computers which handled data serially bit by bit with a single processor to those manipulating parallel bit groupings or words, albeit still with only one processor. Parallelism as described here is concerned with the use, in a variety of approaches, of multiple processors to act upon either single or multiple streams of data. A number of factors have permitted the research and development of parallel processing architectures, which previously had not been cost-effective.

The development of VLSI (Very Large Scale Integration) circuits has allowed tremendous progress to be made in the miniaturization of computer components, most significantly in terms of processor and memory chips, but although users have felt the benefits of significant speed improvements, they have not been of the same order. They continue to improve, but it has been apparent for some time that the power needs of some applications go beyond single processor systems. It is also recognized that the greatest increases in speed can be obtained through changes in system architecture. The RISC (Reduced Instruction Set Computer) approach is already bringing about significant benefits, but parallel architectures, despite the particular difficulties they present for the design of software which can take full advantage, probably hold the greatest potential for radical performance gains. Parallel hardware is, of course, only half the solution and it must be also possible to write programs that can execute in parallel. The Occam programming language developed by Inmos, addresses the special requirements of writing code for arrays of *transputers* (see later).

Architectural approaches to parallelism

The following sections provide information on some of the ways in which degrees of parallelism may be achieved.

Pipelining

This term refers to the activities of a pipeline of processors each of which performs a mathematical operation on a *single vector stream* of data. The approach is based on the premise that any arithmetic process incorporates a number of distinct stages which can be separately allocated to individual processors.

Each processor has an associated register, isolated from the rest, and permitting parallel computation on the data. A clock pulse synchronizes the activities of all processors in the pipeline, so that the data moves through it, step by step with each clock pulse. As an illustrative example, floating point addition requires the performance of a sequence of three operations, namely to: (i) equalize the exponents, adjusting one mantissa as necessary; (ii) add the mantissas; (iii) normalize the result.

New sets of numbers to be added can be fed into the pipeline as each set moves through it to produce the sum.

Instruction pipeline

Pipeline processing can also be applied to the instruction stream. Using the buffering principle, consecutive instructions are read from memory into the pipeline, while preceding instructions are executed by the processor. Complications arise when an instruction causes a branch out of sequence, at which point the pipe must be cleared and all instructions read from memory, but not yet processed, are discarded. The overall effect of such *queuing* is to reduce the average memory access time for reading instructions.

Although pipelining can be described as a parallel architecture, the processors are only operating on a single vector stream of data and the acronym SISD (Single Instruction Single Data-stream) is frequently used to describe its mode of operation. A major advantage of pipeline architecture is that program code developed for von Neumann architecture, that is *serial code*, can be run without modification, whilst improvements in the performance of programs particularly suited to pipeline processing can be changed accordingly. This requires the identification of discrete processing stages and the division of particularly processor-hungry sections of code for allocation to separate processors. A number of manufacturers have produced powerful machines of this type.

Processor arrays

Processors connected in a pipeline can be described as forming a linear array, but the following section is concerned with two and three-dimensional processor arrays, for which the Inmos transputer was specifically designed.

SIMD (single instruction multiple data-stream)

In a two-dimensional array, for example, 4096 processors may be connected in a 64×64 square, so that each one has 4 neighbouring elements.

Known as SIMD architecture, each program instruction is transmitted *simultaneously* to all the processors in the array, so each can then execute the instruction using its *locally* stored set of data. Because all processors are executing the same instruction at any one time, existing serial code can be used, provided the data can be conveniently divided. By the parallel processing of large numbers of data sets at one time, massive increases in job processing speed can be achieved. Of course, not all processors in the array are necessarily concerned with a particular processing stage and data may have to be passed on to the next relevant processor via a number of array elements which have no interest in the data. The length of such communications paths can have a significant effect on system performance and in efforts to reduce the number of processors handling data with which they have no concern, a number of geometrical designs (beyond the requirements of this text) are in use.

MIMD (multiple instruction multiple data-stream)

This also permits the parallel processing of separate sets of data, but each processor is at a different stage in the program's execution. More complex than the SIMD approach, it requires firstly, the vectoring of the program code into separate processes, each with the potential for execution on a separate processor and secondly in some systems, the division of data into *local* (available to a particular processor) and *global* (available to all). Each processor can be viewed as dealing with a particular part of the overall program and a particular data set, as well as having access to certain data available globally to all processors. In order that they can be executed in parallel, each of the processes should be substantially independent of the rest, although in general, they need to communicate with one another. If global memory is used for such communication, co-ordination difficulties can arise. In the Cray 2 system for example, passing data from one processor to another via global memory, requires the synchronization of the write operation by the transmitting processor and the subsequent read by the receiving one. The *transputer* incorporates serial links which allow communications between processors and the concept of global memory is not used.

Parallel processing applications

A number of applications likely to benefit particularly from parallel processing are outlined below.

- *Weather forecasting*, which requires number crunching operations on huge volumes of data, gathered globally and from monitoring satellites, in time to produce accurate weather forecasts, rather than comments on existing weather conditions!

- *Graphics applications*. Ray tracing, for example, where a set of descriptors of three-dimensional objects in three-dimensional space is mapped onto a flat screen complete with shadows, refraction and reflections, needs considerable computation to trace where the light on each screen pixel came from. The application is most easily implemented on pipeline architecture, where it benefits from both the faster maths and the faster communication. With about 10 million calculations to generate a single screen picture, speed is vital when generating sequences of images. A major application is in aircraft flight simulators, where the scenes to be shown are not known exactly in advance, as they depend on the pilot's actions. To be of any use they need to be generated virtually instantaneously in real-time.

- *Simulation*. Engineering design problems benefit hugely from computer simulation. The designers of North Sea oil platforms could ill afford to build prototypes to test to destruction, so they carry out all the structural analysis on a Cray supercomputer costing around 20 million; the process only takes about 9 hours, but the time taken still makes extensive prototyping very expensive. A car body designer using a 1 million mainframe has to wait about 20 hours for a typical run to complete. These lengthy run-times mean that computer simulation tends to be used to validate designs already completed, rather than as a development tool.

- *Image processing*. A particularly exciting example involves the use of computers to assist the plastic surgeon in the repair of facial injuries or deformities. The patients head is scanned by cameras and the image digitized for display on a computer screen. This image can be rotated or tilted on screen by the surgeon and experimental cuts made, the results of which can then be viewed on screen from any angle. In this way, a plastic surgeon can study the results of a variety of strategies before making a single mark on the patient. The complexity of such image processing requires parallel processing if rapid response to user input is to be achieved. Industrial processes frequently require robots which can recognize different shaped components and possess sufficient spatial awareness to allow accurate assembly to take place. Artificial intelligence techniques are applied to both these areas, so that robots can learn and the power of parallel processing greatly enhances the opportunity for such developments.

- *Speech recognition* is an enormously complex process if a system is to be capable of handling a wide range of vocabulary, pronunciation and intonation, let alone the meaning of phrases and even sentences. Artificial intelligence techniques are being applied to the speech recognition process and parallel processing power greatly improves the opportunities for its evolution.

- *Financial and economic system modelling.* To make realistic assessments of the effectiveness of various economic strategies requires the processing of huge volumes of raw data.

Multi-processing

Parallel processing should not be confused with multi-processing architectures which allow the simultaneous running of several separate programs, but with each program only having control of one processor at a time.

Transputers

The Transputer is effectively a building block for parallel processing architectures; while it contains its own memory and processing elements, it also features unique serial links which allow it to communicate with other Transputers. A matrix of Transputers can be created with each one solving a small part of a complete task. The addition of extra Transputers to a system incrementally adds the full power of each unit to the overall system performance. In theory, if one Transputer operates at 10 million instructions per second (mips), then two will give a system performance of 20 mips, 10 will give 100 mips and so on. In practice, the problem still remains of splitting computer processing problems into separate parts for each of the transputers to handle.

Buses

As explained in Chapter 6, all computers have the same basic functional components, but the architectural details in some are far more complex than in others. A particular area of variation relates to the arrangement of the bus systems which permit communication between the various parts of the computer system. A number of features concerning buses can be identified:

- a bus is a group of parallel wires, one for each bit of a word, along which data can flow (as electrical signals);

- the *system* bus comprises a number of such communication channels, connecting a computer's processor and its associated components of memory and input/output(I/O) devices;

- a single bus may carry data for different functions at separate times or it may be dedicated to one function. A computer will usually have several buses, used for specific purposes, for example, the I/O bus or main memory to processor bus;

- some buses are *bi-directional*, that is by the enabling and inhibiting of *gates* (Chapter 5), data can flow in one direction or the other;

- the *width* of a bus determines the length of word which can be handled at one time. For example, a processor which used a 16-bit bus, but required a 32-bit word to address memory, would have to concatenate two 16-bit words in two separate fetch operations.

Communication is required within a processor, to allow movement of data between its various registers, between the processor and memory and for I/O transfers. In a *single* bus system, both I/O and memory transfers share the same communication channel, whereas in a *two-bus* system, I/O and memory transfers are carried out independently; similarly, in small systems with few I/O devices, they usually share the same bus, but a larger system requires several I/O buses to ensure efficient operation.

Each of the separately identified functions of memory, register-to-register and I/O transfers (assuming that the I/O bus is shared by a number of devices), must have the use of:

- a *data bus*, for the transfer of data subject to processing or manipulation in the machine;

- an *address bus* which carries the address of, for example, a memory word to be read (the details of memory addressing as part of the fetch-execute cycle are described in Chapter 4), or the output device to which a character is to be transmitted;

- a *control bus*, which as the name suggest, carries signals concerning the timing of various operations, such as memory write, memory read and I/O operations (this latter aspect of control is examined in more detail in Chapter 14).

All signals on a bus follow strict timing sequences, some operations taking longer than others.

Bus architecture

This concerns the internal structure of a computer, that is the way in which the various components are connected and communicate with one another. As technological advances improve the performance of certain components, so the architecture has to change to take advantage of these improvements. A brief summary of some architectural standards folows. These have been developed and used in recent years, with the aim of improving overall system performance.

- IBM's Micro Channel Architecture (MCA); despite the commercial power of IBM, this standard has not found general acceptance;

- Extended Industry Standard Architecture (EISA);

- Local Bus (VESA and PCI).

Micro channel architecture (MCA)

MCA aimed to overcome the limitations of the old, Industry Standard Architecture (ISA), IBM AT (Advanced Technology) machines as well as a myriad of clones produced by IBM's competitors. IBM used MCA in their 32-bit PS/2 (Personal System 2) range.

System bus width and system performance

One of the many differences with the MCA approach concerns the width of the *system bus*. This bus is a communication link between the processor and system components and is an essential, but passive, part of system architecture. The active components, such as the processor, disk controller and other peripherals are the primary determinants of system performance. As long as the data transfer speed along the bus matches the requirements of these devices and does not create a bottleneck, the bus does not affect system performance. The MCA bus is 32 bits, compared with the AT's 16 bits, and the wider data path allows components within the system to be accessed twice as quickly. The MCA bus also uses bus-mastering controllers to handle data transfers more quickly. The wider bus is also compatible with the 32-bit external bus used on more recent processors. The bus can be controlled by separate *bus master* processors, relieving the main processor of this task.

MCA is also radically different from AT architecture in many other respects. For example, the expansion slots in the PS/2 range which allow the user to insert extra features, perhaps for networking or for extra memory, are physically different from those in the AT and PC machines and their expansion cards will not fit in the PS/2 machines. The problem for existing AT and PC users is that they cannot buy new PS/2 machines and still make use of their existing expansion cards. This incompatibility has also meant that few manufacturers have produced MCA versions of their expansion cards. IBM and Apricot are the biggest proponents of the MCA standard, but the fact that IBM is continuing to release ISA models is possibly an admission that MCA is unlikely to become the dominant architecture.

Extended industry standard architecture (EISA)

A consortium of IBM's competitors including Compaq, Zenith, NEC and Olivetti amongst others, established a new architecture (EISA - Extended Industry Standard Architecture) which aims to give the benefits of MCA and to retain compatibility with existing AT expansion cards. EISA also uses a 32-bit bus, thus providing the same data transfer benefits as MCA, particularly for hard disk controllers (a very important contributor to overall system performance).

Both EISA and MCA machines are more expensive than the ISA-based microcomputers, and tend to be used where extra power is needed, as *file servers* (Chapter 10) in networked systems. Most small business users find that ISA machines are adequate for their needs, particularly as the use of *local bus* technology is further increasing their power.

Local bus

A local bus is a high speed data path connecting the processor with a peripheral. Local bus design is used, primarily, to speed communications with hard disk controllers and display adapters. The need for local bus derives from the imbalance between the clock speed of a 32-bit processor (typically, in excess of 100MHz) and the ISA 16-bit system bus (operating at 8 MHz). The ISA system is illustrated in Figure 7.2.

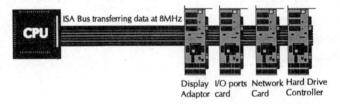

Figure 7.2. *ISA 8MHz bus and high speed processor imbalance*

This imbalance can result in the processor idling while waiting for data to be transferred from disk, or the display adapter waiting for screen data. The widespread use of Windows, a *graphical user interface* and software packages which make intensive use of the hard disk (such as databases) and screen graphics (computer-aided design), has highlighted the deficiencies of such imbalanced computer systems. A local bus provides a wider data path, currently 32 bits and an increased clock speed, typically 33MHz or more. The first local bus systems appeared in 1992, with manufacturers following a standard referred to as *VL-bus*, developed by VESA

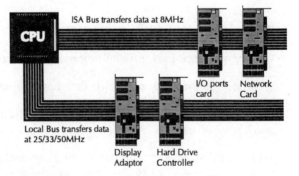

Figure 7.3. *Local bus to high speed display and hard drive devices*

(Video Electronics Standards Association). Figure 7.3 illustrates the broad principle of a local bus system. In 1993, Intel backed the development of a new industry standard called *PCI*.

The standard is in competition with VL-bus and aims to encourage the development of computer systems which allow local bus connection to any high-speed peripheral. Apart from speeding communication with screen graphics controllers, PCI local bus can be used with, for example, hard disk, network and motion video controllers (up to 10 devices in total).

Expansion slots

These are slots into which expansion boards or cards can be plugged, to add extra features to a system. For example, a user may wish to install a sound card, to allow full use of multi-media software, or an additional serial port (see Chapter 11) to connect to a modem. Expansion slots are connected to the system bus (it makes electrical contact), so when an expansion card is plugged in, it becomes part of the system.

I/O ports and interfacing

To allow an I/O device to communicate with the I/O bus, for example, to place data entered through a keyboard onto the data bus, requires the use of an I/O port. A number of I/O ports are usually available, the number and types depending on the range of devices which the system is designed to support. Each port has an *interfacing* role which must convert the data signals, as presented by the connected device, into the form required by the processor, as well as the converse for output data. Thus, for example, the *external* ASCII code used for data storage on a particular tape storage system, will probably have to be converted by the interface into the machine's particular *internal* code (Chapter 2).

Exercises

1. What is *cache memory* and why is it used?

2. What do the abbreviations *CISC* and *RISC* stand for?

3. Why may a 'clock-doubled' processor not necessarily double the speed of the overall computer system?

4. What is meant by *parallel processing*?

5. What significance have parallel processing architectures for the way software is designed?

6. What are the functions of the: (i) data bus; (ii) address bus; (iii) control bus?

7. Describe examples of architectural changes which have sought to overcome the performance restrictions of the ISA bus.

8. Research PC magazines for differing computer configurations and draw up a table which compares their specifications (RAM size, type, processor type, speed etc.). Judge the suitability of each for particular kinds of application (graphic design, word processing, accounts etc.).

Chapter 8

Input and Output Devices

Input devices

Input devices provide a convenient means of transferring information into a computer so that it may be processed in some way or stored permanently on magnetic media. Whatever its particular purpose, each type of input device is an *interface*, a means of bridging the gap between the human user and the electronic computer. For example, an input device such as computer *keyboard* converts the pressing of a key into an electrical signal representing a particular binary code; this code could represent a character within a word processing document, or it could be part of a response to a question posed by the current computer program. An interactive device such as a *mouse* or a *touch screen* provides a convenient method of communicating actions to a computer. Other input devices, such as *scanners* and *optical mark readers*, allow typed or hand-written documents to be read into a computer. In this section we describe several categories of input devices, namely *interactive devices*, *analogue to digital converters*, and *document readers*.

Interactive input devices

Interactive input devices are used in conjunction with visual display units so that the user is provided with immediate feedback on the task being performed by the computer. For example, the movement of a mouse or tracker ball is shown by a pointer on a display screen, and when a key is pressed on a keyboard, the appropriate character appears on the screen.

Computer keyboard

The main section of a typical computer keyboard is similar to a typewriter keyboard, with the usual alphabetic and punctuation characters. The *shift* keys are used to switch between upper case (capital) letters and lower case (small) letters. The *control* keys are sometimes used to change the operation of a normal key. For example, holding down one of the control keys while hitting the *F* key might activate a menu. The separate *numeric keypad* is useful when data includes a high proportion of numeric characters. The *function* keys are used by application programs for special purposes, so the operation of a function key will often be different from one program to another, but quite frequently function key *F1* is used to gain access to a help facility if one is provided.

A keyboard is usually detachable, enabling the operator to position it to suit personal comfort, but it remains physically connected by a coiled cable. The desirable qualities of a keyboard are reliability, quietness and light operating pressure and in these terms keyboards vary considerably.

Keyboards are commonly used for the following types of tasks:

- entering alphanumeric information (that is, combinations of alphabetic, numeric and special characters such as punctuation marks) into the computer. A typical example of this is the use of a keyboard for word processing;

- interactively communicating with a program which asks the user questions and responds to the answers. A good example of this is an expert system (see Chapter 12) which provides advice on some area of interest after asking the user a sequence of questions;

- controlling animated graphics characters in computer games;

- entering commands to an operating system such as MS-DOS.

Concept keyboard

In specialist applications, the standard keyboard is not always the most convenient method of input. In a factory, for example, a limited number of functions may be necessary for the operation of a computerized lathe. These functions can be set out on a touch sensitive pad and clearly marked. This is possible because all inputs are anticipated and the range is small. The operator is saved the trouble of typing in the individual characters which form instructions.

Concept keyboards also have application in education, particularly for the mentally and physically handicapped. Instead of specific functions, interchangeable overlays, which indicate the functions of each area of the keyboard allow the user to design the keyboard to particular specifications.

Mouse

A mouse is a small, hand-held device which the user can move on a flat surface to direct a pointer on the computer screen. It has two or more buttons which work in conjunction with software packages, allowing the user to draw, erase, select and format textual and graphical images. The most common type incorporates a ball which makes contact with the flat surface on which the mouse is moved and turns two rollers, one tracking vertical movements on screen, the other horizontal. The movement of the rollers is detected by sensors which continually send electrical signals through the mouse cable to the computer, reporting the location of the mouse. The software then uses these signals to adjust the pointer's position on the computer screen so that the pointer follows the movement of the mouse. Another type of mouse detects movement purely by optical sensors which work in

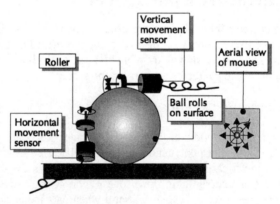

Figure 8.1. *How the mouse movement is detected*

conjunction with a special mouse pad, and some are cable-less, using infra-red to transfer signals to the computer in a way similar to the use of remote controls for TVs.

Most computer systems are equipped with a mouse facility and many packages, including those for art, design, word processing and desktop publishing can only be operated effectively with a mouse. Graphical user interfaces (GUIs - see Chapter 12) such as Microsoft Windows also depend heavily on its use.

Tracker ball

A tracker ball is another variation of a mouse and is used for the same purposes. A tracker ball is a bit like an upside-down mouse, with the ball visible on the top of the base. To use a tracker ball you simply move the ball in the required direction using your fingers. Buttons are supplied, as with a mouse.

Figure 8.2. *Tracker ball*

Like joysticks, tracker balls have the advantage over mice, in that a flat surface is not required for its operation, and for this reason they are often used with portable computers.

Touch screen

A touch screen is a touch-sensitive display, used to read the position of a fingertip. The screen displays options which a user can select simply by touching them. The computer detects the position touched and performs the appropriate action. The range of input values which can be selected will normally be small (a finger is not a very precise pointing device), so a touch screen might typically be used by a tourist agency to allow visitors to request information on, for example, local accommodation, entertainment and tourist attractions, or by a bank to allow customers to view details of banking services. The main components of a touch screen are a special film coating on the surface of the screen and a controlling microprocessor which determines the co-ordinates of the finger's contact point and displays the required information.

Digitizing tablet

A *digitizing tablet* consists of a flat surface, containing an active area, typically 250mm square, which has a grid of very fine horizontal and vertical wires embedded into it. Attached to the tablet is a *stylus* which produces a magnetic field at its tip. The grid of wires allows the position of the stylus on the tablet to be determined very accurately (the grid can contain up to 1000 points per inch), so that the computer can track and store the movement of the stylus. As the user draws on the tablet the results appear on the computer screen. Drawings are stored in the computer's memory so that they can be manipulated or displayed.

Digitizing tablets are useful for entering drawings consisting of lines - engineering drawings or maps for example - into the computer. The line drawing can be placed on the tablet and the stylus used

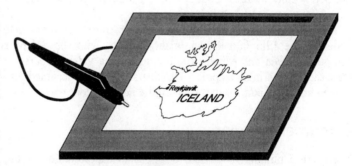

Figure 8.3. *Digitizing tablet with stylus*

to trace the outline or locate key points. Usually the tablet can also be used as a device for selecting options in a similar way to the concept keyboard described earlier, but with the capability of providing many more options. Computer-aided drawing programs often allow templates of pre-defined shapes - electrical circuit components for example - to be overlaid on the tablet so that the user can select a shape which will then appear on the screen ready to be used in a drawing.

Light pen

A light pen has an optical sensor in its tip and can only be used in conjunction with a *cathode ray tube* (CRT) display which creates images on screen through the use of a scanning electron beam; as the beam creates the screen images line by line (see the section on Visual Display Units), the light pen's optical sensor detects the exact moment when the beam passes beneath it and, from this, its position at any particular moment. By displaying functions at particular locations on the screen, the controlling program can allow the light pen to be used to make selections from several alternatives. It may also be used in conjunction with a drawing package to create, edit or manipulate images on screen. Though similar to the operation of a graphics tablet and stylus, a light pen is not capable of the same high accuracy, but it is generally cheaper. LCD (liquid crystal display) displays used in laptop, notebook and palmtop computers do not make use of electron beam scanning and cannot, therefore, support the use of light pens.

Analogue to digital converters (ADCs)

Data is often not in *digital* format but is instead a measurement of, for example, temperature or light intensity. These are called *analogue* forms of data and, before they can be used by a digital computer, they must be converted into digital format. A device which converts analogue data into digital data is called an *analogue to digital converter*(ADC).

If, for example, a certain micro-processor-controlled washing machine allowed you to select several temperature settings for the water, it might use a temperature sensor in conjunction with an ADC to convert water

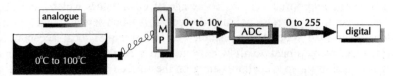

Figure 8.4. *Example of analogue to digital conversion*

temperatures between 0°C and 1000°C to a binary signal in the range 0 to 255, as illustrated in Figure 8.4. The diagram shows a temperature sensor immersed in the water. This will produce a small electrical signal, proportional to the water temperature, which must be amplified so that it produces a voltage in the range 0 volts to 10 volts, for example. The ADC then converts this voltage to a binary signal in the range 0 to 255 (11111111 in binary), so that 0°C is represented by 0 and 100°C is represented by 255. Thus a temperature of 25°C would produce about 2.5 volts from the amplifier and this would translate to binary 63 (00111111).

The term *digitizer* is usually reserved for more complex ADCs used for converting whole frames of photographic film into digital images which, with the aid of suitable software, can be displayed on a computer screen and edited. The output from a video camera, or medical scanning equipment can also be digitized for use in a computer. Digitizers which are designed for textual or graphical documents are usually termed *scanners* and are described in the next section.

Document readers

There are a number of devices designed to capture information, in the form of pictures or text, already printed on paper. Examples of such devices are *scanners, optical character readers* (OCRs), *optical mark readers* (OMRs), *magnetic ink character readers* (MICRs) and *bar code readers*

Scanners

Scanners allow whole documents to be scanned optically and converted into digital images. These vary from small hand-held devices which are manually moved slowly over the document (Figure 8.5), to machines which allow whole sheets of paper to be fed in and scanned automatically (Figure 8.6). Versions of both of these types of scanners are capable of dealing with colour images as well as black and white, though these machines tend to be significantly more expensive. Special scanners are available to convert textual

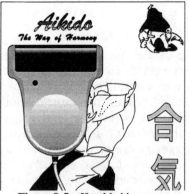

Figure 8.5. *Hand held scanner*

Figure 8.6. *Flat bed scanner*

documents, typed or hand-written, into the sort of format used by word processors. These devices perform *optical character recognition*(OCR*)* and have special software which processes the images once they have been converted into a computer-processable form. The software which can handle handwriting tends to be distinct from that for typed text, and is now commonly available for pen-based portable computers as described in a later section in this chapter.

Optical character reader

As described earlier, these devices perform *optical character recognition* (OCR), the process of converting images of printed or hand-written material into a format suitable for computer processing. Figure 8.7 shows the main components of an optical character reader designed for printed documents. The document is illuminated and scanned by a strong light source and the lens concentrates the documents image onto a detector. The detector passes the image data to the OCR software which processes each character of the image, individually matching each character against stored data of the character set. Non-text regions containing graphics for example are often separated out and saved separately from the text which is output in

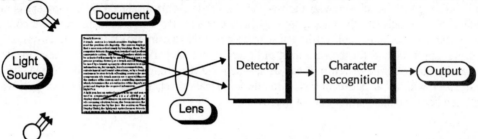

Figure 8.7. *The components of an OCR system*

a format which can be processed by an application program such as a word processor. Most commercial general-purpose OCR devices read machine-written text, but a few can cope with hand-printed text. Special-purpose OCR readers are available for such tasks as reading data on pre-printed forms or processing gas and electricity meter readings.

Optical mark reader (OMR)

An OMR is designed to read simple marks placed in pre-set positions on a document. The document is pre-printed and the values which can be entered are usually limited to marks made in specially placed boxes. Thus, a suitable application for OMR is a multi-choice examination paper, where the answer to each question has to be indicated by a pencil mark in one of several boxes located after the question number. The OMR scans the answer sheet for boxes containing pencil marks and thus identifies the answers, allowing the associated software to determine automatically the grade which the candidate has obtained. Optical mark readers can read up to 10,000 A4 documents per hour.

Magnetic ink character reader (MICR)

This particular device is employed almost exclusively by the banking industry, where it is used for sorting and processing huge volumes of cheques. The millions of cheques which pass through the London Clearing System could not possibly be sorted and processed without the use of devices such as MICRs. Highly stylized characters, such as those illustrated below, are printed along the bottom of the cheques by a special printer, using ink containing iron oxide.

The characters are first magnetized as the cheque passes through the MICR which then electronically reads the magnetized characters. A high degree of reliability and accuracy is possible, partly because of the stylized font, but also because the characters are not affected by dirty marks. This is obviously important when cheques may pass through several hands before reaching their destination. Such marks could cause problems for an optical character reader.

Bar code readers

A *Bar code* usually consists of a series of black bars of varying thickness with varying gaps between. These bars and gaps are used to represent data, which are often printed underneath in human-readable form. Using a laser scanner, the beam passes over the code noting the occasions when light is reflected by a bar and when it is absorbed by a space; the feedback is then converted by the scanner to a computer-readable code. Several standard codes are in use, each having particular features which are appropriate to certain application areas. One very common code is the Universal Product Code (UPC), a purely numeric code which, as the name suggests, is associated with supermarkets and general product distribution.

Bar codes are commonly used to store a variety of data such as prices and stock codes relating to products in shops and supermarkets. A sticker with the relevant bar code (itself produced by computer) is attached to each product, or alternatively, the packaging may be pre-coded. By using the data from the code, the cash register can identify the item, look up its latest price and print the information on the customer's receipt. Another useful application is for the recording of library issues. A bar code sticker is placed inside the book cover and at the time of issue or return it can be scanned and the library stock record updated. By providing each library user with a bar-coded library card, the information relating to an individual borrower can be linked with the book's details at the time of borrowing.

Output devices

Just as input devices allow human beings to communicate with computers, so output devices allow computers to present electronically stored, binary coded data in a form which we can comprehend. In this section we describe *visual display units*, a number of different types of *printers*, two types of *plotters, computer output microform (COM)* and *voice processing* and *sysnthesis*.

Visual display unit

The most commonly used device for communicating with a computer is the *visual display unit* (VDU). Input of text is usually by means of a full alphanumeric keyboard and output is displayed on a viewing screen similar to a television. The term VDU *terminal* is normally used to describe the screen and keyboard as a combined facility for input and output. On its own, the screen is called a *monitor* or *display*. So that an operator can see what is being typed in through the keyboard, input is also displayed on the screen. A square of light called a *cursor* indicates where the next character to be typed by the operator will be placed. Keyboards are described in the section on input devices.

Dumb and intelligent terminals

A dumb terminal is one which has no processing power of its own, possibly no storage, and is entirely dependent on a controlling computer. Where a terminal is connected via a telecommunications link, each character is transmitted to the central computer as soon as it is entered by the operator, making editing extremely difficult and slow; for this reason, they are not generally used for remote data entry.

An intelligent terminal has some memory and processing power and as such, allows the operator to store, edit and manipulate data without the support of the computer to which it is connected. The processing facility is provided by an internal processor, usually a microprocessor and storage is normally in the form of buffer memory in which numerous lines of text can be held and manipulated before transmission. The facility may also include local backing storage and a printer.

A number of text editing tasks involve the use of control codes and these can be built into ROM (Read Only Memory) or magnetic bubble memory, both of which are non-volatile. Typical control codes are those which, through single key-presses, execute functions such as clearing the screen, moving the cursor up or down, and homing the cursor to the top-left of the screen. Function keys for these and other functions are generally specifically marked. It is also likely that the terminal is programmable thus allowing specific routines to be developed for validation of data. Microcomputer systems are often used as intelligent terminals.

Text and graphics modes

All modern display screens operate in either *text* or *graphics mode*. Text consists of letters (upper and lower case), numbers and special characters such as punctuation marks. Most applications require some text display, although it is safe to say that even basic word processors rely almost entirely on the graphics capability of modern screens to permit the use of various character styles or *fonts*. Despite this, the term *graphics* generally refers to picture images, such as maps, charts or drawings produced using graphic design programs, or even photographic images captured with an appropriate *digitizing* device (see section earlier in this chapter).

Text mode dot matrix characters

In text mode (see preceding section), characters are formed using a matrix of pixels, as shown in Figure 8.8, and the clarity of individual characters is determined by the number of pixels used. Selected dots within the matrix are illuminated to display particular characters. A 9 x 16 matrix obviously gives greater clarity and definition than an 8 x 8 matrix. Although both upper and lower case can be accommodated in a particular size matrix, it is usual to add extra rows for the tails of lower case letters such as *g*, *p*, *y* and *j*. There are two main text modes, each defined according to the number of characters which can be displayed on a single line and the number of rows accommodated within the screen's height; they are, 40 characters x 25 rows and 80 characters x 25 rows. The highest *resolution* (see next section) display standard uses 132 characters by 25 or 43 rows.

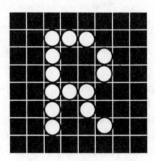

Figure 8.8. *Dot matrix character*

Screen resolution and size

A screen's *resolution* determines the clarity or sharpness of the displayed text or graphics characters. The achievement of high quality graphics generally requires a higher resolution or sharper image than is required for text display. Images are formed on the screen with pixels or tiny dots of light and the density with which they are packed determines the screen's resolution. A typical high-resolution screen provides a pixel density of 1024 columns by 768 rows, a total of 786,432 pixels.

Most microcomputer screens are 14-inch (across the diagonal) but larger screens are often used for applications such as computer-aided design (CAD), where the level of detail on some designs cannot be properly seen on a standard screen, and desktop publishing (DTP) to allow a complete page to be displayed at one time using characters of a readable size. Typical screen sizes are 15, 17, 20 and 21-inch.

Graphics display with bit mapping

To provide maximum control over the screen display, each pixel can be individually controlled by the programmer to give maximum flexibility in the design of individual images. Several *bits* of memory store the colour information for each pixel on the screen; the more colours which are required to be displayed, the more bits which are required per pixel, and the total amount of memory needed for a complete screen depends on the screen resolution, that is, the number of pixels to be displayed. An image, built up in memory pixel by pixel, is used to automatically generate the screen display. This is termed *bit mapping*, which is illustrated in Figure 8.9. With black and white images for example, only one bit per pixel is needed: logic 0 to represent black and logic 1 for white; with four colours, black, red, yellow and white for instance, two bits are needed (00=black, 01=red, 10=yellow, 11=white); three bits are necessary for eight colours, and so on.

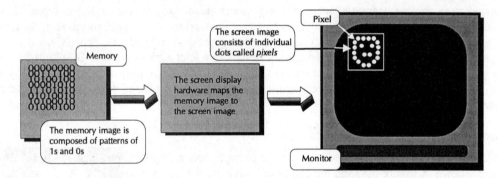

Figure 8.9. *How a bit mapped image is formed*

Where movement is required, for example in computer games, this is achieved in a similar manner to filmed cartoons - smooth movement is simulated by altering the contents of the appropriate memory locations to make small changes to the shape and location of the image. In addition to animation, bit mapping allows the drawing of extremely detailed and life-like pictures and is therefore used by many graphic design and drawing packages. Even word processors or other text-orientated packages make use of bit mapping to allow the display of different character styles and sizes as well as the *icon* images commonly used in WIMP-based *graphical user interfaces* or GUIs (see Chapter 12).

Monochrome and colour

A monochrome screen uses one colour for the foreground and another for the background. White on black is not generally used because of indications from various research studies which say that users suffer greater eye fatigue than is the case with combinations such as green on black or amber on black.

Colour displays require more memory than monochrome, and as explained earlier, the greater the number of colours available for a particular screen resolution, the more memory that is needed. However, a greater range of colours can obtained by using a process called *dithering*. Close to one another, two different colours appear to merge into a new colour, so by carefully mixing pixels of different colours on the screen, many new colours can be created from the true ones available. Though colour displays require a great deal of memory, over recent years the fall in memory costs and the improvements in screen resolution and quality are making them the norm rather than the exception.

Ferroelectric liquid crystal display (FLCD)

The growing market for portable devices, such as laptop and notebook computers and personal digital devices (PDAs) has increased the need for flat screen displays with low power consumption (portable devices are examined at the end of this chapter). Ferroelectric liquid crystal display or FLCD fulfils these requirements and is the most widely used technology for portable devices. It uses ferroelectric materials as bistable (two state) devices. Computer components use bistable devices to indicate a binary 1 or 0. Binary coding is used throughout a computer system to represent every kind of information which it handles; such information could be, for example, text, numbers or bit mapped (see earlier) screen images. The ferroelectric bistable device remains in one of two stable states until an electric field is applied. The field causes the material to switch to its second state; this state remains until another electric field is applied. The full display consists of FLC cells, sandwiched between two glass plates. When a positive charge is applied to a cell, light is blocked and the image appears dark. A negative charge changes the orientation of the molecules in the FLC cell and light is able to pass through. Cells are arranged in rows and columns, like the pixels (picture elements - the dots which make up the screen image) on a CRT display. Filters are used to provide colour images.

Display quality cannot yet match that of the CRT screen, but power consumption is very low. A CRT screen image is updated (scanned) 50 to 60 times per second (Hz), whereas the refresh rate for an FLC display can be as low as 10Hz. Low power consumption is an important quality for battery powered devices, such as notebook computers. The need for 'greener' (less environmentally damaging) computer systems is likely to advance the cause of this type of display. Larger FLC displays (up to 21 inches) are available, but they are expensive and, currently, do not provide serious competition for the desktop computer's CRT display.

Printers

Printers are classed as being either *impact* or *non-impact* devices, but within these two categories there are large variations in speed of operation and quality of print. Speed of operation is largely dependent on whether the printer produces a character, a line or a page at a time. Impact printing uses a print head to strike an inked ribbon which is located between the print head and the paper. Individual characters can be printed, either by a *dot-matrix* mechanism, or by print heads which contain each character as a separate font (*solid font* type). Non-impact printers do not use mechanical hammers. Though non-impact *ink* and *bubble jet printers* use dot matrix heads similar to some impact printers, the method of transferring the ink to the paper is different, and *laser printers* work on a different principle entirely, a technology closely related to that used in photocopiers.

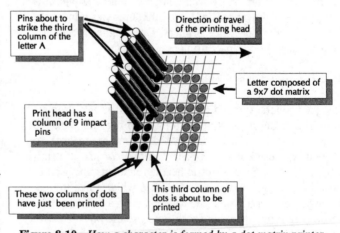

Dot matrix printers

Characters can be formed from a matrix of dots (see the section on VDUs) and the density of the matrix largely determines the quality of the print. The impact is carried out by a number of tiny pins (typically nine or twenty-four) each of which can be pro-

Figure 8.10. *How a character is formed by a dot matrix printer*

jected or withdrawn according to the pattern which is required. The mechanism is illustrated in Figure 8.10. A *ROM* (*Read Only Memory*) chip inside the printer provides it with one or more character sets, and character styles, or *fonts*. Other fonts may be provided by plug-in cartridge or by software. Most printers now provide a range of print qualities and styles which can be selected through a keypad on the casing.

Increased density of print is achieved by passing the print head over a line twice (*double-striking*). Because the individual pins of dot matrix printers can usually be controlled by software, such printers are capable of producing graphical images as well as text. Some matrix-dot printers have special mechanisms and ink ribbons which enable them to produce colour images.

Barrel printer

The barrel printer has a band with a complete set of characters at each print position, of which there are usually 132. Each print position has a hammer to impact the print ribbon against the paper. The mechanism is illustrated in Figure 8.11. One complete revolution of the barrel exposes all the characters to each print position, so a complete line can be printed in one revolution. The characters on the barrel are arranged so that all characters of the same type are in the same horizontal position. Thus, for example, any required *A*s can be printed, then *B*s and so on, until the complete line is printed. The barrel revolves continuously during printing, the paper being fed through and the process repeated for each line of print. Typical printing speeds are 100 to 400 lines per minute. Barrel printers are used for high volume text output.

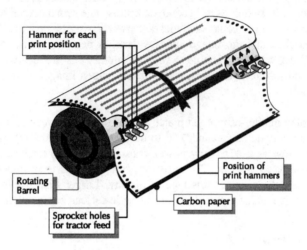

Figure 8.11. *How a barrel printer works*

Line printers are expensive compared with character printers but may be necessary where large volume text output is required. Printing speeds of up to 3000 lines per minute are achieved with impact line printers. Even higher speeds are possible with non-impact printers.

Ink jet printers

Ink jet printers spray high-speed streams of ink droplets from individual nozzles in the print head onto the paper to form characters. There are two different approaches to propelling the ink onto the paper. In *thermal* ink jet printers (see Figure 8.12) electric heating elements are used to heat the ink and form vapour bubbles, which force the ink through fine nozzles onto the paper; the empty nozzles then refill. The other main approach is to use the *piezo-electric effect*. Here, a small electrical signal causes a special type of crystal to alter in size, thus creating a pump-like action which forces the ink through the nozzle. Otherwise, the action of this printer is essentially the same as for the thermal type. As for a impact dot matrix printer, characters

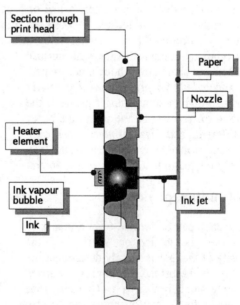

Figure 8.12. *Part of the print head of an inkjet printer*

are formed by the print head printing a number of columns of dots, but because the ink nozzles can be made so small, the separation of the individual dots is much smaller, thus producing much higher quality output. (Typically, there are between 40 and 60 such nozzles). By a series of passes and adjustments to the head's position, graphical images can be produced.

Ink jet printers produce output much more slowly than laser printers. However, printing quality is very high and they provide a relatively cheap alternative to the laser printer, particularly so when colour output is required.

Laser printers

Laser printers use a combination of two technologies: electro-photographic printing used in photo-copying, and high-intensity lasers. Figure 8.13 illustrates the operation of a laser printer. Once the image to be printed has been transferred to the printer's memory, a microprocessor inside the printer converts the image, line by line, into a sequence of signals which switch a laser beam on and off. Each laser beam pulse, representing a single dot of the image, is reflected by a rotating mirror to the surface of a drum. The special surface of the drum is given an electrical charge wherever the laser beam strikes. After a horizontal line of the image has been transferred to the drum in this manner, the drum rotates so that the next line can be built up. As the drum rotates, it comes into contact with plastic ink powder, called *toner*, which is attracted to the electrically charged areas of the drum. Because the printer paper has been given an electrical charge greater than that of the drum, the toner is transferred to the paper as the latter comes into contact with the drum. Finally, the toner is permanently bonded to the paper by means of heated rollers.

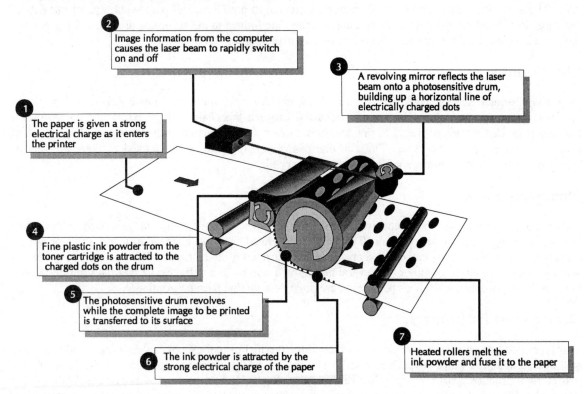

Figure 8.13. *How a laser printer works*

Achieving print speeds of 500 pages per minute (ppm), the most expensive laser printers are used in very large systems which require exceptionally high speed output. Effectively, complete pages are printed at one time.

Although more costly than dot matrix and ink jet printers, laser printers offer greater speed and quality. Typically, speeds range from 6 to 26 pages per minute. Printing definition, or *resolution*, is measured in *dots-per-inch* or *dpi*; until recently the norm has been 300 dpi but more expensive machines producing 600 dpi are becoming increasingly common. The high quality of the printed image makes the laser printer highly suitable for producing the camera-ready copy used in book and magazine publishing.

Other types of printers

Liquid crystal shutter printer

A liquid crystal shutter uses a very similar technology to that of a laser printer, but instead of a laser it contains a powerful halogen light source. In laser printers, the laser is fixed in one position, so to complete an image the width of a page, the beam is reflected from a rotating mirror which moves the laser beam horizontally across the drum (see previous section). This scanning action involves some complicated mechanical machinery which, together with the laser, form a major part of the component costs. Liquid crystal shutter printers, on the other hand, use a halogen light bulb as their light source and an array of liquid crystal shutters (the same technology used for liquid crystal displays (LCD) on watches and portable computer display screens) to control which positions on the photo-sensitive drum are exposed at any one time. Typically, the array contains 2400 shutters, sufficient to produce a full page-width line of ink dots at one time. In a liquid crystal shutter printer, moving parts are limited to the revolving drum and the paper and this makes the machine simpler and cheaper to service than its laser counterpart.

Chain printer

In a chain printer several complete sets of characters are held on a continuous chain which moves horizontally across the paper. The ribbon is situated between the chain and the paper and an individual hammer is located at each of the 132 print positions. A complete line can be printed as one complete set of characters passes across the paper. Thus, in one pass as many lines can be printed as there are sets of characters in the chain. Printing speeds are therefore very high.

Thermal printers

Characters are burned onto heat-sensitive thermographic paper, which is white and develops colour when heated above a particular temperature. The heat is generated by rods in the dot-matrix print head. By selective heating of the rods, individual characters can be formed from the matrix. Printing can be carried out serially, one character at a time or, by several heads, on a line-by-line basis. Serial thermal printing is slow but speeds of more than 1000 lines per minute are possible with line thermal printing.

Electro-sensitive printers

This type produces characters in a similar fashion to the thermal printer except that the paper used has a thin coating of aluminium which covers a layer of black, blue or red dye. Low voltage electrical discharges in the matrix rods produce sparks which selectively remove the aluminium coating to reveal the layer of dye underneath. Operated as line printers with heads at each print position, printing speeds of more than 3000 lines per minute are achieved.

Summary of printers

Generally, smaller, low-speed character printers are of use with microcomputer systems, but the increasing popularity of the latter has demanded increased sophistication in small printers. Features which have improved speeds of character printers include *bi-directional* printing (in two directions) and *logic-seeking,* which allows the printer to cut short a traverse across the paper if only a few characters are required on a line. The most popular printers for microcomputers are impact dot-matrix, ink-jet and laser.

Plotters

A plotter is a device designed to produce charts, drawings, maps and other forms of graphical information on paper. The images may be produced by *pens*, *electro-statically* or *ink jets* (see Printers section). Electrostatic plotters are quicker but the quality of the image is inferior to that produced with the pen type. Ink jet plotters, though expensive, produce the best quality drawings. Pen plotters use an ink pen or pens to create images on paper. There are two types, *flatbed* and *drum.*

Drum plotter

A drum plotter has a different drawing mechanism. Instead of the paper remaining still, it moves to produce one of the lateral movements whilst the pens move to execute the other movements. To control the paper, the drum plotter uses sprocket wheels to interlock with the paper. The main advantage of the drum plotter is its ability to handle large sheets of paper. The operation of a drum plotter is illustrated in Figure 8.14. Plotters are commonly used in conjunction with computer-aided design (CAD) systems for the production of engineering and architectural drawings.

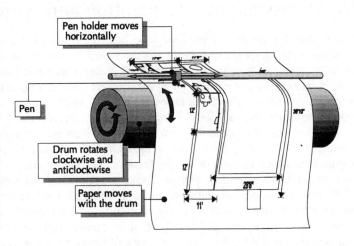

Figure 8.14. *How a drum plotter works*

Flatbed plotter

This type of plotter looks like a drafting board with pens mounted on a carriage which moves along guide tracks. The paper is placed on the bed. The pens can be raised or lowered as the image being created requires and different coloured pens can be brought into use at various stages of the process. Drawing movements are executed by movement of the carriage along the tracks and by the pens along the carriage. The size of paper which can be accommodated is limited by the size of the plotter bed, but this can be extremely large. Figure 8.15 illustrates its principles of operation.

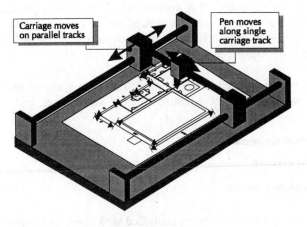

Figure 8.15. *A flatbed plotter*

Special-purpose output

Computer output microform (COM) recorders

COM recorders record information from computer storage onto microfilm or microfiche, by conversion of the digital information into human-readable images. COM equipment is very expensive, but bureau organizations will generally provide a recording service. Microfilm is a continuous reel, whereas microfiche is a sheet of film with a matrix of squares or pages. Either form can be viewed with a magnifying viewer. COM can result in large savings in paper costs, storage space and handling. For example, a 4 inch × 6 inch microfiche sheet can store the equivalent of 270 printed pages. Computer-aided retrieval (CAR) systems are available to automate the archiving and retrieval of microfiche frames.

COM is particularly useful for the storage of large amounts of information which do not need to be updated frequently. The information can be viewed with the use of a special magnifying projector. Large financial institutions use COM together with CAR to allow rapid retrieval of customer account statements.

Voice processing - recognition and synthesis

The recognition process is used for input and the synthesis for output. Human speech varies in accent, personal style of speech and pitch and the interpretation of the spoken word makes the development of systems capable of handling the full range of spoken communication a difficult process. In normal conversation, humans make assumptions about the listener, often cutting sentences short or emphasizing a point with a facial expression. There are however, devices which can be trained to recognize a limited number of words spoken by the individual doing the training. Devices can be used to give commands for machinery control, for example, up, down, left, right, fast, slow etc. Paralysed persons can control a wheelchair or lighting and heating through a voice recognition device controlled by a microprocessor. There are also applications which operate effectively because the communications are highly specialized and the conversation requirements extremely limited. Banks provide telephone banking through interactive voice response (IVR) systems; customers can obtain account balances, order statements or cheque books and make money transfers by spoken commands or by tone entry with the telephone keypad. Interaction is very carefully controlled by the system and callers must be interrogated for precise information, such as their account number. By using a highly structured series of questions and answers, IVR systems only need to recognize key values such as the digits from 0 to 9 and the words 'yes' and 'no'. A caller's spoken request for information is digitized and sent to the host computer; the response is converted into synthesized speech and read out to the caller. IVR systems speak by forming pre-recorded words and phrases into sentences and playing them. For example, a request for an account balance may bring the response "Your balance is", followed by a series of digits which were recorded separately, interspersed by the word "pounds" and "credit" or "debit", as appropriate.

Other systems using voice recognition and voice synthesis include robot operation, telephone answering and information provision concerning the time, share prices, and railway timetables.

Exercises

Exercises for this chapter are combined with those for Chapter 9, Storage Systems.

Chapter 9
Storage Systems

All backing storage systems consist of two main elements, a *device* and a *medium*. For example, a tape drive is a device, but magnetic tape is the associated storage medium. Under program control, the storage device reads from or writes to the medium. The most popular kinds of backing storage devices are those using magnetic tape and magnetic disk, although optical systems are playing an increasingly important role.

Magnetic tape

Despite the continued evolution of disk storage, magnetic tape continues to be used in most large scale computer installations as a cheap and secure method of storing large volumes of data which are normally processed in a serial fashion, as occurs, for example, in the processing of an organization's payroll. It is also useful for the storage of historical or archival files where rapid access to individual records is not essential. The Police National Computer system in Hendon, for example, stores inactive records off-line on magnetic tape, whilst millions of records of current criminal activities are kept on-line and are directly accessible from magnetic disk. When an archived record needs to be retrieved, the relevant tape is placed on-line and searched until the required record is found. It would be inefficient and expensive to keep all records, no matter how old, on-line all of the time.

General features of magnetic tape

The tapes used on mainframe and minicomputer systems are stored on large detachable reels. Tapes are made of plastic and are covered with a coating which can be magnetized and by which means data is encoded.

A particular type of cartridge tape, which looks like a cassette tape but is slightly larger, is often used as a backup for hard disk on microcomputer systems. These *streamer* tapes have huge capacity and can copy the complete contents of a hard disk in several minutes. The rest of this section concentrates on large reel-to-reel systems.

Processing tapes

A tape must be mounted on an on-line tape unit when it is to be used by a computer system. During processing, the tape is propelled past separate read and write heads at high speed. As is explained in Chapter 15 data is transferred between tape and main memory in physical blocks, each one being separated by an inter-block gap (IBG), to allow the tape to decelerate and stop and accelerate again to the correct speed for data transfer. Data transfer has to be carried out in block sizes which can be accommodated by main memory and provide for the quickest possible processing of a complete file.

Data storage on magnetic tape

Figure 9.1 shows how data is stored on magnetic tape. The coding system used is either ASCII or EBCDIC, the latter being used on IBM equipment. The coding systems are binary and in the case of EBCDIC, each character is represented by a group of 8 binary digits (bits), either 0 or 1, plus a parity bit (for checking transmission errors), across the width of the tape. As Figure 9.1 shows, each 0 or 1 bit is accommodated in a single track and each group of bits representing one character occupies one frame across the tape.

The method of representing a 0 or 1 bit depends on the recording system in use but simplified examples are as follow:

- the presence of a magnetic field to represent 1 and the lack of a magnetic field to represent 0;

- the 0 and 1 bits are represented by magnetic fields of opposite polarity, say north for 1 and south for 0.

The tape unit reads across the nine tracks in a frame to identify the character represented.

Blocking data on magnetic tape

As explained in Chapter 15, a file is made up of a number of *logical records*. For example, a stock file contains a logical record for each commodity in stock. Generally, a logical record will not be large enough to constitute a physical record or block, so a number of logical records are grouped for transfer at one read or write instruction. The number of logical records in each block indicates the *blocking factor*. Large blocks save space (fewer inter-block gaps) and speed processing, although memory size is a limiting factor on the size of blocks.

Application of magnetic tape

Typically, one magnetic tape reel can store up to 40 million bytes or

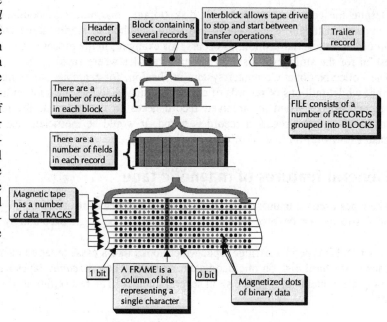

Figure 9.1. *Data storage on magnetic tape*

characters, allowing for header and trailer labels and inter-block gaps; the frequency of the latter will determine the practical capacity of any particular reel. The *data transfer rate*, the rate at which data can be transferred between tape and main memory, is commonly in excess of half a million bytes per second.

These features, together with the media's relative cheapness when compared with magnetic disk, make it appropriate for applications requiring mass storage. However, magnetic tape does not permit direct access to records and this limits its use to applications requiring sequential access only; the most common usage of magnetic tape is for storing back-up files and the archiving of files from magnetic disk storage.

Magnetic disk

Many computer applications require quick, direct access to individual records within a file and this facility is provided by magnetic disk. For this reason, magnetic disks are the most important backing storage media in use today. There are two main types of magnetic disk: *hard* and *floppy*.

Hard disk

The disk is usually made of aluminium with a coating of a magnetizable material on which data can be recorded. Records are stored in concentric rings or *tracks*. The method of encoding is fundamentally the same as that for tape, except that the magnetic states representing binary patterns are stored in single-file around the tracks. Each track is divided into a number of *sectors*, each having the same storage capacity. These features are illustrated in Figure 9.2. Each track and sector has a physical *address* which can be used by software to locate a particular record or group of records. A read/write mechanism is provided for each surface of a disk. The central area of the disk is not used, because to do so would necessitate a higher packing density than can be read or recorded by the read/write head. The number of tracks and sectors is known as the disk's *format*. The sector size can either be fixed permanently or can be altered by software. The former is known as hard sectoring and the latter as soft sectoring.

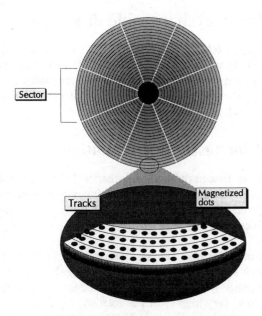

Figure 9.2. *Data storage on magnetic disk*

- *Hard sectoring*. The position of each sector can be indicated by a slot or reflective marker which can be detected by sensors in the drive unit. As the smallest unit of data transfer between disk and CPU is a sector (block), this means that any application is restricted to the disk's block size. Consider, for example, an application which uses logical records of 64 bytes, stored on a disk with 512 byte hard sectors. A minimum of 8 logical records needs to be transferred to memory even if only one is required out of the sector.

- *Soft sectoring*. This method allows the sectors to be set by software. All microcomputer systems use soft sectoring.

Disk pack

To increase storage capacity, disks may be formed into a pack, with a common access mechanism. The disk pack is generally loaded from the top of the disk unit. Because the disk pack can be removed and exchanged, the heads remain in their retracted position when the pack is not in place and when the disks are not revolving at their full operating speed.

Disk cylinder

The concept of the cylinder is explained in Chapter 15. Briefly, if there are ten possible recording surfaces with 200 tracks per surface, there are 200 imaginary, concentric cylinders, each consisting of ten tracks. Each vertical plane of tracks is a cylinder and as such is equivalent to a track position to which the heads on the access mechanism can move. All the read/write heads are fixed to a comb so that each is in the same cylinder at any one time. Sequential files are applied to a disk pack on a cylinder-by-cylinder basis so that all records in a cylinder can be processed with the heads in one position.

Single exchangeable disk

Single exchangeable disks are also known as *cartridge* disks and can be inserted into the front of the disk unit, in which case, part of the disk cover automatically slides to one side to allow the read/write heads to move in, or it can be top loaded and the plastic cover removed by the operator once the disk is in place. As is the case with the exchangeable disk pack, the moveable heads remain in the retracted position except when the disk is revolving at full speed.

Winchester disk technology

When first introduced, Winchester disks were designed for large computer systems and are still popular on such systems. They are now an integral component of all microcomputer systems. Winchester disks provide a much greater volume of on-line storage and faster access to programs and data than is possible with floppy disks.

Winchester disk systems consist of packs of hard disks, stacked in the same way as the exchangeable disk pack systems described earlier. The disks are not removable and are hermetically sealed in the storage units together with the read/write mechanism. The contamination-free environment in which the disks are stored allows very high speeds of rotation, typically, 3600 revolutions per minute. Storage capacities are increasing as technology advances, but commonly available systems for microcomputers can provide almost limitless storage, 50 to 100 megabytes being common.

Disk access time

Access time is the interval between the moment the command is given to transfer a data block (sector) from disk to main memory and the moment the transfer is completed; three processes can be identified.

- *seek time*. Suppose, for example, the read/write head unit is in cylinder 5 and that data is required from cylinder 24. To retrieve the data, the mechanism must move inwards to cylinder 24, the time taken to accomplish this movement being known as the seek time.

- *rotational delay*. When a read or write instruction is issued, the head is not usually positioned over the sector where the required data are stored, so there is some rotational delay while the disk rotates into the proper position. On average, the time taken is half a revolution of the disk pack. This average time is known as the latency of the disk.

- *data transfer time*. This is the time taken to read the block of data into main memory.

Various strategies can be used to reduce disk access time. One solution is to store related records in the same cylinder so that head movement is minimized, a strategy usually adopted for sequential files where records are to be accessed sequentially. Even with random files it is sometimes possible to group related records in the same cylinder. Another solution is to use fixed head disks, which provide each track with its own read/write head and involve no seek time. It has to be said, however, that this second option is no longer used in disk drive systems, primarily because of their high manufacturing costs. Other techniques of speeding disk performance are described below.

Storage capacity and performance

Storage capacity is measured in megabytes or Mb (roughly 1 million bytes) or gigabytes (Gb -approximately a thousand million bytes). At the time of writing, typical storage capacities range from 120 Mb to 2 Gb. *Disk array* systems offer even larger capacity, measured in hundreds of gigabytes. Traditionally, track recording density (the amount of data packed into a single track) is dictated by the amount of data which can be recorded in the innermost (the shortest) track. All the other tracks then use the same recording density. A technique called *variable zone recording* or *zoned-bit recording* (ZBR) stores more information in the longer, outer tracks. In this way, the storage capacity of the entire hard disk is radically increased.

The performance of a particular drive involves a measurement of its *overall response time*, measured in milliseconds. Different kinds of *disk access* take different times, so a quoted response time should be an aggregate of the time taken for a range of typical operational activities. In practice, this means running a system with a range of commonly used applications; currently, this includes use of MS-DOS and Windows applications. Typical response times range, approximately, from 19 ms to 10 ms.

Hard disk performance may be improved with the use of:

- a hardware caching controller;

- software caching;

- de-fragmentation software;

- RAID (redundant array of inexpensive disks).

Hardware caching controller

A hardware caching controller improves the rate at which data can be *written* to or *read* from a hard disk. As an electro-mechanical component of the computer system, the hard disk can access data at speeds measured in milliseconds (thousandths of a second), compared with the processor and main memory speeds, which can be measured in nanoseconds (thousand millionths of a second). A high performance processor may remain idle while waiting for the hard drive to complete a write or read operation. A hardware caching controller uses a separate memory chip, plugged into the drive's controller board. The cache memory is used to store data in anticipation of a read or write operation.

- *Write caching* is the drive's attempt to accept data before the write head is correctly positioned to record it. A write operation starts with the computer signalling the drive that it has begun the process. Instantly, the drive starts to move the read/write heads over the correct track. At the same time, the data to be transferred is copied from main memory to the RAM cache within the drive. Once the copy has been completed, the system is free to continue with other tasks, leaving the drive to complete the write operation (using the copy of the data held in the RAM cache). The write operation completed signal is issued while the drive is still recording (as soon as the copy to the cache is completed); otherwise, the system would still be delayed while the cache copy is written to disk. There is a theoretical risk of data loss, but, for most applications, there is none. Write caching is particularly effective for sequential file processing, where data is recorded into contiguous locations on disk (a complete track is filled before the head moves to the next track). Several write operations can be carried out without any head movement and seek time (the most significant contributor to the slowing of access speeds) is minimized. The opportunities for overlapping write operations are maximized.

- *Read caching*. The drive attempts to fetch data before the application requests it. The principles are the same as for main memory caching (see Chapter 7).

The memory chip used as the RAM cache is held within the drive unit and does not, therefore, take any part of the system's main memory capacity. A hardware caching controller can radically improve the performance of a hard drive, although other advances in design, such as increased rotation speed may be more significant.

In any event, improvement in hard disk performance leads to a speed imbalance within the typical microcomputer. Computer systems using the ISA standard (see Bus Architecture) *system bus* and a high performance hard drive are not well balanced. Many hard drives can handle data up to five times faster than the ISA bus. This can lead to a system bottleneck, which local bus technology (see Bus Architecture) seeks to overcome.

Software caching

A hard disk without a hardware caching controller will probably slow down a system, which in other respects is classed as a high performance system. An effective alternative, commonly used for systems operating Microsoft Windows, is to use a software caching system, such as SmartDrive, Super PC-Kwik and Norton NCache. This uses part of the computer's own main memory as the cache and thus reduces the amount available for applications software and data. Without a hardware caching controller, software caching is an essential component for must business systems.

De-fragmentation

The MS-DOS operating system, for example, keeps track of every stored file by following chains of *clusters* through a *file allocation table* (FAT). A cluster is a group of, up to, 32 sectors, which the operating system uses as a file *allocation unit*. A filename entry in the FAT is followed by the address of the first cluster containing the file. If the file occupies more than one cluster, the first cluster contains a pointer to the next, which contains a pointer to the one after that, and so on, until the end of the file is reached (the last cluster contains a special marker). This system was adopted to allow disk space to be taken by new files when old ones are deleted. If a file cannot be fitted into a vacant space, it becomes *fragmented* (distributed over different parts of the disk). The operating system is still able to keep track of the complete file through the cluster linking mechanism, but read and write times become extended. This is because of the increased head movement (see Seek Time).

De-fragmentation software re-organizes the disk space, such that each file occupies contiguous (no gaps) clusters. The frequency with which de-fragmentation should be carried out depends on the level of file activity and the application. If the application results in frequent changes to the size of files, system performance may be noticeably affected as fragmentation increases.

RAID (redundant array of inexpensive disks)

RAID systems aim to overcome the performance limitations inherent in single disk systems and to improve reliability. A number of different RAID configurations are commonly in use, each one concentrating on improving either *performance* (speed of access to data) or *reliability*. Five such configurations are known as RAID-0, RAID-1 through to RAID-5.

The idea is illustrated by reference to a RAID-0 system; there are two main parameters which can be adjusted - the *block size* and the *number of disks* (known as the *stripe width*) used. The performance of a RAID-0 system can be set by adjusting the values of these parameters. Data is recorded in the following way; for example, if a company's accounting records are to be spread over several physical disks (a *logical volume*), the data is written to each disk block by block, the first going to the first disk, the second to the second disk and so on. It follows from this that an input-output operation, which requires the accessing of more than one block of data, will need the services of multiple disks. To improve performance, the block transfers are carried out *concurrently*, over multiple data paths. Once all the relevant blocks are transferred the logical input-output operation is completed. Buffers are used to accumulate the blocks and assemble them in the correct order. The improvement in performance is achieved by overlapping the block transfers from several disks, instead of serially from a single disk. A problem with a RAID-0 configuration is that the failure of one disk prevents use of the entire volume. Other RAID configurations use techniques, such as mirroring, which provides an entire duplicate of each disk.

Application of magnetic disk

On large computer systems, exchangeable disk packs constitute the most popular form of backing storage, because despite being more expensive than magnetic tape, the provision of direct as well as sequential access, gives magnetic disk an overwhelming advantage. Its support of a variety of file and database organization methods make it appropriate for any application. Typically, a single disk pack can store hundreds of megabytes, or several gigabytes (1 gigabyte = 1024 × megabyte) and although a single CPU can only access one surface in one disk pack at a time, a system may have a number of drive units, each containing a similar disk pack, permanently on-line. Other files may be held on additional disk packs held off-line, but these can be placed on-line as and when required, by exchanging them with those held in the drive units. A multi-processor system could, of course, access several on-line disk packs at the same time. Direct access times will vary, depending on the amount of head movement required (this will depend on the method of file organization and the mode of access) and the performance characteristics of the disk system in use.

Floppy disks or diskettes

Floppy disks are physically and operationally different from hard disks. They are flexible and encased in a square plastic protective jacket, in which the diskette revolves at approximately 360 revolutions per minute, more slowly than a conventional disk. The jacket is lined with a soft material which helps to clean the diskette as it revolves. The read/write heads make contact with the diskette surface when data transfer is in progress and withdraw at other times to reduce wear, but a diskette will eventually wear out after about 500 to 600 hours of contact. The diskette does not rotate continuously and access times are considerably inferior to those of hard disk systems.

Types of floppy disk

Floppy disks are available in two sizes according to diameter - 5.25 inches and 3.5 inches, although the larger size is now virtually obsolete. The 3.5 inch disk is stored in a rigid plastic casing which makes it more robust than its 5.25 inch forerunner (now virtually obsolete). A metal sliding shutter, which covers the recording surface access slot, slides open when the disk is placed in the drive unit. The greater protection provided by this casing allows data to be recorded more densely on a 3.5 inch disk (typically 1.44mb) than is generally practicable on the 5.25 inch variety. A diskette has 80 tracks on each side but the number of sectors can be varied (soft-sectoring is used). If a diskette is formatted into 9 sectors, there are 720 addressable locations. Soft sectoring is used because the operating systems of different computers use different addressing formats. Thus, in principle, standard diskettes can be sold which only require formatting to be used on a particular machine (some are pre-formatted). The formatting procedure also sets up a *directory* which is maintained by the computer system to keep track of the contents of each location. Other types of floppy disk, with larger storage capacities and quicker access times are described next.

Storage densities

Typically, track density is 135 tracks per inch (tpi). A high density disk can store twice as much data as a double density disk, by doubling the number of sectors per track. It is important for users to ensure that good quality high-density disks are used, as inferior disks will not support the required recording densities, resulting in unreliable data storage.

Application of floppy disk

Storage capacities are only a tiny fraction of the hard disk drive systems which are integral to all microcomputers and their slower revolution rate also makes access times so slow that they are only of use for backup purposes and installation of software packages (see also CD-ROM later). Floppy disk systems have the advantage of providing extremely cheap storage.

Alternative backing storage devices and media

Magnetic tape and disk systems account for a very large proportion of all storage systems in use, but there are a number of alternatives.

The conventional disk systems described previously account for a very large proportion of all storage systems in use, but there are a number of products which present alternatives, particularly for back-up and storage expansion purposes. They are all removable, disk-based systems (some hard, some floppy), but both the devices and the media used in them make use of a variety of technologies. The systems described here are: m*agneto-optical*; *floptical*; *Bernoulli*; *magnetic cartridge*; *docking*.

Magneto-optical drives

Like conventional disk drives, magneto-optical devices use magnetism to write data onto the disk, but in combination with laser technology. The recording head does not come into contact with the disk surface, but flies above it. This reduces the risk of head crashes and the problem of wear and tear associated with conventional floppy disk systems, which require contact for both reading and writing. Briefly, a magneto-optical drive operates in the following way:

- To write to the disk involves a two-stage process. First, the laser is used to heat the surface of the disk to a temperature of about 180^{0}C and the write head is set to record bit-0s in the required location. Once the surface is heated the write head causes the magnetic polarity within the current disk location to change and when the surface cools (which it does quickly), the polarity condition is retained. A second recording pass reverses the polarity of those bit positions which are to represent 1s.

- Read operations use the laser at a reduced intensity to detect the bit-1s and bit-0s. They are then translated into the equivalent electrical signals for transmission through the device to main memory. There is no magnetic read head involved in the process.

Disks used in magneto-optical drives require heating before the polarity of stored magnetic fields can be altered. This means that data cannot be corrupted by magnetic fields emanating from, for example, a telephone placed on top of the disks or from nearby electric cabling. Data stored on conventional floppy disks can be corrupted in such circumstances. Reading data only requires the detection of changes in polarized light reflected from the surface of the disk. The manufacturers claim that provided the surface is not scratched, then spilling coffee onto it, for example, would only require that the surface is wiped with a special cleaning kit before it is re-used. To avoid over-heating during the writing process, a small, electric fan is attached to the back of the drive; for the same reason most magneto-optical drives are designed to be attached externally.

The 3.5 inch magneto-optical cartridge has a storage capacity measured in hundreds of megabytes and although the drive units and the media are more expensive than conventional floppy disk (1.44 Mb per diskette) systems, the cost per megabyte of storage is lower. The two-stage writing process means that two revolutions of the disk are required before it is complete and this results in average seek times (see earlier section on disk access time) which are somewhat slower than those for a conventional hard disk drive. Speeds are being improved and because the media are removable, magneto-optical drives could become a cost-effective way of increasing a system's primary backing storage capacity.

Floptical drives

A floptical drive uses floppy disks and makes some use of optical technology. However, unlike the magneto-optical drive, it uses the magnetic heads for both reading and writing and is thus similar to a conventional floppy disk drive. Where the floptical drive differs is in the mechanism which positions the read/write heads over the individual tracks on the diskette; an optical sensor in the drive unit detects an optical positioning pattern on the specially produced floptical diskette, allowing more precise placing of the heads and more densely packed tracks. With the use of very thin heads, data can be packed much more densely and a capacity of 21Mb per disk is typical. A major benefit of the floptical drive is that it is also able to read and write standard 720 kilobyte (Kb) and 1.44 Mb floppy disks.

Unfortunately, the drives revolve the disk at normal floppy drive speeds and provide similar access times. Also, like conventional diskettes, data stored on a floptical disk can be corrupted by nearby magnetic fields. Their storage capacity is small when compared with the magneto-optical variety and their slow access times mean that it is not feasible to use them as an extension to conventional hard disk storage.

Bernoulli drives

The removable disk cartridge used in a Bernoulli drive uses air pressure caused by the disk's revolution to flex the disk towards the read/write head as it passes. It is named after Daniel Bernoulli, an eighteenth century mathematician who first documented the particular airstream effects which are applied in this type of drive. In a conventional Winchester hard disk drive (see earlier section), the read/write heads fly over the surface of the revolving disk and when power is removed may crash onto it, causing severe damage to both and loss of data. Equally, jolting the unit may cause the heads to bounce onto the disk surface and result in similar damage. In the Bernoulli drive, the disk surface is pushed towards the heads which are at a fixed height, so the risk of head crashes is virtually nil. The robustness of the cartridge makes it a popular choice for users wanting removable storage which can be sent through the post. However, the cost per megabyte of storage is relatively high when compared with, for example, magneto-optical drives.

Magnetic-cartridge drives

A magnetic-cartridge drive makes use of a conventional hard disk enclosed in a removable cartridge. The read/write heads are an integral part of the drive and move out over the disk surfaces when the cartridge is inserted. A standard hard drive is sealed and provides a clean operating environment which permits the read/write heads to pass very close to the surface of the disk; this is not the case with a removable cartridge and the dustier environment requires the gap between heads and surface to be greater and this in turn reduces the possible recording density. Nevertheless, a single cartridge can store around 100 Mb and average seek times are better than those for magneto-optical drives (see earlier section).

Docking drives

Docking drives are, effectively, removable standard hard drive units and provide identical access times and storage capacities. However, they are equally delicate, which for a removable device is a significant disadvantage. If security is vital, then the ability to remove and lock up a file storage system is an obvious benefit. Docking drives are expensive and could be used as the primary backing storage facility in place of an integral hard disk system, if the security advantages justify the additional costs.

Optical disk

An optical disk uses laser beam technology to allow data to be recorded and read using bit-densities several times greater than a typical magnetic disk. Data are recorded as bit-patterns, using high-intensity laser beams to burn tiny holes into the surface of the disk. The data can then be read from the disk using a laser beam of reduced intensity.

There are two main types of optical disk system presently available

- CD-ROM;

- WORM.

CD-ROM (compact disk/read-only memory)

As the title suggests this type of disk only allows the computer to read data from the disk which is pre-recorded by the manufacturer. Typically, a single CD-ROM disk can store an enormous 600 Mb of data, sufficient space for storing video sequences and digitized sound such as speech. It is of no use for the storage of data which requires updating, its main application being for Interactive Video Disk systems, which can store text, images and audio signals for use in advertising, training and education. Sequences of film and sound can be retrieved under computer control. The majority of CD-ROM drives, just like domestic CD music players, are only capable of reading CDs, but more expensive machines exist which allow reading and writing, and it is likely that in the near future they will become as common as the current read-only drives.

WORM (write once, read many)

The large storage capacity of optical disks means that the writing facility can be used for a considerable period before all the space is filled. Storage capacities are measured in gigabytes (thousands of millions of characters), way beyond the capacity of any magnetic disk systems. Optical disk systems which provide an erase facility are available but are still too expensive for most users.

Apart from its vast storage capacity, the optical disk is less prone to environmental hazards such as dust, largely because the read signal is more intense and the laser head can be fixed 2mm from the disk surface, allowing dust and other particles to pass underneath.

Application of optical disk

The lack of an overwrite or erase facility is a significant drawback in respect of most common data processing systems and MIS (management information systems), but there are some specialist areas where it can be used to advantage, including databases where updating is infrequent and the prime requirement is for information retrieval. CD-ROM systems are largely used for vocational Computer Based Training (CBT). CD-ROM drives are an essential component of the modern microcomputer, particularly those configured as *multi-media* (Chapter 6) systems.

Mass storage

These storage systems provide massive storage capacity at the cost of relatively slow access times; the financial cost per record unit is low, which is an attractive feature to governments and large commercial organizations.

All mass storage systems are off-line, with an automatic facility for placing units of storage on-line, as necessary. The unit of storage may be, for example, an optical disk or a magnetic tape cartridge. One IBM mass storage system consists of a honeycomb of locations, each containing a tape cartridge with a capacity of 50 megabytes. When a cartridge is needed, it is retrieved by a robot mechanism under program control and the contents are copied onto on-line magnetic disk, from where information can be accessed immediately; the cartridge is then automatically replaced in its proper location.

Magnetic bubble memory

Unlike disks and tapes, which are electro-mechanical devices, magnetic bubble memory has no moving parts at all.

Bubbles are formed in thin plates of magnetic material as tiny cylindrical domains. The presence of a bubble in a location represents a 1-bit and the absence of a bubble, a 0-bit. The bubbles can be moved within the magnetic layer by tiny electrical forces, thus altering the bit patterns. Bubbles can be created and destroyed by similar forces. Because there are no moving parts, bubble memory is potentially more reliable than its electro-mechanical counterparts but as yet it has not been brought into general use for a variety of reasons.

Firstly, storage capacities and access times for magnetic disks are continually being improved. Secondly, except for very small systems, magnetic bubble memory is more expensive per bit of storage, than magnetic disk and this is likely to remain the case until increased volume of production brings down production costs. Its non-volatility makes it a possible alternative to the small disk memories used on some microcomputer systems, but currently, magnetic disk provides better access times.

The main applications of magnetic bubble memory are for memory units in terminals, microcomputers, robots and telecommunications equipment where the memory capacity required is not large. It appears that magnetic bubble memory has failed to make any real impact on storage systems.

Exercises

The exercises which follow also refer to topics covered in Chapter 8.

1. What do the following abbreviations represent: OMR; OCR; MICR? Give an example of an application for each.

2. List the names of hand-held, input devices, which provide alternatives to a keyboard. Briefly describe circumstances when each device may be essential or desirable.

3. (i)   In the context of screen displays, differentiate between *text* and *graphics mode*.

    (ii)   What is meant by *screen resolution*?

    (iii) Explain why colour displays require more memory than monochrome displays.

    (iv)   Why is FLCD (ferroelectric liquid crystal display) used instead of CRT (cathode ray tube) for *portable* computers?

4. Research computer magazines for *types of printer* and produce a table comparing costs, speed and quality. Suggest the kind of application for which each type may best be suited.

5. Suggest applications where *voice processing* (recognition and synthesis) is essential.

6. (i)   Differentiate between *data storage* on magnetic tape and disk.

    (ii)   Which factor is generally the most important when choosing between magnetic tape and disk?

7. (i)   Identify the processes which jointly determine to *disk access time*.

    (ii)   Which process is likely to most significant in slowing access time:

           a. when randomly accessing a randomly organized file;

           b. when sequentially accessing a sequentially organized file.

8. Explain the role of each of the following in improving disk performance:

    (i)   *hardware caching* controller;

    (ii)   *defragmentation*.

9. Why is CD-ROM storage vital to multi-media systems?

Chapter 10
Computer Networks

Networking computer systems has the effect of decentralizing computer processing and improving communications within and between organizations and between organizations and individuals. Some computer networks use dedicated intelligent terminals or microcomputer systems to permit some independent processing power at sites remote from the *host* computer, to which they are connected. Other networks distribute even more processing power by linking microcomputer, minicomputer, mainframe and supercomputer systems. They are sometimes referred to as *distributed processing* systems. Networks can be configured to suit almost any application, from the provision of a world-wide airline reservation system to home banking. *Nodes* (connection points in the network) may only be a few feet apart and limited to a single building, or they may be several thousand miles apart.

Local and wide area networks

Computer networks can be classified according to their geographical spread. A network confined to, say, one building, with microcomputer workstations distributed in different rooms, is known as a *local area network* (LAN). One particular type, known as a ring network can extend over a diameter of around five miles. A computer network distributed nationally or even internationally makes use of telephone and sometimes, satellite links, and is referred to as a *wide area network* (WAN). In large organizations with several branches, it is common practice to maintain a LAN at each branch for local processing requirements and to link each LAN into a WAN covering the whole organization. In this way, branches of an organization can have control over their own processing and yet have access to the organization's main database at headquarters. In addition, inter-branch communication is possible.

Network architecture

The architecture of any network includes definition of: its *components*, both hardware and software, identified by *name* and *function*; the ways the components are connected and communicate with one another.

The architecture of wide area networks (WANs) is described in Chapter 11 and the following primarily relates to local area networks (LANs). However, the section on Network Topologies does relate, in part, to WANs.

LAN architecture

It is important that the components are combined in such a way that the LAN can be: *extended*. The LAN must be capable of providing for new users and new equipment, as the need arises; *upgraded* to take advantage of new technologies which can improve network performance; *connected* to other LANs, both local and remote and Wide Area Networks.

LAN architecture comprises hardware and software, both for the control of the LAN communications and as an interface between the LAN and its users. In order that all components are compatible and operate as a coherent system, it is important that they conform to agreed standards (Chapter 11). This means that LAN producers have to take account of generally agreed standards for equipment linking and data communications, so that as new products come onto the market, the user is not left with a system which cannot take advantage of them. Unfortunately, a number of different standards exist and this means that the decision on which type of LAN to purchase is not always straightforward.

Hardware components

Figure 10.1 shows a simple *client-server* LAN and identifies the main hardware components: *workstation*; *file server*; *printer server*; network *cabling*. The way in which they are connected defines its general *topology* or physical shape.

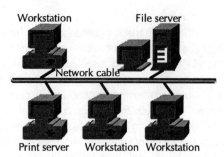

Figure 10.1. *Main components of a client server network*

LAN Workstation

A *workstation* gives a user access to a LAN and its facilities. A workstation comprises a *microcomputer* with a *network card*, which fits into an *expansion slot* inside its system casing. The network card enables workstations to communicate across the network, and with the *file server* (see later). The card converts computer-generated data into a form suitable for transmission over the LAN and as such is an *interface* (Chapter 14). The card is operated with a network card *driver*.

Servers

The general function of servers is to allocate shared resources to other nodes on the network. There are a number of different types of server, which can be categorized according to the resources they control.

File server

The file server is usually a specially configured microcomputer, with a network card, more memory and disk storage, as well as a more powerful processor than is needed for a workstation. It has to control access to shared storage, directories and files. In addition, it controls the exchange of files between network users. Most network software provides *multiple device* support. This means that file servers can support several disks, allowing file storage capacity on the LAN to be increased beyond that of the file server's integral hard disk. A LAN can also consist of several file servers; indeed except for the smallest of networks, this is normally the case.

Print server

A print server (there may be several) accepts and queues jobs from workstations; the user may be informed when printing is complete. The print server may also provide certain print management functions, for example, to attach priorities to different print jobs so that certain jobs are printed before others, no matter what their positions in the queue. A print server will be configured to:

- support the use of particular printers;

- service particular printer *queues*; users with the right to use a particular print queue can then place their jobs in that queue.

Communications server

If a LAN is to have access to external networks or databases, a communications server is required. Generally, the communications server can establish a temporary link with remote computers or users on other networks (see Remote Inter-networking).

Network topologies

Computer networks can be categorized according to their physical shape or topology. Each terminal in a network is known as a *node*. If a central computer controls the network it is known as the *host* computer. The topology of a network is the *arrangement* of the nodes and the ways they are interconnected. The communication system within a network is known as the *subnet*. Data can be transmitted around the subnet either on a *point-to-point* basis or through a *broadcast* channel. If point-to-point transmission is used, the data passes through each device in the network. Thus, if two devices wish to communicate, they must do it indirectly, via any intervening devices. Each device must have the facility to store the entire message and forward it when the output channel is free. If a broadcast channel is used, a common communication channel is shared by all devices in the network. This means that any message sent by a device is received by all devices. The message contains the address of the device intended to receive it, so that the other devices can ignore it. There are a number of recognized network topologies and some of the most common are described below.

Star network

A star topology means that each node is connected, by separate connections to a computer at the centre, known as the *hub*. Figure 10.2 shows a LAN in a star topology. It is also a popular topology for a WAN. In this structure, all messages pass through the host (probably a mainframe or minicomputer) computer, which interconnects the different devices on the network. So, in this topology the host computer at the hub has a *message switching* function. Messages are transmitted point-to-point. The topology is particularly useful for intercommunications between pairs of users on the network (via the host). The network may consist of numerous computer systems (the nodes), connected to a larger host computer which switches data and programs between them.

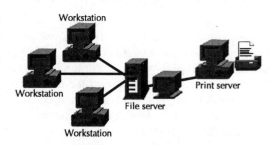

Figure 10.2. *Star network topology*

The star computer network is by far the most popular for WANs, because most large organizations start with a central computer at the head office, from which branch computer facilities are provided through the telephone network. The main aim is to provide computer communication between the branches and head office. Most other network topologies aim to provide communication between all devices on a network. The star topology can also be used for a LAN. The *advantages* of a star network topology are as follow:

- It is suitable for WANs where organizations rely on a central computer for the bulk of processing tasks, perhaps limiting the nodes to their local processing needs and the validation of data, prior to transmission to the central computer;

- Centralized control of message switching allows a high degree of security control;

- Each spoke in the star is independent of the rest and a fault in a link or device in one spoke, can be identified by the computer at the hub;

- The data transmission speeds used can vary from one *spoke* (a link from the hub to a node) to another. This is important if some spokes transmit using high speed devices, such as disk, whilst others transmit from low speed keyboard devices. The method of transmission may also vary. For example, one node may only require access to the network at the end of each day, in which case a *dial-up* connection may be sufficient. A dial-up connection uses the public telephone network and the user only pays for the time taken for transmission. Alternatively, other nodes may require the link for most of the working day, in which case a permanent *leased line* is appropriate. Leased lines provide a more reliable transmission medium and also allow higher speeds of data transmission.

The main *disadvantages* inherent in star networks are as follow:

- The network is vulnerable to hub failures which affect all users. As a distributed processing system, some processing is still possible at the nodes but inter-node communication is lost when the host computer fails;

- For a WAN, the control of communications in the network requires expensive technology at the hub, probably a mini or mainframe computer. Complex operating and communications software is needed to control the network.

Ring network

The ring topology is specifically designed for use with a LAN and is not suitable for a WAN. A ring network connects all the nodes in a ring, as illustrated in Figure 10.3. The *Cambridge Ring*, developed at Cambridge University, has no host computer and none of the nodes need have overall control of access to the network. In practice, a monitoring station is used for the control of data transmission in the network. Messages in a ring network flow in one direction, from node to node.

The ring consists of a series of repeaters, which are joined by the physical transmission medium (twisted pair, co-axial, or fibre-optic cable - see Chapter 11). The choice of medium depends on the distances to be covered and the desired transmission rates. Fibre-optic cable allows the greatest distances to be covered and the highest transmission rates. Repeaters are used to regenerate messages as they pass around the network. The use of repeaters allows a ring network to cover larger distances than is possible for other topologies. In fact, recent developments using fibre optic cable allow a ring with a

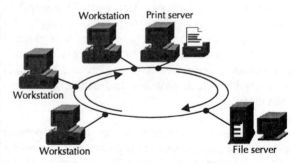

Figure 10.3. *Ring network topology*

range of about 100 kilometres, which makes it a *metropolitan area network* (MAN). The user devices are connected to the repeaters. A message from one node, addressed to another, is passed continually around the ring until the receiving node flags that it is ready to accept it. Acceptance of a message is determined by its *destination address*, which is examined by each node it passes. If the destination address matches the node's own address, the node takes the message; otherwise, the node repeater regenerates the signal to be passed to the next node in the ring. Data is transmitted in mini-packets of about 40 bits and contains the address of the sending node, the address of the destination node and some control bits. A variation on the Cambridge ring is the IBM ring, which uses a different protocol to allow better control of message flow on the network; the two protocols, *empty slot* and *token passing* are described in the section on Network Access Protocols. The ring network presents particular advantages:

- There is no dependence on a central host computer as data transmission around the network is supported by all the devices in the ring. Each node device has sufficient intelligence to control the transmission of data from and to its own node;

- Very high transmission rates are possible; 10 megabits/sec is typical;

- Routing between devices is relatively simple because messages normally travel in one direction only around the ring;

- The transmission facility is shared equally amongst the users.

The main disadvantages are as follow:

- The system depends on the reliability of the whole ring and the repeaters, although it can be designed to bypass any failed node;

- It may be difficult to extend the length of the ring because the physical installation of any new cable must ensure that the ring topology is preserved.

Star/ring network - IBM token ring

The *IBM Token Ring* Network is a star-based topology, with a hub or *multiple access unit* (MAU) to which all the workstations are connected. The movement of data is, however in a *logical ring*. All signals between workstations are through the MAU. The star/ring structure has a major advantage over the basic ring. If one workstation breaks down, or the connection with the MAU is broken, other workstations are not affected (except that they cannot communicate with the damaged workstation). Failure of the MAU will prevent operation of the network. The Cambridge ring structure, described earlier, is prone to complete failure if one workstation fails (the continuous ring is broken).

Bus network

With a bus topology, the workstations are connected to a main cable (known as the *bus* or trunk), along which data travels. The ends of a bus are not connected, so that data has to travel in both directions to reach the various nodes on the network. The bus topology makes the addition of new devices straightforward, either by attachment to the existing cable or to cable which can be added at either end. The main bus standard is known as *Ethernet*. The term *station* tends to be used rather than node for this type of network. The communications subnet uses a *broadcast* channel, so all attached stations can hear every transmission. As is the case in the ring network, there is no host computer and all stations have equal priority in using the network to transmit. The maximum length of a single bus *segment* is 500 metres and 100 stations can be attached to it. Segments can be specially linked to form larger configurations, up to a maximum of about 12 kilometres. Transmission speeds of 10 megabits/second are obtainable. The topology is illustrated in the Figure 10.4.

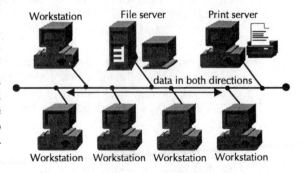

Figure 10.4. *Bus network topology*

The bus network provides certain benefits:

- If a node malfunctions, it simply stops communicating; it doesn't prevent the rest of the network from working;

- The attachment of devices is straightforward and the cable can be extended, if necessary; additional *segments* can be linked to extend the network.

The main drawback is that:

- If a part of the Ethernet cabling develops a fault, the whole network (assuming it consists of a single segment) fails.

Mesh network

The nodes of a mesh network are fully interconnected. The mesh topology is not found in LANs, but is typical of the public switched telephone network (pstn) and WANs. Its complexity requires the use of switching techniques to route data through the network (see Packet Switching in Chapter 11).

Network cabling - the transmission medium

In order to share resources on a network, servers, workstations and other devices must be connected; although wireless radio media are possible, most LANs use physical cabling, which acts as the *transmission medium*. The physical layout of the cabling should conform to one of the basic *topologies*: star, ring or bus. The type of cable used depends on the chosen topology and the rules governing the transmission of data through the cable (the *protocol*). The cabling standards of Ethernet and Token Ring, described below, are also LAN protocols.

Ethernet cabling

Ethernet is one the two most widely accepted standards (the other is Token Ring) for specifying how data is placed on and retrieved from a LAN. An Ethernet-equivalent standard is IEEE 802.3 (see Chapter 11, Standards Authorities), which also uses Ethernet cable, but packets data slightly differently for transmission through the cable. Ethernet cable falls into three main categories:

- *Thick Ethernet* coaxial cable, with a diameter of 10mm has a solid copper core conductor. A single network segment can be 500 metres and supports the attachment of 100 devices. The cabling conforms to the IEEE 802.3 Type 10Base5 standard. The transmission rate is 10 megabits (1,000,000 bits) per second (Mb/s).

- *Thin Ethernet*, which is 10 millimetres in diameter, has a core of stranded cable. The maximum length of cable which can be used in a single network segment is around 180 metres and the maximum number of workstations is around 30. The cabling conforms to the IEEE 802.3 Type 10Base2 standard. The cable supports a maximum transmission rate of 2 Mb/s.

- *10BaseT* Standard Ethernet. The T stands for *twisted pair*. This cable is much cheaper than the thick Ethernet cabling, but provides the same transmission rate of 10 Mb/s; being the same as most telephone cabling, it is easier to install.

Token ring cabling

Used in *IBM token ring* networks use twisted pair cabling, either two pairs or four, depending on data transmission requirements. A single IBM Token Ring network will support up to 260 network devices at rates of 4 Mb/s or 16 Mb/s. Up to eight rings can be connected using *bridges*.

Fibre-optic cabling

See Chapter 11. Cable of this type is available for use with any of the network types, but provides greater *bandwidth* and permits transmission over greater distances, without the use of *repeaters*.

Cable bandwidth

There are two different methods of utilising a LAN cable for the transmission of data; *baseband* and *broadband*.

- Baseband. In a baseband network, a transmitting device uses the whole bandwidth (frequency range), so only one signal can be carried at any one time. This means that, for a brief moment, a transmitting device has exclusive use of the transmission medium. In general, broadband networks are suitable for networks which only transmit data signals.

- Broadband. Broadband networks provide a number of frequency bands or channels within the total bandwidth (*frequency division multiplexing*) and thus allow simultaneous use by different devices on the network. Generally, one channel is dedicated to the user workstations, leaving others free for transmitting video pictures for the security system, voice communication, television pictures and so on.

Cable-device connection

A number of different devices are used to make the connection between network devices, such as workstations and servers, and the transmission medium. The particular components used will depend on the type of network (for example, Ethernet or Token Ring); even for the same type of network, there are a range of connection alternatives.

This paragraph only details the main categories of connection component, which are: (i) *network card* (adapter), which is the *interface* for linking a network device to all other resources on the network; this is fitted into an expansion slot inside each workstation and other network devices. A device attaching to a Token ring network needs a different type of network card, from one attaching to an Ethernet network. A notebook or portable computer can be connected using its PCMCIA (Personal Computer Memory Card International Association) slot and a special network adapter; (ii) *Ethernet transceiver*; this device implements the CSMA/CD access protocol (see Access protocols). It is external from the network device and is connected to the network card and the Ethernet network cable. Although most network cards already contain a transceiver chip, *thick* Ethernet connections need an external transceiver. Thin Ethernet connections simply use the transceiver chip on the network card; (iii) *BNC connector*. Figure 10.5 illustrates its appearance; this is one of several types of connector used for *thin* Ethernet cable. There are BNC male and female connectors for linking sections of cable and T connectors for attaching devices to the cable. *Thick* Ethernet cabling uses a stronger screw

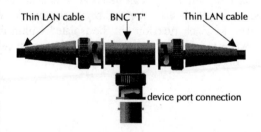

Figure 10.5. *BNC "T" connector*

coupling for cable connections (N-series connectors); (iv) *Terminator*; this is an electrical resistor which must be attached to each end of an Ethernet network segment (see Bus Topology); (v) *Multiple Access Unit* (MAU). This is the central component of a star/ring topology and is used in the IBM Token Ring network (see Star/Ring Network).

Connecting and extending LANs

Although there are limitations to the range of a LAN and the number of devices which can be attached, imposed by the performance ability of the network transmission medium, networks can be connected to one another and extended. LANs set up separately can be connected permanently, or data transmission between them can be restricted, for special user or system requirements. The functions of the main devices used in this area of LAN architecture are described below.

Repeater

Repeaters allow the effective length of an Ethernet segment to be increased. The maximum length of an Ethernet segment is restricted because of signal loss and distortion which occurs as a data packet travels along the cable. A repeater re-strengthens, that is, *re-amplifies* the signal and resets its timing, so that the effective length of the segment can be increased. It is also used to enable a signal to travel to another segment of a network. A repeater can normally connect any kind of cable medium: thick or thin Ethernet, twisted pair or optical fibre. Figure 10.6 illustrates the role of a repeater in connecting a thick Ethernet backbone, to thin Ethernet segments. In relation to the Open Systems Inter-connection (OSI) model, referred to in Chapter 11, a repeater works at the Physical level and only needs to know how to interact with the physical transmission medium.

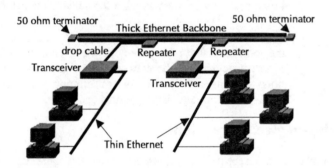

Figure 10.6. *Use of thick and thin Ethernet*

Bridge

A bridge is used to connect two LANs of the same type, that is, two token ring or two Ethernet LANs. This is known as *local inter-networking*. Packets crossing such a link are *forwarded* by the bridge device. Bridges are *protocol transparent*. Thus, the otherwise similar networks can be using different protocols, for example, IPX (Novell) or TCP/IP (Macintosh). They can also divide large networks into smaller segments. Segmenting large networks can improve administrative control and the performance of the separate segments. In the latter case, the bridge can be configured such that only data which needs to cross the bridge actually does. For example, if there are two segments, one for the Sales department and the other for Accounts, the data traffic for each function will be isolated within the respective segments, except when data needs to travel between the two. This improves the performance of each segment and thus the effectiveness of the whole network.

Software components

Apart from the physical components identified in the previous section, the following software in needed to run a network (see Chapter 13 for more detail):

- a *network operating system* resident in the file server. A major commercial example is Novell Netware;

- a *local operating system* within each workstation, for example, MS-DOS, MS Windows, OS/2, UNIX or Apple Macintosh.

- *network connection software*; this must be loaded at a workstation before it can communicate with the network.

Network operating system

A network operating system typically includes functional components to set-up, monitor and administer:

- The *directory* and *file* system on the server; directories are used to organize the storage of programs and data held on the file server's hard drive(s). Some directories are for the storage of the network operating system; others contain application programs and some directory space is allocated for the storage of user's data. Chapter 13 provides an example of a file server's directory structure; each directory is labelled to identify the nature of the files it contains.

- *User login* and activity. A user must be identified by the network operating system before being given access to the network. The supervisor *creates* users and assigns a user-id to each. A user may also be assigned to a *user-group*, for example, Sales or Marketing. To access a network, a user must login at a workstation, which will require the entry of a *user-id* and possibly, a *password*. The precise conditions can be set by the network supervisor; certain time periods can be set when users are not allowed to log into the network; the time restrictions can be applied to all users, specific groups or individuals. The resources available to any given user can also be controlled through the login procedure.

- *User access* to applications and data files. Typically, users are assigned *rights*, sometimes as individuals, but more usually as members of a group. These rights relate to directories and files; in other words, the rights determine whether, for example, a user is allowed to delete or copy files in a particular directory. Access rights to *network executables*, that is application programs, only allow the programs to be run.

- *Network printing*; users can be given access to a shared printer, through a print *queue*; each queue is controlled by a printer server, which directs the jobs to a network printer under its control.

- *Electronic messaging*; this is a LAN version of electronic mail and provides a mailbox facility for inter-user communication.

- *Network backup*. This task, although important to users, because it may prevent the loss of important work, or network facilities, is a task carried out on a regular basis by the network supervisor.

All these tasks are the responsibility of the *network supervisor* or *administrator* who has special rights of access, not available to others. Usually, these tasks are carried out through a system console; any computer on the network can be used for this purpose, but, usually it will be secure in a separate location. Although printing, electronic messaging, applications and limited file management are available to users, their rights should not extend to the amendment of these facilities.

Workstation operating system

Each workstation has its own local operating system, such as MS-DOS or Windows95 to control processing; once an application is retrieved from the file server, the workstation must be able to run it.

Network connection software

The network connection software must be loaded into the workstation RAM (usually from the its integral hard drive, during start-up), before the workstation can be logged onto the network. This software remains in the workstation RAM as long as it is logged onto the network. A program which remains resident like this is referred to as a TSR (terminate and stay resident) program. There are usually several components to the connection software, each having a separate function. Two major functional components are the:

- *Communication protocol*. This is the set of rules for transmitting data through the network; it ensures that devices can successfully communicate with one another by using the same language. Example protocols are: IPX (Novell Netware); TCP/IP (Macintosh); SNA (IBM).

- *LAN driver*, which controls the network card fixed inside the workstation. LAN drivers which conform to the ODI (Open Data-link Interface) standard can accept data from the network in any of the standard communication protocols, listed in the previous paragraph. This means that workstations of different operating system types (MS-DOS, Macintosh, UNIX etc.) can be attached to the same LAN and share its resources.

Network access protocols

Empty slot technique

This system is appropriate for networks in the shape of rings or loops, where messages are passed point-to-point in one direction. One or more empty *slots* or *packets* circulate continuously around the ring. When a device has information to transmit, it loads it into the slot, which carries it to its destination. At the time of loading, the destination address is placed in the slot and a full-empty flag is set to full. As the slot is passed from one repeater to another, no attempt will be made to load the slot as long as the flag is set to full. When the slot reaches the destination device, the devices repeater reads the information without clearing the slot. Before passing it on, the repeater sets a received message flag in the slot. When the slot again reaches the sending device, the flag is set to empty. The destination device can check that the message was received by checking the received flag. If the message was not successfully received, perhaps because the destination device was not listening, the sender device can check the acknowledgement flag and re-transmit in the next slot.

Token passing technique

This technique is also used for ring networks. An imaginary *token* is passed continuously around the ring. The token is recognized as such by the devices, as a unique character sequence. If a device is waiting to transmit, it catches the token and with it, the authority to send data. As long as one device has the token, no other device can send data. A receiving device acknowledges the receipt of a message by inverting a 1-bit field. Token Ring (IEEE 802.5 Standard) employs this access method.

Carrier sense multiple access (CSMA)

This method of access control is used on broadcast systems such as the bus network. Each device is theoretically free to transmit data to any other device at any time. Before attempting to transmit, a device's network card polls the network path to ensure that the destination device is free to receive data and that the communications channel is free. A device wishing to transmit must wait until both conditions exist. Generally such delay will be no more than a few millionths of a second.

- CSMA *Collision Detection* (CSMA-CD). Because of the possibility of collision through simultaneous transmission, a collision detection mechanism is used. When collision does occur, the devices involved cease transmission and try again some time later. In order to avoid the same collision, each device involved is made to wait a different time. If a number of retries prove unsuccessful, an error will be reported to the user. Ethernet (IEEE 802.3 Standard) networks (see Network Cabling) use a form of CSMA/CD.

- CSMA *Collision Avoidance* (CSMA-CA). This strategy attempts to improve on that of CSMA-CD, which allows a device to place a packet onto the network path as soon as its network card detects it as being free. In the time between the test (measured in fractions of a microsecond) and the placing of the packet onto the path, another device's network card may have detected the path as free and be about to place another packet onto it. CSMA-CA seeks to remedy this problem by requiring a device's network card to test the path *twice*, once to see if the path is free and a second time, after alerting the device that it may use the network, but before the packet is placed onto the path.

Remote inter-networking

The term inter-networking is used to describe the formation of integrated network systems, through the connection of separate networks, locally and remotely. This enables organizations to construct organization-wide information and communications systems, even if sections of it are a few or thousands of miles apart. This section looks at the devices used to make connections between LANs which are remote from one another and necessarily therefore, between LANs and wide area networks; these may be, for example, public switched telephone and data networks (see Chapter 11). In general, these devices deal with the:

- connection of networks operating on different protocols;

- connection of LANs to WANs;

- connection of networks of different architecture, cabling and protocol;

- routing of packets along the most efficient path;

- conversion between different packet formats, protocols and transmission speeds.

Computer networking is a relatively new industry and terminology is not entirely standardized. For this reason, definitions of terms, such as bridge, router and gateway can vary from one manufacturer's specification to another. Some devices, for example, combine the features of bridges and routers and are referred to as bridge/routers. Bearing this in mind, the following definitions are generally accepted.

Gateway or router

A gateway, or router, is used to connect two LANs of different (they do not have to be) type ; thus, for example, an Ethernet LAN can be connected to a Token Ring LAN, or the connection may be Ethernet to Ethernet. The LANs may be remotely connected through, for example, British Telecom's Kilostream (Chapter 11) WAN, with a gateway at each LAN's entry point to the WAN.

The term *router* is used to signify that the device is more intelligent than a bridge (see Connecting and Extending LANs), in that it makes decisions about the route a data packet (by reference to its destination address) should follow to reach its destination; in this way, packets can be made to take the most efficient path. It may determine an alternative route for a packet, in the event of, for example, congestion or breakdown on a particular link. Networks may have different architectures and protocols.

A LAN using IPX (Novell) protocol can use a gateway to allow users access to, for example, a remote IBM network, which uses SNA protocol, through the Kilostream packet (X.25 protocol) switching network.

Multiplexer

Low speed terminals, such as those with keyboards, transmit at about 300 bps, whereas voice-grade telephone lines can support transmission speeds of up to 14,400 bps. A multiplexer allows a number of low-speed devices to share a high-speed line. The messages from several low-speed lines are combined into one high-speed channel and then separated out at the other end by a demultiplexor.

In two-way transmissions, both these functions are carried out in one unit at each end of the higher speed channel. The operation of a multiplexer linking several remote terminals to a host computer is illustrated in Chapter 11. Multiplexers use different methods to combine signals and separate them out: *frequency division multiplexing* (FDM) and *time division multiplexing* (TDM).

Concentrator

A concentrator greatly increases data throughput by increasing the number of low-speed channels and instead of transmitting a null character, empties the contents of the next full register. The data from each low-speed device is identified by extra identification bits and this constitutes an overhead.

Front-end-processors (FEP)

A front-end-processor is the most sophisticated type of device for communications control and is usually a minicomputer held at the site of a mainframe host computer. Its main task is to handle all the communications traffic, leaving the mainframe free to concentrate on other processing tasks. Its main tasks include:

- parity checking;

- stripping of overhead characters from serial transmission, start-stop bits and SYN (synchronous transmission - see Chapter 11) characters;

- conversion from serial to parallel transmission and vice versa;

- network control;

- network accounting;

- character conversion.

Benefits of computer networks

The general benefits are:

- sharing of appropriate *software*, *hardware resources* and common *data*;

- sharing of *processing* activity;

- *connectivity*; this is a very broad term used to categorize facilities and devices which support connection and communication between otherwise incompatible systems or devices. For example, a *terminal emulation* card, which enables a microcomputer to communicate with a remote IBM host computer, falls into this category;

- accessible services for *security*, *user support* and *system maintenance*.

Sharing hardware and software

In a LAN, particularly, there are opportunities to share hardware and software. This is because resources tend to be distributed over a small area; it is reasonable to ask users to share a printing resource if the printers serving them are within the same room, or perhaps in an adjacent room. It could be argued that the rapid fall in hardware costs has, to a certain extent, reduced the need for sharing peripherals, such as hard disk drives and printers. Although the prices of hard drives have fallen, the heavy demands of modern software and the increasing number of applications, ensures matching increases in demand for on-line storage. It is now common for microcomputer systems, even at the cheaper end of the market, to have their own hard disk storage with capacities measured in hundreds of megabytes. Although printers are becoming much cheaper, an increasing number of users are demanding the high quality output (and sometimes colour) provided by top quality printers; printers at the top of the quality range are still relatively expensive.

In summary, a number of factors concerning computer usage, storage and printing confirm that resource sharing remains a major purpose of a LAN.

- Applications. The range of computer applications and the number of users is continually increasing.

- Software packages. The increasing sophistication of software means that large amounts of disk space are needed for each package. Network versions of a package are cheaper (per user) than those for stand-alone systems.

- Storage technologies. Optical storage and high performance hard drives are capable of storing thousands of megabytes (gigabytes or gb) and are still relatively expensive. Individual users, each with their own hard disk-based microcomputer, are unlikely to make use of the several hundred megabytes available on each machine. A shared, large volume, hard or optical drive can satisfy the storage needs of all users.

- Printers. Most users require only occasional use of a printer, so there is little point in providing one for each. This is particularly the case for colour printers. A laser printer can produce the high quality output demanded by many applications and it operates at speeds which allow sharing to take place, without unreasonable delay for users.

- Other devices, such as scanners and plotters are relatively expensive and are likely to be used only occasionally.

Sharing data

A major benefit of all types of network concerns the sharing of data, frequently from centralized databases. This purpose is made particularly clear by the expansion of *Internet*, the world-wide network described in Chapter 37.

Data can also be regarded as a resource, so sharing it can bring similar benefits to those available from sharing hardware. For example, a common data store supports the use of a *database* system, which itself reduces the need for data duplication. Traditional computer processing methods require that each application has its own files and this results in the duplication of many data items and the updating process. For example, in a retail business both the stock control and purchasing departments make use of commodity details such as Stock Codes, Descriptions and Prices; if separate files are maintained by each department, a change in, for example, the Price of a commodity requires more than one input.

A database system allows these details (a single copy of each commodity's Stock Code, Description and Price) to be shared by all departments that need them. Even if database methods are not used, the storage of the various application files in a common disk store, means that they can, if desired, be made available to all users on a network. For an organization with numerous branches, each with its own processing facility, there needs to be a central resource, where the results of processing at branches can be merged (and possibly re-distributed) to give corporate (across the organization, as a whole) information.

Limiting access to shared storage

The sharing of data files presents some problems which need to be tackled. Firstly, access to some data may have to be restricted to particular users. Although the aim of networks is to provide computer access to as many users as possible, procedural and software controls can be built in to limit entry to the system, or to particular files or processes. Network software allows the network administrator to vary the rights of users, according to the kinds of access they require to particular applications or files.

Another problem with sharing files is that several users may attempt to update the same data at the same time. This can lead to corruption of data. To combat this problem, network software usually provides a facility for locking individual records while they are being updated. Thus, if a particular record is being altered, it is locked and made inaccessible by any other user until the updating process is complete.

Sharing processing activity

Host computer with intelligent terminals

A host computer with intelligent terminals allows processing to be carried out at remote sites; as such it comes under the heading of WAN. The distribution of processing work may be very limited, such that the majority is processed by a central computer. For example, terminals connected to a remote host computer often have their own processing power, file storage and printing facilities. Usually, before being transmitted to the host computer for the updating of files, *transaction* data will require some *validation* and other accuracy checks and this can be done at the terminal. Microcomputers equipped with suitable software are often used to *emulate* mainframe intelligent terminals, with the added advantage of being useable as stand-alone systems, when not communicating with the mainframe.

Alternatively, the work may be equally shared amongst a number of powerful computer systems, which then merge the results of their separate efforts.

Client-server network

A *client-server* LAN aims to exploit the full processing power of each computer in the network, including the *file server* and the user workstations or *clients*. This is effected by dividing the processing tasks between a client and a server. The client, a microcomputer in its own right (as opposed to the *dumb* terminal found in older mainframe systems) provides the user with a completely separate facility for running applications. The file server which could be a microcomputer, minicomputer, or mainframe, enhances the client component by providing additional services.

These services are traditionally offered by minicomputer and mainframe systems operating a *time-sharing* operating system; they include shared file management, data sharing between users, network administration and security. The major benefit of a client-server network is that the power of the client and server machines is used jointly to carry out the processing of an application. Interactive activities, for example, construction of a spreadsheet or the word processing of a report, are carried out by the client machine; having logged onto the network, the user can load the required applications software from the file server.

Matters of backup and file sharing security, relating to the application, can be handled by the server. Printing tasks can also be queued and handled as a shared printer becomes available. This task is handled by one or more *print servers*, which can be dedicated devices, or microcomputers assigned to the task. Except for very small LANs, most operate on the client-server principle.

Peer-to-peer network

With a peer-to-peer configuration, it is not necessary to have a file server; instead all the workstations on the network contribute to the control of the network. Thus, any workstation can supply or use resources of others, as required. Unfortunately, this has the effect of slowing performance; in addition it means that files are not held centrally and this complicates file management. *Novell Personal Netware* and *LANtastic 6.0* are popular examples of peer-to-peer networking products.

The peer-to-peer approach is highly suitable for very small networks, but both the products mentioned allow the system to be developed to introduce some file server control. Facilities are also included to allow users to share resources in groups; the name of another peer-to-peer networking product illustrates this feature: *Windows for Workgroups*; up to 10 users can be networked.

Network administration

Achieving efficiency and reliability

In aiming for such efficiency and reliability, an organization may use the following guidelines and suggestions for network administration, staff training and the use of fault control systems:

- Use hardware and software which conforms to a Standard; this should ensure that equipment from different sources is compatible and works properly with other network components.

- Obtain a service and support contract with the supplier of the network, or some other organization which specializes in the system in use; the call out response times, to attend to faults or repairs, should meet the needs of the network owner.

- Ensure that fully trained staff are employed to install, configure, monitor, and develop the network.

- Make use of devices to protect against, for example, power failure; an Uninterruptible Power Supply or *UPS* device automatically provides several minutes of power, in the event of a power cut, to allow work to be saved and the network to be shut down safely.

- Train users to use the system properly and not to, for example, attempt to reconfigure a workstation's network software.

- Employ security to prevent unauthorized access, and entry of viruses to the file server. Virus protection software can help, but users should not be able to bring disks or software from machines at home or other locations; diskless workstations can be used to prevent such abuse of the network.

- Ensure regular *backup* of the file server, using, for example, tape streamer devices.

- Use a technique, such as *disk mirroring*, whereby two file server disks operate in tandem. Each block of data written to the main disk is also written to the mirror disk; if one fails, the other continues supporting the network without interruption.

Support of mixed traffic

Mixed traffic is a collective phrase to describe the different kinds of information which may be transmitted over computer networks and telecommunications links. These different kinds of information include, audio and video images, as well as computer data (text, numbers and other characters). If an organization wishes to have a mixed traffic system, it will require a *broadband* (see Broadband) network.

Monitoring activity levels

The word activity is used to refer to various aspects of network use and operation, for example, traffic volumes and patterns. There may be particular times when the volume of data moving around the network significantly reduces its performance; this may indicate a need to re-organize the work patterns of users or to modify the network structure (perhaps by dividing it into smaller segments according to user function, for example Sales and Accounts - see Bridge).

System reporting

A network operating system will normally include various software *utilities* to allow the system administrator or supervisor to monitor and receive reports on various network conditions. For example, the system may report when a workstation has become inoperable or a fault has been detected on the server, or that certain system files have become corrupted and need repair. System reporting can help to ensure network reliability in that the supervisor is notified of such conditions.

Storage control

An important aspect of network management is the control of file storage space on the network. In a client-server (see Client Server Network), applications and data files are held on the file server and its space needs to be managed efficiently to ensure that required files remain accessible and that redundant files are removed (*purged*) and, if necessary, *archived* (copies held on another disk or tape medium, in case they are needed). If redundant files are not removed, space is wasted and the task of retrieving other files becomes more difficult (searching through redundant files for those required).

System configuration

Any network has a particular *configuration*; that is to say, particular types of components are used, they are connected and communicate in a particular way, and particular facilities are provided. The configuration of a network affects the way it works, not only electronically in terms of its hardware and software components, but also in its relationship with users. Thus, the network can be configured concerning:

- *User passwords*. A user may be required to enter a *password* before he or she is logged onto the network and given access to its resources.

- *User access rights*. The supervisor can assign rights to users in respect of particular directories or files on the file server. Such rights determine what a user can do with those resources. For example, in their own user directories, users may be able to create, copy, delete and rename data files; this would be essential if users were able to store work produced with various applications packages. In contrast, users' rights within the directory containing applications software (*executable* files), would be very restricted and only suffi-cient to allow them to run the programs. Some groups of users may have no rights to particular applications programs. For example, a sales clerk would be unlikely to have rights to run the personnel management software.

- *Job queues*. The shared servers (print and communications servers, for example) can be assigned work from particular users or groups of users, through a system of queues. Thus, a print server manages print queues, which are jobs from users awaiting printing on a shared printer. The configuration determines the printing devices to which jobs are assigned and their priority, if any, in a queue. Access to, for example, a laser printer, may be restricted to a small group of users.

Exercises

1. Identify the main *components* of a LAN and briefly explain the function of each.

2. Identify one advantage and one disadvantage of each of the following network topologies: *star*; *ring*; *bus*.

3. How does the *IBM Token Ring* network seek to overcome a weakness of the basic ring topology?

4. Name the main *Ethernet cable standards*, and the performance specification of each.

5. (i)   Differentiate between *baseband* and *broadband* networks.

   (ii) Suggest, by reference to applications, why broadband networks will become increasingly important.

6. Differentiate between the terms *repeater*, *bridge* and *router* (or *gateway*).

7. Identify four functions of a *network operating system*.

8.   What is meant by a workstation's *local operating system*?

9.   In the context of network connection software, briefly describe the functions of the:

    (i)   *communication protocol*;

    (ii)   *LAN driver*.

10.   Outline the operation of the following network access protocols:

    (i)   *empty slot*;

    (ii)   *token passing*;

    (iii)   *CSMA/CA*.

11.   What is meant by the term *remote inter-networking*?

12.   Briefly describe the function of a:

    (i)   *multiplexer*;

    (ii)   *concentrator*;

    (iii)   *front-end-processor* (FEP).

13.   A major benefit of a network is its facilities for *resource sharing*. Identify the particular resources which can be shared and the benefits such sharing brings for an organization and its users.

14.   Differentiate between a *client-server* and *peer-to-peer* network operating system.

Chapter 11

Data Communications

Telecommunications and data communications

The word *telecommunications* can be applied to any system capable of transmitting text, sounds, graphical images or indeed, data of any kind, in electronic form. The signals may travel along wires or they may be radio signals, which require no wires, but can travel through the atmosphere and space. Currently, not all aspects of telecommunications system are digital, so sometimes, data may be transmitted in *analogue* form. Computer data is represented in *digital* form, so where the telecommunications systems support it, data is moved between remote computer systems as digitized signals. The topic of analogue and digital signals is dealt with later. The combination of computer and telecommunications technologies has profoundly affected the way computer systems are used. To a computer, text, sounds and graphical images all constitute data, which it represents digitally, using the *binary* coding system. Although not all transmissions of digital data involve general-purpose computers, they are often generated and controlled by digital computer technology. Data generated by a computer is already in digital form, but other data (the term is used in its broadest sense), such as sounds of human speech, or a photograph, need to be digitally encoded before transmission over a digital network. The term *data communications* can be applied to systems that combine the use of telecommunications and computer technologies.

Standards authorities

The data communications industry has always had to deal with problems of *incompatible* standards. As explained later, standards have to do with all aspects of a communications system, including, for example, the *hardware devices*, the *encoding* of data and the forms of *signals* used. At first, the only computer systems available for use in data communications systems were mainframes and later, minicomputers. These computer systems were produced by a small number of very large manufacturers, the most important being IBM; they also produced the communications devices that worked with their computers. In competition with one another, each manufacturer set the standards for use with its equipment. These *closed* systems prevented a customer from using equipment, produced by different manufacturers, in the same data communications system.

The huge expansion in the uses of data communications, both nationally and internationally has been made possible through the adoption of some common standards. Common standards lead to *open* systems, which allow users to use components from more than one manufacturer. A number of bodies are concerned with the establishment of international standards and these are listed below. Frequently, a standard arises initially from the work of a particular manufacturer, and then, often because of the importance of the manufacturer, it is included in the recommendations of the standards authorities.

- CCITT. This is an acronym for Comité Consultatif Internationale de Télégraphie et Téléphonie an organization that has its headquarters in Geneva, Switzerland. It is part of the United Nations International Telecommunications Union (ITU). The CCITT makes recommendations on most aspects of data communications, for example, modems (see Data Circuit Termination Equipment), networks and facsimile transmission or FAX and publishes them every four years. These recommendations usually obtain world-wide acceptance. CCITT's

'V' series of standards cover equipment used on telephone lines and its X series relate to digital packet transmission standards. Some examples of these standards are mentioned later in this element.

- ANSI is the acronym for American National Standards Institute. ANSI has long maintained a strong influence on standards in the computer and data communications industries. It is formed from industrial and business groups and is a member of the International Standards Organization (ISO). Examples of its influence can be found in the fields of computer hardware and programming languages. For example, by conforming to ANSI standards, the FORTRAN, COBOL and C languages enable the production of computer software, which is largely *portable*. In other words, because each language is more or less universal, a program written in, for example, COBOL can be readily translated for use on any make of computer. In the area of microcomputer hardware, the ANSI standards define the SCSI (an acronym for Small Computer System Interface) parallel interface, for the connection of peripherals, such as disk drives and printers. The institute is also responsible for the ANSI.SYS *device driver*, a program that provides facilities for greater control of a computer console (screen and keyboard), than is possible with the MS-DOS operating system (see Chapter 13).

- IEEE is the acronym for the Institute of Electrical and Electronic Engineers. The organization has set numerous standards for various aspects of telecommunications and computing. Notably, the IEEE has defined standards for local area network (LAN) protocols (see Chapter 10).

- The ISO (International Standards Organization), has its headquarters in Geneva, Switzerland and is responsible for the definition of the Open Systems Interconnection (OSI) model. This model aims to ensure that any computer terminal is able to connect to any network and communicate with any other terminal, whether it is connected to the same or any other linked network. The OSI model is examined in greater detail in the section on Communications Protocols.

Public telecommunications authorities

The main telecommunications network in the United Kingdom is the public switched telephone network (*pstn*), which is owned by British Telecom (BT). Although BT owns the network, Mercury Communications (a competitor *public telecommunications operator* or PTO), is able to use the pstn to provide telephone and network services. Increasing competition is being provided from the independent providers of cellular telephone services.

Types of communications networks

Public switched telephone network (pstn)

The *pstn* is the main telecommunications network for the United Kingdom. It was originally designed for voice transmission, using analogue electrical signals; these electrical signals represent what is spoken and heard at each end of a link. A telephone mouthpiece contains a diaphragm, which vibrates when struck by sound waves. The vibrations are converted into electrical impulses and are sent over the network to the earpiece on the receiving telephone; a diaphragm in the earpiece converts the impulses back into sound.

Much of the pstn is now digital, in particular the national trunk network and call switching exchanges; the analogue connections are mainly confined to the pstn's local links to homes and businesses. Digital voice transmission uses coded patterns of digital impulses, which are similar to those used to represent computer data. To transmit computer data over analogue sections of the pstn, requires use of a *modem* (see Data Circuit Termination Equipment or DCE). This device converts the computer's digital signal into an appropriate analogue form before transmission; a modem at the receiving end converts the analogue signal back to the digital form required by the computer.

Types of telecommunications lines

Dedicated lines

These can be leased from British Telecom and provide a permanent connection for devices in a network. They provide high transmission rates and are relatively error-free. They are only cost-effective for high volume data transmission, or when a permanent link is vital to the users. Charging is by a flat rate rather than when calls are made.

Dial-up or switched lines

These are cheaper, but support lower transmission rates than leased lines. They are more cost effective than leased lines for low-volume work and allow the operator to choose the destination of transmissions.

Digital network systems

Public switched data network (psdn) or switchstream

The psdn, owned by British Telecom (BT) and named *Switchstream*, is a *packet switching* (see later) network. Modems are not required and transmission performance is better than that achievable over the partially analogue pstn. Switchstream is one of four digital services, collectively known as X-Stream; the other services are Kilostream, Megastream and Satstream.

Switchstream conforms to the CCITT (see Standards Authorities) standard known as the X.25 protocol; for this reason, the network is often referred to as the X.25 network. A major benefit of using this CCITT standard is that the network can be used for international communications.

Circuit switching

In any network, setting up a connection between two devices may involve circuit switching. For example, if a network is busy a connection may be established through a series of switches, from one circuit to another, over an alternative route. Thus the actual distance the signals travel may be greatly in excess of the geographical distance between the two points. Charges, whether the connection is for voice or data, will be made according to the geographical distance between the devices (local, medium, long distance), rather than the distance the signals actually have to travel through the various switches.

Packet switching

The main components of a packet switching network are: high speed data lines; packet switching exchanges (PSEs); packet assembler/disassembler (PAD); packet terminal.

With the use of a specialized computer, called a *packet terminal*, a customer can create the packets and connect directly to the network through a dedicated dataline. If the customer is not using a packet terminal, a dial-up connection is used and the data has to go through a *packet assembler/disassembler* (PAD). This device converts data to and from the networks protocol as it enters and leaves the network. Figure 11.1 illustrates these features.

The principles of packet switching are as follow. Messages are divided into data packets, which are then directed through the network to their destination under computer control. Besides a *message* portion, each packet contains data concerning:

- the destination address;

- the source identification;

- the sequence of the packet in the complete message;

- the detection and control of transmission errors.

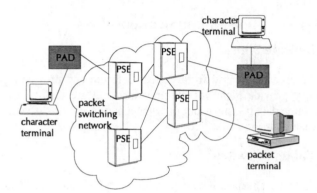

Figure 11.1. *Packet switching network*

The progress of a packet is monitored and controlled by *packet switching exchanges* (PSE) located at each *node* in the network. A node is a junction of network lines, which could be a computer or a computer terminal or other device.

As a packet arrives at a node, the exchange checks the addressing instructions and unless it corresponds to its present location, forwards it on the most appropriate route. Each node has an *input queue*, into which all arriving packets are entered (even those which are addressed to the node itself) and a number of *output queues* (to allow for the possibility of network congestion).

The route on which a packet is then transmitted may be determined by one of a number of *routing strategies*:

- hot potato. The packet is sent as quickly as possible to the shortest output queue; such packets are not unduly delayed, although they may not be transmitted on the most direct route;

- pre-determined routing. With this method, the routing details are included in the packet itself, each switching exchange forwarding the packet according to the embedded instructions;

- directory routing. Each switching exchange has a copy of a routing table to which it refers before forwarding each packet. The appropriate output queue is determined from the table and the packet destination.

Network traffic information is continually transmitted between the various nodes, so that each switching computer has information to allow, for example, the avoidance of congested routes. Figure 11.3 illustrates how a network structure provides alternative routes by which a packet may reach its destination.

If a network is structured as shown in Figure 7.3, a packet sent from terminal T(2) to terminal T(6), would go into the input queue of packet switching exchange PSE (a). Depending on the routing strategy and network traffic conditions, the packet could be directed to an output queue leading to any of the other PSEs. If PSE (e) was inoperative, the alternative routes would be cut drastically; in fact the packet would either have to go through PSEs (b), (c) and (d), in that sequence, or direct from PSE (a) to PSE (d). Packet switching allows packets relating to a single message, to be transmitted on different routes. This may be necessary, either because of the breakdown of some routes, or because of variations in traffic conditions over different routes.

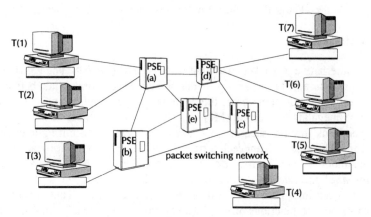

Figure 11.2. *Routing in a packet switching network*

Message switching

As the name suggests, this type of network deals with identifiable and complete messages, in contrast to a packet switched system where the destination user nodes are responsible for re-assembling their packets into complete messages upon receipt. A number of points can be made when comparing and contrasting packet switching and message switching networks:

- both use a store and forward principle; each node in the network has storage facilities for the accumulation of data prior to its onward transmission and the intelligence to examine the destination data before forwarding it;

- packet switching networks treat data transparently. Individual packets generally do not contain complete messages and the network does not recognize connections between packets, except from identification of their destination. The destination user nodes are left with the responsibility of re-assembling individual packets into complete messages;

- the store and forward facilities in message switching networks need to be much larger than those for packet switching systems, because complete messages must be accumulated at each point of transfer in the network;

- message switching requires increased processing time at intervening nodes while messages are accumulated before onward transmission;

- message switching provides users with greater confidence that messages will be transmitted and received in complete form.

X.25 protocol

As already mentioned, the psdn uses a packet switching protocol, known as X.25. The CCITT (see Standards Authorities) provide the X.25 protocol for interfacing terminals with a psdn. The protocol provides users with the following facilities.

- Division of a message into packets.

- Error checking and re-transmission of any packet effected by an error.

- An addressing format that allows international transmission.

- The PSEs control the transmission of packets through the network.

Kilostream

An alternative to packet switching is to use *multiplexing*. The Kilostream service uses this technique for data transmission. The service provides a high speed direct link between two points. Data can pass in both directions at the same time; this is known as *full duplex* mode. The main link can transmit data at a rate of 2048 megabits per second (Mbits/s); this allows a number of low speed terminals to be connected to the high speed link through separate low speed links, each transmitting at either 128 kilobits per second (Kb/s) or 64 Kb/s. The signals from each terminal can then be merged for transmission along the high speed link, using a technique known as *time division multiplexing* (TDM). The process of multiplexing is carried out by a *terminal multiplexer*. At the receiving end of the link, the signals are separated out for transmission along low speed lines connected to their respective terminals. The terminal multiplexer at each end of the link can carry out the functions of multiplexing (combining signals) and demultiplexing (separating the signals). The is obviously necessary for full duplex operation.

Multiplexers fall into two broad categories according to the methods used to combine signals and separate them:

- *Frequency Division Multiplexing (FDM)* differentiates between the data signals sent from different devices by using a different *frequency range* for each. This can be likened to tuning a radio or television to receive particular programmes. So that any given radio programme does not interfere with the transmissions of another (although, they sometimes do), it is assigned a frequency that is not too close to the other assigned frequencies. In the same way, when a data transmission channel is multiplexed to accommodate signals from separate devices, some space must be left between the frequency ranges to avoid confusion of signals. Spaces between the different frequency ranges are know as *guard bands*.

- *Time Division Multiplexing (TDM)*, as the term suggests, provides a *time slice* on the higher-speed line for each terminal. The multiplexer has a number of registers, one per low-speed channel. Each register can store one character. The multiplexer scans each register in sequence, emptying the contents into a continuous stream of data to be transmitted. A multiplexer will send a null character whenever it finds an empty slot.

Figure 11.3 illustrates the multiplexing of signals from three terminals to a remote mainframe computer.

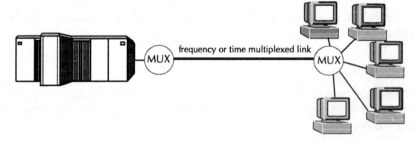

frequency or time multiplexed link

Figure 11.3. *Multiplexers used to allow several terminals to use a single link*

Connecting to a remote mainframe

In organizations with mainframe computers, it is often desirable for staff with microcomputers on their desks to be able to communicate with the mainframe via those systems. With non-IBM systems, where the host computer uses asynchronous transmission, the connection can be made via the RS232C (this refers to a standard used in most serial communications) serial transmission port, located at the back of the microcomputers system casing. However, the most common mainframe systems, IBM and ICL in particular, use synchronous communications, so special terminal emulation cards are required.

Thus, microcomputer workstations can be converted to mainframe terminals using a technique called emulation. A terminal emulation card is fitted into one of the expansion slots in the microcomputers system casing. If there are a number of terminals to be connected, the microcomputer is then connected, via a coaxial cable, to a terminal cluster controller. The controller is linked to a front-end processor (usually a minicomputer, dedicated to handling incoming and outgoing communications for the mainframe), which is itself connected to the mainframe computer. In this way, a microcomputer can, for example, be converted into an emulation of an IBM 3270 terminal.

The advantage of using a microcomputer as a mainframe terminal is that it can also be used on a stand-alone basis for local processing tasks, such as word processing or spreadsheet work. The terminal emulation package ensures that the mainframe responds in the same way as it would to a dedicated terminal. Security mechanisms, such as passwords, prevent users of emulated terminals from carrying out processes which are forbidden to users of dedicated terminals. However, the microcomputer's facility for local storage and processing can present serious security problems for the mainframes data and various mechanisms have to be included to prevent unauthorized updates.

Where emulated terminals are to be linked to a mainframe via a wide area network, adapter cards are available which combine the terminal emulation with the gateway software, to access the intervening network.

Megastream

This service is similar to Kilostream, except that no terminal multiplexing equipment is provided. Data can be transmitted at 2.048, 8, 34 or 140 Mbits/s. A user can choose to use the high speed circuit directly or multiplex the circuit, such that a number of low speed channels are made available across the link. Each separate lower speed channel can then be used to carry data or some may be left for the transmission of digitized speech.

Satstream

This digital data service provides customers with a small dish aerial to allow radio transmission of data, through a communications satellite. Customers are thus able to connect with networks in Western Europe.

Integrated services digital network (ISDN)

Many forms of data, including text, voice and video images, can be digitized and an Integrated Services Digital Network (ISDN) is designed to allow the *integrated* transmission of these various data forms over the same network. An Integrated Services Digital Network exists in various forms in different countries, although the ultimate aim is to achieve an international system. It is defined as a wholly *digital* system, with end-to-end digital connections and digital exchanges throughout. ISDN has become achievable because the telephone network has become largely digital. The public telephone network is, by far, the largest communications network, so once it is fully digitized, every business and home user will have access to ISDN services. British Telecom's ISDN began with a pilot scheme in 1985, which was extended in 1986 and has continued to develop since. The network provides three types of access:

- *single-line* IDA (integrated digital access). The user gains access with *Network Terminating Equipment* (NTE);

- *line adapter module* (LAMs). A LAM allows two terminals to simultaneously share the same, two-wire, connection; this could provide a cheap method of communicating with a remote computer system;

- *multi-line* IDA, which provides 30 independent channels, each being capable of transmitting voice or data.

Broadcast networks

Data communications networks also support:

- television and radio broadcasting;

- cellular telephone systems.

Television and radio broadcasting

When a television studio broadcasts a programme, the signals are carried to television receivers through a network of transmitters; radio programmes are broadcast from a studio in a similar fashion. An out-of-date term for a radio is a wireless; thus the transmissions in these broadcast networks are all carried out without the use of wires, that is, as *radio waves*. Radio waves vary in *frequency* and different frequency bands are used for different kinds of broadcasting. It is beyond the scope of this text to go into detail concerning these frequency bands, but the abbreviations VHF (very high frequency) and UHF (ultra-high frequency) should be familiar. The term *broadcast* is used because the radio wave signals can be received by any number of receivers within the broadcast area. The geographical area which can be reached by a broadcasting station depends on which method is used, namely:

- *cable* connections; this is an exception here as it clearly involves the use of wire or cable;

- *terrestrial* transmitters;

- *communications satellites*

A broadcasting company may use a combination of cable, terrestrial and satellite transmitters to distribute its programmes. For example, the American company WTBS, in Atlanta, Georgia uses satellite to transmit low-cost sports and entertainment programmes to cable systems across the USA. Cable broadcasting, as the term indicates, uses physical cabling and is only economic over a limited area, such as a large city. However, in combination with satellite broadcasting, cable television plays an important role. Although terrestrial transmitters allow a much larger broadcast area than cable, satellites are essential to modern television broadcasting. Within the UK, pictures and monophonic sound are transmitted as analogue signals. The BBC has developed and transmits, NICAM stereo sound, using digital encoding techniques.

Television broadcasting allows the transmission of *moving pictures*, *sound* and *data* to television receivers within the area served by a broadcasting station. Database services provided by television are *one-way* only, to television receivers and are collectively known as *Teletext* (see Network services). The BBC teletext service is known as Ceefax. To access these services a television receiver must have a Teletext *decoder*.

Microwave transmissions and communications satellites

Microwaves are super-high frequency (SHF) radio waves and can be used where transmitter and receiver are not in sight of one another. The communication path must be relatively obstruction-free. Microwaves can also be transmitted, through earth transmitters, to communications satellites; microwaves can penetrate cloud. Earth stations must be no more than 25-30 miles apart, because humidity in the atmosphere interferes with microwave signals. Each station in a communication path acts as a *repeater* station. Obviously, it is impractical to build sufficient repeater stations to deal with all transmissions, so communications satellites are essential. Once a satellite has received a signal, it amplifies it and sends it back to earth. Satellite communications are now fairly common and provide a cheaper and better trans-ocean transmission medium than undersea cable. Apart from television broadcasting, satellites form an essential part of the international telephone network. Voice and data messages are digitally transmitted as packets (see Packet Switching). Numerous transmission channels can be created using *frequency division multiplexing* (see Kilostream).

Cellular telephone networks

These networks use *cellular radio* communications, which operate in the UHF (ultra-high frequency) band. Local *base stations* allow cellphone (hand-held or vehicle-based) users to access the pstn. Each base station covers a *cell site*, an area within which it can pick up cellphone signals. Within the UHF band, signals can penetrate buildings and other barriers, but a user must be within a few miles of a transmitter, particularly in urban areas, where the largest numbers of users tend to be found. Thus, a base station in a rural area, serving fewer users, can cover a larger cell site than is possible in an urban area. Computers are used to allow links to be maintained even while the caller is moving from one transmission area to another. Thus, when a base station receives a signal from a cellphone, it monitors the strength of the signal continuously to determine if it is still the most suitable base station to handle the transmission. Obviously, if the user is driving while making a call, a different base station may be handling the call at different points on the journey. The only effect of these changes is a brief (about one-fifth of a second) interruption to the call as the switch is made to a different base station. Two major cellular radio operators in the UK are Cellnet and Vodaphone.

Modes of data communication

Direction of transmission

Communications media can be classified according to whether *two-way transmission* is supported.

- *Simplex* mode allows communication in one direction only.

- *Half-duplex* supports communications in both directions, but not at the same time; in other words there is only a single channel and the direction is switched after completion of transmission in the other direction.

- *Duplex* mode allows communication in both directions at the same time, as there are two channels permanently available. In interactive systems, where two way communication is continuously required, duplex is the only suitable mode.

- *Asymmetric duplex* is the same as duplex, except that the transmission speed in one direction is different from that of the other.

Devices differ in the ways they communicate or talk with each other. One such difference is in the number of *conductors* or lines they use to transmit data.

Serial transmission

With serial transmission, the binary signals representing the data are transmitted one after another in a serial fashion. Serial data transmission is normally used, except for very short connections between a peripheral and a computer, where parallel techniques are employed. The technique is illustrated in Figure 11.4.

Figure 11.4. *Serial transmission between two devices*

Parallel transmission

As the term makes obvious, data bits are transmitted as groups in parallel; Figure 11.5 illustrates this form.

This is obviously quicker than sending them serially, but it is only practicable over short distances. Communication between a computer and its nearby peripherals can be carried out using parallel transmission, which is particularly important where high-speed devices, such as disk

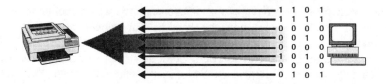

Figure 11.5. *Parallel transmission between a computer and a local printer*

or tape units, are concerned. Microcomputer systems often use parallel transmission to communicate with a nearby printer. The number of lines needed for a parallel connection defines its *bus width*. As explained in the later section on Connectors or Interfaces, each line has a particular function. Thus, apart from the 8 bits needed for the data (see Data Representation), *handshaking* signals are needed to control the transfer of data between a computer and a terminal, which operate at different speeds. Additional handshake lines are needed to carry these signals.

Asynchronous serial transmission

When a sending device transmits characters at irregular intervals, as does for example, a keyboard device, it is said to be transmitting *asynchronously*.

Although the characters are not sent at regular intervals, the bits within each character must be sent at regularly timed intervals. An example of asynchronous character format is shown in Figure 11.6. It can be seen that the line has two electrical states, representing 1 and 0. Between characters, the line is in the *idle* state, a 1 or *mark* condition.

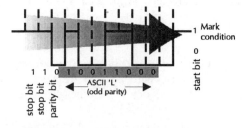

Figure 11.6. *Asynchronous character format*

The first or *start bit*, set to 0, indicates the start of a character, whilst a *stop bit* marks the end. The receiving machine listens to the line for a start bit. When it senses this it counts off the regularly timed bits that form the character. When a stop bit is reached, the receiver switches back to its listening state. The presence of start and stop bits for each character permits the time interval between characters to be irregular, or asynchronous.

Synchronous serial transmission

The start and stop bits used in asynchronous transmission are wasteful, in
that they do not contain information.
With higher speed devices or *buffered*
low-speed devices, data can be transmitted in more efficient, timed, or
synchronous blocks. Figure 11.7 illustrates the technique.

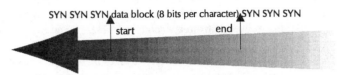

Figure 11.7. *Synchronous character format*

A variety of formats may be used, each having their operating rules or protocol. Communications protocols
are dealt with later in this chapter.

In synchronous transmission, a data stream may be very long, so it is vital that the timing between
transmitter and receiver is synchronized and that individual characters are separated. This is done by using a
clock lead from the transmitter. Synchronization (*syn*) characters are placed at the beginning of each data
block and, in case timing is lost by line disturbance, several syn characters may be situated at intervals within
the data block. Thus if timing is lost, the receiver can re-time its bit groupings from the last syn character.
Like the start and stop bits used in asynchronous transmission, syn characters constitute an overhead and
have to be stripped out by the receiver. Synchronous transmission is generally used for data speeds of 2400
bps or more. Some VDU terminals are designed for high speed data transmission and use synchronous
transmission; many others use asynchronous transmission.

Parallel-serial conversion (UART and USRT)

As data moves around a computer system in parallel form, it needs to be converted to serial form for
transmission though a telecommunications link and from serial to parallel, when the transmission is inward.
These conversion processes are carried out by a hardware device called a *universal asynchronous receiver
and transmitter* (UART) or *universal synchronous receiver and transmitter* (USRT), depending on the type
of computer being used.

Devices

Data terminal equipment (DTE)

All the external devices attached to a network may be referred to collectively as data terminal equipment
(DTE). Examples of DTE equipment are: computer terminals, including microcomputers used for that
function; minicomputers; bank cash dispensers; printers.

Dumb terminal

The DTE may be a *dumb* terminal, that is, one which has no processing power of its own, possibly no
storage, and is entirely dependent on a controlling computer. As soon as each character is entered by the
operator, it is transmitted over the communications link, to the controlling computer; this makes editing
extremely difficult and slow. The remote computer, to which the terminal is connected, has to use an *input
buffer* (small amount of memory assigned to that purpose) to store characters as they arrive. Because the
terminal is dumb, the remote computer must regularly *poll* the line to determine the presence of data.

Intelligent terminal

An *intelligent* terminal (it may be a microcomputer) has memory and processing power, so an operator can use it to store, edit and manipulate data, independently of any other connected computer. For example, a document could be retrieved from a remote computer, be edited within the intelligent terminal and then, in its updated form, be transmitted back to the remote computer. The intelligent terminal's processing facility is provided by an internal processor, usually a microprocessor; its internal memory allows data to be held and manipulated before transmission. The facility may also include local backing storage and a printer. Intelligent terminals can use either EBCDIC or ASCII code (see Standards for Data Representation), but a dumb terminal can only use ASCII.

Two points need to be made concerning the methods used to transmit data and the type of terminal used.

- Dumb terminals, having no processing power and no buffer memory have to use a *point-to-point* connection with the remote, controlling computer. Such terminals transmit data asynchronously. The characters are not evenly separated, because the transmission of characters is determined by the typing speed of the operator and the characters will obviously not be transmitted at precise, regular intervals.

- Intelligent terminals, having a buffer store, can accumulate the keyed characters and send them in blocks or streams. The remote computer signals when transmission of a data stream can begin, thus allowing line sharing by numerous communicating devices. Such line sharing is carried out by multiplexing, a technique described in the earlier section on Packet Switching Networks.

Data circuit termination equipment (DCE)

The intervening connections of a network are leased from the main telecommunications provider, which in the UK is British Telecom. The equipment that allows the DTE to be connected to and interfaced with the network is known as *data circuit termination equipment* (DCE). The CCITT (see Standards Authorities) use the term *data communication equipment* (also DCE). An example of DCE is a *modem*, which allows computer data to be transmitted over sections of the pstn (usually local connections to homes and businesses) which still use analogue signalling.

Modem

Even though much of the public switched telephone network (pstn) uses digital transmission techniques, local connections to homes and businesses still use analogue signals. To allow transmission of computer data (which is digital) over these analogue links, a device called a *modem* is needed to *modulate*

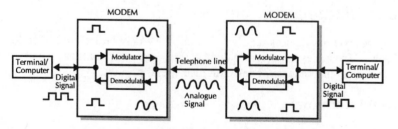

Figure 11.8. *Modems in a data communications link*

and *demodulate* the computers signals. The modem for the transmitter device has to modulate the digital signal into the corresponding analogue form for transmission along the telephone line. The modem at the receiver device has to carry out the reverse operation. Modems are capable of both functions, so that two way communications are supported. Modems are examined in more detail in the section on Protocols. Figure 11.8 illustrates the role of the modem in a data telecommunications link.

Telephone-modem connections

To allow computer communication through a telephone line, the user must obtain a modem, of which there are two main types:

- asynchronous (irregularly transmitted characters) serial modems. Each character requires *start* and *stop bits* to separate one character from another.

- synchronous (regularly timed transmission of data blocks) serial modems. Start and stop bits are not required, because the transmitting and receiving modems are synchronized.

Modem speeds

Baud rate indicates the number of signal changes or pulses per second supported by a communication link. The term used to be synonymous with *bits per second* (bps), but improved data encoding (compression) techniques mean, for example, that a 28,800 baud link can support data transfer rates up to 115,200 bps. Different modems provide different data transmission rates, measured in bits per second (bps). The data compression and error correction standards are set by standards bodies (see start of chapter).

Computer-modem connection

To make use of a modem, the microcomputer should have a serial communication (RS232) port. However, there are two possible alternatives; an adapter card with a serial port capability; a communications board (this fits in an expansion slot, located inside the computer's system casing), which combines the functions of the serial port and the modem.

Interfaces

Interface devices (or connectors - the terms are interchangeable) are designed to allow various pieces of equipment to work with one another. For this reason, they normally conform to certain standards, of which there are a number. For example, to connect a computer to a modem requires an interface that will allow:

- the movement of data, in both directions, between the two devices;

- selection of the transmission rate for data to pass through the telephone line;

- synchronization of the two devices (with clock timing signals).

Standards (usually recommended by one of the Standards Authorities), applied to the design of the interface, may relate to, for example, the number and arrangement of pins, their functions and the signals that are applied to each. This topic is examined further in the following section. The following sections examine several types of interfaces. Interfaces can be categorized according to whether they are designed to handle *serial* or *parallel* transmission of data.

Data communications standards

Data representation

Before transmission, characters must be coded into a code recognized by the sending and receiving devices. Almost all terminals are designed to use either the ASCII or EBCDIC codes (Chapter 2).

The ASCII (American Standard Code for Information Interchange) code uses seven binary digits (*bits*), plus a *parity bit* (see Error Detection) to represent a full range of characters. It is defined by the International Standards Organization (ISO). The 8-bit EBCDIC (Extended Binary-coded Decimal Interchange Code) character code has a 256 character set and is generally used with IBM and IBM-compatible equipment.

Communications protocols

A protocol is a set of rules for the transmission of data between two devices. A protocol may include rules to deal with:

- the establishment of which device currently has *control of the communications link*;

- *error detection and correction*;

- *data flow control*; this is to ensure that data transmission flows smoothly, that the communications channel is not overloaded and that the transmitting device does not send data more quickly than the receiver can handle.

Protocols are often developed by manufacturers and then become recommended by Standards Authorities, but sometimes, they are developed by the latter. Not all protocols cover all three items listed above. For example, the V24 (CCITT standard) and RS232 protocols, which are computer-modem interfaces (see Connectors or Interfaces), do not provide error detection facilities; they are *low level* protocols. Similarly, the X25 interface is a protocol and interface standard for connection to a packet switching network; there are a whole series of X protocols established by the CCITT relating to packet switching networks. A higher level protocol, such as V42 (see Example Protocols) includes error detection and correction facilities. The rest of this section aims to give a brief introduction to this very complex area of data communications.

The OSI (open systems interconnection) model

Many computer devices are now designed for use in networked systems. Manufacturers are now tending to conform to standard protocols that make their equipment compatible with a variety of user networks. *Closed* networks, that are restricted to one manufacturer's equipment and standards, are not attractive to the user, because it restricts the choice of equipment which can be used. The aim of standardization is to achieve more open systems which allow users to select from a wider range of manufacturers' products. A Reference Model for Open Systems Interconnection (OSI) has been under development by the International Standards Organization (ISO) since 1977. Other standards, including SNA (IBM's System Network Architecture) and Ethernet, are largely incompatible with one another. Certain standards in the OSI model have been set by manufacturers as their commercial products have gained in popularity.

The OSI reference model for communications protocol identifies a hierarchy of seven layers. The layers and their functions are briefly described below.

Application layer

This is the highest layer in that it is closest to the user. It supports the transfer of information between end-users, applications programs and devices. Several types of protocol exist in this layer, including those for specific applications and those for more generalized applications, such as accounting, entry control and user identification. The applications layer hides the physical network from the user, presenting a user-orientated view instead. For example, the user need not know that several physical computers are involved when accessing a database.

Presentation layer

This layer covers standards on how data is presented to the end-user devices. The aim is to ensure that different devices, which may be using data in different formats, can communicate with one another. The presentation layer can, for example, handle conversions between ASCII and EBCDIC character codes. It may also carry out encryption to ensure data security during transmission over vulnerable telecommunication links. The presentation layer also attempts to deal with conversions between terminals which use different line and screen lengths and different character sets.

Session layer

The session layer is concerned with the exchange of information between different applications and users; it is the users' interface into the network. When a user requests a particular service from the network, the session layer handles the dialogue.

Transport layer

The data transmission system on any network will have its own peculiarities and the function of the transport layer is to mask out any undesirable features which may prevent a high quality transmission for the network.

Network layer

The function of the network layer is to perform the routing of information around the network and also to connect one network to another. The software can also carry out accounting functions to enable the network owner to charge users.

Data link layer

The physical data transmission media used in a network are subject to interference which can corrupt data and other signals. The data link layer handles data transmission errors and thus improves the quality of the network. The techniques used, for example, for the receipt and acknowledgement of data by a receiver device, are determined by the data link layer. The CCITT V42bis protocol, with its error detection and correction facilities falls into this level.

Physical layer

The physical layer provides the means to connect the physical medium and is concerned with the transmission of binary data within the communication channel. Standards are set regarding the mechanical, electrical and procedural aspects of interface devices. For example, standards are set for the number of pins a network connector should have and the function and position of each pin. The RS232 and V24 protocols are within this level.

Handshaking

Synchronization of data transmission between communicating devices is essential, primarily because they often operate at different speeds, and sometimes, a device may have to wait because the other device is not ready. For example, if a file is being transferred from a remote terminal to a receiving computer, and the file is too large to fit into the computer's memory, then it will have to save sections of the file at intervals. If the computer has no multi-tasking capability, then data may be lost if it is transmitted during a save operation. To prevent such data loss, the flow of data has to be controlled and the activities of the communicating devices need to be properly synchronized.

Handshaking is necessary for both parallel and serial transmissions and involves acknowledgement signals between devices that they are ready to communicate with one another. The process of handshaking can be software or hardware controlled. A hardware handshake, for example, between a computer and a printer, involves the exchange of signals, through dedicated lines or conductors; the signals indicate the readiness of each device to send or receive data. A software handshake, usually employed for serial transmissions through modems, enables each device to establish the particular protocols which will be used for transmissions. Error control and data compression (to improve the transmission rate) can be built into the modems specification and thus be hardware controlled, or they can be provided by a communications package.

Flow control

Flow control enables communicating modems to pause and restart data transmission, as necessary. The need for pauses and restarts stems from the fact that a receiving modem has to use buffer memory (of limited capacity) and may not be able to empty it (pass it on) as quickly as it is being filled. This could be because the computer to which it is connected is busy with another task, such as printing. If transmission is not paused once the buffer is full, data will be lost. To exert flow control, the receiving modem must signal the sending modem that transmission has to be temporarily interrupted. This can be done, either by the modem or the terminal software.

Error detection

Block check characters (BCC)

The idea of even and odd parity bits for each character is introduced in Chapter 2 and is shown to be inadequate for the detection of even numbers of bit errors. Block check characters (BCCs) aim to conquer this problem by checking the parity of blocks of characters within a data transmission stream. BCCs may carry out *longitudinal* or *cyclic* redundancy checks.

Longitudinal redundancy checking (LRC)

By reference to Table 11.1, the principles of LRC can be explained as follows. Each BCC consists of a group of parity bits which carry out LRC. However, each LRC bit is a parity check on the corresponding bits in all the characters in a block. Thus, the first parity bit in the BCC relates to the bits which occupy the first position in each character in the block, the second parity bit in the BCC relates to the second position bits in each character in the block and so on. LRC ensures that multiple errors, whether even or odd, are likely to be discovered, so at the receiver end of the transmission, the parity of individual characters and blocks of characters is checked.

VRC (bit-7) on each character	7	6	5	4	3	2	1	0
	0	1	0	0	1	0	1	1
	0	1	0	0	1	1	1	0
	1	1	0	0	1	1	1	1
	1	1	0	1	0	1	0	0
	1	1	0	1	0	1	0	0
	1	1	0	1	0	1	1	1
	0	1	0	0	0	0	0	1
	1	1	0	0	1	0	0	1
	1	1	0	1	0	1	0	0
	1	1	0	0	0	1	0	1
	0	1	0	1	0	0	1	1
	1	1	0	1	0	1	1	1
BCC to check LRC parity (per block)								

Table 11.1. *Vertical (VRC) and longitudinal redundancy checks (LRC)*

Cyclic redundancy checking (CRC)

The BCCs described previously treat a data block as a set of characters, whereas cyclic redundancy checking (CRC) uses a BCC which views each data block as a continuous *stream* of bits.

Firstly, the data block is regarded as one large binary number. That number is divided by another agreed binary number, the quotient is discarded and the remainder (sometimes referred to as a *checksum*) is attached to the data block as a BCC. Upon receipt of the data block, the receiver repeats the calculation used to generate the BCC and compares the result with the BCC attached by the transmitter; any difference between them indicates some corruption of the block.

Hamming code

Certain codes can be used, not only to detect the occurrence of an error, but also to identify its precise location. In addition, some errors can be rectified.

The Hamming code described here utilizes three *code* bits and four *data* bits, making seven in all, although there are circumstances when more bits may be used. Figure 11.9 illustrates the format which positions each code bit (C_2, C_1 and C_0) in a column position which equates with its binary weight. The data bits (D_3, D_2, D_1 and D_0) occupy the other positions. Thus, C_0 ($2^0 = 1$) is in column 1, C_1 ($2^1 = 2$) in column 2 and C_2 ($2^2 = 4$) in column 4.

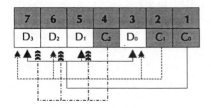

Table 11.2. *Hamming code format*

Table 11.2 shows that parity is maintained in sub-groups, such that the C_0 relates to D_3, D_1 and D_0, C_1 to D_3, D_2 and D_0, and C_2 to D_3, D_2 and D_1. Thus, each sub-group of data bits has a single code bit. This is illustrated further in Table 11.3.

group	7	6	5	4	3	2	1
C_0	D_3		D_1		D_0		C_0
C_1	D_3	D_2			D_0	C_1	
C_2	D_3	D_2	D_1	C_2			

Table 11.3. *Association of code and data bits*

The three code bits produce a unique pattern when any single bit is corrupted. A parity output of 000 would indicate the absence of any errors. To correct the word only requires the inversion of the bit position which is in error. The processes are illustrated in Figure 11.4.

7	6	5	4	3	2	1	explanation of pattern
D_3	D_2	D_1	C_2	D_0	C_1	C_0	with each group using even parity
1	0	0	1	1	0	0	C0, C1, C2 groups all maintain even parity
0	0	0	1	1	0	0	column 7 error - parity error in each group
1	0	0	1	0	0	0	column 3 error - parity error in C$_1$, C$_0$ groups

Table 11.4. *Code patterns with example errors*

Table 11.4 shows three code patterns, the first one being correct and the other two being in error. The location of the erroneous bit is identified by the creation of a 3-bit pattern. Each bit, starting with the least significant is used to flag the parity status of of the C_2, C_1 and C_3 groups, respectively. Even parity is maintained in each group in the first example, so the flag pattern is 000. In the second example, parity is lost in each group, resulting in a flag pattern of 111, which indicates that the erroneous bit is in column 7 (111_2). Checking the third example, reveals that even parity is maintained in the C_2 group, but is lost in the other two; the resulting flag pattern of 011 indicates that the bit in column 3 (011_2) is wrong.

This method does not enable detection of double errors, but the limitation can be removed by the inclusion of a single parity bit across the whole word. However, double bit errors are not correctable.

Echoplex (echo checking)

Echoplex is used in asynchronous communications, for low speed, *dumb* (see Devices) terminals connected to a remote host computer. When a character is transmitted (in other words, when a key is pressed) the host device immediately sends it back to be displayed on the dumb terminal's screen. If the displayed character does not match the character selected from the keyboard, the operator should detect this; the host device can be advised, by the terminal operator, to ignore the incorrect character, by the sending of an agreed *control* character. Clearly, the method is slow and crude. A character could have been received correctly by the host device and an error could corrupt it on its way back. The operator has no way of knowing how and at what point an error occurred. Another disadvantage is that error correction is manual; in an interactive system, the user needs to rely on automatic error control and correction.

Error correction

Automatic repeat request (ARQ)

When a receiver detects an error it must tell the sending device to re-transmit the erroneous data; this is known as *automatic repeat request* (ARQ). The technique is most appropriate to the handling of data streams, that is, synchronous communications, in conjunction with cyclic redundancy checking (CRC - see earlier). ARQ can take one of three forms:

- *Stop and wait ARQ* or *ACK and NAK*. With this form the receiver acknowledges every block of data, with ACK if it detects no error and NAK if an error is detected. The sending device cannot send the next block until an acknowledgement is received. Any NAK block is re-transmitted repeatedly, if necessary, until an ACK is received.

- *Go-back N ARQ*. With this form, a block is only acknowledged if an error is detected. The sending device can continue transmitting without waiting for an acknowledgement. When a NAK is received, the block in which the error occurred is identified and that block, plus any transmitted since (N blocks), must be re-transmitted.

- *Selective-repeat ARQ*. This is the most sophisticated form of ARQ, in that blocks transmitted since the erroneous block (correct ones are not acknowledged), do not have to be sent again. Thus the sender only re-transmits the identified block and then continues from where it left off, when the NAK was received.

File transfer protocols

File transfer is the process of transmitting complete files from one computer to another. To achieve a successful transfer, both sending and receiving devices must establish the protocol (the set of rules) by which they will communicate. Various protocols are commonly recognized, but they vary in their performance and suitability for particular tasks. Some examples are described below.

ASCII

This is only appropriate for *text* files, which contain no control characters. Thus it cannot be used to transfer files produced with a word processor, spreadsheet or graphics package. Neither can it transfer command (COM) or executable (EXE) files, or files in compressed (ZIP, for example) form. Apart from this, the protocol is not good at controlling errors.

Xmodem

This is a file-transfer protocol used for asynchronous communications. It is commonly used in communications packages. The Xmodem protocol transfers data in blocks of 128 bytes, giving each transmitted *frame* a sequential block number; this number is used to identify the location of errors. A *checksum* (see Block Check Characters) is attached to each block to check transmission errors. Its ability to find and correct errors makes it suitable for the transfer of files, which must retain their integrity, such as program files.

Zmodem

This is one of the most advanced protocols, being much faster than Xmodem. Its error correction controls are absolutely reliable.

CCITT V42bis

This protocol includes a *data compression* (through encoding, data is reduced in volume) technique and error detection and correction. Both the sending and receiving modem must possess the error correction facility.

Transmission media

When data is transmitted between two hardware devices in a network, a communication medium is used. The commonly used media are, *twisted-pair* cable, *coaxial* cable and *optical fibre*. Where a physical connection is not practical, then radio, infra-red, microwave and laser technologies may be used.

Twisted-pair cable

Twisted-pair cable is formed from strands of wire twisted in pairs. It predates any other method and is still extensively used for standard telephone or telex terminals. Each twisted pair can carry a single telephone call between two people or two machines. Although twisted-pair cable is generally used for analogue signal transmission, it can be used successfully for digital transmission. Variation in the lengths of wire within pairs can result in signals being received out of phase, but this can be overcome by the frequent use of repeaters. The repeaters refresh the signal as it passes to maintain its consistency. Although transmission rates permitted by such cable are lower than for some other media, they are acceptable for many computer applications.

Coaxial cable

Coaxial cable is resistant to the transmission interference which can corrupt data transmitted via twisted-pairs cable. It thus provides a fast, relatively interference-free transmission medium. Its construction consists of a central conductor core which is surrounded by a layer of insulating material. The insulating layer is covered by a conducting shield, which is itself protected by another insulating layer. During network installation, the cable can be cut and connections made, without affecting its transmission quality. The quality of cable can vary and some low quality cable is unsuitable for data transmission over long distances. On the other hand, high quality cable can be quite rigid and difficult to install in local networks, where space is limited. Despite this difficulty, it is an extremely popular choice for LANs.

Optical fibre cable

Optical fibre cable consists of thousands of clear glass fibre strands which transmit light or infra-red rays instead of electrical signals. The data is transmitted by a light-emitting diode (two-state signals) or injection-laser diode. Transmission speeds of billions of bits per second are achieved. Repeaters are only required after several miles. The other end of the cable has a detector which converts the light pulses into electrical pulses suitable for the attached device. Optical fibre cable is more expensive than electrical cable but is finding increasing use in LANs. However, its main application is for long-distance communications.

Network services

Many networks, both private and public, provide additional services which give them the collective name of *value-added networks* or VANs. Switchstream, Megastream and Satstream (see Digital Network Systems) are VANs provided by British Telecom. Other VANs provide specific services, such as *videotext* (see later), electronic mail, facsimile transmission, bulletin boards and bibliographic databases, for use by academics and researchers.

Gateways

Gateways allow different types of computer to communicate with one another, even if they use different communications protocols or transfer data at different speeds. For example, the mainframe computers of the main holiday tour operators can be accessed by travel agents, through a Prestel gateway.

Bibliographic databases

These databases provide information on specialized or widely ranging topics. For example, BLAISE, which is provided by the British Library, gives information on British book publications. Euronet Diane (Direct Information Access Network in Europe) provides information extracted from publications, research documents and so on, which may be of interest to specialists, such as scientists, engineers, economists and lawyers. Each extract provides the relevant bibliographic references to allow users to access the original sources more fully.

Bulletin boards

A bulletin board (BB) is simply a means by which, users can, for example, exchange ideas, pass on information and buy or sell items to one another. Frequently, no charge is made. Chat lines are often included; this means that two users can carry on a conversation, through the use of screen and keyboard. Where more than two users are conversing, a form of *teleconferencing* can occur; any user wishing to contribute to the discussion has their contribution placed in a queue, from where it will be displayed on each contributor's screen.

Telex

Telex is a well established communications system which, rather like the public telephone network, allows subscribers to communicate with one another. There are over a million subscribers in this country at present. Each subscriber is given a telex code (you will often see it at the top of business letter headings next to the telephone number) and must have a teleprinter which is a combination of keyboard and printer. There is no screen, so all messages sent or received are printed onto hard copy. The transmission rate of approximately 6 characters per second is slow compared with more modern telecommunications systems, but the limitations of keyboard entry and printer speed on the teleprinter, make any faster speed unnecessary. The main benefit of telex is that a permanent record of communications is kept and the receiver does not have to be on the spot when the message arrives. Its main disadvantage is that there is no storage facility for messages. Any transmission has to be printed as soon as it is transmitted so that if the receiver is faulty, the system comes to a halt. Although it is inferior to e-mail (see next section), it is still the only method (apart from telephone) of instant communication with less developed countries, where Telex machines are still widely used.

Electronic mail (e-mail) services

E-mail systems based on computer networks are paper-less (except when a user requires hard copy). A major advantage is the facility for message storage if a destination terminal is busy, or has a temporary fault. When it is free, the message can be transmitted.

Certain basic features can be identified as being common to all e-mail systems:

- a terminal for preparing, entering and storing messages. The terminal will be intelligent, possibly a microcomputer, mainframe terminal or dedicated word processor. In any event, it should have some word processing or text editing facilities to allow messages to be changed on screen before transmission. A printer may also be available for printing out messages received over the system;

- an electronic communication link with other workstations in the network and with the central computer controlling the system;

- a directory containing the electronic addresses of all network users;

- a central mailbox facility (usually the controlling computer) for the storage of messages in transit or waiting to be retrieved.

Ideally, the following facilities are available to e-mail users:

- messages are automatically dated upon transmission;

- messages are automatically acknowledged as being received when the recipient first accesses it from the terminal;

- multiple addressing, that is the facility to address a message to an identified group, without addressing each member of the group individually;

- priority rating to allow messages to be allocated different priorities according to their importance.

Networks require two particular features in order to support e-mail:

- a message storage facility to allow messages to be forwarded when the recipient is available;

- compatibility with a wide range of manufacturers' equipment. Devices attached to a network have to be able to talk to the communications network using protocols or standards of communication.

Benefits of e-mail

The following major benefits are generally claimed for e-mail systems:

- savings in stationery and telephone costs;

- more rapid transmission than is possible with conventional mail;

- e-mail can be integrated with other computer-based systems used in an organization;

- all transmissions are recorded, so costs can be carefully controlled;

- e-mail allows staff to telework, that is, to work from home via a terminal;

- the recipient does not have to be present when a message is sent. Messages can be retrieved from the central mailbox when convenient.

Teletex

Teletex is nothing to do with teletext systems, such as Ceefax and Oracle (see Videotex). Teletex is similar to Telex, except that transmissions are quicker and cheaper and text is not restricted to upper case characters. It uses the pstn, but can also access packet switching networks and the Telex system through *gateways*. Teletex standards have been internationally agreed through the CCITT (see Standards Authorities) and Teletex is now used in many countries throughout the world.

Electronic data interchange (EDI)

Similar to E-mail, EDI allows users to exchange business documents, such as invoices, delivery notes, orders and receipts over the telephone network. EDI can drastically reduce the volume of paperwork and business can be transacted much more quickly than is possible through the normal postal system. UK examples of EDI systems are:

- Tradanet, linking manufacturers, wholesalers, distributors and retailers;

- Brokernet, which links insurance companies and brokers;

- Drugnet, linking medical practices to pharmaceutical companies, allowing the provision of current information on various products;

- Factornet allows firms to deal with *factors* who buy outstanding customer bills at a discount; the factors then obtain payment from the debtor. Small firms find this service particularly useful as it enables them to improve their cash flow.

EFTPOS (electronic funds transfer at point-of-sale)

This service provides for the automatic debiting of customers' bank accounts at the checkout or point of sale. Many garages now have a device for reading the magnetic strip details on bank and credit cards. The system saves considerable time when contrasted with payments by cheque and as an alternative to cash, reduces the likelihood of theft. The retailer also has the assurance that the payment is authorized before the sale is made. Usually, a retailer will have a floor limit, or amount above which a telephone call needs to be made to the credit card company for authorization of payment.

EFT (electronic funds transfer)

This system is used to transfer money between the branches of the same bank and between different banks. In the UK, the system is known as the Bankers Automated Clearing Service (BACS). The service is not restricted to bank use; organizations can pay their employees salaries directly into their bank or building society accounts. Business accounts can also be settled through this EFT system. Apart from the banks, other users usually link into the pstn through a dial-up connection (unless the volume of data justifies a leased line).

Remote job entry (RJE)

RJE systems make the simplest use of data communications to transmit bulk data rapidly to a central computer; transmission is one-way, from an RJE terminal located at the remote site to the central computer, which is probably situated at the head office of the organization. In a wholesaling organization, for example, each distribution warehouse could transmit details of stock changes and requirements via an RJE terminal, at the end of each day via a simplex dial-up communications link. In the 1960s, RJE terminals commonly consisted of a card or paper tape reader and printer; more recently, transmission would be direct from a key-to-disk or key-to-tape system.

Facsimile transmission (FAX)

This service allows the transmission of facsimiles or exact copies of documents or pictures through a data communications network. Using a fax machine connected to a telephone line, the user simply dials the fax number of the recipient, waits for the correct signal and the document is fed though the fax machine and transmitted. The fax machine sends picture elements or pixels obtained by scanning the document in a series of parallel lines; a synchronized fax machine at the other end prints a facsimile from those pixels.

Teletext

Teletext systems, such as Ceefax and Oracle, provide a public service based on a central computer database, which users can access via an ordinary television set with special adapter and keypad. The database consists of thousands of pages or frames of information which are kept up to date by Information Providers. Pages can be accessed and displayed on the television screen through the use of the keypad, directly via page number or through a series of hierarchical indexes. Major subject areas include Sport, News, Business, Leisure and Entertainment, Finance and Travel. Pages are transmitted using spare bandwidth unused by television pictures, in carousels or groups. The user may have to wait some time while the carousel containing the required page is transmitted. Its major drawback is that communication is *one-way*. The user cannot send messages to the database, only receive.

Viewdata or videotex

A viewdata system is based on a central computer database, which provides pages of information on a variety of subjects, including sport, travel and business, for access by subscribers. As an *interactive* system, users typically access services using simple, low cost, viewdata terminals, or microcomputer systems equipped with special software. Users connect with a viewdata *gateway* through the public telephone network. The major public viewdata system in the UK is *Prestel*. It uses the Teletext *alpha mosaic* character set. The graphics it produces appear similar to Lego building blocks. Developed by British Telecom, Prestel is now technologically out of date and is used, mainly, as a *gateway* to third party databases, for example, Electronic Yellow Pages, and CitiService (a financial database). Apart from information provision, the following services may be available through a viewdata system:

- Electronic mail. Viewdata users can transmit electronic messages to other users in the system, using such things as bulletin boards and chat lines. The British Campus 2000, which links together schools in Britain and other countries is an example of a viewdata electronic mail system.

- Paying bills, purchasing tickets, ordering goods and other such transactions.

- The distribution of computer programs. Centrally stored computer programs can be transferred to users' microcomputer systems so that they can later be used independently of the viewdata system. This is sometimes referred to as *telesoftware*.

In France, a combined teletext and viewdata system is called Antiope, and another viewdata system, available since 1984, is called Teletel. The latter system is very widely used, with more than eight million terminals attached to the system. The US service is called Prodigy and in Japan it is called Captain.

File transfer

A file can be a data file or a program file; the data could be a document prepared on a word processor and a program file could be a program of any kind. A file transfer service allows the use of one computer to retrieve a file from another computer, through a telecommunications link. Equally, a file can be transmitted in the opposite direction. E-mail is a special kind of file transfer facility, but to most users, the facility is used to retrieve documentary information from remote databases, or software from, for example, bulletin boards. To be transferred correctly, and this is particularly important in the case of program files (it can not be executed if the code is corrupted), requires the use of file transfer protocols. A modem suited to the purpose will use a particular file transfer protocol and whatever communications package is used, it must be able to use that protocol.

Internet

The Internet (Chapter 37) is a world-wide network derived from DARPANET (Defense Advanced Research Projects Agency Network) which was developed, during the 1960s, initially as a military defence project for the U.S. Department of Defense. Later, with universities and other academic institutions making unauthorized use of the network for private electronic mail, the name was changed to ARPANET. A packet switching protocol called NCP (network control protocol) had its initial development in the UK and this was adopted as the network protocol. Since 1984, the number of host computers connected to the network has grown from 500 to more than 3 million; it is estimated that the number of users, world-wide is over 30 million. This figure is likely to increase exponentially.

World wide web (WWW)

Although accessing the network is not difficult, finding specific information can be, considering the number of host computers connected to it. In 1990, the European Laboratory of Particle Physics in Switzerland, developed a *hypertext* based user interface. This interface allows a user to move from one Internet resource to another by way of, for example, topic searches, without knowing in advance, the precise location of each piece of information.

Service providers

To gain access to Internet, microcomputer users need to use a *service provider*. These are organizations which not only provide the necessary software to gain access to the network, but provide some of the additional services outlined in the previous section; in particular, the services cover e-mail, file transfer and access to bibliographic databases. Some of the main UK service providers are:

- BBC Networking Club;

- CityScape;

- CIX (Compulink Information Exchange);

- Demon Internet;

- EasyNet.

A major American service provider is CompuServe.

Exercises

1. (i)   Name three *standards authorities* for the data communications industry.

    (ii)   What is meant by the phrases *open systems* and *closed systems*?

2. Differentiate between the *pstn* and the *psdn*.

3. What types of user would be likely to use a:

    (i)   *dedicated* line;

    (ii)   dial-up connection.

4. Differentiate between *message* and *packet switching*, identifying any advantages one has over the other.

5. (i)   What is the purpose of *multiplexing*?

    (ii)   Name a commercial service which uses multiplexing?

    (iii)   Briefly differentiate between *time division* and *frequency division* multiplexing.

6. What is the ISDN?

7. Explain the terms *asynchronous* and s*ynchronous serial* transmission.

8. Define the terms *simplex*, *half-duplex* and *duplex* transmission.

9. Describe the operation of *cyclic redundancy checking* (CRC).

10. What are the functions of a *modem*?

11. In the context of modem communcations, what is meant by *flow control*?

12. Identify and briefly describe the three main forms of *automatic repeat request* (ARQ), for error checking.

13. Name the seven layer of the *OSI* (open systems inter-connection) model.

14. Identify and briefly describe four *network services*.

Chapter 12
Computer Software

The term *software* is used to describe the complete range of computer programs which convert a general purpose digital computer system into one capable of performing a multitude of specific functions. The term software implies its flexible, changeable nature, in contrast to the more permanent characteristics of the hardware or equipment which it controls.

The particular piece of software controlling the computer system at any particular moment determines the manner in which the system functions. For example, a certain type of software might cause the computer to behave like a word processor; another might allow it to perform accounting or stock control functions, or any one of a huge variety of other useful tasks. Whatever the task, it is software which directs the computer system.

Computer programs

The terms software and program tend to be used interchangeably so what precisely is meant by the term *computer program*?

At the level at which the computer operates, a program is simply a sequence of numeric codes. Each of these codes can be directly converted by the hardware into some simple operation. Built into the central processing unit (CPU - the heart of the computer) is a set of these simple operations, combinations of which are capable of directing the computer to perform complex tasks. Computer programs, in this fundamental form, are termed *machine code*, that is code which is directly understandable by the machine.

The numeric codes of the program are stored electronically in the main memory of the computer. Because this memory is volatile (its contents can be changed), it is possible to exchange the program currently held in the memory for another when the computer is required to perform a different function. For this reason the term *stored program* is often used to describe this fundamental characteristic of the modern digital computer.

Programming languages

When it is considered that a typical program might contain tens of thousands of machine code instructions it might seem that programming is a formidable task, well beyond the capabilities of all but the most determined and meticulous of computer professionals. Indeed, if machine code were the only computer language in use, it is extremely unlikely that society would today be experiencing such a widespread presence of computers in almost every aspect of industrial, commercial, domestic and social life.

Fortunately for the computer industry, programming techniques have evolved along with advances in hardware. There is now a proliferation of programming languages designed to allow the programmer to concentrate most of his or her attention on solving the problem, rather than on the tedious task of converting the solution to machine code form. Such computer languages are termed *high-level languages*. High-level languages provide a method of specifying complex processing tasks in a form relatively easy to use and understand by programmers, but not immediately understandable by a computer; the computer itself, using another program called a *language processor* or *translator*, performs the task of converting the high-level instructions into a usable form. Examples of commonly used computer languages are COBOL, Pascal, BASIC and C.

Categories of software

The tree diagram shown in Figure 12.1 below illustrates the different categories of software and, to some extent, their relationships to each other. This section begins by examining the distinction between *systems software* and *applications software*.

The term systems software covers the collection of programs usually supplied by the manufacturer of the computer. These programs protect the user from the enormous complexity of the computer system, and enable the computer to be used to maximum effect by a wide variety of people, many of whom will know

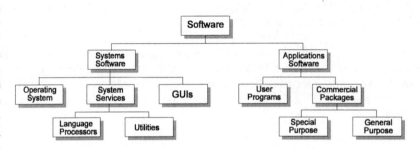

Figure 12.1. *Categories of software*

very little about the inner workings of computers. Without systems software a modern digital computer would be virtually impossible to use; as computer hardware has evolved, so systems software has been forced to become more and more complex in order to make effective use of it.

Broadly speaking, systems software consists of three elements:

- those programs concerned with the internal control and co-ordination of all aspects of the computer system, namely the *operating system* (Chapter 13);

- a number of other programs providing various services to users. These services include *translators* for any languages supported by the system and *utility programs* such as program editors and other aids to programming;

- *graphical user interfaces* (GUIs) providing intuitive, easily learned methods for using microcomputer systems.

Applications software refers to programs which have some direct value to an organization, and will normally include those programs for which the computer system was specifically purchased. For example, a mail order company might acquire a computer system initially for stock control and accounting purposes, when its volume of business begins to make these functions too difficult to cope with by manual means. Applications programs would be required to record and process customers' orders, update the stock file according to goods sent or received, make appropriate entries in the various accounts ledgers, etc. Commercially produced applications software falls into two main categories:

- *special-purpose* packages, such as a company payroll program used to store employee details and generate details of pay for each individual employee;

- *general-purpose* packages which may be used for a wide variety of purposes. An example of a general-purpose package is a *word processor*, a program which allows the computer to be used somewhat like an electronic typewriter and is therefore appropriate to numerous text processing tasks.

User programs are written by people within the organization for specific needs which cannot be satisfied by other sources of software. These program writers may be professional programmers employed by the organization, or other casual users with programming expertise.

Systems software

First generation computers are normally defined in hardware terms, in that they were constructed using valve technology, but another important characteristic of this generation of computers was the equally primitive software support provided for programmers and other users. Modern computers perform automatically many of the tasks that programmers in those days had to handle themselves: writing routines to control peripheral devices, allocating programs to main store, executing programs, checking peripheral devices for availability, as well as many other routine tasks.

In subsequent generations of computers, manufacturers started addressing themselves to the problem of improving the programming environment by providing standard programs for many routine tasks. Many of these routines became linked together under the control of a single program called the *executive*, *supervisor*, or *monitor*, whose function was to supervise the running of user programs and, in general, to control and co-ordinate the functioning of the whole computer system, both hardware and software. Early programs of this type have evolved into the sophisticated programs collectively known as *operating systems*.

Systems software has four important functions:

- to make it easier to run user programs;

- to improve the performance of the computer system;

- to provide assistance with program development;

- to simplify the use of the computer system for users other than computer specialists.

The operating system takes care of the first two requirements, system services provide assistance with program development and graphical user interfaces (GUIs) simplify the use of the computer system.

Operating systems

If a computer system is viewed as a set of resources, comprising elements of both hardware and software, then it is the job of the collection of programs known as the operating system to manage these resources as efficiently as possible. In so doing, the operating system acts as a buffer between the user and the complexities of the computer itself. One way of regarding the operating system is to think of it as a program which allows the user to deal with a simplified computer, but without losing any of the computational power of the machine. In this way the computer system becomes a virtual system, its enormous complexity hidden and controlled by the operating system and through which the user communicates with the real system.

The main functions of operating systems

Earlier it was stated that the function of an operating system is to manage the resources of the computer system. These resources generally fall into the following categories:

Central processing unit (CPU)

A *multi-user* computer system can be accessed by several users, simultaneously; since only one program can be executed at any one time, access to the CPU must be carefully controlled and monitored. In a *timesharing* multi-user system each user is given a small time-slice of processor time before passing on to the next user in a continuously repeating sequence. Another common scheme is to assign priorities to users so that the system is able to determine which user should have control of the CPU next.

Memory

Programs (or parts of programs) must be loaded into the memory before they can be executed, and moved out of the memory when no longer required there. Storage space must be provided for data generated by programs, and provision must be made for the temporary storage of data, caused by data transfer operations involving devices such as printers and disk drives.

Input/output (I/O) devices

Programs will request the use of these devices during the course of their execution and in a multi-user system conflicts are bound to arise, when a device being utilized by one program is requested by another. The operating system will control allocation of I/O devices and attempt to resolve any conflicts which arise. It will also monitor the state of each I/O device and signal any faults detected.

Backing store

Programs and data files will usually be held on mass storage devices such as magnetic disk and tape drives. The operating system will supervise data transfers between these devices and memory and deal with requests from programs for space on them.

Files

These may be regarded as a limited resource for multi-user systems, in the sense that several users may wish to share the same data file at the same time. The operating system facilitates access to files and ensures restricted access to one program at any one time for those files which are to be written to.

Resource allocation is closely linked to one part of the operating system called the *scheduler* (Chapter 13). The term *scheduling* refers to the question of when, in a multi-user system, should a new process be introduced into the system and in which order the processes should be run.

The above is by no means a full list of the functions of an operating system. Other functions include:

- interpretation of the command language by which operators can communicate with the operating system;

- error handling. For example, detecting and reporting inoperative or malfunctioning peripherals;

- protection of data files and programs from corruption by other users;

- protection of data files and programs from unauthorized use;

- accounting and logging of the use of the computer resources.

System services

Often a manufacturer will provide a number of programs designed specifically for program or application development. Some examples of such aids are as follow.

Language processors

These are computer programs designed to convert high-level language programs into machine code, that is, into a form directly usable by a computer. Common types of language processors are *compilers* and *interpreters*.

Utility programs

As part of the systems software provided with a computer system there are a number of utility programs specifically designed to aid program development and testing. These include the following.

Editors

These permit the creation and modification of source programs and data files. The facilities offered by these programs usually include such things as character, word and line insertion and deletion, automatic line numbering, line tabulation for languages which require program instructions to be spaced in a specific manner, the storage and retrieval of files from backing storage, and the printing of programs or other files.

Debugging aids

Programs in which the appropriate translator can find no fault will often contain errors in logic, known as bugs, which only become apparent when the program is run, producing results which are contrary to expectations, or even causing the computer to cease functioning. These bugs are often very difficult to detect and may lead to long delays in the implementation of the program. Debugging aids help programmers to isolate and identify the cause of bugs.

File managers

These simplify and facilitate a number of operations connected with program development and maintenance such as:

- keeping backup copies of important files;

- deleting files and creating space for new ones;

- merging files;

- providing details of current files held on backing storage;

- sorting file names into specified orders.

Without the help of such dedicated programs, operations such as these could be extremely time-consuming and consequently expensive.

Graphical user interfaces (GUIs)

The vast majority of microcomputer users are interested merely in using a computer as a tool, without any real interest in the technical details of its operation. A typical user will probably want to run one or more common general-purpose applications, organize files into directories, delete files and format disks. Though the operating system will provide these services, the user needs to have a certain amount of technical knowledge to perform these tasks. *Graphical user interfaces* (or GUI, pronounced *Gooey*) provide a more intuitive means of performing common tasks. They usually make use of a pointing device, typically a *mouse* (see Chapter 8), by means of which a *pointer* is moved around the monitor screen on which small pictures (or *icons*) are displayed. These icons represent, among other things, programs which can be run by moving the mouse pointer over the icon and then clicking one of the buttons on the mouse. Applications run in their own self-contained areas called *windows*. In addition, it is usually possible to activate *pull-down menus* which provide access to standard functions. When a GUI uses Windows, Icons, Mouse, Pointers and Pull-down menus, it is referred to as a *WIMP* environment. Figure 12.2 shows an example of a GUI produced by Microsoft, namely, Microsoft Windows.

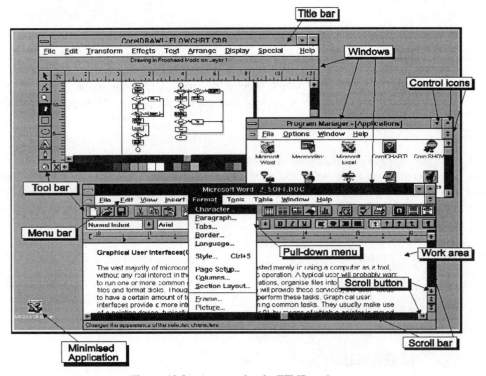

Figure 12.2. *An example of a WIMP environment*

Three windows are shown in the figure:

- a window running a Program Manager containing icons which represent available applications programs. An application is run by positioning the pointer over the application's icon and clicking one of the mouse buttons, a very simple, easily remembered operation. This is really a utility window rather than an application;

- a window running CorelDraw, a graphic design program (see later);

- a window running the word processor, Microsoft's Word for Windows.

Only Microsoft Word, in the window with the black title bar, is active, that is, currently in use. Either of the other two can be made the active window by merely positioning the pointer in the window and clicking the mouse. Thus it is possible to be working on several applications at the same time, switching from one to the other very quickly and with minimum effort.

All such windows, no matter what the application, have a number of common features, including:

- a title bar with the name of the particular application and the name of the document being edited or created by that application;

- a menu bar containing the names of a number of pull-down menus;

- horizontal and vertical scroll bars providing access to parts of the document not shown in the window;

- a number of control icons for sizing, maximizing (making the current window occupy the whole screen), minimizing (reducing the window to an icon such as that shown in the bottom left-hand corner of Figure 12.2) and closing the window;

- a tool bar containing icons which, when selected, perform frequently required tasks, such as saving documents to disk or printing documents as in the case of Word for Windows, or drawing tools in the case of CorelDraw;

- a help facility accessed from the menu bar and providing detailed information on the operation of all aspects of the application on the screen while the application is running.

The major advantage of applications having these common features is that, having learned how one application operates, it is possible to use much of the same knowledge with other windows applications, thus significantly reducing the time required to become proficient in the use of unfamiliar applications.

Applications software

An analysis of the uses to which companies and individuals put computers would reveal that the same types of tasks appear time and time again. Many organizations use computers for payroll calculations, others to perform stock control functions, accounting procedures, management information tasks and numerous other common functions.

These types of programs are classed as *applications software*, software which is applied to practical tasks in order to make them more efficient or useful in other ways. Systems software is merely there to support the running, development and maintenance of applications software.

An organization wishing to implement one of these tasks (or any other vital to its efficient operation) on a computer has several alternatives:

- Ask a software house, that is, a company specializing in the production of software, to take on the task of writing a specific program for the organization's needs.

- Use its own programming staff to produce the software in house.

- Buy a commercially available program off the shelf and hope that it already fulfils, or can be modified to fulfil, the organization's requirements.

- Buy a general purpose program, such as a database or spreadsheet package, that has the potential to perform the required functions.

The final choice will depend on such factors as the urgency of the requirements, financial constraints, size of the company and the equipment available. It is beyond the scope of this chapter to enter into a discussion regarding either the strategy for making such a decision or to investigate specific items of software available for specific applications; but, with the immense and growing, popularity of general-purpose packages, particularly for personal microcomputer systems, it is worth looking in more detail at this category of software.

General-purpose packages for microcomputers

Discussion of this class of software will be restricted here to the following headings, though they are not intended to represent an exhaustive list of all the categories of general purpose packages which are available:

- word processors;

- spreadsheets;

- databases;

- graphics packages, including desktop publishing (DTP), business graphics, graphic design and computer aided drawing (CAD).

What characterizes these software types as belonging to the category of general-purpose packages is that they have been designed to be very flexible and applicable to a wide range of different tasks. For instance, a spreadsheet can be used as easily for simple accountancy procedures as for stock control; a database can be used with equal facility to store information on technical papers from journals, stock item details and personnel details for payroll purposes. In fact, particularly in respect of modern personal computer software, the trend is for general-purpose packages to do more and more. For example, recent word processors, such as Microsoft's Word for Windows and WordPerfect, include facilities, once only found in desktop publishing packages, for drawing diagrams and for producing graphs, in addition to the normal functions associated with a word processor; the graphic design package CorelDraw, includes some word processing functions and graph drawing functions; the spreadsheet Excel has a number of facilities normally associated with database packages. Fierce market competition has resulted in the major software houses continually improving on their last version of a piece of software, attempting to outdo their competitors.

The suitability of a particular general-purpose package for a specific application will be largely dependent on the particular characteristics of the package. Though the general facilities afforded, for instance, by different database packages may be roughly equivalent, each manufacturer will adopt its own style of presentation and will provide certain services not offered by its competitors. A prospective buyer should have a clear idea of the main uses for which the package is to be purchased right at the outset, because some packages may be much more suitable than others.

Some advantages of general-purpose software compared to other forms of applications software are as follow:

- Because large numbers of the package are sold, prices are relatively low;

- They are appropriate to a wide variety of applications;

- As they already have been thoroughly tested, they provide a great reduction in the time and costs necessary for development and testing;

- They are suitable for people with little or no computing experience;

- They are very easy to use;

- Most packages of this type are provided with extensive documentation.

Some of the disadvantages are:

- Sometimes the package will allow only a clumsy solution to the task in question;

- In the case of a spreadsheet or database, for example, the user must still develop the application. This requires a thorough knowledge of the capabilities of the package, which are frequently extensive, and how to make the best use of them;

- The user will need to provide his own documentation for the particular application for which the package has been tailored;

- Unless the software is used regularly, it is easy to forget the correct command sequences to operate the package, particularly for people inexperienced in the use of computer software of this type;

- The user must take responsibility for security measures to ensure that vital data is not lost, or to prevent unauthorized personnel gaining access to the data.

Word processors

The word processor performs much the same function as a typewriter, but it offers a large number of very useful additional features. Basically, a word processor is a computer with a keyboard for entering text, a monitor for display purposes, one or more disk drives for storage of files produced by applications and a printer to provide the permanent output on paper. A word processor is really nothing more than a computer system with a special piece of software to make it perform the required word processing functions; some such systems have hardware configurations specifically for the purpose (such as special keyboards and letter-quality printers) but the majority are merely the result of obtaining an appropriate word processor package.

Word processors can be used to produce:

- letters;

- legal documents;

- books;

- articles;

- mailing lists;

and in fact any type of textual material.

Here are some of the advantages they have over ordinary typewriters:

- typing errors can be corrected before printing the final version;

- the availability of such automatic features as page numbering, the placing of page headers and footers and word/line counting;

- whole document editing, such as replacing every incidence of a certain combination of characters with another set of characters. For instance, replacing each occurrence of the name Mr. Smith by Mrs. Jones;

- printing multiple copies all to the same high quality;

- documents can be saved and printed out at some later date without any additional effort.

However, word processors do have some drawbacks. For instance, prolonged viewing of display monitors can produce eyestrain. They are generally considerably more expensive than good typewriters, and to be used properly, a certain amount of special training is required. Word processors are now firmly established in the so-called 'electronic office' and there is no doubt that their use will not continue to expand.

Typical word processor facilities

A typical word processing package will provide most of the following facilities:

Word wrap. As text is typed, a word is moved automatically to the start of a new line if there is insufficient room for it at the right-hand margin. With this facility, the only time that the Enter key needs to be pressed, to move the cursor to the beginning of a new line, is at the end of paragraphs or when a blank line is required.

Scrolling. Once the bottom of the screen is reached during text entry, the top of the text moves, line by line, up out of view as each new line of text is entered. This ensures that the line being entered is always visible on screen. The directional arrow keys on a standard keyboard allow scrolling to be carried out at will to view various parts of the document.

Deletion. This facility allows the deletion of characters, words, lines or complete blocks of text.

Insertion. This is concerned with the insertion of single letters or a block of text.

Block marking. A special function key, or more usually, by dragging the mouse pointer, allows the marking or highlighting of text to be dealt with separately from the rest of the document. The marked text may be moved, deleted, copied or displayed in a different style - in italics or bold print, for example.

Text movement or copying. The user may need to move or copy a marked block of text to a different part of the document.

Tabulation. Markers can be set to allow the cursor to be moved directly to column positions with the use of the TAB key. This is useful when text or figures are to be presented in columns.

Formatting. Text can be *aligned left*, with a straight left margin and a ragged right margin:

xxxx xxx xxxxx x xxxx xxxxxxxxxx xxx xxxxxxx xxxx xxxxxxx xxx xxxxxx xx xxxxxxx x xxxxx
xxxxxxx xx xxxx x xxx xxxxxxxxxxx xxx xxx xxxxxxx x xxxxxxx xxx xxxxx xxxxx x xxxx x xx xxxxxx
x xxxx xxxxx xxx x xxxxxxxxxx xxxxx xxx xxxxxxxx xx xxxxxxxxxxxxxx xxxx x.

or it can be *justified* so that it has a straight left and right margin:

xxxx xxx xxxxx x xxxx xxxxxxxxxx xxx xxxxxxx xxxx xxxxxxx xxx xxxxxx xx xxxxxxx x xxxxx xxxxxxx
xx xxxx x xxx xxxxxxxxxxx xxxxxxxxxxxxxx xxx xxxxxxx xx xxxxxx xxx xxxxxx xxxx xxxxxxxxx xxxx
xxxxx xxx x xxxxxxxxxx xxxxxx xxx xxxxxxxxx xx xxxxxxxxxxxxxx xxxx x.

or it can be *right aligned* with a straight right margin only:

xxxx xxx xxxxx x xxxx xxxxxxxxxx xxx xxxxxxx xxxx xxxxxxx xxx xxxxxx xx xxxxxxx x xxxxx
xxxxxxx xx xxxx x xxx xxxxxxxxxxx xxx xxx xxxxxxx x xxxxxxx xxx xxxxx xxxxx x xxxx x xx xxxxxx
x xxxxxxxxxxxxxx xxx xxxxxxx xx xxxxxx xxx xxxxxx xxxx xxxxxxxx xxxx xxxxx xxx x xxxxxxxxxx
xxxxxx xxx xxxxxxxxx xx xxxxxxxxxxxxxx xxxx.

or it can be *centred*:

xxxx xxx xxxxx x xxxx xxxxxxxxxx xxx xxxxxxx xxxx xxxxx xxx xx xxxxxxx x xxxxx xxxxxxx xx xxxx
x xxx xxxxxxxxxxx xxx xxx xxxxxxx x xxxxxxx xxx xxxxx xxxxx x xxxx x xx xxxxxx x
xxxxxxxxxxxxxx xxx xxxxxxx xx xxxxxx xxx xxxxx xxxx xxxxxxxx xxxx xxxxx xxx x xxxxxxxxxx
xxxxxx xxx xxxxxxxxx xx xxxxxxxxxxxxxx xxxx x.

Printing styles

Text can be printed in a variety of styles, including **boldface**, *italic,* ~~strike-through~~, underscored superscript or subscript. Most word processors allow these styles to be displayed on the screen as well as on the printer and are known as WYSIWYG (What You See Is What You Get) packages.

Various fonts and sizes of characters

Different character fonts, that is variations in the shapes of characters, and sizes of characters can be mixed in the same document:

This is called CG Omega 12 pt

This is Courier New 10 pt

This is Times New Roman 14 pt

THIS IS UMBRELLA 14 PT

Mailing lists

This allows a user to personalize standard letters. The mailing list is, in effect, a file of names and addresses, details from which can be inserted into marked points in a standard letter. The word processor prints multiple copies of the standard letter selected by the user and personalizes each with data extracted from the mailing list.

Additional features

These include facilities for the checking of spelling (and sometimes its automatic correction as you type) in a document by reference to a dictionary held on disk, the import of text and figures from other packages such as spreadsheets, the incorporation of graphics and the export of text to other packages.

Windows-based word processors

Programs like Microsoft's Word for Windows and other windows-based word processors are have taken over from those that do not operate in a windows environment. These latest word processors allow the use of a mouse to move the cursor around documents quickly, to edit text and to provide easy access to commonly used functions such as saving and printing work, opening existing documents and creating tables. All the other advantages of windows-based programs also apply. Figure 12.3 shows part of a document produced using Word for Windows, to give you an idea of what can be achieved with this type of word processor.

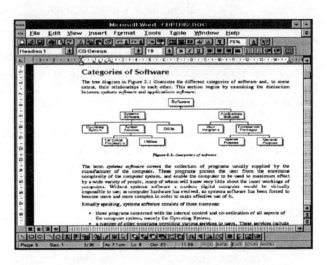

Figure 12.3. *A document produced using Word for Windows*

Spreadsheets

Just as word processors are designed to manipulate text, spreadsheets are designed to do the equivalent with numerical information. A spreadsheet program presents the user with a blank grid of cells each of which is capable of containing one of three types of information:

- a label consisting of alphanumeric characters;

- a number;

- a formula, which usually will make reference to other cells. These allow calculations to be performed on data in other cells, or on the results from other formulae.

These three types of information are sufficient to allow a wide range of applications to be implemented in a very convenient and easily understandable way. For example, suppose that a small business, Acme Computers, dealing in the sale of personal computer systems wishes to use a spreadsheet to record on a monthly basis, the sales of its four salespersons. The spreadsheet might be set up as shown in Figure 12.4.

Column A contains labels describing the systems purchased. Columns C and D, E and F, G and H, I and J show respectively, the sales and commissions for each of the four salespersons. The commission is calculated automatically by means of a formula stored in the commission columns D, F, H and J.

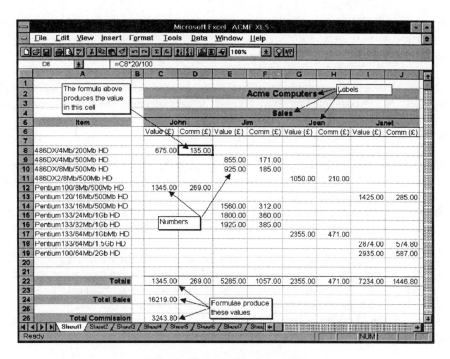

Figure 12.4. *An Excel spreadsheet*

Formulae are used to produce the calculated values. Thus John's sale of the 486DX costing £675 is entered in cell C8 and the commission is calculated using the formula '=C8*20/100'. This calculates 20% of the retail price. The actual value of the commission is displayed in cell D8.

The column totals, shown in cells C22 to J22, were calculated using a built-in function '=SUM(range)' which calculates the sum of a range of cells. For example, John's total commission, shown in cell D22, was calculated using the formula '=SUM(D8:D20)'. Note that empty cells are treated by formula as having a value of zero.

Any changes in the data on the spreadsheet would cause all the calculations to be repeated. This automatic calculation facility gave rise to the expression 'what if' which is often used to describe an important capability of spreadsheets. It is possible to set up complex combinations of inter-dependent factors and see what happens to the final result if one or more of the factors is changed. The spreadsheet, once set up, takes care of all the recalculations necessary for this type of exercise.

The earliest program of this form was called 'Visicalc' and it ran on an Apple microcomputer. Many such programs now exist, having capabilities far exceeding those of Visicalc, but they still closely resemble the original concept in appearance and operation.

Typical spreadsheet facilities

Apart from the entry of labels, numbers and formulae, a spreadsheet package normally allows the user to use various facilities from a menu to handle the data stored on the worksheet. Typically, spreadsheets offer the following facilities:

Copying. This allows the copying of fixed values or labels, or formulae which are logically the same in another part of the worksheet. Thus, for example, in the earlier worksheet sample, the formula

'=SUM(C8:C20)', which totalled a group of values for John, could be copied to succeeding columns to the right as '=SUM(D8:D20)', '=SUM(E8:E20)', '=SUM(F8:F20)', and so on. The formula is logically the same but the column references change, according to the position of the formula.

Formatting. A cell entry can be centred, or left or right justified within a cell. Numeric values can be displayed in a variety of formats including fixed decimal, integer, percent and scientific or as money values prefixed by a $ or £ sign to 2 decimal places. Individual formats can be selected globally, that is throughout a worksheet or for selected ranges of cells.

Functions. These include =SUM(range) , which adds the contents of a specified range of cells, '=AVER-AGE(range)', which calculates the average value in a specified range of cells, '=MIN(range)', which extracts the minimum value held in a specified range of cells, and '=SQRT(cell)', which returns the square root of a value in a specified cell. The full range of functions usually includes those used in mathematics, trigonometry, finance and statistics. These are examples of functions found in Excel.

Macros. Groups of regularly used key sequences can be stored and then executed by one key press in combination with the Alt key, for example, Alt C; alternatively, a macro can be assigned to a new button on the tool bar and executed by clicking it. Macros can be useful when the spreadsheet has been tailored for a particular application which may be used by inexperienced users. Without macros, each user would have to be completely familiar with the spreadsheet commands needed. With macros, one experienced user can tailor the spreadsheet so that training time for other staff is minimized.

Graphs. Numerical data can be displayed in a variety of graphical forms, including bar charts, line graphs, scatter diagrams and pie charts. All modern spreadsheet packages provide graphical output directly and also allow numerical data to be exported to another package for graph production. The range and quality of graphs vary greatly from one package to another. With the use of a colour printer, very attractive and presentable graphs can be produced to illustrate business reports.

Consolidation. This feature allows the merging of several worksheets into a summary sheet, whilst keeping the original worksheets intact. Consolidation adds together cells with the same co-ordinates in the various worksheets.

Other Facilities. These include, amongst others, cell protection facilities to prevent alteration of certain entries, the alteration of individual column widths and the display of cell contents as formulae instead of the results of their calculation.

Spreadsheets have a number of attractive features compared to traditional programming solutions to processing needs:

- designed for laypersons;

- easy to learn and use;

- wide range of uses;

- relatively cheap;

- easily modified;

- well tried and tested;

- provide quick development time.

On the debit side:

- they tend to be too general-purpose and therefore tend to provide satisfactory rather than ideal solutions;

- the problem must still be analysed and a solution method identified.

Database

At one time, database programs, or Database Management Systems (DBMS) as they are often called, were restricted to mainframe computers because of the large memory requirements demanded of such applications. Currently, however, even personal business microcomputers have sufficient internal memory to make such applications not only feasible but also extremely powerful. These programs allow files, comprising collections of records, to be created, modified, searched and printed.

Here are just a few examples of database applications:

- names and addresses of possible customers for a mail order firm;

- details of the books in a library giving author, title and subject covered by each book, to aid with locating books of a certain type;

- details of the items stored in a warehouse, giving location, cost, number currently in stock and supplier;

- lists of people on the electoral register for a certain region;

- details of the employees of a large firm.

Typical database facilities

A typical database program will offer, as a minimum, the following facilities:

- user-definable record format allowing the user to specify the fields within the record;

- user-definable input format to allow the user to define the way the data is to be entered into the computer;

- file searching capabilities for extracting records satisfying certain criteria from a file;

- file sorting capabilities so that records can be ordered according to the contents of a certain field;

- calculations on fields within records for inclusion in reports;

- user-definable report formats, so that different types of reports containing different combinations of record fields may be produced.

Database packages for microcomputers

These packages fall broadly into two groups, *card index* and *relational* (Chapters 24 and 25). Generally, card index systems are simpler to set up and operate but they provide less sophisticated data manipulation and search facilities than do the relational type. Further, the relational type provide a programming language which allows the development of user friendly, tailored applications. Thus, a user can be protected from the complexities of package operation by being presented with, for example, a menu-driven system with options for record insertion, modification, deletion and retrieval and perhaps the production of summary reports. The card index type cannot be programmed in this way, so the user must have a more detailed knowledge of package operation. On the other hand, card index packages tend to be easier to use. The superior data management facilities provided by the relational type tend to be under-used unless professional database designers and programmers are involved in the development of the database application. The business executive who plans to use the database as a personal tool without such professional help, will probably be well advised to purchase a card index package rather than a relational database package. Another factor to be considered when choosing a database, is disk space and access speed. In contrast with spreadsheet packages, database packages require frequent disk accesses when carrying out sorting and retrieval operations. Floppy disk access times tend to be too slow and their storage capacity inadequate for anything but the simplest application. A package should also allow sorting with the use of indexes, so that files do not have to be physically sorted. Indexed sorts are much quicker and a number of different indexes can be set up so that the database can be displayed in a variety of logical orders without re-organizing the data on disk.

Graphics packages

Common types of graphics packages provide facilities for: business graphics; graphic design; desktop publishing; computer-aided design. Some graphics packages will to a greater or lesser degree cater for all of these applications, but many are designed specifically for one of them.

Business graphics

Business graphics packages allow the production of such things as bar charts, line graphs and pie diagrams, that is, diagrams of a statistical nature likely to be included in business reports. An examples of this type of diagram is shown in Figure 12.5.

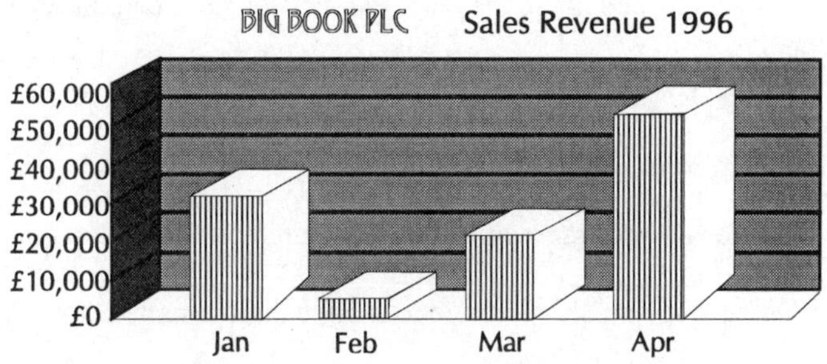

Figure 12.5. *Example of business graphics*

Graphic design

Packages for *graphic design* consist of a collection of special functions aimed at aiding the graphic designer. The artist uses the screen as a canvas and a light-pen, mouse or equivalent device as a brush. They generally allow work of professional quality to be produced in a relatively short amount of time, and include such facilities as:

- large colour palette;

- geometric figure drawing, e.g. lines, rectangles, circles;

- filling areas with colour or patterns;

- undoing mistakes;

- moving/copying/deleting/saving areas of the screen display;

- choice of a variety of character fonts;

- printing the finished design;

- a large number of pre-drawn pictures for inclusion in designs. This is called 'clip-art'.

Figure 12.6 shows a typical graphic design program with the user in the process of editing a picture.

Figure 12.6. *A painting package*

The drawing tools shown down the left-hand side are used to produce a variety of effects. They include tools for:

- cutting out rectangular or irregularly shaped areas of the drawing so that they may be moved or erased;

- spraying colour;

- producing text;

- erasing parts of the drawing using a variable-size eraser;

- filling areas with colour;

- brushing colour onto the screen using brushes of different sizes and shapes;

- drawing filled or unfilled shapes, such as rectangles and circles.

Colours are selected by clicking with the mouse pointer on the colour palette along the bottom of the screen, and other functions can be chosen from the menus along the top of the screen. Drawings can be stored on disk or printed.

Desktop publishing

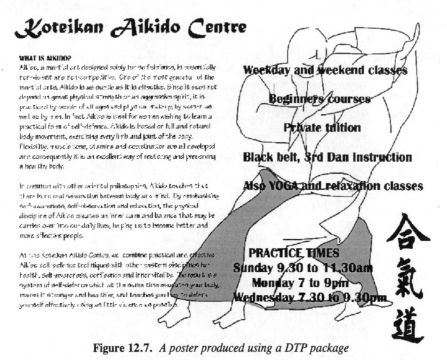

Figure 12.7. *A poster produced using a DTP package*

Desktop publishing programs are designed to produce such things as posters, illustrated articles, books and other documents which combine large amounts of text with illustrations. As such they tend to contain a number of facilities in common with graphic design packages, but emphasize layout and printing. These packages place a lot of emphasis on being able to experiment with arranging sections of the document and seeing its overall appearance. Text is also given more importance; a rudimentary word processor may be provided, or text may be imported from a prepared file, and the user is generally able to experiment with different type fonts on text already displayed on the screen. Typically, a DTP package will have facilities for:

- modifying text by means of using different fonts and type styles;

- importing text from word processors;

- displaying text in columns;

- importing pictures/diagrams from graphic design packages;

- re-sizing pictures;

- producing simple geometrical shapes such as lines, rectangles and circles;

- mixing text and graphics;

- automatically numbering pages;

- producing contents pages, lists of figures and indexes.

Figure 12.7 is an example of a poster produced with a DTP program. Notice that the poster contains a mixture of graphics objects and text of various sizes and fonts. All of these components can be repositioned, re-sized and modified very easily using a mouse.

Computer-aided design

Computer-aided design constitutes perhaps one of the most widely used commercial applications of computer graphics. Here the user simulates real-world geometrical objects using various software drawing tools. Often these tools are selected and used in a WIMP style environment. Sometimes a graphics tablet is used in conjunction with a pressure-operated stylus, or a light-pen might be used to draw electronically on the VDU screen. Whatever the physical method of using the system, the types of software tools and facilities available are fairly standard, providing tools for operations such as:

- drawing common objects (lines, curves, circles, ellipses, rectangles, polygons etc.);

- editing objects (modifying or deleting objects);

- filling shapes with patterns or colours;

- generating three-dimensional objects; Figure 12.8 shows some examples.

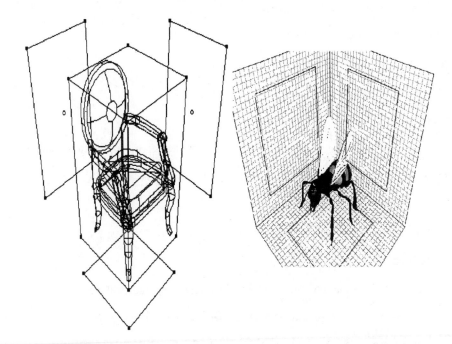

Figure 12.8. *Computer-produced CorelDream ™ 3-dimensional images*

- rotating two-dimensional and three-dimensional objects;

- viewing three-dimensional objects from different directions;

- displaying three-dimensional objects in wireframe or solid form;

- applying different texturing effects to solid objects.

Applications of CAD programs include: engineering drawing; architectural design; interior design; printed-circuit and integrated circuit design; advertising material; computer animation for tv advertising; special effects in films.

Exercises

1. Why is a *translator program* required for a high-level language?

2. Explain the difference between a *compiler*, an *interpreter* and an *assembler*.

3. Name three *high-level languages*.

4. Define the following terms:

   (i)   *Systems software*;

   (ii) *Operating system*;

   (iii) *GUI*;

   (iv) *Applications software*.

5. Name three main functions of an operating system.

6. What does WIMP stand for?

7. What is an *icon*?

8. Name four commonly used *general-purpose* (that is, content-free) applications packages.

9. List three advantages and three disadvantages of general-purpose software.

10. List four uses of *word processors*.

11. Give three advantages of a word processor over a typewriter.

12. Give two disadvantages of word processors.

13. What three types of information can be stored in a single spreadsheet cell?

14. Give three advantages of a spreadsheet over a specially written program.

15. Give two disadvantages of spreadsheets.

16. List three uses of a spreadsheet.

17. List three applications of a database program.

Chapter 13
Operating Systems

If a computer system is viewed as a set of resources, comprising elements of both hardware and software, then it is the job of the collection of programs known as the operating system to manage these resources as efficiently as possible. In so doing, the operating system acts as a buffer between the user and the complexities of the computer itself. One way of regarding the operating system is to think of it as software which allows the user to deal with a simplified computer, but without losing any of the computational power of the machine. In this way, the computer system becomes a virtual system, its enormous complexity hidden and controlled by the operating system and through which the user communicates with the real system.

The central core of an operating system, which remains in memory permanently when the computer is running, is the executive (also known as the supervisor or kernel); as the terms suggest, it has a controlling function, its major function being to carry out system requests from applications programs in such a way that conflicts between them are avoided. The remainder of the operating system is normally held on a direct access medium, from where parts of it can be called as and when required.

Main functions of operating systems

The introduction states that the function of an operating system is to manage the resources of the computer system. These resources generally fall into several categories.

Central processing unit (CPU) or processor

Since only one program can be executed at any one time, computer systems which allow several users simultaneous access (multi-user) must carefully control and monitor use of the processor. In a timesharing multi-user system each user receives a small time-slice from the processor before it passes on to the next user in a continually repeating sequence. Another common scheme is to assign priorities to users so that the system is able to determine which user should next have control of the processor.

Memory

Programs (or parts of programs) must be loaded into the memory before they can be executed, and moved out of the memory when no longer required there. Storage space must be provided for data generated by programs, and provision must be made for the temporary storage of data, caused by data transfer operations involving devices such as printers and disk drives.

Input/output (I/O) devices

Programs will request the use of these devices during the course of their execution and in a multi-user system, conflicts are bound to arise when a device being utilized by one program is requested by another. The operating system controls the allocation of I/O devices and attempts to resolve any conflicts which arise. It also monitors the state of each I/O device and signals any faults detected.

Backing storage

Programs and data files are usually held on mass storage devices such as magnetic disk and tape drives. The operating system supervises data transfers between these devices and memory, and deals with requests from programs for space on them.

Files

These may be regarded as a limited resource in the sense that several users may wish to share the same data file at the same time. The operating system facilitates access to files and ensures that only one updating program can retrieve a particular record at any one time.

The above is by no means an exhaustive list of the functions of an operating system. Other functions include:

- interpretation of the command language by which operators can communicate with it;

- error handling, such as detecting and reporting inoperative or malfunctioning peripherals;

- protection of data files and programs from corruption by other users;

- protection of data files and programs from unauthorized use;

- accounting and logging of the use of the computer resources.

Categories of operating system

Single-stream

As the term suggests, single-stream operating systems are designed to handle only one job at a time. Today, the only operating systems which are likely fall into this category are those designed for microcomputer systems, for example MS-DOS (really, it is a *single-user* system- see also *multi-tasking*), but in the late 1950s the then state of the art mainframe systems could only handle jobs singly. These early systems automated the running of their jobs under customized *control programs* (initially punched onto cards), which were the forerunners of operating systems.

Batch processing systems

The concept of batch processing is explained in detail in Chapters 16 and 17. The early single-stream operating system was improved with the use of an *executive* which queues a number of separate jobs, *schedules* them according to allocated *priorities* and *executes* them, one after another. Some jobs will be required more urgently than others and will be allocated priority accordingly; jobs are loaded and executed according to their priority rating, not their position in the queue, so additional jobs can be added at any time.

Such systems are very inefficient for various reasons. Each job must be completed before commencement of the next; the fact that most jobs comprise a great deal of I/O and very little processing means that the processor is idling for much of the time. This feature is exacerbated by the imbalance between the operating speed of the processor and the data transfer rate of the associated disk and tape drives; the imbalance is even greater where printed output is required. Thus, when the overall system's speed is dictated by the speed of the I/O peripheral, rather than the processor, the system is described as being *I/O bound*. The technique of *off-lining* was introduced in the late 1950s to help deal with the problem of very slow peripherals, such as card readers and printers.

Batch multi-programming systems

Optimization of resource usage

Multi-programming describes the running of several jobs in main memory, apparently simultaneously, although in reality, the processor's attention is being repeatedly switched from one to another under the control of the executive. This makes much better use of the processor's time than the single stream batch processing described previously. Thus, the objective of a batch multi-programming operating system is to *optimize the use of processor time and the rate of system throughput*.

Dynamic resource allocation

With single-stream processing, computer resources (processor time, main memory space, file storage and peripherals) can be allocated to each job and remain fixed for the duration of each job. In contrast, the concurrent processing of several jobs inherent in a multi-programming environment, with the likelihood that the mix of jobs will change as some are completed and new ones are initiated, requires an executive capable of allocating resources *dynamically* to each job.

Job priority

Jobs will vary according to:

- the amount of I/O involved;

- the types and speeds of I/O devices used;

- the amount of processor time needed.

After consideration of these factors, each job is given a *priority rating*, which will determine how frequently and how much processor time it receives. The allocation of priorities can be a complex process but simplistically:

- high priority will be given to a job requiring a large amount of I/O and a relatively small amount of processor time. When I/O operations are being carried out, processor attention is not required after the initial I/O command is given. Conversely, when it does require attention, a high priority will ensure that its small processing requirements are attended to promptly and fully, following which it can return to I/O;

- a low priority job will tend to be one which requires a large amount of processor time; a high priority would result in it hogging the processor and preventing largely I/O jobs from receiving what little attention they require.

Scheduling

High-level scheduler

It is a function of a high-level scheduler to determine which programs in the job queue should next be loaded into main memory. Before loading a job, the following criteria must be satisfied:

- there is sufficient room for it in main memory;

- all associated input files are on-line;

- the necessary peripherals are also on-line.

If priorities are allocated then, subject to fulfilment of the above criteria, these will be used by the high level scheduler to decide the order in which jobs are removed from the job queue.

Dispatcher or low-level scheduler

The dispatcher allocates the processor amongst the various processes in the system. To understand the operation of the dispatcher, it is useful to differentiate between the concept of a *program* and a *process*. A process is a sequence of actions produced through the execution of program instructions. Processes carried out within the system include, for example, interrupt handling, error handling, I/O control and so on; each process may involve one or more programs.

To do this the dispatcher must record the current *status* of each process selecting from the following possibilities:

- it is runnable, that is, free to run;

- it is running; in other words, it has the attention of the processor;

- it is unrunnable or suspended, perhaps because it is awaiting completion of an I/O operation.

A *process descriptor table* records the status of each process in the *processor queue*. The dispatcher must refer to it before deciding on re-allocation of the processor to a process in the queue; such a decision needs to be made each time there is an *interrupt* (see Chapter 14 and later in this chapter). The dispatcher will choose the process with the highest priority, from those which are runnable, unless the process which was running at the time of the interrupt still outranks them.

The dispatcher is invoked under the following circumstances:

- whenever the current process cannot continue; this may result, for example, from a programming error or a switch to I/O, **or**

- when an external interrupt changes the status of a process, for example, following completion of data transfer; it thus becomes runnable.

Batch processing systems collect all input data in a file, from where it is loaded and processed to completion by the relevant application program, storing any output data in another on-line file; the executive then directs the printing program to print any hard copy results from the output file. Prominent features of such systems are:

- lack of any communication or interaction with the user;

- the delay in producing results of processing.

The following categories of operating system allow results of processing to be obtained, frequently on a VDU screen, directly after their entry. They are categorized according to the techniques used to manage the computer resources (the ways in which the systems are used are described in the Chapter on Processing Methods):

- time-sharing;

- multi-tasking;

- multi-user;

- real-time.

Time-sharing

The term time-sharing refers to the allocation of processor *time-slices* to a number of user programs in a multi-programming environment. The aim of a time-sharing operating system is to *keep the users busy*; this contrasts with the batch multi-programming system which aims to keep the processor occupied. The time slices are controlled and synchronized by a real-time clock which generates frequent, regularly timed pulses; each time-slice is extremely short, say 100 milliseconds.

Round robin system

With this method, the operating system works sequentially through the list of programs being run, giving each process an equal slice of processor time.

If all current programs can be accommodated in main memory at one time, users should not experience poor response times. Unfortunately, the total main memory requirements of all current users may exceed the capacity of main memory, making it necessary to swap programs or program segments in and out from backing storage as the processor switches its attention from one to another. The number of such data transfers can be reduced by extending the length of each time slice, but at the cost of reducing the frequency with which the processor transfers its attention from one process to another. Optimizing system performance requires a balance to be struck between these two objectives.

Unless the processor is overloaded, perhaps because there are too many users or because the applications require a large amount of processor time (for example, program compilation - see Chapter 27), each user should feel that he or she is the sole user of the system.

Priority system

Instead of giving single time-slices on a round robin basis, they are allocated according to a system of priorities. This means that some programs will receive a number of time slices in succession before another is attended to. The priority rating of each program will not normally remain static but will be adjusted in relation to the relative amount of processing time it receives in comparison with the other programs in operation.

Time-sharing systems are used *interactively* in that users communicate directly with the computer through VDU terminals. A common use of a time-sharing operating system is to provide *multi-access* to one or more programming languages for the purposes of program development. Other systems may provide users with access to various applications programs which can be run apparently simultaneously.

Multi-tasking

Multi-tasking is a technique which allows a computer to carry out tasks in a similar fashion to a human worker. For example, the Financial Director of a business may be composing a financial report which requires the use of a dictaphone, occasional reference to various financial summaries and telephone calls to other executive staff in the business. Although these tasks are not carried on at exactly the same time, the director is rapidly switching from one to another, and they all contribute to the completion of the financial report. At certain times, an unrelated task may have to be completed, for example, the answering of a brief query from a member of staff. This does not require complete abandonment of the other tasks in hand and the main work continues from the point at which it was left.

Computer multi-tasking requires that the system can accommodate several tasks in memory at one time and that these tasks can be run *concurrently* by rapidly switching the processor's attention between them. The principles of resource management are similar to those employed in multi-programming, except that they relate to a *single user*, are controlled interactively and must be executed in ways which maintain response times acceptable to the user.

Multi-user

A multi-user system is invariably multi-access (although it is possible to provide multi-user facilities within a single stand-alone microcomputer, but only one user at a time) in that it provides a number of users with concurrent access to shared computing resources, which may be part of a computer network or may comprise a centralized computer with multiplexed terminals. Additionally however, the multi-user operating system must protect each user's (or user group's) files from access and/or corruption by other users, either within memory or on backing storage. This is achieved through dynamic memory partitioning and directory-based file management respectively. Later in this chapter, the *Novell network operating system* is used to illustrate aspects of a multi-user operation.

Real-time

A real-time system is one which reacts to inputs sufficiently rapidly to permit tight control of its environment. A computer system's environment can be defined as the application or activity it is controlling. Real-time operation is essential for computerized *process control* (Chapter 35), for example, in chemical production. Such activities require continual control so that parameters of, say pressure and temperature, are adhered to. Inputs from the process, collected through *transducers*, are digitized, input and processed, to provide immediate feedback to the system's controllers, which for the previous example may be a heating mechanism and air pressure control.

Some business information systems also require real-time control (Chapters 16 and 35). Typical examples include airline booking and some stock control systems where rapid turnover is the norm.

The mechanisms used by a real-time operating system to control the system resources are beyond the scope of this text.

Further functions and facilities

Command language interpretation

An important function of the operating system is to interpret the command language which allows the user/operator to communicate with it. Two types of language are generally recognized:

- command language;

- job control language.

Command language

A *command line interpreter* (CLI) accepts command lines, checks them for syntax errors and passes on the relevant requests to the operating system. Such requests may be, for example, to display directory contents on screen, delete files from disk, or copy them from one disk to another. Simple, ad hoc requests will generally be made via a keyboard but lengthy, regularly used sequences of commands may be stored in a command or batch file. The MS-DOS operating system (see later) provides such a facility.

Today, the *graphical user interface* (GUI) is preferred to the command line interpreter. GUIs are examined in Chapter 12. Operating system utilities are selected, with a mouse, from representative icons on the screen; the GUI communicates these requests in the systems command language and the CLI interprets and passes them on to the operating system in the normal way. The GUI is another level of interface between the user and the CLI.

Job control language (JCL)

Associated with batch processing operating systems, JCLs allow details of job requirements to be specified to the operating system. An example JCL sequence is given below.

```
BEGIN
JOB 3367
COMPILE payroll.cbl (disk 1)
LOAD payroll.obj (disk 1)
RUN
END
```

This sequence of commands identifies the job, compiles a COBOL (cbl) source program, loads the resultant object program and executes it.

I/O handling

The executive part of the operating system controls data transfers to and from peripherals, normally through a system of interrupts. The topic of I/O is dealt with in Chapter 14. Other causes of interrupts are dealt with in the following section.

Interrupt handling

Apart from I/O operations, interrupts are necessary to notify the operating system of a variety of other system events, including:

- hardware failure, for example, through power loss or a memory parity error;

- program termination;

- peripheral data transfer failure, for example, because a printer is out of paper or the directory on a disk has been damaged;

- an attempt to access a non-existent memory address;

- in a time-sharing or real-time system, a clock pulse indicates completion of time slices;

- program instruction error, for example, an attempted division by zero or an attempt to communicate with a non-existent device;

- an externally generated command from the operator.

As explained in Chapter 14, when such events occur, the *interrupt handler* routine must establish the cause/source of the interrupt and call the appropriate *interrupt service routine*.

Error handling/trapping

It is important that events which would ordinarily upset or crash the computer system, are *trapped* and handled in an orderly way. Thus, for example, upon encountering an illegal application program instruction, an interrupt is generated, followed by entry to an appropriate interrupt service routine in the executive. The application program is aborted and the service routine displays an error message on screen, detailing the nature of the error. Arithmetic errors, such as an attempt to divide by zero, and I/O errors should also be trapped and treated in a similar fashion. Although data lost as a result of programming errors may not be recoverable by the operating system, any loss caused by abnormal operational interrupt of an I/O activity should be preventable by an appropriate routine to restore the data.

Of course, applications software should, wherever possible, anticipate possible system errors such as disk read errors and other peripheral faults, and protect the user from contact with the operating system by producing its own user friendly messages. Further, in the same way that the operating system prevents system crashes, applications software should, if the fault can be corrected, be robust enough to allow its continuance without loss of data.

File management and security

The major facilities provided by an operating system for file management relate to:

- creating and deleting files;

- allocating space on storage media;

- identifying and keeping track of files on storage media;

- editing the contents of files;

- protecting files from hardware malfunction;

- protecting files from other applications or users;

- protecting files against unauthorized access.

More details of file management and security are illustrated by reference to the Novell and MS-DOS operating systems, described later in this chapter.

Accounting and logging

An important part of system control is that the operator should have a record of all operator communications, error conditions and applications which have been run; the operating system keeps a log of such events and either outputs the relevant messages to the operator's console printer or records them on backing storage for later printing.

Multi-access operating systems normally provide an accounting facility which identifies and records terminal usage, including basic details such as user-id, time logged on and off, and processor time used; in this way, users or departments of an organization can be charged for computer time.

Memory management

Single user operating systems such as MS-DOS do not provide particularly sophisticated memory facilities, as only one application is *resident* at one time. There is one special case, that of the graphical user interface (GUI) which stays resident in memory; it must advise the operating system of its storage needs, in order that it is not corrupted by subsequent loading of applications.

Multi-programming and multi-tasking systems require quite complex memory management facilities in order to accommodate and maintain the *integrity* of the several programs and associated data which may be resident at any one time. Memory requirements do not remain static because the mix of programs being run may vary from moment to moment; the space left by a program swapped out of memory may not be large enough to accommodate an incoming program, requiring the *relocation* of programs already there.

Memory partitions and relocatable code

To fulfil these requirements, the operating system must be able to partition memory *dynamically* and adjust those partitions as programs and data are relocated. This latter point means that all software should be capable of relocation and not be tied to *absolute* addresses in memory. This is effected with the use of *relative addressing* instructions which are examined in more detail in Chapter 4. The relocatable code is allocated to the absolute memory addresses by the executive, the relative addresses of each instruction being added to the *base* address of the relevant memory partition. Subsequent relocations can be carried out by re-specification of the base address.

Segmenting and interleaving

Where large programs are concerned, it may be possible to divide them into *segments*, which can be rolled in and out of memory from direct access storage as required. As only one segment of a particular program need be resident in memory at any one time, any replacement segment will simply *overlay* it.

In a multi-programming environment, segments from different programs are in memory at one time and are said to be *interleaved*.

Virtual memory

Although main memory and direct access backing storage are physically separate, it is possible to present their joint capacity as being available to run programs. Such virtual memory can be used to accommodate much larger programs, as well as expand the level of multi-programming. A programmer can regard the addressable memory space as being beyond the physical capacity of main memory. Programs are automatically divided into *pages* (a fixed unit of virtual storage) and when one is loaded, its virtual memory addresses are mapped to the absolute memory addresses by the executive. The addresses of each page are held in main memory and during program execution, they are paged-in and paged-out as required.

Operating system case studies

This section looks at a variety of operating systems which provide a single-user, multi-tasking and/or multi-user environments.

MS-DOS

Command line and shell interfaces

All MS-DOS commands can be entered through the *command line* (C:\> prompt), or through the operating systems *shell*. Figure 13.1 illustrates the graphical nature of the shell interface. Instead of keying in a command, character by character, a user can select it from the range of menu options. An on-line, Help facility can be accessed as required. The shell is regarded as user friendly and supports the use of a mouse. The command line tends to be used only by experienced users. Commands are available for the control of every aspect of the computer system's resources. The most commonly used commands are concerned with the management of file storage space and the running of applications. The function of some of these commands are described in this chapter. Where example commands are given, they relate to the use of the C:\> prompt, rather than the operating system's shell. All operating system commands are dealt with by the *command line interpreter*. Some commands

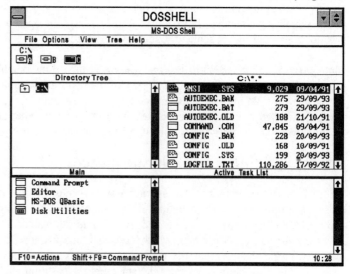

Figure 13.1. *DOS shell interface*

are *memory resident* or *internal* and are continually available once MS-DOS has been loaded. Other, less frequently used commands, are called from disk as required.

File management

Each *filename* is held in a *directory* together with its size (expressed in bytes) and the date and time it was created or last modified (the previous figure shows a typical directory listing). Most microcomputer systems keep track of the current date and time (even when the machine is switched off) with CMOS memory (Chapter 7). Directories are used to divide disk space into a number of user or application areas. A floppy disk with 1.44Mb (megabytes) capacity may contain, say, 60 or 70 files at most, so it is possible for a user to scan a single directory in the search for a particular file name. A hard disk, with a capacity of hundreds of megabytes, may contain thousands of files and managing them all in a single directory is virtually impossible. For this reason, MS-DOS allows the creation of *sub-directories* to which groups of files can be assigned. When the operating system's attention is directed to a particular directory, it is known as the *current* or *working* directory. MS-DOS keeps track of files on disk with the use of a *file allocation table* (FAT). When a disk is formatted, MS-DOS initially sets up two system areas, one for the FAT and the other for the main or *root* directory. The FAT has an entry for each *cluster* (a cluster is group of sectors). Clusters containing only part of a file have a FAT entry which points to the next cluster relating to that file, or, if it is the last part of a file, a special indicator. Thus, MS-DOS can find a complete file by reference to the pointers in each cluster containing a part of it. Empty clusters have a zero entry in the FAT.

File operations

Viewing directories

As explained earlier, it is essential to organize file storage space and to allocate files relating to a single application into, at least, one separate sub-directory. To view the contents of a particular directory may require the entry of commands to:

- select the *drive letter*. If a system has a hard disk and two floppy disk drives, these are labelled as C, A and B, respectively. Sometimes, if the hard disk is partitioned into several areas (or there are other drives attached to the system), additional drive letters may be used - D, E, F and so on;

- switch to the working directory.

Figure 13.1 shows the DOS shell views of drives and directories. Note that each row details, from left to right, the filename, *extension* (for example, autoexec.bat), size of file in bytes and the date it was last modified. The file extension indicates the file type. For example, BAT indicates a *batch file* (see later) and EXE an *executable* program file. Applications packages add their own file extension to any file created with the package. For example, if a user creates a worksheet with the Excel package and names it BUDGET, the file will appear in the directory as BUDGET.XLS. The details of a named file can also be viewed by the command

```
dir a:budget.xls
```

Using a wild card

A wild card allows the user to broaden the scope of a command. For example, to display details of files beginning with the file name TEST, on drive B, could be entered as

```
dir b:test*
```

The wild card can be used with some other commands, including the COPY command, which is explained in the next section.

Other file and disk commands

- `erase` - to remove a named file (or, using the wild card, group of files) from disk. `del` has the same effect.

- `undelete`. Available with MS-DOS 5.0 (and later versions) this command recovers a file which has been accidentally deleted. Deleted files are only marked as such and are recoverable with this command, unless MS-DOS has subsequently used the area for another file. The command cannot be used if the directory which contained the deleted file has been removed (see later).

- `copy` - to copy a named file or group of files to another disk and/or directory.

- `attrib` - protects a file by making it read only. Thus, `attrib +r budget.xls` prevents any write operation of the named file (`attrib -r budget.xls` removes the protection).

- `comp` - compares the contents of two files or two groups of files.

- `diskcomp` - compares the contents of two disks on a track-by-track basis, rather than by reference to particular files.

- `diskcopy` - allows the copying of a complete disk onto another. It is generally used to carry out security backups.

- `format` - formats the disk in the specified drive. All new disks must be formatted to accept MS-DOS files before use (a similar command exists in all operating systems). The command initializes the directory and file allocation tables on disk. It destroys any existing files as the complete disk contents are wiped. File protection attributes provide no protection. The only protection against accidental formatting of diskettes is to use the appropriate write protection mechanism. Hard disks cannot be write-protected but more recent versions of MS-DOS provide more user warnings if the specified drive contains the hard disk. The accidental wiping of a 200 megabyte hard disk could be catastrophic.

- `print` - initiates a primitive form of spooling and prints a named text file on the attached printer while other commands are processed.

- `recover` - recovers a file or entire disk containing some bad or corrupted sectors. The command causes MS-DOS to read the file sector by sector and skips the bad sectors, marking them to ensure that they are not used again. Thus, the uncorrupted parts of a file can be recovered.

- `type` - displays the contents of a file on screen. For example, `type a:test.dat`, displays the contents of the file named `test.dat` and stored on drive `A:\>`. A wild card cannot be used with this command.

Directory creation and handling

If a computer is used by more than one user, or a single user is working on a number of different projects, it is advisable to organize work files accordingly into different directories. This is similar to separating manual files by placing them into different drawers or sections of a filing cabinet. Although it may be common practice to maintain all files in the root directory of a floppy disk, it is virtually essential, if any proper control is to be maintained, to organize work files on hard disk into different directories. Systems and applications programs must be installed into separate directories because, in addition to the need for organization, many have the same filenames and therefore must be separated. For example, there may be one directory (and several sub-directories) for a spreadsheet program, another for the word processing program and another for the accounts programs. Regarding work files, a user has to decide what logical divisions need to be made. MS-DOS organizes files in what is termed a *multi-level directory structure*. Figure 13.5 in the Novell Netware section shows this type of structure. Each of the directories and sub-directories may contain a number of files. A multi-level directory structure looks rather like an up-turned tree with a single root at the top and branches growing from it. The root directory is created when the disk is formatted, but other directories have to be created by the user. Any directory with sub-directories beneath it is called a *parent* directory. Once directories have been created, any file can be directed to its relevant directory, either directly with the use of MS-DOS commands or (more usually) through the applications software.

Directory commands

The command mdir (or simply md) stands for make directory and is used for the creation of directories. For example, md\dos creates a directory called dos for the storage of the operating system files. Similar commands can be used to create directories for applications packages (this is usually done automatically when a package is installed) and associated files and the users work files. The backslash (\) symbol is used to separate directories names, the first backslash indicating separation from the root directory which is inferred within the command. The series of directory names and backslashes indicates the path to be taken by the operating system to access particular files.

The command chdir (or cd) is used to move from one working directory to another. For example, cd\dos changes to the dos directory. The command cd\ always returns control to the root directory from any point in the structure. Directories can be removed with rmdir (or rd). A directory can be deleted only when it is empty.

Accessing external commands

External commands are those operating system commands which have to be called from disk whenever they are required. Internal commands are the most commonly used and remain resident in memory after the operating system has been loaded. A user may be working in any one of a number of directories, so the operating system needs to be given a path to the directory containing the external commands (in case any are needed during processing). If the directory is called dos, then the command path\dos must be executed. This is done automatically at system start-up, by including the command in the autoexec.bat (see later), which is stored in the root directory. The automatic execution of commands through batch files is dealt with in a later section.

Redirecting input and input

Unless commanded otherwise, MS-DOS assumes that input is through the keyboard and that output is to be directed to the screen. With appropriate commands, input can be accepted from a disk file, rather than from the keyboard. Similarly, output can be directed to a printer instead of the screen. Sometimes, output from one process is required as input for another and this redirection of output can be effected with the use of a *pipe*.

An MS-DOS command normally directs output to the screen. For example, `dir` displays, on screen, the directory listing of the disk in the currently active drive. By adding a greater-than (>) sign and a filename, the directory listing can be written to a disk file of that name. For example, `dir > file.lst` creates a file called `file.lst` and writes the directory to it.

To append output to an existing file, two greater-than symbols are used. For example, `dir >> file.lst` sends the directory listing to the named file and appends the data to the existing file contents. If the file doesn't exist, then MS-DOS creates it.

To call input from a channel other than the keyboard, requires the use of the less-than symbol (<). For example, `newfile.txt < input. txt` causes `newfile.txt` to receive its input from the file `input.txt`, rather than the keyboard.

Filters

Filter commands are used to transform an input file in some way, before it is sent to an output device. For example, filter commands can be used to read a file from disk, sort it and then display the sorted file on screen. MS-DOS provides three commonly used filters:

- `find`, which searches for specified text in a named file;

- `sort`, which sorts a text file. For example, a directory listing could be sorted before being displayed on screen;

- `more`. When displaying a text file on screen, `more` allows it to be output one screen at a time.

Pipes

Pipes permit the use of more than one operating system command at a time. Each command is separated by a vertical bar sign |. For example, `dir|sort|more` sorts the working directory and displays it on the screen. If the listing occupies more than the length of the screen, the user is prompted to continue after each section of the list fills the screen.

Batch files

Batch files are special files used for the automatic execution of regularly used sequences of commands. Any valid sequence of commands can be included and the operating system will execute them in the same way as if they had been entered one at a time from the keyboard. To be recognized by the operating system as a batch file, MS-DOS requires the filename extension .BAT to be used. To execute a batch file, only the filename, without the extension .BAT, is typed. One particular type of batch file called `autoexec.bat` has a special significance which is explained later in this section. A batch file is created with a text editor.

Batch file example - file copying

A batch file called `movfile.bat` could also be used to automate a file copying operation. The following sequence of commands creates a new directory called `second`, copies a file `bumph.dat` from its location in the directory called `first`, deletes the original and then displays the contents of directory `second` (which now contains bumph.dat). The word rem means remark or comment and is used to document the file; rem is ignored by MS-DOS.

Listing 13.1.   Batch file to copy a specific file

```
rem prevents command execution of screen
@echo off
rem creates the new directory
md c:\second
rem copies the bumph.dat file to the new directory
copy c:\first\bumph.dat c:\second
rem deletes the original file
erase c:\first\bumph.dat
rem displays the contents of the new directory
dir c:\second
rem displays the message shown
echo Here is the file in the new directory
```

The drawback of the batch file shown in Listing 13.1, is that it only deals with two particular directories and one named file. MS-DOS allows replaceable parameters to be entered with the batch file name. This means that movfile.bat can be modified to allow the user to specify directory names and filenames before the batch file is executed. The modified commands are shown in Listing 13.2. The replaceable parameters are represented by %1 and %2.

If the command, movfile c:\second c:\first\bumph.dat, is entered, MS-DOS executes the batch file named movfile and replaces %1 with c:\second and %2 with c:\first\bumph.dat. If these replacements are traced through the command sequence in Listing 13.2, it can be seen that its effect is the same as that in Listing 13.1. Of course, entry of different parameters enables the batch file to be used for any new directory and file, or files to be moved to it. For example, movfile c:\newplace c:\old-place*.doc would move a set of files, with the same file extension .doc, from the existing directory oldplace to the new directory newplace.

Listing 13.2.   Batch file with replaceable parameters

```
echo off
md %1
copy %2 %1
erase %2
dir %2
echo Contents of new directory
```

Function of autoexec.bat file

An autoexec.bat file can be used to customize a computer for a particular purpose at system start up. Thus, for example, a computer which is used for one particular package can be automated to load that package when MS-DOS is started. Because the autoexec.bat file is executed when the operating system is first loaded, it must reside in the root directory.

The automatic starting of the Windows GUI (see later) provides a popular example of such customization. This is because users of the GUI tend to use software packages which are controlled by it. Autoexec.bat files can include numerous, advanced command sequences, but a simple example is provided in Listing 13.3.

Listing 13.3.   An example `autoexec.bat` file

```
echo off
rem loads UK keyboard driver
keyb uk
rem provides path to DOS commands and programs
path c:\dos;c:\word
rem loads mouse driver
mouse
rem opens the MS-DOS shell
dosshell
```

Function of config.sys file

The `config.sys` file is also stored in the root directory and is automatically executed when the system is switched on. It contains commands which configure the computer system for particular installation requirements. Listing 13.4 shows a sample `config.sys` file.

Listing 13.4.   Sample config.sys file

```
rem identifies the mouse driver
device=c:\mouse\mouse.sys
rem sets number of files which can be open at any one
rem time. Normal set-up allows only 8. An application
rem which requires more is likely to indicate the fact.
files =20
rem these are disk buffers in which MS-DOS can hold data
rem being read from or written to disk, when the amount
rem of data is not an exact multiple of sector size. Word
rem processors which use the disk intensively perform
rem better with 10 to 20 buffers. If a large number of
rem directories is created, then 20 to 30 buffers
rem may improve performance.
buffers=20
rem this selects the time, date and currency format.
rem The code 044 is for the UK.
Country=044
```

OS/2

OS/2 Version 1.0 was announced by IBM and Microsoft in April 1987, as a *multi-tasking* operating system. Since then the collaboration between these two companies has broken down and Microsoft has produced its highly successful Windows GUI. Numerous improvements have been made to the original version of OS/2, but it is still failing to make any significant impression in the PC software market. In an effort to take an increased share of this market, IBM has ensured that OS/2 is able to run applications developed for MS-DOS and Windows, as well as OS/2 itself.

Workplace shell - the OS/2 GUI

Workplace Shell has the main features of a conventional GUI, with windows that can be moved and re-sized, scroll bars (for viewing different areas of work within the available window), dialogue boxes, etc. Unlike the Windows GUI, it does not allocate file management to a separate component. Instead, users are encouraged to view data files as the entry point for applications (rather than the other way around). Workplace Shell can be described as *object orientated*. An object can be a program, a data file, a folder (directory) or device (such as a printer). When an object is selected, a pop-up menu offers options appropriate to the object. For example, a program object menu includes a run option. Similarly, a data file object provides options concerning, for example, the printing or copying of the file. When running Microsoft Windows applications, the desktop is presented accordingly, with the Program Manager window.

32-bit applications

For brevity, OS/2 Version 2.1 is referred to simply as OS/2. As a 32-bit operating system, OS/2 can take full advantage of the current 32-bit processors and 32-bit software. Handling data in 32-bit units, rather than 16 bits at a time, contributes to quicker system performance. To ensure its compatibility with a huge section of the PC software market, OS/2 can run 16-bit software; virtually all MS-DOS and a few Windows applications are designed to retain backward compatibility with the 16-bit 80286 processor. Windows 3.1 also runs 32-bit applications (using an i386, or later, processor), when it is operating in *enhanced mode*.

Multi-tasking

OS/2 allocates a separate, private, area of memory to each application. It also provides facilities to protect one application from the activities of another. Device drivers (disk controllers, screen and printer drivers) operate at a higher level of privilege within memory, because they have to remain accessible to all current applications.

OS/2 uses *pre-emptive* multi-tasking. This means that the operating system controls the amount of processor time each application receives, before switching activity to one of the others. The amount of time received by a task, depends on its urgency (the user can specify priorities). OS/2 can *multi-thread* separate processes; for example, it can initiate the printing of a document by a word processor and then immediately return to its previous task. The user can continue working on another task, while the document is being printed in the background.

File management

OS/2 offers two file management systems. Users have to choose which one to install. The choice depends largely on the capacity of the drive and whether or not MS-DOS applications are to be used.

- an enhanced File Allocation Table (FAT) system, which can be read by MS-DOS;

- a High Performance File System (HPFS).

The HPFS is completely different from the FAT system and is designed to manage, more effectively, the higher capacity (measured in gigabytes) hard drives. HPFS file names can be up to 254 characters in length (compared with the 8 permitted by MS-DOS). Both filing systems allow up to 64Kb of *attribute data* to be attached to each file; the data can comprise text and images. This permits extensive labelling of a file, describing its contents and perhaps associations with other files or applications. Effectively, this means that longer file names can also be used with the enhanced FAT system.

Both systems (like Windows 3.x) support *write caching* (see Chapter 9), which means that writing to disk can be delayed if the processor is busy. The mechanism can be disabled, as there is a small risk that data may be lost (while it waits in the cache memory) if there is a sudden power cut.

A short history of Microsoft Windows

Microsoft's Windows was initially developed as a front-end to DOS-based applications. It allowed novice computer users to use an IBM-compatible PC without having to learn the rather cryptic DOS commands. However, it was not really until 1990 that it became a serious alternative to DOS. The history of Windows is briefly traced, from its rather inauspicious first appearance in 1985, to its huge popularity today.

Five releases preceded Windows 95, the latest version of the Microsoft Windows operating system. The first version, version 1.0 released in 1985, was beset with problems. The main reason for this was that the hardware generally available at the time did not lend itself to a graphical user interface. The combination of an under powered processor (the Intel 8086), low-resolution graphics and lack of internal memory conspired to produce a piece of software that was not very well received by the computer industry. Though it did make a PC easier to use for non-technical users, being text-based it was not what is recognized today as a true graphical user interface.

However, the success of Apple's Macintosh personal computer, with its intuitive, graphical user interface, encouraged Microsoft to continue in competition and the result was Windows 2.0. Still text-based, this version was not a great deal better than the previous one, though the Windows/386 version released in 1988 did offer multi-tasking as a direct result of the increased processing power that the Intel 80386 processor provided. It was not until 1990, when Windows 3.0 provided an attractive, user-friendly graphical interface and several other enhancements, that Windows was recognized as providing a real alternative to DOS-based application. Windows 3.0 offered improved memory management so that applications could do more; it made extensive use of icons and it provided the Program Manager utility, shown in Figure 13.2, which simplified the management of applications.

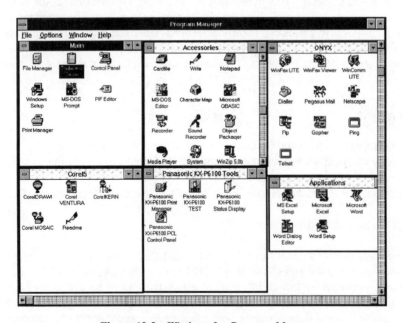

Figure 13.2. *Windows 3.x Program Manager*

This version of Windows also allows several tasks to run at the same time. However, partly as a result of its attempt to make Windows 3.0 backwardly compatible with other versions and also with DOS applications, Microsoft introduced too much instability into the operating system. This manifested itself in system crashes which announced themselves with the notorious Unrecoverable Application Error message box. Version 3.1 addressed these problems by fixing known bugs in version 3.0 and, more importantly, by more carefully monitoring the behaviour of applications to trap possible problems before they caused the system to 'hang'. Moreover, in version 3.1 Microsoft introduced the facility to utilize disk space as virtual memory, thus releasing the user from having to be too careful about the amount of memory that was required by an application.

The next main development in the evolution of Windows was the release of Windows for Workgroups 3.11. This release represented Microsoft's efforts to support small organizations using small Local Area Networks. The new features included in Windows for Workgroups allowed a number of PCs to be linked by installing a network card and some cable. Network features such as meeting scheduling and e-mail were also provided. The reliability of Windows was further improved in this version.

Windows NT

Microsoft's Windows NT operating system first became available in September 1993. It is a 32-bit multi-tasking operating system and competes directly with OS/2. Its hardware requirements are greater than those needed for the Windows 3.1 GUI and it is not seen as a replacement for it. Windows NT needs a minimum of 12Mb of main memory and 75Mb of free disk space. Machines based on RISC processors (Chapter 7) require 16Mb of main memory and 92Mb free disk space to run Windows NT. The operating system includes facilities for *networking*, enabling machines to be used as print and file *servers* (Chapter 10), and *multi-user/multi-access* operation.

There are three main parts to Windows NT:

- NT *executive*, which is the operating system and controls the hardware;

- Win32 sub-system, which the NT executive runs as an application. Win32 provides the Windows GUI;

- MS-DOS, OS/2 and Portable UNIX sub-systems, which allows the running of software written for these operating systems. Concerning OS/2, only applications written for the character-based interface are supported. Software written for Windows 3.# will also run under Windows NT. These sub-systems can only operate through the Win32 sub-system.

Figure 13.3 illustrates the main components in the structure and their relationship one with another and to the hardware.

- The Virtual Memory Manager controls the allocation of main memory to applications and ensures that each is protected from other processes. When there is insufficient main memory space, some memory contents are paged to disk (*virtual memory*) until room becomes available (when they are paged back in). This protection does not apply to Windows 3.# applications (run through the Windows sub-system) which can, at times, clash for memory space and crash.

- The Process Manager controls the multi-tasking process. Windows NT (like OS/2) can carry out fine grained multi-tasking. This enables the concurrent processing of tasks within the same application. For example, new records could be entered into a database, while a database sort is being executed in the background.

- The Input/Output Manager handles file reading and writing operations, at the physical machine level. It provides a File Allocation Table (FAT) system, compatible with the MS-DOS system and a High Performance File System (HPFS) to handle OS/2 applications. NT's own file system (NTFS) allows the use of long file names and the storage of files up to 17 billion gigabytes in size.

- The *kernel* handles signals from the hardware, indicating conditions such as, the completion of data transfer through a communications port.

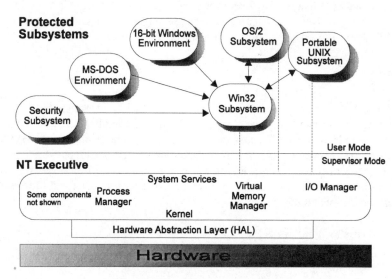

Figure 13.3. *Windows NT structure*

Portability

The MS-DOS and OS/2 operating systems are designed to make particular use of the Intel series of processors (Chapter 7). Apart from the kernel, the Windows NT operating system does not relate specifically to the architecture of any particular processor; to some extent it is processor independent and can be used on non-Intel processor machines. This independence is achieved with the use of a Hardware Abstraction Layer (HAL), which comes between the hardware and the NT Executive.

Windows95

Based on Windows NT, Windows 95 offers a PC operating system that also does not rely on DOS for its operation. Though it is not regarded as a replacement for the more powerful NT operating system, Windows 95 nevertheless has a number of major improvements over previous versions of Windows. These include:

- improved speed;

- improved reliability;

- better user interface;

- better networking capabilities;

- 'plug and play' capability;

- support for long file names.

The speed improvement results from the fact that Windows 95 uses 32-bit code to perform much of its work and that it uses *pre-emptive multitasking* to control applications. As mentioned earlier in this chapter, multi-tasking allows several applications, or *tasks*, to be running simultaneously, but with pre-emptive multi-tasking it is the operating system rather than the tasks, that controls the resources that are available. This ensures that each current task is allowed its fair share of the resources that it requests.

Improved reliability has resulted mainly from removing Window's dependence on DOS. Many of the instability problems experienced in previous versions of Windows were directly related to its use of DOS which allowed applications to take complete control of the computer system. When more than one application is running in a multi-tasking environment, then each application must restrict itself to using only certain resources, especially memory, otherwise conflicts arise which cause the machine to crash. DOS applications can still run in Windows 95, but they are restricted to a virtual machine that emulates earlier processor architectures such as that of the 8086 family. This greatly reduces the possibility of a DOS application 'misbehaving'. Additional stability resulted from more 'bug fixes'. The new user interface is shown in Figure 13.4.

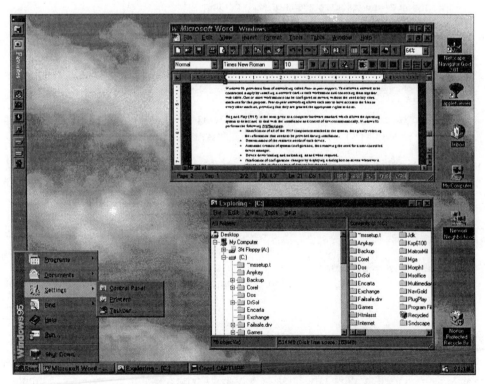

Figure 13.4. *The Windows 95 new user interface*

'Explorer' replaces in a single application the previous versions' Program Manager and File Manager utility programs. It provides a very flexible way of organizing files and programs using 'folders' which are similar to directories. A *task bar* at the bottom of the screen has a 'Start' button which is used to activate pop up menus, and applications currently available, either running or idle, are shown as separate named buttons. By clicking on the name of an application on the task bar, that application's window becomes the current focus, thereby allowing access to the application's controls.

Note also the application shortcuts on the right, represented by icons and the shortcut bar on the left; both features add to the flexibility and ease of use of the system.

Windows 95 provides a form of networking called *Peer-to-peer* (Chapter 10) support. This allows a network to be constructed simply by installing a network card in each workstation and connecting them together with cable. One or more workstations can be configured as servers, without the need to buy extra machines for this purpose. Peer-to-peer networking allows each user to have access to the files on every other machine, providing that they are granted the appropriate rights to do so.

Plug and Play (PNP) is the term given to a computer hardware standard which allows the operating system to detect and to deal with the installation and control of devices automatically. Windows 95 performs the following PNP facilities:

- identification of all of the PNP components attached to the system, thus greatly reducing the information that needs to be provided during installation;

- determination of the resource needs of each device;

- automatic creation of system configuration, thus removing the need for a user-controlled device manager;

- device driver loading and unloading as and when required;

- notification of configuration changes by displaying a dialogue box on-screen whenever a change in the number or type of devices has changed.

Because of their dependency on DOS, previous versions of Windows required the familiar 8.3 format (*filename.ext*) for file names; Windows 95 now allows filenames of almost any length to be used, including embedded spaces.

Novell Netware

Novell Netware is the most widely used local area network operating system and provides a high level of multi-user provision and security. This section looks in some detail at the filing system and the facilities for multi-user administration.

Filing system

The file server contains the shared file storage system and handles requests for access to it. Like any filing system, it has to be organized to allow efficient access to and management of the resource. Commonly, such organization is *hierarchical* and the Netware system provides a typical example. Figure 13.5 shows how the file system might be structured.

Volumes

Referring to Figure 13.5, the server (FS1) disk storage may be divided into *volumes*; a volume is a physical amount of storage, which can be a section of one storage device or it may incorporate several devices. Volumes can be used to divide the network's filing system according to separate organizational requirements. For example, separate volumes may be assigned to Accounts, Manufacturing and Personnel. One reason for such separation is security; security backups can be carried out separately on each volume and allocation of users to the separate organizational functions is made easier. However, these volumes are still part of the same network filing system and a user can be allowed to access more than one, when necessary. For simplicity, Figure 13.5 shows that the server has only one volume (SYS:, which is automatically created when Netware is set up). A workstation accesses a volume by a drive letter (F:\ for example).

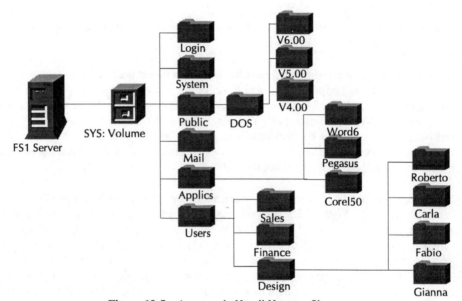

Figure 13.5. *An example Novell Netware file system*

Directories and sub-directories

Directories are subdivisions of a volumes space. Referring to Figure 13.5 and volume SYS:, a number of different types of directory can be identified:

- *system*; there are four (Login, System, Public and Mail), created when the file server's network software is installed;

- *DOS* (a sub-directory of Public). Each version of the MS-DOS operating system, used by workstations attached to the network, has a sub-directory; one workstation may be using version 6.0, whilst others may be using version 5.0 or 4.0 and if applications are to run correctly, they must have access to the appropriate operating system commands;

- *applics*; these contain the executable files of applications software. There are three sub-directories within this directory: Word6 (word processor); Pegasus (accounting); Corel50 (graphics);

- *users*; the workspace allocated to user data files. Figure 13.5 shows three main sub-divisions of users: Sales; Finance; Design. The Design group has four separate user areas allocated to it: Roberto; Carla; Fabio; Gianna. The other user groups of Sales and Finance may well be similarly sub-divided, but this is not shown in the figure.

The highest level (the top row) in this *tree* structure contains a number of *system* directories. Figure 13.5 shows four:

- *login*; this directory contains programs concerning the login procedure;

- *public*; this holds Novell network (as opposed to MS-DOS) operating system commands and utilities which can be accessed by users;

- *system*; files and programs used by the network operating system and the network supervisor are held in here;

- *mail*; this contains a sub-directory relating to each network user and containing their *login script*. A *user login script* can be used to tailor the network environment for a particular user, such as the display of a special applications menu or greeting. More usually, the *system login script* is used for all users; programming statements, such as IF ...THEN ...ELSE can be used to determine the network environment for different users or groups of users. Thus, for example, the Sales, Finance and Design groups may each have a different menu, giving access to a different set of applications.

The *network supervisor* (the person in charge of network administration) needs to create other directories, for the applications and data areas. Figure 13.5 shows an *applics* (applications) directory, which is divided into three sub-directories, one each for word processing, accounting and graphic design packages. The *users* directory is divided into a series of sub-directories, one data or work area for each user; each of these, usually identified by the user name, is the allocated workspace for a user. A data directory may be shared by a number of individual users, belonging to the same group, such as Finance. Alternatively, as in the case of the four Design users, each may have their own data directory. Upon login, the user name is used to *map* the workstation to the user's own data directory; this is done through the *login script* (similar to a batch file in MS-DOS).

User directory and file management

When a user logs in the workstation is *mapped* to their user directory. Thus, at the MS-DOS prompt, user ST001 may see the following.

```
F:\USERS\ST001
```

Within that directory ST001 has full directory and file rights (see later), which means that he or she can:

- create and modify a structure of sub-directories, within their user directory, to suit the division of their own work;

- read, write, copy, delete or rename any files stored within that structure.

Access rights

Network storage is shared, so access to it needs to be carefully controlled. Thus, users should only be able to gain access to those directories and files which they need and are authorized to use.

There are a number of different rights, each of which permits a certain operation to be carried out in respect of a file or directory. The rights for files and directories are the same. The directory and file operations available to a user are determined by their rights. Rights only relate to the use of network storage and are not relevant to the integral drives of a workstation. The examples given here relate to the Novell Netware operating system. Every user has certain rights which they can invoke when they login in:

- network applications (*executables*), which can only be accessed and run;

- access to their default user directory and data files within it. These are broadly unrestricted, although the physical space allocation is likely to be set. Creation and modification of a directory structure is allowed and the user is given full housekeeping rights concerning the files within that structure.

	Right	Meaning
S	Supervisory	Unrestricted in the directory. Can grant rights to other users.
R	Read	Can open files, read contents and run programs in the directory.
W	Write	Can open and alter the contents of files in the directory.
C	Create	Can create new files and sub-directories in the directory.
E	Erase	Can erase directory, sub-directories and files contained in them.
M	Modify	Can alter file attributes or names.
F	File Scan	Can see files and directories covered by this right.
A	Access Control	Can give rights (same as own) to other users in the directory.

Table 13.1. *Novell Netware directory and file access rights*

Table 13.1 lists the directory and file rights, which can be assigned with the Novell Netware operating system. Following the table are brief explanations on the significance of each type for network operation and security. The 8 rights shown in the table can be granted in respect of a given *directory* and will thus be restricted to that directory (except in the case of *inherited rights* - not dealt with in this text). Rights can also be related to specific *files*. Table 13.2 gives typical circumstances when a user needs some of the rights in Table 13.1.

Operation	Rights needed
Create a new directory	Create
Execute a program (an *executable* file)	Read, File Scan
Erase a file	Erase
See a filename	File Scan
Look through a directory for files	File Scan
Copy files to another directory	Write, Create, File Scan
Rename a file or directory	Modify
Create a file and write to it	Create

Table 13.2. *Rights needed for example directory and file operations*

Default rights

When a Novell server is set up, a SUPERVISOR user is created, with S(upervisory) rights in all directories. A user group called EVERYONE is also created, to which all new users are assigned, unless the supervisor creates other groups in which to place them. The EVERYONE group members are given the following default rights:

- *C(reate)* in the SYS: MAIL directory, which contains a sub-directory for every user (not their data directory). Each sub-directory contains the relevant users *login script* (see Directories and Sub-directories).

- R(ead) and F(ile Scan) in the SYS:PUBLIC, which holds the executable network operating system commands for users (for example: NDIR and NCOPY).

Additional rights need to be assigned to allow users to run applications software. From Table 13.2, it can be seen that a user would need R(ead) and F(ile Scan) rights to the directory containing the required applications. The methods by which users can be assigned rights are dealt with in the next section.

User administration

Four categories of *Novell user* need to be identified:

- *SUPERVISOR.* This user has unrestricted access and operational power in any part of the network server for which he or she is responsible. The network administrator will be the only SUPERVISOR user.

- *Console Operator. Security equivalence* enables a user to be given the same rights as another, so although there is only one SUPERVISOR user for a Novell file server, another person can be given the same rights by being given supervisor equivalence. *Console Operator* is the term given to a person given supervisor equivalence.

- *Workgroup Manager.* The network administrator can create this category of user if it is necessary to give another person *supervisory* rights over a particular volume or directory. This is useful if another person is to be given responsibility for their own users and data.

- *User.* This is the ordinary user, who has no supervisory rights and whose access to any part of the network is controlled by user *account restrictions*. Accounts also exist for the special users: SUPERVISOR; Console Operator; Workgroup Manager. When a new user is installed, he or she becomes part of the group EVERYONE, every member of which is assigned R(ead) and F(ileScan) rights to the SYS:PUBLIC directory and SYS:MAIL. Additional rights can be assigned directly to the user, or by making him or her a member of a group, which has additional rights. Alternatively, additional rights can be given to all users by altering the rights of the group EVERYONE.

Groups

Network administration can become very complex if file and directory rights are separately assigned to each user. A much better method is to create groups. By making a user a member of a particular group, the rights of that group are automatically assigned to that user. Most users can be dealt with in this way. Suppose, for example that a business allocates directories for Sales, Finance and Design. Clearly, the staff in the Accounts department are going to need access to the same files (customer Sales Ledger, for example), which are held in the Finance directory. Equally, they are likely to need access to the same accounts applications and will need R(ead) and F(ile Scan) rights in the Accounts software directory (this contains executable files for the accounts software). By creating a group called ACCOUNT, and assigning the appropriate rights to it, staff in the Accounts Department can be added to the group and gain the necessary rights automatically. If a member of the Accounts department moves to another job within the business, they can be transferred to another group (with rights to access other directories and files) and their rights will be modified accordingly.

How rights can be assigned

The ways in which a network administrator can assign rights are illustrated in Figures 13.6, 13.7 and 13.8. Unless a user has very particular requirements, then the most appropriate method (Figure 13.7) of giving rights is to assign users to a group which has the assigned rights he or she needs. Another useful method of giving a user or group the same rights as

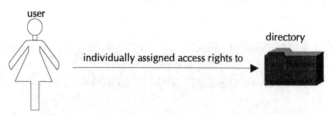

Figure 13.6. *Individual rights assigned directly to user*

another is to use *security equivalence* (Figure 13.8). This is the method used by the network administrator to give a console operator the same rights as the SUPERVISOR user (the network administrator).

Trustees

Each directory and file on a file server has a *trustee list*, which specifies the users who can use that storage area. The rights granted to a trustee, by whatever method, dictate the kind of access the trustee is allowed to have. A user or group of users can be trustees of multiple directories and files, but the rights they have in each may be different. Thus, for example, SALES user group may be a trustee of the Accounts directory, but their access rights may be limited to R(ead) and F(ile Scan). This would allow members of that group to view, for example, customer details and amounts owing, but not modify them or erase them. The SALES group may also be trustee of the Orders directory, with the additional rights of C(reate), W(rite) and E(rase). Each member of the user group, would also be a member in

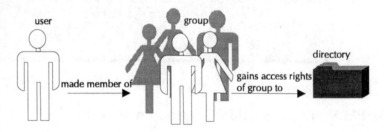

Figure 13.7. *Assigned rights through group membership*

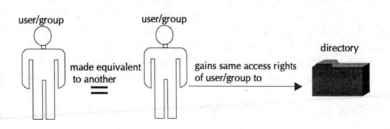

Figure 13.8. *Assigned rights by user/group equivalence*

his or her own right, and have full rights, within their default data directory.

Figure 13.9 shows a directory's trustee list, together with the access rights of each trustee. The letters in the Rights column are the initial letters of the access rights detailed in Table 13.1.

Trustee List	
Trustee	Rights
Artists	[RWCEFMA]
Marketing	[R F]
Peter	[WCE]
Pablo	[RWCEFMA]

Figure 13.9. *A trustee list*

Creating users with SYSCON (system console)

The Novell Netware operating system provides a utility called SYSCON, primarily for use by the network administrator. The opening screen appears as shown in Figure 13.10.

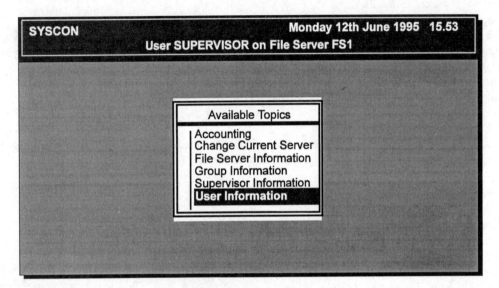

Figure 13.10. *SYSCON utility main menu*

SUPERVISOR user and workgroup managers

SYSCON and other utilities, such as FILER (for network storage management) are held in a Private directory, which is not visible to users generally. The network administrator is a special user, referred to in Novell Netware as SUPERVISOR, who has access to all the network utilities. The network administrator can make the SYSCON utility available to a Workgroup Manager, who is another special type of Novell user. A Workgroup Manager can create users or groups and manage their accounts, but does not replace the SUPERVISOR user, who still has full rights to manage all user accounts. Existing users and groups cannot be controlled by a Workgroup Manager, unless he or she has been given User Account Manager status by the SUPERVISOR user. The User Account Manager status will only apply to the users and groups assigned by the SUPERVISOR user. For security reasons, a Workgroup Manager is only given S(upervisory) rights in a specific volume or directory, enabling him or her to assign trustee rights to the users in that area only. For example, a Workgroup Manager may have control over the Design directory.

Setting account restrictions

Two options are of particular importance in controlling a users access to the network: *account restrictions*; *change password*. Each user account includes properties which place limits on the user's initial access to the network (during login). Login security is supported through:

- the allocation of a user name;

- the requirement for a password of minimum length; the settings may also require, for example, periodic password change. A user can be allowed or prevented from making their own password changes;

- the restriction of times during which a user can login.

A *change password* option allows the Supervisor to initially set and subsequently alter a user's password. By setting default account restrictions, from the Supervisor options menu, all users can be controlled by basic settings. If special controls are required for individual users, then this can be done separately.

Enabling file sharing

There may be occasions when a user wishes to make their own files available to another user or user group. This can be achieved by making the user or user group a *trustee* of the relevant directory. Normally, a user has all rights in their own directory. To make another user, or group, a trustee of that directory requires use of the A(ccess Control) right. This can be achieved with the GRANT command (at the command line prompt). The format of the command is as shown below.

```
GRANT rightslist . . . [FOR path] TO [USER | GROUP] name
```

The word ALL can follow GRANT, if all rights held by the directory owner (users cannot assign rights they do not have) are to be assigned to the trustee user or group. If the command is being issued from the user's default directory, no *path* needs to be specified. An example command is shown below.

```
GRANT r w c e m TO USER gianna
```

The REVOKE command can be used to remove Gianna's trustee rights, as shown below (specific rights may be listed if some are to remain).

```
REVOKE ALL FROM USER gianna
```

User identification

Before allowing login, the network operating system requires identification of the user, through entry of the user name and password. An organization can set standards concerning both. These standards will be implemented through user account restrictions, which allow the setting of:

- user name formats; standards could determine a strict format for the assignment of user names. For example, each user name may have to begin with a 3 character code, which identifies their department;

- a minimum password length. The organization may set a standard minimum length and this can be enforced through the network user's account. The longer the password, the less likely it is that others will guess it, or identify it from watching the keys that the user presses;

- requirement for a periodic password change or a unique password (can only be used once). The organization may require each user to renew his or her password every week. Infrequent changes increase the likelihood that passwords will not remain secret. Unique (once only) passwords are appropriate for users who only have occasional need to access the network. Each occasion is specially authorized though the assignment of a unique password;

- login restricted to certain days or times of day; if the network remains active after normal office hours, for a restricted group of users, other users can be excluded by placing time limits on their accounts;

- number of grace logins after expiry of the users password; a user may be allowed, say, three logins after password expiry and if the password is not renewed within that period, the user is locked out. Reference then has to be made to the network supervisor to regain entry. The organization's standards may require that such circumstances are reported to, for example, the relevant Head of Department, before the user account is unlocked.

Exercises

1. Briefly describe two functions of an *operating system*.

2. What is meant by *dynamic resource allocation*?

3. When jobs are *scheduled* in a batch multi-programming system, what factors regarding each job can be used to determine each job's priority in the schedule?

4. Distinguish between the *high-level scheduler* and the *low-level scheduler*, or *dispatcher*.

5. Under what circumstances is the dispatcher invoked?

6. (i)   Define the term *time-sharing*;

    (ii)   Briefly describe two methods of allocating the processor in a time-sharing environment.

7. Distinguish between a *multi-tasking* and a *multi-user* operating system.

8. Suggest why the *graphical user interface* (GUI) has virtually eclipsed the *command line interpreter* (CLI) as a means of communication between the user and the operating system.

9. (i)   Define the term *interrupt*.

    (ii)   Identify four *events* which may trigger an interrupt.

10. Why are dynamic *memory partitions* and *relocatable code* essential to a multi-programming operating system?

11. With reference to the MS-DOS operating system, what is a *batch file*?

12. Define the term *pre-emptive multi-tasking*.

13. Identify the various methods used by a network operating system, such as Novell Netware, to *control access* to network resources.

Chapter 14
Input/Output Control

Figure 14.1 illustrates the *architecture* of the communication system which allows data transfers between the various elements of a computer system. This chapter examines the various methods of implementing and controlling input/output (I/O) operations. Some well-known I/O interface standards are also examined. One major problem for I/O control concerns the speed imbalance between the operation of the processor and communicating peripheral devices; various techniques used to compensate for such imbalance are described.

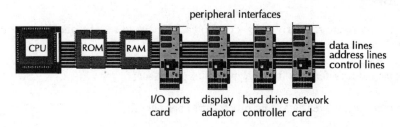

Figure 14.1. *Computer communication architecture*

A number of components can be identified:

- *Bus* or *highway*. A bus consists of a number of wires, one for each bit making up the unit of data transfer. A common I/O bus connects all I/O peripherals to the processor, so only one peripheral can use the bus at a time. This is not normally a restriction because the processor can only handle one instruction at a time, but most computers have an I/O bus which is independent of that used for processor/main memory transfers. Those machines using a common bus for I/O and processor/memory data movements are referred to as single bus systems;

- *Interface*. This is a hardware device containing electronic components, which connects an I/O peripheral to the computer. The chapter on Data Representation describes the use of internal and external codes for internal computer and external peripheral operations respectively; one of the functions of an interface is to carry out the conversion process between the two codes, according to whether data is being transferred to or from the peripheral;

- *Device controller*. This device is fundamentally the same as the interface, except that it is associated with the control of data transfers to and from storage devices, such as magnetic disk and tape drives.

Methods of I/O control

The transfer of data to and from a peripheral device can take place either:

- under the control of the host machine's processor; this is *programmed input/output* or *PIO*;

- or, under the autonomous control of the device; most commonly, this is *direct memory access* or *DMA*.

Programmed input/output (PIO)

Most microcomputers still use PIO for the control of data transfers. This means, for example, that the computer's processor controls each stage of data transfer between the system's hard disk drive and itself. PIO can be effected in one of two ways: *software polling*; *hardware interrupts*.

Software polling

The operating system software regularly *polls* (checks) each device to see if it requires attention. To achieve I/O transfers by this method, instructions are needed:

- for *input* - to transfer data from peripheral to processor;

- for *output* - to transfer data from processor to peripheral;

- to *set* individual control flags in the I/O interface unit;

- to *test* individual flags in the I/O interface unit.

A peripheral device is attached to an interface unit by a cable. The interface unit (usually inside the computer) is connected to one of a number of I/O slots, each of which has a fixed address, by which a peripheral can be identified for input or output. There are 3 basic elements in an interface unit which is polled by software:

- a control bit or *busy* flag - used to signal a device to start input or output. This cannot be set by the device as it is under control of the processor;

- a flag bit or *done* flag - this is set by the device when the data transfer is complete and can be tested or cleared by program instructions;

- a *buffer register* for the storage of data transferred into (read by) or to be transferred from (written by) the device.

When a 'start read' instruction is given, one character is transferred between the interface buffer register and the device. A single character is transferred in the opposite direction if a 'start write' instruction is given. A processor instruction commands the device to operate by setting the busy flag and then repeatedly tests the done flag to discover when the transfer is complete. The major difficulty with software polling is that the repeated testing of the done flag is carried out at the same time as it continues with some other computation. This means that the program instructions currently being executed (probably the program that issued the I/O instruction) must be interleaved with the regular issue of instructions to test for completion of the transfer. The last operating system to use software polling was CP/M (Control Program/Microcomputer) which was used on some early microcomputer systems, but is now obsolete. An example instruction sequence for software polling may be as follows:

For *input* from a specific device:

- instruction to interface to set the busy flag for 'start transmit';

- send instruction to test done flag. If the flag indicates that the transfer is complete, skip next instruction;

- branch to previous instruction;

- issue instruction to transfer character from buffer register into processor accumulator;

- issue store instruction to transfer character from accumulator to main memory.

For *output* to a specific device:

- issue instruction to transfer character from processor accumulator into buffer register of interface device;

- issue instruction to set busy flag to start transfer;

- issue instruction to test done flag and if set, skip the next instruction;

- branch to previous instruction.

The repetitive flag-test loop is necessary to ensure that a character transfer is completed before the next one is transmitted. A more efficient method of PIO control is to use hardware interrupts.

I/O using hardware interrupts

An I/O interrupt is a signal from an I/O device to the processor to indicate that:

- data is waiting to be read;

- an I/O error has occurred;

- a previous I/O transfer is complete.

To enable I/O devices to initiate requests for service from the processor, an I/O bus includes interrupt request (IRQ) lines, typically 15. All the IRQ lines go to every expansion slot in the I/O bus, so when a device adapter card (for example, a disk drive controller) is plugged into a slot, the specific IRQ line it is to use can then be set, by configuring the card, either through utility software or by physical switches on the card. The device then uses that IRQ line to signal the processor that it requires service. A processor has only one interrupt pin, which is set when an I/O interrupt occurs, to indicate the presence of an interrupt, but not its source. An interrupt handler routine (part of the operating system software) is executed when an interrupt is detected, to establish its source. On a typical microcomputer, interrupts are used by the keyboard, mouse, disk and the COM ports.

Establishing the source of an interrupt

The source of the interrupt is determined by checking each IRQ line to see if it has been set. If more than one device has set its IRQ line, the handler routine will select the one with the highest priority. Once the source has been identified, the interrupt handler calls the relevant *interrupt service routine*. Following completion of the service, control of the processor must be returned to the original process. The checking of the processor's single I/O interrupt register is carried out at the start of each instruction, as part of the fetch-execute cycle.

Executing the interrupt

Before entry to the relevant interrupt service routine, the current state of the machine must be saved. This includes storing the state of the current process and the contents of the Program Counter (PC) in a separate location; the PC value is then replaced by the starting address of the interrupt service routine and the routine is executed. Once the interrupt has been serviced, control of the processor must be returned to the appropriate point in the original program by copying its stored continuation address back into the PC. An interrupt-on/off flag in the processor must be set to off prior to acceptance of an interrupt and then cleared to on as soon as control has been returned to the original program, in order to prevent an interrupt from another device being accepted until the original program has resumed control.

Interrupt priority

Interrupts may emanate from a variety of sources (I/O and others) and for a number of different reasons (Chapter 13 Operating Systems); the operating system can be used to allocate different priority ratings to particular events and devices.

Nested interrupts

Some systems may leave the interrupt mechanism enabled so that an interrupt service routine may itself be interrupted by a higher priority request; this may happen repeatedly, requiring the nesting of interrupts. A LIFO (Last In First Out) stack (Chapter 32 Data Structures) can be used to store the return addresses and accumulator contents relating to these nested interrupts so that they can be retrieved in reverse order. If a higher priority interrupt occurs during I/O there is a danger of data being lost. Each peripheral is allocated a given priority rating which must be compared with that of the current process, before the interrupt routine is entered. As a general rule, low speed devices are given high priority, because frequent interruptions to relatively slow data input may result in there being insufficient data to continue processing. Where the interrupting peripheral has a priority rating lower than or equal to that of the current activity, it is kept waiting; otherwise the interrupt takes place.

Masking device interrupts

Where the interrupt mechanism is left enabled, it may be desirable to selectively mask out certain low priority devices from that facility. This can be achieved by using a register as an interrupt mask (Table 14.1), with bit positions corresponding to individual devices in the interrupt request register; devices are masked out by setting the relevant bits in the mask to 0 and carrying out a logical AND operation between the mask and the interrupt request register.

	interrupt request register						
device	1	2	3	4	5	6	
interrupt status	1	0	1	1	0	1	AND
interrupt mask	1	0	0	0	0	1	
device	1	2	3	4	5	6	
interrupt status	1	0	0	0	0	1	

Table 14.1. *Masking device interrupts*

With the current mask settings, only devices 1 and 6 are allowed to request interrupts.

A number of other system conditions, some with higher priority than I/O requests, may generate interrupts and these are examined in Chapter 13 on Operating Systems.

Direct memory access (DMA)

Not all data transfers between peripheral devices and the processor are carried out under continual program control (programmed input/output or PIO). Other schemes such as DMA allow data transfer to or from high speed storage devices such as tape or disk to be effected without continual processor control. Data is transferred in blocks, as opposed to character by character. DMA is possible because of the ability of peripheral devices to operate autonomously, that is, after the initial input or output instruction has been given by the processor, the peripheral is able to complete the data transfer independently. To allow the memory to be accessed directly by a peripheral, instead of via the processor, hardware known as a DMA controller is needed. For transfers from main memory to peripheral, the processor supplies the DMA controller with the start address in memory of the data block to be transferred and its length. A transfer from, for example, a disk pack to memory would require the processor to tell the DMA controller the relevant disk address and into which memory locations the data is to be copied. The DMA controller 'steals' memory cycles from the processor while the data transfer is taking place. Meanwhile, the processor can continue execution of its current program, although its operation is slowed slightly by the cycle stealing. DMA is not as quick as PIO, but is an essential component to any computer system working in multi-programming mode.

I/O interface standards

Centronics parallel interface

This interface has become a world-wide standard for parallel data transmission between computers and peripherals. It was originally developed by the American printer manufacturer Centronics, Inc. The Centronics parallel interface includes eight parallel data lines and additional lines for control and status information. The eight data lines are the minimum required for transmission of one complete character at a time; an ASCII coded character consists of 8 bits (including the parity bit). The control and status lines are needed for the 'conversation' between the device and the computer. For example, when a printer is on-line it sends a ready signal to the computer and when the computer is ready to send a character, it initializes the printer, which clears the printer's buffer memory. A character printer (ink jet or dot matrix, for example) has a small amount of memory called buffer memory, which it uses to temporarily store a line of characters, before they are printed. Laser printers, which print a complete page at a time, need sufficient buffer memory to store all the data (both text and graphics) on a page, before the page is printed. The signals and processes that enable printing through a Centronics interface are, briefly, as follow.

- Once the printer is on-line, it sends a ready signal to the computer.

- The computer sends a response, which initializes the printer; this has the effect of alerting the printer and clearing its small buffer memory.

- After the printer is initialized, the computer places the data bits (8), for the first character to be printed, on the data lines.

- The computer sends a strobe signal, which sends the 8 data bits, in parallel, to the printer's buffer memory.

- Once the data is received by the printer, it is acknowledged with an acknowledge signal to the computer.

The process continues, until the computer has no more characters to send. The printer may, at times, send a busy signal, if it is not ready for the next character; the computer then has to wait for the all clear, before sending the next character. A printer may also interrupt the process, if, for example, it is out of paper.

SCSI and IDE interfaces

SCSI (pronounced 'scusi') stands for Small Computer Systems Interface. It is a high speed, parallel interface (or device controller) standard, defined by ANSI (see Standards Authorities in Chapter 11). SCSI interfaces are widely available for connecting microcomputers to a range of peripheral devices, including hard disks and printers; SCSI interfaces are also used for connecting computers to one another, and to local area networks (Chapter 10). Separate ports (a port is a location for passing data in or out of a computer) do not have to be used for each attached device. Instead one device can be connected directly to a SCSI port in the computer and other devices (a maximum total of seven) can be linked to the first, in a "daisy chain". Only one device can communicate through the SCSI port at any one time, so each device in a chain is given a separate logical address, which indicates its priority. The device with the highest address is given top priority. Macintosh computers and some computers in the IBM range include an SCSI port as standard. IBM PCs and 'compatibles' could be upgraded to include an SCSI port, with the use of an expansion card. The SCSI interface was of particular value for the attachment of high speed devices, such as hard disk drives, because it allowed more rapid data transfer than was the norm for the IDE (Industry Device Electronics) based hard drives, used in most PCs. The IDE interface has become most popular with PCs (formerly referred to as IBM compatibles) because it is cheaper and easier to install than the SCSI interface. IDE performance has now been increased to that of a SCSI interface. A newer standard, the Enhanced IDE now provides superior *transfer rates* (Chapter 9) to those of SCSI.

Serial interfaces

Serial interfaces are used for the connection of modems, terminals and printers. Physically, they are recognizable by the shape of the plug and socket, which are D-shaped. The most common are the 9-pin and 25-pin.

RS232 and V24 serial interfaces

Both these standards (Chapter 11) relate to an interface for serial transmission between a computer or terminal and a modem. RS232 is a Recommended Standard (RS) of the American Electrical Industries Association (EIA). There have been 4 versions of this standard, the most recent being the RS232D (sometimes known as EIA 232D), although the previous version, RS232C is still the most widely used. The main purpose of the revision was to bring it into line with V24, which is the CCITT's equivalent of the RS232C. The V24 standard does not define the physical characteristics of the connection (the RS232 standard does), but only the characteristics of the control signals (see Flow Control) and how they are to be used; the V24 standard is usually used with the 25-pin D-connector. This connector is defined by the International Standards Organization (ISO - see Chapter 11).

Other I/O techniques

Off-lining

Early computer systems used punched cards as the initial form of input and to speed processing a technique of off-lining was introduced. Data would be transferred from punched cards to magnetic tape under control of a separate processor. The operator could then place the magnetic tape file on-line, from where it could be accessed and processed by the application program. The hugely superior data transfer rate of magnetic tape radically improved processing times and went some way to countering the speed imbalance between the input device and the processor. The same technique was also applied to printed output, which could be directed to magnetic tape and then printed from there under control of a separate processor.

Buffering

Buffering is a technique which helps compensate for the speed differences between the processor and the various input and output devices which communicate with it. To speed processing, many computer systems contain special high-speed memory areas called buffers. An input buffer acts as a waiting area within memory for a block of data transferred from a peripheral; from there it can be quickly accessed and processed by the processor. An output buffer stores data which has been processed by the processor and is awaiting output. Most peripherals have the facility for autonomous operation, leaving the processor free for other tasks; buffering and the use of autonomous peripherals allows the simultaneous operation of several of the latter.

Double buffering

In the case of storage devices, double-buffering makes use of two buffers which work in 'tandem' to speed processing. If the records are blocked the systems software initially places the first block into buffer 1 and the second into buffer 2. Read instructions from the applications program retrieve the data from these buffers. The processor can retrieve logical records faster from the buffer than from tape. As soon as all logical records from buffer 1 have been processed, the reading process transfers to the logical records in buffer 2. Meanwhile, the next block on tape can be transferred into buffer 1 and so on. The principle is also used with peripherals in general, including input and output devices, to help redress the radical imbalance between the processor's speed and that of the device with which it is communicating. This imbalance is less significant in respect of storage devices, which have significantly faster data transfer rates than most input and output devices, particularly where direct memory access (DMA) - see earlier section, is employed.

Spooling (simultaneous peripheral operation on-line)

This is a development of the off-lining technique described earlier and is used to speed data throughput. Multi-programming (Chapter 13 Operating Systems) allows data to be transferred from slow peripherals to fast backing storage devices as a background process. The process is facilitated by autonomous peripherals which can carry out data transfers independently of the processor after it has initiated the read or write instruction.

Multiplexing

Multiplexing is a technique which enables inputs from several devices to be directed through one channel to a computer; the reverse process is known as de-multiplexing. A multiplexer normally has the facilities to carry out both operations. Figure 14.2 illustrates its principal function.

Asynchronous terminal multiplexer

Any multi-terminal computer system will include a local multiplexer to allow a number of terminals to use one interface to the computer. Apart from the benefit of removing the need for numerous separate physical interfaces, a multiplexer can support I/O devices with different data transfer rates.

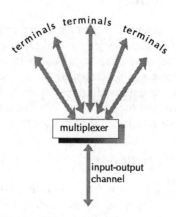

A multiplexer has buffer registers for the temporary storage of characters before onward transmission, either to or from a connected device. In order to identify individual terminals, each one is given an individual address within the common interface. A multiplexer's operation is based on the realistic assumption that the data transfer rates from the various terminals will be well within the capacity of the computer's I/O interface. Typically, a single local multiplexer will support 16 terminals; even if, for example, each asynchronous (characters are sent at irregular intervals) terminal is transmitting continuously, with a transfer rate of 2400 bits per second (bps), then the resulting 38400 bps from the multiplexer to the interface would

Figure 14.2. *Multiplexed terminals*

be well within the capacity of a typical minicomputer's bus transfer rate of one million bps. In practice, it is unlikely that all terminals would be transmitting continuously at that rate.

In order to give attention to each of the transmitting terminals, the multiplexer may address each terminal in a round robin polling sequence. Each terminal is checked to see if there is a character waiting in its buffer and if there is, the character plus the terminal's line number are removed. Once an input character from a particular terminal has been dealt with, the multiplexer checks to see if there is a character to be output to that same terminal and if so the character is fetched from memory and output. The multiplexer then directs its attention to the next terminal in the sequence and repeats the process. The scanning process is implemented by hardware and is, therefore, very quick. Multiplexers can also operate synchronously, that is, transfer characters at a regularly-timed frequency. The topic of remote multiplexing is dealt with in Chapter 11 on Data Communications.

Exercises

1.   Distinguish between the terms *programmed input/output* (PIO) and *direct memory access* (DMA).

2.   What is the main disadvantage of *software polling* to control input/output?

3.   What is the function of an *IRQ line*?

4.   Define the following terms: *spooling*; *buffering*.

5.   What is the function of an *asynchronous terminal multiplexer*?

Chapter 15
Computer Files

This chapter deals with the ways in which computer files are stored, organized and processed.

Files, records and fields

In data processing, it is necessary to store information on particular subjects, for example, customers, suppliers or personnel and such information needs to be structured so that it is readily controllable and accessible to the user. In traditional data processing systems, each of these 'topics' of information is allocated a file. Figure 15.1 illustrates the structure of a book file.

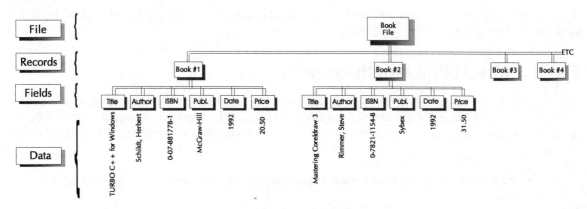

Figure 15.1. *File structure*

The *file* is a collection of *records*, one for each book. Each record contains details of the book's title, its author(s), ISBN number, publisher, date of publication and cost; each of these *data items* is allocated physical space, known as a *field*, within the record. Figure 15.1 shows a sample record, with the Title field (each one is identified by its *field name)* containing the value 'Turbo C++ for Windows' and the other fields containing values associated with that book.

Types of file

Files can be categorized by the ways in which they are used and there are generally recognized to be four such categories.

Master files

They are used for the storage of *permanent*, or *semi-permanent*, data which is used in applications such as stock, sales or payroll. Some of the fields tend to contain data which is fairly static, for example, customer name and address, whilst data in some fields is continually changing, for example, customer balance, as transactions are applied to the file. Such *updating* is carried out, either through the direct entry (on-line) of individual transactions, or from an accumulated set of entries stored on a *transaction* file.

Transaction files

These are transient and only exist to allow the updating of master files. Each transaction record contains the *key field value* of the master record it is to update (to allow correct matching with its relevant master record), together with data gathered from source documents, for example, invoice amounts which update the balance field in customer accounts.

Reference files

These contain data used for reference or look-up purposes, such as price catalogue and customer name and address files.

Archival or historical files

These contain data which, for legal or organizational reasons, must be kept and tend to be used on an ad hoc basis and may be referred to only occasionally.

Fixed and variable length records

The extent to which the information in a particular file can be standardized and categorized will determine whether each record in the file can be fixed or variable in length. The length of the record is the number of character positions allocated to it within the file. In Figure 15.1 the file would probably contain *fixed* length records because:

- the number and types of data items required in this case are likely to be the same for each book;

- the number of character positions for each field can be fixed or at least set to a maximum. For example, the ISBN is fixed at 13 character positions and Title could be set to a maximum of 30, provided that no book title exceeded this length.

Variable length records may be used in files which have storage requirements markedly different from those referred to above, for instance:

- some records could have more fields than others. In a personnel file, for example, each record may contain details of previous jobs held and as the number of previous jobs may vary considerably from one employee to another, so the number of fields would be similarly varied;

    or

- the number of character positions used for individual values within a field is variable. For example, in a library system each record may contain a field for data which describes the subject of the book and the amount of text needed to adequately describe this may vary from book to book.

Listed below are some of the advantages of *fixed length* records.

- Fixed length records are simpler to process, in that the start and end points of each record can be readily identified by the number of character positions. For instance, if a record has a fixed length of 80 character positions, a program reading the file from the start will assume that the second record starts at the 81st character position, the third at the 161st character position and so on, making easier the programming of file handling operations.

- Fixed length records allow an accurate estimation of file storage requirements. For example, a file containing 1000 records, each of fixed 80 characters length, will take approximately 80000 characters of storage.

- Where direct access files are being used, fixed length records can be readily updated 'in situ' (in other words the updated record overwrites the old version in the same position on the storage medium). As the new version will have the same number of characters as the old, any changes to a record will not change its physical length. On the other hand, a variable length record may increase in length after updating, preventing its return to its home location.

There are some instances when *variable* length records are more appropriate. For example:

- where records in a file contain highly variable quantities of information, variable length records may be more economical of storage space;

- when the saving in storage space makes the introduction of more complex file handling techniques worthwhile.

Record identification - primary and secondary keys

In most organizations, when an information system is operational it will be necessary to identify each record uniquely. In a Personnel File, for example, it might be thought that it is possible to identify each individual record simply by the employee's Surname and this would be satisfactory as long as no two employees had the same surname. In reality, many organizations will have several employees with the same surnames, so to ensure uniqueness, each employee is assigned a unique Works Number. The works number field is then used as the primary key in the filing system, each individual having his or her own unique Works Number and so a unique primary key.

There are certain circumstances when the primary key may be a *composite key*, that is, one made up of more than one field and the following example shows how a pair of fields, which individually may not be unique, can be combined to provide a unique identifier.

Table 15.1 shows an extract from a file which details suppliers' quotations for a number of different products. There is a need for a composite key because there may be a number of quotations from one supplier (in this case, SupplierNo 41192) and a number of quotations for the same part (in this instance, PartNo A112). It is necessary, therefore, to use both SupplierNo and PartNo to identify one quotation record uniquely.

SupplierNo	PartNo	Price	DeliveryDate
23783	A361	2.59	31/01/96
37463	B452	1.50	29/01/96
40923	A112	3.29	30/01/96
41192	A112	3.29	28/01/96
41192	C345	2.15	30/01/96

Table 15.1. *Extract from quotation file with composite primary key*

Uniqueness is not always necessary. For example, if it is required to retrieve records which fulfil a criterion, or several criteria, *secondary keys* may be used. Thus, for example, in an information retrieval system on Personnel, the secondary key Department may be used to retrieve the records of all employees who work in, say, the Sales Department.

File storage media

This topic is examined more fully in Chapter 9. File storage media may be classified according to the kind of access they provide:

- serial access;

- direct access.

Serial access media

Serial access means that in order to identify and retrieve a particular record, it is necessary to 'read' all the records which precede it in the relevant file. The standard medium for serial access is magnetic tape. One of the difficulties with this medium is that there it has no readily identifiable physical areas which can be addressed. In other words, it is not possible to give a name or code and refer this to a particular location. It is said to be *non-addressable*. To find an individual record, the software needs to examine each record's *key field*, starting from the beginning of the file, until the required record is found.

Direct access media

Storage media such as floppy or hard disks allow *direct* access to individual records, without reference to the rest of the relevant file. They have physical divisions which can be identified by computer software (and sometimes hardware) and are *addressable*, so that particular locations can be referred to by a name or code to retrieve a record which is stored at that location. Retrieval of an individual record stored on such a medium is achieved (depending on the way the file is organized) by specifying the relevant *primary key field value*, thus providing the software with a means of finding and retrieving the specific individual record directly.

File organization methods

Another function of the *primary key* is to provide a value which can be used by computer software to assign a record to a particular position within a file. The file organization method chosen will dictate how individual records are assigned to particular *logical* positions within a file. Serial access media are limited in the file organization methods they permit because they are non-addressable. Direct access media are more versatile in that they allow a variety of file organization methods, in addition to those allowed by serial access media. The different types of file storage media are discussed in some detail in the next section.

Magnetic tape - a serial access medium

Physical and logical records

Because of the physical characteristics of magnetic tape it is necessary, when processing a file, that the tape unit (the device onto which a tape is loaded for processing) starts to read the tape at the beginning of the reel. The take-up spool receives the tape from the feed spool via a read/write head in the unit which can either record information onto or read information from the tape as it passes. As there are no specific physical locations on the tape which can be identified and referred to by the computer (except of course the beginning and end), the only way it can find a particular record is by reading the whole file. Unless the whole tape is to be processed, it may only be necessary to read up to the point where the specific record it is seeking is found. There may well be more than one

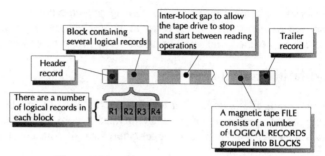

Figure 15.2. *Magnetic tape file organization*

logical file on a tape but these will have to be read in the sequence that they appear on the tape. As the tape is read, the computer will compare the key field value of each record which it comes to, with the specified key value, until the required record is found. Figure 15.2 illustrates the way in which a file is arranged on tape both *logically* and *physically*.

You should note from Figure 15.2 that records R1, R2, R3 and R4 are instances of logical records. For example, if this were a stock file, each logical record would relate to one commodity held in stock. On the other hand each physical record consists, in this illustration, of 4 logical records. The reason for making the distinction between logical and physical records stems from the fact that data is transferred between the computer's internal memory and the tape storage medium in manageable *blocks*, the optimum size of each depending on factors such as the size of the computer's internal memory.

Each physical record is referred to as a block of data. Between each block transfer, the tape has to stop while the previous one is processed by the computer. In order to give the tape time to stop and then restart for the next block, there is an *inter block gap* (IBG), a blank area of tape between each block. It is unlikely that the optimum block size will coincide with the actual length of a single logical record, so it is necessary to transfer a number of logical records between tape and internal memory at one time. Thus, a physical record or block will often consist of a number of logical records.

The example of a stock file is used again to illustrate this point further. Assume that each block contains 3 logical stock records (in other words three individual commodities). If the first record to be processed is stored in the fifth block, then the first four blocks have to be read in sequence into memory and each logical stock record examined for its key field value, without any records actually being used. When the fifth block is eventually read into memory each of the three logical stock records is then examined for its key field value until the required key and thus logical record, is identified.

File organization methods on magnetic tape

There are two ways in which a file can be organized on tape: *serially*; *sequentially*.

This restriction stems from the fact that magnetic tape is a *serial* access medium. As is noted earlier, this means that it has no addressable locations, so records have to be traced by reading the file from beginning to end.

The processing of tape files can only be carried out satisfactorily if they are organized in the sequence of their primary keys. This restriction applies to both master and transaction files. Serial files, which are out of sequence, are only useful as an interim measure, prior to processing.

Generally, when a transaction file is being created on tape, for example, when customer orders are received, they are written to tape in the order in which they are received, thus creating a serial file. Before the master file can be updated, the serial transaction file has to be sorted by the computer to become a sequential file.

Updating the master file

When a tape file is updated, a new master file must be created on a new reel of tape because the tape drive unit cannot guarantee to write an updated record to the exact position from which it was read (it is *non-addressable*). There is a danger, therefore, of adjacent records being corrupted or completely overwritten.

The following procedures are followed during the update (assuming that no new records are to be inserted). For the sake of clarity, some complexities are not mentioned.

- A transaction is read into memory.

- A master record is read into memory. If the record keys do not match, the master record is written, unchanged, to the new reel. Master records continue to be read, examined and written in the original sequence to the new reel until a match for the transaction is found.

- Once the match is found, the master record is updated in main memory and then written to the new reel.

These steps are repeated until all transactions have been processed and the complete updated master file has been written to the new reel. If the transaction files were not sorted into the same sequence as the master file, it would be necessary to rewind the master file whenever a transaction required a master record which had already passed through the system; clearly, this would be both inefficient and impractical. The process is illustrated in the chapter on System Controls.

Magnetic disk - a direct access medium

Addressing magnetic disk

Magnetic disk provides file storage facilities which are more flexible and powerful than those provided by magnetic tape. As an *addressable* medium, the surface of the disk is divided into physical locations which are illustrated in Figure 15.3. The address of any one physical location on a single disk incorporates a *track* number, and within that track, a *sector* number. A sector is the smallest physical area on the disk which can be addressed, each addressable unit being referred to as a *block* or *physical record*. The size of the blocks is normally determined by the systems designer through the use of systems software, although some disk storage systems use *hard sectoring* (the block size cannot be altered). The number of logical records which can be accommodated in a particular block obviously depends upon the physical size of the block and the length of each logical record. The maximum number of logical records which can be fitted into

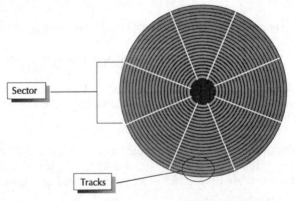

Figure 15.3. *Addressing structure of magnetic disk*

a block is known as the *blocking factor*. Considerations regarding the determination of block size are beyond the scope of this text, but some of the design factors can be readily explained as follows.

Example

If a disk's block size approximates to the storage of 500 characters and a stock file has logical records, each with a fixed length of 110 characters, then the maximum number of records which can be stored in a block is 4. To retrieve one logical stock record requires the software to address the relevant block and retrieve the physical record. This means that it will retrieve all the logical stock records in the block. Therefore, the larger the number of logical records stored in any specific block, the less selective the software can be in retrieving them but the faster the complete file is processed.

Operational features of magnetic disk

Although there are many variations in the capacities and sizes of disk that are available, there are certain physical characteristics which are common to all.

On smaller computer systems disks tend to be handled singly on individual disk drive units. On larger systems a number of disks may be mounted on a central spindle. This is shown in Figure 15.4. To transfer data to or from the disk pack it is necessary to mount it on a disk drive unit which rotates the pack at high speed. Data is recorded magnetically on disk in a similar fashion to the recording on magnetic tape. Special read/write heads are mounted on moveable arms within the disk drive unit in such a way that they move in synchronization across the disk surface. The software positions the heads for the writing or retrieval of records.

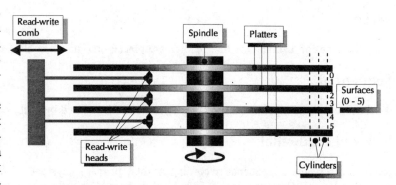

Figure 15.4. *Disk pack illustrating cylinder concept*

Further disk addressing concepts

Cylinders

If the Figures 15.3 and 15.4 are considered together it can be seen that, in a disk pack, a specified track on one disk (track 0) is vertically above other tracks on lower disks which are also specified as track 0. In other words, all the track 0s are in the same vertical plane. Such a grouping is known as a *cylinder* or *seek area*. Similarly, all track 1s form another cylinder, as do track 2s and so on. It can be seen therefore, that there are as many cylinders as there are tracks on each disk surface.

The fastest way of reading or writing records on disks is achieved by minimizing the movement of the read/write arms. This is achieved by positioning associated records, which are likely to be needed as a group (they may form a complete file), into sequence (as a sequential file) on tracks in the same cylinder. Records are written to the disk pack, such that track 0 on surface 1 is filled first, followed by track 0 on surface 2 and so on, until all number 0 tracks are filled (the first cylinder). Then, if the file requires more than one cylinder, adjacent tracks are filled to form further cylinders, until the file is complete.

When access is required to the file it is quickest, in terms of keeping read/write head movement to a minimum, to deal with one cylinder of records at a time. Thus, a complete cylinder of records is processed before any head movement is required. A cylinder is also known as a seek area, because all records in a cylinder can be accessed by the read/write heads whilst they are positioned in that cylinder.

Buckets

The minimum amount of data which can be transferred between the backing store of the computer and its internal store is the *block*. However, there are occasions when a larger unit of transfer is required and on such occasions the concept of the *bucket* is used; a number of blocks (up to the maximum of one track) is given the same disk address (this is usually the address of the first block in the bucket) and any logical records held within such a bucket are retrieved when that disk address is used.

File organization methods using magnetic disk

Magnetic disk supports the following file organization methods.

Serial

As is the case for a serial tape file, records are placed onto disk one after another in no particular sequence.

Sequential

As for a sequential tape file, records are stored on disk ordered by each record's primary key.

Indexed sequential

Records are stored in sequence according to their primary keys and an *index* is produced when the file is created, allowing direct retrieval of individual records. The software searches different levels of the index (a *multi-level index*): cylinder index; track index; bucket (or block index), before positioning the read/write heads to retrieve the block containing the required record.

The indexes may be structured as shown in Table 15.2, using a five-digit primary key in the range 00001 to 50000. The table represents an extract only.

Cylinder index		Track index for cylinder 55		Sector/block index for track 3	
cylinder	highest key	track	highest key	sector	highest key
1	00452	1	26000	1	26071
2	00940	2	26063	2	26076
3	01650	3	*26120*	3	26080
.....	.....	4	26185	4	26087
55	*26500*	5	26242	5	26095
56	27015	6	26320	6	26104
.....	.....	7	26426	7	26112
115	50000	8	*26500*	8	*26120*

Table 15.2. *Extract from multi-level index*

The indexes are constructed as the records are written sequentially (according to the primary key) to the disk pack. As each sector is filled, the primary key of the last record to be placed in the sector (the highest key) is recorded in the *sector index* and once all sectors in a track have been filled, the last key to be entered is added to the *track index*, the completion of a cylinder causing the highest key field in it to be recorded in the *cylinder index*. This process is repeated with subsequent cylinders until the file is complete.

The retrieval of records requires a *serial search* to be made of the cylinder, track and sector indexes respectively, unless a complete track is to be read, in which case the sector index is not used. Referring to the Table 15.2, suppose that the record with primary key 26085 is required; the indexes may be used as follows:

- a serial search of the cylinder index is made until a highest key entry is found which is equal to or greater than the required key. The entry which meets this requirement is 26500, indicating that a search of the track index for cylinder 55 is needed;

- a serial search of that track index, again looking for an entry greater than or equal to record key 26085, reveals that the record is to be found in track 3, where the highest key field is 26120;

- searching the sector index for track 3 returns the entry of 26087, the highest key field entry for sector 4.

Unless record 26085 has been placed in an *overflow area*, owing to a full sector, it can be retrieved by reading in the block of data occupying the address - sector 4, track 3, cylinder 55.

The cylinder index for a given file will normally be read into main memory when the file is first opened and held there until processing is complete. Each track index is normally held in the cylinder to which it relates and will be read into main memory as required. Similarly, the sector index is usually held within its relevant track.

The preceding procedures and mechanisms only illustrate the main principles of index construction and usage, as the detail is likely to vary considerably from one system to another. To facilitate updating, space will normally be left in sectors, tracks and cylinders to allow for the insertion of new records.

This method allows the efficient sequential processing of the file as well as direct retrieval of records using the indexes. Indexes can become quite large and the file may need to be re-organized periodically so that new records can be inserted in the correct sequence. Records which are marked for deletion need to be removed from the file and the indexes then have to be reconstructed. The frequency with which such re-organization is necessary depends on the level of file activity and the number of insertions and deletions. File re-organization is a *house-keeping* activity.

Overflow

Where new records, or variable length records which have been extended by updating, cannot be inserted into their correct sequenced positions, they are assigned to overflow areas.

Local overflow areas include any located within the same cylinder as their associated home locations; thus, local overflow areas may be located within each track or sector of a cylinder, or at the end of the cylinder. These overflow areas have the advantage that access to them requires no head movement and therefore, no increase in seek time.

Global overflow areas may be formed from a separate cylinder or cylinders and will tend to be used when local overflow areas are full. The main disadvantage is that access to an overflow record requires additional head movement.

A file may use either local or global overflow areas, or a combination of the two; the use of global overflow only, tends to be less wasteful of space but with the disadvantage that the retrieval of any overflow record will require additional head movement.

If frequent reference is required to overflow records, *performance degradation* (a worsening of the system's response times) is likely to be noted by users and file re-organization will be beneficial.

Random organization

This is a method which is impractical in any non-computerized situation. However, in a computerized system it is feasible to place records onto disk at random. The procedure for placing specific records in a particular position on disk may simply relate the primary key *directly* to its disk address, for example,

> *disk address = primary key*
> *disk address = primary key + index value*

With *absolute* and *indexed addressing*, each record has a unique address and can be retrieved directly with its own primary key. A major disadvantage of this method is its orientation towards the needs of the computer; the values needed for disk addressing may well be inappropriate for use as meaningful (to the user) primary keys for logical records. Further, the unique link between a disk address and a particular logical record means that any vacated space cannot be used by another record unless it adopts the same key as the previous occupant record.

Hashing algorithms

A more usual method of addressing uses a mathematical formula called a *hashing algorithm*, which generates a disk address from the record's primary key. The hashing algorithm operates on the primary keys within a given range to produce pseudo-random numbers which may then be used as bucket addresses, to which the logical records are allocated. Each pseudo-random number could refer to an address where a single record is stored, but it is more economical for it to refer to an area where a group of records is stored; thus a *bucket address* will normally contain a number of logical records.

Overflow

An uneven distribution of records means that some buckets overflow and cannot accommodate all the logical records allocated to them, whilst others remain empty or are seriously under-used. Excessive overflow slows the access time for any record which cannot be allocated to its home address. To achieve a reasonably even spread, the selection of a particular algorithm requires consideration of the following factors:

- the pattern and range of the primary keys within the file;

- the size of each bucket and the number available;

- the *packing density* required (number of records, divided by the total record capacity of the available buckets).

The topics of bucket size and packing density are dealt with in more detail in the section on overflow handling.

Example algorithm

Prime number division. The primary key is divided by the largest prime number which is less than the number of available buckets. The remainder of this calculation is taken as the *relative* bucket number, that is, the number of buckets after the first. For example:

> *available buckets 2000*
> *prime number 1999*
> *primary key 22316*
> *22316/1999 = 11 remainder 327*

The relative bucket number is thus 327.

The same mathematical formula is used to subsequently retrieve records, which is ideal in situations where random enquiries are the norm and there is little need for sequential processing. Randomly organized files can be processed sequentially but with less efficiency than sequentially organized files. An advantage of this method is the lack of large indexes which tend to take up considerable storage space on the disk.

The aim of any randomizing or hashing algorithm is to achieve an even distribution of records over the disk space allocated to a file. Most random files allow more than one logical record to occupy a single bucket, as any given algorithm will normally generate the same disk address from several different primary keys; conversely, any hashing algorithm is likely to leave some buckets with no allocated records. Any record which is stored in the address allocated to it by an algorithm is referred to as a *home record*.

Synonyms and collisions

If an address can only hold one record, the first one to be allocated to it, then subsequent records have to be stored elsewhere; such records are referred to as *synonyms* and the circumstances causing their re-allocation, as *collisions*. Synonyms increase access times for affected records, so one aim of an algorithm is to minimize their occurrence. Other factors to be considered by the file designer include, *bucket size* and *packing density* (see previous section). A large bucket size (the maximum is one track) will obviously reduce the number of synonyms, but at the cost of reduced precision in the retrieval of individual logical records. It is fairly unlikely that, in a random file, more than one logical record from the same bucket will be required at the same time, so a number of records are read unnecessarily. In deciding on the packing density (the percentage of the file space occupied) for any particular file, the designer has to consider the *volatility* or activity of the file. It is generally recognized that 50 per cent is probably the minimum packing density and is appropriate only for highly volatile files where a large number of record additions is likely; most files are designed to be 75 to 80 per cent packed when they are set up. A low packing density will further reduce the likelihood of synonyms, but at a cost of increased storage space.

Overflow handling techniques

As can be seen from the previous sections, overflow is a problem encountered with both indexed sequential and random files. There are three methods of tracking the location of overflow records: progressive overflow; chaining; tagging.

Progressive overflow

This is the most simplistic method, in that synonyms are placed in the next available bucket following their home bucket; there are no pointers from home buckets to the appropriate overflow locations. Retrieval of an overflow record requires a serial search of buckets following the home bucket, such simplicity bringing the disadvantage that a request for a non-existent record would not be rejected until the whole file had been searched. Further, if a record is deleted from its home area, a search has to be made to discover if any synonyms of that record exist and if one is found, it must be placed in the vacant home area; if this is not done, and the area is left vacant, it will appear that no synonyms for that address exist.

Chaining

A chain is a data structure which enables items to be accessed by a series of *pointers* leading from the first in the chain, to the second, to the third and so on until the last one is reached. A *link field* in each chained record provides the necessary pointer. Thus, once a bucket is full, the last record to be placed in it is chained to the next record to be assigned to that bucket - the first synonym; each subsequent synonym is linked to its predecessor. Chained overflow records may be held in a separate overflow area, or more efficiently, in the next available bucket. This method combines the benefits of progressive overflow with those of chaining. The main disadvantages of progressive overflow, described in the previous paragraph, are thus removed.

Greater efficiency can be obtained by ensuring that chain lengths are kept to a minimum; this can be effected by moving synonyms into home buckets as and when vacancies occur through deletions. Figure 15.5 illustrates the chaining technique. Removing and adding synonyms to a chain requires the adjustment of pointers, a process described in Chapter 32 on Data Structures.

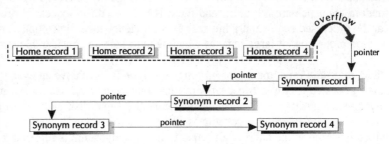

Figure 15.5. *Chained overflow*

Tagging

This method ensures that each synonym can be accessed directly after reference to its home bucket, the address of each overflow record being directly referenced or tagged from its home bucket. The technique is illustrated in the Figure 15.6.

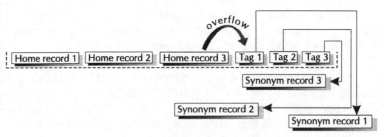

Figure 15.6. *Tagged overflow*

The maintenance of tags in home buckets takes up space, so the number of synonyms should be kept to a minimum. Performance degradation is likely to be minimized with tagging, the most effective of the overflow tracing techniques.

Accessing disk files

Serial files

As with magnetic tape, the only way to retrieve records is serially, in other words, one after another.

Sequential files

The addressing features of disk are not used and the method is the same as that for sequential tape files.

Indexed sequential files

There are 3 methods of retrieving such records:

- *sequentially*. Transactions are sorted into the same sequence as the master file. This is suitable when a large proportion of the records in the file are to be processed in one run, that is, when the *hit rate* (the percentage of master records in a file, for which there are transactions) is high. Minimal use is made of the index. The cylinder index and track index may be searched, then the whole track is read into memory, sector by sector, without reference to the sector index;

- *selective* or *skip sequentially*. When records are sequentially organized by key, not every record need be read when scanning the file. The transactions are sorted into master file sequence and the indexes are used, so that only those blocks containing master records for which there is a transaction are read into memory. This is suitable when the hit rate is low;

- *randomly*. Transactions are not sorted. They are processed in the order in which they occur, the indexes being used to find the relevant master records as they are required. The read/write heads have to move back and forth through the file and so head movement is greater than with sequential methods of processing. This method is appropriate when records are updated immediately after the transaction occurs or, for example, when there is a need for random enquiries of a stock file.

Random files

Transactions or enquiries need not be in any logical sequence. Records are retrieved by generating the physical address from the record key. The software uses the same hashing algorithm it used to assign the record to its address in the first place.

Choice of file organization method and storage medium

Choice should be based on the type and purpose of the system to be used. For example, an on-line enquiry system or stock control system needing frequent, rapid, direct access to individual records within large files will best be served by a randomly organized file, using hash addressing. Very large files, of an archival nature are probably best held off-line on magnetic tape; the medium's lack of an addressing facility would necessitate such files being maintained sequentially. It may be reasonable to hold sections of such archival data, those which are most in demand, on magnetic disk and organized as indexed sequential files. An illustration of this is provided by the Police National Computer system, which holds more recent data on magnetic disk, with older files held on magnetic tape. Systems which do not require direct access, for example, monthly payroll files, can be efficiently stored and processed on magnetic tape and even if the computer system only has disk storage, sequential organization is still likely to be the chosen method. Applications which require both sequential and direct access are generally best served by indexed sequential files.

Typically, the only files which are held serially, are temporary files, such as transaction files prior to sorting for a sequential update run.

Exercises

1.   Distinguish between *master*, *transaction*, *reference* and *archival* files.

2.   Using a suitable example, illustrate the meaning of the terms: *data*; *field*; *record*; *file*.

3.   With the aid of an example, explain when records are likely to be of *variable*, rather than *fixed* length.

4.   Using examples, distinguish between the terms *primary key* and *secondary key*.

5.   Why are the *logical records* in a sequential file, usually grouped into *blocks*?

6.   Why must a *transaction file*, stored on magnetic tape, be *sorted* before it can update the master file? What will determine its sequence?

7.   Define the term *blocking factor*.

8.   Distinguish between *block* and *bucket*.

9.   (i)   What is a disk *cylinder*?

    (ii)   Why is a *sequential disk file* stored cylinder by cylinder?

10. An indexed sequential file consists of a *multi-level index*, *home* area and *overflow* areas.

    (i)   What *index levels* may exist and what would they contain?

    (ii)   Briefly explain how a *new record* would be *inserted* into this file; your explanation should allow for there being no room for the record in its home location.

    (iii) Apart from new records, under what other circumstances may overflow handling be necessary?

    (iv)   What housekeeping routine would be needed if numerous records had to be placed outside their home areas.

    (v)   Distinguish between *local* and *global overflow*.

11. In the context of *random* file organization:

    (i)   Explain, with the aid of an example, the term *hashing algorithm*.

    (ii)   A hashing algorithm should have two main aims. What are they?

    (iii) Define the terms *synonyms* and *collisions*.

12. Compare and contrast the following methods of overflow handling: *progressive*; *chaining*; *tagged*, pointing out their comparative benefits and drawbacks.

Chapter 16

Processing Methods

Data handling systems make use of one or more processing methods, depending on the requirements of the application. The methods can be categorized according to the ways in which data is controlled, stored and passed through the system; the major categories are: *batch* processing; *on-line* processing, which includes *real-time* and *time-share* processing; *distributed* processing and *centralized* processing; *database* systems (a separate chapter is devoted to this topic). To allow particular methods of processing a computer must have the necessary *operating system* software (Chapter 13); thus any particular computer system is equipped with, for example, a batch processing or real-time operating system, or even a combination of types, depending on the needs of the user organisation.

Batch processing

Such systems process *batches* of data at regular intervals. The data is usually in large volumes and of identical type. Examples of such data are customer orders, current weekly payroll details and stock issues or receipts. The procedure can be illustrated with the example of payroll, which is a typical application for batch processing. Each pay date, whether it is every week or every month, the payroll details, such as hours worked, overtime earned or sickness days claimed, are gathered for each employee (these details are referred to as *transactions*) and processed in batches against the payroll *master file*. The computer then produces payslips for all employees in the company. A major feature of this and similar applications is that a large percentage of the payroll records in the master file are processed during the payroll 'run'. This percentage is known as the *hit rate*. Generally, high hit rate processing is suitable for batch processing and if, as is usual, the master file is organized sequentially, then the *transaction file* will be sorted into the same sequence as the master file. In the case of magnetic tape, transactions must be sorted because the medium only allows *serial* (one record after another in their physical order) access.

The batch processing method closely resembles manual methods of data handling, in that transactions are collected together into batches, sent to the computer centre, sorted into the order of the master file and processed. Such systems are known as traditional data processing systems. There is normally an intermediate stage in the process when the data must be encoded using a *key-to-tape* or *key-to-disk* system.

A disadvantage of batch processing is the delay, often of hours or days, between collecting the transactions and receiving the results of processing and this has to be remembered when an organisation is considering whether batch processing is suitable for a particular application. Conversely, batch processing has the advantage of providing many opportunities for controlling the accuracy of data (Chapter 17) and thus is commonly used when the immediate updating of files is not crucial.

On-line processing systems

If a peripheral, such as a Visual Display Unit or keyboard, is *on-line*, it is under the control of the computer's processor or Central Processing Unit (CPU). On-line processing systems therefore, are those where all peripherals in use are connected to the CPU of the main computer. Transactions can be keyed in directly. The main advantage of an on-line system is the reduction in time between the collection and processing of data. There are two main methods of on-line processing: *real-time* processing; *time-share* processing.

Real-time processing

Process control in real-time

Real-time processing originally referred only to process control systems where, for example, the temperature of a gas furnace is monitored and controlled by a computer. The computer, through an appropriate sensing device, responds immediately to the boiler's variations outside pre-set temperature limits, by switching the boiler on and off to keep the temperature within those limits.

Real-time processing is now used in everyday consumer goods, such as video cameras, because of the development of the 'computer on a chip', more properly called the *microprocessor*. An important example of the use of the microprocessor is the engine management system, which is now standard on an increasing range of cars. A car's engine performance can be monitored and controlled, by sensing and immediately responding to, changes in such factors as air temperature, ignition timing or engine load. Microprocessors dedicated to particular functions are referred to as *embedded systems*. Further examples of the use of microprocessors can be found on the automated production lines of engineering works and car plants, where operations requiring fine engineering control can be carried out by *computer numerical controlled* (CNC) machines. The important feature common to all real-time applications is that the speed of the computer allows almost immediate response to external changes.

Information processing in real-time

To be acceptable as a real-time information processing system, the *response-time* (that is the time between the entry of a transaction or enquiry at a VDU terminal, the processing of the data and the computer's response) must meet the needs of the user. The delay or response time may vary from a fraction of a second to 2-3 seconds depending on the nature of the transaction and the size of the computer. Any delay beyond these times would generally be unacceptable and would indicate the need for the system to be updated. There are two types of information processing systems which can be operated in real-time: *transaction processing*; *information storage and retrieval*.

Transaction processing

This type of system handles clearly defined transactions one at a time, each transaction being processed completely, including the updating of files, before the next transaction is dealt with. The amount of data input for each transaction is small and is usually entered on an *interactive* basis through a VDU. In this way, the user can enter queries through the keyboard and receive a response, or the computer can display a prompt on the screen to which the user responds. Such 'conversations' are usually heavily structured and in a fixed format and so do not allow users to ask any question they wish. A typical example of transaction processing is provided by an *airline booking system* and the following procedures describe a clients enquiry for a seat reservation.

(i)   A prospective passenger provides the booking clerk with information regarding his/her flight requirements.

(ii)   Following prompts on a screen, the clerk keys the details into the system, so that a check can be made on the availability of seats.

(iii)   Vacancies appear on the screen and the client can confirm the booking.

(iv)   Confirmation of the reservation is keyed into the system, usually by a single key stroke and the flight seating records are immediately updated.

(v)   Passenger details (such as name, address, etc.) can now be entered.

Such a system needs to be real-time to enable reservations to be made at once, while the client is there (or on the telephone) and so that the seating records accurately reflect availability at all times.

Information storage and retrieval

This type of system differs from transaction processing in that, although the information is updated in real-time, the number of updates and the number of sources of updating is relatively small.

Consider, for example, the medical records system in a hospital. A record is maintained for each patient currently undergoing treatment in the hospital. Medical staff require the patient's medical history to be available at any time and the system must also have a facility for entering new information as the patient undergoes treatment in hospital. Sources of information are likely to include a doctor, nurses and perhaps a surgeon, and new entries probably do not number more than one or two per day. This is an entirely different situation from an airline booking system where the number of entries for one flight record may be 200-300 and they could be made from many different booking offices throughout the world.

Time-share processing

The term *time sharing* refers to the activity of the computer's processor in allocating *time-slices* to a number of users who are given access through terminals to centralized computer resources. The aim of the system is to give each user a good *response time*. These systems are commonly used where a number of users require computer time for different information processing tasks. The processor time-slices are allocated and controlled by a time-share operating system. The CPU is able to operate at such speed that, provided the system is not overloaded by too many users, each user has the impression that he or she is the sole user of the system.

A particular computer system will be designed to support a maximum number of user terminals. If the number is exceeded or the applications being run on the system are 'heavy' on CPU time the response time will become lengthy and unacceptable. Time-share systems are possible because of the extreme speed of the CPU in comparison with peripheral devices such as keyboards, VDU screens and printers. Most information processing tasks consist largely of input and output operations which do not occupy the CPU, leaving it free to do any processing required on other users tasks.

Distributed processing

As the term suggests, a distributed processing system is one which spreads the processing tasks of an organisation across several computer systems; frequently, these systems are connected and *share resources* (this may relate to common access to files or programs, or even the processing of a single complex task) through a data communications system (Chapter 11). Each computer system in the network must be able to process independently, so a central computer with a number of remote intelligent terminals cannot be classified as distributed, even though some limited validation of data may be carried out separately from the main computer. Examples of distributed systems include mini or mainframe computers interconnected by way of *wide area networks*, or a number of *local area networks* similarly linked.

Distributed systems provide a number of benefits:

- *Economy*. The transmission of data over telecommunications systems can be costly and local database storage and processing facilities can reduce costs. The radical reduction in computer hardware costs has favoured the expansion of distributed systems against centralized systems.

- *Minicomputers and microcomputers*. The availability of minicomputer and microcomputer systems with data transmission facilities has made distributed processing economically viable. An increasingly popular option, in large multi-sited organisations, is to set up local area networks of microcomputers at each site and connect them through communications networks to each other and/or to a central mainframe computer at the Head Office. This provides each site with the advantages of local processing power, local and inter-site communications through *electronic mail* (Chapters 11 and 37) and access to a central mainframe for the main filing and database systems.

- *Local management control*. It is not always convenient, particularly where an organisation controls diverse activities, to have all information processing centralized. Local management control means that the information systems will be developed by people with direct knowledge of their own information needs. Responsibility for the success or otherwise of their division of the organisation may be placed with local management, so it is desirable that they have control over the accuracy and reliability of the data they use.

Centralized systems

With this type of system, all processing is carried out centrally, generally by a mainframe computer. The continuing reduction in hardware costs and the increase in computer power has led the move towards distributed processing systems. This is achieved through computer networks.

Exercises

1. Define the term *hit rate* and explain its significance in file processing.

2. Distinguish between *batch* and *transaction processing*, using example applications to illustrate your answer.

3. With the aid of an example, describe the main features of an information storage and retrieval system

4. Briefly describe the operation of a *time-sharing* system.

5. Use an example to describe the meaning of *distributed processing*.

Chapter 17
System Controls

Computerized information systems present particular problems for the control of data entering the system, because for much of the time this data is not in human-readable form and even when it is stored, the information remains invisible unless it is printed out or displayed on a VDU screen. If proper system controls are not used, inaccurate data may reach the master files or unauthorized changes to data may be made, resulting in decision-making which may be based on incorrect information. System controls can be divided into three main types, according to the purposes they serve: data control; auditing; data security.

Data control

A number of data control mechanisms, including for example, the validation of input data, can be employed. Controls should be exerted at all stages in the data processing cycle, which commonly recognizes the following stages: (i) data *collection*; (ii) *input*; (iii) *processing*, including file processing; (iv) *output*.

Controls can be implemented by clerical and software procedures. It is only through the combined application of both clerical and software controls that errors can be minimized, although their entire exclusion can never be guaranteed.

Data collection and input controls

Before describing the controls it is necessary to outline the activities which may be involved in the collection and input of data. Depending on the application these may include one or more of the following:

- Source document preparation. To ensure standardization of practice and to facilitate checking, data collected for input, for example, customer orders, are clerically transcribed onto source documents specially designed for the purpose.

- Data transmission. If the computer centre is geographically remote from the data collection point, the source documents may be physically transported there, or be keyed and transmitted through a terminal and telecommunications link to the computer.

- Data encoding and verification. This involves the transcription, usually through a keyboard device, of the data onto a storage medium such as magnetic tape or disk; a process of machine verification accompanied by a repeated keying operation assists the checking of keying accuracy. *Key-to-disk* and *key-to-tape* systems are used for encoding, commonly making use of diskette and cassette tape storage, from which media the data is then merged onto a large reel of magnetic tape or a disk pack for subsequent rapid input.

- Data input and validation. Data validation is a computer controlled process which checks the data for its validity according to certain pre-defined parameters, so it must be input to the computer first. The topic of validation is examined in more detail later.

- Sorting. In order to improve the efficiency of processing, input data is sorted into a sequence determined by the *primary key* of each record in the relevant master file (Chapter 15 Computer Files); this is always necessary for efficient sequential file processing, but direct access files allow records to be processed by transactions in the same order that they are received.

Collection and input controls

Transcription of data from one medium to another, for example, from telephone notepad to customer order form, or from source document to magnetic disk, provides the greatest opportunity for error. A number of strategies can be adopted to help limit data collection input errors, including:

- minimizing transcription. This may involve the use of automated input methods such as bar code reading (Chapter 8). Another solution is to use *turnaround documents*, which are originally produced by the computer and later become input documents, for example, remittance advices which, having been sent to customers, are then returned with their payments. Because these remittance advices already show customers' details, including account numbers, only the amounts remitted need to be entered for them to become complete input documents;

- designing data collection and input documents in ways which encourage accurate completion;

- using clerical checking procedures such as the re-calculation of totals or the visual comparison of document entries with the original sources of information;

- using codes with a restricted format, for example, customer account numbers consisting of two alphabetic characters, followed by six digits, permits easy validation;

- employing *batch* methods of input which allow the accumulation and checking of batch control totals, both by clerical and computerized methods;

- using screen verification before input data is processed and applied to computer files. Screen dialogue (the form of conversation between the computer and the user) techniques, which allow data verification and correction at the time of entry, can be used to provide this facility;

- checking input data with the use of *batch* or *interactive* screen validation techniques;

- ensuring that staff are well trained and that clerical procedure manuals are available for newly trained staff;

- controlling access to input documents. This is particularly important where documents are used for sensitive applications such as payroll. For example, input documents for changing pay rates should only be available to, say, the Personnel Manager.

File processing controls

Once validated data has entered the computer system, checks have to be made to ensure that it is; (i) applied to the correct files; (ii) consistent with the filed data.

Header records

Files can have header records which detail the function, for example, Sales Ledger, *version number* and *purge date*. The purge date indicates the date after which the file is no longer required and can be overwritten. Thus, a file with a purge date after the current date should not be overwritten. Such details can be checked by the application program to ensure that the correct file is used and that a current file is not accidentally destroyed.

File validation checks

Some validation checks can only be made after data input when reference can be made to the relevant master file data. These are described in the later section on data control in batch processing systems.

Data integrity

The printing of all master file changes allows the user department and auditors to check that all such changes are *authorized* and *consistent* with transaction documents. All data used by applications for reference purposes should be printed periodically; price lists, for example, may be held as permanent data on master files or in table form within computer programs.

Output controls

It might reasonably be supposed that input and file processing controls are sufficient to ensure accurate output. Nevertheless, a number of simple controls at the output stage can help to ensure that it is complete and is distributed to the relevant users on time. They include:

- the comparison of *filed* control totals with *run* control totals. For example, when an entire sequential file is processed, the computer counts all processed records and compares the total with a stored record total held in a *trailer record* at the end of the file;

- the *conciliation* of control totals specific to the application, with totals obtained from a related application. For example, the sales transactions total posted to the Sales Ledger for one day should agree with the total sales transactions recorded in the Sales Day Book or Journal;

- the following of set procedures for the treatment of error reports;

- the proper checking and re-submission of rejected transactions.

Data control in batch processing

It is extremely important that all relevant data is processed and that accuracy is maintained throughout the data processing cycle. The controls which are used will depend on the type of processing method in operation, but batch processing provides the greatest opportunity for exerting control over the data, from the input stage through to the output stage. Amongst the control methods outlined above, there are two which are particularly important - *verification* and *validation*. These control methods can be used to maximum advantage in a batch processing system and typical procedures are described below.

The stages involved in a batch processing *system cycle* are illustrated in Figure 17.1 with a systems flowchart for a payroll run. The following controls can be used at certain stages within the cycle.

Clerical controls

These can be used at any stage in the cycle when the data is in a human-readable form. The types of check include:

- visual checking of source documents to detect missing, illegible or unlikely data values, an example of the latter being a total of 100 in the weekly overtime hours entry for an individual worker;

- the verification of entries by checking them against another source, for example, the price catalogue for the price of a stock item on an invoice;

- the re-working of calculations on a source document, for example, the checking of additions which make up the total quantity for an item on an order form.

Verification

Before processing, data has to be transcribed from the source documents onto a computer input medium, usually involving a keying

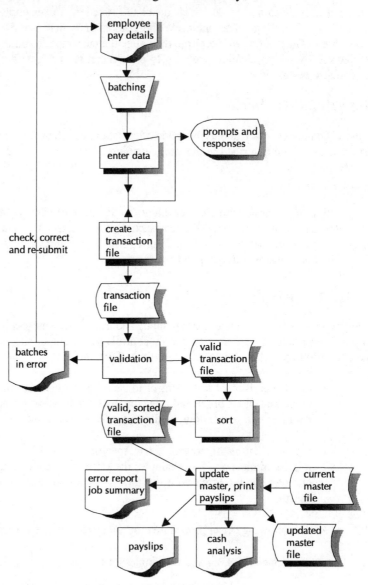

Figure 17.1. *System flowchart of batch payroll system*

operation to encode the data onto magnetic tape or magnetic disk. This stage can be prone to error, particularly if large volumes of data are involved and verification, which is usually a machine-assisted process, can ensure that data is encoded accurately. Magnetic tape encoders (*key-to-tape* systems), for example, can operate in two modes, *record* and *verify*. The operation involves one person keying the data in the record mode, after which a second person re-keys the data with the machine in verify mode. In effect the machine reads the data from the first keying operation and then checks it against the second keying as it occurs. The machine signals if characters do not agree, thus indicating a possible transcription error. *Key-to-disk* systems operate on a similar principle, either with stand-alone workstations or through terminals linked to a minicomputer and usually incorporate some facility for *validation* of data.

Validation

This process is carried out after the data has been encoded onto the input medium and involves a program called the *data vet* or *validation program*. Its purpose is to check that the data falls within certain parameters defined by the systems analyst. A judgement as to whether or not data is valid is made possible by the validation program, but it cannot ensure absolute accuracy. That can only be achieved by the use of all the clerical and computer controls built into the system at the design stage. The difference between *validity* and *accuracy* can be illustrated by the following example.

Example of validation

A company has established a Personnel file. Each record in the file may contain a field for the Job Grade. The permitted values of job grade are A, B, C or D. An entry in an individual's record may be *valid* and accepted by the system if it is recorded as A,B,C or D, but of course this may not be the *correct* grade for the individual worker concerned. Whether or not the grade is correct can only be established by the clerical checks discussed earlier.

Types of validation check

Character, field and record checks

- *Size*. The number of characters in a field is checked. For example, an account number may require 6 characters and if there are more or less than this, then the item is rejected.

- *Mode*. It may be that particular fields must contain particular types of character, for example alphabetic or numeric. If the system is programmed to accept only numbers then letters would be rejected.

- *Format*. This refers to the way characters within a field are organized. For example, an Item Code may consist of 2 alphabetic characters followed by 6 numeric characters, so the system would reject any entry which did not correspond to this format.

- *Reasonableness*. Quantities can be checked for unusually high or low values. For example, a gas consumer with one small appliance may have a meter reading appropriate to a consumer with a large central heating system and a reasonableness test could be used to reject or highlight it.

- *Presence*. If a field must always have a value then it can be checked for existence. For example, the field 'Sex' in a Personnel record would always have to have an M(ale) or F(emale) entry.

- *Range*. Values are checked for certain upper and lower limits, for example, account numbers may have to be between 00001 and 10000.

- *Check digit*. An extra digit calculated on an account number can be used as a self checking device. When the number is input to the computer, the validation program carries out a calculation similar to that used to generate the check digit originally and thus checks its validity. This kind of check will highlight transposition errors caused by, for instance, keying digits in the wrong order.

The following example serves to illustrate the operation of one such check digit method.

Modulus 11 check digit example

Consider a stock code consisting of six digits, for example 462137.

The check digit is calculated as follows:

(i)   Each digit of the stock code is multiplied by its own weight. Each digit has a weight relative to its position, assuming the presence of a check digit in the rightmost position. Beginning from the check digit position (x) the digits are weighted 1, 2, 3, 4, 5, 6 and 7 respectively, as shown in Table 17.1

Stock Code	4	6	2	1	3	7	(x)
multiplied by weight	7	6	5	4	3	2	(1)
product	28	36	10	4	9	14	

Table 17.1.

(ii)   The products are totalled. In this example, the sum produces 101.

(iii)   Divide the sum by modulus 11. This produces 9, remainder 2.

(iv)   The check digit is produced by subtracting the remainder 2 from 11, giving 9.

Whenever a code is entered with the relevant check digit, the validation software carries out the same algorithm, including the check digit in the calculation. Provided that the fourth stage produces a remainder of zero the code is accepted as valid. This is proved in Table 17.2, using the example in Table 17.1.

Stock Code	4	6	2	1	3	7	9
multiplied by weight	7	6	5	4	3	2	1
product	28	36	10	4	9	14	9

Table 17.2.

The sum of the products in Table 17.2 is 110, which when divided by 11, gives 10, with a remainder of 0. Therefore the number is valid.

If some of the digits are *transposed* (swap positions) the check digit is no longer applicable to the code and is rejected by the validation program because the results of the algorithm will not leave a remainder of zero. This is shown in Table 17.3. The sum of the products equals 111, which when divided by 11, gives 10 with a remainder of 1. The number is, therefore, invalid.

Stock Code	6	4	1	2	3	7	9
multiplied by weight	7	6	5	4	3	2	1
product	42	24	5	8	9	14	9

Table 17.3.

All the above checks can be carried out prior to the master file updating stage. Further checks on data can be made through the use of a validation program at the *update* stage, by comparison with the master file. They are as follow:

- *new records*. When a new record is to be added to the master file, a check can be made to ensure that a record does not already use the entered record key .

- *deleted records*. It may be that a transaction is entered for which there is no longer a matching master record.

- *consistency*. A check is made that the transaction values are consistent with the values held on the master record which is to be updated. For instance a deduction for pension contributions by an employee who is not old enough to be in a pension scheme would obviously be inconsistent.

Validation using batch controls

Batch totals

The purpose of batch totals is to allow a conciliation of manually produced totals for a batch with comparable computer-produced totals. Differences are signalled and the batch is rejected for checking and re-submission. Following the arrangement of source documents into batches of say 30 in each batch, totals are calculated on add-listing machines for each value it is required to control. On an order form, for example, quantities and prices may be separately totalled to provide two control totals. Totals may also be produced for each account number or item code simply for purposes of control although they are otherwise meaningless. For this reason such totals are called hash or nonsense totals. The totals are recorded on a *batch control slip* (Figure 17.2), attached to the batch, together with a value for the number of documents in the batch and a batch number. The batch number is kept in a register held by the originating department so that missing or delayed batches can be traced. It should be noted that *hash totals* may produce a figure which has a large number of digits, so extra digits over and above the original length of the data item are truncated.

Figure 17.2. *Batch control slip*

Reconciliation of batch totals

The details from each batch control slip are entered with each batch of transactions at the encoding stage. The serial transaction file which results may be arranged as in Figure 17.3.

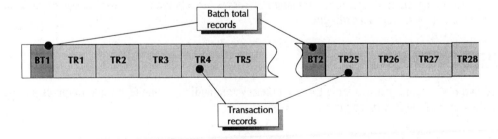

Figure 17.3. *Arrangement of serial transaction file, with batch totals*

The serial transaction file is processed from beginning to end by the validation program. The sum of the transaction records relating to each batch should match the batch total. If any validation error is detected, either by differences in batch totals or through the character of field checks described earlier, the offending batch is rejected to be checked and re-submitted. The rejected batches are reported on a computer printout.

Validation during updating

Checks can be made in the manner described earlier, on transactions for deleted or new records, or on data which is inconsistent with the relevant record on the master file. These controls can be used in conjunction with proper clerical procedures to ensure that as far as possible, the information stored on the master files is accurate.

File controls

In addition to controlling the accuracy of data entering the system it is essential to check both that the data is complete and that all relevant data is processed. This can be done through the use of file controls on the transaction file.

Following the validation of the batches of transactions, correct batches are written to another file to be sorted and used for updating the relevant master file. During validation, the validation program accumulates totals for all the correct batches. These can be used during the update run to ensure that the whole transaction file is processed.

Validation in on-line systems

On-line systems, as described in the Chapter 16 on Processing Methods, tend to be interactive and transactions are processed immediately against the master files at the data entry stage. The main controls which can be introduced to such systems include:

- the character, field and record validation checks described earlier. Error messages are displayed on the screen at the time data is entered and require immediate correction at that time;

- visual verification. At the end of each transaction entry, the operator is given the opportunity to scan the data on the screen and to re-enter any incorrect entries detected. This usually takes the form of a message at the bottom of the screen which is phrased in a way such as "Verify (yes or no)";

- the use of well-trained data entry operators. They should have sufficient knowledge of the data being entered and the application it serves, to respond to error messages and make corrections to data accordingly.

Auditing

There are two main techniques available for computer system auditing. One technique involves the use of *test data* and the other of *audit enquiry* programs.

Test data method

With this method, the auditor runs the target application with test data, the expected processing results of which are already known. In this way, the computation of for example, payroll figures, can be tested for accuracy in a variety of circumstances. The logical outputs of the program can also be verified. In fact, the method is similar to that used by systems designers prior to a system's implementation. The test data may be recorded on a batch of source documents, in which case, the input will not only test the application's computerized processing and controls, but also the suitability of the source document design for input purposes. The auditing process may also include the testing of batch preparation and input data verification procedures. Software validation checks should be subjected to testing with *normal* and *exceptional* data. Normal data includes the most general data which the software is designed to handle. Exceptional data includes any which the software is not designed to accept. The software should demonstrate that it can reject all such data and continue its normal operation. Test data runs may take one of the following forms.

Live data testing

The auditor selects examples of live data from the system which fulfil the conditions to be tested. The results are calculated manually and checked against the computer-produced outputs. It is essential that manual calculations are made, as a casual assessment of the accuracy of processing can often lead to errors being overlooked. A severe disadvantage of this approach is that the auditor may be unable to find examples of all conditions to be tested in the available live data. It is also quite possible that examples of exceptional or nonsensical data will not be found at the time of the audit and it is important that such conditions are tested. 'Murphy's law' will probably ensure that such exceptional data appears the day after the audit. The testing can only give a 'snapshot' of the system's performance which may be radically different on other occasions.

Historical data testing

Sampling of transactions which have already passed through the system is an important part of internal auditing. It is important that the original transaction documents are made available for inspection to allow the auditor to check their *validity*, *authorization* and *consistency* with associated results. Results can be calculated manually and then compared with any printed results. If results were not printed at the time, then use may be made of a *file dump utility* to access the appropriate historic file.

Dummy data testing

With this method, the auditor constructs fictitious or dummy data which contains the conditions to be tested. To ensure that such test data is not applied to the application's operational files, it is also usual to set up dummy files, for example, customer or supplier files, specifically for audit purposes. If such data is used in an actual processing run, and the entries are not reversed out in time, there is a danger that the results will be taken as real by users. There are a number of apocryphal stories concerning lorries which delivered goods to non-existent addresses as a result of such fictitious entries. For this reason, it is always advisable to make use of specially created audit files or copies of the master files.

In summary, the test data method is useful for the audit of:

- data preparation procedures, such as batching;

- data verification and validation controls;

- an application's computational and logical processes.

A number of drawbacks and limitations of the test data method of auditing can also be identified:

- it only provides a snapshot view of the system at the time of the audit. On the other hand, it may be used repeatedly in order to cover a more extended period of assessment;

- it may involve the setting up of dummy files if fictitious data is to be used;

- source documents and batch totals have to be prepared for fictitious data which is not of operational use to the business;

- the computer system has to be made available to the auditor for the period of the test. During this time it is not available for operational use.

Audit enquiry programs

These programs overcome many of the disadvantages inherent in the test data method and are an essential audit tool, particularly for external auditing which requires the examination of live data already processed. Audit enquiry programs vary in sophistication but generally provide facilities to:

- examine the contents of computer files;

- retrieve data from computer files;

- compare the contents of files. Thus, for example, two versions of identical files may be compared to ensure that the structure has not been altered, perhaps to include an extra field or record type;

- produce formatted reports according to the auditor's requirements.

A major benefit to the auditor is that any data stored on computer file can be retrieved. Many financial packages update files 'in situ', so that each updating transaction causes the overwriting of the relevant master record with new values. Thus, there may be circumstances when the results of processing individual transactions can only be established in terms of the cumulative effect of a group of transactions on a particular record. For example, during one day, a stock record may be updated by several transactions but the values held in the stock record at the end will not show their individual effects. However, provided that the source documents are retained or the transactions are logged onto a separate file (see Transaction Logging in the next section on Security), the auditor can still reconcile their expected effect on the master file with the actual values held there.

Audit trails

An audit trail should allow the tracing of a transaction's history as it progresses from input through to output. Computerized systems present particular difficulties in that the trail disappears as it enters the computer system. The auditor may ignore the computer system and pick up the trail at the output stage (auditing around the computer). This has obvious limitations in that the auditor cannot trace a transaction which does not result in printed output. Although audit enquiry programs allow the auditor to examine the contents of files, not every transaction effect is recorded permanently on computer file. Audit trails have to be designed into the system in such a way that intermediate stages of a transaction's progress are recorded for audit purposes.

Data security

The controls used have several main functions:

- to prevent loss of data files caused by software or procedural errors, or by physical hazards;

- to protect data from accidental or deliberate disclosure to unauthorized individuals or groups;

- to protect the data from accidental or deliberate corruption or modification. This is known as maintaining *data integrity*;

- to protect the rights of individuals and organizations to restrict access to information which relates to them and is of a private nature, to those entitled or authorized to receive it. This is known as *data privacy*.

Security against data loss

The loss of *master files* can be an extremely serious occurrence for any organization so properly organized security procedures need to be employed. Among commercial organizations that have lost the major part of their information store, a large percentage subsequently go out of business.

The main causes of data loss are as follow:

- environmental hazards such as fire, flood and other natural accidents;

- mechanical problems, for example the danger of disk or tape damage caused by a drive unit malfunction;

- software errors resulting from programming error;

- human error. A wrong file may be loaded, the wrong program version used, a tape or disk mislaid, or physical damage caused to tape or disk;

- malicious damage. It is not unknown for staff to intentionally damage storage media or to misuse programs at a terminal.

The standard solution to such problems is to take regular copies of master files and to store the copies in a separate secure location. It is also necessary to maintain a record of transactions affecting a file since the last copy was taken, so that if necessary they can be used to reconstruct the latest version of the file.

Magnetic tape file security

When a tape master file is updated by a tape transaction file the physical nature of the medium makes it necessary for a new tape file to be produced. As Figure 17.4 illustrates, the updating procedure provides a built-in security system referred to as the Grandparent, Parent and Child (*generation*) system.

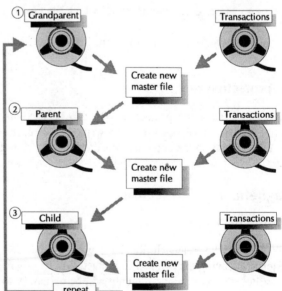

Figure 17.4. *Generation security system for tape files*

In the first run, Master File 1 is updated by the transactions file to produce Master File 2 as its Child. Master File 1 is the Parent. Should the Child file be damaged and the data lost, it can be re-created from the Parent master file and the relevant transactions. At the end of the second run, Master File 1 becomes the Grandparent, Master File 2 becomes the Parent and Master File 3, the Child. Each generation provides security for subsequent files. The number of generations used will depend on the policy of the organization. Three generations are usually regarded as providing sufficient security and the oldest files are re-used by being overwritten as each cycle of generations is completed.

Internal header labels

Internal header labels are designed to deal with two major areas of concern:

- It is important that the correct file is used in a file processing operation to ensure correct results. Thus, the *subject* of the file and the *version* must be identifiable. For example, it is no good producing monthly payslips using information from a payroll master file three months out of date.

- A tape file must be protected against accidental erasure. This may occur because tapes are re-usable and when a file is no longer required it can be overwritten by new information.

To ensure that the correct file is used for any particular job, a tape file usually has an internal header label. The label appears at the beginning of the tape and identifies it. The identifying information in the label is usually recorded under program control or by a data encoding device.

A tape header label usually contains the following items of information:

- file name e.g. Payroll, Stock, Sales;

- date created;

- purge date - the date after which the tape is no longer required and may be re-used.

The label is checked by the program, before the file is processed, to ensure that the correct tape is being used.

File protection ring

A device called a file protection ring can be used to prevent accidental erasure. When tapes are stored off-line, the rings are not fitted. To write to a tape, the ring must first be fitted to the centre of the reel. A tape can be read by the computer whether or not a ring is fitted. The simple rule to remember is 'no ring, no write'.

Magnetic disk file security

Security back-ups

Disk files can be treated in the same way as tape files in that the updating procedure may produce a new master file leaving the original file intact. On the other hand, if the file is updated *in-situ* (which in so doing overwrites the existing data), then it will be necessary to take regular back-up copies as processing proceeds. The frequency with which copies are taken will depend on the volume of transactions affecting the master file. If the latest version of the master file is corrupted or lost, then it can be re-created using the previous back-up together with the transaction data received since the back-up.

Transaction logging

In an on-line system, transactions may enter the system from a number of terminals in different locations, thus making it difficult to re-enter transactions for the re-creation of a damaged master file. One solution is to log all the transactions onto a serial transaction file at the same time as the master file is updated. Thus, the re-creation process can be carried out without the need for keying in the transactions again. The systems flowchart in Figure 17.5 illustrates this procedure.

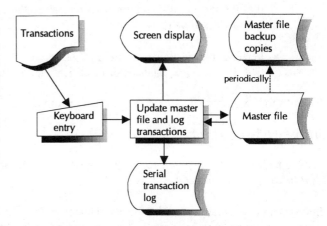

Figure 17.5. *Backup and transaction logging*

Access controls

Unauthorized access to a system may: provide vital information to competitors; result in the deliberate or accidental corruption of data; allow fraudulent changes to be made to data; result in loss of privacy for individuals or organizations.

To avoid such hazards an information system should be protected *physically*, by *administrative procedures* and *software*. To detect any unauthorized access or changes to the information system:

- users should require *authorization* (with different levels of authority depending on the purpose of access);

- the computer should *log* all successful and attempted accesses;

- users should be *identifiable* and their identity *authenticated;*

- the files should be capable of being *audited;*

- the actions of *programmers* should be carefully controlled to prevent fraud through changes to software.

Physical protection

These include the use of security staff, mechanical devices, such as locks and keys and electronic alarm/identification systems.

Computer systems with terminals at remote sites present a weak link in any system and they must be properly protected and here software plays an important protection role. Disk and tape libraries also need to be protected, otherwise it would be possible for a thief to take file media to another centre with compatible hardware and software. A variety of methods may be used to *identify* and possibly *authenticate* a system user. They include:

- Identity cards. Provided that they cannot be copied and have a photograph, they can be effective and cheap. The addition of a magnetic strip which contains encoded personal details including a *personal identification number* (PIN), which the holder has to key in, allows the user to be checked by machine. This method is used to allow access to service tills outside banks. Of course, the user of the card may not be the authorized holder, possession of the PIN being the only additional requirement; the following methods allow authentication as well as identification.

- Personal physical characteristics. Voice recognition or fingerprint comparison provide effective, if expensive, methods of identification and authentication.

Such methods are only effective if the supporting administrative procedures are properly followed.

Software protection

Ideally, before a user is given access to a system, the log-in procedures should check for: *authorization*; *identification*; *authentication*.

Authorization is usually provided by an account code, which must be keyed in response to a computer prompt; similar prompts may appear for a user-id *(identification)* and a password *(authentication)*. Examples of these controls are provided in the section on Novell Netware in Chapter 13.

Further control can be exerted with *fixed terminal identifiers*, whereby each terminal and its location is physically identifiable by the controlling computer, thus preventing access from additional unauthorized locations. Such controls can also be used to restrict particular terminals to particular forms and levels of access.

Password controls

Access to files can be controlled at different levels by a series of passwords, which have to be keyed into the terminal in response to a series of questions displayed on the screen. For example, a clerk in a Personnel Department may be given authority to display information regarding an employee's career record but only the Personnel Manager is authorized to change the information held on file.

Passwords should be carefully chosen, kept secure (memorized and not divulged) and changed frequently. Using people's names, for example, may allow entry by trial and error. Characters should not be echoed on screen as the password is entered.

Handshaking is a technique which requires more than a simple password and may be used between two computers or a computer and a user, as a means of access control. In the latter case, the user would be given a pseudo-random number by the computer and the expected response would be a transform, of that random number. The transform may be to multiply the first and last digits of the number and add the product to a value equal to the day of the month plus 1. Provided the transform is kept secret, handshaking provides more security than simple passwords.

One-time passwords. With this method, the computer will only accept a password for *one access occasion*; subsequently, it will expect the user to provide a different password for each additional access, in a pre-defined sequence. Provided the password list and their expected sequence list are kept separate, then possession of one list only will not be of any assistance.

The number of attempts at logging-on should be controlled, so, for example, after three unsuccessful attempts, the user should be locked out and a record kept of the time and nature of the attempt.

Authorization tables

These are held with the relevant files and detail the kinds of access permitted by particular users or groups of users - read only, read and write or delete (see Novell Netware in Chapter 13). Control may also be exerted at a record or field level.

Data encryption

If data signals being transmitted along the telecommunication links are not properly protected, *hackers* can pick up the signals and display them on their own machines. To prevent such intrusion, data encryption methods are used to protect important financial, legal and other confidential information during transmission from one centre to another. Encryption scrambles the data to make it unintelligible during transmission. As the power and speed of computers has increased, so the breaking of codes has been made easier.

Code designers have produced methods of encryption which are currently unbreakable in any reasonable time period, even by the largest and most powerful computers available. An example of such an elaborate coding system is illustrated by the operation of the Electronic Funds Transfer (EFT) system. This is used by banks and other financial institutions to transfer vast sums of money so these transmissions are protected by the latest data encryption techniques. The Data Encryption Standard (DES) was approved by the American National Bureau of Standards in 1977, but as costs of powerful computers have fallen and come within the reach of criminal organization, EFT makes use of the DES standard, plus additional encryption techniques.

Security to maintain data integrity

Data integrity refers to the accuracy and consistency of the information stored and is thus covered by the security methods outlined above. A major threat to data integrity comes from a variety of computer viruses.

Computer viruses

A computer virus is program code designed to create nuisance for users, or more seriously, to effect varying degrees of damage to files stored on magnetic media. Generally, the code

- is introduced through portable media, such as floppy disks, particularly those storing pirated or shareware programs; files downloaded from *bulletin boards* on the Internet (Chapter 37) may be infected and uncontrolled use of these services is likely to result in the receipt of viruses;

- transfers itself from the infected medium into the computer's main memory as soon as the medium is accessed;

- transfers from memory onto any integral storage device, such as a hard disk and commonly conceals itself in the boot sector (and sometimes in the partition sector where it is less likely to be traced), from where it can readily infect any other media placed on line in that computer system, whether it be stand-alone or networked. Naturally, any write-protected media cannot be infected.

Some virus codes are merely a nuisance, whilst others are developed specifically to destroy, or make inaccessible, whole filing systems. They pose a serious threat to any computer-based information system, but a number of measures can be taken to minimize the risk:

- only use proprietary software from a reliable source;

- write-protect disks being used for reading purposes only;

- use virus detection software, although this is only effective in respect of viruses using known storage and proliferation techniques;

- use diskless workstations on networks;

- control access to portable media and forbid employees to use their own media on the organization's computer system.

Security to maintain privacy of data

The rights of individuals and organizations concerning their confidential records are similarly protected by the security controls outlined earlier. In addition, legislation by parliament (the Data Protection Act 1984 - see Chapter 39) attempts to exert some control by requiring persons or organizations holding personal information on computer files to register with the Data Protection Registrar. Some countries have 'Freedom of Information Acts' which allow the individual to see any personal information stored in their own files, except where national security is thought to be threatened. It is generally accepted that the Data Protection Act falls far short of complete freedom of information.

Exercises

1. Distinguish between *verification* and *validation*.

2. Using batch order processing as an example:

    (i)   suggest four *data collection controls* to control the accuracy of data entering the system;

    (ii)   suggest three *validation checks* which could be applied to customer order details;

    (iii) indicate any *file processing controls* which could be employed.

3. Draw a *system flowchart* to illustrate the batch processing of customer orders and the updating of stock, order and customer files.

4. With the aid of an example, describe how a *check digit* is generated and subsequently used to check the validity of a code number.

5. In the context of auditing, distinguish between *live*, *historical* and *dummy data testing*, pointing out the relative benefits and drawbacks of each.

6. What is an *audit trail* and why is it useful?

7. With the use of an example, describe the *generation system* of security for tape files.

8. What is transaction logging?

9. With the aid of an example organization, describe methods to prevent *unauthorized access* to data.

Chapter 18

Systems Analysis - an overview

Systems analysis can be defined as *a disciplined process which begins with the establishment of user requirements for a given application and concludes with the implementation of a fully operational system.* The work of systems analysis has been carried out by trained professionals since the introduction of early mainframe computers but its processes are equally appropriate to the task of computerizing small business applications. Many businesses will not employ specialist staff capable of carrying out an analysis of their computer requirements and may employ the services of an outside consultant. The main stages of systems analysis are often referred to as the *system life cycle.* The following sections give a brief overview of their functions within the systems analysis process.

Feasibility study

The aim of this stage is to establish whether or not a proposal for the computerization of a particular application is worthwhile or feasible. In simple terms, the feasibility study has to answer questions such as follow: "Will computerization achieve the users' objectives?"; "What type of system will be most suitable?"; "Will it be financially worthwhile?"

System investigation and design

Assuming that the feasibility study produces a recommendation to proceed with computerization of an application (there may, of course, be several), then before any system specification is produced, an analysis has to be made of the processes and procedures involved in the application under consideration. For example, an analysis of Sales Order Processing should identify how orders are received, the order forms used and the procedures necessary to fulfil orders. Analysis is not simply the recording of an application as it currently operates. Through a variety of information gathering methods such as interviewing and observation, the requirements of a new system should be identified.

Although the needs of the organization are of obvious importance, employees are more likely to be concerned with matters of job satisfaction and working conditions. Successful implementation of a computerized system requires a great deal of work, involvement and willingness to co-operate by everyone concerned. If staff feel that their views have been considered such co-operation is more likely. Although users' views are important an outside observer can often identify problems with current practice which have never been questioned. A systems analyst from outside the firm needs therefore, to possess qualities of tact and diplomacy if his or her views are to be considered.

The process of design should produce a complete picture of the input, processing, storage and output requirements of the new system. The picture will include narrative descriptions, as well as flowcharts illustrating clerical procedures, data flows and the role of the computer in broad outline. The design of a computerized system should include as many improvements suggested in the investigation stage as is practicable and it will almost certainly be necessary to question users further when, for example, problems arise in the implementation of particular system requirements. Compromises will have to be made between what is desirable and what is practicable. Management and users may have specified requirements during the investigation stage which prove either too expensive or extremely difficult to satisfy.

System implementation

System implementation or 'going live' involves a range of preparatory activities, although the importance of each will depend on the type and size of the project and the number of people involved. The main activities are as follow:

- Development and/or testing of software. If an 'off the shelf' system is chosen, then no development time is necessary, but testing is still vital.

- File conversion. This is probably the most time-consuming activity in that all data relating to the application, which is currently held in manual files, has to be encoded onto the chosen magnetic storage medium. Although a laborious task, accuracy is obviously vital and both software and clerical checking procedures should be employed.

- Staff training and education. This may take a variety of forms but may be part of the proposals put forward by the chosen supplier. It is an extremely important activity if the system's effectiveness is to be maximized and if staff are to feel happy and confident in its operation.

- Introduction of new clerical procedures. The computer software which has been developed or purchased forms only part of the whole information processing system and if the whole system is to function correctly, the computer processing aspect has to be supported by the clerical procedures designed to work with it. Part of staff training, therefore, has to be dedicated to purely clerical tasks such as the preparation of input data or source documents.

- Choice of a changeover or 'going live' plan. A number of alternatives are available and each has costs and benefits associated with it. *Parallel running*, for example, requires that the old and new systems are operated alongside one another until the new system is fully tested. Although this minimizes the risks consequent upon system failure, it is an expensive option in that it involves a great deal of staff time. *Direct changeover* is obviously less expensive if the new system works but failure could mean catastrophe for the business. The plan used will depend on a number of factors, for example, the importance of the system to the success of the business.

System maintenance

After its initial introduction a system should be flexible to the changing needs of the business. An allowance for the business's expansion should be made in the original system specification and the supplier should be able to satisfy those expansion needs as and when necessary. Equally, advances in hardware technology and the sophistication of software mean that a system soon becomes outdated. Even if a business chooses not to take advantage of improved software, hardware is likely to become less reliable and will need replacement after about five years of business use. Agreements on software and hardware maintenance should be established with the supplier and formalized in the contract signed by purchaser and supplier.

Chapter 19
The Feasibility Study

Introduction

The traditional purpose of a feasibility study is to determine whether or not the purchase of a computer system can be justified. The study has to answer two fundamental questions: "Can the envisaged applications be carried out by a computer system more efficiently than with existing facilities?"; "Will a computer system be economically viable?".

Since the early 1970s, prices of all types of computer system have fallen dramatically and their power has increased to such a degree that, for example, microcomputers challenge the minicomputer in their range of applications. This may be part of the reason why many organizations find it difficult to justify undertaking a detailed feasibility study and argue that no matter how limited their needs there is a computer system to satisfy them at a cost-effective price; it is only necessary to decide on its best application(s). Although this is an understandable view, it should be remembered that any item of equipment should be justified in terms of its costs and benefits to the business and that a computer system should be no exception. Although there are few businesses which cannot benefit from computerization at all, the process of carrying out a feasibility study disciplines the purchaser to think carefully about how it is to be used. In modifying the purpose of a feasibility study, the previous questions can be replaced by the following: "Which applications can be computerized to give most benefit to the organization?"; "What type of computer will be required?"; "What are the likely acquisition and running costs?"; "What are the likely implications, especially those concerning personnel and organizational procedures?".

Pressures for computerization

There are many and various pressures which can 'trigger' the thought of using a computer, either for the first time or, where a computer is already installed, for other applications still operated manually. Some examples are as follow:

(i)   A business is expanding and to cope with the increased workload it appears that the only the alternative to computerization is increased staffing.

(ii)   A business is growing at such a rate that more information is needed to manage it properly. To obtain the information manually is too time-consuming and by the time it has been gathered is probably out-of-date.

(iii)   Staff are being asked to work regular and increasing amounts of overtime and backlogs of work are building up.

(iv)   Customers are complaining about the speed and quality of the service provided.

(v)   Where stock is involved, it is difficult to keep track of stock levels and while some customer orders cannot be filled because of stock shortages, other stock is 'gathering dust' on the shelves.

(vi)   A great deal of advertising literature is constantly reminding business management that they are out-of-date and at a disadvantage with their competitors.

(vii)   Other businesses providing a similar service use a computer.

Examples (i), (ii) and (iii) suggest that the business is operating successfully and needs to take on extra staff or streamline its systems. Examples (iv) and (v) may be symptomatic of generally poor business management and in such cases, computerization alone may not solve the problems. Examples (vi) and (vii) may tempt the management to computerize simply 'to keep up with the Jones's'. Although a computerization programme resulting directly from one or more such pressures may be completely successful and worthwhile, the pressure itself should not be the reason for computerization. Instead, management should establish the organizational objectives they wish to achieve through computerization.

Establishing objectives for computerization

It is important for management to establish what they are trying to achieve in terms of the overall objectives of the business and in the light of this, the objectives of the systems which contribute to their achievement. For example, two major business objectives may be to improve the delivery of customers' orders and to minimize the stock levels which tie up valuable cash resources. The achievement of these objectives may involve contributions from several different information processing systems and the list may include the following.

- Stock Control - records stock movements and controls stock levels.

- Purchasing - responsible for the ordering of new supplies from suppliers.

- Sales Order Processing - receives customers' orders and initiates the process of order fulfilment.

- Purchase Ledger - the accounting record of amounts owed and paid to suppliers of stock.

- Invoicing - the production of invoices requesting payment from customers for goods supplied.

- Sales Ledger - the accounting record of amounts owing by and received from customers for goods supplied.

These and other applications within a business are interconnected by the information which flows between them. Such connections can be illustrated with the use of data flow diagrams (DFD), which are described in Chapter 23.

Establishing priorities for computerization

It is not generally advisable or even practicable to attempt the computerization of more than one or two applications at the same time, even if they are closely linked. In any case, it is likely that some applications make a greater contribution to the achievement of the required business objectives than do others. Thus, the applications which are going to bring greatest benefit to the business should be computerized first.

Establishing individual system objectives

Before any single application can be computerized, it is necessary to establish its objectives clearly because users may have become so used to its procedures that they no longer question their purpose. It is self-evident that before any informed judgements can be made on the design of a computerized system, the objectives of the relevant application must first be clearly understood.

The following list for stock control serves to illustrate the definition of such objectives.

- To maintain levels of stock which will be sufficient to meet customer orders promptly.

- To provide a mechanism which removes the need for excessively high safety margins of stock to cover customer orders. This is usually effected by setting minimum stock levels which the computer can use to report variations below these levels.

- To provide automatic re-ordering of stock items which fall below minimum levels.

- To provide management with up-to-date information on stock levels and values of stocks held.

The Feasibility Report

The Feasibility Report should contain the following sections:

Terms of reference

These should set out the original purpose of the study, as agreed by management and detail the business objectives to be achieved, for example: (i) the improvement of customer service, such that orders are delivered within 24 hours of order receipt; (ii) the provision of more up-to-date management information on current stock levels and projected customer demand; (iii) a tighter control of the business's cash resources, primarily through better stock management.

Applications considered for computerization

The applications which may assist the achievement of the business objectives set out in the Terms of Reference are listed, for example: stock control; purchasing; sales order processing; invoicing; accounts.

System investigations

For each application under consideration there should be:

- a description of the existing system;

- an assessment of its good and bad points. For example, the sales order processing system may be slow to process customer orders and this results in poor delivery times, which in turn causes customers to take away their business;

- an estimate of the costs of the existing system. For example, apart from the cost of staffing, an estimate has to be made of the cost of lost business, which could be avoided with an improved system.

Envisaged system requirements

This section should detail, in general terms, those aspects of each application which need to be improved and a broad outline of how each system may operate following computerization. Of course, it is still possible that not all applications will benefit from computerization but can be improved by other methods.

Costs of development and implementation

These will include both capital costs and revenue or running costs. Capital costs are likely to be incurred for the following: (i) computer hardware; (ii) systems software and software packages (either 'off-the-shelf' or 'tailor-made'); (iii) installation charges for hardware and software; (iv) staff training. Revenue costs include those for the maintenance and insurance of the system. In addition, unless there are existing computer specialists in the organization, additional suitable staff may need to be recruited.

Timescale for implementation

This will depend on the scale of the operation, the type of application and whether or not packaged software is to be used.

Expected benefits

These are more difficult to quantify than the costs but may include, for example:

- estimated savings in capital expenditure on typewriters and photocopiers;

- more efficient stock management allows customer service to be maintained whilst keeping stock levels lower. This releases valuable cash resources and reduces possible interest charges on borrowed capital;

- expansion in business turnover, without the need for extra staff and reduced overtime requirements.

Other considerations

The staff have to support any development for it to be properly successful and this usually means consultation at an early stage in the feasibility study and the provision of a proper staff training programme. Customers must also be considered. For example, when a customer receives a computer-produced invoice it should be at least as easy to understand as the type it replaced. Assuming that the feasibility study concludes that the proposed computerization is worthwhile, according to the criteria set out in the report, then more detailed investigation and design can follow.

Chapter 20
System Investigation and Design

Introduction

If the feasibility report gives the go-ahead to the computerization project, then a more detailed investigation of each candidate system begins. The facts gathered about each system will be analysed in terms of their bearing on the design and implementation of a computerized version. The objectives of the analysis are to gain a thorough knowledge of the operational characteristics of the current system and to settle, in a fair amount of detail, the way in which a computerized system will operate. It is extremely important that the new system does not simply computerize existing procedures. The design should, as far as possible, ignore existing departmental structures which may inhibit the introduction of different and improved procedures. For example, it may be that customer credit limits are fixed by the Accounts Department and that Sales staff have to refer to the Accounts Department before accepting a customer order. A computerized system may allow Sales staff to access credit limits directly without reference to the Accounts Department. This method could be used in most cases and the computer could indicate any customer accounts which needed to be specially referred to the Accounts staff. The aim of the investigation and design process is to produce a specification of users' requirements in documented form. This is referred to as the Statement of User Requirements and will be used to tender for supply of hardware and software.

Fact-finding methods

There are several methods which can be used to gather facts about a system: (i) interviewing; (ii) questionnaires; (iii) examination of records and procedure manuals; (iv) examination of documents; (v) observation. Each method has its own particular advantages and disadvantages and the method or methods chosen will depend on the specific circumstances surrounding the investigation, for example, the size of the business, the number of staff employed and their location and distribution.

Interviewing

This method has much to recommend it, in that the facts can be gathered directly from the person or persons who have experience of the system under investigation. On the other hand, a business with a number of geographically distributed branches makes the process of extensive interviewing expensive and time-consuming. Further, interviewing skills need to be acquired if the process is to be effective. The interviewer needs to know how to gain the confidence of the interviewee and ensure that the information which is given will be of value in the design of the new system. Questions need to be phrased unambiguously in order that the interviewee supplies the information actually required and a checklist of points will help to ensure that all relevant questions are asked. Of course, the interview may need to stray from the points in the checklist, if it becomes apparent that the interviewee is able to provide relevant information not previously considered. For example, clerical procedures may be designed quite satisfactorily but may be made less effective because of personality conflicts between staff. Such tensions may only be revealed through personal interview.

The interviewer also needs to detect any unsatisfactory responses to questions and possibly use alternative methods to glean the required information. Unsatisfactory responses include:

- Refusal to answer. Such refusal may indicate, for example, that set procedures are not being followed and that the member of staff does not wish to be 'incriminated'.

- Answer with irrelevant information. It may be that the question is ambiguous and has to be re-phrased in order to elicit the required information.

- Answer with insufficient information. If a system is to be designed which covers all foreseeable user requirements and operational circumstances, it is important that the analyst has all relevant information.

- Inaccurate answer. The interviewer may or may not be aware that an inaccurate answer has been given but it is important that other sources of information are used to cross-check answers.

Questionnaires

Questionnaires are useful when only a small amount of information is required from a large number of people, but to provide accurate responses, questions need to be unambiguous and precise. The questionnaire has a number of advantages over the interview:

- each respondent is asked exactly the same questions, so responses can be analysed according to the pre-defined categories of information;

- the lack of personal contact allows the respondent to feel completely at ease when providing information, particularly if responses are to be anonymous;

- questionnaires are particularly suited to the gathering of factual information, for example, the number of customer orders received in one week;

- it is cheap, particularly if users are scattered over a wide geographical area.

A number of disadvantages attach to the use of questionnaires:

- questions have to be simple and their meaning completely unambiguous to the respondents;

- if the responses indicate that the wrong questions were asked, or that they were phrased badly, it may be difficult to clarify the information, particularly if the respondents were anonymous;

- without direct observation it is difficult to obtain a realistic view of a system's operation. The questionnaire often provides only statistical information on, for example, volumes of sales transactions or customer enquiries.

Examination of records and procedure manuals

If existing procedures are already well documented, then the procedure manuals can provide a ready-made source of information on the way procedures should be carried out. It is less likely, however, that procedures will be documented in the smaller organization. In any event, it is important to realise that procedures detailed in manuals may not accord entirely with what actually happens. The examination of current records and the tracing of particular transactions can be a useful method of discovering what procedures are carried out.

Special purpose records which may involve, for example, the ticking of a box when an activity has been completed, can be used to analyse procedures which are causing delays or are not functioning efficiently. The use of special purpose records imposes extra burdens on staff who have to record procedures as they happen and the technique should only be used when strictly necessary.

Examination of documents

It is important that the analyst examines all documents used in a system, to ensure that each:

- fulfils some purpose, that is, it records or transmits information which is actually used at some stage. Systems are subject to some inertia, for example, there may have been a 'one-off' requirement to record and analyse the geographical distribution of customers over a single month and yet the summary document is still completed because no-one told the staff it was no longer necessary;

- is clear and satisfies its purpose, for example, a form may not indicate clearly the type of data to be entered under each heading. In any case, it may well require re-designing for any new system which is introduced.

The documents, which should include, for example, source documents, report summaries, customer invoices and delivery notes, help to build a picture of the information flows which take place from input to output.

Observation

It is most important to observe a procedure in action, so that irregularities and exceptional procedures are noticed. Observation should always be carried out with tact and staff under observation should be made fully aware of its purpose, to avoid suspicions of 'snooping'.

The following list details some of the features of office procedures and conditions which may usefully be observed during the investigation:

- office layout - this may determine whether the positioning of desks, filing cabinets and other office equipment is convenient for staff and conducive to efficient working;

- work load - this should indicate whether the volume of documents awaiting processing is fairly constant or if there are peak periods of activity;

- delays - these could show that there are some procedures which are constantly behind schedule;

- methods of working - a trained observer can, through experience, recognize a slow, reasonable or quick pace of working and decide whether or not the method of working is efficient. It is important that such observations should be followed up by an interview to obtain the co-operation of the person under observation;

- office conditions - these should be examined, as poor ventilation, inadequate or excessive temperatures, or poor lighting can adversely affect staff efficiency.

Often the observation will be carried out in an informal way but it may be useful on occasion to, for example, work at a user's desk, so as to observe directly the way that customer orders are dealt with. It is important to realise that a user may 'put on a performance' whilst under observation and that this reduces the value of the information gathered.

Documenting the results of analysis

A number of standard approaches, apart from narrative description, can be used to document the result of the system analysis, including: *data flow diagrams* (DFDs); *organization charts*; *system flowcharts*. Their applications are illustrated in the following section, which examines the categories of information which need to be gathered and recorded during a system investigation; data flow diagrams are further examined in Chapter 23.

Categories of system information

The major categories of information which need to be gathered involve: (i) functional relationships and data flows; (ii) personnel and jobs; (iii) inputs; (iv) processes; (v) outputs; (vi) storage.

Functional relationships and data flows

A business has a number of functional areas, such as Sales, Accounts, Stock Control and Purchasing, each having its own information system. However, the computerization of a system in one functional area cannot be carried out without considering its effects on the rest of the business. Information systems within a business interact with and affect one another. The business, as an entity, also interacts with and is influenced by individuals and organizations in the surrounding environment and the business's individual information systems should be co-ordinated to allow the achievement of overall business objectives. The data flows between individual functional areas can be illustrated with the use of a *data flow diagram* (Chapter 23).

Personnel and jobs

It is possible to design a computerized system without involving staff, but it is likely to be less successful, partly because users can provide valuable insights into the practical aspects of system operation and partly because they will feel less motivated if they have had little or no influence on the final design. A formal organization chart can be used to gain an overall picture of staff relationships and responsibilities but it should be borne in mind that designated and actual job responsibilities can differ radically. For example, it may turn out that a junior sales clerk is carrying out the checking of orders, which should be the responsibility of the sales supervisor. Thus, it may be necessary for the analyst to draw an alternative informal organization chart to show the actual working relationships of staff. An example is given in Figure 20.1.

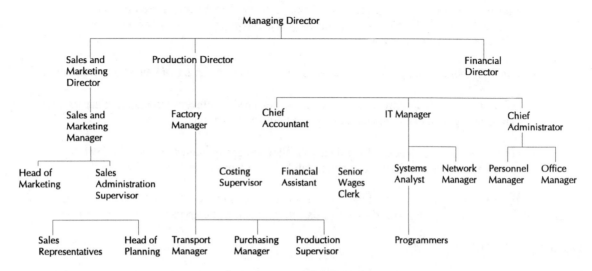

Figure 20.1. *Organization chart*

Apart from identifying working relationships between staff, it is useful to draw up brief job descriptions so that consultation on individual system procedures can take place with the appropriate staff. For example, a job description for a sales clerk may include the following activities: completion of standard order forms; checking stock availability; notification of orders to accounts.

Therefore, although the sales departmental manager may have knowledge of such procedures, the sales clerk will have practical experience of their operation and should be consulted.

System inputs

A number of details concerning the data inputs to a system need to be established:

- *source*. It may, for example, originate from a customer, a supplier, or another department in the business;

- *form*. The data may arrive, for example, by telephone, letter, or a standard form such as an order form or supplier's invoice;

- *volume* and *frequency*. For example, the number of orders received each day or week;

- *contents*. For example, the individual items of data which appear on a supplier's invoice.

Such information will allow the analyst to make recommendations on the most appropriate methods of computer input. The design of appropriate input methods also has to take account of several tasks involved with the collection and entry of data to a system:

- *recording*. For example, the completion of a customer order form following receipt of a customer order by telephone;

- *transmission*. For example, the order details may need to be transferred to another department or branch of the business for encoding and computer processing or they may be keyed in directly at the point of collection;

- *visual checking*. It may be, for example, that a customer order has no quantities entered;

- *encoding*. Verification procedures need to be designed to prevent transcription errors when data is encoded onto a computer storage medium for processing;

- *validation*. Data is checked by a data validation program against set limits of validity, for example, account numbers may have to fall between a particular range of values.

Thus, decisions need to be made concerning: (i) data collection procedures; (ii) methods for the transmission of data to the place of processing; (iii) data entry, data verification and data validation procedures.

Data collection

The designer needs to be aware of the available input technologies. These can be divided into two categories, keyboard entry and data capture technologies such as bar code reading, optical character reading (OCR) and optical mark reading (OMR), which allow direct input to the computer from specially designed input forms.

Keyboard entry

This is the most common method of input and requires the transcription of data from source documents. These can be designed to minimize the possibility of transcription errors at the data collection stage.

Direct input

Bar codes are pre-encoded and are thus immune from errors of transcription (assuming that the bar code is correct in the first place). Optical mark reading requires that pencil marks are used to indicate particular values from a limited set on a pre-designed form. Although no keyboard entry is required, mistakes may be made by the originator of the document and good design is therefore important.

Data transmission

It may be that no data transmission is necessary because the data is processed at the point of collection. For example, customer orders may be recorded on order forms at the sales desk and then taken into the next room for keying into the computer. Alternatively, the data may have to be transmitted some distance, perhaps to another floor of the building or to another building some miles away. A fundamental decision has to be made, whether to localize processing at the points of collection, or to use a central facility with data communications links from each location.

Data entry

The data entry method chosen will depend on the data collection methods used and may involve keyboard transcription from source documents or data may be captured directly from bar codes, OCR or OMR type documents. Where keyboard transcription is used, verification and validation procedures are likely to be interactive, in that the data entry operator has to respond to prompts on screen and make corrections as and when the system indicates. Most small business computer systems will be used for on-line processing, where transactions are processed immediately with master files at the data entry stage. Consequently, validation and verification have to be carried out immediately prior to the processing of each transaction.

On-screen verification

At the end of each transaction entry, the operator is given the opportunity to scan the data on the screen and to re-enter any incorrect entries detected. This usually takes the form of a message at the bottom of the screen which is phrased in a way such as Verify (yes or no).

On-screen validation

Character, data item and record checks, such as range and mode checks, can be made each time the RETURN key is pressed during data entry. For example, the screen may prompt for the entry of an account number, which must be 6 digits long and be within the range 000001 to 500000. Any entry which does not conform with these parameters is erased and the prompt re-displayed for another attempt. Appropriate screen dialogue to allow the data entry operator to enter into a 'conversation' with the computer is a crucial part of the input design process and is dealt with as a separate topic in Chapter 21.

Batch data entry

The type of keyboard transcription used will be affected by the type of input data. Where, for example, files only need to be updated weekly, transaction data may be batched and entered onto magnetic disk for processing at a later stage in one update program run.

System processes

All the clerical and machine-assisted processes, which are necessary to achieve the desired output from the given inputs, need to be identified. This will allow the systems analyst to determine the role of the computer in the new system, the programs necessary to take over the processing stages and the changes needed to clerical procedures, before and after computer processing. There are many instances when the processing requires not only the input data but also data retrieved from files. For example, to generate a customer invoice requires: (i) input data concerning commodity codes and quantities ordered; (ii) data from the stock master file concerning prices of items ordered by reference to the input commodity codes; (iii) customer details from the customer master file.

The above processes can be completely computerized but other processes may require human intervention. For example, before a customer order is processed, the customer's credit status may need to be checked and referred to a supervisor before authorization.

Non-standard procedures

Most processes will follow standards suitable for their particular circumstances. For example, before an order is processed, stock items ordered are checked for availability. It is important, however, that the investigation identifies and notes any non-standard procedures. For example, what procedure is followed when there is an insufficient quantity of an ordered item to completely fulfil a customer order? It may be that some customers will take part-orders, whilst others require the full quantity of an item or none at all. If non-standard procedures are needed, it is important to know their complexity, how often they are used and what extra information is required. Ideally, a system should be designed to cope with all possible circumstances, but cost sometimes forces a compromise. If cost prohibits the inclusion of certain system features, for example, the ability to deal with part-orders, then it is important that the business is aware of such limitations so that it can modify its business objectives.

Document flow

System flowcharts can be used to model the movement and interaction of documents and the data they record, as well as the processes involved, as they pass from one functional area or department of the business to another. In order that the involvement of each section, department or personnel grouping in the processes can be identified, the system flowchart is divided into columns representing these divisions of responsibility. A system flowchart may use a range of standard symbols which are illustrated in Figure 20.2. A number of standards exist for the drawing of system flowcharts and the range of symbols used depends on which stage of the investigation and design process has been reached. For example, in the early stages of investigation of an existing manual system, there will be no representation of computer methods of input, processing, output or storage. At a later stage, when computer methods are being considered, it will be necessary to use suitable symbols in the flowchart. Figures 20.3, 20.4 and 20.5 show example system flow-

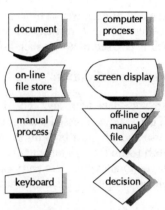

Figure 20.2. *Flowchart symbols*

charts. Figure 20.3 illustrates a manually operated order processing and invoicing system.

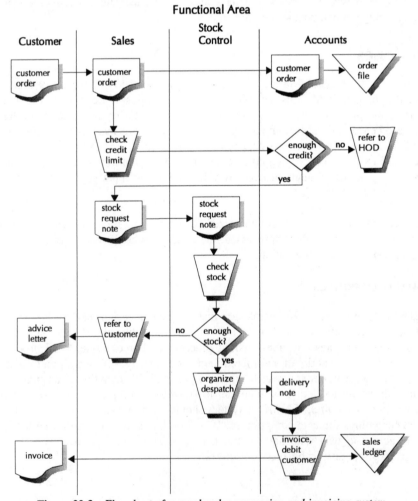

Figure 20.3. *Flowchart of manual order processing and invoicing system*

Figure 20.4 represents a batch processing update of a stock master file. Notice the sorting and validation stages, which are essential to batch processing systems. (Chapter 17).

Most business systems require alternative actions to be taken dependent upon some variable condition or circumstance. For example, 15 per cent customer discount may be allowed if the invoiced amount is paid within, say, 14 days of the invoice date, after which time all discount is lost. In order that computerized and non-computerized processes can be properly designed, the investigation must identify all: decisions made during system operation; conditions and circumstances which lead to alternative decisions; actions to be taken following a decision.

Figure 20.5 represents the computerized aspects of a similar system, but does not detail procedures needed to prepare, for example, the data for input or the distribution of output. A computerized system must have the necessary clerical procedures to support it. Some decisions and consequent actions will need to be documented for clerical procedure guidelines, whilst others which involve computer processing will form part of program specifications used in program writing or as bases for choice of packaged software.

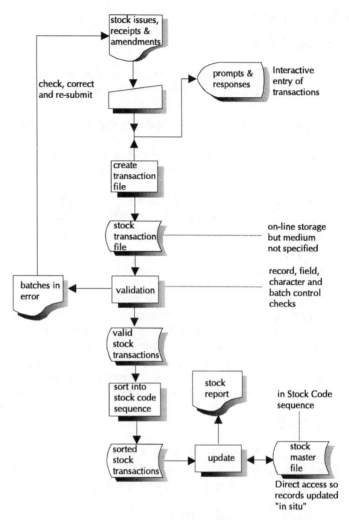

Figure 20.4. *System flowchart for batch processing, stock file update*

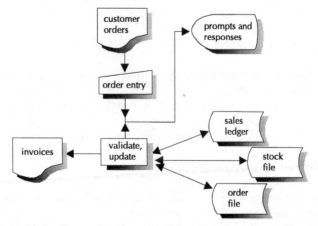

Figure 20.5. *System flowchart - on-line order processing and invoicing*

System outputs

Output design first requires identification of the following:

- data items required as output. Some may be revealed in the existing system, whilst others may be requested by users as being desirable in any new system;

- form of the output, for example, whether or not printed copy is required;

- volume of data with each output and the frequency of the output. This information assists decisions on the type and number of output devices required.

Based on the above information, the following tasks can be carried out: (i) selection of an appropriate output device to display or communicate the outputs. Available technologies are described in Chapter 8; (ii) designing output screen and document layouts. This topic is examined in more detail in Chapter 21.

System storage (files)

The storage of historic and current information is a vital part of any business system. For example, to produce a payslip not only requires transient input data concerning hours worked and sickness days but also data on rate of pay, tax code, deductions of tax and superannuation to date etc., which are held in the payroll master file stored on magnetic disk. Information on the contents of files will be gathered from existing manual files, together with responses from users regarding the output requirements of any new system. If packaged software is to be used then the contents of files will be dictated by the package, in which case some data item types may be surplus to requirements, whilst others which are required may not be available.

File contents

Each file consists of a number of logical records, each of which has a number of associated data items. For example, each stock record in a stock master file may include: Stock Code; Description; Unit Price; Minimum Stock Level; Re-order Quantity; Quantity in Stock.

File organization and access

This concerns the logical ordering of records within a file. The available file organization and access methods are described in Chapter 15.

Database management systems (DBMS)

An increasingly popular alternative to traditional file processing systems is to construct databases controlled by a DBMS. The design process requires that data is analysed according to subject area, for example, raw materials or staffing, rather than by department or functional area. The tools and techniques for database design are examined in Chapter 24; the structured analysis and design techniques examined in Chapter 23 are relevant to both database and non-database systems.

Choice of storage device

Choice is concerned with storage capacity, mode and speed of access. A full description of the various storage technologies is given in Chapter 9.

Chapter 21
User Interface Design

The movement from centralized to distributed systems and the expansion in microcomputer usage has spawned the need for a variety of approaches to the design of *user interfaces* (UIs) which fulfil the requirements of an increasing population of computer users, the majority of whom are not computer specialists. When all computer processing was controlled by small numbers of experts, in centralized data processing departments, there was little pressure for UI design to be particularly 'friendly'. This is probably a major reason why many people used to regard computers with some suspicion and apprehension. UIs are also variously known as *human-computer* and *man-machine* interfaces. UI design is now recognized as being of critical importance and is usually the yardstick by which a system is judged; poor UI design can seriously affect a user's view of a system's functionality.

Several design principles can be identified:

- it should be a product of collaboration between the designer and the users;

- user, not designer, convenience should be paramount;

- the interface should be of consistent design throughout the system;

- built-in help and advice should be accessible at different levels, depending on the degree of assistance required.

Interface metaphors

Through the use of metaphors, an interface can present a system's facilities in a form familiar to the user. A number of metaphors are commonly employed.

Desktop metaphor

As the term indicates, the UI relates everyday desktop or office facilities to routine computer tasks such as loading, saving or deleting files. The following representations are usual:

- filing cabinets for disc drives;

- documents for files;

- folders for directories;

- waste paper baskets for the deletion of files from backing storage.

Control panel metaphor

A screen control panel may include a variety of elements, such as: *buttons* for initiating actions, for example, print; *switches* for setting options on and off, for example, a grid on a spreadsheet; *radio buttons* for choosing from ESGs (exclusive selection groups), for example, A5/A4/A3 documents sizes; *sub-panel menu* of buttons or switches to select, for example, system default settings; *lights* to indicate some active event, for example, printing; *signs* displaying, for example, which file is currently active; *sliders*, to vary for example, RGB (red green blue) colour mixes.

WIMP interfaces

An acronym for Windows, Icons, Menus, Pointing (alternatively, Windows, Icons, Mice and Pull-down menus), the WIMP concept stems from original work by Xerox PARC Laboratories in the mid-1970s and was first employed on Apple Lisa and Macintosh computer systems. Since then a number of WIMP orientated UIs have been developed, notably, GEM, MS-Windows, ARC and Sun.

Such interfaces have a number of characteristics and features:

- the necessary skills are easy to grasp and the systems are easy to use;

- multiple windows for switching between tasks (multi-tasking);

- full-screen interaction allows quicker command execution than is usually possible through a *command line interpreter* (Chapter 13);

- control panels (see previous section).

However, as a relatively new concept, there are no standards for the design of WIMP-based products. Certain difficulties in their design may be experienced:

- although multiple windows are useful for task switching, too many windows can be confusing;

- designing icons which unambiguously tell the user of specific functions can be difficult and some may need to be augmented with text support, perhaps in a help window.

Menu systems

A menu of options is displayed, from which a user can make a selection. Menus are only appropriate where a limited range of options is available at any one time, although the selection of an item may cause the display of a further sub-menu. Commonly, each option is identified by a single letter or number which has to be keyed to select the option. Some packages, typically those running under the MS-DOS operating system, use a menu system which allows selection of an option either by highlighting the option with the cursor and pressing the 'enter' key or simply by keying the first letter of the option (without the need for confirmation). The problem for all such systems is to design each menu such that the first letter of each option is unique in that menu. The use of main menus which give access to sub-menus, each of which in turn may provide access to further sub-menus, follows a hierarchical structure.

A number of design principles may be employed:

- Provided a simple mechanism is available for the user to return to the main menu, then several levels of menu can be used without the user becoming 'lost'. Commonly, the Esc key allows the user to work backwards from lower level menus to the main menu. Alternatively, each sub-menu may include an option 'Return to Main Menu'.

- The designer of a menu structure should limit the number of options displayed in a menu to a maximum of about eight, at which point, a sub-menu should be considered for further options. An excessive number of options on screen at one time looks untidy and may be rather intimidating to the user.

Pull-down menus

This method generally displays the main menu along the top of the screen and is popularly associated with WIMP orientated systems. When an option is selected with the cursor or mouse pointer, the range of sub-options associated with it are 'pulled down' and displayed.

Menu systems provide a number of benefits:

- all possibilities are presented as a command list;

- minimal typing is required;

- error trapping is simple;

- inappropriate choices can be withheld from the user;

- context sensitive help can be provided.

The drawbacks are that:

- they can be tedious for experienced users;

- an extended hierarchy of menus can be difficult for the user to follow;

- a large number of choices may require the use of several screens, as is the case, for example, with viewdata systems.

Form-fill dialogue

This type of dialogue requires that the screen layout matches the associated input document as closely as possible. The operator is then able to make the entries in the same logical progression as the hand-filled form.

A number of features are usually evident:

- boxed in areas indicate fields for data entry;

- form headings are protected and cannot be overwritten by the user;

A number of design features can be applied to the data entry process:

- with fixed length data items, for example, a 6-digit account number, the cursor skips automatically to the next field as soon as the last character is entered;

- with variable length data items, the TAB key is pressed by the user when an entry is complete. This causes the cursor to skip to the next field;

- when all entries have been made, the user scans the screen to ensure all entries appear correct and the confirms them by pressing 'return';

- if errors are discovered before the 'return' key is pressed, a mechanism is available to enable corrections to be made.

The form-fill method is inappropriate when system responses are displayed which may obscure the screen headings or entries. Thus, if an invalid entry is made, the system should 'bleep' to indicate that a correction is required, without displaying an error message or display the message in a status line at the bottom of the screen; users should be well trained and aware of the valid data formats, so the need for help messages should be minimal.

Instruction and response

This design of dialogue is particularly appropriate for inexperienced users, where the main task is to input data. Examples are given in Figures 21.1 and 21.2. For more experienced users, the dialogue in Figure 21.1 would seem laboured and extremely frustrating, in which case it could be modified, as shown in the second figure, to omit many of the prompts.

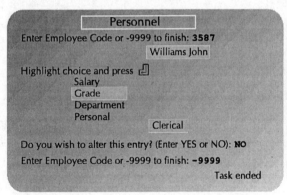

Figure 21.1. *An instruction and response dialogue*

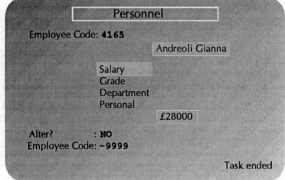

Figure 21.2. *Dialogue for a more experienced user*

Natural language dialogue

This type of dialogue is frequently used in database systems to allow users to specify their requirements in a 'natural' language style. The construction of the language is a complex process and many systems only allow the use of strictly limited syntax and sentence construction. Thus although the language can be described as 'natural', there is limited flexibility to allow different users to form requests in a way which is natural to each. As a result, the casual user may become frustrated by having to rephrase requests in attempts to resolve ambiguities. Queries tend to be verbose and speech recognition may provide useful support in the future.

Mnemonic driven dialogue

This design is suitable for highly trained users carrying out specialized tasks. Virtually no explanatory prompts are provided. A typical example can be found in airline reservation systems. The operator can carry out a variety of tasks relating to seat reservations using only brief mnemonic (memory aid) representations for the input. For example, in response to a customer enquiry, the operator requests a list of flights which may satisfy the customer's requirements. These may be:

```
Departure Date: 23rd June
Departure Time: 2.30pm
Departure From: London
Destination City: New York, USA
```

The operator's screen entry may appear as follows:

```
? A23JUNLHRNYCJFK1430
```

The string of characters is in strict sequence according to function. Thus: A = Available; 23JUN = 23rd June; LHR = London, Heathrow Airport; NYCJFK = New York City, John F. Kennedy Airport; 1430 = 2.30pm or up to one hour earlier or later. The system then displays any flights which satisfy these criteria, together with details of seats available, arrival times, type of aircraft etc. The operator can, if requested, immediately make a reservation for the customer with a similar mnemonic command.

Command line interface

The user enters a command to initiate action, to access information, or to call up a sequence of other commands. Still available with operating systems such as MS-DOS, a number of advantages and disadvantages are evident.

Advantages

- easy to implement with low resolution alphanumeric displays;

- the language processing techniques used with the command line interpreter (CLI) are well developed in the related area of compiler design and CLI's are thus cheap to produce;

- the power of the interface can be extended with macro commands;

- the brevity of commands, although not particularly user friendly, is ideally suited for rapid expert use.

Disadvantages

- unsuitable for inexperienced users;

- the command language must be learned and remembered;

- system interaction is restricted to the keyboard.

Some design considerations

- When designing command mnemonics, trying to achieve clarity of meaning tends to conflict with the aim of making them brief enough for rapid use.

- It may be helpful to use a two-tier system, providing menus for novices, leaving the 'hot key' facilities for experiences users.

Communication of errors

Where data validation is to be performed at the time of data entry, it is important that the interface facilitates error detection and correction. Before designing error dialogues, the following points should be noted.

- A screen which leaves error messages on screen and re-displays the prompt beneath is untidy and confusing to the user

- Repeated rejection of data without any explanation can be extremely frustrating. Such systems are only suitable for properly trained users who know the forms of input expected.

- Validation alone cannot ensure accuracy. Proper input document design, staff training and clerical checking are also vital. Users should be made aware of what validation is and its limitations, otherwise they may come to think of the system as infallible.

- It can save considerable frustration if the system is 'transparent' in terms of upper and lower case characters. In other words, entries are not made invalid simply because they are upper or lower case. Even if characters are to be output in only one case, the conversion can be carried out by the software.

- Where inexperienced users are involved, it may be useful if the system produces appropriate help messages from a file on disk. This facility is provided with many general-purpose packages.

- Error messages should be concise but detailed enough to allow the user to correct the error.

- Whilst using an application program, the user should not be presented with an error message directly from the operating system; as far as possible, all errors should be capable of being handled by the application and communicated via it to the user.

Other design considerations

It is important that the interface presents screen prompts and responses in a way which aids interpretation and to this end:

- any dialogue should follow a logical progression appropriate to the user, the activity and in the case of data entry, to the input document;

- spacing is important. Full use should be made of the screen space available;

- the interface should, as far as possible, be consistent across all applications in a given user area. This is particularly desirable when several packages are being used in a general application area such as accounts. The dialogue for sales ledger, purchase ledger, stock control and so on, should follow a similar structure. Many integrated packages allow the user to learn basic dialogue structure which allows rapid transfer of skills from one part of the package to another;

- techniques of highlighting such as brightness variation, blinking and colour coding should be used sparingly. Brightness variation should be limited to two levels, bold and normal as other variations will be difficult to detect. The blinking of a field on screen to attract the user's attention can be useful provided it does not continue once appropriate action has been taken.

Chapter 22

System Implementation, Maintenance and Review

There are several clearly identifiable areas which require attention in the implementation of a new system, including: file conversion; system testing; staff training; changeover plan - going live.

File conversion

All records to which the computer requires access must be transferred to the appropriate backing storage medium. Records may include those concerning, for example, customer accounting and stock control. The encoding of large files is a time-consuming process and because live transaction data will be continually changing the values in the master files, they may need to be phased into the computer system in stages. In a stock control system, for example, records for certain categories of stock item may be encoded and computer processed, leaving the remainder to be processed by existing methods and encoded at a later stage. If a business has inadequate staffing to cope with the encoding exercise, a computer bureau may be used. Where possible, the bureau's staff should carry out the work on site because the records will be needed for the continued operation of the business. In favourable circumstances, a large scale encoding exercise may be undertaken to initially create the file and then, through an application program, transactions which have occurred since the encoding began can be used to update the file to reflect the correct values. Users will have to be made aware of which records have already been encoded into the system, so that they can properly update them as transactions occur. An additional problem is that records in their existing state may not conform with the file layouts designed for the new system and the data may have to be copied onto special-purpose input forms to assist with accurate encoding.

System testing

Before a system is made fully operational it should be thoroughly tested, generally in stages. If reputable and popular packaged software is being used, then provided it is being used with a wholly compatible hardware configuration, its reliability can probably be assumed. It is essential, however, that the user tests the system with real data from the business. With tailor-made systems, the testing needs to be more complex and lengthy. Once the reliability of the system has been tested, the user should run it with historical data, for which the results of processing are already known. The computerized results can then be checked for accuracy and consistency against the known manual results; software testing is examined in detail in Chapter 28.

Staff training

The education and training of the users of a system is vital if it is to be operated correctly and the full benefits are to be obtained.

Generally, although managerial staff will not carry out routine data entry, except in the event of staff sickness, they should possess skills in the operation of a terminal, desk-top or notebook microcomputer, to allow them, for example, to make database enquiries. The supplier should provide training for everyone connected with the computer system, so that they are aware of its functions and are confident in its use. In the main, this will consist of computer operating skills for data entry staff, but those receiving computer output need to know what to expect and to be able to interpret it readily. Deciding when to carry out the training can be difficult. If too early, some staff will have forgotten what they have been taught by the time the system is introduced. If too late, staff may feel panicked because they have not been properly prepared.

System changeover

Switching from the old to the new system can be carried out in stages or all at once. There are three generally recognized approaches to going live: parallel running; pilot running; direct changeover.

Parallel running

With this approach, the old and new systems are run concurrently and the results of each are compared with the other for accuracy and consistency. The old system is not abandoned until the user has complete confidence in the reliability and accuracy of the new one. Obviously, parallel running places a great administrative strain on the business, in that staff are effectively doing many of the jobs twice. Any inconsistencies in results have to be cross-checked and the source of errors located (they may result from the old or the new system). The major advantage of parallel running is that the old system can be used whenever the computer system crashes or fails to function as it should. However, the two systems cannot operate together indefinitely and Murphy's Law will probably ensure that some errors only become apparent after the old system has been abandoned. In conclusion, it can be said that parallel running provides a safe, but expensive and time consuming, method of switching systems. It is unlikely that many businesses will use it for any extended period, except where system failure would be completely catastrophic.

Pilot running

This strategy requires that only a portion of live transactions go through the new computerized system, the rest being processed by the old method. Thus, for example, the transactions for one section of the business, or a sample of transactions from the whole business, could be used to test the system. This is a reasonably safe strategy but again, the transactions which cause errors may be amongst those which do not pass through the computer system.

Direct changeover

This is the riskiest option in that the new system completely replaces the old, without any interim parallel or pilot running. Its major benefit is the lack of administrative costs experienced with the other two methods. The potential costs can be severe, in that system failure could mean complete loss of data access and business failure. To minimize these risks, changeover should be preceded by careful system testing and thorough staff training. It is also helpful if the changeover is carried out during a slack period so that staff are not under pressure. The considerable cost of parallel and pilot running mean that this, the riskiest strategy, is often used in small businesses.

System maintenance

Following its initial introduction, a system will not remain static and dealing with the necessary changes is termed *system maintenance*. Problems will probably become apparent as the system is operated but even if they do not, the information needs of the business will probably change after a time. Some changes will come from within the business, as staff and management identify new possibilities for the system, whilst others may be forced upon the organization because of changes in the strategies of competitors or government legislation. The most important catalyst for change is probably the desire for better and more timely information by management, to assist their decision-making and planning. Maintenance may concern updating of hardware or amendment of software. The hardware purchased should be expansible and the software should, ideally, be flexible enough to allow amendments to be made. Often, where packaged software is used the manufacturer provides, either free or more usually for an additional payment, upgraded versions of the software with extra features (this can be a supplier-led method of system maintenance).

System review

Three to six months after system implementation, a review should be undertaken to assess the performance of the system against the suppliers specification. This should be agreed with the supplier beforehand to help avoid dispute. Following the review, the user can agree deficiencies with the supplier and hopefully have them remedied.

Case Study

This case study is the basis for the systems analysis exercise, which follows it. **Barford Properties** is a small firm of estate agents, with three partners, each one specializing in a particular aspect of the business. The specialisms are:

- property valuation;

- mortgage, insurance and conveyancing;

- marketing.

There are five sales negotiators and a potential buyer or vendor is assigned to one sales negotiator. The partner responsible for marketing has an assistant. These staff are directly responsible to the partners. An office manager is responsible for two accounts staff and one administrative clerk. Two secretaries are also employed, with a range of duties including general correspondence, and the production of property descriptions (including photographs).

The agency operates a number of functions, as follows:

- Property valuations. When a client first approaches the agency with a request to handle the sale of their property, the responsible partner visits the property to assess its market value. The establishment of a selling price is usually a matter for negotiation. The client has a minimum figure in mind, which may coincide with the valuation assessment by the agency. If the valuation is less than the minimum figure put forward by the client, they are advised to lower the asking price accordingly. However, the final decision is made by the client. The asking price may be reviewed, depending on the response or otherwise of potential buyers. In making the assessment, the agency draws on its local experience, but also on data concerning regional and national trends in the housing market.

- Property sales. Once an asking price is agreed, fees are settled. Charges vary according to the value of the property, as the agency takes a percentage of the ultimate selling price, plus costs of advertising. Other charges for conveyancing work are also made. The sales negotiator assigned to a vendor handles their routine enquiries and correspondence to keep them informed of progress. If a client is not satisfied with progress and wants a different asking price, for example, he or she is referred to one of the partners.

- Marketing. This section deals with the placing of advertisements in local and national newspapers and property journals. It also organizes the window displays and property details leaflets which are given out to interested buyers.

- Mortgage, conveyancing and insurance services (the agency acts as a broker). Buyers of properties handled by the agency are offered these services, and many clients make use of them, particularly if they are first-time buyers. The agency does not have Independent Financial Adviser status and mortgages are arranged with the Barford and Bamford Building Society. Property, mortgage protection and endowment insurances are obtained from the Buzzard Life Insurance Company.

- Financial accounting. This section handles all the customer accounts and deals with receipts and payments flowing between the agency, building societies, solicitors and insurance companies.

A brief outline of the procedures involved in a property sale is given below.

1. The initial request from a client wishing to sell a property is dealt with by the responsible partner, who makes an appointment to visit the property. Details of location, type, agreed asking price, number of rooms and so on are recorded. Photographs are also taken.

2. The property details are transcribed onto one of two standard forms, depending on whether the property is residential or business. This process is carried out in the Property Sales section.

3. The staff categorize the property according to basic criteria, including property location, type, size, quality, number of rooms and price range. These basic details are transcribed onto record cards, which are the initial point of reference when a potential buyer makes an enquiry.

4. To match prospective buyers with properties for sale, a Buyer Clients file is maintained. Details of suitable properties are sent (using a mailing list) to potential buyers.

5. When a buyer expresses an interest in a property, a viewing appointment is arranged between the buyer and the vendor (if the property is empty, one of the partners will accompany the buyer).

6. If a buyer expresses interest, they are asked to make an offer, which is then put to the vendor for consideration. Apart from the offer price, other factors are considered; for example, whether the buyer has a property to sell.

7. Once a sale is agreed, solicitors take over the process of carrying out the various conveyancing operations and agreeing a completion date, when payment is made and the property ownership changes hands. When this is completed, the agency requests payment of the fees by the vendor. Buyers are not charged by the agency, although they do incur conveyancing costs.

Exercise

This *systems analysis* exercise relates to topics covered in Chapters 18 to 22 and is based on the preceding Barford Properties case study. To extend the exercise, you may carry out some additional research into the operation of an estate agency in your area. It is proposed that the Property Sales system is computerized.

1. Produce a plan of the *systems analysis stages*, which you will need to follow. Explain the purpose of each stage and the general activities it involves.

2. Identify the users who would be expected to have access to the records and assess their requirements.

3. Undertake a *feasibility study* of the proposal. Define the *purpose* of the Property Sales System and establish its *objectives*. Other systems within the estate agency, which may interact with it, also need to be identified.

4. Briefly describe the standard techniques for gathering users system requirements. Select the technique(s) you consider most appropriate for the estate agency proposal and your choice. Prepare a *questionnaire* for gathering information from buyers. The aim of the questionnaire is to establish which types of information on houses they most need, in the initial stages of an enquiry and the form(s) in which they would like the information to be presented to them. You also want to know which types of house and price ranges are most in demand and the number of houses each respondent has bought. Most people have bought at least one house, so you should obtain around 20 *responses*.

5. Draw an *organization chart* to represent the divisions of responsibility in the agency.

6. Analyse the Property Sales system, and a produce a *systems analysis report* on the existing manual system. Use systems flowcharts, where appropriate. Your analysis should detail the current:

   - data collection methods and inputs;

   - documents used;

   - operations and decisions;

   - storage;

   - system outputs.

Also, include in your report, *recommendations* for a computerized system. These should:

   - describe the different types of system (for example, batch processing, transaction processing, information storage and retrieval) and make an argued recommendation for a particular type;

- detail *input* (including form, source and collection method), *processing* (form of processing activity), *storage* and *reporting* requirements of the system; you should also detail expected *volumes* of data and *frequency* of input and outputs;

- identify *expectations* of the system.

- assess likely *costs* and *savings* of a new system, identifying necessary resources.

Chapter 23

Structured Systems Development Techniques

The value of structure and methodology in programming is well recognized. Jackson's Structured Programming (JSP), described in Chapter 28 on Program Design is one such methodology which defines the structure of the data to be processed, determines the programming processes based on those structures and then defines the necessary tasks to be performed in more detail.

The task of analysing and designing a complete system comes within the framework of the system life cycle, described in Chapter 18 Systems Analysis - an Overview. The main drawback of the traditional analysis and design approaches, is that progress tends to be incremental and problems discovered at one stage frequently necessitate a return to an earlier stage to deal with them. The data modelling techniques described in this chapter and in Chapter 24 on Databases seek to improve on the traditional approach and like JSP, the approach described here is data-driven and typified by Entity-Relationship Modelling (ERM), which forms part of the data analysis technique developed by Chen in 1976. Methodologies developed since then have adopted the data driven approach or used ERM as a basis for another, such as the SSADM (Structured Systems Analysis and Design Methodology). The following sections describe the main tools and techniques used in data-driven methodologies.

Database modelling tools and techniques

Data analysis

Data analysis is a technique primarily concerned with determining the *logical structure* of the data, its *properties* and the *processes* needed to make use of it. Its objective is to produce a model which represents the information needs of a particular information system or sub-system and it should be understandable by users as well as analysts, in order to provide a basis for discussion and agreement. The main tool used within data analysis is the *Entity-Relationship Model (ERM)*, which classifies information into:

- entities;

- attributes;

- relationships.

Entities are objects which are of interest or relevance to the organization, for example, Supplier, Customer, Stock. An entity will normally equate with a database table; an *entity occurrence* is normally synonymous with a *record* within that table.

Attributes comprise those properties of an entity which are identified as being of interest to users. It may be helpful to equate attributes with fields in a conventional record, but it is important to note that in database systems (where the term data item type is sometimes used), it is not always necessary to have all the attributes for an entity stored in the relevant record in the database; it is necessary, however, to ensure that all attributes relevant to a particular entity can be associated with it. This point is explained in Chapter 24.

Relationships exist between entities. For example, an Employee works for a particular Department and a Purchase Order is sent to one particular Supplier. The degree of the relationship may be: one-to-one; one-to-many; many-to-many.

One-to-one relationship

Figure 23.1 provides an example of a one-to-one relationship. Each hospital patient develops a unique medical history and each medical history can only relate to one hospital patient.

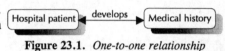

Figure 23.1. *One-to-one relationship*

One-to-many relationship

Figure 23.2 illustrates that an order may comprise one or many order lines, but each order line will be unique to a particular order. Note the double arrow head to indicate the *many* side of the relationship. By many, we mean one or more, whereas one means one only.

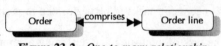

Figure 23.2. *One-to-many relationship*

Many-to-many relationship

A stock item may be ordered in a number of purchase orders and a single purchase order may include a number of stock items. This is symbolized in Figure 23.3.

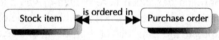

Figure 23.3. *Many-to-many relationship*

Some of the practical implications of these relationship types are explained in the *Stock Control* case study in Chapter 25 (Editing Tables through Query Dynasets).

An ERM for a given information system or sub-system may consist of a number of entities, the attributes associated with each and the relationships between those entities. The modelling process requires that any given model is continually refined until its efficiency in satisfying users' needs is optimized and its structure is in a form dictated by the requirements of the RDBMS in use.

An ERM for an Academic database

Figure 23.4 shows a normalized (3NF) entity relationship model (ERM) for the *Academic* database outlined in Chapter 24. The diagram can be interpreted as follows.

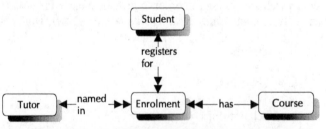

Figure 23.4. *Normalized ERM for Academic database*

- Each student registers for one or more enrolments, but each enrolment relates to only one student. This is a one-to-many relationship, the enrolments being the many side. The single arrow head indicates the one side and the double headed arrow, the many side.

- Each tutor is named in many enrolments, but each enrolment only names one tutor; this is also a one-to-many relationship. Although tutors are assigned students, the process is carried out through the enrolment entity, so there is no direct relationship between the Student and

Tutor entities; instead the connection is through the Enrolment entity. This structure is arrived at through the normalization process.

- Each course has many enrolments, but each enrolment only concerns one course. Therefore, there is a one-to-many relationship between the Course and Enrolment entities.

An ERM for a Personnel database

Figure 23.5 is an ERM for the *Personnel* database, used as a case study in Chapter 25.

The diagram shows the following relationships between the three entities.

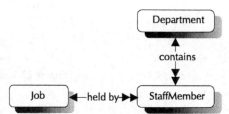

Figure 23.5. *Normalized ERM for Personnel database*

- Each department contains many staff, but each member of staff is based in a single department. There is a one-to-many relationship between Department and StaffMember.

- Each job (job title or grade) is held by one or more members of staff, but each member of staff has only one job title. The relationship between Job and StaffMember is also one-to-many.

The ERMs shown in Figures 23.4 and 23.5 illustrate database structures after data normalization. They can be drawn at various stages of the modelling process, to help clarify the entities which are needed and the relationships which arise between them. Thus, an ERM drawn for the Academic database after the first stage of normalization (1NF), would only show the Student and Enrolment entities (see Chapter 24). The second and third stages of normalization are fine-tuning the structure, but it must be in first normal form (no repeating groups) before you can attempt to construct a database. Entity relationship modelling can be a complex process, which requires much training and experience, so at this stage, you are likely to be constructing databases from fully normalized ERMs.

Functional analysis

This activity is concerned with identifying the data requirements, processes and activities relevant to each business function which is to use the data model established in the data analysis stage.

Data flow diagrams (DFDs)

Figure 23.6 shows some typical, standard symbols for the drawing of data flow diagrams. DFDs are used to illustrate, in a diagrammatic form, the logical data flows between entities, accompanying processes and any file storage or data stores. DFDs can be used at various stages in the analysis and design process. In the early stages, they will be at a high level and may, for example, show little detail except for a department's general function, such as sales accounting or stock control; later, DFDs may be drawn at a lower, more detailed level, to

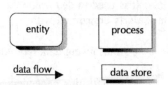

Figure 23.6. *DFD symbols*

show for example, the checking of a customer's account before sending an invoice reminder or statement of account. Figure 23.7 shows a *high level* DFD for a typical trading organization. More details on the data flows in its Sales Order Processing system are shown in the low level DFD in Figure 23.8.

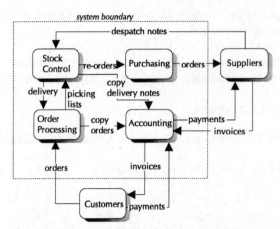

Figure 23.7. *High level DFD for trading business*

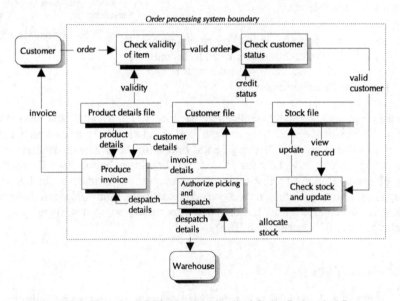

Figure 23.8. *Low level DFD showing detail of Order Processing System*

Normalization

Normalization (see Chapter 24) is a technique which is particularly useful in the design of relational database models. It is used to determine the validity of the logical data model produced in the data analysis stage and is particularly concerned with:

- minimising data redundancy or duplication;

- establishing dependencies between data items and grouping them in the most efficient way;

- obtaining a measure of data independence, such that a database can be supplemented with new data without changing the existing logical structure and thus the applications programs.

Prototyping

A prototype is, in effect, a first try at manufacturing a newly designed product; it is not expected to be perfect, but will form a basis for future development and design improvements. Car manufacturers do this when trying to incorporate revolutionary features and technologies into a new car. A prototype of an information system allows users to test it for achievement of their desired objectives. Prototyping can take place at various stages of the system development cycle, but its use must be planned and anticipated to ensure maximum feedback is obtained from users. In the early stages, a prototype may be developed to test the appropriateness of screen dialogues, without constructing the main files, whilst later it may include a section of database and some applications software. Prototyping is expensive, in terms of time and resources and is unlikely to be used where user requirements are well established or the system is fairly standard.

CASE (computer-aided software engineering) tools

Software engineering is a concept which recognizes the fact that the principles of engineering normally applied to other disciplines, can be highly relevant to the `engineering' of information systems; the parameters for the effectiveness and quality of an information system have to be set at the design stage, if users' needs are to be properly met.

A CASE tool can loosely refer to any software tool used in the development of information systems, for example:

- language processors (compilers and interpreters);

- fourth generation languages (4GLs);

- graphics programs to allow analysts to draw DFDs or ERMs.

A more precise definition of the term requires reference to the typical features of CASE proprietary software; complete CASE packages or toolkits are commercially available to aid the systems analyst and/or programmer in system development. A CASE toolkit would normally contain components for:

- diagram construction;

- data dictionary development and control;

- interface generation;

- source code generation;

- project management.

Diagram construction

This tool is essential for the support of a structured systems methodology. The graphical facilities allow the drawing, storage and modification of diagrams and charts, such as data flow diagrams (DFDs), entity-relationship models (ERMs) and data structure diagrams (for program development).

Data dictionary

Being particularly important in the development of database systems for the control and consistency of data, the function of data dictionaries is described in Chapter 24 on Databases.

Interface generation

Interface generators support the preparation of prototypes of user interfaces, such as screen dialogues, menus and reports.

Source code generation

These tools allow the automated preparation of computer software, in other words, the conversion of a system specification into the source code of a chosen programming language, which can then be compiled into executable object or machine code. CASE tools for code generation are general purpose and are, as a consequence less efficient in the production of source code than specialized applications generators; most code generators will only produce, say, 75% of the code automatically, leaving the rest to be hand-coded by a programmer.

Project management

Such tools support the scheduling of analysis and design activities and the allocation of resources to the various project activities.

Integrated CASE tools

CASE tools can be used as separate, discrete elements or as a complete system. The integrated use of CASE tools can best be managed through windowing software, which allows, for example, the simultaneous viewing of data flow diagrams and data dictionary entries on screen. Integration also has the benefit of allowing data from one component of the toolkit to be transferred to another, for example, data dictionary entries to entity-relationship diagrams.

Exercises

1. Identify the *entities*, *attributes* and *relationships* in each of the applications:

    (i)   patient records in a General Medical Practice;

    (ii)   a library lending system;

    (iii)   an estate agency's 'houses for sale' monitoring system.

2. Draw an *entity-relationship model* (ERM) for each application.

3. Define the terms: *prototyping*; *normalization*; *data dictionary*.

Chapter 24
Database Design and Construction

The term database is often used to describe any large collection of related data, but to understand the concepts which follow, it is necessary to establish a more precise definition. More specifically a database is *a collection of data, generally related to some subject or topic area and structured so as to allow relationships to be established between separate data items according to the various needs of users*.

From this definition it is possible to identify specific features of a database:

- A database contains data of use in a *variety* of applications.

- The data is *structured* to allow separate data items to be connected, to form different *logical* records according to the requirements of users and hence, to applications programs.

- A database will normally be used for different applications, but those applications must have some *common interests* concerning the data items they use. For example, sales, purchasing, stock control and production control applications are likely to use common data in respect of raw materials or finished goods. On the other hand, a database containing data on both materials and personnel may be difficult to justify; even then connections between the separate databases can be facilitated if the information requirements so justify.

Controlled redundancy

One feature which is not specifically referred to in the definition is that of *controlled redundancy*. Effectively, this means reducing to a minimum the number of data items which are duplicated in a database. In traditional computerized filing systems, each department in an organization may keep its own files, which results in a massive amount of duplication in the data that are stored. Although the removal of duplicated items is a desirable aim in terms of keeping database volume to a minimum, there are occasions when duplication is necessary to provide efficient access to the database.

Physical storage and data independence

Periodically, the *physical* database needs to be changed to accommodate variations in user requirements. However, there is no need to alter all applications programs, because the way the data is *physically* stored on the storage medium is independent of the *logical* record structures required by applications programs. In a traditional computerized system, if a data file is changed, then any program accessing it needs to be changed also. In a database, records can be stored essentially in two different ways.

- Independently - the primary key is used to decide the physical location of a record; frequently this is effected through a *randomizing* process to distribute records efficiently on the storage medium.

- In association - records are stored according to their relationship with other records and connections may be made between them with the use of *pointers* (Chapter 32 on Data Structures). A *physical pointer* gives the address where a record is stored and can be used to relate records anywhere in the database; a *logical pointer* is a value from which the physical address can be calculated.

The physical and logical database

A database has to satisfy the differing information needs of many users, generally through specially written applications programs. Therefore, it is often necessary to add further data items to satisfy changes in users needs. The software which controls the database must relate to the data at data item rather than at record level, because one programmer's logical record requirements may contain some data items which are also required for another programmer's logical record description. The physical database must allow for both. It must be possible for data items to be connected into a variety of logical record forms.

Creating the database

A special language called a *data description language* (DDL) allows the database to be created and changed and the logical data structures to be defined.

Manipulating the database

A *data manipulation language* (DML) enables the contents of the database to be altered by adding, updating or deleting records. The language is used by programmers to develop applications programs for users of the database. The functions of both these languages are combined, together with a query language facility in *Structured Query Language* (SQL), which is dealt with later in the chapter.

Database storage

Because the database must allow for various user applications programs accessing it at the same time, direct access storage must be used. There are many ways of physically organizing the data which are dealt with in the chapter on Data Structures, but whatever method is used it must allow for the variety of logical record forms needed by applications programs. The applications programmer does not need to know how the data is physically stored. The programmer's knowledge of the data held in the database is restricted to the *logical view* required for the program. The complete or global logical database is termed the *schema*. The

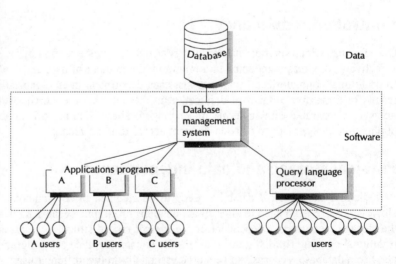

Figure 24.1. *Relationship between database, DBMS, applications and users*

restricted or local logical views provided for different applications programs are termed *subschemas*.

Database management systems (DBMS)

So that each application program may only access the data which it needs for processing or retrieval (that data which is defined in its subschema), a suite of programs referred to as the Database Management System (DBMS) controls the database and prevents accidental or deliberate corruption of data by other applications programs. An application cannot access the database without the DBMS. Figure 24.1 illustrates the relationship between users, application programs, the DBMS and the database.

A DBMS has the following functions.

- It is the common link between all applications programs and the database.

- It facilitates the use and organization of a database and protects the database from accidental or deliberate corruption.

- It restricts a programmer's logical view of the database to those items of data which are to be used in the applications program being written.

Types of database

The logical structure of a database can be based upon one of a number of natural data structures which the Database Management System (DBMS) uses to establish links between separate data items. Physical pointers inform the DBMS where the next logical record is to be found. In certain types of database the logical organization of the database is constrained by whatever data structure is used and can therefore be described as *formatted*. Two main categories of data structure are used in such databases: (i) *Hierarchical* or *tree* structure; (ii) *complex* and *simple plex* structure (often called *network* structures). To avoid some of the restrictions inherent in formatted databases, a popular method of database management is to use a *relational* approach. To provide a basis for comparison with relational databases it is useful first to examine the data structures used in formatted databases.

Hierarchical or tree structure

A hierarchical or tree structure is illustrated in Figure 24.2. Each element is called a *node* and the only node which is not a *member* in any relationship is the *root* at the top of the tree. Three features of this structure need to be identified:

- only *one-to-many* relationships are supported;

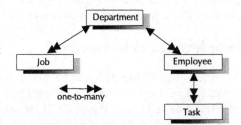

Figure 24.2. *Hierarchical structure*

For example, in the Figure 24.2, each Department can have many Employees, but each Employee can only belong to one Department. Similarly, each Employee may have more than one Task but each Task can only be carried out by one Employee.

- the highest level in the hierarchy has only one node called the *root;*

- each node is a member in exactly one *relationship* with a node on a level higher than itself, except for the root node at the top of the tree.

For example, Job and Employee each relate to only a single *parent node* (Department); the root node, Department, is not a member in any relationship. The main problem with the hierarchical structure is that not all databases fit naturally into it; a record type may require more than one parent. For example, a library database may require a book to be a member in more than one book category, say, Geology and Geography.

Network data structures

There are two types of network or plex data structures: *complex*; *simple*.

Complex plex structure

A complex plex structure is illustrated in Figure 24.3. This structure supports *many-to-many* (complex) relationships. Thus, a Student may be enrolled on one or more (many) Courses and each Course may have many Students.

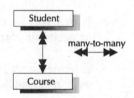

Whether or not such data structures can be used depends on the data description language (DDL) being used. IBMs DDL called DL/I supports any plex structure but the Codasyl DDL (described later) does not and cannot therefore, be used to describe complex plex structures.

Figure 24.3. *Complex plex*

Simple plex structure

A simple plex structure is illustrated in Figure 24.4. This structure supports *one-to-many* or simple relationships and unlike the tree structure, a node can have more than one parent. Thus, for example, a Quotation record may be owned by both one Builder and one Job record, but each Builder and Job record could own many Quotation records.

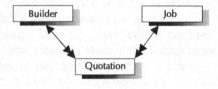

Figure 24.4. *Simple plex*

A complex plex structure can be reconstructed if the available software does not support such a structure. For example, the complex plex structure in Figure 24.3 can be converted to a hierarchical structure or to a simple plex structure. These reconstructions are shown in the Figures 24.5 and 24.6 respectively.

Complex plex to hierarchical

The structure in Figure 24.3 can be converted to two hierarchical or tree structures by duplicating Course and Student as follows in Figure 24.5; the course and student data will only be duplicated *logically*, not physically.

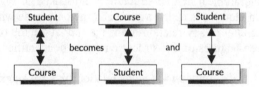

Figure 24.5. *Complex plex to hierarchical*

Complex plex to simple plex

The simple plex structure in Figure 24.6 is achieved through the creation of another record, which avoids the need to duplicate the Student and Course data. The relationships are now one-to-many rather than many-to-many. The new record Enrolment must contain the information necessary to establish the relationship between the original Course and Student records; as in this example, the record identifiers are generally used for this purpose.

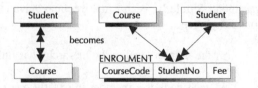

Figure 24.6. *Complex plex to simple plex*

An example of a DBMS which supports *simple plex* structures is the CODASYL database management system. The Codasyl logical schema in Figure 24.7 serves to illustrate this method of database organization.

Codasyl database schema for a large company

The schema can be explained in terms of *sets* as follows.

There are 4 record types:

1. DEPARTMENT

2. STAFF MEMBER

3. SECTION

4. PREVIOUS JOBS

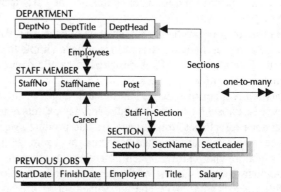

Figure 24.7. *Example Codasyl schema*

Each of 1, 2 and 3 can be retrieved directly by its *record key*, DeptNo, StaffNo and SectNo respectively. Record type 4 is only accessible through the STAFF MEMBER type record. This is reasonable as it would be unusual to search for a PREVIOUS JOBS record without first knowing the identity of the member of staff. There are 4 *sets*, each of which has an *owner* record and one or more *member* records. For example, one DEPARTMENT will have a number of STAFF MEMBERs (a one-to-many relationship). The sets are:

Employees	*(owner*, DEPARTMENT/ *member*, STAFF MEMBER)
Sections	*(owner*, DEPARTMENT/ *member*, SECTION)
Staff-in-Section	*(owner*, SECTION/ *member*, STAFF MEMBER)
Career	*(owner*, STAFF MEMBER/ *member*, PREVIOUS JOBS)

Diagrammatically, a set can be pictured as shown in Figure 24.8. For example, referring to Figure 24.7, Department 4 (an owner record) may have a number of Section (member) records.

Data Manipulation Language statements could be used to retrieve a Section record directly using its SectNo or through its Sections Set (owned by Department Record). For example, if the section is in Department No 12, it may be found through the following steps.

```
1 move 12 to DeptNo
2 find any Department
3 show Section
4 find next Section
5 show Section
```

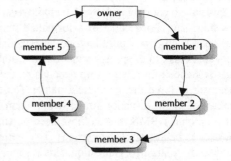

Figure 24.8. *Codasyl set*

Steps *4* and *5* are repeated until the correct Section record is found or the end of set is reached. It should be noticed that a PreviousJobs record can *only* be found through the Career set and the appropriate StaffMember record. As with any database, a Codasyl DBMS organizes and accesses the logical database through the schema description. In all formatted databases, the structure defines the route which can be taken through the database, but the programmer/user must know what linkages have been established to be aware of how and what data can be accessed.

Relational database management systems

This section examines the principles of database design and definition, as well as the role of a *relational database management system* (RDBMS) package. RDBMS software packages are designed for the construction and control of *databases*. Packages, such as dBase, Paradox and Access, are often loosely referred to as databases. Strictly and to avoid confusion, they are database management systems (DBMS).

A fair amount of jargon is associated with database theory but the ideas represented are straightforward and simple to understand. A relational DBMS is designed to handle data in two-dimensional, *table* form and a single database is likely to contain a number of separate, but related, tables. This tabular view of data is easy to understand; everyday examples include telephone directories, train timetables and product price lists. An example of tabular data is given in Table 24.1. For information and clarity, when referring to other texts on relational databases, some of the jargon is defined below, by reference to Table 24.1. The underlined terms are not used further in this text.

PART_SUPPLIER		
PartCode	**Price**	**SupplierNo**
012	3.25	14
015	0.76	07
016	1.26	14
018	7.84	05

Table 24.1. *Tabular data*

- A table is sometimes referred to as a a *relation* and each entry in the table is a single data item value. For example, PartCode 012 is a data item value consisting of 3 characters.

- Each column in the relation contains values for a given *data item type*. We will use the word *field*. The set of values for a given data item type is called its *domain*. A domain is identified by its description, that is, the name for the data item type. For example, in Table 24.1 the set of values in the second column is called the Price domain.

- Each row in a relation is a record occurrence and is called a *tuple*; we use the more usual word, *record*. The terms record and field are defined in Chapter 15.

Establishing relationships

The power of a relational DBMS lies in its facility to allow separate tables to be manipulated and combined in a variety of ways to establish new tables. Thus, for example, a table containing details such as the names and addresses of a firm's employees can be combined with a table detailing the make and registration numbers of cars owned by the employees, to produce a new table containing the names of employees owning, say, Ford cars. In a formatted database using a simple plex structure, for example, connections between such data would have to be established when the database is constructed; a relational database can leave this task to the programmer or the Database Administrator (DBA). The important thing to realise is that the existence of a relationship depends on the presence in both tables of a field value or values; they may not necessarily have the same field name. Tables in a relational database are related dynamically through the values of the information found within them, rather than through inbuilt physical links. In the simplest types of relational DBMS, that is those used on small business systems, it is the responsibility of the programmer or user to be aware of the existence of common values to link tables together. In a mini or mainframe system owned by a larger organization, this responsibility may lie with the DBA, whose task is to control database usage by programmers and users.

The need for common values to establish relationships requires some duplication of data (see later examples) and thus some *controlled redundancy*.

Benefits of a relational DBMS

The attraction of the relational approach is that logical record structures and connections between them are not constrained by pointers using rigid formats such as those provided by the tree and plex structures described earlier. Instead, with some duplication of data or controlled redundancy, a programmer can establish any relationships that need to be made for output specified by users. New relations can be added or existing relations modified as user requirements change.

Database design

Design is an important pre-requisite for database construction. For example, a common mistake is to create one table, containing all the data items required by the applications programs. Consider the Product table in Figure 24.9. Additional fields could be included for suppliers' names and addresses, but, on the assumption that many products come from one supplier, much data would be needlessly duplicated. It is more useful to create a separate table for the suppliers' names and addresses, as shown in Figure 24.10. Note that the Supplier table also contains a Supplier Code field; this allows a *relationship* to be established with the Product table. Similarly, a database for the maintenance of student records, may contain a single table consisting of twenty or thirty data items ranging from student name, address, and date of entry, to all assignment and exam grades for all subjects studied within a given course. Clearly, such a database is unwieldy when, for example, a list of student names and addresses is all that is required by a particular user. The following sections describe some of the more important concepts and techniques relating to proper database design.

PartCode	Description	Price	Quantity	SupplierCode
A123	Table (Cottage)	£23.50	15	KSU518
A124	Chair (Cottage)	£42.23	36	KIT518
A125	Stool (Cottage)	£28.15	6	KIT518
A133	Bar Stool	£33.55	4	KSU518
A136	Bread Bin (wood)	£14.25	4	KIT518
A139	Bread Bin (metal)	£10.25	6	KSU518
B122	Spanner (adjustable)	£8.25	4	BCS436
B126	Step Ladder (small)	£19.50	6	PAR116
B129	Screw Driver (ratchet)	£15.55	13	BCS436
B133	Ladders (aluminium)	£85.66	2	STA436
B136	Spirit Level	£13.55	6	STA436
B145	Step Ladder (medium)	£31.25	4	PAR116
B181	Hammer (medium claw)	£6.75	12	STA436

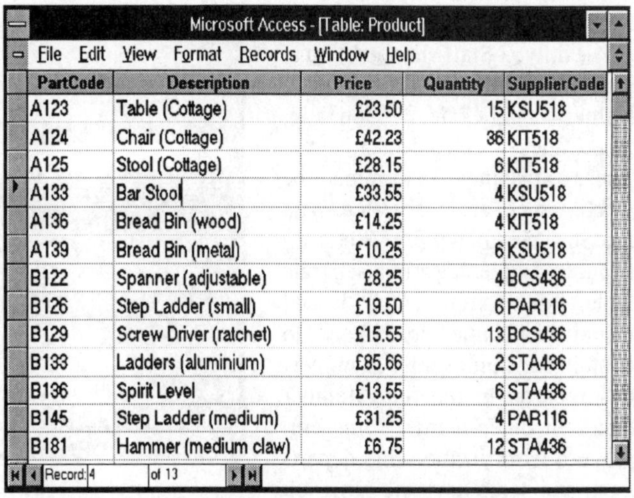

Figure 24.9. *Product table*

PartCode	Description	Price	Quantity	SupplierCode
A123	Table (Cottage)	£23.50	15	KSU518
A124	Chair (Cottage)	£42.23	36	KIT518
A125	Stool (Cottage)	£28.15	6	KIT518
A133	Bar Stool	£33.55	4	KSU518

SupplierCode	SupplierName	SupplierAddress
ABC123	ABC Supplies	Transit Row, Darlington
KIT518	Kitchen Systems	28 Holmeside, Sunderland, SR3 4ST
KSU518	Kitchen Supplies	112 High Street, Darlington, DL1 4SJ
PAR116	Parsons Ltd	Parsons House, Market Place, York YO4 3NS
STA436	Stapleton	36 Warwick Place, Darlington, DL4 6AJ

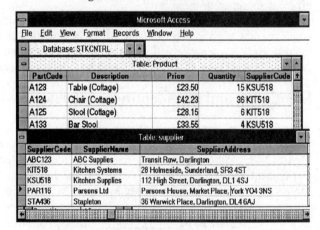

Figure 24.10. *Product and Supplier tables*

Entities

A database should contain a number of logically separate tables, each corresponding to a given subject or part-subject (an *entity*). In the example of the product database (Figure 24.10), two logically separate tables (one for the Product entity and the other for the Supplier entity) are constructed. *Entities* are the objects of the real world, which are relevant to a particular information system.

Attributes

An entity has a number of related *attributes*, which are of interest to users. Consider, as an example, a Personnel database (see also *Personnel* case study in Chapter 25). An entity, StaffMember, may have the attributes of StaffCode, Name, JobCode, JobTitle, DeptCode, DepartmentName. These attributes determine the *fields* which are associated with the StaffMember *table*. Some attributes may be kept in a separate table. For example, JobTitle and DepartmentName are likely to contain the same values in numerous records in the StaffMember table. In other words, some employees work in the same department and some have the same job title. With an RDBMS, it is more efficient to separate these attrib-

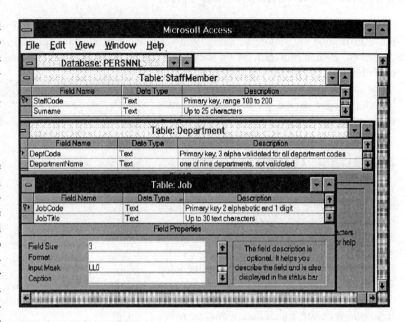

Figure 24.11. *Tables for StaffMember, Department and Job entities*

utes, through the creation of separate tables (one for Department and the other for Job). Although an employee has a given job title and works in a particular department, these attributes are also of separate interest; each is a separate *entity*. For example, a new job title may be identified before an employee has been assigned to it. Figure 24.11 shows the tables which represent these entities.

Identifying and non-identifying attributes

Some attributes, for example, Name and JobTitle, are descriptive. Another (StaffCode) may serve as a unique identifier. Attributes can be classified, therefore, as being either *identifying* or *non-identifying*. In Figure 24.11, StaffCode acts as the unique identifier (or *primary key field*) for a StaffMember record; Department and Job records use DeptCode and JobCode, respectively. These entity and attribute structures can be expressed in the form shown in Figure 24.12. Unique identifiers are underlined.

```
StaffMember (StaffCode, Name, JobCode, DeptCode)
Job(JobCode, JobTitle)
Department(DeptCode, DepartmentName)
```

Figure 24.12. *Entity structures*

Sometimes, more than one attribute is needed to uniquely identify an individual record; such attributes form a *composite identifier* or *key*. An example of such a key is given below.

```
. Order Line (OrderNo, ItemNo, Description, Price, Quantity)
```

Figure 24.13. *Entity structure using composite primary key*

An order form usually has several lines, each relating to a separate item which a customer wants. The same item may be ordered by other customers, so the OrderNo and ItemNo are needed to identify a particular order line, relating to a particular customer order.

Relationships and link fields

Notice that, in Figure 24.12, the JobCode and DeptCode fields also remain in the StaffMember table. This is necessary to allow relationships, or links, to be established between the tables. Suppose, for example, that a user wishes to view a list of employee details, which includes Name, DepartmentName and JobTitle. The list is obtained by *querying* (see Database Construction and Operation) the database. To process the query, the RDBMS needs to extract information from more than one table. An examination of the entity structures in Figure 24.12 reveals that all three are needed (StaffMember, Job and Department). The user must specify which fields are used to link the tables to one another. Figure 24.14 illustrates these links.

DeptCode is the primary key for the Department table, but the same attribute also appears in the Staff-Member table. When the two are linked, DeptCode in the Staff-Member table is acting as a *foreign key*. JobCode in the StaffMember table also serves as a foreign key when it is used to link with the Job table.

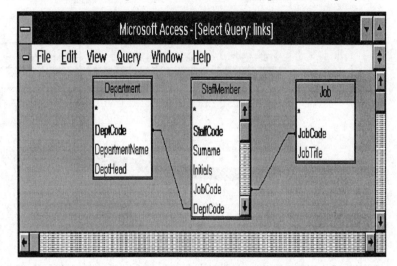

Figure 24.14. *Link fields to establish relationships between tables*

Data analysis

This process (see Chapter 23) is concerned with establishing what the entities, attributes and links (*relationships*), for any given database, should be. To make such an analysis, it is obviously necessary to have knowledge of the organization to which the information relates, because there will be certain items of information which only have significance to that particular organization. For example, in an Academic database, the following entities may be identified and a table established for each.

```
Student; Course; Tutor; EducationHistory; ExamGrade
```

Normalization

Normalization is a technique established by E.F. Codd to simplify the structure of data as it is *logically viewed* by the programmer or user. The data requirements for a database are systematically analysed to establish whether a particular attribute should be an entity in its own right, or simply an attribute of some other entity. When an attribute is identified as a separate entity, the link or relationship must be maintained with the original entity. Normalization is a step-by-step process for analysing data into its constituent entities and attributes. Its main aim is to improve database efficiency. There are three stages of normalization described here, though there are others which are beyond the scope of this text. To illustrate the process of normalization, the example of an *Academic* database is used. When a student enrols for one or more courses, a registration form is completed. An example is shown in Figure 24.15.

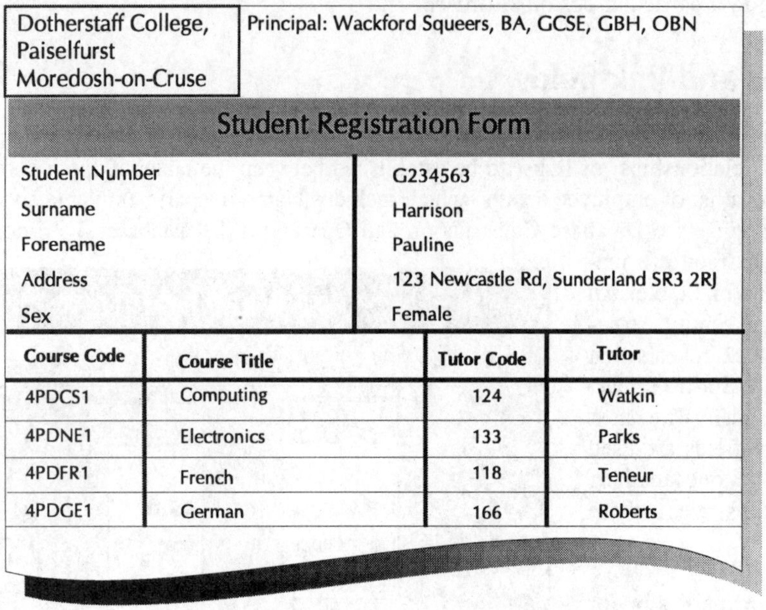

Dotherstaff College, Paiselfurst Moredosh-on-Cruse	Principal: Wackford Squeers, BA, GCSE, GBH, OBN

Student Registration Form

Student Number	G234563
Surname	Harrison
Forename	Pauline
Address	123 Newcastle Rd, Sunderland SR3 2RJ
Sex	Female

Course Code	Course Title	Tutor Code	Tutor
4PDCS1	Computing	124	Watkin
4PDNE1	Electronics	133	Parks
4PDFR1	French	118	Teneur
4PDGE1	German	166	Roberts

Figure 24.15. *Extract from student registration form*

First normal form (1NF)

Treated as a single entity, the structure could be described, initially, as shown in Figure 24.16.

```
Student (StudNo, Surname, Forename, Address, Sex, [CrseCode, CrseTitle,
TutNo, TutName])
```

Figure 24.16. *Structure of Student entity*

The unique identifier (primary key), StudNo, is underlined. Each student registration form (see Figure 24.15) may show enrolments on several courses. Thus, the attributes [CrseCode, CrseTitle, TutNo and TutName] can be identified as a *repeating group*.

The first stage of normalization demands the removal of any repeating groups. This is achieved by creating a new entity. The attributes in question relate to the activity of enrolment, which is of separate interest and an entity in its own right. The new entity is called Enrolment-1 and is used to store details of individual enrolments; each enrolment will be a separate record in the Enrolment table. Neither StudNo nor CrseCode, on its own, uniquely identifies an individual enrolment. A *composite key*, using both attributes, is used to uniquely identify a single enrolment. The two entity descriptions are shown in Figure 24.17.

```
Student-1(StudNo, Surname, Forename, Address, Sex)
Enrolment-1(StudNo, CrseCode, CrseTitle, TutNo, TutName)
```

Figure 24.17. *Entity structures after conversion to first normal form (1NF)*

The entities are now in first normal form (1NF) and this is indicated by suffixing each entity name with a 1. The unique identifier is underlined in each entity description. Note the *composite key* in the Enrolment entity.

To relate the Enrolment records to the relevant Student records requires that StudNo (as the link field) appears in both the Student and Enrolment tables in the Academic database. Thus, to ensure that entities and attributes are in first normal form requires the removal of repeating groups of attributes, rewriting them as new entities. The identifier of the original entity is always included as an attribute of any such new entity, although it is not essential for it to form part of the identifier of the new entity (it could be a non-identifying attribute). Some necessary *data redundancy* is created by including StudNo in both entities, to allow a given student to be connected with a particular enrolment. Such duplication of data does not necessarily mean an increased use of storage because normalization is concerned with the *logical structure* of the data and not with the ways in which the data is physically organized.

Second normal form (2NF)

The second stage of normalization ensures that all non-identifying attributes are *functionally dependent* on the unique identifier (the primary key); if the identifier is composite (comprising more that one attribute), then non-identifying attributes must be functionally dependent on the whole of the identifier. This rule is best explained by example. Consider the 1NF entity descriptions, produced from the first stage of normalization (Figure 24.17). Referring to the Enrolment entity, it can be seen that TutNo and TutName each depend on both parts of the composite identifier. For example, if a student enrols on more than one course, he or she has a different tutor for each course. To identify a tutor in an enrolment record, requires specification of both values (StudNo and CrseCode). However, CrseTitle is not functionally dependent on the whole of the

composite identifier, only on CrseCode; the title of a course could be found through entry of the CrseCode value alone. Figure 24.18 illustrates both these points with a diagram. An arrowed line connects the box, which surrounds the composite identifier, to TutNo and TutName. CrseTitle is connected only to CrseCode. The second stage of normalization is achieved by the creation of a new entity, Course-2, with the attributes CrseCode (the identifier) and CrseTitle. The entity descriptions now appear as in Figure 24.19. The suffix 2 indicates that all entities and attributes are now in second normal form.

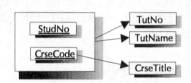

Figure 24.18. *Functional dependency*

```
Student-2(StudNo, Surname, Forename, Address, Sex)
Enrolment-2(StudNo, CrseCode, TutNo, TutName)
Course-2(CrseCode, CrseTitle)
```

Figure 24.19. *Entity structures in second normal form (2NF)*

Benefits of 2NF

Conversion of entities and attributes to second normal form brings advantages apart from the avoidance of some data duplication. The entry of new data into the database is also facilitated. Suppose, for example, that a new course is to be added to the database and that the data is stored as arranged after the first stage of normalization. The new course entry could not be made until the first enrolment for that particular course. Also, if a particular course has no enrolments, then information concerning the course is not held in the database.

Third normal form (3NF)

At this stage we are concerned with finding any *functional dependencies* between non-identifying attributes. These can be identified from Figure 24.19 as TutNo and TutName and are illustrated in Figure 24.20. Again, the problem is solved by the creation of a new entity, Tutor-3. The entity contains TutNo as the identifier and TutName as a non-identifying attribute. The entities are in third normal form (indicated by the suffix, 3), as shown in Figure 24.21.

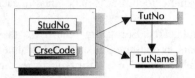

Figure 24.20. *Functional dependencies*

```
Student-3(StudNo, Surname, Forename, Address, Sex)
Enrolment-3(StudNo, CrseCode, TutNo)
Course-3(CrseCode, CrseTitle)
Tutor-3(TutNo, TutName)
```

Figure 24.21. *Entity structures in third normal form (3NF)*

Defining a database structure

Each entity structure, shown in Figure 24.21, must be defined as a table in the *Academic* database. In the case of Student-3, it would be beneficial to sub-divide Address into separate attributes of, say, Street, Town and PostCode. Each definition includes reference to *primary keys*, *field names*, *data types* and *field lengths*. All these terms are explained, through examples, in Chapter 25 on Database Case Studies, but are briefly defined below.

Primary keys

In the Academic database, for example, StudentNo, CrseCode and TutorNo, act as primary keys for the Student, Course and Tutor tables, respectively. Although an Enrolment record can be identified through the combined use of StudNo and CrseCode, you could add an additional field, such as EnrolmentNo, to act as the primary key.

Data types

A typical RDBMS provides the following data types.

Character, text or alphanumeric

This is for a field which may contain text, or a mixture of text, symbols and numbers. Sometimes a field may only contain numeric digits, perhaps an account number or telephone number. If it is not treated numerically, but as text, character type is normally used.

Numeric

This type must be used for fields containing numerical values (such as money amounts or quantities) to be used in calculations.

Logical (yes/no)

This type allows the entry of two possible values, indicated by *true* or *false*. Sometimes, *yes* and *no*, respectively, may be used instead. For example, the Student table in the academic database contains a field to record the sex of a student. Use of the field name Male means that Yes is entered for a male student and No for a female. If the field name Female is used, No is entered for a male and Yes for a female student. The name of the field determines whether an affirmative or a negative (Yes or No) is entered.

Date

Although character type may be used for the storage of dates, the *date* type allows the correct sorting of dates. Also, in defining queries, date type fields enable the database to compare dates held in records, with a specified date. This is not practical with a character type field.

Field lengths

Logical and *date* type fields invariably have a pre-determined length, typically, 1 and 8 respectively. For a character field, a maximum length must be specified (allowing for the number of digits, letters or symbols to be accommodated within it). Numeric fields are defined according to the number range which needs to be accommodated and the number of decimal places.

Abbreviating and coding data

There are a number of benefits to be gained if data can be abbreviated or coded, without obscuring its meaning. Some are described below.

- *Saving space*. Codes and abbreviations take up less space, but must be of sufficient length to allow the entry of unique values. The minimum length of such a field is determined by the number of different values which need to be represented.

- *Query expressions* can be shorter. As long as users are aware of what the codes mean and are happy with using them, much time and keying effort can be saved.

- *Data entry*. If there are a large number of records to be keyed in, the procedure is extremely time-consuming and tedious. Coding and abbreviating data may reduce the time and labour requirements considerably.

Querying a database

A query is a request for information from a database. Queries can include *criteria* for the selection of information. For example, the Academic database could be queried for details of all male students, or students on a particular course. If the query requires that the RDBMS takes data from more than one table, appropriate link fields must be indicated. Suppose, for example, that a report is required listing the names of all students, together with the name(s) of the course(s) on which they are enrolled. It is assumed that no criteria are specified. Student names are held in the Student table, the course code is in the Enrolment table, and the name of the course is in the Course table. Therefore, to process the query requires that these three tables are used. The QBE form of the query is shown in Figure 24.22.

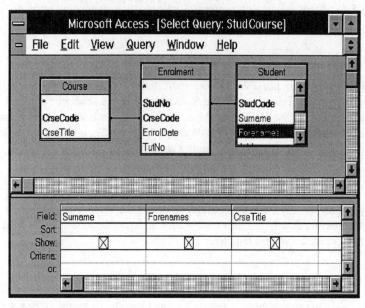

Figure 24.22. *Query (QBE form) using three tables from Academic database*

The query can also be expressed in *Structured Query Language* (SQL), as shown in Figure 24.23.

```
SELECT DISTINCTROW Student.Surname, Student.Forenames, Course.CrseTitle
FROM Student INNER JOIN (Course INNER JOIN Enrolment ON Course.CrseCode =
Enrolment.CrseCode) ON Student.StudCode = Enrolment.StudNo;
```

Figure 24.23. *Structured Query Language (SQL) form of query in Figure 24.22*

The use of SQL and QBE is dealt with in Database Construction and Operation. The query produces more than one record per student, but this is because a student may be enrolled on more than one course. The output appears in Figure 24.24.

Secondary keys

Apart from the primary keys, which are used to identify records uniquely, an important function of an RDBMS is to allow the querying of the database, by reference to *secondary key* values. Thus, in the Academic database, useful secondary keys could be CrseTitle, and TutName (if neither code was available). Secondary keys can also be used as foreign keys (see Relationships and Link Fields), when joining tables in a query.

Surname	Forenames	CrseTitle
Pallister	Robert	Electronics - Foundation
Atkinson	Fiona	French - Foundation
Wilson	John	German - Foundation
Cancello	Carla	German - Foundation
Williamson	Peter	Art - Foundation
Adamson	Rachel	Art - Foundation
Erikson	Karl	Art - Foundation
Pallister	Robert	German - Intermediate
Laing	Alan	Electronics - Advanced
Pompelmo	Paolo	Electronics - Advanced

Figure 24.24. *Output from query in Figure 24.22*

Structured query language (SQL)

Many new RDBMS packages provide a Structured Query Language (SQL). Practical examples of SQL are given earlier in this chapter and in Chapter 25. Developed by IBM, SQL is a *non-procedural* language and as such belongs to the group of programming languages known as 4th Generation Languages (4GLs); this means that programmers and trained users can specify what they want from a database without having to specify how to do it. Procedural languages such as COBOL, Pascal and C, require the programmer to detail, explicitly, how a program must navigate through a file or database to obtain the necessary output. The programmer must, for example, code procedures such as read the first master record, process it, read the next, process it and so on until the end of the file is reached. As explained below, SQL is an attempt to provide a language which includes the facilities normally provided separately by a *data description language*, a *data manipulation language* and a *query language* (to allow on-demand queries by users).

Features of SQL

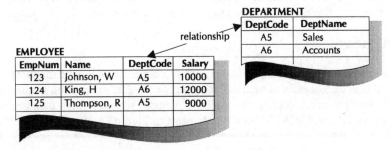

Figure 24.25. *Extract from company database*

The example database extract in Figure 24.25 is used here to illustrate some of the main features of SQL by showing how a programmer or trained user could use SQL to access a database without specifying procedures.

Selection by criteria

Referring to Figure 24.25, if the Name and Salary of EMPLOYEE 124 is required, the SQL statements may take a form similar to the example in Figure 24.26).

```
SELECT Name, Salary
FROM EMPLOYEE
WHERE EmpNum = 124
```

Figure 24.26. *SQL statement to extract details of Employee 124*

The output would be as in Figure 24.27.

Name	Salary
King, H	12000

Figure 24.27. *Output from query in Figure 24.26*

SQL supports all the functions expected of a *relational* language including, for example, the operators, JOIN and PROJECT.

Updating the database

SQL can also change values in a database; for example, to give all employees in the A5 (Sales) department a 6 per cent pay increase, the statements shown in Figure 24.28 may be used:

```
UPDATE EMPLOYEE
SET Salary = Salary * 1.06
WHERE DeptCode = A5
```

Figure 24.28. *SQL update query*

SQL has built-in functions and arithmetic operators to allow the grouping or sorting of data and the calculation of, for example, average, minimum and maximum values in a particular field.

Defining the database

As a multi-purpose database language, SQL can be used to define, as well as manipulate and retrieve data. This definition function is traditionally carried out using a separate data description language (DDL) but SQL incorporates this facility for implementing the logical structure (*schema*) for a database. For example, to create a new table called QUALIFICATIONS the statements in Figure 24.29 may be entered:

```
CREATE TABLE QUALIFICATION
(EmpNum CHAR (3)
Qual VARCHAR (20));
```

Figure 24.29. *SQL statement to create a table*

The table would contain two fields, namely, EmpNum with a fixed length of three characters and Qual with a variable number of characters up to twenty. Following creation of the table, data can be entered immediately if required.

Modifying the database definition

Tables can be modified to allow for the removal or addition of fields, according to changes in user requirements. Existing data does not have to be re-organized and applications programs unaffected by data changes do not have to be re-written. The independence of the logical database from the applications programs is known as *logical data independence* and constitutes one of the main features of a relational database.

Two major aims are inherent in the design of SQL:

- As a non-procedural language it is expected to increase programmer productivity and reduce the time and costs involved in application development.

- SQL allows easier access to data for the purposes of on-demand or ad hoc queries.

Techniques for Database Administration

Database administrator (DBA)

A database administrator (DBA) appointed with a corporate function has special responsibility for:

- database design and development;

- selection of database software;

- database maintenance;

- database accuracy and security.

A DBA should have a working knowledge of both the DBMS and the organization. A DBA will supervise the addition of new data items to the database (changes to the schema). Supervision of the data dictionary is also the DBA's responsibility (see next paragraph). The DBA has to ensure the consistent use of data across the whole database. For example, a functional area may request new data to be added to a database, when it already exists. This can happen when different departments in an organization refer to a field by different names. For example, a Sales department may refer to the name Product Code, whilst the Warehouse staff may use the term Stock Code, when referring to the same field. During database development, it is easy to forget the precise definitions given to a field and when adding the field to another table, introduce inconsistencies.

Data dictionaries

A data dictionary system is a data processing department's own information system, with the database administrator, systems analysts and programmers as the main users.

An essential part of the database design process is to maintain a data dictionary. Its main function is to store details of all the data items in a database. Such details can be wide ranging, but should include, as a minimum:

(i)   field names and the table(s) in which they occur;

(ii)   field definitions, including field types and lengths;

(iii)   additional properties, concerning, for example, data formats and validation controls;

(iv)   synonyms. Sometimes, the same field occurs in more than one table, but using different names. Generally it is better not to use synonyms.

The dictionary's main role is to ensure consistent data usage; if synonyms are used (different data names may be used by different functional areas of an organization to refer to the same field), the dictionary must record their use accordingly to prevent duplication.

Database recovery

Recovery techniques can be used in certain circumstances to recover lost data when a database is corrupted. Most recovery techniques depend on making a *dump* (copy) of the whole (or a selected part) of the data in the database. Recovery of a database requires:

- that the cause of the failure be diagnosed and remedied;

- replacement of the corrupted database with the most recent dump of the database;

- updating of the database with all the transactions and amendments which occurred since the last dump until the time of the database's failure.

Difficulties are apparent in this procedure; re-processing may take a long time and all updating transactions which have taken place since the last dump must be recorded, together with their sequence of entry, since the order of processing can determine the eventual state of the database. To allow for this, a DBMS will record each entry in a sequential file or transaction log; re-processing can then take place in the correct sequence, without the need for any re-keying of data.

Data sharing and data integrity

Sharing of data by different users is fundamental to the database concept and the DBMS has to allow for it, whilst at the same time protecting the *integrity* of the database. Such access may be through different applications programs or through the same one. Database integrity is not affected by accesses which only read data; no matter how many users are reading the same data, its integrity will not be affected. *Concurrent* updates present the possibility of updates being lost.

Consider, for example a database schema which held the following stock record type.

```
STOCK(Item#, Item-Description, Quantity-held)
```

Two applications programs PR1 and PR2 are updating the Quantity-held for Item# 3254; following the delivery of units of that item, PR1 is to increase the balance by 200, whilst PR2 is to reduce it by 150 in respect of stock issues. If the initial value of Quantity-held is 200, then the following sequence of events could occur:

(i)   PR1 reads Stock record, Item# 3254;

(ii)   PR2 reads Stock record, Item# 3254;

(iii)   PR1 increases Quantity-held by 200 and re-writes the record to the database;

(iv)   PR2 decreases Quantity-held by 150 and re-writes the record to the database.

At this stage, Stock record, Item# 3254, would show a Quantity-held value of 50, when it should be 250. This error has occurred because PR2 read the record before PR1 had re-written its updated version to the database.

With the use of *integrity locks*, a DBMS can ensure that any program which reads a record for the purpose of updating, must result in the *locking* of that record against access by any other updating program, until the updated version has been re-written to the database. Programs accessing the record for *reading purposes only*, are not prevented access by an integrity lock.

Integrity locks can be implemented through the use of an additional data item within a record, the value of which can be set to *on*, as and when required. Integrity locks can present their own problems, but they are not of concern in this text.

Database security

Security is concerned with controlling access to data, both to prevent its accidental or deliberate corruption and, in the case of confidential data concerning individuals or organizations, to maintain appropriate privacy.

Access control mechanisms

Identification, authentication and authorization

Before being granted access to a database, users must identify themselves, normally with an assigned account number or identification code. Authentication of a user's identity normally requires provision of a password, known only to the system and its legitimate users; the Chapter on System Controls examines the topic of passwords in more detail. The system holds information, supplied initially by the database administrator (DBA), on each user or category of user. This information is held to allow the system to carry out its identification and authentication procedures and to determine the level of authorization - the kinds of access any particular user is permitted.

Another mechanism for controlling access uses access control locks and access control keys. Consider the following example of how a very simple access lock could work; the extracts of a schema description and application program are coded in the Codasyl Data Description Language and Data Manipulation Language.

Schema extract
```
     RECORD NAME IS CLIENT
     CLIENT-NUM PICTURE 9 (8)
     DATE-OF-BIRTH PICTURE 9 (6)
     BALANCE PICTURE 9 (6) V99
     ACCESS CONTROL LOCK FOR GET IS `ZEBRA'
```

Program extract
```
     MOVE `ZEBRA' TO KEY-CHECK
     USE FOR ACCESS CONTROL ON GET FOR CLIENT
```

The character string 'ZEBRA' is declared as being the access control lock on the command GET for the data item BALANCE, only. Thus, the Balance data cannot be used by an application program unless the access control key 'ZEBRA' is provided and transferred to the location called KEY-CHECK, where it is compared by the DBMS with the access control lock. If the values do not agree then access is prevented to the Balance data. This is a fairly trivial example and not particularly secure, as a glance at the schema listing would reveal the access control lock's value; more sophisticated ways of assigning the access control lock are generally used.

Levels of authorization

A fundamental principle of security is that access is limited to those persons who require it and that the degree of access is limited to that which is necessary to their jobs. For example, authorization to alter schema or sub-schema descriptions may be limited to the DBA; user A may be given access to particular data for enquiry, but not for alteration purposes, whilst User B may be the only person authorized to change prices in the Stock File.

Benefits and drawbacks of databases in general

The following list details some of the generally accepted advanatages and disadvantages.

- Apart from controlled redundancy, there is no unnecessary duplication of data as occurs in traditional filing systems. Apart from the economic advantage, this means that transactions can update all affected areas of the database through a single input.

- Because of the single input principle, there is less chance of inconsistency as may occur if the same transaction is keyed in several times to different files. Equally, of course, an incorrect entry will mean that all applications programs using the data will be working with the wrong data value.

- The opportunities for obtaining comprehensive information are greatly improved with a central pool of data.

- On-demand or ad hoc enquiries are possible through the use of a query language.

- Security opportunities are enhanced because access to a single database can be more readily controlled than is possible with a system based on numerous separate files. On the other hand, database design and creation is a complex process and the failure of a database affects all applications which make use of it.

Exercises

1.   Distinguish between the *physical* and *logical* database.

2.   Define the terms *schema* and *subschema*, illustrating your definition with examples.

3.   Suggest three applications for which a *hierarchically* structured database would be unsuitable.

4.   (i)   If the relationship between 'cinema' (with multiple screens) and 'film' is *complex plex*, what does this mean?

     (ii)   Illustrate a method of converting the relationship in (i) to a *simple plex* structure and explain the new structure.

     (iii)   Why would the conversion in (ii) be necessary for a relational database structure?

5.   What kind of structure is supported by a Codasyl database management system?

Chapter 25
Relational Database Case Studies

The Overview section takes you through the main facilities provided by an RDBMS (relational database management system), using a simple database example. Then there are three database case studies to provide varied illustrations of RDBMS usage. They are: *EuroTent*, holding information on European campsites; *Personnel*, which stores staff details for Pilcon Electronics; *Stock Control*, which records details of products and suppliers. In Chapter 24, another case study, *Academic*, is used to illustrate the design process for a relational database.

Overview of RDBMS operation

When you use an RDBMS, you need to be familiar with the purpose and functioning of a number of components, which are described in the following paragraphs. A simple Products database is used to illustrate the descriptions.

Tables

An RDBMS is designed to handle data structured in two-dimensional *table* (the term relation is also used) form. A single database may contain one or more tables. The *EuroTent* database has only one table, which holds all the information on the European campsites it has in its brochure. The *Personnel* database separates the data into three separate tables, each being concerned with a different aspect of staff information. Thus, there is a table holding staff names, department codes, job codes and salaries; the other two tables contain further information on jobs and departments. *Stock Control* is a database comprising two tables, one for product and the other for supplier details. The *Academic* database (see Chapter 24) places information on enrolments, students, courses and tutors into four separate tables. The idea of dividing information into separate tables is fundamental to the operation of an RDBMS and is explained fully, in Chapter 24. Although the information may be in more than one table, it is related and can be brought together as and when you require, by linking or joining the tables. It is anticipated that you will work through the EuroTent example first, as this will allow you to develop your skill in the practical operation of the RDBMS package, without concern for relational database theory. To fully understand the Personnel and Stock Control examples you should first have studied Chapter 24. You will use tables in two ways:

(i)   to *define the structure* of the data which is to be held within it; you need to do this before you can enter any data into the database;

(ii)   to *enter* and subsequently *view* and *edit* the data within a table.

Figure 25.1 shows data held in a Product table.

Each column in Figure 25.1 corresponds to a particular type of data and is referred to as a *field*. A name which identifies a particular field is known as a *field name*. There are five fields in the Product table, called PartCode, Description, Price, Quantity and SupplierCode, respectively. Each row in the table is a *record* occurrence. The PartCode field is used to uniquely identify an individual product and is know as the *primary key* field. For example, PartCode 'A125' allows unique identification of the 'Stool(Cottage)' record and the information contained within it. The Product table will contain a record for each product. Figure 25.2 displays the definition of the Product table.

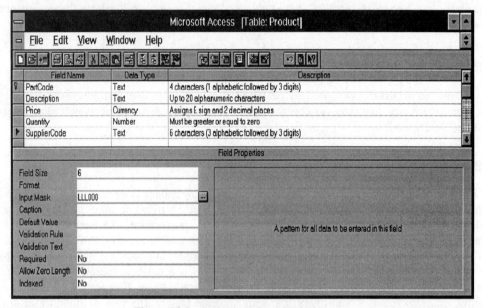

Figure 25.1. *Product table with sample records*

Figure 25.2. *Definition of product table*

A number of table features can be identified from Figure 25.2. There are three columns in the upper part of the window. From left to right, the columns are used for:

- *Field names*. You enter a field name for each item of data you are going to store concerning the table topic. In Figure 25.2, the table defines a product *record* which comprises five fields: PartCode; Description; Price; Quantity and SupplierCode.

- *Data types*. You can define the kind of data which is to be stored in a field. For example, in Figure 25.2, you can see that the Description field allows the entry of *text*; this means any characters, alphabetic or numeric. Obviously, the Quantity field is defined as *number*, because it will contain numeric quantities only. The definition of the Price field as *currency* ensures that a £ sign and 2 decimal places are automatically assigned to each price entered. Thus, for example, if you enter the value 3.5, it will be altered to £3.50. Other data types include date and logical, but these will be described in more detail later.

- *Field descriptions*. These are not used by the RDBMS and are simply there to allow you to document some aspect of the field.

Field Properties

The lower half of the window is for the specification of *field properties*. Figure 25.2 displays the additional properties set for the SupplierCode field:

- *field size* has been restricted to 6 characters;

- an *input mask* ensures that each supplier code is entered as 3 letters followed by 3 digits. You should also note that *validation* parameters can also be set. For example, the Quantity field prevents entry of values less than zero.

Forms

You can use a form to tailor your view of information held in a table. A form is always associated with a particular table and allows you to enter, edit and view the data held within it. A form is not a separate store of data, but simply an alternative view of its associated table. A major benefit of a form is that it allows you to view or edit one record at a time; a table displays as many records as can be accommodated within its window. Figure 25.3 shows a form associated with the Product table in Figure 25.1. It was created using a Form Wizard, in the Access RDBMS.

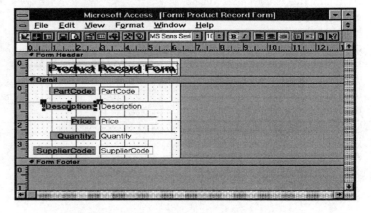

Figure 25.3. *A form for Product records*

You can begin with a blank form and design your layout, or more easily, you can produce one with a wizard and then modify it to your requirements. Figure 25.4 shows the Product Record Form in design mode, with the 'Description' field label selected. You can see from the figure that a form consists of a number of objects, including field labels and data entry points. Each data entry point uses the field name defined in the table definition and ensures that each entry point on the form is associated with the correct field in a record.

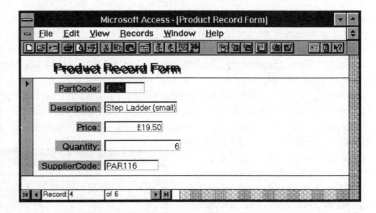

Figure 25.4. *Product Record form in design view*

As a consequence, field names should not be altered on the form (unless they are also altered in the table definition). Field labels, on the other hand can be altered; the field names are used by default, unless you specify otherwise. The form design is divided into sections: *header* (for titles); *detail* (for the field names and data entry points); *footer* (for additional comments, perhaps to guide the data entry process).

Queries and dynasets

A query is a request for information from a database. You can use a query to:

(i)   display all the records in a table;

(ii) display information from several tables by *joining* them (see Personnel, Stock Control and Academic Case Studies);

(iii) display limited information by specifying that only certain fields are displayed;

(iv) use *criteria* to *filter* records from one table or from several joined together.

The data extracted by a query is known as a *dynaset*. Referring to (iv), you may want to query, for example, a Product database for all products supplied by a particular supplier; alternatively, you may wish to identify products within a particular category. Each of these is an example of a *criterion*. If you specify more than one requirement, such as products from a particular supplier, under a particular price, then you are using two *criteria*. When criteria are used in a query, a filter is being applied; only those records which satisfy the criteria pass through the filter. If you want to identify an individual record, you will normally use the primary key; in the case of the Product table, this would be the PartCode. To retrieve groups of records, such as products from a particular supplier, you can use the SupplierCode, which is an example of a *secondary key*. You can only identify products within a particular category if there is a field in the table which allows for it. In the Product table in Figure 25.1, you can see that the PartCodes beginning with 'A' are connected with items of furniture, whereas, the 'B' items are do-it-yourself or DIY items. Assuming this is the intended categorization, you could use the first letter of the PartCode for such a query. In this case, the PartCode field will be serving as a secondary key; this is because only part of it (the first character) is being used. A query can be made on a single table or, as demonstrated in the Personnel, Stock Control and Academic examples, on more than one. Queries can be expressed in one of two forms:

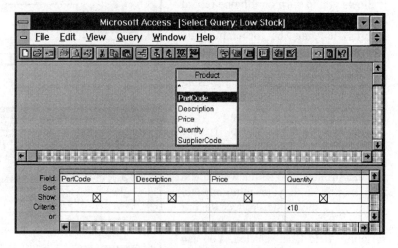

Figure 25.5. *Query by example to retrieve products with quantity less than 10*

(i)   *query by example (QBE)*. With this method, queries are carried out according to the criteria you provide, in the form of examples. The query in Figure 25.5 uses the Product table from Figure 25.1. By entering the expression '<10', which means 'less than 10', under the Quantity field, you are effectively applying a filter; only records which satisfy the criterion pass through the filter and are selected by the query.

Figure 25.6 shows the result of running the query. Compare it with Figure 25.1 to see the effect.

(ii) *structured query language (SQL).* This method requires that you know the form of the language, to write the query expressions. However, if you create a query using the QBE method (which is the simplest), you can request the RDBMS to show you the SQL equivalent. Figure 25.7 displays the SQL equivalent of the QBE example in Figure 25.5. For most queries you will use QBE, but SQL is needed if the query you want to make is not possible with QBE.

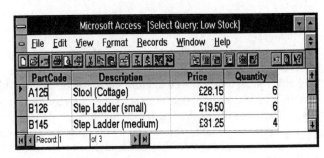

Figure 25.6. *Dynaset from query in Figure 25.5*

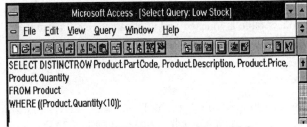

Figure 25.7. *SQL for query in Figure 25.5*

A number of component parts can be identified in the SQL statement in Figure 25.7. The lower case words are table and field names. The upper case words: SELECT; DISTINCTROW; FROM; WHERE, are all SQL *reserved words*. Like any programming language, they have a particular meaning to the language processor and can only be used for a specified purpose. Briefly, each has the following use:

- SELECT. This is used to select individual or groups of records from named table(s); it is followed by the fieldnames (each prefixed by its table name) to be displayed when the query is executed;

- DISTINCTROW. This prevents the selection of duplicate (values are the same in the fields selected for the query) records;

- FROM is used to identify the table(s) to which the query is directed; in Figure 25.7, the named table is Product;

- WHERE is followed by the criterion which, in Figure 25.7, is that the Quantity is less than 10. The field name is prefixed by the name of the table (Product). This is because a criterion can be directed at a different table from the one identified in the FROM clause.

Sorting

Although a table or query output may have a particular sequence, perhaps in the order of the primary key, there will be occasions when you want to change the sequence. If for example, you are viewing a list of personnel, you may wish the list to be in alphabetical order by surname. Alternatively, you may prefer to see them first grouped into departments (which you also want in alphabetical order) and then, within each department, ordered alphabetically by surname. Before executing a sort, you need to indicate which column or field is to dictate the sequence; apart from this, you can choose ascending or descending order. Indexing (see below) can be used to speed the sorting process.

Indexes

Indexes are used to speed the sorting and retrieval of records. If you index (see Table definition in Figure 25.1) a field, this speeds the sorting and retrieval of records, using that field as a key. The effect will only be noticeable with databases containing hundreds of records. The RDBMS creates an index file for each field you index and has to update it every time you modify the contents of the table to which it relates. Indexes take up space and because of the need for their updating, may have the effect of slowing data entry and editing. For this reason, you should avoid using them indiscriminately. An index file contains all the values taken from the indexed field. For example, if you indexed the SupplierCode field in the Product table in Figure 25.1, each value in that column would be in the index file. Each value would then have a pointer which indicated the physical location of the record containing that value. Referring to Figure 25.1, you can see that some supplier code values are duplicated; this is necessary because numerous products may be supplied by a single supplier. You can choose that the index allows for duplicates. The primary key in the Product table is indexed and duplicates are not permitted; this is obvious, because the purpose of the primary key is to uniquely identify a record.

Reports

Report facilities allow you to decide what information from a table or query is visible when you view it or print it. Reports are usually categorized as:

- *Single column*. Records are displayed in full down the side of the page or screen, rather than across the page in columns.

- *Multiple column*. A column is provided for each field you specify and records are placed one after another. You can allow the field names to be used as column headings, or design your own.

- *Grouped*. If the information can be grouped into different levels, then the report can be presented in this way, with sub-totals or other calculations on numeric or currency fields, at the end of each group or subgroup.

Figure 25.8 shows a report on screen, generated with a 'report wizard', using the Product table from Figure 25.1. The sequence is by Description and this was specified as part of the report construction process. Like *forms*, you can design reports from scratch or use a wizard and then modify the design (see Figure 25.4 for Form design) as necessary.

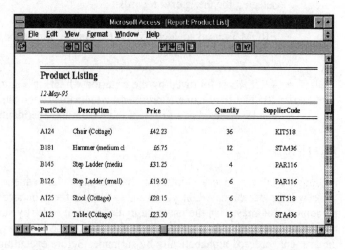

Figure 25.8. *Column report on contents of Product table*

EuroTent database case study

EuroTent is a small holiday agency, specializing in a range of French campsites, details of which are published in its brochure. It also provides a ferry and site reservation service. Some clients have no clear idea about the sites they wish to use and sometimes are not even sure which region they want to visit. For these clients, the main criteria for selection are price and campsite rating. Campsites charge on a nightly basis, but the price varies according to the season. There are two charging periods: Low Season (from March to May and September to October) and High Season (from June to August). Most campsites are closed outside those periods. A computer database would allow flexible retrieval of information, using criteria, such as price range or region. Also, amendments, perhaps to site ratings or prices, could be recorded. This would allow checks to be made on the current situation, where the printed brochure may be out of date. EuroTent decide to create a single table database to manage the campsite information. A database named EuroTent is created and the task for defining the campsite table begins.

Defining the Campsite table

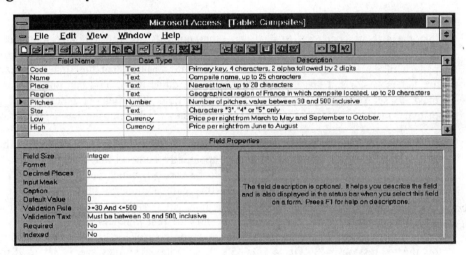

Figure 25.9. *Definition of Campsites table in Eurotent database*

Figure 25.9 shows the table definition, including field names, data types and field descriptions. The lower half of the figure, shows the field properties chosen for the Pitches field. Note that:

(i)   you can see that the selected data type is number and that the field size is *integer* (whole number only). Other optional field sizes allow for the storage of *real* numbers (they can have a fractional element) at different levels of precision (more or fewer significant digits);

(ii)   a validation rule has been set, using the expression '> =30 And < =500'. This ensures that only values between 30 and 500 are accepted; the validation text is the message which appears when an attempt is made to enter a value outside this range.

The properties for three of the other fields are shown in Figure 25.10 and the entries are explained below. The Name, Place and Region fields are all text fields of varying lengths, with no other properties specified.

	Code	Star	Low
Field size	4	1	Currency
Format			
Input mask	LL00	0	
Validation rule		='3' Or '4' Or '5'	>=7 And <=25
Validation text		Characters 3, 4 or 5	Must be £7 to £25
Required	Yes	No	No
Indexed	Yes (no duplicates)	No	No

Figure 25.10. *Field properties for Code, Star and Low fields*

(i) Code field. As you can see from Figure 25.9, this is a text field. Figure 25.10 shows that the size has been set to 4. If no other controls are exerted, any four characters can be entered. However, an *input mask* ensures that the data must have a particular pattern of entry. 'LL00', in the Access RDBMS, ensures that the first two characters are letters (A-Z) and that the last characters are digits (0-9). You can only use an input mask to set patterns for a *text*, *date* or *time* field. The field is indexed, but as the primary key for the table, it allows no duplicates (each campsite has a unique code).

(ii) Star field. This stores a 'star' rating for a site. You can see from Figure 25.9 that this is a text field, even though the input is apparently numeric (sites are rated as '3', '4' or '5' Star). This enables an input mask to be used (0) which ensures entry of a single digit between 0 and 9. You cannot do this with a numeric field. A byte field, for example, which allows storage of values between 0 and 255 (an integer field allows –32,768 to 32,767) will not prevent the entry of real numbers, but will simply round them to the nearest whole number. The validation control for the Star field is completed by the expression ='3' Or '4' Or '5'. A suitable error message is set to display if any other characters are entered.

(iii) Low field. This stores the price of a pitch (per night) during the less popular seasons. The High field stores the high season price. It will hold prices in sterling and the currency format ensures that if values are entered without a £ sign or without 2 decimal places, it is altered to this format. A validation rule is included to restrict values to the range 7 to 25 (you do not enter the £ sign in the expression, but it is shown in the validation text message). The High season price field has similar settings except that the prices are from £10 to £28.

Form data entry

Figure 25.11 shows some sample records in the Campsite table. As explained in the Overview section, you can use a *form* to enter, view and edit records. You can do the same in the table's 'data view', but you have no control over the layout or the fields which are displayed. Figure 25.12 shows a form generated with a form wizard; it has then been modified, in design mode, to include different entry labels. Unless you specify otherwise, the field names from the table definition are used.

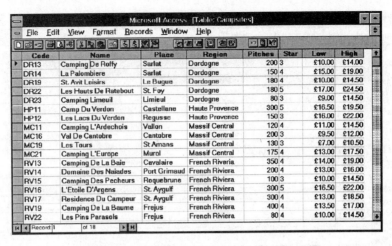

Figure 25.11. *Sample contents of Campsite table*

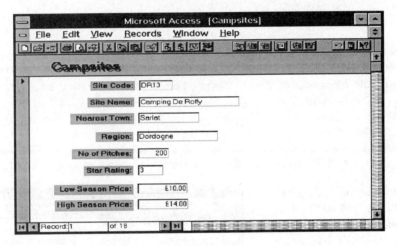

Figure 25.12. *Form with modified entry labels*

Database queries

EuroTent query 1 - Low Season Prices

The design of the first query, 'Low Season Prices', is shown in Figure 25.13. A customer is visiting France during March, which is part of the low season and is willing to consider any area at the moment. Therefore, a list of all sites is appropriate, but only showing the prices for the relevant season. As the figure shows, the Campsites table is selected for the query (as it happens, the database only has one table at present). Then the fields to be included in the query (Name, Place, Region, Star and Low) are placed in the relevant row in the QBE grid. If the query is to be used in a report, you can alter the order of the fields through the report design.

This query does not filter records with criteria, because a list is required of all sites in the database. However, not all details are needed and as Figure 25.13 reveals, only five field names have been placed in the QBE grid. The query is also sorting the records into ascending alphabetical order, by region.

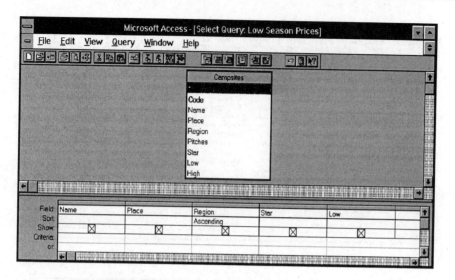

Figure 25.13. Design of Low Season Prices query

The query, expressed in SQL, is shown in Figure 25.14.

```
SELECT DISTINCTROW Campsites.Name, Campsites.Place, Campsites.Region,
Campsites.Star, Campsites.Low
FROM Campsites
ORDER BY Campsites.Region;
```

Figure 25.14. *SQL form of Query 1 to display low season prices of sites*

The SQL reserved words 'SELECT', 'DISTINCTROW' and 'FROM' have already been used and defined in the Overview. The phrase 'ORDER BY' means sequence, or sort, using the named field; in this case it is 'Region' and is prefixed by the name of the table. Every time you use a field name in an SQL statement, you need to prefix it with its table name. This is despite the fact that the EuroTent database has only one. Note from Figure 25.13 that the table used in the QBE query has to be selected first. The table must always be named, because you can use the same field name repeatedly, pro-

Name	Place	Region	Star	Low
Les Hauts De Ratebout	St. Foy	Dordogne	5	£17.00
St. Avit Loisirs	Le Bugue	Dordogne	4	£10.00
Camping Limeuil	Limieul	Dordogne	3	£9.00
La Palombiere	Sarlat	Dordogne	4	£15.00
Camping De Roffy	Sarlat	Dordogne	3	£10.00
Residence Du Campeur	St. Aygulf	French Riviera	4	£13.00
Camping Des Pecheurs	Roquebrune	French Riviera	3	£10.00
Camping De La Baie	Cavalaire	French Riviera	4	£14.00
Camping De La Baume	Frejus	French Riviera	4	£13.50
Les Pins Parasols	Frejus	French Riviera	4	£10.00
L'Etoile D'Argens	St. Aygulf	French Riviera	5	£16.50
Domaine Des Naiades	Port Grimaud	French Riviera	4	£13.00
Les Lacs Du Verdon	Regusse	Haute Provence	3	£16.00
Camp Du Verdon	Castellane	Haute Provence	5	£16.50
Les Tours	St Amans	Massif Central	3	£7.00
Camping L'Europe	Murol	Massif Central	4	£13.00
Val De Cantobre	Cantobre	Massif Central	3	£9.50
Camping L'Ardechois	Vallon	Massif Central	4	£11.00

Figure 25.15. *Dynaset from Low Season Prices query*

vided each occurrence is in a different table. The output from the Low Season Prices query is shown in Figure 25.15.

EuroTent query 2 - Pitches 150 or less, Low Season, 4 to 5 Star

Customers visiting France when campsite prices are lower can afford to be more selective and frequently choose small, but good quality sites. This query (Figure 25.16) is designed to produce the kind of information they require.

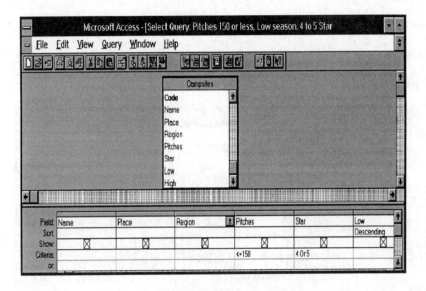

Figure 25.16. Design of Query 2

The SQL form of Query 2 is shown in Figure 25.17.

```
SELECT DISTINCTROW Campsites.Name, Campsites.Place, Campsites.Region,
Campsites.Pitches, Campsites.Star, Campsites.Low
FROM Campsites
WHERE ((Campsites.Pitches<=150) AND (Campsites.Star="4" OR
Campsites.Star="5"))
ORDER BY Campsites.Low DESC;
```

Figure 25.17. *SQL form of Query 2*

The meaning of the SQL statement, shown in bold, should be quite clear when you compare it with the criteria used in the QBE form in Figure 25.16. The reserved word WHERE is followed by two criteria; the first is that the Pitches field must contain a value of 150 or less; the second criterion is that the Star field must contain either '4' OR (used as a *logical operator*) '5'. The AND logical operator means that both criteria must be satisfied, before a record is selected. The final statement in this SQL query contains the reserved word DESC, which means *descending* (order). The

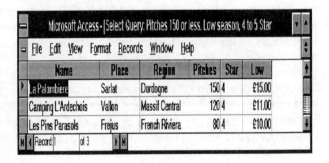

Figure 25.18. *Dynaset from Query 2*

output from Query 2, showing the smaller, better quality sites, with low season prices, is shown in Figure 25.18.

EuroTent query 3 - French Riviera £14 to £19

This query is in response to a more precise request for information. A family wish to stay in the Riviera region during the High season and are willing to pay between £14 and £19 a night. The query design is displayed in Figure 25.19.

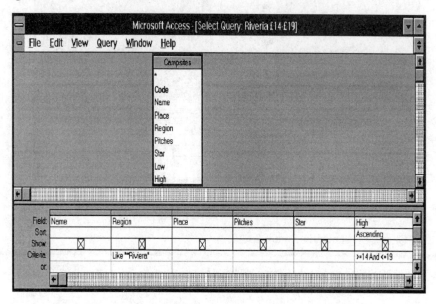

Figure 25.19. *Design of query for Riviera sites between £14 and £19*

The main point to note is that there are two criteria, one concerning the Region and the other, the High season price. The latter is similar to the criterion used in Query 2. The criterion that the Region should be the French Riviera could have been expressed fully, in the form = 'French Riviera'. QBE does not require the use of an ' = ' sign, so you could simply type 'French Riviera' as the criterion. In Figure 25.19, a wild card (*) is used, thus: *Riviera. The RDBMS takes this as being a request for any string of characters which ends with 'Riviera' and prefixes it with 'Like', which is the proper form of the expression. If there were other occurrences of the string 'Riviera' in the Region column, such as 'Italian Riviera', you would have to be more specific.

The SQL form of Query 3 is displayed in Figure 25.20.

```
SELECT DISTINCTROW Campsites.Name, Campsites.Region, Campsites.Place,
Campsites.Pitches, Campsites.Star, Campsites.High
FROM Campsites
WHERE ((Campsites.Region Like "*Riviera") AND (Campsites.High>=14 And
Campsites.High<=19))
ORDER BY Campsites.High;
```

Figure 25.20. *SQL form of Query 3*

The results of running Query 2 are displayed in Figure 25.21.

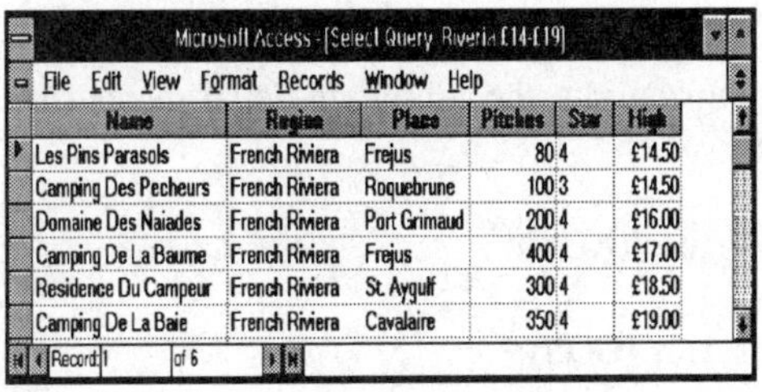

Name	Region	Place	Pitches	Star	High
Les Pins Parasols	French Riviera	Frejus	80	4	£14.50
Camping Des Pecheurs	French Riviera	Roquebrune	100	3	£14.50
Domaine Des Naiades	French Riviera	Port Grimaud	200	4	£16.00
Camping De La Baume	French Riviera	Frejus	400	4	£17.00
Residence Du Campeur	French Riviera	St. Aygulf	300	4	£18.50
Camping De La Baie	French Riviera	Cavalaire	350	4	£19.00

Figure 25.21. *Dynaset from query for Riviera sites at £14 to £19 per night*

A grouped column report

Query 1 produces the full list of campsites, ordered alphabetically by Region. Since there are several sites in each region, each regions name is repeated. A grouped column report only displays each group name once. Figure 25.22 shows a grouped report on the output from EuroTent's Query 1.

EuroTent		*14-May-95*	Low Season Prices	
Region	**Name**	**Place**	**Rating**	**Price**
Dordogne				
	Camping Limeuil	Limieul	3	£9.00
	St. Avit Loisirs	Le Bugue	4	£10.00
	Camping De Roffy	Sarlat	3	£10.00
	La Palombiere	Sarlat	4	£15.00
	Les Hauts De Ratebout	St. Foy	5	£17.00
French Riviera				
	Camping Des Pecheurs	Roquebrune	3	£10.00
	Les Pins Parasols	Frejus	4	£10.00
	Residence Du Campeur	St.Aygulf	4	£13.00
	Domaine Des Naiades	Port Grimaud	4	£13.00
	Camping De La Baume	Frejus	4	£13.50
	Camping De La Baie	Cavalaire	4	£14.00
	L'Etoile D'Argens	St. Aygulf	5	£16.50
Haute Provence				
	Les Lacs Du Verdon	Regusse	3	£16.00
	Camp Du Verdon	Castellane	5	£16.50
Massif Central				
	Les Tours	St Amans	3	£7.00
	Val De Cantobre	Cantobre	3	£9.50
	Camping L'Ardechois	Vallon	4	£11.00
	Camping L'Europe	Murol	4	£13.00

Figure 25.22. *Grouped report on output for Query 1*

Personnel database case study

This case study demonstrates the use of a relational database by using multiple tables to store the information. Pilcon Electronics is organized into the following departments (the abbreviation in brackets is used in the database as the DeptCode):

- Accounting and Finance (ACC);

- General Office Services (GOS);

- Management Information Services (MIS);

- Personnel (PER);

- Production (PRO);

- Purchasing (PUR);

- Research and Development (RAD);

- Sales and Marketing (SAL);

- Warehousing (WAR).

The Personnel database holds basic information on individual staff, departments and job grades; the database has three tables, one for each of these categories of information. They are named: StaffMember; Department; Job. The database allows the staffing in the departments to be monitored, in terms of salary costs and the individuals who are employed in them. It is also useful to be able to monitor the structure of staffing by grouping staff according to job titles; this analysis can be carried out across Pilcon Electronics, as a whole, or it can be specific to one department. Each table has to be separately defined, in the same manner as the Campsites table in the EuroTent case study. The definition of the StaffMember table is displayed in Figure 25.23.

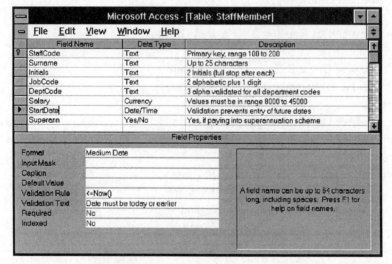

Figure 25.23. *Definition of StaffMember table*

StaffMember definition

The field properties of the StaffMember table are shown in Figure 25.24.

property	StaffCode	Surname	Initials	JobCode
field size	3	25	4	3
input mask	000			LL0
validation rule	$>=100$ And $<=200$			
validation text	Range 100 to 200			
required	No	No	No	No
indexed	Yes(no Duplicates)	No	No	No

property	DeptCode	Salary	StartDate	Superann
field size	3			
format			Medium	Yes/No
input mask	LLL			
validation rule		$>=8000$ And $<=45000$	$<=$Now()	
validation text		Range 8000 to 45000	Invalid date	
required	No	No	No	No
indexed	No	No	No	No

Figure 25.24. *Field Properties in Staff Member table*

The lower half of Figure 25.23 shows the field properties chosen for the StartDate (the date a member of staff's employment with Pilcon began) field and you should note the following:

(i)   The data type is *date/time* and the format is *medium date*. This means that data can be entered as, for example, 1/4/95 and it will be displayed as 01-Apr-95, or similar. Formatted as long date, it would appear as 1 April 1995.

(ii) A validation rule is used to ensure that the starting date for an employee must not be in the future. A function 'Now()' returns the system date (the current date and time is stored in the computer) and the expression '$<=$Now()' means 'less than or equal to today's date'.

Most of the other field properties, shown in Figure 25.24, have already been introduced in Figure 25.10 and are explained thereafter. One detail not given in Figure 25.24 is the validation rule for DeptCode. It is as follows.

```
=ACC Or GOS Or MIS Or PER Or PRO Or PUR Or RAD Or SAL Or WAR
```

The expression checks that the DeptCode is one of the three character strings listed; these are the abbreviations for each of the departments (see earlier). The Superann (Superannuation Scheme Member) field is a *logical* or *yes/no* field. It is used as a true/false indicator. Thus, with a field name Superann, 'yes' indicates that the person is a member of the company superannuation scheme; 'no' obviously means he or she is not a member.

Department definition

The DeptCode and Department-Name fields in Figure 25.25 need little explanation. You should notice that the DeptHead field has the same format as StaffCode in the StaffMember table definition; the same input mask is used. DeptHead and StaffCode are *synonyms*; they are different names, but they have the same meaning. You could make the DeptHead field size, say 25, and store the names of heads of departments in the Department table. There is no point however, because as members of staff, their names are already held in the StaffMember table. As shown later, information can be drawn from several tables in a database, provided there are *link fields* to establish *relationships* between them.

Job definition

In Figure 25.26, you can see that JobCode is the primary key for the Job table. You should recognize that the field of the same name in the StaffMember table enables access to the job titles in the Job table. The fields have exactly the same pattern, so the same input mask is used (LL0 - two alphabetic and one digit) to control input to the JobCode field.

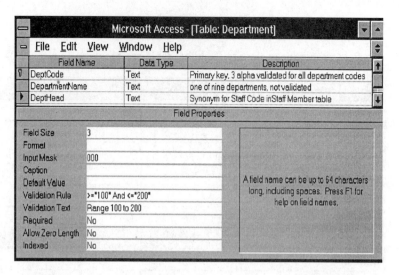

Figure 25.25. *Department definition showing properties for DeptHead*

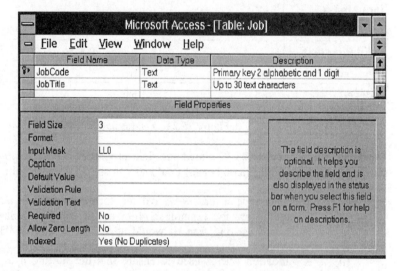

Figure 25.26. *Definition of Job table*

Contents of Personnel database

Figures 25.27, 25.28 and 25.29 show sample contents for the StaffMember, Department and Job Tables, respectively.

StaffCode	Surname	Initials	JobCode	DeptCode	Salary	StartDate	Superann
100	Picket	W.	CL2	ACC	£15,000	23-Jan-77	Yes
101	Ringwood	K.	HD1	PRO	£33,000	14-May-95	Yes
103	Clacket	D.	CL0	GOS	£13,500	01-Jan-86	No
106	Boreham	L.	SS1	ACC	£23,000	23-Sep-72	Yes
108	Winkle	R.V.	SU1	WAR	£18,000	01-Sep-88	Yes
110	Dickens	C.	OP1	PRO	£8,000	14-May-95	No
115	Cratchit	B.	CL2	ACC	£8,500	01-May-94	No
118	Boffin	C.	HD1	RAD	£38,000	01-Sep-66	Yes
123	Heap	U.	HD1	SAL	£37,500	31-Oct-93	Yes
124	Miggins	M.	SU1	GOS	£14,500	31-Oct-93	Yes
126	Squeers	W.	SS1	PER	£17,500	13-Jun-88	Yes
128	Chiseller	M.	HD2	ACC	£43,000	01-Apr-83	Yes
131	Marley	J.	OP1	PRO	£8,600	16-Jun-91	No
133	Server	I.	HD1	WAR	£32,000	01-Sep-60	Yes
136	Grabbit	U.	HD2	PUR	£45,000	12-Apr-66	Yes
138	Stackit	I.	OP1	WAR	£9,200	03-Apr-68	No
139	Broaket	H.E.	OP2	PRO	£13,000	17-Apr-76	Yes
145	Ramidos	Z.	SU1	MIS	£17,900	12-Jun-88	Yes
149	Machem	I.	HD2	PRO	£40,000	01-Apr-90	Yes
155	Pusher	P.	HD2	GOS	£44,000	01-Feb-60	Yes
159	Nervey	M.	OP1	WAR	£10,000	01-Apr-95	No
160	Surcoat	I.	HD2	MIS	£40,000	02-May-66	Yes
168	Sached	U.R.	HD2	PER	£38,000	01-May-82	Yes
172	Tefal	B.	HD2	RAD	£37,000	02-Mar-66	Yes
180	Leavmey	B.	HD2	SAL	£42,000	01-Oct-72	Yes
187	Lostem	I.	HD2	WAR	£32,500	31-Oct-88	Yes

Record: 11   of 26

Figure 25.27. *StaffMember records*

DeptCode	DepartmentName	DeptHead
ACC	Accounting and Finance	128
GOS	General Office Services	155
MIS	Management Information Services	160
PER	Personnel	168
PRO	Production	149
PUR	Purchasing	136
RAD	Research and Development	172
SAL	Sales and Marketing	180
WAR	Warehousing	187

Record: 3   of 9

Figure 25.28. *Department records*

JobCode	JobTitle
CL0	Clerical - Trainee
CL1	Clerical - Junior Grade
CL2	Clerical - Middle Grade
CL3	Clerical - Senior
HD1	Assistant Head of Department
HD2	Head of Department
LS1	Production Line Supervisor
OP1	Machine Operator
OP2	Machine Maintenance Technician
SS1	Section Supervisor
SU1	Supervisor
SU2	Supervisor - Senior

Record: 4   of 12

Figure 25.29. *Job records*

Database queries

Queries can be applied to single tables or to more than one. Multiple tables can be queried because *relationships* exist between the tables. For example, the relationship between the Department table and the StaffMember table is through the DeptCode field, which exists for that purpose in both tables. The relationship is *one-to-many*; this means that each StaffMember record relates to only one Department, but each Department record relates to many StaffMember records. Similarly, the relationship between Job and StaffMember is one-to-many. There is no direct relationship between Job and Department; this is only possible through the StaffMember table, which relates to both.

Personnel query 1 - Department Heads and Salaries

In preparation for a meeting of Pilcons Board of Directors, details of the salaries earned by the Heads of Department are required. The information should comprise, each Head's surname, salary and their Departments name; the output is to be in descending numerical order, by Salary. The names and salaries of Heads of Department are held, with those of the rest of the staff, in the StaffMember table and the Department names are in the Department table. This means that the query has to join these two tables. The full details of the query design (using QBE) are shown in Figure 25.30. You might be surprised that no criterion is necessary to select the JobCode 'HD2', which

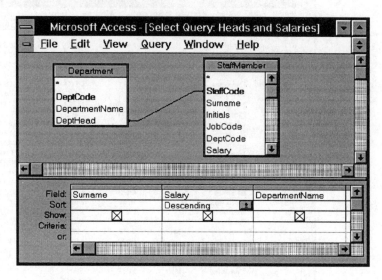

Figure 25.30. *QBE to extract Heads of Department details*

identifies Heads of Department. This can be explained as follows. You can see from Figure 25.30 that a *relationship* is established between DeptHead in the Department table and StaffCode in the StaffMember table (remember these field names are synonyms). This ensures that, when the tables are *joined* in the query, data is only used from those records where the value in StaffCode matches with the value in its synonym, DeptHead. The latter field is an example of a *secondary foreign key*. A link could also be established between the DeptCode fields in each table, but it is unnecessary; having linked the tables through StaffCode and DeptHead, the DepartmentName details are made accessible. The query, expressed in SQL is displayed in Figure 25.31.

```
SELECT DISTINCTROW StaffMember.Surname, StaffMember.Salary,
Department.DepartmentName
FROM Department INNER JOIN StaffMember ON Department.DeptHead =
StaffMember.StaffCode
ORDER BY StaffMember.Salary DESC;
```

Figure 25.31. *SQL form of Query 1 to display Heads of Department details*

Much of the SQL in Figure 25.31 is used in earlier examples. The new points to note relate to the second statement. Joining tables establishes relationships or links between them. Figure 25.31 shows two such relationships. 'INNER JOIN' is the most commonly used operation which merges information from two tables where values in the link fields are common to both tables. The SQL word 'ON' is followed by the table names and fields to be joined. As can be seen from the QBE form of the query in Figure 25.30 and the SQL statement in Figure 25.31, records are combined when the DeptHead (Department table) value equals the StaffCode (StaffMember table) value.

The dynaset from Query 1 is shown as a report in Figure 25.32. Note that the report design process automatically inserts a SUM formula to calculate and display the total for the Salary column (see Figure 25.33 for report design screen). Note also the use of the *Now()* function to display the current date.

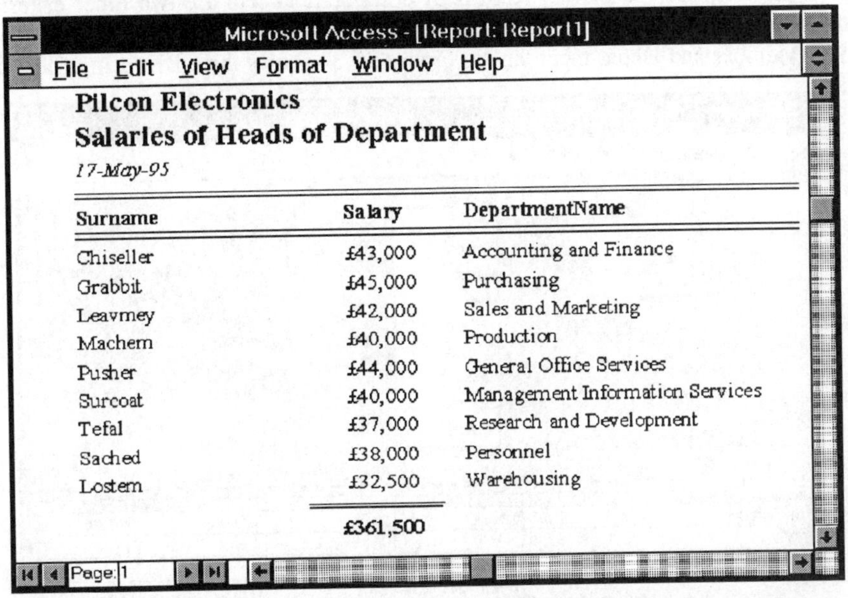

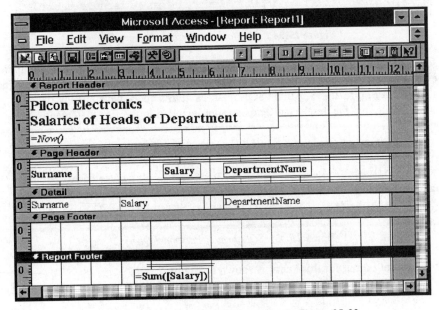

Figure 25.32. *Column report on Heads of Department query*

Figure 25.33. *Design screen for report in Figure 25.32*

Personnel query 2 - Non-HODs in Superannuation scheme

This query uses the criterion '<>HD1' And '<>HD2', which means 'staff who are not Heads or Assistant Heads of Department', to extract records of other staff. There are two other criteria: member of Superannuation scheme; appointed on or before 1st January 1990. To produce this information requires the joining of the StaffMember and Department tables. Figure 25.34 shows the QBE form of this query.

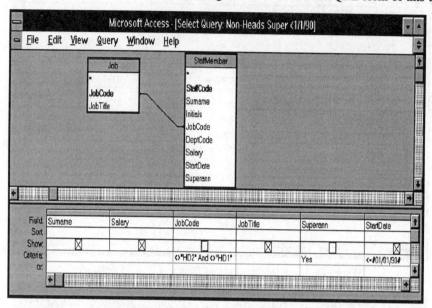

Figure 25.34. *QBE form of Personnel Query 2*

Note that the JobCode and Superann fields are needed in the QBE grid to allow entry of the appropriate filter criteria. However, they do not need to displayed, so the 'Show' check boxes are deselected. The SQL form of the query is shown in Figure 25.35. All the SQL features in this query have already been met, so it should be self-explanatory. Note that the deselected fields are not included in the first statement.

```
SELECT DISTINCTROW StaffMember.Surname, StaffMember.Salary, Job.JobTitle,
StaffMember.StartDate
FROM Job INNER JOIN StaffMember ON Job.JobCode = StaffMember.JobCode
WHERE ((Job.JobCode<>"HD2" And Job.JobCode<>"HD1") AND
(StaffMember.Superann=Yes) AND (StaffMember.StartDate<=01/1/90#));
```

Figure 25.35. *SQL form of Personnel Query 2*

The simple table form of output for this query is shown in Figure 25.36.

Figure 25.36. *Dynaset for Personnel Query 2*

Personnel Query 3 - Operator and Clerical Staff

This query (see Figure 25.37) involves the use of all three tables. To enable selection of operators and clerical staff, the JobCode is needed. Note that a wild card is used to pick up the various grades in each group. Thus, *Like 'CL*'*, will find CL0, CL1 and CL2. Similarly, *Like 'OP*'* picks out OP1 and OP2.

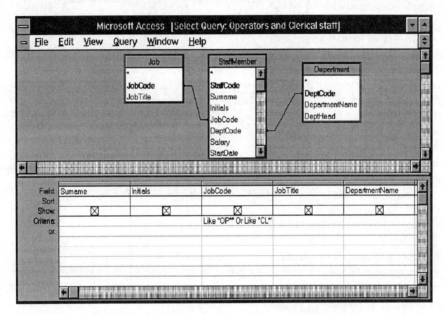

Figure 25.37. *QBE form of query to identify operator and clerical staff*

The SQL form of the query is shown in Figure 25.38.

```
SELECT DISTINCTROW StaffMember.Surname, StaffMember.Initials,
StaffMember.JobCode, Job.JobTitle, Department.DepartmentName
FROM (Job INNER JOIN StaffMember ON Job.JobCode = StaffMember.JobCode) INNER
JOIN Department ON StaffMember.DeptCode = Department.DeptCode
WHERE ((StaffMember.JobCode Like "OP*" Or StaffMember.JobCode Like "CL*"));
```

Figure 25.38. *SQL form of Personnel Query 3*

The output is displayed in Figure 25.39.

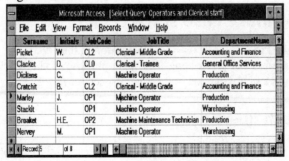

Figure 25.39. *Dynaset for Query on operator and clerical staff*

Personnel query 4 - updating Salaries

Figure 25.40 is an example of an *update query*. Using this type of query you can update groups of records with a single operation. Of course, the update has to be of a form which allows group updating, such as a percentage increase in salaries. The salary increase of 10% is effected with the expression *[Salary]*1.1*. On performance, Pilcon have decided not to increase the salaries of Heads and Assistant Heads of Department (see criteria in Figure 25.40). If you did increase their salaries, you would first have to alter the validation rule for the Salary field, which restricts values to the range 8000 to 45000.

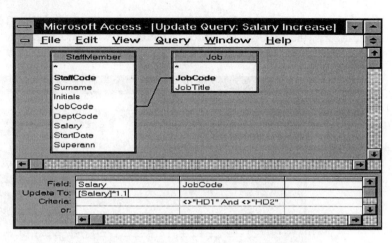

Figure 25.40. *Update query to increase salaries by 10%*

The SQL form of this update query is displayed in Figure 25.41.

```
UPDATE DISTINCTROW StaffMember INNER JOIN Job ON StaffMember.JobCode =
Job.JobCode SET StaffMember.Salary = [Salary]*1.1
WHERE ((StaffMember.JobCode<>"HD1" And StaffMember.JobCode<>"HD2"));
```

Figure 25.41. *SQL form of update query*

The main points to observe from Figure 25.41 are as follow:

    (i)   Instead of SELECT, the first SQL word is UPDATE;

    (ii)   The INNER JOIN is carried out ON a SET of records, WHERE JobCode is not equal to 'HD1' and not equal to 'HD2'.

Viewing the StaffMember table would reveal that all salary figures (except those of Heads and Assistant Heads) are increased by 10%.

Stock Control database case study

This example makes use of the Product table, used for illustration in the Overview, plus a Supplier table. The full definitions of the database are not given here. The main purpose of the Stock Control case study is to illustrate editing tables through a query dynaset and further aspects of *forms*.

Editing tables through query dynasets

The contents of the Product and Supplier tables are shown in Figures 25.42 and 25.43, respectively.

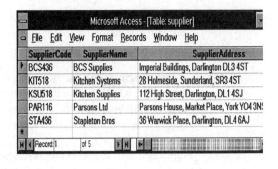

Figure 25.42. *Sample contents of Product table*   **Figure 25.43.** *Sample contents of Supplier table*

Suppose, for example, that you wish to view and edit the combined information from both tables. You could join the tables in a query, the design of which is shown in Figure 25.44.

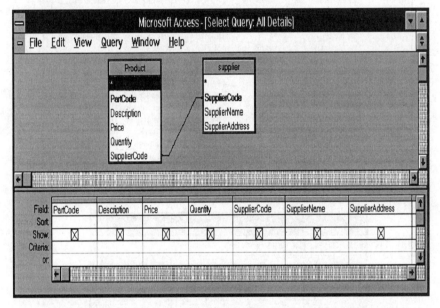

Figure 25.44. *Query to join information from Product and Supplier tables*

The simple datasheet view of the resulting dynaset is shown in Figure 25.45. You should notice that each supplier name and address is repeated several times. The relationship between the Supplier and Product tables is one-to-many, which means that many products are bought from a single supplier, but each product is ordered from a single supplier. Although the information from both tables can be viewed, only certain fields can be edited to update the tables, upon which the query is based. In the case of a one-to-many relationship, changes can only be made to dynaset fields which come from the *many* side of the relationship. Two important points need to be understood.

(i)   Referring to Figure 25.44, if the query uses the SupplierCode from the Product table, you will be able to alter the Supplier codes in the dynaset shown in Figure 25.45. The name and address will then change accordingly (by using the relationship established with the Supplier table). The changes to the supplier details will be applied to the underlying Product table. Changes affect the many side of the relationship, only. Figure

25.46 shows that the supplier of the 'Hammer (medium, claw)' is now 'Parsons Ltd', instead of 'Stapleton', as shown in Figure 25.45. This is achieved by altering the SupplierCode for that record.

(ii)   If, in designing the query in Figure 25.44, you use the SupplierCode from the Supplier table, the RDBMS would not let you edit it through the dynaset. In this example, this means that you can edit the Product table (the *many* side), but not the Supplier table (the *one* side), through the query dynaset.

If the underlying tables have a one-to-one relationship there are no editing restrictions through the dynaset. If you want to prevent any editing through a dynaset, the RDBMS provides an option to disable the facility. There are other circumstances when dynaset editing is restricted, but they are beyond the scope of this text.

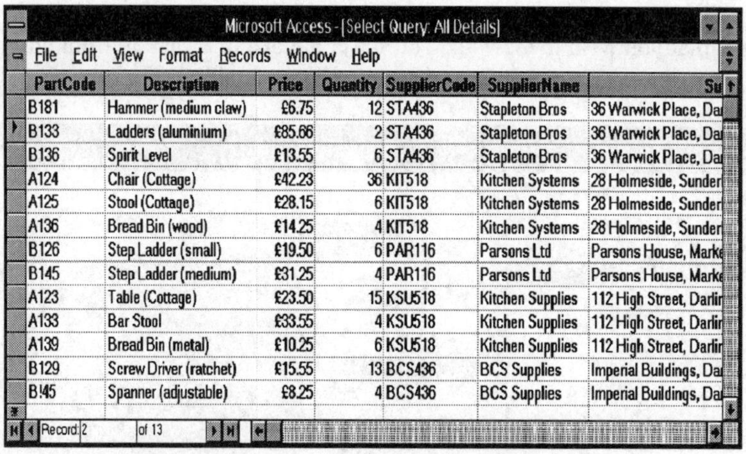

PartCode	Description	Price	Quantity	SupplierCode	SupplierName	Su
B181	Hammer (medium claw)	£6.75	12	STA436	Stapleton Bros	36 Warwick Place, Da
B133	Ladders (aluminium)	£85.66	2	STA436	Stapleton Bros	36 Warwick Place, Da
B136	Spirit Level	£13.55	6	STA436	Stapleton Bros	36 Warwick Place, Da
A124	Chair (Cottage)	£42.23	36	KIT518	Kitchen Systems	28 Holmeside, Sunder
A125	Stool (Cottage)	£28.15	6	KIT518	Kitchen Systems	28 Holmeside, Sunder
A136	Bread Bin (wood)	£14.25	4	KIT518	Kitchen Systems	28 Holmeside, Sunder
B126	Step Ladder (small)	£19.50	6	PAR116	Parsons Ltd	Parsons House, Marke
B145	Step Ladder (medium)	£31.25	4	PAR116	Parsons Ltd	Parsons House, Marke
A123	Table (Cottage)	£23.50	15	KSU518	Kitchen Supplies	112 High Street, Darlin
A133	Bar Stool	£33.55	4	KSU518	Kitchen Supplies	112 High Street, Darlin
A139	Bread Bin (metal)	£10.25	6	KSU518	Kitchen Supplies	112 High Street, Darlin
B129	Screw Driver (ratchet)	£15.55	13	BCS436	BCS Supplies	Imperial Buildings, Da
B145	Spanner (adjustable)	£8.25	4	BCS436	BCS Supplies	Imperial Buildings, Da

Record 2 of 13

Figure 25.45. *Dynaset from query joining Product and Supplier tables*

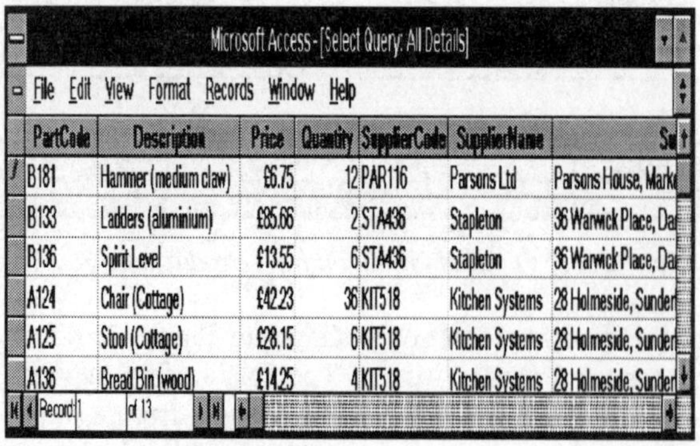

PartCode	Description	Price	Quantity	SupplierCode	SupplierName	Su
B181	Hammer (medium claw)	£6.75	12	PAR116	Parsons Ltd	Parsons House, Marke
B133	Ladders (aluminium)	£85.66	2	STA436	Stapleton	36 Warwick Place, Da
B136	Spirit Level	£13.55	6	STA436	Stapleton	36 Warwick Place, Da
A124	Chair (Cottage)	£42.23	36	KIT518	Kitchen Systems	28 Holmeside, Sunder
A125	Stool (Cottage)	£28.15	6	KIT518	Kitchen Systems	28 Holmeside, Sunder
A136	Bread Bin (wood)	£14.25	4	KIT518	Kitchen Systems	28 Holmeside, Sunder

Record 1 of 13

Figure 25.46. *Change of Supplier for Hammer (medium, claw) record*

Viewing and editing with main/sub forms

Figure 25.45 shows a dynaset which provides a view of all the information in both the Product and Supplier tables. The main drawback is that the suppliers' names and addresses are repeated several times. In addition, as a dynaset, the Supplier table (the *one* side of the one-to-many relationship) cannot be edited through it. Editing could be carried out using a separate form for each table, or more effectively, with the main/sub form shown in Figure 25.47.

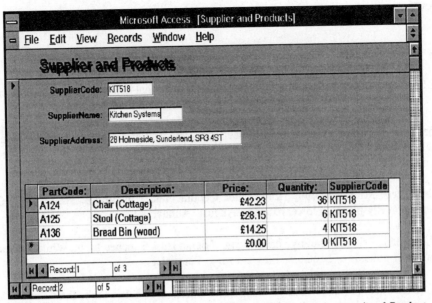

Figure 25.47. *Main/sub Form showing one Supplier record and the associated Products*

The form can be created using a form wizard, but you can start with separate forms and then combine them, making the Product form the sub. As you scroll through each Supplier record (you can see that there is a scroll bar for each part of the form), all the associated (through the SupplierCode relationship) Product records appear in the lower, sub form. You can edit or add new Supplier Records, by using the upper, main form. Figure 25.48 shows a new supplier record entered within the main form, but before entry of any product records for that supplier. Entry of a new supplier code would mean that there would be no Product records in the sub form; you could then enter any details of products supplied by the new supplier. Similarly, you can edit or add new Product records in the sub form, for an existing supplier. Remember, changing a SupplierCode in the Product section of the form (the *many* side) will not affect records in the Supplier table (the *one* side).

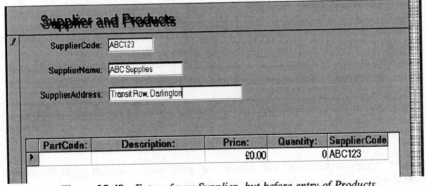

Figure 25.48. *Entry of new Supplier, but before entry of Products*

Forms for dynasets

The rules which apply to dynaset editing, detailed already, also apply to editing through a form. Thus, creating a form for the dynaset shown in Figure 25.45, does not alter the restrictions concerning the editing of any underlying table on the 'one' side of a one-to-many relationship.

Exercises

Each of the following exercises is to be implemented with a relational database. In each case, ensure that the data is in third normal form (3NF) and produce an entity-relationship model (ERM).

1. As a member of local botany group, you have been given the task of designing and creating a wild flowers database. It will be used as a central resource for members. Details of flowers will be added as they are spotted by members. The following sample data is provided.

- Chaffweed. Primrose family. Latin name Centunculus. 1 inch high. Pink flower. Grows in damp gravelly places. Flowers June to August. Annual.

- Chickweed. Primrose family. Latin name Trientalis. 4-6 inches high. White flower. Abundant in Highlands of Scotland. Flowers June. Perennial.

- Sea-Milkwort. Primrose family. Latin name Glaux. 3-6 inches high. Pink flower. Common on sea shore and salt marshes. Flowers June to August. Perennial.

- Viper's Bugloss. Borage family. Latin name Echium. 1-2 feet high. Red then blue flower. Walls, old quarries and gravel pits. Flowers June to August. Biennial.

- Lungwort. Borage family. Latin name Pulmonaria. 1 foot high. Pale purple flower. Woods and thickets, rare. Flowers April, May. Perennial.

- Comfrey. Borage family. Latin name Symphytum. 1-3 feet high. White, pink or purple flower. Water places and banks of rivers, common. Flowers May to August. Perennial.

- Borage. Borage family. Latin name Borago. 1-2 feet high. Deep blue flower. Waste ground. Flowers June to September. Biennial.

- St. John's Wort. St John's Wort family. Latin name Hypericum. 1 foot high. Yellow flower. Gardens and shrubberies. Flowers July to September. Perennial.

(i)   Identify the main entities, their associated attributes and set up the appropriate tables.

(ii)   Consider the different kinds of reports which could be generated from this database and design and construct it accordingly. If you can gather information concerning other wild flowers, it would help to expand the database.

(iii)   Print the complete database and check the information against your manual lists. Use the database editing facilities to correct any errors.

(iv)   Generate a number of reports, which you think may be useful to the botany group. For example, you could list those flowers which fall into the same family. Make use of whatever report design facilities are provided by your database package.

2. The following description is taken from a brochure which advertises hundreds of holiday properties (throughout Europe) for rent. Several different agents are represented.

> ***Casa Girasole, Castagneto, Tuscany, Italy.*** *Sleeps 6. This delightful farmhouse, set amid 8 acres of rolling pasture land and terraced olive groves, is 2 miles from the quaint hilltop village of Castagneto Carducci and only 9 kilometres from the nearest beach at Marina di Castagneto. The owners live in one part of the property and guests have their own entrance and terrace. The accommodation, comfortably furnished, is on two floors with a large, fully equipped kitchen and spacious living room. The bedrooms, on the first floor, are small. Children would delight in exploring the estate and discovering the livestock on this small working farm. There are very good views from the bedroom windows. The unmade road to the property is rough in parts.*
>
> *Accommodation. Ground floor: Entrance from terrace into kitchen/dining room. Shower/WC, washing machine. Sitting room, fireplace. First floor: 2 bedrooms: 1 double, 1 small room with bunkbeds. Bathroom/WC.*
>
> *Situation/facilities. Castagneto Carducci 2 km. All facilities. Seaside 9 km. Volterra 70 km. San Gimignano 95 km. Pisa 70 km.*
>
> *Agent: Italia Vita, 23 Hemingway Road, Malvern, Worcestershire, WR13 9PN. Tel. 0435 364782*

(i) Identify the main entities, their associated attributes and set up the appropriate tables.

(ii) Analyse the description and define a suitable database structure. Use similar property descriptions to create a holiday home database.

(iii) Identify and generate reports which may be useful for clients who are seeking property to rent.

3. This activity concerns the patient records held by a medical practice. Information is held concerning: patient name and address; date of next visit; details of visits over the past five years; doctor to whom the patient is assigned; current medication (if any); medical history, including stays in hospital and medication given by the practice; allergies to medication; risk factor to particular illnesses, such as heart disease.

(i) Identify the main entities, their associated attributes and set up the appropriate tables.

(ii) Design and construct a suitable database structure. You should be able to identify further entities or attributes to extend the database.

(iii) Enter sufficient records to allow demonstration of the database.

(iv) Generate those reports which you think may be of use to the medical practice. Make use of any report design facilities provided by the package.

4. Borsettshire College of Further and Higher Education runs a wide range of vocational and non-vocational courses for both full-time and part-time students. It is generally accepted and generally stipulated by external course validating bodies such as BTEC, that full-time vocational courses should include a period of relevant work experience for each student. Borsettshire College offers full-time vocational courses in, for example, catering, hotel management and reception, computing, business studies, nursery nursing and social work. During the year, the total number of students requiring work placement of one sort or another is around 500. Approximately 30 academic staff are involved in organizing the work placements, and many use the same employers.

It has been agreed that, as a first step, information on work placements should be centrally available to all interested staff. Before approaching an employer, a member of staff would be expected to refer to the centrally held information, to see who else used the employer and to determine if there are likely to be any clashes. If any further information is required, the other member(s) of staff responsible for work placements with the same employer, can be consulted directly.

The database is to contain information concerning the employer, the type of work placements offered, official contacts and details of the relevant college staff.

- (i)   Identify the entities, attributes and primary keys. Ignore any requirement for the identification of college tutors with particular employers.

- (ii)   Define and save the database structure.

- (iii) Enter sufficient records to illustrate the operation of the database. Print the contents of each table.

- (iv)   Query the database, for three useful output reports, establishing any necessary links between the tables in the database. Save each query.

- (v)   Define a suitable report layout for each query and execute the queries. Print the results of each query, using the appropriate report layout.

Chapter 26

Programming in High-level Languages

The general characteristics of high-level languages (HLLs) are discussed briefly in Chapter 12. Here we consider the common characteristics of HLLs in more detail before examining a number of languages in depth. Like computer hardware, computer languages can be categorized according to *generations*, from the first to the latest fifth generation languages. The five generations may be summarized as follow.

First generation

Appearing in the 1960s, these languages were based on the architectures of the current computers. Control structures were very basic, closely related to the instruction set of machines such as the IBM 704. Data structures were similarly based on the internal representations used for numbers and characters. The rather rigid syntactic structure of first generation languages was influenced by the constraints arising from the use of punched cards as the main input medium for programs. Fortran is typical of this generation of languages.

Second generation

These elaborated on the structure of first generation languages in a number of important ways. Firstly, block structuring (see later) was introduced, facilitating program design. Secondly, there was a move towards structured programming by the introduction of more structured control constructs. Thirdly, the syntax of the languages became more flexible, allowing statements to be expressed in a freer format. Algol-60 is typical of this generation.

Third generation

User-defined data structures became available, allowing a more application orientated approach to programming to be adopted. Control structures were modified to make them simpler and more efficient than those of the previous generation, and new, application oriented control structures such as the case statement, were added. These changes resulted in third generation languages becoming much more independent of computer hardware. Pascal is a good example of third generation languages.

Fourth generation

Such languages continue the tradition of reducing the work of the user and increasing the load on the computer. The terms Fourth Generation Language, and its contraction, 4GL, are subject to a wide variety of interpretations and definitions, but they all have a number of characteristics in common:

- easier to use than existing high-level languages, particularly by non-specialists;

- allow quick solutions to data processing tasks;

- more concise than existing high-level languages;

- the language is closer to natural language;

- user-friendly;

- non-procedural.

Two examples of current software systems which fit this loose definition of a 4GL are Structured Query Languages (SQLs) and Program Generators.

Fifth generation

These languages break away from the conventional imperative language format in ways which facilitate implementation on alternative computer architectures. For example, the declarative nature of the fifth generation language PROLOG allows programs to be implemented using parallel processing techniques. Object oriented languages and functional languages also allow this possibility, while still usable on conventional computers. LISP and Smalltalk are two further examples of fifth generation languages. Though all HLLs can be applied to a wide variety of programming tasks, and are in that sense general-purpose languages, most high-level languages have been designed specifically for particular application areas. For example, Fortran's syntax facilitates modelling mathematical problems, COBOL allows data processing and file handling applications to be coded in a convenient manner, and LOGO was written to encourage children to approach problem solving logically and to explore mathematical concepts. Table 26.1 summarizes the characteristics of a number of well-known languages. All of the languages below are to a greater or lesser extent general-purpose, so only special application areas are mentioned. The code *c* means 'Compiled', *i* means 'Interpreted' and *t* means 'Threaded Interpretive Language'.

language	date	type	application areas
Ada	1979	c	Real-time systems programming; embedded systems.
ALGOL	1960	c	General-purpose.
APL	1966	i	Scientific/mathematical problems inc vectors and matrices.
BASIC	1963	i,c	Teaching programming; for casual users rather than serious professional programmers.
C	1972	c	Systems programming.
COBOL	1960	c	Data processing.
Forth	1969	t	Control of servo-driven devices.
FORTRAN	1954	c	Mathematical/scientific problems.
LISP	1960	i	Artificial intelligence.
Logo	1967	i	Helping children with problem solving; artificial intelligence.
Modula-2	1979	c	Systems programming.
Pascal	1970	c	Teaching program/algorithm design.
PL/1	1965	c	General-purpose.
PROLOG	1972	i	Artificial intelligence.
Smalltalk	1972	c	Object oriented programming.
SNOBOL	1966	i	Text processing.

Table 26.1.

All of these languages, and many others, have a considerable number of similarities; most programming problems require data to be stored, calculations to be performed, values to be read from some external source or displayed in some form, alternative sets of operations to be executed depending on some condition arising, sections of programs to be repeated a specified number of times, and so on. For convenience, these similarities can be grouped under a number of headings:

- reserved words and keywords;

- identifiers;

- data structures;

- operations on data;

- input/output operations;

- control structures;

- file handling;

- functions and procedures;

- reserved words and keywords.

All high-level languages contain a number of words having special meanings. For example, in Pascal begin, end and while are such words. These are called reserved words because the programmer is not allowed to use them as identifiers; they are used only in specific contexts and their meanings are recognized by the language compiler. In languages such as COBOL, having over 300 reserved words, this constitutes something of a problem for programmers.

An alternative approach, one used by some early HLLs, notably Fortran, is to use keywords which are only recognized by the compiler as being special words if they are used in prescribed circumstances; used in any other context they are assumed by the compiler to be identifiers. Most modern HLLs use reserved words as this method is less prone to ambiguity.

Identifiers

In addition to reserved words or keywords, programs contain names created by the programmer. Names are given to program variables or constants; names are assigned to subprograms or program modules; names are given to user-defined data structures. These names are collectively called *identifiers*. They comprise groups of alphanumeric characters, typically beginning with a letter, which allow programmers to give convenient names to program items.

Data items whose values are allowed to change during the execution of a program are called variables; constant data items retain their values throughout the execution of the program. In some HLLs, variables, constants, procedures and functions have to be declared before they can be used, usually at the start of the program or subprogram in which they appear. Declarations are used to define the form or type of identifiers.

Scope of variables

The term scope refers to the degree of accessibility of a variable. For example, variables declared within the main program are often accessible to any part of the whole program, whereas the accessibility of variables defined within a subprogram (see later) is restricted to that subprogram only. The former are termed *global* variables, and the latter *local* variables. The precise rules governing scope vary according to the particular language.

Data structures

The commonest data types are:

- *numerics*, either Integers (e.g. 255) or Reals (e.g. 1.45);

- *characters* (e.g. 'a') and Character Strings (e.g. 'Freddy');

- *booleans*, which can take only one of two values (e.g. TRUE or FALSE);

- *pointers*, which contain the location of other data items.

These *primitive* data types can be combined to form data structures, the commonest of which are:

- *arrays* or lists of data of one specific type, with individual elements referenced by means of one or more subscripts;

- *records*, which allow collective names to be assigned to groups of variables of different types;

- *files*, which are collections of identically structured records.

A number of HLLs, notably Pascal and C, allow new user-defined data types to be constructed from primitives or other (previously declared) user-defined data types, in order to create data structures of almost any complexity.

Operations on data

The operations available in an HLL normally include:

- arithmetic operations involving addition, subtraction, multiplication and division;

- logical operations, usually the operations 'AND', 'OR', 'NOT' and 'EOR'(exclusive OR).

Results of such operations may be stored in variables by means of assignment statements taking the form of mathematical identities. For example, an assignment statement in Fortran looks like this:

```
Sum = A + B
```

The variable Sum would be assigned the value corresponding to the sum of the values of the variables A and B. The normal rules of precedence apply, and brackets may be used freely as in ordinary algebra.

Input and output operations

Most HLLs provide special input statements for capturing data from a standard input device such as a keyboard for allocation to a specified variable, and special output statements for displaying data on a standard output device such as a VDU.

Control structures

Control structures are the means by which the normal top to bottom execution order of statements may be modified. The basic control constructs are:

- *Selections*, such as IF..THEN..ELSE, CASE, ON X..GOSUB, allowing the current states of specified variables to determine the next action to be taken by the program; in other words, the means by which alternative courses of action may be taken.

- *Iterations*, such as FOR..NEXT, REPEAT..UNTIL, WHILE..DO, allowing blocks of instructions to be repeated.

Note that certain HLLs, for example Prolog, do not explicitly have the above types of control structures; the reason for this is explained later in the section on Logic Programming.

File handling

High-level languages invariably provide a set of instructions for manipulating files held on backing storage devices such as magnetic disks. By means of these types of instructions, blocks of data may be transferred to and from backing storage. A typical set of file-handling instructions might include instructions for:

- opening files ready for use;

- closing files;

- reading records from a sequential file;

- writing records to a sequential file;

- reading records from a random file;

- writing records to a random file.

Other languages, COBOL for example, provide facilities for processing indexed-sequential files. Sometimes a language will provide low-level file-handling instructions for reading/writing single bytes, single numbers or strings from backing-storage. C is such a language.

Functions and procedures

Languages such as Pascal and C allow the programmer to create subprograms (also called subroutines or modules) which may be referenced by name in the main program. Broadly speaking, a subprogram is a self-contained section of program code which performs some identifiable task. This facility is invaluable when designing large programs because it allows the programmer to split a large, complex task into a collection of smaller, simpler tasks.

Subprograms are usually allowed to contain local variables, which are declared within the subprogram, and whose scopes are restricted to the extent of the subprogram. These variables are usually dynamically created when the subprogram is invoked and are destroyed, that is, their memory areas are released, on completion of the subprogram.

Subprograms, are frequently called procedures or functions. Simply speaking, a procedure is a subprogram which when invoked, or called, from the main program (or another subprogram) performs some task and then returns control to the place from which it was called; a function does much the same thing but, in addition, returns a value to the calling program or subprogram.

The difference between procedures and functions is best illustrated by means of an example. Suppose, as part of a large program which has been produced as an aid in the design of buildings, a subprogram is required to display a rectangle, of given dimensions, on the VDU. Then this would probably be written as a procedure invoked by a statement such as

```
procedure draw_rectangle(10, 5)
```

where the numbers in the brackets are parameters specifying the dimensions of the rectangle to be drawn. The code for the procedure draw_rectangle would exist either within the program or on some backing storage medium, such as a magnetic disk, accessible to the language compiler. The code would be executed, causing a rectangle of the required dimensions to be drawn, and the program would continue with the next instruction following the call.

Suppose now that another subprogram is required to calculate the area of building material required to produce a rectangular shape of the same dimensions. This task would most probably be implemented as a function of the form

```
area = function calc_area(10, 5)
```

Again two parameters are passed to the function, but this time it is expected to calculate and, on completion, return a value which is to be stored in the variable area.

This is a rather simplistic view of procedures and functions; in practice there are many variations and enhancements of these basic ideas. Pascal and C both make extensive use of subprograms assuming a variety of different forms.

Block structuring

Earlier it was mentioned that some languages require that variables are defined prior to their use by means of declarations. When such declarations are made in subprograms, the declared variables are usually termed local variables. This means that their values are defined only when the subprogram is being executed, and otherwise, as far as the main program is concerned, they do not exist. The scope of these variables, depends on the language. In C, the scope of such variables, that is the area of the program able to recognize them, is restricted to the subprogram only; in Pascal it is restricted to that subprogram and any other subprograms defined within it. Variables which are defined in the main program have global scope, that is they are accessible to the whole program, including its subprograms. Such variables are called global variables.

A number of languages allow the use of compound statements, where a number of statements can be grouped together to form a block. For example, in C a block starts with the delimiter { and ends with the delimiter }. Within these block delimiters it is possible to declare variables whose scope is restricted to the block, as if they had been defined as local variables within a subprogram. Indeed, a block in this context is a kind of open subroutine, that is a subprogram which is inserted where it is required rather than being referenced by name, with the actual code appearing elsewhere in the program. Blocks may be nested to any depth.

Languages which exhibit these types of structures, that is nested subprograms or compound statements containing declarations of variables in addition to program statements, are called block-structured languages. In Pascal, Modula-2 and Ada the block-structuring is implemented by means of nested procedure definitions, whereas in C nested compound statements, with similar scoping rules, are used.

Parameters

An important characteristic of procedures and functions is the ability to pass parameters to and from them. Parameters are frequently shown as variables enclosed within brackets after the name of the procedure/function, as illustrated in an earlier section. Parameters allow the programmer to use the same subprogram to process different values, without the necessity of repeating the code for the subprogram wherever it is needed. Two types of parameters are in common use: *value* parameters and *variable* parameters.

With value parameters, the transfer of data is one way only - from the calling program to the subprogram. A copy of the value to be passed to the subprogram is made before transfer takes place, and therefore the original is unchanged by whatever processing occurs within the subprogram. This is often termed a *call by value*.

In the case of variable parameters, the subprogram uses an alias (ie a different name) for the variable passed as a parameter; this means that the subprogram can alter the value of the variable even though it may use a different name for the variable. This is often termed a *call by value-result*. Pascal supports both of these systems of parameter passing.

Summary of high-level languages

The following sections give a brief introduction to a number of well-known high-level languages. A number of other languages, PROLOG as an example, are dealt with elsewhere because of their special natures. All of the languages in this section are conventional high-level languages in the sense that they were designed for use on computers based on Von Neumann's model of a digital computer. A growing number of other high-level languages, regarded as being fourth or fifth generation, have been developed with other computer architectures in mind. Languages such as PROLOG, Ada, and Modula-2 fall into this category.

BASIC

BASIC was developed at Dartmouth College, in the USA, in 1963 and was intended to be easy to learn and appropriate for a wide variety of applications. Its popularity has been largely the result of its ease of implementation on microcomputers, and it is frequently supplied with them. There is a standard for BASIC, just as there are standards for Fortran and COBOL, and most versions of BASIC adhere to this standard, but each version usually has additional features, many of which are specific to the particular version. Fortunately, however, having learnt one version makes it easy to adapt to a different one.

In the past, BASIC has been heavily criticized for its tendency to encourage bad programming habits. Initially, few versions of BASIC had control structures to encourage or facilitate the use of structured programming techniques, and consequently large programs tended to be difficult to understand and modify. Some recent versions, however, have rectified this deficiency to greater or lesser extents by incorporating Pascal-like facilities.

Originally BASIC was an interpreted language, a feature which contributed to its suitability for novices, but over the past few years, such has been its popularity, that a significant number of software houses have produced BASIC compilers which allow programs to be run independently of an interpreter and with the usual speed and security benefits provided by compiled languages.

C

C is a programming language developed by Bell Laboratories of the USA around 1972. It was designed and written by Dennis Ritchie who was at the time working on the development of the UNIX operating system. UNIX was designed to be particularly useful to the software engineer by providing a wide variety of software tools. In fact, the UNIX operating system was written in C, and even the C compiler is now written in C.

It was designed to be easy to learn and use, powerful and reliable and it has many characteristics of structured languages such as Pascal. Its roots are based in the language Algol, and C retains many of its features, but C's strength lies in its simplicity, the facility with which complex programs may be built from simple building blocks.

Because Dennis Ritchie worked in the field of systems software, C is orientated to such applications as operating systems, computer language development and text processing. Its suitability for these areas is largely attributable to the fact that it is a relatively low-level language which facilitates very efficient programming, yet at the same time it retains the advantage of high-level languages to hide the details of the computer's architecture.

COBOL

On the whole, data processing applications involve a great deal of input and output operations with a relatively minor amount of calculation in between. The data operated upon generally consists of files comprising a large number of records. For example, a computerized stock control system for a wholefood warehouse would contain details of each item held: description of item, sale price, unit size, number currently in stock etc. This collection of data is termed a record, and together all these records form the stock file. Each time an item of stock is sold, the record for that item would need to be changed by reducing the stock level for that item. In terms of the data processing requirements of this type of operation, it would be necessary for the computer to read the details of the sales, find the appropriate stock records, subtract the appropriate amounts from the current stock levels and store the modified records. This sequence would be necessary for each sale recorded on a sales file.

COBOL is ideally suited to this type of application; it was designed to facilitate the manipulation of large amounts of data requiring fairly simple processing operations. Programs written in COBOL tend to be lengthy compared to other languages capable of performing similar processing tasks, the reason being that it requires the programmer to identify the purpose of the program, the computing equipment to be used, and the format of the files to be processed, as well as the procedure to be adopted for processing the files. All this information must be contained within the program itself. Subsequently, COBOL is often criticized for being very cumbersome, but on the credit side, all this detail helps to make a COBOL program easy to read and understand.

A COBOL program is divided into four areas termed DIVISIONS which appear in the order IDENTIFICATION division, ENVIRONMENT division, DATA division and PROCEDURE division. Each division comprises a number of SECTIONS and these are further divided into SENTENCES.

The IDENTIFICATION DIVISION allows the programmer to describe the whole program in general terms by supplying, under appropriate headings, such information as the name of the program, its author, when it was written and what it does. Some of this information is optional and none of it has a direct effect on the program's operation.

In the CONFIGURATION SECTION of the ENVIRONMENT DIVISION are details of the computers on which the program was developed and is intended to be run, and the INPUT-OUTPUT SECTION specifies the peripheral devices to be used for reading or writing the files which will be defined later in the program.

The DATA DIVISION contains a FILE SECTION in which each file named in the INPUT-OUTPUT SECTION is given a File Description (FD). The FD contains the file name and one or more record names. The structure of a record is defined hierarchically using LEVEL numbers starting at 01 and getting progressively bigger for finer definitions. The WORKING-STORAGE SECTION of the DATA DIVISION contains definitions of other data items specifically referenced in the PROCEDURE DIVISION of the program but which are not part of any file.

Finally, the PROCEDURE DIVISION defines precisely how the processing is to be performed. The programmer may give PARAGRAPH names to groups of SENTENCES to which reference may be made from other parts of the program, and these paragraphs may be grouped together into SECTIONS.

Each SENTENCE, terminated with a full stop, defines one or more basic operations to be performed on data; in keeping with the general philosophy of making a COBOL program easily readable, the instructions often read like ordinary English sentences as, for example, the SENTENCE

```
ADD vat TO cost GIVING total
```

Forth

Forth was developed around 1969 by Charles H. Moore who, dissatisfied with the traditional languages available to him, designed Forth as an interface between himself and the computers he was programming at the time. He developed the final version of the language while working on an IBM 1130 regarded, at the time of its introduction, to be an advanced 'third generation' computer. The resulting language seemed to him to be so powerful that he regarded it as a 'fourth-generation' language. He therefore would have liked to call it 'Fourth' but the 1130 would only allow five-character identifiers, so he settled for 'Forth'.

Because Forth is a threaded interpretive language, as described in Chapter 27, it offers a combination of fast execution time and interactive program development. Forth is an extensible language in the sense that the programmer is allowed to add new facilities to the language by defining them in terms of the basic operations that are originally supplied. These new facilities may be temporary or permanent features depending on how they are defined by the programmer.

The language makes extensive use of a data structure called a stack (see Chapter 32) and arithmetic operations are defined in Reverse Polish Notation. (In this form of notation an expression such as $A\times(B+C)$ would be written as $ABC+\times$, where the arithmetic operators $+$, $-$, $\times$ and $/$ follow their arguments rather than separate them).

A program is defined in a modular fashion in which sections, called words, of a program are defined in terms of basic operations; further words can make reference to words defined previously in a hierarchical structure.

FORTRAN

FORTRAN was designed by John Backus of IBM in 1953 for the science and engineering field. A compiler for the language first appeared in 1955 for an IBM machine, and since that time it has enjoyed widespread popularity as a powerful software tool. Since its introduction, FORTRAN has steadily evolved, giving rise to such versions as WATFOR (developed at the university of WATerloo, Canada) and WATFIV as well as FORTRAN IV.

Mainly orientated towards scientific/mathematical/engineering applications, many of its statements resemble and provide for numerical calculations. A FORTRAN program may be defined as a subroutine (subprogram) which may be referred to (called) by other programs in order to perform some standard or common operation. By forming libraries of these subroutines a programmer is able to reduce the amount of work required to write a new program; where possible, his program will make reference to these pre-written modules which will be combined with his code when the program is compiled. The language has many standard mathematical functions, such as SIN, COS, and SQRT, built in.

Pascal

Devised by Professor Niklaus Wirth in 1970 and named after the gifted 17th century mathematician and philosopher Blaise Pascal, Pascal is a general-purpose language based on Algol-60. Because Pascal, like BASIC, was designed as a teaching language, it is a very easy language to learn. Moreover, being orientated towards structured programming, it encourages the clear expression of the logical structure of the program. This makes Pascal a very easy language to write programs in, and is particularly suitable for the development of large programs. For these reasons it is widely used in teaching, and is being adopted by more and more establishments of further and higher education as the main programming language for computing courses. Many people believe Pascal to be superior to any other general-purpose programming language in use today, and its expanding use in all sectors of industry is evidence in support of this claim. Each Pascal program consists of a declarations section in which the structure of the data to be processed and produced is defined, a section for the definition of functions and procedures which are referenced in the program body section. The program body defines the operation of the program in a precise series of steps. Functions and procedures may be called from the program body whenever required.

Recursive programming

The term recursion is used to refer to the process of subprograms calling themselves. This is best explained by means of an example. The pseudocode program in Listing 26.1 uses a recursive call to print integers starting at 1 up to a given value.

Listing 26.1.

```
{Print consecutive integer values}
  read number
  call print_upto(number)                    {call the procedure}
{end}
```

```
select
  when N > 1
    call print_upto(N-1)              {procedure calls itself}
  when N <= 1
    next statement                    {ie do nothing}
endselect
write N
return
```

The recursive procedure is called `print_upto(number)` taking, as a parameter, the integer variable `number` which is read at the start of the program and is the upper limit for the integers to be printed.

Notice that, in the procedure `print_upto(N)`, the parameter N enclosed in brackets is automatically local to the procedure; this property of procedures, vital to recursive programming, is illustrated by the program trace which follows (the value of `number` is taken to be 3).

Depth of Recursion

Step		0	1	2
1	call	print_upto(3)		
2		when 3 > 1 call	print_upto(2)	
3			when 2 > 1 call	print_upto(1)
4				write 1
5				return
6			write 2	
7			return	
8		write 3		
9		return		
10	end			

Step *1*:   the procedure is called from the main program passing as a parameter the value of number (taken to be 3 in this example).

Step *2* :   the first line of the procedure tests the value of the parameter (called N in the procedure) and, because it is greater than 1, calls itself, this time passing a parameter value of N-1, that is 2. Because the procedure has not yet been completed, local variables (in this case just N) are saved to a stack so that when control eventually returns, the values of the local variables can be restored.

Step *3* :   the process is now at a recursion depth of 1 because the procedure has called itself once. The parameter N now has a value of 2, which is still greater than 1. Because the condition tested is true, the procedure calls itself once more. The current value of N (i.e. 2) is saved to a stack before the procedure is called.

Step *4* :   the process is now at a recursion depth of 2 because the procedure has called itself twice. The parameter N now has a value of 1, which is not greater than 1. Because the condition N > 1 is not true this time, the procedure ignores the call statement and goes on to the next statement in the procedure which prints the current value of N (i.e. 1).

Step *5* :   the return statement causes local variables to be discarded and their memory space reclaimed before program control is returned to the calling (sub)program. This process of returning back through recursive calls is often termed *bottoming out*.

Step *6* :   the process resumes at recursion depth of 1 having returned from the call statement invoked in Step *3*. The values of all local variables are restored from the stack. The write statement displays the value of local variable N (i.e. 2).

Step *7* :   this is identical to step *5*.

Step *8* :   the process arrives at the first invocation of the procedure having returned from the call statement in Step *2*. The values of all local variables are restored from the stack. The print statement prints the value of local variable N (i.e. 3).

Step *9* :   this is identical to steps *5* and *7*.

Step *10*:   finally, the program terminates.

Problems that lend themselves to recursion are often definable in terms of simpler versions of themselves as illustrated above: printing the numbers 1, 2, 3, 4 is just a simpler version of the problem of printing the numbers 1, 2, 3, 4, 5; printing 1, 2, 3 is just a simpler version of the problem of printing 1, 2, 3, 4, and so on. A number of data structures, including trees and linked lists, lend themselves to recursive processing techniques for this reason. The next examples further illustrate the point.

Two simple examples of recursive algorithms

The algorithm in Listing 26.2 calculates the value of an integer number, base, raised to certain positive integer power, exp.

Listing 26.2

```
{Calculate base raised to power}
  read base, exp
  write power(base,exp)
{end}

function power(b,e)
  local v
  select
    when e = 0
      v = 1
    when e <> 0
      v = b * power(b,e-1)
  endselect
return(v)
```

Table 26.1 contains examples of the values returned by the algorithm in Listing 26.2.

base	exp	result	
10	0	1	$=10^0$
10	3	1000	$=10^3$
2	0	1	$=2^0$
2	5	32	$=2^5$

Table 26.1

The example in Listing 26.3 uses a very similar method to calculate the factorial of a positive integer.

Listing 26.3.

```
{Calculate a factorial}
  read fac
  write factorial(fac)
{end}

function factorial(f)
  local v
    when f = 0
      v = 1
    when f <> 0
      v = f * function factorial(f-1)
    endselect
  return(v)
```

Table 26.2 shows some factorials calculated by the algorithm in Listing 26.3.

factorial	result	
0	1	
1	1	
2	2	$= 2 \times 1$
3	6	$= 3 \times 2 \times 1$
4	24	$= 4 \times 3 \times 2 \times 1$
5	120	$= 5 \times 4 \times 3 \times 2 \times 1$

Table 26.2.

Tracing through these algorithms in the same way as illustrated for the first example in this section should help to clarify the mechanisms used to obtain the desired results.

Advantages and disadvantages of recursive programming

Recursive solutions to programming tasks are often elegant and concise. They tend to be most effective when the solution to a problem may be expressed in terms of a simpler version of itself.

When a subprogram is executed, its data area is stored on a stack, so that if a subprogram calls itself a number of times, there will be a number of similar data areas on the stack at the same time, one for each recursive call. Therefore there is always the possibility of running out of stack space when executing recursive programs.

Another not insignificant problem with recursive programming is understanding how it works sufficiently well to be able to write programs which use recursion; being able to appreciate a recursive solution to a programming task is often very much easier than originating such a solution. Furthermore, detecting and correcting bugs in recursive programs may not be as straightforward as debugging more traditional, iteration-based programs.

Recursion is one of the central features of logic and functional programming languages both of which are discussed in later sections.

Declarative vs imperative languages

The languages discussed so far are often classified as *imperative* or *procedural* languages. These terms are used to describe high-level languages which require the programmer to show explicitly the order in which program statements are to be executed, and precisely how the programming solution is to be reached. The sequence of commands in a program is a key feature of imperative languages such as Pascal, FORTRAN and COBOL, since they are based on the Von Neumann computer model in which a stored program is executed by sequentially stepping through instructions stored in the immediate access store of a computer. Store locations are modified as a direct result of the action of the program. Similarly, imperative languages achieve their objectives by modifying program variables using assignment statements, and by causing sequential execution of program statements. Because imperative languages are so closely related to the operation of conventional computers, they are relatively efficient. However, other computer architectures, such as those using parallel processing, give rise to different types of programming languages.

Declarative languages rely on a different mechanism for solving programming problems. In these languages the emphasis is on defining the problem to be solved, not on the detailed sequence of instructions that are required in order to achieve the desired solution. It can be argued that a language such as Pascal is less procedural, and therefore more declarative, than an assembly language because there is less need for the programmer to define precisely how to do standard processing tasks such as input/output or arithmetic operations. For example, in an assembly language, it would require quite a complex sequence of instructions to perform the Pascal floating point calculation

```
x := (-b + sqrt(det))/(2.0*a);
```

Yet in Pascal it is merely a matter of specifying the calculation to be performed and allowing the compiler to determine how to organize the instructions required to do it. Thus languages that are predominantly procedural have elements of non-procedural characteristics. Declarative languages take this a stage further, allowing the language translator to do much more of the work, so that the programmer can concentrate on specifying what the problem is rather than how to solve it.

Because declarative languages do not rely on the programmer specifying precisely in which order instructions are to be executed, it is often possible to process a number of instructions in parallel if the mechanism exists to allow this. In the next section we examine the logic programming language PROLOG which is generally regarded as a good example of a predominantly declarative, or non-procedural, language. Functional languages, LISP for example, also essentially declarative, are described in a later section. Both PROLOG and LISP have features which allow them to take advantage of alternative computer architectures.

Logic programming

PROLOG, PROgramming in LOGic

Invented by Alain Colmerauer in the early 1970s, PROLOG was first implemented in Marseilles in 1972. It provided a means of allowing the programmer to specify a problem in terms related to formal logic rather than procedures.

The language has been adopted as the basis of software development for the Japanese fifth-generation project because of its relevance to research in artificial intelligence. It has been used extensively in the development of expert systems because it includes facilities ideal for this type of application.

PROLOG is said to be goal oriented, that is to say the programmer specifies the problem to be solved in terms of a goal, and is not expected to provide detailed instructions regarding the achievement of the goal. A goal is defined in terms of subgoals, the achievement of which will lead to the final solution. A subgoal may be a simple statement which evaluates to logical true or false, or may depend on its own subgoals which PROLOG will try to evaluate. Since there may be alternative sets of subgoals for a particular goal, PROLOG may, having failed to successfully resolve one combination, backtrack and try another combination. It will continue to try different combinations until either a solution is reached or there are no further combinations of subgoals to try. The power of PROLOG lies in its built-in ability to select goal combinations and to backtrack; in other languages this would have to be programmed explicitly.

Programming in PROLOG involves defining objects to be manipulated and relationships between them. A program consists of facts and rules (or clauses): facts are taken to be true statements about objects and rules declare that statements about objects are true if certain conditions (subgoals) are true. Executing a PROLOG program involves stating a goal to be achieved and allowing PROLOG to determine whether the goal can be achieved with the current facts and rules.

As an example, to represent the relationships between the members of a family spanning three generations as illustrated by the family tree shown in Figure 26.1.

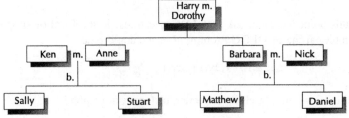

Figure 26.1. *Family tree*

This shows that Harry and Dorothy had two daughters, Anne who married Ken, and Barbara who married Nick. Anne and Ken had a son, Stuart, and a daughter, Sally. Barabara and Nick had two sons, Daniel and Matthew. Not shown on the diagram are Nick's parents, Raymond and Margaret.

These facts could be represented as follows in PROLOG:

```
male(raymond).
female(margaret).
male(harry).
female(dorothy).
male(nick).
female(barbara).
male(ken).
female(anne).
female(sally).
male(stuart).
male(matthew).
male(daniel).
parent(raymond,nick).
parent(margaret,nick).
parent(harry,barbara).
parent(dorothy,barbara).
parent(harry,anne).
parent(dorothy,anne).
parent(nick,daniel).
parent(nick,matthew).
parent(barbara,daniel).
parent(barbara,matthew).
parent(anne,sally).
parent(anne,stuart).
parent(ken,sally).
parent(ken,stuart).
```

The first type of fact concerns the sex of each member of the family:

```
male(raymond).
```

This asserts that raymond belongs to the set male. Similarly, barbara belongs to the set female. The other type of fact, parent, asserts that, for example, nick is a parent of daniel.

At this point we could ask PROLOG questions, in the form of simple goals, about this small database. For example, at the PROLOG prompt, '?−', we could type

```
?- parent(X,barbara).
```

PROLOG would search its collection of facts and respond

```
X = harry
More(y/n)?
```

Having found one value of variable X satisfying the goal, PROLOG displays this and asks if the search is to continue for another fact satisfying the goal. If we answered 'y', PROLOG would respond

```
X = dorothy
More(y/n)?
```

This is the only other solution to the goal and if we responded 'y' again, PROLOG would answer with 'No', indicating that there were no more solutions to the goal.

The goal

```
?- parent(anne,X).
```

would return values 'X = stuart' and 'X = sally', that is, the children of Anne.

Moreover, the goal

```
?- parent(X,Y).
```

would return all of the parent/child pairs in the database in the form

```
X = nick, Y = daniel
```

Rules could be added to the database in order to establish connections between facts. For example, the rule

```
childof(Y,X)  :- parent(X,Y).
```

says that Y is a childof X if X is a parent of Y.

If we wanted to find out from the collection of facts all the children of Dorothy, at the PROLOG prompt (?-) we would type

```
?- childof(y,dorothy).
```

PROLOG would regard this as a goal to be achieved and would try to find a fact or rule satisfying this goal. Because childof is a rule consisting of one subgoal, parent, PROLOG tries to find a value of X such that parent(X,dorothy) succeeds. It therefore produces 'Y = anne' and 'Y = barbara' as solutions to the goal.

The slightly more complex rule

```
mother(X,Y)  :- parent(X,Y), female(X).
```

establishes that X is the mother of Y if X is the parent of Y and X is also female.

Suppose we wished to establish whether Barbara is the mother of Matthew. We would pose the question

```
?- mother(barbara,matthew).
```

Substituting for X and Y, PROLOG would generate the two subgoals

```
parent(barbara,matthew), female(barbara).
```

Since both of these facts exist in the database, both goals could be achieved and PROLOG would answer 'Yes'.

Posing the question

```
?- mother(X,sally).
```

would again generate two subgoals, this time of the form

```
parent(X,sally), female(X).
```

Now PROLOG would first find a solution to the first subgoal in the form parent(ken,sally), and then attempt to satisfy the second subgoal, female(ken) which would fail. PROLOG would then backtrack to search for another solution to parent(X,sally). It would find parent(anne,sally) as a solution and then search for female(anne), this time succeeding. Finally, PROLOG would respond with 'X = anne'.

As a further example, the rule

```
grandparent(X,Z) :- parent(X,Y), parent(Y,Z).
```

establishes the condition for X to be the grandparent of Y.

Recursion plays a prominent role in PROLOG programs. Consider, for example, a rule which generalizes the previous rule for a grandparent:

```
predecessor(X,Z) :- parent(X,Z).
predecessor(X,Z) :- parent(X,Y), predecessor(Y,Z).
```

This time there are two clauses associated with the same definition: the first is necessary to halt the recursion exhibited in the second. To understand how this works, suppose that we posed the question

```
?- predecessor(X,daniel).
```

We would expect the solutions to be X = nick, X = barbara (these are parents), X= raymond, X = margaret, X = harry and X = dorothy (grandparents).

PROLOG would start by finding solutions to the first rule and simply find X = nick and X = barbara. The second rule would also be used as a goal, generating the subgoals

```
parent(X,Y), predecessor(Y,daniel).
```

One solution to parent(X,Y) is parent(raymond,nick), so PROLOG would try to find predecessor(nick,daniel). This recursively generates the subgoal parent(nick,daniel) from the first rule for predecessor, and this succeeds producing in effect

```
parent(raymond,nick), parent(nick,daniel)
```

allowing PROLOG to exit from the recursion. PROLOG would therefore state 'X = raymond' as another solution.

PROLOG has been used extensively as a database language and in AI (artificial intelligence) for natural language processing, expert systems and applications requiring knowledge representation.

PROLOG's suitability as a database language can be attributed to three main characteristics:

- A database defined in Prolog can be extended readily without any special provision for this growth needing to be made. This is in contrast to languages such as BASIC and COBOL where new information or requirements might necessitate a complete software revision.

- Databases can be merged or pooled with great ease; systems can be extended without the necessity for extensive forward planning.

- The language has, built in, the facility for drawing logical conclusions from a user's inputs, and for extracting information embedded in complex sequences of rules. This obviates the need for a special database query language.

Since natural language has a large number of rules regarding the composition of sentences, PROLOG is well suited to natural language processing where it is necessary to reduce sentences into their constituent parts. For example, in BNF notation a simple sentence can be represented by

```
<sentence>  ::=<noun phrase><verb phrase>
<noun phrase>  ::=<determiner><noun>
<verb phrase>  ::=<verb><noun phrase>
<determiner>  ::= the|a|an
<noun>  ::= dog|man
<verb>  ::= bit|fed
```

This is sufficient to successfully parse the sentences

```
The dog bit the man,
A man fed the dog
```

Notice the close similarity with PROLOG: the facts are <determiner>, and <noun>, and the rules are <sentence>, <noun phrase> and <verb phrase>. Natural language is of course much more complex than shown by this example, but PROLOG's suitability for this type of problem should be quite obvious.

Expert systems and other knowledge-based systems also require collections of facts combined with rules for establishing connections between them, again just what PROLOG is designed to handle.

Knowledge-based systems

A knowledge-based system embodies human knowledge in a form amenable to processing by a computer program. Such a system will store facts about a certain subject area, and relationships, often in the form of rules, which will allow conclusions to be drawn from the facts. A PROLOG program such as that provided in the previous section is a good example of a knowledge base, and a PROLOG translator executing such a program could be classed as a knowledge-based system.

The most common type of knowledge-based system is the expert system, and this is discussed in some detail in the following section.

Expert systems

Pure research in the field of artificial intelligence has had a number of practical spin-offs. One such spin-off has been the development of programs known as Expert Systems, or Intelligent Knowledge Based Systems. These are programs designed to be able to give the same sort of help or advice, or make decisions, as a human expert in some narrow field of expertise. For instance, a program called PROSPECTOR is capable of predicting the existence of mineral ores given various pieces of information gathered from physical locations. In the same way that, given certain evidence, an expert might say that a particular site looked favourable for containing ore, PROSPECTOR indicates the probability of the existence of the ore. PROSPECTOR is in fact attributed with the discovery of an extremely valuable quantity of molybdenum which had previously been overlooked by human experts. Expert systems have been developed in numerous areas which traditionally have been the province of human experts. For example, several expert systems have been developed to aid medical diagnosis and treatment. However, decisions in areas such as this are often so critical that it would be foolish to blindly accept the pronouncement of a computer. For this reason, expert systems have the built-in ability to justify the chain of logical reasoning leading to any conclusion, so that it can be checked and verified (or rejected) by a human. Another characteristic of many expert systems is the use of *fuzzy logic* which allows degrees of uncertainty to be built in to logical deduction processes. Such expert systems are able to state conclusions which are qualified by a probability value indicating the probability of the conclusion being correct.

Other successful expert systems include:

> MYCIN - diagnosis of infections;
>
> HEURISTIC DENDRAL - identifies organic compounds;
>
> XCON - for configuring (VAX) computer systems;
>
> SACON - for advice on structural analysis.

An expert system has three main components:

- a *knowledge base* consisting of rules which use facts supplied by some external source, typically a user;

- an *inference engine* which processes the knowledge base;

- a *user interface* to facilitate communication with the user.

As an example, the following knowledge base is for a simple botanical expert system to identify whether a particular plant is a shrub, tree, herb or vine. Four rules are to be used:

```
1   IF      STEM IS GREEN
    THEN    TYPE IS HERB.
2   IF      STEM IS WOODY
    AND     ATTITUDE IS CREEPING
    THEN    TYPE IS VINE.
3   IF      STEM IS WOODY
    AND     ATTITUDE IS UPRIGHT
    AND     ONE MAIN TRUNK IS TRUE
    THEN    TYPE IS TREE.
4   IF      STEM IS WOODY
    AND     ATTITUDE IS UPRIGHT
    AND     ONE MAIN TRUNK IS FALSE
    THEN    TYPE IS SHRUB.
```

This forms the knowledge base.

The inference engine starts by attempting to satisfy a primary goal, in this instance to determine the TYPE of the plant. To this end, it searches its knowledge base for the goal by looking for a rule containing the word TYPE in the conclusion part of the rule (after the THEN part of a rule). This process of examining conclusions to rules while attempting to resolve goals is called *backward chaining* (or *goal-driven inference*).

Rule 1 satisfies this requirement, but in order to establish if the plant is a HERB, the system must obtain information regarding the STEM. Initially this information will not be available and must be supplied by the user. Consequently, obtaining the STEM information is added to a list of subgoals to be evaluated, along with rule 1, and the system looks for another rule containing the goal in its conclusion. The subgoal list also notes the rule which generated the subgoal in question.

After the remaining rules have been processed in a similar fashion, the system must then attempt to satisfy the subgoal list. Consequently, the user interface is invoked. This generates a question of the form

```
IS THE STEM OF THE PLANT GREEN?
```

Let us suppose that the plant is a SHRUB (which has a woody stem, grows upright, and has more than one main trunk). The user answers 'NO' which is stored as a fact relating to the stem of the plant.

Having succeeded with a subgoal, the inference engine again searches for a rule conclusion containing TYPE. It can attempt to evaluate the first rule now that it has all the necessary information. The rule does not produce a conclusion since the STEM is not green. This rule is therefore discarded since it can never cause the primary goal to succeed in this particular consultation.

Examination of the second rule reveals to the inference engine that it cannot be resolved until the ATTITUDE of the plant is in its list of facts, so this is added to its list of subgoals.

Eventually, all the necessary facts are available and the inference engine is able to discard all rules except rule 4 which establishes that the plant is a SHRUB.

In the course of a consultation the user might wish to know why the system is asking a certain question. The information required to answer this question is easy to find: the subgoal generating the question being asked was stored along with the rule from which it came, and this contains all the necessary information. For example, if the inference engine was attempting to resolve rule 4 by asking about the number of TRUNKS, the user interface might respond,

```
I am trying to determine the TYPE. I know that the STEM
is woody. I know that the ATTITUDE is upright. If ONE MAIN
TRUNK is false then I will know that the TYPE is SHRUB.
```

Expert system shells

The term 'Shell' is given to expert systems which have been given no specific knowledge base, only the inference engine and user interface; the knowledge base has to be provided by the user. A single expert system shell can thus be used to provide advice or help in a number of areas of expertise, providing it is given the appropriate knowledge base for each area.

For example, an expert system shell could be used to give advice on the procedures and sequence of steps necessary for selling a house (what solicitors call 'conveyancing'), or to give advice about possible causes and cures of diseases in houseplants, or diagnosing faults in cars. Not only could these applications be of practical use, but they could also be instructive because the user could ask for and obtain the reasons behind any conclusions.

One of the problems of using such shells is the determination of the rules which represent the wisdom of a human expert; many experts are not consciously aware of the precise reasoning processes they themselves use in order to come to some conclusion, yet in order to produce an expert program, these processes must be defined in a form that is usable. The process of determining the knowledge base rules is known as 'knowledge elicitation' or 'knowledge acquisition' and is performed by 'knowledge engineers'.

Functional languages

The pseudocode function, range, shown in Listing 26.4 determines the range of three numbers by finding the difference between the largest number and the smallest number.

Listing 26.4.

```
function range(x, y, z)
  a = max(x, y)
  b = max(a, z)
  c = min(x, y)
  d = min(c, z)
  r = b - d
return(r)

function max(m, n)
  select
    when m > n
      return(m)
    when otherwise
      return(n)
  endselect
{end}

function min(m, n)
  select
    when m < n
      return(m)
    when otherwise
      return(n)
  endselect
{end}
```

Notice that function `range` uses a number of assignment operations for intermediate calculations, and that these calculations must be executed in the order specified because they occur on consecutive lines. In fact, all of these assignment statements can be eliminated by writing the `range` function in the following way (the word function has been omitted from functions `max` and `min` for the sake of clarity);

```
function range(x, y, z)
return(max(max(x, y), z) - min(min(x, y), z))
```

This is the function-based version which eliminates all assignment statements and no longer specifies the order in which intermediate calculations are to be executed. Moreover, the max and min functions may be executed in parallel since neither depends on the other.

Functional languages such as LISP and, to a lesser degree, LOGO use this nested function approach, thereby allowing more flexibility in the implementation of programs. However, these languages take the use of functions a stage further than that shown in the example. In LISP, for instance, the same program might appear as shown in Listing 26.5.

Listing 26.5.

```
(defun max(m n)
  (cond((greaterp m n) m)
  (t              ) n)

]
(defun min(m n)
  (cond((lessp m n) m)
  (t              ) n)

]
defun range(x y z)
(- (max (max x y) z) (min (min x y) z)
]
```

All functions, which are defined using defun, are enclosed in brackets and return a value. Thus the built-in function greaterp returns t (true) if m is greater than n.

The selection function, cond, takes the form

```
(cond (exp₁ val₁)
      (exp₂ val₂)
      .  .
      (expₙ valₙ))
```

and it returns the value (val) corresponding to the first true expression (exp) in the list of value/expression pairs. So, for example, the pseudocode

```
select
  when exp
    return(val₁)
  when otherwise
    return(val₂)
endselect
```

translates in LISP to

```
(cond (exp val₁ )
      (t    val₂ ))
```

where t is boolean true. Thus if exp is true, val_1 is returned from cond, else val_2 is returned since t is always true.

The subtraction function is merely the '–' sign. So, to subtract the two values a and b we would write

```
(– a b)
```

where a and b could be numbers or functions returning values.

As a final note of explanation, the terminating square bracket, ']', is used to represent any number of close parentheses, ')'; with complex nested expressions it is quite difficult sometimes to determine the correct number of ')', and easy to get it wrong, so the ']' is provided to prevent this occurring.

The following two sections describe in very general terms the main characteristics of LISP and LOGO as examples of functional languages.

LISP

Though LISP is one of the oldest computer languages (nearly as old as FORTRAN) it is used extensively in one of the most innovative of today's research areas: artificial intelligence. As its popularity increases it is becoming available on more and more machines; most main-frames and an increasing number of micros support a version of the language.

LISP was designed as a purely functional language. By this we mean that statements in LISP look like functions. For instance, the function which adds numbers in LISP is called PLUS and is written

```
(PLUS 2 3)
```

The function PLUS operates on the 'arguments' 2 and 3. All statements are written in this way.

However, LISP is primarily a language for manipulating symbols rather than performing complex numeric calculations. It treats all forms of data as being elements of lists and has facilities for conveniently manipulating these lists in various ways. Moreover, the language is extensible in that the user is able to create his own functions to be used like any of those supplied.

Programs in LISP are developed interactively. Typing the name of a function, followed by its arguments, causes the function to be performed and the result displayed. In the addition example above, LISP would return the number 5 as soon as the function had been entered. This characteristic is one of the strengths of the language in that programs are written in small, easily testable steps, the effects of which can be seen immediately.

LOGO

Designed as a language to provide a very early and easy route into programming, LOGO is probably best known as the first language to use 'turtle graphics'. When running LOGO, the turtle appears as a graphics cursor which can be instructed to move across the screen using commands such as FORWARD 20 or RIGHT 30. Remotely controllable devices can also be connected to the computer and controlled by the same commands.

The 'turtle' commands have been designed to be appealing and to motivate children to write programs to make the turtle perform visually pleasing manoeuvres. Seymour Papert, the American mathematician who designed the language, was largely influenced by Piaget's well-known ideas on intellectual development in children. Consequently LOGO is emerging as an important educational tool. Unlike much educational software currently available in which the computer is the teacher, and the child reacts to it, LOGO offers a completely different approach to computer assisted learning. With LOGO the roles are reversed, the child teaching the computer what to do.

In his book, 'Mindstorms', Seymour Papert explains the philosophy of LOGO, how it was developed and how it works.

LOGO, however, is more than a language just for children. It is based on LISP and shares many of its features. Like LISP it is extensible, based on list processing, and allows recursion. Because it is interpreted, it is easy to use and allows programs to be edited without difficulty. In fact it is a surprisingly powerful language, as well as being easy to learn. It is by no means a 'toy' language and is attracting much interest in all kinds of areas, including artificial intelligence applications.

Here are two simple subprograms in LOGO to enable the turtle to draw a box of side L screen units.

```
TO SIDE :L
FORWARD :L
RIGHT 90
END

TO SQUARE :L
REPEAT 4 [SIDE :L]
END
```

The first subprogram, `SIDE`, instructs the turtle to move forward L units and then turn right by 90 degrees.

The second subprogram, `SQUARE`, draws a square of side L by repeatedly calling `SIDE`.

The turtle would be instructed to draw a square of side 100 units with the command

```
SQUARE 100
```

The functional nature of the language is illustrated by the manner in which arithmetic is performed. For example, to add two numbers and store them in the variable, `S`, we would write:

```
MAKE S SUM :A :B
```

where `SUM` is the function taking two arguments, in this case the values of variables `A` and `B`.

As a second example, the calculation $x = a + b*c$ would become

```
MAKE X SUM :A PROD :B :C
```

Object oriented programming (OOP)

Object oriented programming attempts to simulate the real world by means of objects which have characteristics and functions. Object oriented languages are classed as fifth generation languages.

As its name suggests, object oriented programming is based on the idea of an object. An object is a combination of local variables and procedures, called *methods*, together forming a self-contained programming entity. The term *encapsulation* is sometimes used to describe the combination of a data structure and the methods which manipulate it in an object. Invoking a method is called passing a message to an object.

The individual variables in an object together form a data structure which exists intact throughout program runtime. This is not the case with similar structures such as subprograms whose variables are in effect destroyed on completion of the subprogram. An object can retain *state information* even while it is inactive.

Information hiding is another characteristic of object oriented programming. The idea is that the programmer needs to know only what an object does, not how it does it, in order to use it in a program.

By means of *inheritance*, new objects may be derived that inherit data and methods from one or more defined objects. Further data structures and methods may be redefined or added to the derived objects, hence forming a hierarchy of structures and reducing the code required to define a new object.

These ideas need to be clarified by means of an example. Borland's Turbo C++, an object oriented extension of C, will be used as the vehicle for the example which involves part of an interactive drawing program. Suppose that we wish to provide a facility for drawing a dot of a certain colour. The dot object could be defined as shown in Listing 26.6.

Listing 26.6

```
class point
{
  private:
    int X,Y;
    int colour;
  public:
    int getX() {return X;}
    int getY() {return Y;}
    int getcolour() {return colour;}
    void setcolour(int c) {colour=c;}
    void plot() {putpixel(X,Y,colour);}
}dot;
```

The declarative class allows objects to be defined. In addition, class allows the use of the word private, which restricts access to the variables (X, Y and colour in this case) exclusively to the object's methods, and public which allows access to variables and methods by functions external to the object being defined.

Five methods are defined: the first three allow external functions to obtain the position of the point and its colour, the fourth allows the point's colour to be set at some integer value, and the final one displays the dot using a predefined function, putpixel(). Notice that the methods are defined within the object, that is in-line, though C++ also allows them to be defined elsewhere if required.

In order to obtain dot's X co-ordinate we would invoke method getX() using a statement such as

```
x_coord = dot.getX();
```

To change its colour to 1 would require

```
dot.setcolour(1);
```

and it could be displayed using

```
dot.plot();
```

It is important to note that the only way to use the dot object is by means of the appropriate method; this means that if any of the methods are changed, there will be no need to alter any other part of the program which makes use of the object. This is a very important characteristic of object oriented programming. Furthermore, there is no possibility of an object's variables being corrupted inadvertently elsewhere in the program since, having been declared as private, the only functions allowed to access them are the object's methods. Together, these two features characterize information hiding mentioned earlier.

Notice also that the dot object's state information, that is, its co-ordinates and colour, is retained throughout the execution of the program, unlike local variables within a subprogram.

Object oriented programming languages usually allow defined objects to be the basis of derived objects, in which variables and methods may be inherited. For example, we could use the point object as the basis of a more general dot which would allow its co-ordinates to be changed. This would involve defining the new dot in terms of point and adding two more methods, one to set X and the other to set Y.

This type of situation, where a base object may be used to derive a special object, occurs frequently in programming tasks. A car object, for instance, could be the basis of a number of different types of cars, such as sports, saloon, hatchback, and so on, each inheriting the basic car characteristics and adding to or modifying them according to special data/functional requirements. A convenient way to start when using object oriented design is to state the system requirements in narrative form and identify key nouns which relate to object classes, and key verbs which correspond to object methods. For example, consider the outline system specification below:

> The temperature control system regulates the temperature of a number of <u>rooms</u> in the building. Each room has a <u>minimum temperature</u> and <u>maximum temperature</u> and the system **keeps** the temperature of the room between these two limits. The limits may be **changed** by means of the <u>system console</u>, which also **shows** the <u>current temperature</u> of each room in the form of a <u>dynamic display</u>.

<u>Nouns</u> are shown underlined and **verbs** in bold.

Thus the nouns identify a room object which requires temperature regulation, and a system console object for data input and display purposes. As a preliminary step we might therefore identify the following object classes and associated operations.

```
Object class:      Room
Operations:        Detect temperature
                   Increase temperature
                   Decrease temperature
```

```
Object class:        System Console Keyboard
Operations:          Get new/initial temperature limits
                     Communicate with user


Object class:        System Console Display
Operations:          Update room temperatures
                     Display room temperatures
```

This would provide a reasonable starting point for the detailed design which would follow.

Implementation languages

A number of computer languages have features which facilitate object oriented design without having been specifically written for this purpose. These languages include Simula, Ada, Modula-2, C++ and some versions of Pascal. Smalltalk on the other hand was designed specifically as a language which could be used to implement an object oriented design directly.

Smalltalk was developed by the Xerox Corporation following an idea by Alan Kay regarding the development of personal computers. The original research in the 1970s involved the development of a notebook computer called a 'Dynabook'. To this end, a windows-based, graphical user environment was developed, with the underlying control of the system being achieved by Smalltalk. The system was highly interactive, having been influenced by the type of user interface employed by Logo.

Since object oriented design encourages software re-usability, Smalltalk provides a large library of basic object classes which may be used directly or tailored to specific needs. Since it was originally designed to be used with powerful personal computers supporting WIMP environments, its use is likely to increase, particularly with the increasing speed and memory size of personal computers we are currently experiencing.

Advantages of object oriented programming

We have already seen that communication between objects is via messages, eliminating the need for shared data areas such as sets of global variables, and removing the possibility of accidental modification to data shared by a number of functions or programs. This is particularly important when a large programming project is being developed by a team of programmers simultaneously working on different aspects of the job, because it ensures that the work of one programmer will not interact in unforeseen ways with that of any other.

Furthermore, access to an object's methods are exclusively by means of a well-defined, unchanging interface. The way that an object performs its characteristic functions is of no interest to users of the object, and any internal changes to its structure will be invisible. This ensures that modification of an object, being independent of other objects, will have no effect whatsoever on any other part of the program.

The inheritance property of object oriented programming languages allows the hierarchical structuring of objects, reducing coding effort and simplifying the program structure.

Because objects are self-contained entities which may be used sequentially or in parallel, an object oriented design offers substantial flexibility in its implementation; decisions regarding the use of processing method, whether serial or parallel, need not be made immediately, and programs may be converted to a different processing method without the necessity for a complete rewrite.

Disadvantages of object oriented programming

Object inheritance can produce significant run-time overheads, reducing the execution speed of a program. A complex hierarchical object structure might involve a substantial number of cross-referenced objects, giving the program extra work to do.

An object oriented design is not always the most appropriate solution. Sometimes a more functional approach can simplify the programming task, particularly where system state information does not need to be retained by a program. Remember that an object can retain state information during the execution of a program, unlike the values of variables in subprograms which are lost as soon as the subprogram is exited; in certain applications this may not be required. For example, the common cash dispenser comprises a screen, a numeric keypad and a number of function keys such as Withdraw cash, Obtain balance, Proceed, Cancel request. The customer, having entered his or her PIN (personal identification number), selects a function by pressing the appropriate function key.

A natural program design would be to assign a subprogram to process each function. Since each function operates independently of the others, there is no need to retain any sort of state information. An object oriented approach could of course still be used, but there would be no particular advantage in doing so.

Exercises

1.   Briefly describe the main characteristics of the five generations of computer languages.

2.   What are reserved words and how do they differ from keywords?

3.   The text describes the main features of a number of popular languages. Research and summarize, in a similar fashion, the following languages, which are not covered in the text:

(i)   C++;

(ii)   Visual C++;

(iii)   Visual Basic;

(iv)   Delphi;

(v)   Java;

(vi)   Perl;

(vii)   Python.

4.   Explain the difference between Declarative and Imperative computer languages. Give an example of each of these two types of languages.

5.   What is meant by recursive programming?

6.   What are the main components of an expert system?

7.   Name two languages associated with artificial intelligence work.

Chapter 27

Language Processing

The definition of computer languages

Fundamental to the design of a computer language is the idea of a grammar which precisely defines the syntax of program statements. This section describes two notations commonly employed to specify such grammars; they are *Backus-Naur form* and *syntax diagrams*. All languages, whether computer languages such as Pascal or Prolog, or natural languages such as English or Japanese, have a number of rules governing the syntax of well-formed statements or sentences. The collection of these syntax rules is called the grammar of a language. The grammar of a natural language is very difficult to state precisely, and might require several hundred syntax rules to define it even approximately, but, because computer languages are relatively simple and unambiguous, they can be defined exactly using a relatively small set of rules. Two common methods of describing the grammar of languages are:

- Backus-Naur Form (BNF), named after the two men that developed this notation for defining Algol;

- syntax diagrams.

These are examples of *meta-languages*, that is, languages which are used to describe other languages.

Such formal definitions of computer languages are useful for a number of reasons:

- they provide the means to determine whether a given sequence of characters constitutes a valid statement in the language;

- they allow us to break down a statement into its constituent parts, that is, parse the statement, so that it can be converted into a machine-sensible form;

- they can be used to generate well-formed statements.

Backus-Naur form (BNF)

As a simple example of the use of BNF notation, consider a grammar which defines the form of integers of any length:

$$< integer > ::= < digit > \mid < integer > < digit >$$

$$< digit > ::= 0 \mid 1 \mid 2 \mid 3 \mid 4 \mid 5 \mid 6 \mid 7 \mid 8 \mid 9$$

<integer> and <digit>, are called *non-terminals* because they are defined in terms of other non-terminals or elementary symbols called *terminal* symbols. Thus the symbols 0 to 9 are terminal symbols. The ::= notation is read as 'is defined as' and the symbol | means 'or'. So the first rule reads

'*integer* is defined as a *digit* or an *integer* followed by a *digit*'.

The second rule reads

'*digit* is defined as the symbol 0 or 1 or 2 ... or 9'.

integer and *digit* are termed *syntactic entities* since they each define a separate part of the grammar.

We can use these rules to generate integers by repeatedly replacing the left-hand syntactic entities by the right-hand terminals and non-terminals. For example, replacing *digit* by 5 produces

<integer> ::= 5   (from the rule, <integer> ::= <digit>)

This is one instance of an integer, according to our grammar. But the grammar also states that <integer> ::= <integer> <digit>, so we can replace <integer> on the right-hand side by 5 and <digit> by, say, 2 to give

<integer> ::= 52

By repeating this procedure we can produce any integer value; for this reason, rules are also called *productions*. Notice that the *recursive* nature of the first rule enables this simple grammar to generate an infinite number of integers. Not all grammars are recursive, but those that are describe infinite languages. A (simplified) recursive grammar for an arithmetic expression in a high-level language such as C could be expressed as:

<expr>	::= <term> | <expr> <expr operator> <term>
<term>	::= <factor> | <term> <term operator> <factor>
<factor>	::= <variable> | <integer> | (<expression>) | –<factor>
<variable>	::= A | B |..... | Z
<integer>	::= <digit> | <integer> <digit>
<digit>	::= 0 | 1 | 2 | 3 | 4 | 5 | 6 | 7 | 8 | 9
<expr operator>	::= + | –
<term operator>	::= * | /

Using this grammar, examples of valid arithmetic expressions are:

A + B

P – Q/2

X + Y*(Z + 1) – W

L*M + 3*(A*A – B/4)

A compiler could use this grammar to determine the syntactic validity of an expression within a program statement by attempting to establish that the expression conforms to the rules of the grammar. *Parsing*, this process of analysing a string of symbols using the production rules of the grammar, is discussed later in the section devoted to the structure and function of compilers.

Syntax diagrams

A more graphical approach to language definition is the use of *syntax diagrams*. For example, the BNF definition of an unsigned integer given in the previous section is equivalent to the syntax diagram shown in Figure 27.1. The different paths that may be taken through the diagram are indicated by the arrows.

Figure 27.1.

Here, *digit* represents one of the symbols 0–9 as before and shown in Figure 27.2.

Figure 27.1 shows that, by following a single left-to-right path, an integer can be a single digit; by following the loop path two or more times, an integer can contain two or more digits.

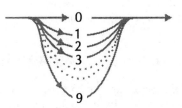

The arrows in Figure 27.2 indicate that only one of the digits 0-9 may be selected in going from left to right, meaning that a digit is one of the symbols 0,1,2...9. Syntax diagrams are read by following

Figure 27.2.

the routes indicated by arrows, adding the symbols indicated in the circles or oval boxes to build up strings representing valid syntactic structures. So, in the example above, we could select '8' as the first digit, and by following the loop back around once more, and this time choosing '5', we would have generated the integer 85. Figure 27.3 defines the rules for the formation of the Roman numerals for 1-10:

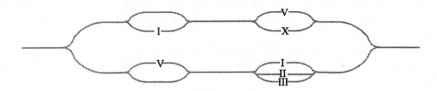

Figure 27.3.

The ten possible different routes through the diagram generate the numerals: I, II, III, IV, V, VI, VII, VIII, IX, X. As a final example, the syntax diagram in Figure 27.4 shows the overall structure of a Pascal program. When used for this purpose, three different symbols are used:

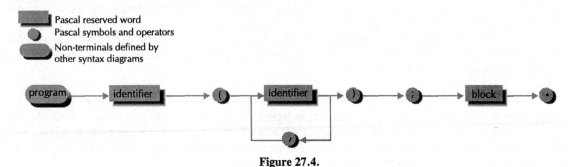

Figure 27.4.

Examples of valid program identifiers, according to this definition, are

> program example1(input,output); < block >.

where *example1*, *input* and *output* are identifiers and < block > is a non-terminal which is defined by its own syntax diagram.

> program eg2(file1,file2,file3);.

Here *eg2*, *file1*, *file2* and *file3* are identifiers and < block > is again a non-terminal.

Syntax diagrams have the added advantage of succinctly describing the complete set of syntactic constructs of a computer language, thus providing a convenient source of reference for programmers.

Computer language translators

The general function of *translators* (or *language processors*) is to convert program statements written in one programming language into another, most commonly into machine code. This chapter examines the function and operational characteristics of the three main types of translators, namely *assemblers*, *compilers* and *interpreters*.

Assemblers

In the history of programming languages, one of the first significant innovations was the development of assembly languages. A program written in an assembly language is much more readable and understandable than its equivalent in machine code; the problem arises, however, that it is no longer directly executable by the computer. An *assembler* is a computer program which carries out the necessary translation.

The assembler accepts an assembly language program as data, converts *mnemonic* operation codes (op-codes) to their numeric equivalents, assigns *symbolic addresses* to memory locations and produces as output the required machine code program.

The assembly language program is termed the *source program* and the final machine code program is the *object program*.

Though it is true that by far the majority of computer programming today is in high-level languages such as Pascal, C or COBOL, programming in assembly languages is still essential for certain tasks. The reason for this, despite continual improvements in compiler design, is simply that the programmer, having total control over the structure of the machine code generated by the assembler, is able to write much faster and more efficient code than that produced by a compiler. The very nature of high-level languages, allowing us to deal with a greatly simplified, virtual machine, often precludes the programmer from being able to fine-tune code according to particular circumstances.

For example, a commonly used method of increasing the speed of a machine-code program is to utilize internal registers as much as possible in preference to memory locations, in order to minimize relatively slow memory accesses. While this type of code optimization is perfectly feasible in any assembly language, most high-level languages do not allow the programmer this degree of control (C is a notable exception, allowing identifiers to be specifically allocated to general purpose registers).

A consequence of the one-to-one correspondence between an assembly language instruction and its equivalent machine-code instruction is that assemblers are *machine dependent*, producing machine code for a specific type of processor. For instance, the machine code generated by an Intel 8086/88 assembler could not be used directly by a computer with a Motorola 68000 processor. For this reason, there is no single, archetypal assembler; rather, each assembler is related to the architecture of the processor for which it has been designed. Thus, if the processor supports two-address machine-code instructions (Chapter 4), this will be reflected in the format of the assembly language instructions.

In the following sections a number of fundamental characteristics, common to most assemblers, are introduced. Assembly language programming is discussed in Chapter 31, using a hypothetical microprocessor and associated assembly language to illustrate simple programs and including an example program to illustrate the assembly process described in this chapter.

Assembler tasks

Early assemblers did little more than convert instruction mnemonics to their equivalent numeric machine codes, but current assemblers do much more. Some of the most common assembler tasks are described below:

- *Op-code translation*. Numeric operation codes replace the mnemonic op-codes used in the source program.

- *Absolute address allocation*. Each instruction or data word in the source program must be allocated an absolute machine address (its physical location). The assembler maintains a *location counter* (sometimes referred to as a *load pointer*) which, having been set to an initial base address, is incremented by the length of each data or instruction word as it is assembled.

- *Symbolic operand conversion*. This refers to the assembly process of substituting any symbolic addresses, that is, user identifiers used in place of memory locations, with numeric machine addresses. A symbol table records each symbolic operand together with its corresponding absolute address; a similar table logs labels and their machine addresses. If relative addressing is used, labels and symbolic addresses are converted to offsets from the location counter; this enables a program to be relocatable (See Chapter 4).

- *Converting constants to their internal forms*. This will involve conversion from textual (ASCII, for example) representations of decimal, hexadecimal, octal or binary to pure binary.

- *Replacing identifiers by user-defined macros*. If the assembly language supports the use of *macro* instructions (a shorthand used by a programmer to express sequences of regularly used instructions by a macro name), any such macro must be expanded by the assembler and inserted into the source program prior to assembling it.

- *Obeying directives*. Many assemblers support the use of *pseudo-operations*, or *directives* which are instructions not directly translatable into machine instructions. These involve such things as reserving space for data, defining the values of identifiers used in the program and defining where the program is to be located in memory.

- *Generating error messages*. If the assembler detects any syntax errors in the source program, it must be able to issue a message indicating the source and nature of the problem.

- *Producing source-code listings*. These may take various forms including listings of the source-code, object-code and symbol table.

Assembly

The assembly process usually involves the assembler in executing several passes of the program's source code, each one carrying out certain of the tasks described above. The problem of forward referencing (an instruction uses a symbolic operand which is not defined until later in the program, so its address has not been allocated at that point and cannot be included in the instruction) means that assemblers usually carry out a minimum of two passes.

Two-pass assembly

Pass 1. Any macro instructions are expanded as part of the pass or as a separate initial pass, making three in all. All instructions are examined and checked for syntactical correctness; any errors are recorded in a table. After each instruction has been dealt with, the location counter is incremented, and a symbol table is constructed to link any symbolic operands and labels with their corresponding absolute addresses.

Pass 2. By reference to the symbol tables, the assembler generates and outputs the object code.

In Chapter 31 a three-pass assembly is illustrated with a simple program, showing how the object program is generated at each stage in the assembly process.

Cross assembler

This is an assembler which carries out the translation of an assembly program on one machine to produce object code for execution on another. For example, a certain cross assembler running on an IBM PC might assemble a source program to produce Motorola 68000 machine code for use on an Apple computer.

Compilers and interpreters

There are two main types of high-level language translators (or language processors as they are often known): (i) compilers; (ii) interpreters.

Since the choice of translator has implications regarding program development time, debugging and testing, memory requirements, execution speed and program security, it is important from a programming point of view to be quite clear about the difference between the two types.

A compiler accepts a *source program*, that is, a program written in some high-level language, Pascal for instance, checks that it is correctly formed and, if so, generates the equivalent *object program* in a low-level language. The translated program may be in the form of an assembly language, in which case it must first be assembled before it is executed, or it may be in machine code, allowing it to be executed directly without further modification. If any errors are detected during compilation, they will be reported and, if serious enough, may prevent the compiler from completing the translation process. A compiler will often have access to a library of standard routines and special routines appropriate to the application area for which the source language was designed; this collection of subroutines is called the *run-time library*. Included in this library of machine code subprograms will be routines for performing arithmetic operations, input/output operations, backing storage data transfers and other commonly used functions. Whenever the source code refers to one of these routines specifically, or needs one to perform the operation specified, the compiler will ensure that the routine is added to the object program.

Note that the final object code is independent of both the source code and the compiler itself. That is, neither of these two programs needs to be resident in main store when the object code is being executed. However, any alterations to the program subsequent to its compilation will necessitate modification and re-compilation of the source code prior to executing the program again.

An interpreter uses a different method to translate a source program into a machine-sensible form. An object program is not generated in this form of translation, rather the source program, or an intermediate form of it, is scanned statement by statement, each in turn immediately being converted into the actions specified.

The source code statements are translated and executed separately, as they are encountered, while the source code is being processed by the interpreter. The object code actually executed is held within the interpreter; the latter merely identifies from the source statement which piece of machine code is relevant and causes it to be performed. On completion of a statement, control returns to the interpreter which then processes the next logical statement in the program sequence.

It might seem, therefore, that an interpreter has a big advantage over a compiler. In terms of the amount of effort required in obtaining an executable program, this is certainly true, but there are a number of other factors which favour the use of a compiler. For example, an interpreter must do a considerable amount of work before it can even begin to cause a source statement to be executed (error checking, for instance); on the other hand, a compiler has already done this work during compilation. Moreover, should a section of source code be repeated one or more times, an interpreter must re-interpret the section each time. Consequently, interpreted programs tend to run significantly slower than equivalent compiled programs, and for time-critical applications this might be a major concern. Furthermore, because the translation and execution phases are interwoven, the interpreter must be resident in memory at the same time as the source code. If memory space is at a premium, this can be a severe limitation of an interpreted language. Languages designed for use by children or for teaching purposes are often interpreted. Logo, for example, originally designed as a language for children, is interpreted to facilitate its interactive nature. Similarly, BASIC is interpreted in order to simplify its use for programming novices.

A possible compromise is to provide both an interpreter and a compiler for the same language; this allows rapid development time using the interpreter, and fast execution obtained by compiling the code.

Compilers

The compilation process can be broken down into a number of stages:

(i)   lexical analysis - the source code is scanned and converted into a form more convenient for subsequent processing, and a symbol table is partially constructed;

(ii)   syntax analysis and semantic analysis - the output from the lexical analyser is analysed for grammatical correctness, the symbol table is completed, error messages are generated if errors have been detected, and the program is further transformed ready for the next stages;

(iii)   intermediate code generation - the output from the parser is put into an internal form permitting easier conversion into object code;

(iv)   code optimization - the intermediate code is made more time or space efficient using a number of different techniques;

(vi)   code generation - the object code, which may be either machine code or assembly language, is generated.

These stages are discussed in more detail in the following sections.

Lexical analysis

Most programming languages allow a certain amount of redundancy in the preparation of the program. For example, spaces can often be inserted to aid readability of the source code, and comments are used to explain the function of the program and sections of code. A section of the compiler, called the *lexical analyser* or *scanner*, removes such redundancies and performs other modifications of the source code prior to passing it to the next stage of compilation.

The lexical analyser takes the source code and translates it into a string of characters, which is to be passed to the *syntax analyser*, or *parser*. The process of lexical analysis identifies *lexemes*, that is, the basic lexical units of the source language, such as reserved words, operators, identifiers, constants and literals, and associates them with specific integer values or *tokens*. For example, each reserved word would be represented by a unique integer, say in the range 256-511, all identifiers would have a certain code such as 512, constants perhaps 513, and special symbols such as '(' or '*' would probably retain their ascii values. Additionally, each identifier would be replaced by a pointer to its position in a *symbol table* containing details of its characteristics. The lexical analyser thus preprocesses the source code to facilitate subsequent stages in the compilation process. In addition, it provides an interface between the programmer and the computer, allowing some limited flexibility in the layout of the source code.

Syntax and semantic analysis

These analysers do the actual hard work of breaking the source program into its constituent parts. The complete source program is analysed into blocks, which are then broken down into statements, which are further analysed into instruction words, variables and constants. Each variable used in the source program is placed in a symbol table, together with a declaration of its attributes - type (numeric, string etc.), where it is to be located in memory (its object program address) and any other information required for object code generation.

The syntax analyser, or parser, takes the output from the lexical analyser and determines syntactic correctness of the program using the grammatical rules for the language.

The *syntax* or grammar of a programming language consists of a set of rules which define a legal program statement, as opposed to a meaningless string of characters. The rules determine correct sentence structure; the process of checking the validity of sentence structure is known as *parsing*. In English, for example, the sentence

> *the monkey ate the banana*

can be determined as grammatically correct by reference to the rules of English grammar. Conversely, the rules can be used to determine that

> *monkey the ate banana the*

is grammatically incorrect.

Similarly, the grammar or syntax of the Pascal programming language can be used to determine that the program statement

```
net := gross - deductions;
```

is correct, and that

```
gross - deductions := net;
```

is not.

However, even the first statement, though syntactically correct, might still be invalid on *semantic* grounds. For instance, if any of the variables `net`, `gross` or `deductions` had not been previously declared, or if any of them had been declared as having `type char` (character), the statement would be meaningless. Returning to our English example, the sentence

The banana ate the monkey.

is still grammatically correct but semantically very suspect because we are aware that one of the attributes of an ordinary banana is that it is a non-carnivorous fruit.

Semantic analysis is therefore concerned with checking the meaning or interpretation to be placed on words in the particular context of their use. Once the parser has confirmed the grammatical validity of a program construct, the semantic analyser can use the symbol table to check that an operation is semantically valid. In addition, the semantic analyser may supplement the work of the parser by using the symbol table to guide the generation of intermediate code. For example, a number of languages use different routines for arithmetic, depending on whether the arithmetic expression involves integer or real values, or a mixture of the two. The semantic analyser will examine the data types of the variables in the expression and determine the appropriate routines to use. Sometimes the parser contains semantic routines which are invoked as the parsing process progresses, sometimes semantic analysis forms a distinct stage after the parser has completed its analysis, but frequently the two methods are combined. During the course of this stage in the compilation process, a number of data structures may be created to facilitate code optimization and generation. The symbol table has already been mentioned, but in addition a *parse tree* will be created, representing the structure of the complete program split into a hierarchy of its components, and arithmetic expressions may be converted into a more convenient internal form such as *postfix*, also known as *Reverse Polish*, notation. The next few sections examine these data structures in more detail.

Parsing techniques

To determine whether a string of symbols such as P − Q/2 represents a valid expression in a simplified version of the grammar defined in the section on BNF:

<expr>	::= <term> | <expr> <expr operator> <term>
<term>	::= <factor> | <term> <term operator> <factor>
<factor>	::=variable | integer | (<expr>) | −<factor>
<expr operator>	::= + | −
<term operator>	::= * | /

Here 'variable' and 'integer' are named terminals, so called because they are identifiers which represent actual terminals. The analysis could proceed as shown below, repeatedly scanning the string from left to right, replacing (at appropriate points) terminals and non-terminals by higher level non-terminals:

1.   P - Q/2

2.   variable < expr operator > variable < term operator > integer

3.   < factor > < expr operator > < factor > < term operator > < factor >

4.   < factor > < expr operator > < term > < term operator > < factor >

5.   < factor > < expr operator > < term >

6.   < term > < expr operator > < term >

7.   < expr > < expr operator > < term >

8.   < expr >

This process of *bottom-up parsing* repeatedly examines the string of symbols and at each pass determines whether a group of syntactic entities may be combined to form another syntactic entity. Thus the group, < term > < term operator > < factor >, can be replaced by < term >, which is a higher level syntactic entity. Since, at stage 8, we arrive at the highest level, that is, < expr >, an expression, the string must be a well-formed arithmetic expression in this grammar. Here is another example, this time illustrating the recursive nature of the grammar: the string to be parsed is X*(Y + Z).

1.   X*(Y + Z)

2.   variable < term operator > (variable < expr operator > variable)

3.   < factor > < term operator > (< factor > < expr operator > < factor >)

4.   < factor > < term operator > (< term > < expr operator > < factor >)

5.   < factor > < term operator > (< expr > < expr operator > < term >)

6.   < factor > < term operator > (< expr >)

7.   < factor > < term operator > < factor >

8.   < term > < term operator > < factor >

9.   < term >

10. < expr >

Though we have used an intuitive method to determine at what point in the parse to make substitutions for syntactic entities, in practice the process is based on precedence relations between adjacent symbols which precisely determine the order in which the components of the input string are processed. However, the precise details of the process are quite complex and they are beyond the scope of this text. An alternative approach is to use a *top-down* parser such as that employed in *recursive descent parsing*. Such a parser uses a set of recursive functions to represent the syntactic structure of the source program. The outline pseudocode for such a recursive descent parser might take the form shown in Listing 27.1.

Listing 27.1. Recursive descent parse

```
function expression()
  token := function term()
  while token = expression_operator
    select
      when "+": token := function term()
        call addition()
      when "-": token := function term()
        call subtraction()
    endselect
  endwhile
  return(token)

function term()
  token := function factor()
  while token = term_operator
    select
      when "*": token := function factor()
        call multiplication
      when "/": token := function factor()
        call division
    endselect
  endwhile

function factor()
  token := function get_next_token()
  select
    when variable: call variable_found()
      token := function get_next_token()
    when integer: call integer_found()
      token := function get_next_token()
    when "(": token := function expression()
      if token < > ")": token := brackets_err
        call error(token)
  endselect
  return(token)
```

The parser assumes that the expression to be parsed is in token form, and that the function `get_next_to-ken()` takes care of keeping track of the next token to be processed and returns this token when called.

Each of the three functions, `expression`, `term` and `factor` corresponds to the appropriate syntax diagram, and each returns a value corresponding to the next token available. The process terminates when a NULL (terminating) token is encountered, or when an error arises during the parse.

The first function, expression(), immediately calls term(), which immediately calls factor() which identifies the current token as being either a variable, an integer or an expression enclosed in parentheses. Appropriate procedures (not detailed here) deal with each of these cases, storing the identified item in a parse tree. Function factor() then returns the next token available, or an error code if an invalid token has been detected. Function term() then looks for a term operator, '*' or '/' and calls factor() again to provide the next operand. This repeats until there are no more factors in the term being processed. A term having been identified, control returns to expression() which looks for an expression operator, '+' or '−', to be returned from term(). If this is the case, expression calls term() again to identify the next term in the expression; the process terminates if a NULL token is returned, or some other token signifying an error condition. In recursive descent parsing, control continually descends through the function nesting to obtain operands, and ascends through the functions in reverse order. The recursive nature of the parse results from the definition of a factor which may be a parenthesized expression, thus causing expression() to call itself. These parsers are relatively simple to implement, being based directly on the language definition. BASIC interpreters frequently use recursive descent to evaluate arithmetic expressions, since such interpreters need to do no preprocessing of expressions (see the case study in the section on interpreters following).

Parse trees

The following Pascal program calculates the area of a rectangle, given its length and width:

```
program pteg (input, output);
var area, len, wid :integer;
begin
  readln (len, wid);
  area := len*wid;
  writeln ('The area is', area)
end.
```

When the program above is processed, the parser builds up a parse tree which identifies all the grammatical categories it encounters. The leaves of the tree are the tokens, that is the smallest grammatical entities, and the interior nodes represent non-terminals. As each non-terminal and token is identified, it is added to the parse tree being constructed until, finally, the whole program has been transformed into an intermediate representation. The parse tree is shown in Figure 27.5.

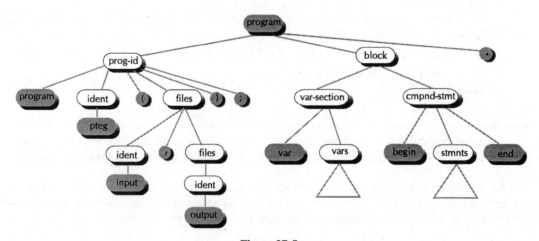

Figure 27.5.

The parts of the tree shown as shaded triangles are expanded in Figures 27.6 and 27.7.

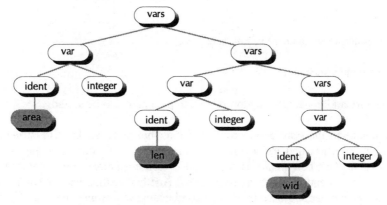

Figure 27.6

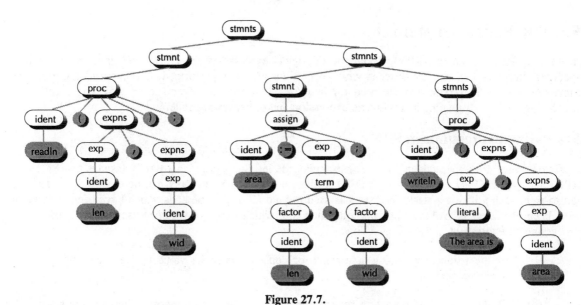

Figure 27.7.

Notice that the parse tree has the same form as the syntax diagrams for the same structures, but it is specific to this program rather than being a generalized specification of Pascal. The parse tree could be conveniently implemented as a tree data structure (see Chapter 32) with each node identifying the appropriate grammatical structure and with pointers to other nodes identifying substructures. In this form, the source program is much easier to handle in the code generation phase of the compilation process.

Symbol tables

Checking for semantic correctness and generating code requires knowledge of the attributes of the identifiers used in the source program. This information is stored in a data structure known as a *symbol table* which plays a central role in the translation process. For each occurrence of an identifier in a source program, the table will be searched for its symbol table entry, new identifiers will be inserted into the data structure, and new information regarding known identifiers will be added.

Typically, the information stored in the symbol table for each variable will comprise:

- name;

- type, for example, integer, real, character etc.;

- memory location allocated.

Subprograms will require additional information related to parameters to be stored.

Because of its importance to the translation process, the symbol table needs to be structured in a manner which allows efficient insertion and extraction of information. Numerous strategies for structuring the symbol table are possible. One commonly used method is to use a *binary tree* organized alphabetically to facilitate access to identifiers and insertion of new nodes. Another method uses *hashing* to speed access to symbol table entries. Yet another approach is to use a combination of *hashing* and *linked lists*. The principles of these three techniques are discussed in Chapter 32.

Reverse Polish Notation

In Reverse Polish Notation (RPN), arithmetic or logical expressions are represented in a manner which specifies simply and exactly the order in which operations are to be performed. All operators are given the same precedence, thus removing the need for brackets. This has the advantage of providing a relatively simple way of both evaluating an arithmetic expression and of generating code.

Evaluating expressions in RPN

Operators come after operands in RPN. For example, the infix expression A+B*C translates to ABC*+ in RPN, and (A–B)/C+D becomes AB–C/D+. Arithmetic expressions in RPN can be evaluated by a single left-to-right scan utilizing a stack. The stack is used to hold all of the operands which have been scanned or have been produced as the result of some operation, but which have not yet been used. The algorithm for processing an expression in RPN is as follows:

(i)   If the scanned symbol is a variable or constant, push its value to the stack and scan the next symbol.

(ii)   If the scanned symbol is a binary operator, pop the two topmost values on the stack, apply the operation to them and then push the result to the stack.

(iii)   If the scanned symbol is a unary operator, pop the top of the stack, apply the operation to this item and then push the result to the stack.

[Note that the term *binary operator* refers to an arithmetic or logical operator which requires two operands, such as * in the expression $a+b*c$; the two operands are b and c. The term *unary operator* refers to an arithmetic or logical operator which requires a single operand, such as '–' in the expression $-b+c*d$; the single operand is b in this case.]

For example, suppose that we wish to evaluate the RPN expression

$$ab \sim cd* + +$$

equivalent to $a+(-b+c*d)$ in usual infix notation, where $\sim$ represents unary $-$. Table 27.1 illustrates how the evaluation would be handled with values $a=2$, $b=3$, $c=-4$ and $d=5$.

scanned symbol	old stack contents	operation	new stack contents
ab~cd*++		push a	[2]
ab~cd*++	[2]	push b	[2,3]
ab~cd*++	[2,3]	–b	[2,–3]
ab~cd*++	[2,–3]	push c	[2,–3,–4]
ab~cd*++	[2,–3,–4]	push d	[2,–3,–4,5]
ab~cd*++	[2,–3,–4,5]	c*d	[2,–3,–20]
ab~cd*++	[2,–3,–20]	–b+c*d	[2,–23]
ab~cd*++	[2,–23]	a+(–b+c*d)	[–21]

Table 27.1.

Table 27.1 shows the symbol being scanned (in bold, the rest being gray), the stack contents prior to this symbol being processed, the operation performed on the appropriate operands and, lastly, the contents of the stack after processing the scanned symbol.

Converting arithmetic expressions from infix to RPN

An algorithm for converting from infix to RPN is as follows. Firstly, we associate numerical values with the relative precedences of arithmetic operators according to Table 27.2.

operator	precedence level
unary + and –	4
^(exponentiation)	3
*, /	2
+, –	1

Table 27.2.

The method also uses a stack, this time for the temporary storage of operators while processing the infix input string. The output from the algorithm is the equivalent string in RPN. The algorithm is based on the following rules which are applied as each symbol in the input string is scanned in turn:

(i)   If the incoming symbol is a variable or a constant, copy it to the output string directly.

(ii)   If the incoming symbol is an operator, and it is of higher numerical precedence than the operator currently on top of the stack, or if the stack is empty, push it to the stack.

(iii)   If the incoming symbol is an operator of equal or lower precedence than the current top of the stack, pop the top of the stack to the output string and go to step (ii) using the current symbol.

(iv)   Left parenthesis, '(', goes on top of the operator stack regardless of the current contents of the the stack, and remains on the stack until released by right parenthesis, ')'.

(v)   Right parenthesis, ')', releases all operators on the stack to the output string until a ')' is encountered, at which point the ')' is removed from the stack.

(vi)   When the end of the input string is reached, any operators remaining on the stack are released to the output string, and the process terminates.

Table 27.3 traces the conversion of the expression a*(b+c)–d/g to RPN.

scanned symbol	current stack	new stack	output string
a*(b+c)–d/g	[]	[]	a
a*(b+c)–d/g	[]	[*]	a
a*(b+c)–d/g	[*]	[*,(]	a
a*(b+c)–d/g	[*,(]	[*,(]	ab
a*(b+c)–d/g	[*,(]	[*,(,+]	ab
a*(b+c)–d/g	[*,(,+]	[*,(,+]	abc
a*(b+c)–d/g	[*,(,+]	[*]	abc+
a*(b+c)–d/g	[*]	[–]	abc+*
a*(b+c)–d/g	[–]	[–]	abc+*d
a*(b+c)–d/g	[–]	[–,/]	abc+*d
a*(b+c)–d/g	[–,/]	[–,/]	abc+*dg
a*(b+c)–d/g	[–,/]	[]	abc+*dg/–

Table 27.3.

Intermediate languages

Having completed the parsing phase, it is quite common for a compiler to produce an intermediate language prior to generating code. One reason for doing this is to facilitate code optimization by tailoring the intermediate code to the needs of the optimization phase. Another reason is that it allows compilers for different target machines to use the same 'front end' stages and machine specific 'back end' stages for code optimization and generation, the intermediate code being the interface between the two ends.

One type of intermediate language consists of a set of *three-address statements*. For example, the C fragment

```
if ( a > max +1 ) a = max + 1;
b = b + 1;
```

might be transformed into

```
    T1 := max + 1
    if a < T1 goto L1
    T2 := max + 1
    a := T2
L1:T3 := b + 1
    b := T3
```

where T1, T2, T3 are temporary variables which are added to the symbol table.

Code optimization

The example of intermediate code shown in the preceding section provides a number of opportunities for optimization. If, for instance, one or more of the variables referenced were allocated to internal CPU registers, the code would become more time efficient since fewer memory accesses would be required. In fact some high-level languages (C for instance) allow the programmer to explicitly allocate variables to registers with declarations such as

```
register int i;
```

Another opportunity for optimization is to use increment/decrement operations rather than addition/subtraction operations. For example, it is faster to increment b in the statement b := b + 1 rather than perform the addition if the target language contains an increment instruction.

Other common optimization techniques include:

- *Constant folding* - where arithmetic operations can be executed at compile time rather than run time. For example, if the term 20*3 appears in an arithmetic expression, it can be replaced by 60 by the compiler, thus removing the need for the multiplication when the program is executed.

- *Algebraic identities* - code can be simplified by taking advantage of a number of algebraic identities such as

  $$x + 0 = x$$
  $$0 + x = x$$
  $$x*0 = 0$$
  $$x*1 = x$$
  $$0/x = 0$$
  $$x - 0 = x$$

- *Dead code elimination* - the compiler detects code that can never be reached during execution.

- *Loop-invariant expressions* - an expression within a loop may be exactly the same each time through the loop, so evaluating it only once outside of the loop will reduce execution time. For example, for i := 1 to m*4 do procX, could be compiled as if it had been written

  ```
  T1 := m*4;
  for i := 1 to T1 do procX;
  ```

Machine-specific compilers may use other techniques which are dependent on the target language, but, though optimization is desirable, care must be taken that optimization does not alter the original intention of the programmer; most compilers are therefore conservative with optimization, and several give the user the option of what optimizations the compiler is to attempt at compile time. As a final note, probably the best optimizations are those produced by careful algorithm design on the part of the programmer, rather than those of the compiler.

Code generation

The final phase of the compilation process translates the optimized intermediate code to either machine code or to assembly language, depending on the particular compiler. Here the actual sequences of code necessary to, for example, call subprograms, add two floating-point numbers, and multiply two integers are emitted.

Because the intermediate form of the source program will be only slightly more abstract than assembly language, a table lookup process can be used to replace each three-address instruction by the equivalent assembly language code. At this time the compiler must determine whether a variable is to be allocated to a register or to main memory, and also take into account the context in which variables are referenced; the symbol table will contain information regarding the nature of each variable, whether it is global or local for instance.

Types of compilers

It is possible to write a compiler that works its way through the source code once only and produces the object code at the end of the pass. This is called a *single-pass compiler*, for obvious reasons. The main problem with this approach is the necessity to deal with *forward references*. For example, the compiler may have to compile an instruction such as

```
goto L1
```

without yet knowing the location of the label L1. The solution is to leave a gap for the address of the label, note that the information is missing by adding an entry to a special list reserved for this eventuality, and then when the information becomes available, filling in the gap after consulting the list.

However, it is generally more convenient to process the source program using a multi-pass compiler in which there are number of passes, each pass performing certain functions and producing a modified version of the program to be used in the next pass. Such compilers have two major advantages over the single-pass compilers:

- The compiler can be written in a modular manner rather than as a monolithic program.

- Decreased memory requirements, since the code for the current pass is all that needs to be memory resident.

The chief disadvantage of the multi-pass compiler is the probable necessity to make frequent disk accesses to read and write the intermediate files required to allow the separate phases to communicate with each other.

Linking

Frequently, the object code produced by the compiler comprises separate modules of machine code which are related to each other via call and return addresses; the separate modules may also share common data. The object code may also make reference to library routines, held externally from the main program block. The function of the linker program, or *linkage editor*, is to incorporate the absolute call and return addresses of any external routines (*closed subroutines*) which are to be used by the program, as well as those needed to link the various modules of machine code produced by the compiler. Sometimes, linking is carried out as part of the compilation process.

Interpreters

Because interpreters do not produce stand-alone object code, they use a number of special processing techniques to optimize the speed at which a program executes. For example, before starting to execute a source statement, an interpreter might first convert it into a more convenient internal form by tokenizing keywords as they are entered so that they are more readily recognizable at run time. Rapid methods of accessing variables must be devised since this will be a major task of the interpreter.

These and other issues are addressed in the following sections using interpreted BASIC as a case study.

A case study - BASIC

The interpreter described here is based on one of Acorn's early BASIC interpreters. It consists of a number of functional components:

- command handler;

- tokenizer;

- statement interpreter;

- expression evaluator;

- heap/stack handler.

These are described in the following sections.

Program statements in BASIC start with a line number and contain one or more keywords such as PRINT or INPUT. These statements are tokenized before being inserted into the current program at the position determined by the line number. The program is executed when the command RUN is entered. However, if a statement is entered without an initial line number, BASIC assumes that the statement is to be treated as a command and executed immediately. Thus the line

```
PRINT 'Hello there'
```

would be treated as a command causing the computer to display 'Hello there' on the monitor, whereas

```
100 PRINT 'Hello there'
```

would cause this line to be inserted at the appropriate point in the current program.

Heaps and stacks

As well as the space required for the program, a BASIC interpreter must also be able to allocate dynamic storage for variables and other needs that arise during the running of a program. BASIC uses two data structures, a *heap* and a *stack* for such purposes.

The BASIC heap is explained in Chapter 32, Data Structures, as an application of a linked list. Briefly, the heap consists of an interwoven set of linked lists, one list for each set of variables starting with the same letter. The heap is located in the memory area just above the program storage area, and it increases in size each time a variable is allocated a value for the first time. A special pointer keeps track of the next free location available for the storage of a *variable information block* which contains the details of a variable. A variable information block contains a pointer to the location in the heap of the next variable with the same initial letter, the name of the variable (except for its initial letter which does not need to be stored) and its value. Locating an established variable involves accessing each node of the appropriate linked list until the required variable information block is located.

Two additional linked lists are included in the heap: one for procedures and the other for functions. The value field in this instance contains a pointer to the location of the start of the procedure or function definition.

The main BASIC stack is used for three main purposes:

(i)   As a temporary storage area for storing intermediate values while the expression evaluator is processing an expression.

(ii)   To store the processor stack when procedures or functions are called. This is necessary if the processor's stack is limited in size because recursive subprograms might cause it to overflow very quickly.

(iii)   As a temporary storage area for parameters and local variables associated with procedures and functions so that they may be restored to their original values when calls are completed.

Two other smaller stacks are used for `repeat...until` and `for...next` loops. These are used to store the locations of the first statements in such loops so that control can repeatedly return to them while loops are in operation.

Tokens and links

When a line has been typed at the keyboard, the command handler sends the line to the tokenizer so that keywords can be *tokenized*. This involves replacing the keyword by a single byte containing a unique value. Tokens serve the dual function of reducing the size of a program by replacing multi-character keywords with a single character, and of speeding up program execution by proving an efficient method of invoking the appropriate keyword handler.

When a keyword token is recognized, it is used as an offset to the start address of a table of pointers to keyword-handling routines. For example, assuming 16-bit addresses, suppose that the keyword FOR had a token value of 5 and the keyword address table started at address 1000, as shown in Table 27.4.

address	keyword handler address(hex)	keyword
1000	BF50	ABS
1001	AEEF	COS
1002	AEE3	DEG
1003	AF32	EVAL
1004	BF78	FN
1005	BF47	FOR
1006	AD45	GET

Table 27.4

Then, in order to access the subprogram that deals with FOR statements, the interpreter needs only to add 5 to the base address of 1000 to obtain the starting address (BF47) of the FOR handler.

The tokenizer will also tokenize initial line numbers, again to save space but also, more importantly, to speed up the location of destination line numbers in statements such as

```
200 GOTO 4560
```

which will entail searching each line number in the program in turn from the start until 4560 is located; tokenized line numbers significantly reduce the amount of time spent in comparing line numbers with the one required, particularly when a large number of statements are involved.

Another device for speeding up searching for particular lines is by using links inserted into program lines. These links are offsets to the start of the next instruction. Thus a program line might have the following format:

> *tokenized line number*
> *length of line*
> *first character of statement*
> *second character of statement*
> *etc*
> *end of line character*
>
> *start of next line*

The *length of line* item allows the line to be skipped by adding its value to the address of the start of the line - this gives the start of the next line. Thus the body of unwanted lines may be ignored, saving a relatively large amount of time when searching for a particular line.

Statement interpreter

When a program is executed, after it has been entered and tokenized, the *statement interpreter* then decides how to handle the line. If it finds a keyword, then it will call the appropriate keyword handler; if it finds a variable name, it calls the assignment handler which in turn calls an *expression evaluator* to provide a value to be assigned to the variable. Failing it finding any valid construct, the statement interpreter will generate an error message to indicate that an unrecognizable instruction has been located at this current line.

Most of the keyword handlers will also call the expression evaluator to obtain the values they require in order to perform their functions; it is therefore one of the major sections of the interpreter.

Expression evaluation

In the earlier section on parsing, a technique called *recursive descent* parsing was described. It was described as being used by a compiler to analyse a source statement and to convert it into an intermediate form. The same method is often used by interpreters to evaluate expressions. The *expression evaluator* divides the expression into several processing levels according to the priorities of the operators it encounters as it scans the expression. Low priority operations are dealt with by the top levels which call lower levels to deal with higher priority operations. High priority results are passed back to the top levels for low priority operations to be completed. So, for example, in the calculation 5 - 8/2, the subtraction is a lower level operation than the division, so the division would be performed first and the result would be passed back to the subtraction routine to complete the evaluation of the expression.

This is exactly the same process as recursive descent parsing, but the interpreter evaluates the expression as it is analysing the expression rather than using it as a compiler would to produce a data structure for use later.

Tracing the expression above, (that is, 5 - 8/2), and using a simplified scheme, would produce the following steps:

(i)   the *expression* evaluator calls a routine *term* to obtain a value corresponding to a term in the expression;

(ii)   *term* calls *factor* to obtain a value;

(iii)   *factor* gets the value 5 which it pushes to a stack before returning to term ;

(iv)   since there are no more factors in the first term, *term* has completed its task and returns control to *expression*;

(v)   *expression* then finds a '-' so it calls *term* again;

(vi)   *term* calls *factor* to provide a value;

(vii)   *factor* obtains the 8 and then pushes it to the BASIC stack;

(viii) *term* needs another factor because of the '/' it finds, so it calls *factor* again;

(ix)   *factor* gets the 2 which it stacks and then returns to *term*;

(x)   *term* performs the division 8/2 and stacks the result, 4, before returning to *expression*;

(xi)   *expression* then pops the 4 and the 2 from the stack and completes the subtraction to give an answer of 1.

The section on recursive descent parsing earlier in this chapter contains an algorithm (Listing 27.1) for the process outlined above.

It is worth mentioning at this point that although interpreters and compilers are the main types of translators used for high-level languages, there are several variations on this theme, two of which are described below.

Threaded interpretive languages (TILs) allow the programmer to define operations in terms of sequences of predefined, primitive operations, called *words* in TIL parlance, such as `add`, `subtract`, `multiply`, `divide` and many of the operations found in other languages. Words may refer to other user-defined (secondary) words which then become new commands extending the language. In fact, typical TIL programs consist of short, progressively defined new words. The final word of the program is entered, to perform the required task.

In one variation of this type of language, the words are linked together using pointers to the location of either a primitive word or a secondary word, depending on how the word has been defined. When executed, an interpreter controls this process by getting the next pointer, jumping to the location pointed to and either executing the machine code found there if the routine is a primitive or repeating the process if it finds another secondary word. Usually there is no theoretical limit to the depth to which these secondary levels may be nested.

Because the interpreter must perform this function at run-time, it must be co-resident with the program in memory, taking up space and slowing down execution time. Other TIL variations overcome the speed restriction to some degree but still operate in much the same way.

An example of a TIL is Forth.

Some languages are processed using a combination of compiler and interpreter. The compiler operates in the normal way, but instead of producing machine code it produces *p-code* (pseudo-code) which is a refined form of the source code. The interpreter must then be used to actually execute the program by interpreting the p-code at run-time. Because the compiler has already performed most of the analysis and error checking of the source code, the interpreter has much less work to do than in a conventional system and can execute the p-code very efficiently.

One of the main advantages of this system is that the language is easier to implement on a variety of different computer systems since the relatively simple interpreter can be tailored to the particular machine.

Again, however, the penalty in using an interpreter is loss of speed; machine code will execute more quickly than p-code.

Some versions of Pascal produce interpreted p-code and BCPL also works on this principle.

Exercises

1. Name and briefly describe two common methods of defining computer languages.

2. Explain the difference between the following types of language translators:

    (i)   assembler;

    (ii)   compiler;

    (iii)   interpreter;

3. With the aid of examples explain the following terms:

    (i)   lexical analysis;

    (ii)   semantic analysis;

    (iii)   bottom-up parsing;

    (iv)   recursive descent parsing;

    (v)   parse tree;

    (vi)   symbol table;

    (vii)   Reverse Polish Notation.

Chapter 28

Program Design

The single most important requirement of a computer program is that it runs without error at all times, since a program that either produces erroneous results or hangs up under certain circumstances is almost useless. Because of this stringent requirement, computer program design and production is a very skilled activity demanding meticulous attention to detail. It is not sufficient to address only the relatively easy problem of designing and implementing a program which produces the correct output when provided with ideal data. Rather, the program must be able to cope with non-ideal data such as that provided by a user who may be unfamiliar with its operation or data input requirements. Such a user might supply inappropriate input by, for example, entering alphabetic instead of numeric characters, and even experienced operators of the program might accidentally enter invalid data on occasions.

In fact there are many ways that a program could be presented with exceptional - that is, invalid or unreasonable - data and it is the responsibility of the program designer to allow for such. Consequently, the program design stage of program production, in which possible problems - and their solutions - are identified, is of vital importance. As a result, there are now a number of established program design methodologies to aid the program designer to produce well-crafted, error-free programs. The design method described here is a form of *structured programming* using *top-down*, *stepwise refinement*. Two forms of notation that we will use to express solutions to design problems are *pseudocode* and *structure charts*; these are called *program design languages* (PDLs). Structure charts provide a graphical representation of a program, allowing its logical structure to be easily appreciated, whereas pseudocode, having a form similar to program instructions, aids program writing and testing.

A number of the programs designed later in this chapter have been converted to Pascal and C are described in Chapters 29 and 30. Many of the ideas presented here are also covered in the those chapters so we recommend that you refer to the appropriate sections in the latter while studying this chapter.

Problem solving

Whether a problem is computer-related or otherwise, the strategy for solving it has essentially the same three main stages: (1) *understand the problem*, (2) *devise a solution*, and (3) *test the solution*. In addition, for program design tasks there is a further stage which is to (4) *document the solution*.

1. Understand the problem

This first stage requires a *thorough* understanding of the problem being addressed so that you can identify what assumptions can be made and what can't in order to test your solution in the correct context.

Some problems are apparently straightforward but, when analysed with a view to producing a program design, become much more complex. As an example, consider the following outline program specification:

> *Write a program to read in a date and convert it to the number of days from the start of the calendar year.*

It sounds simple enough until you start to consider what the problem implies. For example, what format is to be used for the date? - 15th January, 1995 or 15 Jan 95, or 15/1/95, or 15-01-95 or 150195, or 950115, and so on. Is a particular format to be adopted and incorrectly formatted dates to be rejected, or is the program to attempt to interpret different formats? Are leap years to be considered when calculating the day number? Do you assume that the date is for the current year or can the date be for a different year? You may be able to think of more problems that could arise. We will return to this example later in the chapter and provide a possible solution.

2. Design a solution

The method adopted here to design the solution involves tackling the problem in a number of steps. An outline program is designed first, showing the main modules of the program, and the order in which they are to be executed. Each main module is then reduced to a number of smaller, simpler, and more manageable components, and this process of refinement continues until the program designer judges that there is sufficient detail in the design for a programmer to be able to convert the design directly into a programming language. The

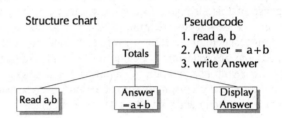

Figure 28.1.   *A simple program design for the addition of two real numbers*

process of reducing components into sequences of smaller components in stages is often termed *stepwise refinement*. Top-down, stepwise refinement encourages program design to be tackled methodically in a number of stages of increasing detail. Although structure charts and pseudocode are both suitable program design languages, we recommend that you adopt our approach of first using structure charts to produce your program designs in outline form and then translating them into detailed pseudocode prior to testing and subsequent conversion to program code.

An example of a simple structure chart and the equivalent pseudocode for the addition of two real numbers are shown in Figure 28.1. (Note that a *real* number is a number with a fractional part such as 23.456, whereas an *integer* is a whole number such as 32). Answer, a and b are called variables which serve a similar function to the symbols used in algebra - they are general, symbolic representations of data that is to be processed. Thus, the pseudocode statement 1 in Figure 28.1 means 'read two values from the input device (such as a keyboard) and call them a and b respectively'. Statement 2 adds the two values and calls the result Answer. Statement 3 displays Answer on the output device (such as a display screen). By using variables rather than actual numbers, this sequence of statements defines how a computer is to deal with the addition of *any* two numbers. In addition to the problem solution itself, another part of the design is a *data table* which defines the purpose and type of the variables used in the solution. The data table (Table 28.1) would identify whether these variables were integers or real numbers and their purpose.

name	description	type
Answer	Holds the sum of the two numbers	real variable
a	First number entered	real variable
b	Second number entered	real variable

Table 28.1.

3. Test the solution

This involves using test data to manually step through the solution statements so that the computed output can be compared with the expected output. For instance, the date example mentioned above should give an answer of 69 for 10th March 1995, assuming that the days are calculated from 1st January, 1995. This value would be compared with that provided by the design - if the answer was different then the apparent design fault would need to be investigated and corrected before continuing with further testing.

4. Document the solution

The documentation contains the following: (i) the problem statement; (ii) the top-level program design; (iii) the final detailed program design; (iv) the data table. These are produced during the course of the first three stages of program design. The examples in later sections show the form of this documentation.

Structured programming

Most current program design methodologies are based on *structured programming* concepts. Structured programming is generally associated with certain basic principles:

1. **Restricted use of control structures.** These are limited to three types: *sequence* consisting of instructions which are performed one after the other in the order that they appear in the program; *selection* of one set of instructions from several possible sets of instructions so that the program is able to deal with a number of different circumstances; *repetition*, or *iteration,* of a set of instructions using some kind of program loop. Restricting design to using only these three constructs does not necessarily produce error-free code, but it does help to produce a program which is clear and relatively easy to test.

2. **Modularity.** This is the subdivision of a program into easily identifiable and manageable segments, or *modules*. Each module should require no more than about one page of code. A module may be realised in the final program as one or more small subprograms (see functions and procedures later in this chapter). Using modules helps to clarify the logical structure of a program for human readers and, by incorporating subprograms, aids its construction.

3. **Top-down, stepwise refinement.** This program design method was described in the earlier section *Problem Solving*.

4. **Clear program format.** This is concerned with the layout of the program instructions. Each page of coding should contain clearly identifiable control structures and blocks of code. One main method of achieving this clarity of structure is by the consistent use of indentation showing the limits of loops, selections and blocks of instructions. Formatting standards apply both to pseudocode and actual program code.

5. **Comments.** The thorough use of comments within the pseudocode design and the actual program in order to explain the purpose of each variable and each few lines of logically related code.

6. **Simplicity.** Where there is a choice between a simple solution to a problem and a slightly more efficient solution which perhaps uses less code, then the simple solution is to be preferred. Straightforward, simple code is easier to test, modify and understand than obscure, 'clever' code.

Basic control structures

As explained earlier, structured programs are constructed using the three control structures sequence, selection and iteration. In order to illustrate how each of these is expressed and used in program design, consider the following programming problem:

> *Read a set of ten positive and negative numbers entered from a keyboard and find the separate totals of the positive numbers and the negative numbers. Print the two totals.*

It is assumed that only valid real numbers such as 1.2, –7.3, 25, –6 will be entered. The program can be considered to be a *sequence* of three simple modules:

1. **Initialise variables.** Two variables will be required: one for the total of the positive numbers and the other for the total of the negative numbers.

2. **Process the numbers.** This involves a loop to read numbers typed in from the keyboard until ten values have been entered. A count will be incremented every time a number is read in.

3. **Display the results.** This will involve writing out the two totals.

This top-level design is illustrated by the structure chart shown in Figure 28.2. The equivalent pseudocode for the top-level design is shown in Listing 28.1.

Figure 28.2.   *Top-level design as a sequence of three modules*

Listing 28.1.

```
{Totals}
1  Initialise
2  Process numbers
3  Display results
```

The first refinement of the design results in the structure chart shown in Figure 28.3.

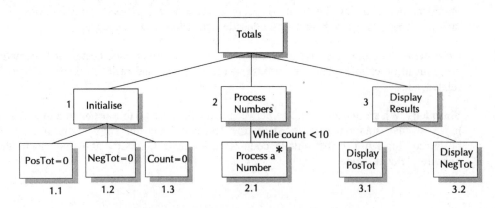

Figure 28.3.   *First refinement showing an iteration*

The loop that reads the ten numbers, in other words the *iteration*, is indicated in the structure chart by an asterisk in the top right-hand corner of the component that is to be repeated. The condition governing the loop is written above this component; in this case the loop continues while the count variable has a value less than ten. The equivalent pseudocode is shown in Listing 28.2.

Listing 28.2.

```
     {Totals}
1.1     PosTot=0
1.2     NegTot=0
1.3     Count=0
2       while Count < 10
2.1        Process Number
2       endwhile
3.1     write PosTot
3.2     write NegTot
```

Each of the Listing 28.1 statements, numbered *1*, *2* and *3*, have all been refined in Listing 28.2; statement *1* (`initialise`) has been replaced by three detailed instruction, *1.1*, *1.2* and *1.3*. Similarly, statements *2* and *3* in Listing 28.1 have also been refined in Listing 28.2. (These statement level numbers reflect the depth of the structure diagram; a single statement level such as *1* indicates a top-level module, a statement number such as *1.2* indicate the second step of a refinement of level *1*. Number *2.3.1* indicates the first step of a refinement of statement *2.3*, and so on. A refinement of a statement is denoted by adding another level to the statement number.) Notice that the end of the loop is indicated by `endwhile` and the instruction inside the loop, `Process Number`, is indented. A loop thus translates into **three** pseudocode statements: one statement for the type of loop and the condition that governs it, another for the item that is to be repeated, and the third for the end of the loop. The final refinement is to expand `Process Number`, since this is the only statement that has not yet been fully defined: we need to show *how* a number is to be processed. The full design is shown in Figure 28.4.

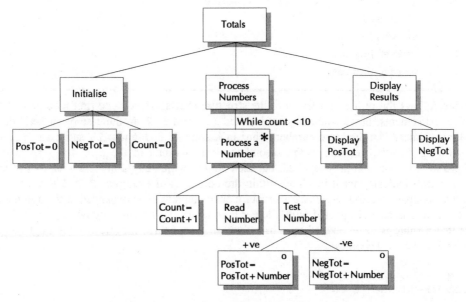

Figure 28.4. *The final refinement showing a selection*

The structure chart shows that the repeated component `Process Number` involves three steps: increment the count, read a number, and test the number to determine its sign. Positive numbers are to be accumulated in `PosTot` and negative numbers are to be accumulated in `NegTot`. The test involves a *selection*, each independent choice being indicated by a small circle in the top right-hand corner of the box. The condition governing each choice is written above the appropriate box as shown.

This version of the design needs no further refinement since it is now in a suitable form for conversion to pseudocode and subsequently to a programming language such as Pascal or C.

The pseudocode in Listing 28.3 uses a `select` statement for the selection. If the condition following the first `select` is true, the statement or statements following are obeyed, otherwise the next `select` is considered. The `endselect` statement must be used to terminate the `select` statement. Note that the number of alternative sets of statements is not limited to two - as many as necessary can be chained together in this way. If some action is necessary when none of the select statements are true then the `select` when `otherwise` statement can be included before `endselect`.

Listing 28.3.   Totalling positive and negative numbers

```
        {Totals}
        1.1      PosTot = 0
        1.2      NegTot = 0
        1.3      Count = 0
        2        while Count < 10
        2.1         Count = Count + 1
        2.2         Read Number
        2.3         select
        2.3.1a         when Number > 0
        2.3.1b             PosTot = PosTot + Number
        2.3.2a         when Number < 0
        2.3.2b             NegTot = NegTot + Number
        2.3         endselect
        2        endwhile
        3.1      write PosTot
        3.2      write NegTot
```

The numbering follows the refinement levels of the structure charts. Thus if the first module is refined as a sequence of two statements, these statements are labelled *1.1* and *1.2*. In the case of an iteration, the start and end statements are given the same number. Thus in Listing 28.3, the `while` and `endwhile` both are labelled 2 showing that the iteration is the second top-level module in the program. The start and end statements of a selection are similarly labelled, but each option, which might involve a number of steps has a small letter added to indicate that it is a step within the option. (For example, *2.3.1a* and *2.3.1b*). In addition, in the examples that follow, where a structure chart step has been expanded in the pseudocode, each part of the expansion is also designated with a lower case letter. This frequently occurs when the structure chart shows that a value is to be entered by a user through a keyboard; the pseudocode might be expanded thus: *5.1* read Number becomes

        5.1a   write 'Enter a number'
        5.1b   read Number

This helps to prevent the structure chart from becoming too detailed and thus unclear. To complete the design, the three variables must be defined in a data table (see Table 28.2).

name	description	type
Count	Counts how many numbers have been entered	integer variable
PosTot	The sum of the positive value numbers	real variable
NegTot	The sum of the negative value numbers	real variable

Table 28.2. *Definition of variables*

Summary

Figure 28.5 summarizes the structure chart and pseudocode notation used for the three basic control structures, sequence, selection and iteration. Iteration is shown in a commonly used alternative form in which the condition is expressed as `re-peat..until <condition>`. In this form the condition is tested at the end of the loop rather than at the beginning; this means that the statements within the loop will be repeated at least once. The `repeat..until` loop is illustrated in the worked examples.

Worked examples

The worked examples presented in the next sections use a combination of structure charts and pseudocode to arrive at the final program design. Structure charts are used for the design refinements in order to express the overall logic in a

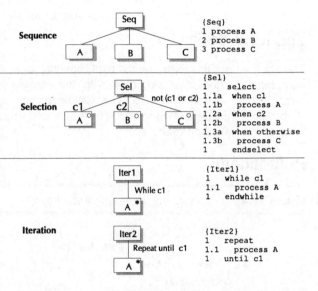

Figure 29.5. *The three basic control structures used in structured programming*

clear, easily understandable form. The design is then presented in pseudocode in order to present it in a form more suitable for testing and subsequent conversion to a programming language. At this stage some fine detail may also be added to the design. Some designs have been converted into Pascal code in the chapters on programming in Pascal and C. Note, however, that the program design technique presented here, rather than being targeted at a particular programming language such as Pascal, is in a form suitable for conversion to any one of a number of quite different high-level languages. Each of the following worked examples is in the format:

(i)   the problem statement;

(ii) any assumptions that have been made;

(iii) structure charts showing the top-level design and any further refinement stages;

(iv) pseudocode for the final design;

(v)   the data table for the complete design;

(vi) comments.

Reading and displaying information

Problem statement

Design a program which will accept from the keyboard a value representing a number of inches and display the equivalent number of centimetres.

Assumptions

1. The input is a valid real number.
2. There is no preferred format for the output.

Top-level design

The top-level design, shown on the right, now requires only minor refinements concerned with the precise form that the output is to take. This can be accomplished conveniently in pseudocode without the need to draw another structure chart.

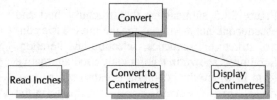

Pseudocode

Listing 28.4.   Converting inches to centimetres

```
{Convert}
1a      write 'Enter the length in inches: ', <newline>
1b      read Inches
2       Centimetres = Inches*2.54
3a      write <newline>
3b      write 'A length of ', Inches, ' inches is equivalent to ',
                        centimetres, ' centimetres', <newline>
```

Data table

name	description	type
Inches	Value entered at the keyboard and converted to centimetres	real variable
Centimetres	The value to be output	real variable

Table 28.4.

Comments

<newline> indicates that the cursor is to move to the beginning of the next line.

Loops - Running totals

One very frequent programming task is to keep a running total when a number of values are read within an iteration (that is, *loop*). This next example illustrates the technique usually adopted to accumulate a total in a variable.

Problem statement

Design a program to read ten numbers from a keyboard and display their sum.

Assumptions

1.   Exactly ten valid real numbers will be entered using a keyboard.

2.   The sum of the numbers is to be accumulated as the numbers are entered, and thus there is no requirement to store them.

Top-level design

The top-level design is a simple sequence of three modules. The second module, `Process Numbers`, involves a loop which is to repeat a known number of times (namely 10). It can therefore be implemented using a count variable as shown in refinement #1.

Refinement #1

The variable `Total` is to be used to accumulate the sum of the ten numbers and therefore must start with an initial value of zero. `Count` is to start at 1 because it must be increased by one each time a new number is read. Each time through the loop a new number is read into the variable `Number` and then added to `Total` which accumulates the numbers. When `Count` reaches 10, the loop terminates.

Refinement #2

The statements required for processing a number and incrementing the loop control variable have been added; this represents the final structure chart form of the design.

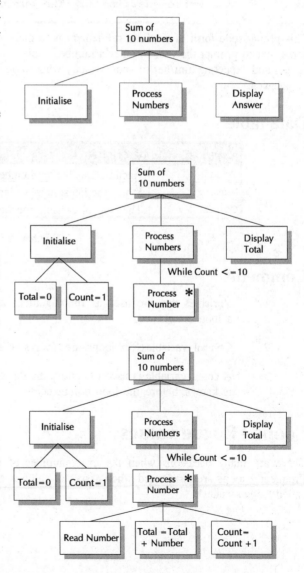

Pseudocode

Listing 28.5.   Keeping running totals

```
{Sum of 10 numbers}
1.1      Total = 0
1.2      Count = 1
2        while Count <= 10
2.1a       write <newline>, 'Enter number #', Count
2.1b       read Number
2.2        Total = Total + Number
2.3        Count = Count + 1
2        endwhile
3        write <newline> , 'The sum of the 10 numbers is: ', Total
```

This pseudocode form of the final refinement is to make the program a little more user friendly by adding some text to prompt the user to enter a number - this is much better than presenting the user with a blank screen and expecting him/her to know exactly what to do. The final instruction adds some text to announce the answer.

Data table

name	description	type
Total	Accumulates the ten numbers	real variable
Number	Stores the latest number input	real variable
Count	The control variable for the loop	integer variable

Table 28.5.

Comments

1. Variables that are used as running totals and counts must always be initialised before a loop commences.

2. Control variables for loops are always of type integer.

3. A count variable is used to control the duration of a loop when the number of repetitions is known before the loop commences.

Loops - Rogue values

There are many occasions when the exact number of repetitions of a loop is not known in advance. Frequently loops are terminated when a special value is entered by the user. Such special values are often called 'rogue values'.

Problem statement

Design a program to read a set of numbers representing the cost of some purchased items. The end of the list is to be indicated by entering 0 for the cost. Display how many items were purchased and the total cost of the items.

Assumptions

1.   The values entered will be valid real numbers

2.   No negative numbers will be entered

Top-level design

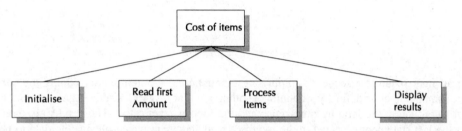

The strategy used in this instance is to read a value before the loop represented by the module, Process Items, is commenced. The condition governing the continuation of the loop will be While Amount > 0 and this means that Amount needs to have been assigned a value before the loop starts. (This is called *reading ahead* and is a common method used for reading files, as we will see later in this chapter).

Refinement #1

This refinement now shows that if the user initially enters zero for the amount, the loop is not executed at all because the condition, Amount > 0, is false. This is a very important characteristic of the while loop and a reason for not using the repeat..until loop construct in this instance.

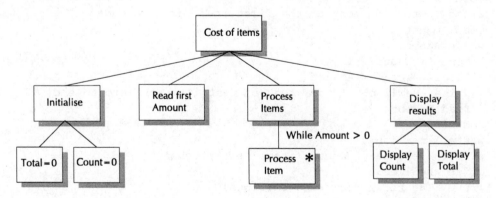

Refinement #2

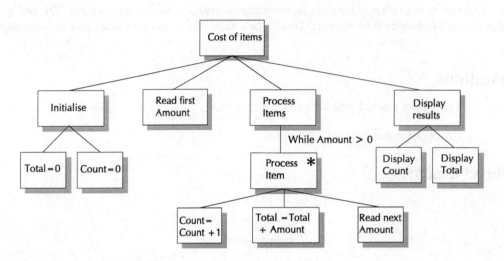

Processing an item requires a sequence comprising incrementing the item count, adding the current item's cost to the running total and finally obtaining another amount. Again, if this latter amount is zero, the condition for continuing the loop becomes false and the loop is terminated. The results are then displayed. Notice that the last statement executed in the loop is a read statement which obtains the data to be processed next. Since no further detail is required for the structure chart, this is the final refinement before writing the pseudocode.

Pseudocode

Listing 28.6.   Entering and totalling costs

```
{Sum of 10 numbers}
1.1     Total = 0
1.2     Count = 0
2a      write 'Enter the cost of the first item, or 0 to end'
2b      read Amount
3       while Amount > 0
3.1       Count = Count + 1
3.2       Total = Total + Amount
3.3a      write <newline>, 'Enter cost of next item, or zero to end'
3.3b      read Amount
3       endwhile
4.1a    write  <newline>,
4.1b    write  <newline>, Count, 'items were purchased'
4.2a    write <newline>
4.2b    write 'The total cost was: £', Total
```

The detail added to the pseudocode is again to improve communication with the user by displaying prompts such as that in statement *2.1* and by using blank lines (that is, write <newline>) to improve the clarity of the output.

Data table

name	description	type
Total	Accumulates the cost of the items	real variable
Amount	Stores the current item's cost	real variable
Count	Counts the number of items	integer variable

Table 28.6.

Comments

Try to avoid using a while condition such as Amount <> 0 (not equal to zero) instead of Amount > 0 because real numbers may not be represented exactly within a computer; the representation of zero might not be **exactly** zero and the condition Amount <> 0 may still be true even when zero is entered for Amount.

Making decisions - the select statement

This example introduces the idea of taking one of several courses of action depending on the value of a variable read in from the keyboard. A loop is again terminated by testing for a rogue value, this time a negative value.

Problem statement

Design a program to accept a number of values representing student examination marks. Each mark is to be displayed as a grade as follows:

Mark	Grade
80 or over	Distinction
60 or over	Merit
40 or over	Pass
less than 40	Fail

A negative value is to be used to indicate the end of the set of marks.

Assumptions

The marks are entered as valid integers.

Top-level design

The third module in this sequence is an iteration which repeatedly reads and grades a mark until a negative mark is entered.

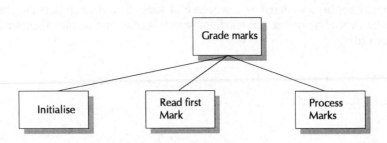

Refinement #1

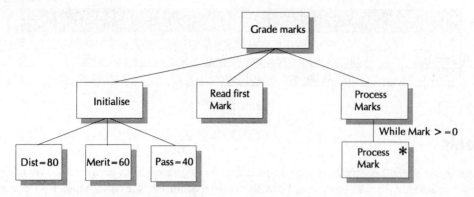

The threshold values for the grades are assigned to integer constants. Any negative value entered will be regarded as the signal to terminate the program.

Refinement #2

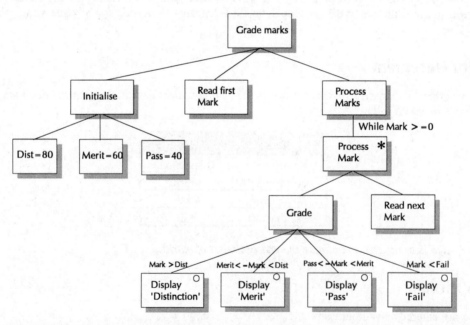

The four actions comprising the selection statement, Grade, which determine the message to be displayed should not be considered as a sequence of tests; the selection notation simply shows which action is to be taken depending on the one condition which is true, and as such the four actions could have been drawn in any order.

Pseudocode

Listing 28.7.   Using selection to convert marks to grades

```
{Grade marks}
1.1       Dist = 80
1.2       Merit = 60
1.3       Pass = 40
2.1a      write 'Enter the first mark(-1 to end):'
2.1b      read Mark
3         while Mark >= 0
3.1          select
3.1.1a         when Mark >= Dist
3.1.1b            write 'Distinction', <newline>
3.1.2a         when Mark = >= Merit and Mark < Dist
3.1.2b            write 'Merit', <newline>
3.1.3a         when Mark >= Pass and Mark < Merit
3.1.3b            write 'Pass', <newline>
3.1.4a         when Mark < Pass
3.1.4b            write 'Fail', <newline>
3.1          endselect
3.2a         write 'Enter the next mark(-1 to end):'
3.2b         read Mark
3         endwhile
```

The three thresholds for the grades are stored in the integer constants Dist, Merit and Pass. The advantage of doing this rather than using the actual values 80, 60 and 40 respectively is that if any of these values need to be modified, they need only be changed in the initialisation module and nowhere else.

Data table

name	description	type
Dist	The distinction mark	integer constant = 80
Merit	The merit mark	integer constant = 60
Pass	The pass mark	integer constant = 40
Mark	The student's exam mark	integer variable

Table 28.7.

Comments

The precise form of a selection statement in a programming language can vary considerably; it is the responsibility of the programmer to choose the most appropriate form available in the target language that exactly represents the required logic.

Decisions - A menu program

Where a program offers a user a number of different options, a menu-based program structure is often employed. The options are displayed and the user is invited to choose one of them by, for example entering its first letter. The program then performs the requested operation and re-displays the menu after it is completed. One of the options always allows the user to exit the program. This example illustrates the structure of a program which presents the user with four options concerned with currency conversion.

Problem statement

Design a menu-based program to allow a user to choose between converting pounds sterling to German marks, American dollars or French francs. The program will ask the user to enter the number of pounds and it will display the equivalent amount in the chosen currency before returning to the menu. The menu is to appear at the top of a blank screen and have the following appearance:

```
Currency conversion program

(M)arks
(D)ollars
(F)rancs
e(X)it

Which currency do you want to convert to Pounds?
```

Assumptions

1. Invalid choices (that is entering a letter other than M, D, F or X) will produce an error message and an invitation to try again.

2. Upper and lower case letters will be allowed.

3. The amount in pounds entered by the user will be a valid real number.

4. A single statement, ClearScreen, is available to blank the display screen.

Top-level design

The top-level design in this instance is very simple: the initialisation module sets the values for the three currency conversion factors and the remaining module, Main, repeatedly displays the user options and executes the one chosen.

Refinement #1

Three constants used for the currency conversion calculations are defined at this point (don't rely on these figures for holiday plans!). Further, the

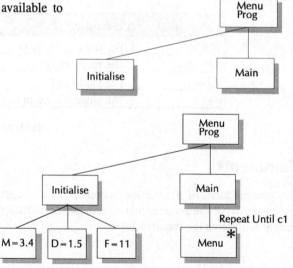

iteration is defined as a `repeat..until` loop with condition `c1`. Logical conditions governing loops and selections can be coded in this way so that defining their precise form can be deferred until the design has been completed. We will see later in refinement #3 that `c1` is the condition that indicates the user has chosen the exit option. Remember that the `repeat` loop causes the statements within the loop to be repeated at least once, and that the test for continuing to repeat the statements is made at the end of the loop.

Refinement #2

This refinement now shows that the loop controls a sequence of two modules. The first, `Display menu`, repeatedly clears the display screen, shows the menu of options and then reads the user's choice. The second module is a selection statement which processes the option chosen. The final refinement defines the operation of each of the options and under what circumstances each is chosen.

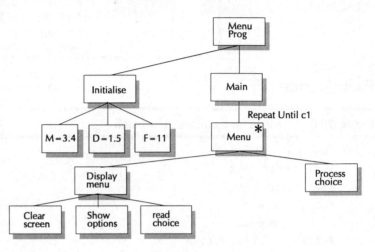

Refinement #3

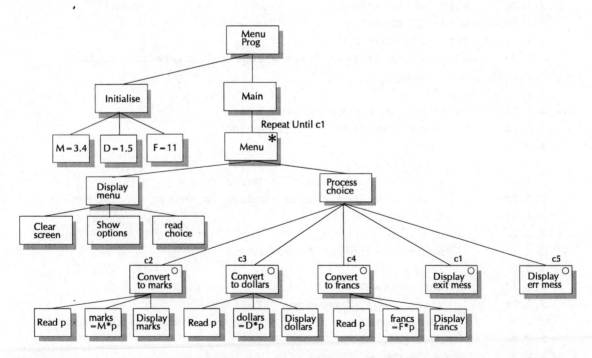

The first three options are concerned with the actual currency conversions. The fourth option displays a message to confirm that the user has chosen to exit the program. The final select statement is only invoked if the user has entered an invalid choice, that is, the letter entered is not 'M', 'D', 'F' or 'X'. The condition codes `c1`-`c5` are defined in the next table.

c1	choice = ('X' or 'x')
c2	choice = ('M' or 'm')
c3	choice = ('D' or 'd')
c4	choice = ('F' or 'f')
c5	choice <> ('X' or 'x')or ('M' or 'm')or ('D' or 'd')or ('F' or 'f')

Pseudocode

Listing 28.8.   Menu for Currency conversion

```
{Menu program}
1.1      M = 3.4
1.2      D = 1.5
1.3      F = 11
2        repeat
2.1.1      ClearScreen
2.1.2a     write 'Currency conversion program', <newline>
2.1.2b     write <newline>
2.1.2c     write '(M)arks'
2.1.2d     write '(D)ollars'
2.1.2e     write '(F)rancs'
2.1.2f     write <newline>
2.1.2g     write 'Which currency do you want to convert to pounds?'
2.1.3      read Choice
2.2        select
2.2.1a       when Choice = ('M' or 'm')
2.2.1b          write <newline>, 'Enter amount'
2.2.1c          read p
2.2.1d          Currency = M*p
2.2.1e          write ' = ', Currency, ' Marks'
2.2.1f          write <newline> 'Press <Enter> to return to the menu'
2.2.1g          read key
2.2.2a       when Choice = ('D' or 'd')
2.2.2b          write <newline>, 'Enter amount'
2.2.2c          read p
2.2.2d          Currency = D*p
2.2.2e          write ' = ', Currency, ' Dollars'
2.2.2f          write <newline> 'Press <Enter> to return to the menu
2.2.2g          read key
2.2.2a       when Choice = ('F' or 'f')
2.2.3b          write <newline>, 'Enter amount'
2.2.3c          read p
2.2.3d          Currency = F*p
```

```
2.2.3e          write ' = ', Currency, ' Francs'
2.2.3f          write <newline> 'Press <Enter> to return to the menu
2.2.3g          read key
2.2.4a      when Choice = ('X' or 'x')
2.2.4b          write 'Exiting program..'
2.2.5a      when otherwise
2.2.5b          write 'Invalid option. Please try again'
2.2.5c          write <newline> 'Press <Enter> to return to the menu
2.2.5d          read key
2.2         endselect
2.3     until Choice = ('X' or 'x')
```

Data table

name	description	type
M	Conversion factor for pounds to marks	real constant = 3.4
D	Conversion factor for pounds to dollars	real constant = 1.5
F	Conversion factor for pounds to francs	real constant = 11
p	The number of pounds to convert	real variable
Choice	The user's menu choice	character variable
Currency	The equivalent value in the currency chosen	real variable
key	Dummy variable to accept the <Return> key	character variable

Table 28.8.

Comments

1. This is a good model for constructing menu-driven programs.

2. The manner of implementing the `select` statement can vary considerably with the target programming language. Pascal provides `if` and `case` statements which each have their particular advantages and disadvantages. The programmer is responsible for choosing the most appropriate selection construct from those available.

File handling

The term *file* can be used to describe a number of different forms of storing data on backing storage. Here are some examples of different types of files:

- *Program source file* - the source code for a program written in a high-level language such as C or Pascal. This is usually a text file such as that produced by an editor or word processor.

- *Executable, or binary, file* - a file, containing compiled program code, which is in a form suitable for running. It could be a word processor or spreadsheet program or a scientific program, for example.

- *Picture file* - a collection of data representing a coloured or black and white picture which can be displayed on a computer screen with the aid of suitable software. It probably would have been created with the aid of a graphic design program.

- *Data file* - a file organised as a collection of *records*, each record comprising a number of fields. Such files are commonly used in data processing applications such as payroll, stock control and accounting.

We will be concerned with this last type of file. Most general-purpose high-level programming languages are able to create, read and modify files organised as collections of records; they provide single program instructions to transfer a complete record as a unit from backing storage into memory, at the same time splitting the record into separate data items called *fields*. The data in the fields are automatically allocated to variables declared for this purpose. This is the process of *reading a record* from a file. Another instruction allows the programmer to transfer a single, complete record as a unit from memory to a backing storage medium. This is the process of *writing a record*. Two other important file-handling operations are (1) *opening a file* in an appropriate mode and (2) *closing a file* that previously has been opened. The open file statement usually involves naming the file to be opened and specifying whether it is to be opened for input (that is, for reading records) or output (that is, for writing records).

The program designs that follow are concerned only with reading and writing sequential files, that is, where the records can be read only in a fixed sequence. Simple examples illustrate the logic required to create, read, search and update sequential files.

Creating a sequential file

Problem statement

Design a program to create a sequential file of car details. Each car record will contain the following data:

Make	*: maximum of 10 characters*
Model	*: maximum of 10 characters*
Insurance group	*: an integer value*
Cost	*: a real value*

Assumptions

1. The data will be stored in the form that it is entered - no validation checks will be performed.

2. A backing storage device such as a hard disk drive or a floppy disk drive is available to store the records of the file.

Top-level design

The top-level design is a sequence of a statement to prepare the file for output, followed by an iteration which allows the user to keep adding records to the file, and finally a statement which closes the file.

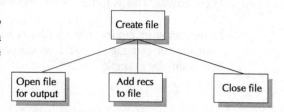

Refinement #1

The iteration is implemented as a `repeat` loop which terminates when the user answers 'no' to the opportunity to add another record to the file. The loop repeatedly (1) requests the user to enter a set of car details (that is, a car record), (2) stores the record if the user consents to it, and (3) then asks if another record is to be entered. The character variable, `Answer`, will contain 'N' if the user wishes to discontinue adding records to the file and this will cause the `repeat` loop to terminate.

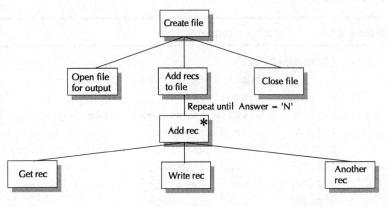

Refinement #2

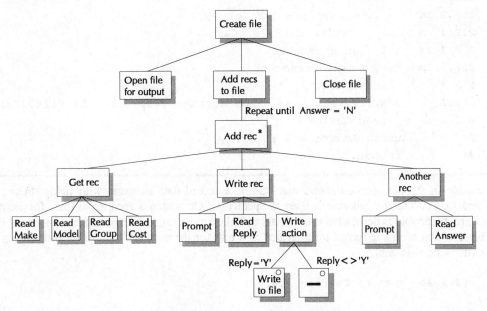

In this final refinement, the detail of the `Add rec` module is added. The selection statement, `Write action`, shows that we are interested only in `Reply` containing the character 'Y' indicating that the car record is to be stored; any other character simply results in no action being taken, which is indicated by the dash in the box.

Pseudocode

Listing 28.9.   Creating a sequential file

```
{Create file}
1            fopen output, Carfile
2            repeat
2.1.1a         write <newline>, 'Make (eg Ford):'
2.1.1b         read Car.Make
2.1.2a         write <newline>, 'Model (eg Escort):'
2.1.2b         read Car.Model
2.2.3a         write <newline>, 'Insurance group (eg 7):'
2.1.3b         read Car.InsGp
2.1.4a         write <newline>, 'Cost (eg 8450.50):'
2.1.4b         read Car.Cost
2.2.1          write <newline>, 'OK to save this record(Y/N) '
2.2.2          read Reply
2.2.3          select
2.2.3.1a         when Reply = ('Y' or 'y')
2.2.3.1b           fwrite CarFile, Car
2.2.3.2a         when otherwise
2.2.3.2b           next statement
2.2.3          endselect
2.3.1          write <newline>, 'Add another record to the file?(Y/N)'
2.3.2          read Answer
2            until Answer = ('Y' or 'y')
3            fclose CarFile
```

The data table in the next section shows that Car is a record data structure with fields Make, Model, InsGp and Cost. The *dot notation* is used to specify a field within a record, so that, for example, the insurance group variable is designated Car.InsGp. This same notation is used in the pseudocode in Listing 28.9. This allows a complete record to be treated as a unit for the purposes of reading and writing records. Thus the file write statement,

```
2.2.3.1b   fwrite CarFile, Car
```

specifies that the current Car record is to be written to CarFile.

The complete list of file-related commands used in this chapter have the following general formats:

```
fopen output, FileName          Opens the named file for writing
fopen input, FileName           Opens the named file for reading
fwrite FileName, RecordName     Writes the named record to the named file
fread FileName, RecordName      Reads the named record from the named file
fclose FileName                 Closes the named file
```

Finally, note that following statement from Listing 28.9,

2.2.3.2b   `next statement`

means, in effect, that no action is to take place at this point and control passes to the next available statement. It is included to make the logic of the selection statement clear and consistent with the structure chart component that it represents.

Data table

name	description	type
`Car`	A car record	record
`Car.Make`	The manufacturer of the car	string field
`Car.Model`	The model of the car	string field
`Car.InsGp`	The insurance group of the car	integer field
`Car.Cost`	The price of the car	real field
`CarFile`	Sequential file of car records	file of Car record
`Reply`	Holds the user's answer (Y or N) regarding whether a record is to be written to the file	character variable
`Answer`	Holds the user's answer (Y or N) regarding whether another record is to be entered	character variable

Table 28.9

Comments

This program is designed to initially create the car file; each time that it is used, the car file would be re-created. A technique for extending a sequential file is presented in a later example.

Reading sequential files

Two variations of reading the records in a sequential file are presented here. The first design is the most general form which assumes that a programming language will detect the end of a file when an attempt is made to read a record after the last one in the file. The read file statement in this instance has an at end clause which allows some action (in our case setting an flag called EOF to boolean true) if an end-of-file condition has arisen. Languages such as C and COBOL handle sequential files in this way.

The second design assumes that EOF is a built-in system function which checks the file and returns a value of true if there are no more records in the file remaining to be read. This is how Pascal handles sequential files.

Problem statement

Print in tabular form the contents of the car file created in the previous progam.

Assumptions

1.   The file is to be printed in the same order in which it was created.

2.   Version A assumes that the variable EOF is set to true when an attempt is made to read past the last record in the file.

3.   Version B assumes that the function EOF becomes true when there are no records in the file remaining to be read.

Top-level design

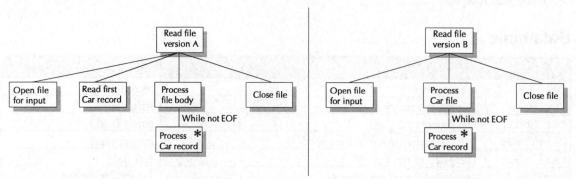

This shows that in version A the first record is read outside the loop, and the final operation within the loop is to read the next record (see refinement #1). In version B, this first read is not necessary.

Refinement #1

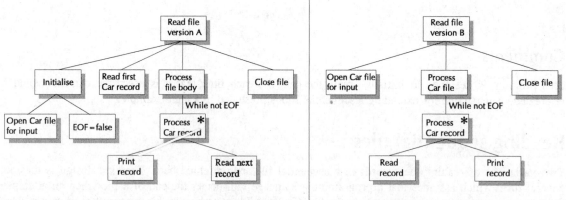

Processing a record in version A requires the current record to be printed before an attempt is made to read the next record. If there are no more records remaining to be read, EOF becomes true and the loop is terminated. With version B, a record is read and then printed. If it is the last record, EOF becomes true and the loop exits.

Pseudocode for version A

Listing 28.10a.   Reading a sequential file - version A

```
{Read file version A}
1.1    fopen input, Carfile
1.2    EOF = false
2a     fread CarFile, Car
2b        at end set EOF = true
3      while not EOF
```

```
3.1      write <newline>, Car.Make, Car.Model, Car.InsGp, Car.Cost
3.2a     fread CarFile, Car
3.2b       at end set EOF = true
3        endwhile
4        fclose CarFile
```

Note the at end option used with the read file statements - if an attempt is made to read past the last record in the file, EOF is set to true.

Pseudocode for version B

Listing 28.10b.   Reading a sequential file - version B

```
{Read file version B}
1        fopen input, Carfile
3        while not EOF(CarFile)
3.1        fread CarFile, Car
3.2        write <newline>, Car.Make, Car.Model, Car.InsGp, Car.Cost
3          endwhile
4          fclose CarFile
```

Here, EOF(CarFile) checks CarFile and if there are no more records remaining to be read, it returns boolean true, otherwise it returns boolean false. When available, this facility simplifies sequential file processing.

Data table for version A

name	description	type
Car	A car record	record
Car.Make	The manufacturer of the car	string field
Car.Model	The model of the car	string field
Car.InsGp	The insurance group of the car	integer field
Car.Cost	The price of the car	real field
CarFile	Sequential file of car records	file of Car record
EOF	Boolean variable used to detect the end of the file	boolean variable

Table 28.10

Data table for version B

This is the same as for version A except that the variable EOF is not used; instead EOF(CarFile) is a system function which returns true if there are no more records to be read in CarFile, otherwise it returns false.

Comments

These two versions should be sufficient to describe the logic of sequential file processing for the majority of commonly used high-level languages.

Searching sequential files

The next example illustrates the logic of extracting details from all the records in a file that satisfy some criterion. In this instance we want to find all the cars that are under a certain price, but the logic would be the same if we were searching for any other characteristic of the data held in the car records. The structure of the design is very similar to that for reading a sequential file, and the structure diagrams should be self-explanatory.

Problem statement

Produce a report of all cars which are within £1000 of a price which the user enters.

Assumptions

1. The EOF(FileName) function described in version B of the previous example is available. Follow the guidelines given for version A if the target programming language does not offer this facility.

2. The complete record of cars matching the criterion will be printed.

Top-level design

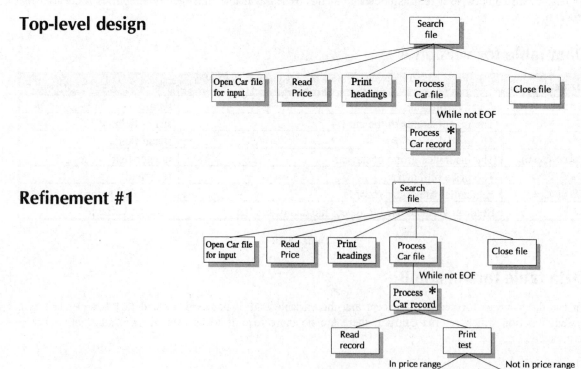

Refinement #1

Pseudocode

Listing 28.11. Sequential file search

```
{Search file}
1       fopen input, Carfile
2a      write <newline>, 'Enter the approximate price of cars to be listed'
2b      read Price
3       write <newline>,'Cars which are within £1000 of £', Price,':'
4       while not EOF(CarFile)
4.1     fread CarFile, Car
4.2       select
4.2.1a      when Price-1000 <= Car.Cost <= Price+1000
4.2.1b        write <newline>, Car.Make, Car.Model, Car.InsGp, Car.Cost
4.2.2a      when otherwise
4.2.2b        next statement
4.2       endselect
4       endwhile
5       fclose CarFile
```

Data table

name	description	type
Car	A car record	record
Car.Make	The manufacturer of the car	string field
Car.Model	The model of the car	string field
Car.InsGp	The insurance group of the car	integer field
Car.Cost	The price of the car	real field
CarFile	Sequential file of car records	file of Car record
Price	Approximate car price entered by the user	real variable

Table 28.11.

Comments

If the target programming language does not deal with sequential files in the same way as Pascal, remember that you must use a variable in the while condition to register the end of the file and terminate the iteration.

Subprograms

One of the characteristics of programming in high-level languages is the use of *subprograms* such as *procedures* or *functions* to allow a large program to be separated into a number of independent units. These subprograms are connected together by means of a main program. A subprogram usually communicates with the main program with the aid of *parameters* which allow data to be passed to and from the main program. Here we show how subprograms can be represented by structure charts and pseudocode.

Structure chart symbols and pseudocode

Figure 28.6 shows the symbols used for subprograms in structure charts and the equivalent pseudocode statement. Diagram (a) shows the simplest case in which component Sub 1 is a procedure which has no parameters. The subprogram has its own structure chart which is drawn separately from the main program. The pseudocode statement which invokes the subprogram is call Sub1. Again, the content of the subprogram is defined as a separate piece of pseudocode.

In diagram (b), Sub 2 has a single value parameter to which the variable X is passed. In pseudocode, brackets indicate that the variables inside are parameters. Sub 3 returns a value to the main program variable Y; in pseudocode this is indicated by putting the variable after the colon, as in call Sub3:Y. Diagram (d) shows how a subprogram which has a variable parameter Z is depicted; the double arrow indicates that Z is passed to the subprogram and that it is also returned to the main program. In pseudocode, a variable parameter is indicated by preceding it with var, as in call sub4(var Z). Finally, diagram (d) shows how a subprogram with more than one parameter and more than a single return value is represented. Notice that in the pseudocode statement call Sub5(var W, X):Y,Z, var only refers to W; X is a value parameter because it is not immediately preceded by var.

In a structure diagram these new symbols appear as illustrated in Figure 28.7. The diagram shows that component A is a simple subprogram with no parameters, subprogram D has a value parameter and accepts a variable X from the main program, and subprogram E returns a value to variable Y. The equivalent pseudocode is shown in Listing 28.12.

Figure 28.6. *Symbols for subprograms*

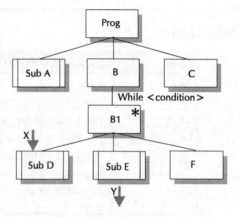

Figure 28.7. *Use of subprogram symbols in structure charts*

Listing 28.12.

```
{Prog}
1      call SubA
2      while <condition>
2.1      call SubD(X)
2.2      Y = call SubE
2.3      F
2      endwhile
```

Notice line *2.2*, in which the call to subprogram E results in a value being returned to the main program variable, Y.

The data table (Table 28.12) for the main program needs to contain entries defining each subprogram. The table shows that SubA is a procedure which has no parameters; SubD is a procedure which requires a string type to be passed as a parameter; SubE is a function which has no parameters but which returns an integer type.

name	description	type
SubA	Procedure to	proc
SubD	Procedure to	proc(string)
SubE	Function to	func:integer

Table 28.12.

Defining subprogram structures

Figure 28.8 shows the structure chart for a subprogram called Sub 2. It shows that a value is passed into value parameter P from the main program and that it returns a value in variable R to the main program (or subprogram) that called it. Notice that a subprogram can itself also contain further subprograms (component D). The pseudocode equivalent to this subprogram is shown in Listing 28.13.

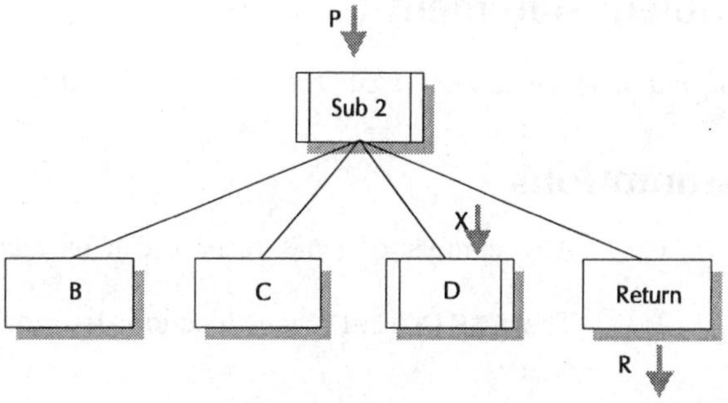

Figure 28.8. *Subprogram*

Listing 28.13.

```
Function Sub2(P)
1    process B
2    process C
3    call D(X)
4    return R
```

The parameters to which values are passed are shown inside the brackets after the name of the subprogram. The value that is returned is named after the word return at the end of the subprogram.

Each subprogram must also have its own data table which must define all of the parameters of the subprogram and any other variables used. For example, the subprogram in Listing 28.13 would require that P and R have entries such as those shown in Table 28.13.

Function Sub2(P):R		
name	description	type
P	Parameter used for ...	integer value parameter
R	Returns ..... to main program	real value parameter
etc.		

Table 28.13.

The following worked example shows the complete design of a program which uses subprograms to extend a sequential file.

Extending a sequential file - putting it all together

We mentioned earlier that when a sequential file is opened for output it must be re-created. In the next example we examine a general method of extending a sequential file without using a special extend-file command. (Some languages, notably COBOL, allow you to open a sequential file in a mode especially for extending it, but this is not generally the case). The method uses a temporary file to which the sequential file is copied. While this temporary file is still open for output, the additional records are added and then the complete temporary file is copied back to the original file.

Problem statement

Design a program to enable car records to be added to the car file.

Assumptions

1.   Any number of extra records can be added to the car file.

2.   The EOF(FileName) function described in previous examples is again available.

Main program

Top-level design

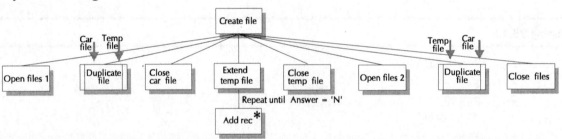

The procedure Duplicate file copies the first-named file to the second file. Thus it appears twice here: the first time to copy the current car file to a temporary file to which the extra records are to be added; the second time to copy the temporary file, now containing the extra records, back to the original file.

Refinement #1

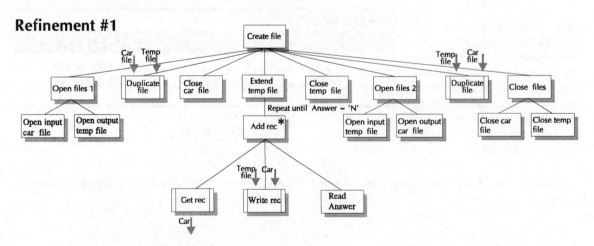

The further detail shows the order in which the two files need to be opened and closed, and also that two further subprograms are used. Get rec is used to get the details of a new car and return this record to the main program. Write rec writes the record to the temporary file. Both the record and the name of the file to which it is to be written are passed as parameters to this procedure.

Pseudocode

Listing 28.14. Extending a sequential file

```
{Extend file}
1.1    open input CarFile
1.2    open output TempFile
2      call DuplicateFile(CarFile, TempFile)
3      close CarFile
4      repeat until Answer = 'N'
4.1      Car = call GetRec
4.2      call WriteRec(TempFile, Car)
4.3a     write <newline>, 'Add another record to the file?(Y/N):'
4.3b     read Answer
4      until Answer = ('N' or 'n')
5      close TempFile
6.1    open output CarFile
6.2    open input TempFile
7      call DuplicateFile(TempFile, CarFile)
8.1    close CarFile
8.2    close TempFile
```

Data table

name	description	type
DuplicateFile	Procedure to copy one sequential file to another	proc(file of Car record, file of Car record)
GetRec	Function which gets and returns a car record	func:Car
WriteRec	Procedure to write a car record to a car file	proc(file of Car, Car)
Car	A car record	record
Car.Make	The manufacturer of the car	string field
Car.Model	The model of the car	string field
Car.InsGp	The insurance group of the car	integer field
Car.Cost	The price of the car	real field
CarFile	Sequential file of car records	file of Car record
Answer	Used to ask the user if another record is to be added to the car file	character variable

Table 28.14

Comments

The data table includes entries for the three subprograms that are called in the main program. These subprograms must also be fully defined using structure charts, pseudocode and data tables.

Procedure - Duplicate file

Top-level design

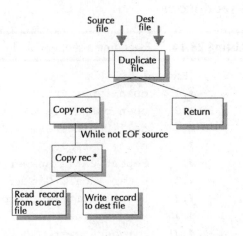

Pseudocode

Listing 28.15.   Duplicating the file

```
Procedure DuplicateFile(SourceFile, DestFile)
1       while not EOF(SourceFile)
1.1        fread SourceFile, Rec
1.2        fwrite DestFile, Rec
1       endwhile
2       return
```

Data table

Procedure DuplicateFile(Sourcefile, DestFile)		
name	description	type
SourceFile	The file to be copied	file of Car records
DestFile	The copy file	file of Car records
Rec	A single car record from the file	Car record

Table 28.15.

Function - Get rec

Top-level design

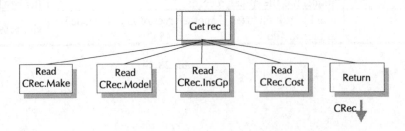

Pseudocode

Listing 28.16.

```
Function GetRec:Crec
1a      write <newline>, 'Make:'
1b      read Crec.Make
2a      write <newline>, 'Model:'
2b      read Crec.Model
3a      write <newline>, 'Insurance Group:'
3b      read Crec.InsGp
4a      write <newline>, 'Cost:'
4b      read Crec.Cost
5       return Crec
```

Data table

Function GetRec:Crec		
name	description	type
CRec	A car record	record
CRec.Make	The manufacturer of the car	string field
CRec.Model	The model of the car	string field
CRec.InsGp	The insurance group of the car	integer field
CRec.Cost	The price of the car	real field

Table 28.16.

Procedure - Write rec

Top-level design

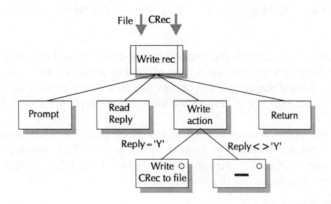

Pseudocode

Listing 28.17.

```
Procedure WriteRec(File, CarRec)
1a      write <newline>, 'OK to save this record?(Y/N) '
1b      read Reply
2       select
2.1a      when Reply = ('Y' or 'y')
2.1b          fwrite File, CRec
2.2a      when otherwise
2.2b          next statement
2       endselect
3       return
```

Data table

Procedure WriteRec(File, CRec)		
name	description	type
File	The file to be written to	value parameter file of Car records
CRec	A single car record from the file	value parameter Car record
Reply	User reply	character variable

Table 28.17.

Program testing, debugging and documenting

Once the program has been written, it must go through two stages in order to remove errors which almost inevitably will be present. No matter how much care has been taken in the design and coding of a program, it is very likely to contain errors in syntax, that is incorrectly formed statements, and almost as likely to contain errors in logic as well. *Debugging* is the term given to the process of detecting and correcting these errors or *bugs*.

The first stage in the removal of errors is the correction of syntax errors. Fortunately for the programmer, modern interpreters and compilers will provide a large amount of assistance in the detection of syntax errors in the source code. Badly formed statements will be reported by a compiler after it has attempted to compile the source code; an interpreter will report illegal statements as it attempts to execute them.

Logic errors, however, are largely undetectable by the translating program. These are errors which cause the program to behave in a manner contrary to expectations. The individual statements in the program are correctly formed and it runs, but the program as a whole does not work as it should; it may give incorrect answers, or terminate prematurely, or not terminate at all.

Hopefully, even the most puzzling logic errors, having been detected, eventually can be removed. But how can the programmer be confident that the program will continue to behave properly when it is in use? The answer is that the programmer never can be absolutely certain that the program will not fail, but by the careful choice of test data in the second stage of the debugging process, the programmer can test the program under the sort of conditions that are most likely to occur in practice. Test data is designed to determine the robustness of the program: how well it can cope with unexpected or spurious inputs as well as those for which it has been designed specifically to process.

The purpose of *documentation* is to provide the user with all the information necessary to fully understand the purpose of the program and how that purpose has been achieved. The precise form that the documentation takes will be determined by a number of factors:

- The type of program.

- Who is likely to use the program.

- Whether it will be necessary to modify the program coding after it has been finally tested and accepted.

General guidelines for the contents of program documentation are given at the end of this chapter.

Detecting logic errors

If, after examining a program listing for a reasonable amount of time, the cause of an error remains a mystery, there are a number of courses of action which will probably be much more productive than continuing to pore over the listing:

1. Ask a fellow programmer to listen while you explain the operation of the program and the way it is behaving. Quite often you will see the cause of the error as you are making the explanation. Alternatively, your helper might recognise the type of error and its probable cause from his/her own experience, or might ask a question which makes you reconsider some aspect of the program which you have assumed to be correct or has no direct bearing on the problem. It is surprising how often this simple approach works.

2. Examine the values of key variables while the program is running by installing temporary lines of code throughout the program to display the values of key variables. Comparison of the values actually displayed with expected values will normally indicate the likely source of the error.

3. Use debugging utilities provided in the language itself or separately in the system software. Several versions of BASIC have a trace facility which, when turned on, displays the line number of statements prior to their execution. Sometimes a particular implementation of a language will provide more sophisticated debugging facilities which will display the values of particular variables as they are encountered during program execution. Some Pascal compilers have similar facilities for tracing a program as it is running. Minicomputer systems and mainframes usually have special debugging software which can be used with any of the languages supported by the system. It is up to the programmer to investigate the debugging aids available and make good use of them.

Test data

When the programmer feels that the gross program errors have been detected and removed, the next stage is to test the program using carefully selected data. The nature of the test data should be such that:

- every statement in the program is executed at least once;

- the effectiveness of every section of coding devoted to detecting invalid input is verified;

- every route through the program is tried at least once;

- the accuracy of the processing is verified;

- the program operates according to its original design specification.

In order to achieve these aims, the programmer must be inventive in the design of the test data. Each test case must check something not tested by previous runs; there is no point in proving that a program which can add successfully a certain set of numbers can also add another similar set of numbers. The goal is to strain the program to its limit, and this is particularly important when the program is to be used frequently by a number of different people.

There are three general categories of test data:

1.   *Normal data.* This includes the most general data for which the program was designed to handle.

2.   *Extreme values.* These test the behaviour of the program when valid data at the upper and lower limits of acceptability are used. The process of using extreme values is called boundary testing and is often a fruitful place to look for errors. For numeric data this could be the use of very large or very small values. Text could be the shortest or longest sequence of characters permitted. A program for file processing could be tested with a file containing no records, or just a single record. The cases where zero or null values are used are very important test cases, frequently highlighting programming oversights.

3.   *Exceptional data.* Programs are usually designed to accept a certain range or class of inputs. If illegal data is used, that is data which the program is not designed to handle, the program should be capable of rejecting it rather than attempting to process it. This is particularly important when the program is to be used by people other than the programmer, since they may be unaware of what constitutes illegal data. A programmer should from the outset assume that incorrect data will be used with the program; this may save a great deal of time looking for program errors which may actually be data errors.

Validation

At some point the programmer must decide that the program has had sufficient testing. He or she will be confident that the program will operate according to specification and without crashing or hanging up under extreme or unexpected circumstances; the reputation of a professional programmer relies on this. Prior to release, the final testing is then performed by the user for whom the program was developed. The programmer may have overlooked areas of difficulty because it is often difficult to view a program objectively or entirely from the point of view of the user. If this is the case then the program will be modified and re-tested until all user requirements are met.

Program documentation requirements

A program which validates a temporary file prior to creating it permanently will probably require a minimum of user interaction and only a small number of instructions for the benefit of the person who will run the program. However, at some later date, it might be necessary for the author of the program, or a different programmer, to modify it. This possibility means that the structure of the program will have to be explained in great detail, and test procedures to ensure its correct operation will have to be provided.

A general purpose program such as a spreadsheet, designed for people who just want to use the computer as a tool, will require extremely detailed instructions regarding its function and use. Such programs are generally accompanied by extremely detailed user manuals and tutorials. On the other hand, users would not be expected (and definitely not encouraged) to modify the program coding; thus no details would be provided regarding the way the program has been written. This latter type of documentation would only be required for the people responsible for producing the program.

In addition to the documentation requirements of users and programmers, there is a third category of person to be catered for. These are people such as managers who are neither likely to use programs extensively nor want to attempt to modify them. They merely need to have an overview of the program - its function, capabilities, hardware requirements etc.

Thus there are many factors governing the coverage of documentation, and for this reason, in the next section, it is only possible to provide a checklist of items which might reasonably be included.

Documentation checklist

The documentation for a simple program generally falls into four sections:

- Identification

- General specification

- User information

- Program specification.

Most users will need access to the first three sections; in general the fourth section will only be needed if the program is to be modified. The amount of detail in each section will depend entirely on the particular application and, to some extent, the implementation language. COBOL, for example, is largely self-documenting. It contains an Identification Division containing all the information listed in the first section below; the Data Division of a COBOL program contains precise details regarding all of the files used by the program and which devices are required; the Procedure Division is written in 'English-like' sentences which are generally easy to understand, even by a non-programmer. Consequently, a program written in COBOL will generally require less documentation than one written in BASIC, a language which is not self-documenting.

The following checklist is a guide to what might reasonably be included in the documentation for a program.

Identification

- title of program;

- short statement of its function;

- author;

- date written;

- language used and version if relevant;

- hardware requirements.

General specification

- description of the main action(s) of the program under normal circumstances;

- file specifications;

- restrictions and/or limitations of the program;

- equations used or references to texts explaining any complex procedures/techniques involved.

User information

- format of input required, e.g. source document or screen mask;

- output produced, e.g. typical printout or screen display;

- detailed instructions for initially running the program;

- medium on which program located, e.g. floppy disk(s).

Program specification

- structure charts/flowcharts/decision tables;

- annotated listing;

- testing procedure including test data and expected output.

Chapter 29

Pascal Programming

Introduction

This chapter addresses the task of developing a piece of software using the programming language Pascal. Here we look at Pascal in enough depth for you to be able to develop your own simple programs, provided of course that you have access to a Pascal compiler. The programs presented in this unit were written and tested using Borland's Turbo Pascal. However, apart from a small number of possible exceptions, the programs should work with any standard version of Pascal. Any special features of Turbo Pascal used in example programs are noted and explained; if you are not using Turbo Pascal, your version will most likely have very similar features that you can substitute, but you will need to refer to the appropriate language reference manual for the precise instruction format required. Turbo Pascal was chosen because it provides an ideal, easy to use environment for developing programs since it combines in one package all the tools required for the task. For example, it has: (i) an *editor* for creating and editing source programs; (ii) a *compiler* to check the syntax of a program, to report and identify errors and to produce object code; (iii) a *linker* to produce executable code; (iv) a *debugger* to help with locating runtime errors; (v) a *file manager* to allow you to quickly save, retrieve and print source programs. Before going on to look at the language itself, we outline all the stages involved in producing a working program to put the process of actually using a Pascal compiler in its correct context.

The structure of a Pascal program

A Pascal program consists of four main parts: (i) the *name* of the program; (ii) a *declarations* section in which the programmer defines global *identifiers*. These are the variables and constants used in the program; (iii) *function* and *procedure definitions*; (iv) The main *procedural* part of the program which defines the sequence of instructions to be performed by the program. This section uses the identifiers, functions and procedures defined in the previous two sections of the program. It starts with the word `begin` and ends with end. Listing 29.1. shows the general structure of a Pascal program.

Listing 29.1.   General structure of a Pascal program

```
program Name(input, output);

   {Declarations of global variables and  and constants}

   {Procedures and functions definitions}

begin
   {The main body of the program containing a sequence of
   instructions to be performed}
end.
```

As a simple example to illustrate these ideas, Listing 29.2 shows a program which calculates the total cost of a purchased item by calculating VAT and adding it to the price of the item. The algorithm on which the program is based is as follows:

1. *Ask the user to enter the price of the item*

2. *Store the price*

3. *Calculate the VAT at 17.5% (i.e. multiply the price by 0.175)*

4. *Calculate the total price by adding the VAT to the price*

5. *Display the total cost on the screen.*

Note that the line numbers preceding each line in the program are included in the example programs presented in this chapter simply for ease of reference to specific lines when describing them. *Line numbers are not part of the Pascal language and should not be included if you intend to compile and run the example programs.*

The operation of program `Example1`

Line *1* declares that this program is called `Example1` and (`input, output`) indicates that the program uses the keyboard for the input of data and the screen for the display of data.

Lines *2* and *3* declare that VAT is a *constant* value.

Listing 29.2.   A simple program to calculate the total cost of a purchase

---

```
1       program Example1(input, output);
2       const
3         VAT = 0.175;
4       var
5         Price :real;
6         Tax :real;
7         TotalCost :real;
8       begin
9         write('Enter price of the item');
10        readln(Price);
11        Tax:= Price*VAT;
12        TotalCost:= Price + Tax;
13        writeln('The total cost is:' , TotalCost:8:2);
14      end.
```

Lines *4* - *7* declare three *variables* `Price`, `Tax` and `TotalCost` (hence the word `var` on line *4*) each as being of type `real`. Variables are used to store data, which in this case are in the form of real numbers, that is, numbers which are not whole numbers. Every variable used in a Pascal program must be declared in this way.

Up to this point the programmer has defined a number of *identifiers* that will be used in the procedural part of the program which follows.

Line *8* indicates the beginning of the procedural part of the program, that is, the section of the program which states what operations are to be performed. This is the part of the program in which the tasks identified by the algorithm are coded.

Line *9* causes the message Enter price of the item to be displayed on the screen.

Line *10* stores causes the computer to pause and accept numeric data typed in to be stored in the variable Price before continuing.

Line *11* stores the result of Price multiplied by VAT in the variable Tax.

Line *12* stores the result of adding Price and Tax in TotalCost.

Line *13* then displays the text, 'The total cost is: ' followed by the value stored in TotalCost. The total cost is shown as a total of eight characters with two figures after the decimal point.

Finally in **Line *14***, the word end followed by a full stop indicates the end of the program.

Some general remarks

Before going on to explore Pascal in more depth, it is worth mentioning a few general points at this stage:

1. Pascal does not distinguish between the use of capitals and lower-case letters. Thus it regards BEGIN, begin and Begin as being exactly the same.

2. Pascal uses the semicolon to indicate the end of an instruction, which is why you will see a semicolon at the end of most of the lines in a program. (You will quickly learn where a semicolon is not necessary). If you forget to terminate a complete instruction with a semicolon, the compiler will 'think' that the instruction is continued on the next line and, more often than not, it will say that there is an error in the next line.

3. It is a good idea to include comment lines (that is, text enclosed between '{' and '}') to describe the purpose of lines or sections of your program. Particularly for large, complex programs, this is very helpful if it is necessary to change the program at some later date.

4. Using spaces, blank lines and indentation can greatly improve the appearance and the clarity of a program, thus making the program easier to read and understand if it has to be modified later for any reason.

5. Programming involves meticulous attention to detail; omitting punctuation marks, including them in the wrong place or making spelling mistakes will usually lead to the compiler reporting syntax errors, but sometimes such slips might cause serious errors which are more difficult to detect, so be very careful to form instructions precisely.

Identifiers and data types

The term *identifier* is a general term used for *variables*, *constants* and other programmer-defined names such as *procedures* and *functions*. Variables and constants are always associated with a data *type*. Pascal requires that variables are given a type such as integer or real so that the necessary amount of memory can be reserved for their use.

Variables

A variable, which represents an item of data such as a single number, has a name and a current value. Variables are given names such as `Amount`, `Total` or `Numb3` and are assigned values by program instructions. These values are stored in the memory of the computer and they are accessed whenever a variable is referenced in a program instruction. So, for example, in the instruction

```
Total := Price + Tax;
```

the value associated with the variable `Price` is added to the value of the variable `Tax` and the sum is then assigned to the variable `Total`. If in a previous instruction total had already been assigned a value, that value would be replaced by the new one.

Constants

Constants too are assigned values but only once after the word `const` preceding the main program. The constant `VAT` in Listing 29.2 is an example. Constants retain their values throughout the execution of a program; Pascal does not allow you to use a constant in an instruction which tries to change the value of the constant. Thus, if in Listing 29.2, you included an instruction such as

```
VAT := 0.2;
```

in the main program, the Pascal compiler would report an error. Notice that a constant is assigned a value using only the '=' sign without the ':'.

Special identifiers and reserved words

Certain words in Pascal are classed as *special,* or *standard, identifiers* because they perform the same function as programmer-defined identifiers but they are recognized by the compiler as being pre-defined and they are therefore to be used only in a certain context. Examples of special identifiers are the words `write`, `writeln`, `read`, `readln`, `input` and `output`. If you use any of these words for identifiers, for example by declaring

```
var
    Read :integer;
```

then Pascal will not necessarily regard this as a mistake, but you will have overridden the standard definition of `read` as an input instruction, and you will have to use it as an integer variable; you will not be able then to use read as an input instruction since, in effect, you will have redefined its function. The moral is to avoid using these special identifier names for your own, programmer-defined identifiers.

Reserved words such as begin, end, real and program are words which are actually part of the Pascal language and are unavailable for use as identifiers. Pascal's reserved words and special identifiers are shown below.

Reserved words

and	array	begin	case	const
div	do	downto	else	end
file	for	function	goto	if
in	label	mod	nil	not
of	or	packed	procedure	program
record	repeat	set	then	to
type	until	var	while	with

Special identifiers

abs	arctan	boolean	char	chr
cos	dispose	eof	eoln	exp
false	get	input	integer	ln
maxint	new	odd	ord	output
pack	page	pred	put	read
readln	real	reset	rewrite	round
sin	sqr	sqrt	succ	text
true	trunc	unpack	write	writeln

Rules for naming identifiers

Pascal imposes a number of restrictions concerning the formation of names for identifiers:

1.   The name must consist only of alphabetic and numeric characters.

2.   The name must start with an alphabetic character.

3.   The name must not be a special identifier or a reserved word.

Examples of valid identifiers

firstNum	NUMBER1	abc31	Counter	x

Examples of invalid identifiers

12abc	(starts with a numeric character)
first-number	(contains a non-alphabetic/numeric character)
var 1	(contains a space)
End	(a reserved word)
READ	(a special identifier)

Data types

As well as having a names and values, variables are also given a *type*. Three commonly used types are integer, real and char (character). Data types are declared before the main program. For variables, the type must be shown after the name of the variable, as illustrated on lines 5-7 of Listing 29.2. More examples of type declarations are shown below.

```
var
    Amount              :real;
    CodeLetter          :char;
    NumberOfItems       :integer;
```

The type `real` means that these variables can be used for numbers such as 123.456, 0.22 or –9.93, that is, *signed* numbers that are not whole numbers. The computer holds `real` numbers in floating-point form so that very large, and very small numbers can be stored.

Signed whole numbers, that is, `integer` values are stored as two's complement binary values in the computer. Some examples of integers are 23, 0, –1, 32767 and –559.

Type `char` means that the named variable (`CodeLetter` in the example above) stores a single character such as 'a', 'D', '6' or '?'.

Turbo Pascal provides a further data type to handle *strings*. A string is simply a number of characters which are collected together and used as a unit. For example, a person's name is a string of alphabetic characters, and a stock number such as 100-234/ABC in a mail order catalogue is a string containing a mixture of alphabetic, numeric and special characters. String variable declarations are illustrated in the examples below.

```
    Surname             :string[20];
    StockNumber         :string[12];
    Address1            :string[30];
```

The number inside the brackets specifies the maximum number of single characters to be handled by the named variable.

A further standard data type is the type `boolean`. This type of variable has only one of two possible values, namely `true` or `false`. A boolean variable declaration is made as follows:

```
    Morevalues      :boolean;
```

Pascal provides the two reserved words `true` and `false` which can be used to assign a value to a boolean variable, as in:

```
    Morevalues:= true;
```

The use of boolean variables will be explored in a later section.

Performing calculations

Probably every program that you will ever write will contain at least one calculation, and this is true of the majority of programs. It is not surprising therefore that Pascal and other high-level languages make calculations easy to perform. Arithmetic instructions simply involve defining what arithmetic operations are to be performed on numeric identifiers and constants. The four common arithmetic operations: add; subtract; multiply; divide, use the symbols +, -, * and /, respectively. The examples of arithmetic operations provided in Table 29.1 assume that the following data declarations have been made.

```
const
  PI      =3.14;
var
  Length, Width, Perimeter          :integer;
  Area, Radius, Gallons, Miles, Mpg  :real;
  a, b, c, x, y                      :real;
```

Expression	Pascal statement
Area = length × width	`Area:= Length*Width;`
Area = πr^2	`Area:= PI*Radius*Radius;`
Perimeter = 2 × (length + width)	`Perimeter:= 2*(Length + Width);`
Mpg = gallons ÷ miles	`Mpg:= Gallons/Miles;`
x = 0	`x:= 0;`

Table 29.1. *Examples of arithmetic operations with real variables*

All of the statements in Table 29.1 involve calculating a value using real or integer variables or a combination of reals and integers. Pascals rules concerning how such calculations may be expressed are called *assignment compatibility* rules. They state that a calculation which involves: (i) a mixture of integers and reals must be assigned to a real variable; (ii) only integers may be assigned to either an integer variable or a real variable. Another point to note is that Pascal provides two divide operators. The '/' divide operator may be used with any values, real or integer,

Operands	Example	Answer	Answer type
real/real	7.3/0.2	36.5	real
	0.5/0.25	2.0	real
real/integer	13.9/5	2.78	real
integer/real	1116/7.2	155.0	real
integer/integer	33/11	3.0	real
	33/10	3.0	real
	3/5	0.6	real
integer div integer	33 div 11	3	integer
	33 div 10	3	integer
	3 div 5	0	integer
integer div real	Not allowed		
real div integer	Not allowed		
real div real	Not allowed		
integer mod integer	33 mod 10	3	integer
	10 mod 33	10	
integer mod real	Not allowed		
real mod integer	Not allowed		
real mod real	Not allowed		

Table 29.2. *Examples of divide operations*

but if both values are integers, the result is a `real` value and must be assigned to a `real` variable. The second divide operator, `div`, is only allowed to be used with integers. If the result of a division does not produce a whole number, the fractional part is ignored. In other words, the result is rounded down to the nearest integer. The remainder when one integer is divided by another is produced by the `mod` operator. Some examples should help to clarify these points and these are shown in Table 29.2.

Listing 29.3 is an example of the use of integer division. The program converts a number of seconds into hours, minutes and seconds.

Listing 29.3.   The `div` and `mod` integer division operators

```
1       program ModAndDiv(input, output);
2          {Program to convert a time given in seconds
3          to hours, minutes and seconds}
4
5       const
6          SECONDSPERMINUTE    =60;
7          MINUTESPERHOUR      =60;
8
9       var
10         Hours          :integer;
11         Minutes        :integer;
12         Seconds        :integer;
13         Duration       :integer;
14         Temp           :integer;
15
16      begin
17         writeln;
18         write('Enter the time in seconds: ');
19         readln(Duration);
20         Seconds := Duration mod SECONDSPERMINUTE;
21         Temp := Duration div SECONDSPERMINUTE;
22         Minutes := Temp mod MINUTESPERHOUR;
23         Hours := Temp div MINUTESPERHOUR;
24
25         writeln;
26         writeln(Duration, ' seconds is: ');
27         writeln;
28
29         write(Hours, ' hours ');
30         write(Minutes, ' minutes ');
31         writeln(Seconds, ' seconds.');
32      end.
```

On line *17* the user is requested to enter the time to be converted from seconds to hours, minutes and seconds. The number of seconds is stored in the variable `Duration`. The first stage in the calculation is to calculate the remainder when `Duration` is divided by the number of seconds per minute stored in the constant `SECONDSPERMINUTE` which has the value 60. Suppose, for example, the user entered the number 6573 when asked for the time in seconds. Line *20* would produce the value 6573 mod 60, that is, 33. This is assigned to the variable, `Seconds`. Next, the temporary variable `Temp` is given the value 6573 div 60, that is, 109. The remainder when this last number is divided by the number of minutes per hour, that is 60, gives the value for Minutes: 109 mod 60 = 49. The number of hours is calculated using 109 div 60 = 1. Thus, when the program is run, it produces the following output:

```
Enter the time in seconds: 6573 ⏎

6573 seconds is: 1 hours 49 minutes 33 seconds.
```

Operator precedence

The term *operator precedence* applies to the order in which the operators in an arithmetic expression are used. For example, to evaluate the expression

$$x = y + 3z$$

z is multiplied by 3 before the result is added to y; the multiply operator thus has precedence over the addition operator. If y had a value of 2 and z had a value of 4, x would be calculated as

$$x = 2 + 3 \times 4 = 2 + 12 = 14$$

The higher the precedence of an operator, the sooner it is used in the evaluation of an expression. The use of parentheses within an expression can alter the way a calculation is performed. So, in the above expression, to force the addition to be performed before the multiplication, we would write $x = (y + 3) \times z$. This would result in y being added to 3 before multiplying by z. Thus,

$$x = (2 + 3) \times 4 = 5 \times 4 = 20$$

In C, the operators *, / and % have equal precedence; this means that in an expression involving two or more of them, they are simply used in the order that they appear in the expression. These four operators all have higher precedence than + and –. Again, + and – have the same precedence. As a further example, consider the program in Listing 29.4.

Listing 29.4. Illustration of operator precedence

```
1    program Example2(input, output);
2    var
3      x1 :real;
4      y1 :real;
5      n :integer;
6    begin
7      n:= 11;
8      y1:= 5;
9      x1:= 1.0/2.0*(y1 + n div y1);
10     writeln(x1:8:2);
11   end.
```

The order of evaluation of line *9* is as follows:

1.	`1.0/2.0`	i.e.	`0.5`
2.	`n div y1`	i.e.	`11 div 5 = 2`
3.	`y1 + n div y1`	i.e.	`5 + 2 = 7`
4.	`1.0/2.0*(y1 + n div y1)`	i.e.	`0.5*7 = 3.5`

Reading and displaying information

Practically every program requires that data are provided by some input device such as a keyboard and that results are produced on an output device such as a monitor. Pascal provides a number of instructions to simplify these operations. The example program in Listing 29.4 used three input-output instructions, namely `readln`, `writeln` and `write`. In this section we examine these instructions in a little more detail.

The `readln` instruction uses data provided by a standard input device such as a keyboard to assign values to variables . The word `input` inside the brackets after the program name at the beginning of a Turbo Pascal program tells the Pascal compiler that a keyboard is to be used to enter character-based data (see Listing 29.4 for an example). You use the readln instruction to read real numbers, integers, single characters or strings into appropriately declared variables. For example, the statement

```
readln(Price);
```

would cause the program to wait for the user to enter a number to be stored in the real variable price. The user presses the ENTER key (⏎) to signify the end of data entry. It is good practice to include a write instruction to precede readln to inform the user what information is required. So, for example, the statements

```
write('Please enter the price of the item: ');
readln(Price);
```

would cause the computer to display

```
Please enter the price of the item:
```

on the display screen and then, with the text cursor remaining on the same line, wait for the user to type in a value and press the ⏎ key. The `writeln` instruction is almost identical to `write`, except that the text cursor is automatically moved to the beginning of the line immediately following the line on which the message is displayed. Which one of the instructions write and writeln you use depends on how you want your output to appear. Listing 29.5 illustrates the use of `write`, `writeln` and `readln`.

Listing 29.5.   Using `write`, `writeln` and `readln` instructions

```
1      program convert1(input, output);
2         {Program to convert inches to centimetres }
3      const
4         CENTIMETRESPERINCH =2.54;
5      var
6         Centimetres   :real;
7          Inches        :real;
8      begin
```

```
 9        write('Enter the length in inches: ');
10        readln(Inches);
11        Centimetres := Inches*CENTIMETRESPERINCH;
12        writeln;
13        write('A length of ', Inches:5:2,' inches');
14        write(' is equivalent to ');
15        writeln(Centimetres:5:2, ' centimetres');
16     end.
```

The program would produce the following output when run:

```
Enter the length in inches: 12 ⏎

A length of 12.00 inches is equivalent to 30.48 centimetres
```

Notice the different form of the `writeln` instruction on line *12*: it simply produces a single blank line when the round brackets are not used. This is useful for making your output clear and easy to read. The output shows that the user entered the number *12* followed by ⏎ when prompted to type in the length in inches.

In line *13*, `write('A length of ', Inches:5:2,' inches');`, the purpose of the numbers after the variable `Inches` is to control the number of characters printed, that is, the *field width* and the number of decimal places of the displayed variable. In this instance the field width, including the decimal point, is to be restricted to five, with two figures after the decimal point. When the variable is of type `integer`, only one figure representing the total number of digits to be displayed is provided. If the field width is larger than the item to be displayed, the output is padded with blanks. Using a field width of zero, as in `Inches:0`, or less than the number of digits in the number, causes the minimum number of digits to be displayed. Table 29.3 contains a number of examples using various output formats.

value	type	format	output	remarks
15.234	real	:10:1	******15.2	Six leading spaces are added
6.6666	real	:10:1	*******6.7	The figure after the decimal point is rounded up
6.6666	real	:0:2	6.67	The minimum number of digits is displayed
−8.3124	real	:0:3	−8.312	As above
234.56	real	:1	2.3E+02	Number is displayed in floating-point form
234.56	real	none	2.3456000000E+02	The maximum number of decimal places is displayed
123	integer	:5	**123	Two leading spaces included in the field
123	integer	:2	123	Minimum number of figures displayed and no leading spaces
'hello'	string	:10	*****hello	Strings are treated like integers
'hello'	string	:0	hello	As above

Table 29.3. *Examples of various output formats and their effects*

Note that the instructions that we have covered in this section, namely `readln`, `write` and `writeln`, are actually implemented as *standard procedures* which are explored later in this chapter.

Loops

A very frequent programming requirement is to perform a set of instructions several times. Rather than writing the set of instructions several times (which is impractical for all but a small number of repetitions), they are controlled by a special instruction which causes them to be repeated as many times as desired. Such program constructs are called *loops*, and each repetition of a set of statements is often called an *iteration*. For example, suppose a program is required to read 10 numbers, add each one to a running total and then display the final total. The program in Listing 29.6 accomplishes this task using a loop.

Listing 29.6.   Using a loop to add numbers

```
1      program RunningTotal2(input, output);
2        {Program to add ten numbers }
3      var
4        Number        :real;
5        Total         :real;
6        Count         :integer;
7      begin
8        Total:= 0;
9        writeln('Enter ten numbers: ');
10       for Count:= 1 to 10 do
11       begin
12          readln(Number);
13          Total:= Total + Number;
14       end;
15       writeln('The total is: ', Total:10:2);
16     end.
```

Listing 29.6 uses a for loop to repeat the two instructions which repeatedly read a number and add it to a running total. The for loop requires that a control variable, called Count in this example, is defined as type integer. The control variable is automatically given the first value specified (1 in this example) and, each time the statements within the loop are repeated, it is increased by 1 until it finally reaches the second value specified (10 in this example). Thus the same program, but with the value 10 replaced by the required number, could be used to add any number of numbers. Statements to be repeated are enclosed between begin and end. Listing 29.7 is a further example of the use of the for loop.

Listing 29.7.   Using a for loop to display a conversion table

---

```
1      program ConvTab(input, output);
2        {Program to display a conversion table for inches to
3          centimetres using a for loop}
4      const
5        CONVERSIONFACTOR =2.54;
6        MAXINCHES =12;
7      var
8        Inches :integer;
9        Centimetres :real;
```

```
10
11    begin
12      writeln;
13      writeln('Inches':20, 'Centimetres':20);
14      writeln('------':20, '-----------':20);
15
16      for Inches:= 1 to MAXINCHES do
17        begin
18            Centimetres:= Inches*CONVERSIONFACTOR;
19              writeln(Inches:17, Centimetres:20:2);
20        end;
21    end.
```

The output produced looks like this:

```
    Inches        Centimetres
    -------        ------------
      1             2.54
      2             5.08
     etc             etc
     12            30.48
```

Notice that the end value in the `for` statement on line *16* is a `constant` called `MAXINCHES`; this could also have been defined as a variable used in a `readln` instruction.

A slight variation in the format of a `for` statement allows the count variable to go down from a high value to a low value. For example, you could write

```
for i:= 12 downto 1 do ....
```

which would cause the variable `i` to start at 12 and go down to 1 in steps of 1.

The `for` statement is a very useful means of implementing a loop, but certain programming problems require a different approach to repeating a set of instructions. For example, consider the following outline program description:

> *Read a set of real numbers representing the cost of a number of items. Accumulate the total cost of the items until a value of zero is entered, then display the number of items purchased and their total cost.*

Here it is not known how many times the loop is to be repeated: the user decides when to terminate the loop by entering a *rogue value*, (zero in this case). The rogue value is used in another type of loop instruction, the `while` instruction. Listing 29.8 shows how a `while` loop can be used in conjunction with a rogue value. The rogue value is defined as a constant on line *5*. Because the user may want to terminate the program immediately, without entering any values, the program asks for a purchase amount before entering the loop starting on line *18*. The `while` instruction requires that a true/false expression is included after the word 'while'. Thus the expression, `Amount > ROGUEVALUE`, will be true if `Amount` entered is greater than zero, and it will be false if `Amount` is not greater than zero, that is if it is equal to, or less than zero. When the expression is true, the statements between the immediately following `begin` and `end`, that is lines *20* to

23, will be executed; as soon as the expression becomes false, the loop terminates and the program goes on to line *26*.

Notice that the last instruction in the lines to be repeated is the `readln` instruction to read another value: this means that because the next instruction to be executed is the `while` instruction, the value typed in by the user is immediately compared with the rogue value. This ensures that the rogue value is not processed as an actual data item.

Listing 29.8.   Using a `while` loop and a rogue value

```
1      program RogueVal(input, output);
2        {program to illustrate the use of a rogue value
3           to terminate a loop}
4      const
5        ROGUEVALUE =0;
6      var
7        Count :integer;
8        Amount :real;
9        Total :real;
10
11     begin
12       Total:= 0;
13       Count:= 0;
14
15       write('Enter the cost of the first item, or 0 to end :');
16       readln(Amount);
17
18       while Amount > ROGUEVALUE do
19         begin
20           Count:= Count + 1;
21           Total:= Total + Amount;
22           write('Enter the cost of the next item, or 0 to end :');
23           readln(Amount);
24         end;
25
26       writeln;
27       writeln(Count, ' items were purchased.');
28       writeln;
29       writeln('The total cost was: £', Total:0:2);
30     end.
```

Here is a typical output from the program:

```
Enter the cost of the first item, or 0 to end :23.45 ⏎
Enter the cost of the next item, or 0 to end :6.12 ⏎
Enter the cost of the next item, or 0 to end :5.99 ⏎
```

```
Enter the cost of the next item, or 0 to end :0 ⏎

3 items were purchased.
The total cost was: £35.56
```

Notice that the assignment instruction on line *20*, Count := Count + 1, is used as a means of counting the number of times the loop is executed. The instruction simply adds 1 to the variable, Count, each time the instructions within the loop are repeated. The true/false expression on line *18* in the while statement uses the *relational operator*, >, meaning 'greater than', to compare Amount with ROGUEVALUE. There are in fact six different relational operators that can be used in such logical expressions, and these are shown in Table 29.4.

relational operator	meaning
>	Greater than
> =	Greater than or equal to
<	Less than
< =	Less than or equal to
=	Equal to
< >	Not equal to

Table 29.4. *Relational operators used in logical expressions*

The operators in Table 29.4 are used according to the relationship to be established between two values. Whatever logical expression is used, the result of the comparison will either be true or false - if true, the while loop will repeat; if false the loop will terminate. More examples of the use of these operators are provided in the next section, which deals with the use of logical expressions in making program decisions.

Decisions

Suppose a program is required to display multiple-choice questions with one correct answer out of three possible choices. For example, one of the questions could be:

```
A BYTE is the name given to

    (a)  Four bits
    (b)  Eight bits
    (c)  Sixteen bits

Your answer is:
```

The program is also required to display the message

```
Correct - well done!
```

if the answer is correct, and display a message such as

```
Sorry, the correct answer is (b)
```

if the answer provided is incorrect.

The program must therefore be able to take two alternative courses of action depending on the answer supplied. An if statement is one possible way of achieving this requirement. The appropriate form of the if statement is illustrated in Listing 29.9 which shows the Pascal code required to display the question above and provide the response appropriate to the letter 'a', 'b' or 'c', typed in.

Listing 29.9.   Using an if statement

```
1        program Decisions1(input,output);
2          {Program to illustrate the use of the if statement}
3        var
4          Answer       :char;
5        begin
6          writeln('Enter the letter corresponding to the ');
7          writeln('correct answer for the following question:');
8          writeln;
9
10         writeln('A BYTE is the name given to');
11         writeln('(a) Four bits');
12         writeln('(b) Eight bits');
13         writeln('(c) Sixteen bits');
14         writeln;
15         write('Your answer is: ');
16         readln(Answer);
17
18         if Answer = 'b' then
19           writeln('Correct - well done!')
20         else
21           writeln('Sorry, the correct answer is (b)');
22       end.
```

The if statement extending over lines *18* to *21* shows how the program can take one of two possible courses of action depending on the value of a variable. We saw in the last section concerning the use of the while statement that logical expressions are either true or false. This is also the case with the logical expression Answer = 'b' in the if statement on line *18*. If the letter stored in the character variable Answer is the letter 'b', then the logical expression Answer = 'b' will be true, otherwise it will be false. If it is true, the statement following the word then is executed (that is, line *19*), otherwise the statement after else is executed (that is, line *21*).

The general form of the if statement is

```
if {logical expression} then
    {statement 1}
else
    {statement 2}
```

Note that {statement 1} is the instruction that is performed if {logical expression} is true; {statement 2} is performed if {logical expression} is false. Note also that either {statement 1} or {statement 2}, or both of them, can be a block of instructions enclosed between begin and end as follows.

```
if Answer = 'b' then
    writeln('Correct - well done!')
```

```
      else
        begin
          writeln('Sorry, the correct answer is (b)');
          writeln('There are eight bits in a byte');
        end;
```

Sometimes it is necessary to choose between more than just two courses of action in a program. For example, Listing 29.10 shows a program which converts a percentage mark to a pass, merit, distinction or fail grade. The program repeatedly accepts marks and converts them to grades until the mark entered is the rogue value –1 (or any negative integer value) signifying the end of the mark inputs. The rules that are used to determine the grade are as follows:

> *For a distinction the mark must be over 80.*
> *For a merit the mark must be greater than or equal to 60 and less than 80.*
> *For a pass the mark must be greater than or equal to 40 and less than 60.*
> *Below 40 is a fail.*

Listing 29.10. The if..else if construction

```
1      program Decision2(input, output);
2      const
3        DIST     =80;
4        MERIT    =60;
5        PASS     =40;
6
7      var
8        Mark       :integer;
9
10     begin
11       writeln;
12       write('Please enter the first mark(-1 to end): ');
13       readln(Mark);
14
15       while Mark >=0 do
16       begin
17         if Mark >= DIST then
18           writeln('Distinction')
19         else if (Mark >= MERIT) and (Mark < DIST) then
20                 writeln('Merit')
21             else if (Mark >= PASS) and (Mark < MERIT) then
22                     writeln('Pass')
23                 else writeln('Fail');
24         write('Please enter the next mark(-1 to end): ');
25         readln(Mark);
26       end;
27     end.
```

The if statement between lines *17* and *23* reflects this logic exactly. It is possible to chain if statements in this way to cope with quite complex lines of reasoning. Added flexibility is provided by the use of the logical and operator used for the the logical expressions on lines *19* and *21*. The and operator requires that both of the minor logical expressions it connects are true for the complete logical expression to be true. If either or both are false, then the whole expression is false. Logical operators are discussed in more detail in the next section.

Here is a typical output from the program:

```
Please enter the first mark(-1 to end):46 ⏎
Pass
Please enter the next mark(-1 to end):68 ⏎
Merit
Please enter the next mark(-1 to end):32 ⏎
Fail
Please enter the next mark(-1 to end):83 ⏎
Distinction
Please enter the next mark(-1 to end):-1 ⏎
```

Logical operators

Logical operators allow you to combine logical expressions. There are three logical operators in Pascal : and, or and not. An example of the use of the and operator was provided in Listing 29.10. The and and the or operators are always placed between two logical expressions, and they each combine these logical expressions to produce a value of true or false. Table 29.5 shows the rules that are applied by Pascal to determine whether a compound logical expression is true or false. This type of table is usually called a *truth table*.

(Expr 1)	(Expr 2)	(Expr 1) or (Expr 2)	(Expr 1) and (Expr 2)
true	true	true	true
true	false	true	false
false	true	true	false
false	false	false	false

Table 29. 5. *Truth table for the and and or logical operators*

Referring back to Listing 29.10 in the previous section, on line *19*, where the compound logical expression (Mark >= MERIT) and (Mark < DIST) is used to determine whether the mark is equivalent to a merit grade. In the expression, (Mark >= MERIT) is an example of (Expr 1) and (Mark < DIST) is an example of (Expr 2) shown in Table 29.5. The next table (Table 29.6) shows how the and operator combines these two logical expressions for a number of cases.

Mark	(Mark > = MERIT)	(Mark < DIST)	(Mark > = MERIT and (Mark < DIST)
45	false	true	false
86	true	false	false
67	true	true	true

Table 29. 6. *Truth table for the and logical operator.*

Thus, both logical expressions must be true for the complete expression to be true; with the or operator, however, only one of the expressions needs to be true for the complete expression to be true. For example, consider the program in Listing 29.11 which reads some text and counts how many vowels it contains. The program uses a for loop to test each letter in turn in the text against each possible vowel. If the current letter is a vowel, that is 'a', 'e', 'i', 'o' or 'u', a count is incremented.

Listing 29.11.   Illustrating the use of the or logical operator

```
1        program Vowels(input, output);
2        var
3          VowelCount        :integer;
4          Letters           :string[80];
5          LengthOfText      :integer;
6          c                 :integer;
7        begin
8          VowelCount:= 0;
9          writeln('Type text followed by ENTER: ');
10         readln(Letters);
11         LengthOfText:= length(Letters);
12
13         for c:= 1 to LengthOfText do
14           if (Letters[c] = 'a') or
15              (Letters[c] = 'e') or
16              (Letters[c] = 'i') or
17              (Letters[c] = 'o') or
18              (Letters[c] = 'u')
19         then
20            VowelCount:= VowelCount + 1;
21
22            writeln;
23            writeln('The text contained ', VowelCount, ' vowels');
24       end.
```

The text is held in a string variable called Letters. Each letter in Letters is accessed by specifying its position within the text. For example, if the text entered was the string 'hello there', then Letters[1] is the letter 'h', Letters[2] is the letter 'e', Letters[3] is the letter 'l', and so on. The for loop control variable, c, starts at 1 and goes up in steps of 1 to the length of the string (11 for the string 'hello there'). The length of the string is determined by the pre-defined Pascal function length(), on line *11*, which requires a string as its single argument. (See the later section on Pascal functions for more detail about functions).

Here is the output from the program when the string, 'the cat sat on the mat' is typed in:

```
Type text followed by ENTER: the cat sat on the mat ⏎

The text contained 6 vowels
```

Note that the program will only work with lower-case text. The reason is that lower-case letters 'a', 'b', 'c', etc are represented in a computer using a different set of codes from the equivalent upper-case letters 'A', 'B', 'C', etc.

The third logical operator is the not operator which simply reverses the logical value of a logical expression. Thus, the logical expression not (x > 3) is true only when x is less than or equal to 3. Similarly, the logical expression not (Balance <= 0) is true only when Balance has a value that is greater than zero. The truth table shown in Table 29.7 defines the operation of the not logical operator.

Expr	not Expr
true	false
false	true

Table 29.7. *Truth table for* not *logical operator*

More control statements

Listing 29.12 draws together two further Pascal control statements, namely the repeat..until and the case statements using a progam which allows you to convert Pounds Sterling into one of three foreign currencies: American Dollars, German Marks or French Francs. The repeat..until statement provides a third method of constructing a loop. It is similar to the while statement in that it uses a logical condition to determine when to exit the loop, but the difference is that the condition appears at the end rather than at the beginning of the loop. This means that the loop will be executed at least once, which is appropriate for this example in which the loop repeatedly executes instructions which display a menu and ask the user to choose one of the menu options. In this example, the repeat statement repeats the statements between lines *13* to *63* until the condition following the word until is true, that is, when the user enters the letter 'X' or 'x' to indicate the desire to exit the program.

Listing 29.12.   Using the case and repeat statements in a menu program.

```
1      program menu1(input, output);
2      uses CRT;
3      const
4         DOLLARS    =1.5;
5         MARKS      =3.4;
6         FRANCS     =11;
7      var
8         Choice     :char;
9         Currency   :real;
10        Pounds     :real;
11     begin
12       repeat
13         clrscr;
14         writeln('Currency conversion program');
15         writeln;
16         writeln('(M)arks');
17         writeln('(D)ollars');
18         writeln('(F)rancs');
19         writeln('e(X)it');
20         writeln;
21         write('Which currency do you want to convert to Pounds? ');
22         readln(Choice);
```

```
23          writeln;
24
25          case Choice of
26             'D', 'd':
27                  begin
28                    writeln('Enter the amount to convert to Dollars');
29                    readln (Pounds);
30                    Currency:=Pounds*DOLLARS;
31                    writeln('You would get ',Currency:0:0,
32                            ' Dollars for',Pounds:0:0, ' Pounds');
33                    writeln('Press ENTER to return to the menu');
34                    readln;
35                  end;
36             'M', 'm':
37                  begin
38                    writeln('Enter the amount to convert to Marks');
39                    readln(Pounds);
40                    Currency:=Pounds*Marks;
41                    writeln('You would get ',Currency:0:0,
42                                ' Marks for ',Pounds:0:0, ' Pounds');
43                    writeln('Press ENTER to return to the menu');
44                    readln;
45                  end;
46             'F', 'f':
47                  begin
48                    writeln('Enter the amount to convert to Francs');
49                    readln(Pounds);
50                    Currency:= Pounds*FRANCS;
51                    writeln('You would get ',Currency:0:0,
52                            ' Francs for ',Pounds:0:0, ' Pounds');
53                    writeln('Press ENTER to return to the menu');
54                    readln;
55                  end;
56             'X', 'x':
57                  writeln('Exiting program..');
58             else
59                  begin
60                    writeln('Invalid option. Please try again');
61                    writeln('Press ENTER to return to the menu');
62                    readln;
63                  end;
64
65       until (Choice = 'X') or (Choice = 'x');
66    end.
```

The case statement is an alternative method to the if statement for choosing between alternative courses of action wihin a program. It has the following general format:

```
case {variable name} of
    value list 1: statement 1;
    value list 2: statement 2;
    etc...
      ......
else statement N
end;
```

The variable name after the word case can be of type integer, character or boolean, but string and real variables *are not allowed*. Pascal matches the value of the variable against the values specified on the subsequent lines; when a match is found, the corresponding statement is executed after which the case statement is immediately exited without considering any remaining values. If there are no values that match the variable, the case statement does nothing unless the else option is used, in which circumstances, the supplied statement (shown as statement N above) is executed. Note that some versions of Pascal may not support the use of the else option: you may need to consult the language manual for your version of Pascal. In Listing 29.12, the case statement is used to select the block of statements corresponding to the menu option chosen by the user. The user can choose one of four options using the letters 'D', 'M', 'F' or 'X'; to allow for the possibility of either upper or lower case letters being entered, both are included in the case statement value lines. Here are some program fragments which should help to clarify the use of the case statement:

Example 1

```
var
  Month, Days   :integer;
.......
.......
case Month of
    1, 3, 5, 7, 8, 10, 12   :Days:= 31;
    4, 6, 9, 11             :Days:= 30;
    2                       :Days:= 28;
end;
```

Month contains a number corresponding to the month of the year, where January = 1, February = 2 ..... December = 12. The case statement is used to store, in the variable, Days, the number of days in the month whose number is stored in Month. Thus if Month contained the number 8 corresponding to August, Days would be assigned the value 31.

Example 2

```
var
  Smoker :boolean;
......
......
case Smoker of
    true :writeln('Smoking seriously damages your health!');
    false :writeln('Good for you!');
end;
```

If the boolean variable, Smoker, has been assigned a value of true prior to the case statement, the health warning will be displayed, otherwise the complimentary message 'Good for you!' will be displayed. This is equivalent to using the if statement

```
if Smoker then
  writeln('Smoking seriously damages your health!')
else
  writeln('Good for you!');
```

Note that it is because Smoker is a boolean variable having a value of true or false, that it can be used as a logical expression in an if statement as illustrated above.

Example 3

```
var
  Letter :char
  VowelCount :integer;
  ConsonantCount :integer;
  .....
  .....
case Letter of
  'a', 'e', 'i', 'o', u : VowelCount:= VowelCount + 1;
  'A', 'E', 'I', 'O', 'U' : VowelCount:= VowelCount + 1;
  ',', '.', ';', ':', '(', ')', ' ':{No action required}
else ConsonantCount:= ConsonantCount + 1;
end;
```

Here the program adds one to a vowel count if Letter contains either an upper or lower case letter; otherwise it adds one to a consonant count. Punctuation marks, brackets and spaces are ignored. Note that using if statements to perform this task would be much more difficult.

Arrays

An *array* is a data structure which allows you to store a number of items of data without having to allocate separate variable names to them. Arrays, like all other identifiers, must be declared before they are used. For example, the following declaration is for an array of five integers:

```
var
  Array1    :array[1..5] of integer;
```

This single declaration is in effect defining five variables called Array[1], Array[2], Array[3], Array[4] and Array[5], each of which can store a single integer value. The integer value inside the square brackets is called the array's index, and it is allowed only to take the range of values specified in the declaration (1 to 5 inclusive in this example). Each of these identifiers can be used just like any ordinary integer variable. For instance, to set each of them to zero could be accomplished as follows:

```
Array[1]:= 0;
Array[2]:= 0;
Array[3]:= 0;
```

```
      Array[4] := 0;
      Array[5] := 0;
```

However, we could accomplish the same operation by using an integer variable as an *index* and by putting a single assignment statement in a for loop:

```
      for i:= 1 to 5 do Array[i] := 0;
```

Now the count variable i takes on the integer values 1 to 5 and again each element in the array is set to zero. The obvious advantage of using a variable for an index is that arrays can then be used very effectively within loops, and they allow the manipulation of as many or as few numbers as appropriate to the task in hand; notice that the same for loop could initialise 5000 array elements as easily as 5 elements:

```
      for i:= 1 to 5000 do Array[i] := 0;
```

This would be an exceedingly difficult task to accomplish without the use of an array.

Listing 29.13 illustrates the use of an array of real numbers. The program reads five numbers into an array and then finds the position within the array of the smallest number. It then swaps this number with the first number in the list before displaying the re-ordered array.

Listing 29.13.   Using an array.

```
1      program TopList(input, output);
2      uses CRT;
3      const
4         MAXNUMS      =5;
5      var
6         Array1       :array[1..MAXNUMS] of real;
7         Temp         :real;
8         i            :integer;
9      begin
10        clrscr;
11        writeln('Enter ', MAXNUMS, ');
12        writeln;
13        for i:= 1 to MAXNUMS do
14          begin
15            write('Enter number ', i, ' and press ENTER :');
16            readln(Array1[i]);
17          end;
18        for i:= 2 to MAXNUMS do
19          if Array1[i] < Array1[1] then
20            begin
21                Temp:= Array1[1];
22                Array1[1]:= Array1[i];
23                Array1[i]:= Temp;
24            end;
```

```
25      writeln;
26      writeln('The new list is as follows:');
27      for i:= 1 to MAXNUMS do write(Array1[i]:10:2);
28   end.
```

Line *2* contains a non-standard statement which allows you to clear the screen by using the pre-defined *procedure* clrscr shown on line *10*. You may have to omit these two lines if you are not using Turbo Pascal. Note that *procedures* and the uses statement are discussed later.

The program first defines a constant MAXNUMS to be the maximum size of the real array, Array1. Lines *11* to *17* are to read in the ten numbers with appropriate user prompts. Thus the first number is read into Array1[1], the second into Array1[2], and so on up to the last number which is read into Array1[10]. The second for loop starting on line *18* compares each number in the array in turn with the first number; if one is found that is greater than the first, they are swapped over. By the time the last number in the array has been compared with the first one, the largest number is in the first position in the array.

A typical output from the program might be as follows:

```
Enter 5 numbers

Enter number 1 :5.7 ⏎
Enter number 2 :3.9 ⏎
Enter number 3 :9.1 ⏎
Enter number 4 :1.7 ⏎
Enter number 5 :98.4 ⏎


The new list is as follows: 1.7   3.9   9.1   5.7   98.4
```

As a final example in this section on arrays, Listing 29.14 shows a program which uses a random number generator to select five lottery numbers in the range 1 to 49.

Listing 29.14.   Using random numbers and an array to generate lottery numbers

```
1      program Lottery(input, output);
2      uses CRT;
3
4      const
5         NUMOFNUMS      =5;
6         MAXNUM         =49;
7      var
8         LuckyNums      :array[1..MAXNUM] of integer;
9         Num            :integer;
10        i              :integer;
11        Count          :integer;
12
13     begin
14        clrscr;
```

```
15        writeln('Lottery random number generator');
16        writeln;
17
18        randomize;
19
20        for i:= 1 to MAXNUM do LuckyNums[i]:= 0;
21
22        for Count:= 1 to NUMOFNUMS do
23          begin
24            Num:= random(MAXNUM + 1);
25            while LuckyNums[Num] <>  0 do
26                 Num := random(MAXNUM + 1);
27
28            LuckyNums[Num]:= Num;
29            write(Num:5);
30          end;
31
32        writeln;
33        writeln;
34        write('Press ENTER to exit program');
35        readln;
36      end.
```

The random numbers are generated using the pre-defined function random(N) which produces a random number in the range specified by its single integer argument, N, within the brackets. For example, random(11) would produce a random number between 1 and 10 inclusively. Thus the statement

```
Num:= random(MAXNUM + 1);
```

assigns a random number between 1 and 49 to the variable Num. The randomize instruction on line *18* simply initialises the random number generator so that it does not produce the same sequence of random numbers every time the program is run. Line *20* initialises each element to zero in the array LuckyNums[] which is to be used to store the five random numbers. The reason for the while loop on lines *25* and *26* is to ensure that the same random number is not used more than once. The loop keeps generating random numbers until it finds one that has not been generated previously. For instance, if the first random number generated on line *24* was the number 36, then this would be stored in Num. The while loop will only generate another random number if Luckynums[36] contains zero, showing that 36 has not previously been generated. As soon as the while loop finds an empty slot, the number is stored in the array and immediately displayed on the screen. The process repeats until five different numbers have been generated.

Pre-defined procedures and functions

High-level languages almost invariably provide libraries of useful pre-written programs that are available to the programmer. These programs, which are often termed *pre-defined procedures* and *functions*, have previously been written, compiled and thoroughly tested so that they can be used by programmers with confidence that they are error-free.

In Turbo Pascal such libraries of programs are declared with the nonstandard instruction, uses, followed by the name the library file, or *unit*, as it is called. We have already used a unit called Crt containing the procedure clrscr which was used to clear the display screen Some library programs require you to provide information in the form of *parameters* at the time they are called. An example of such a program is the delay(T) procedure which requires you to supply a delay, T, in milliseconds inside the brackets. Functions always return an item of information when they are used. For example, in Listing 29.14 we saw that the function random(N) returned to the calling program a random number in the range 1 to N-1, where N is an integer value. Whatever the version, however, Pascal always provides a number of *standard procedures* and *functions* which are available without the need to declare them in programs. They comprise procedures and functions which are considered to be the most frequently used. It was noted earlier that readln, write and writeln are in fact such standard procedures, rather than instructions such as for and if which are integral parts of the Pascal language. Turbo Pascal keeps the standard procedures and functions, plus quite a few more, in a library unit called System which is automatically available when a program is compiled. Pascal's standard functions are described at the end of this chapter, and in addition we have provided further descriptions of a selection of procedures and functions that are available in some of Turbo Pascal's other units.

Simple user-defined procedures

Procedures are often called *subprograms* or *subroutines* because they form only part of a complete program. We saw in the previous section that Pascal provides a number of pre-written functions and procedures that you can use in your own programs, but it is also possible for you to write your own. These are called *user-defined* procedures and functions.

A Pascal procedure is very similar to a Pascal program, the main difference being that a procedure cannot stand by itself - it must form part of another program. Like identifiers such as constants and variables, procedures must also be declared at the beginning of the program before they are used. The structure of a program containing two procedures, called Procname1 and Procname2, would have the outline structure shown in Listing 29.15.

Listing 29.15.   The structure of a program containing two procedures.

```
1    program Progname(input, output);
2    const
3       {Progname constants are declared here}
4    var
5       {Progname variables are declared here}
6
7    procedure Procname1;
8    const
9       {Procname1 constants are declared here}
10   var
11      {Procname1 variables are declared here}
12   begin
13      {Procname1 code goes here}
14   end;
15
16   procedure Procname2;
```

```
17    const
18       {Procname2 constants are declared here}
19    var
20       {Procname2 variables are declared here}
21    begin
22       {Procname2 code goes here}
23    end;
24    begin
25       . . . . . . . .
26       . . . . . . . .
27       Procname1;
28       . . . . . . . .
29       . . . . . . . .
30       Procname2;
31       . . . . . . . .
32    end.
```

The two procedure definitions, shown in the shaded sections of the program, appear after the constants and variables declarations of the main program. The definitions of the procedures look exactly like a main program, each having their own constants and variables declarations (if required) and their own main code between begin and end.

The program in Listing 29.16 illustrates the use of simple procedures to cycle through three rudimentary pictures of faces in order to give the appearance of a face winking alternate eyes. The program uses three procedures, Face1, Face2 and Face3, each of which uses keyboard characters to display a face. The procedures are executed in the main program by simply naming them. Thus line *36* Face1 causes the instructions in procedure Face1 to be executed. The program then continues with line *37* delay(500), a pre-defined procedure which causes a delay of 500 milliseconds.

Listing 29.16.   Using procedures to make a face wink.

```
1     program Winker(input, output);
2     uses CRT;
3     var
4        i      :integer;
5
6     procedure Face1;
7     begin
8        clrscr;
9        writeln('    _ _   ');
10       writeln('  < o o > ');
11       writeln('   | ^ |  ');
12       writeln('    \_/   ');
13    end;
14
15    procedure Face2;
```

```
16    begin
17      clrscr;
18      writeln('    _ _    ');
19      writeln(' < 0 o > ');
20      writeln('  | ^ |  ');
21      writeln('   \_/   ');
22    end;
23
24    procedure Face3;
25      begin
26      clrscr;
27      writeln('    _ _    ');
28      writeln(' < o 0 > ');
29      writeln('  | ^ |  ');
30      writeln('    \_/    ');
31      end;
32
33    begin
34    for i:= 1 to 10 do
35      begin
36        Face1;
37        delay(500);
38        Face2;
39        delay(500);
40        Face1;
41        delay(500);
42        Face3;
43        delay(500);
44      end;
45    end.
```

Each of the procedures uses the pre-defined `clrscr` procedure to clear the screen so that the face stays in the same place and appears to wink. Notice that the logic of the main program is easy to follow by the use of procedures - this is one of their major advantages. Another feature of this program is that although the procedure `Face1` is used twice, the code required for it appears only once in its definition. This economical use of program code is another major advantage of using procedures in programs.

Global vs local variables

Earlier we said that a procedure is allowed to have its own `var` declarations. When this is the case, the variables declared in the procedure are termed *local* variables. This means that these variables only have values while the procedure is being executed; once the procedure has been completed and control has returned to the main program, local variables cannot be accessed. On the other hand, *global* variables which are defined in the main program are always available, even to procedures, while the program is running. Note, however, that if a variable declared in a procedure has the same name as a variable declared in the main program, the local variable only, can be used in the procedure. These ideas are best illustrated with the aid of an example such as that shown in Listing 29.17.

Listing 29.17.   A program to illustrate the difference between global and local variables

```
1      program Scope(input, output);
2      uses CRT;
3      var
4        Greeting1      :string[20];
5
6      procedure Proc1;
7      var
8        Greeting1      :string[20];
9      begin
10       Greeting1:= 'How do';
11       writeln('Proc1':15, 'Greeting1':15, 'local ':15, Greeting1:15);
12     end;
13
14     procedure Proc2;
15     var
16       Greeting2      :string[20];
17     begin
18       Greeting2:= 'Hi ';
19       writeln('Proc2':15, 'Greeting2':15, 'local ':15, Greeting2:15);
20       writeln('Proc2':15, 'Greeting1':15, 'global':15, Greeting1:15);
21     end;
22
23     begin
24       clrscr;
25       writeln('Source':15, 'Variable':15, 'Scope':15, 'Value':15);
26       writeln;
27       Greeting1:= 'Hello ';
28       writeln('Main ':15, 'Greeting1':15, 'global':15, Greeting1:15);
29       Proc1;
30       Proc2;
31     end.
```

The program declares three string variables: Greeting1 which is a global variable defined on line *4*, Greeting1 a variable local to procedure Proc1 and declared on line *8*, and finally Greeting2, a local variable declared in Proc2 on line *16*. The main program assigns a value ('Hello') to Greeting1 on line *27* and displays it. Then, when Proc1 is executed, the local variable Greeting1 is assigned a different value ('How do') on line *10* and then displays that string. Finally, when Proc2 is executed, it displays the contents of the local variable Greeting2 followed by the global variable Greeting1. Note that an attempt to include a line such as

```
writeln(Greeting2);
```

after line *30* in the main program would result in an error since, once Proc2 has terminated, the local variable Greeting2 does not exist. Here is what the program produces as its output:

Source	Variable	Scope	Value
Main	Greeting1	global	Hello
Proc1	Greeting1	local	How do
Proc2	Greeting2	local	Hi
Proc2	Greeting1	global	Hello

Each line of the output indicates the source of the line, that is whether it is generated from the main program or from a procedure, the name of the variable whose value is being displayed, whether the variable is local or global, and the contents of the variable.

Using parameters in procedures

The 'wink' program shown in Listing 29.16 uses the simplest form of procedure which performs a task without any need to communicate with the main program. However, there will be many instances when you will want to use information available in the main program. As we saw in the previous section, global variables provide one means of accomplishing this, but for sound reasons current programming practice discourages the use of global variables for this purpose. Usually a much better method is to use procedures which have either *value parameters* or *variable parameters*.

Value parameters

Listing 29.18 is a modification of the program shown in Listing 29.16. Notice that another procedure, Wink(), has been included. This new procedure uses a *value parameter*, called Eye, which is defined within brackets after the procedure name on line *34*. A value parameter allows you to pass a value to a procedure from the main program or from another procedure. Thus, on line *47*, the value of the for loop variable k is passed to the procedure Wink. k takes the values 1, 2 and 3 which are used to decide which of the three procedures, Face1, Face2 or Face3 to execute. In effect, this causes each of the latter three procedures to be executed in turn. The outer for loop makes this cycle of three procedures to repeat ten times. When one loop is controlled by an outer loop in this fashion, they are called *nested loops*.

Listing 29.18.   A program to illustrate the use of value parameters

```
1      program Winker2(input, output);
2      uses CRT;
3      var
4          i      :integer;
5          k      :integer;
6
7      procedure Face1;
8      begin
9        clrscr;
10       writeln('   _ _    ');
11       writeln(' < 0 0 > ');
12       writeln('  | ^ |  ');
13       writeln('   \_/   ');
```

```
14    end;
15
16    procedure Face2;
17    begin
18      clrscr;
19      writeln('    _ _    ');
20      writeln(' < 0 o > ');
21      writeln('  | ^ |  ');
22      writeln('   \_/   ');
23    end;
24
25    procedure Face3;
26      begin
27      clrscr;
28      writeln('    _ _    ');
29      writeln(' < o 0 > ');
30      writeln('  | ^ |  ');
31      writeln('   \_/   ');
32      end;
33
34    procedure Wink(Eye:integer);
35    begin
36      case Eye of
37        1 :Face1;
38        2 :Face2;
39        3 :Face3;
40      end;
41    end;
42
43    begin
44    for i:= 1 to 10 do
45      for k:= 1 to 3 do
46        begin
47          Wink(k);
48          delay(500);
49        end;
50    end.
```

The number of parameters that you can use in a procedure is not limited to one - you can use as many as you like as long as you declare them in the procedure definition and include them within the brackets when you call the procedure from the main program. For example, suppose that we wanted to include the pre-defined delay procedure on line *48* within the procedure Wink() as shown in the program fragment below.

```
procedure Wink(Eye:integer, Time:integer);
begin
  case Eye of
```

```
        begin
          1 :begin
                   Face1;
                   delay(Time);
               end;
          2 :begin
                   Face2;
                   delay(Time);
               end;
          3 :begin
                   Face3;
                   delay(Time);
               end;
      end;
```

Now Wink() has two value parameters and these would both be included in any call to the procedure, as shown in the example below.

```
        for i:= 1 to 10 do
              for k:= 1 to 3 do Wink(k, 500);
```

An important point about value parameters is that they provide a *one-way transfer of information* from the main program to a procedure. Variables used as value parameters when a procedure is called are unaffected by any processing that has occurred within the procedure; this is not the case, however, with *variable parameters*.

Variable parameters

Listing 29.19 is an example of a program which incorporates a procedure that uses a variable parameter.

Listing 29.19.   A program to illustrate the use of variable parameters.

```
1      program VarParam(input, output);
2      var
3        Smaller     :real;
4        Larger      :real;
5
6      procedure Sort(var a, b:real);
7      var
8        Temp        :real;
9      begin
10       if a > b then
11         begin
12            Temp:= a;
13            a:= b;
14            b:= Temp;
15         end;
```

```
16    end;
17
18    begin
19      write('Enter two numbers: ');
20      readln(Smaller, Larger);
21      Sort(Smaller, Larger);
22      write('The sorted numbers are: ');
23      writeln(Smaller:10:2, Larger:10:2);
24    end.
```

The program simply sorts two numbers into ascending order of magnitude using a procedure. The procedure has two variable parameters, a and b, which it compares: if a is greater than b, the values in a and b are swapped over. The main program asks the user to enter two numbers, it calls the procedure using the two numbers stored in Smallest and Largest, and then displays them when the procedure has finished. Here is a typical run of the program:

```
Enter two numbers: 34.6 17.32 ⏎

The sorted numbers are: 17.32 34.6
```

Notice that the values contained in Smallest and Largest, which were exchanged in the procedure using the variables a and b, have been swapped over. Thus, *variable parameters allow a two-way exchange of data* between a program and a procedure.

User-defined functions

As well as being able to write your own procedures you can also devise your own functions. Functions also accept value or variable parameters, but in addition they require that you declare what type of value they return. So, for a function, you would need to write its first line using the following format:

```
function FunctionName(parameters):return type;
```

In addition, you must assign the return value to FunctionName somewhere within the function. For example, for a function called TriangleType which accepts three positive real numbers, in ascending order of magnitude, representing the three sides of a triangle and which returns an integer value of 0, 2 or 3 indicating how many of its sides are equal, the function definition in Listing 29.20 might be appropriate.

Listing 29.20.   A function to determine the type of triangle represented by three numbers

```
20    function TriangleType(a, b, c:real):integer;
21    var
22      Count      :integer;
23    begin
24      Count:= 0;
25      if a = b then Count:= Count + 1;
26      if b = c then Count:= Count + 1;
27      if c = a then Count:= Count + 1;
28      case Count of
```

```
29        0 :TriangleType:= 0;
30        1 :TriangleType:= 2;
31        2 :{not possible}
32        3 :TriangleType:= 3;
33     end;
34   end;
```

The three sides are passed as value parameters to the variables a, b and c. The if statements on lines *25* to *27* increment Count if any two sides are the same. The values that Count can assume are 0 for no sides equal, 1 if two sides are equal and 3 if all three sides are equal; a value of 2 is not possible when the three sides are arranged in ascending order of magnitude. The number of equal sides is stored in TriangleType by the case statement and it is this value which is returned by the function to the calling program. Note that because a function always returns a value it can be used like a variable in an arithmetic expression or in a logical expression or in a write statement. For example, it would be perfectly valid to write

```
if TriangleType(x, y, z) = 3 then writeln('Equilateral triangle');
```

Writing programs using procedures and functions

Listing 29.21 illustrates the use of user-defined procedures and functions in a program which allows two people to use the computer to play noughts and crosses. The program illustrates the use of procedures and functions appropriate to a variety of situations. The main program alternately gets X and O moves, checking each time for a winning or drawn position. The program terminates when someone has won or after nine moves have been made.

Listing 29.21.   Noughts and crosses game

```
1    program Oxo(input, output);
2
3    {-------------------------------------------------------------------}
4    {A program which makes use of functions and procedures to allow two }
5    {players to play noughts and crosses. The computer checks for a win }
6    {or draw automatically, and ensures that illegal moves are not made. }
7    {The board is a grid numbered 1 to 9. Each Player in turn selects a  }
8    {number and the grid is redrawn with the X or O in that position.    }
9    {X always starts first.                                             }
10   {-------------------------------------------------------------------}
11
12   uses CRT; {The screen handling unit to allow the screen to be cleared}
13
14   var
15      Grid       :array[1..9] of char;
16      Move       :integer;
17      Count      :integer;
18      Winner     :boolean;
19      XMove      :boolean;
20
21   procedure InitGrid;
22   {-------------------------------------------------------------------}
```

```
23  {This sets up the board with the positions numbered from 1 to 9       }
24  {--------------------------------------------------------------------}
25
26  begin
27    Grid[1]:='1';
28    Grid[2]:='2';
29    Grid[3]:='3';
30    Grid[4]:='4';
31    Grid[5]:='5';
32    Grid[6]:='6';
33    Grid[7]:='7';
34    Grid[8]:='8';
35    Grid[9]:='9';
36  end;
37
38  procedure DrawGrid;
39  {--------------------------------------------------------------------}
40  {This draws the current board after every move                       }
41  {--------------------------------------------------------------------}
42
43  begin
44    clrscr;
45    writeln(' ',Grid[1], ' | ', Grid[2], ' | ', Grid[3]);
46    writeln('---|---|---');
47    writeln(' ',Grid[4], ' | ', Grid[5], ' | ', Grid[6]);
48    writeln('---|---|---');
49    writeln(' ',Grid[7], ' | ', Grid[8], ' | ', Grid[9]);
50    writeln;
51  end;
52
53  function CheckMove(Move:integer):boolean;
54  {--------------------------------------------------------------------}
55  {This validates every move to make sure that a number from 1 to 9 is }
56  {chosen and that the selected position is not already occupied by an }
57  {X or O.                                                             }
58  {Parameters: Move - integer value parameter                          }
59  {Return value: boolean - true if valid move, false if invalid move   }
60  {--------------------------------------------------------------------}
61
62  begin
63    CheckMove:= true;
64    if (Move 1) or (Move  9)
65    then begin
66            writeln('Invalid position - enter number between 1 and 9');
67            CheckMove:= false;
68         end
69    else if (Grid[Move] = 'X') or (Grid[Move] = 'O')
70         then begin
71                 writeln('This position has already been used');
72                 CheckMove:= false;
```

```
73                    end;
74    end;
75
76    function GetXmove:integer;
77    {---------------------------------------------------------------------}
78    {This accepts the X move from the player. If the move is invalid, the}
79    {player is required to enter the move again.                         }
80    {Parameters: None                                                   }
81    {Return value: Integer in the range 1 to 9                          }
82    {---------------------------------------------------------------------}
83    var
84      Xpos            :integer;
85      ValidXMove      :boolean;
86    begin
87      repeat
88        writeln;
89        writeln('Enter position( 1 to 9 ) for X move');
90        readln(Xpos);
91        ValidXMove:= CheckMove(Xpos);
92      until ValidXMove;
93      GetXmove := Xpos;
94    end;
95
96    function GetOmove:integer;
97    {---------------------------------------------------------------------}
98    {This accepts the O move from the player. If the move is invalid, the}
99    {player is required to enter the move again.                         }
100   {Parameters: None                                                   }
101   {Return value: Integer in the range 1 to 9                          }
102   {---------------------------------------------------------------------}
103   var
104     Opos            :integer;
105     ValidOMove      :boolean;
106   begin
107     repeat
108       writeln;
109       writeln('Enter position( 1 to 9 ) for O move');
110       readln(Opos);
111       ValidOMove:= CheckMove(Opos);
112     until ValidOMove;
113     GetOmove:= Opos;
114   end;
115
116   function CheckForWinner :boolean;
117   {---------------------------------------------------------------------}
118   {This checks for a line of Xs or Os in one of the 7 possible ways    }
119   {It determines whether a row, column or diagonal contains the same   }
120   {character (ie an X or an O).                                        }
121   {Parameters: None                                                   }
122   {Return value: Boolean - true if there is a winner, false otherwise  }
```

```
123  {-------------------------------------------------------------------------}
124
125  begin
126    if  (Grid[1]=Grid[2]) and (Grid[2]=Grid[3]) or
127        (Grid[4]=Grid[5]) and (Grid[5]=Grid[6]) or
128        (Grid[7]=Grid[8]) and (Grid[8]=Grid[9]) or
129        (Grid[1]=Grid[4]) and (Grid[4]=Grid[7]) or
130        (Grid[2]=Grid[5]) and (Grid[5]=Grid[8]) or
131        (Grid[3]=Grid[6]) and (Grid[6]=Grid[9]) or
132        (Grid[1]=Grid[5]) and (Grid[5]=Grid[9]) or
133        (Grid[3]=Grid[5]) and (Grid[5]=Grid[7])
134    then
135        CheckForWinner:= true
136    else CheckForWinner:= false;
137  end;
138
139  begin   {Main program }
140    InitGrid;           {Call procedure to initialise the board }
141    Count:= 0;          {Counts the number of valid moves made  }
142    Winner:= false;     {Boolean variable which becomes true     }
143                                {when there is a winner           }
144    XMove:= true;       {Keeps track of whose move it is:         }
145                                {true for X move                  }
146                                {false for Y move                 }
147    DrawGrid;           {Display the initial board position       }
148
149    {Loop to repeat the playing sequence                          }
150    while (Count < 9) and not Winner do
151      begin
152        case XMove of
153        true:                  {Do this if it is X's move         }
154              begin
155                Move:= GetXmove;  {Get the X move position        }
156                Grid[Move]:='X';  {Store it in the data structure}
157                XMove:= false;    {Make it O's move next          }
158              end;
159        false:                 {Do this if it is O's move         }
160              begin
161                Move:= GetOmove;  {Get the O move position        }
162                Grid[Move]:= 'O'; {Store it in the data structure}
163                XMove:= true;     {Make it X's move next          }
164              end;
165        end;
166
167        Count:= Count + 1;        {Increment count after every move}
168
169        DrawGrid;                 {Show the current board position }
170
171        {Check to see if the game is a win or draw                }
172        Winner:= CheckForWinner;
```

```
173     if Winner
174       then writeln('End of Game:', Grid[Move], ' has won')
175     else if Count=9
176         then writeln('A draw');
177     end;
178
179     readln;
180 end.
```

The two procedures, InitGrid and DrawGrid, and the four functions, CheckMove, GetXMove, GetYMove and CheckForWinner, used in the program are described in the following sections.

InitGrid

This procedure initialises the character array, Grid[], which is a global array used throughout the program by every procedure and function. The procedure is used once only and does not require any parameters.

DrawGrid

This procedure draws the current board position. Initially the board is displayed like this:

```
     1 | 2 | 3
    ---|---|---
     4 | 5 | 6
    ---|---|---
     7 | 8 | 9
```

The numbers are replaced by Xs and Os as the game progresses.

CheckMove

This function has a single integer value parameter called Move which represents the current player's choice of board position. The function first checks that the integer is in the range 1 to 9 before checking the contents of Grid[Move] to ensure that the position is not already occupied with an X or an O. If the move is valid, the function returns a boolean value of true, otherwise it returns false. CheckMove is used by the following two functions.

GetXMove

This function asks the X player to type in a number from 1 to 9 representing a board position. If the move is valid, the function terminates and the position entered by the player is returned as an integer value; if the move is invalid (see function CheckMove) the player is requested to try again.

GetOMove

This function asks the O player to type in a number from 1 to 9. Otherwise it is structurally identical to GetXMove.

CheckForWinner

This function checks individually the three rows, three columns and two diagonals, to see that they contain the same character. If one of these lines does contain the same character, then one of the players has won. For example, if the diagonal represented by `Grid[1]`, `Grid[5]` and `Grid[9]` all contain an X, then the X player has won.

Advantages of using procedures and functions

All good programmers make full use of procedures and functions, and in fact their use is essential to the development of all but the most trivial programs. There are a number of good reasons for making this statement, including the following: (i) they allow a large, complex program to be built up from a number of smaller of more manageable units. This facilitates a team approach to program development by allowing each unit to be written and tested independently of the rest of the program; (ii) they can reduce the amount of code required for a program. Once a subprogram has been developed, it can be used as many times as required within a program using the same code; (iii) they can reduce the amount of time required to write a program if libraries of re-usable functions and procedures are available. This is much the same as building electronic circuits using standard electronic components.

Screen handling

Turbo Pascal's `CRT` unit contains a number of useful screen handling functions and procedures. We have already used two of the procedures in the unit: `clrscr` to clear the screen and `delay()` to make the computer pause while executing a program. More functions and procedures in the `CRT` unit are described below.

Window procedure

Defines a text window on the screen. The syntax of the procedure is

`Window(X1,Y1,X2,Y2)` where the four parameters are explained by the following diagram.

To set a text window containing ten lines at the top of the screen use

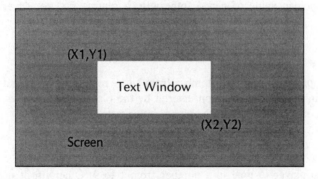

```
window(1,1,80,10)
```

To return the current window to the full screen size use

```
window(1,1,80,25)
```

ClrEol procedure

Clears all characters from the cursor position to the end of the line without moving the cursor. It uses the current text window.

DelLine procedure

Deletes the line containing the cursor in the current text window.

GotoXY procedure

Moves the cursor to X, Y, where X is the column and Y is the row relative to the top left corner of the current window which has the coordinates (1, 1). Thus to move the cursor to row 5, column 10, you would use GotoXY(10,5).

InsLine procedure

Inserts a line in the current text window, above the line that the cursor is on.

TextColor procedure

This sets the colour for subsequently displayed text. There are sixteen colours and you can specify each one by name or by using the equivalent number as shown in the Table 29.8. Thus, to set the text colour to red, you could use either TextColor(Red) or TextColor(4).

By using the pre-defined constant, blink, you can make the text flash, for example, TextColor(Blue + Blink).

colour	value	colour	value	colour	value	colour	value
Black	0	Red	4	DarkGray	8	LightRed	12
Blue	1	Magenta	5	LightBlue	9	LightMagenta	13
Green	2	Brown	6	LightGreen	10	Yellow	14
Cyan	3	LightGray	7	LightCyan	11	White	15

Table 29.8.

TextBackGround procedure

This allows you to set one of sixteen different colours for the text background. The colours are shown in the table. Thus to set the background colour to light grey you could use either TextBackGround(Light-Gray) or TextBackGround(7).

Note that if you clear the screen using clrscr after setting the background colour, the whole of the current text window will change to that colour.

Example program 1

The example shown in Listing 29.22 illustrates the use of text windows and text colours by drawing random windows of different colours.

Listing 29.22.   Using text windows

```
1      program Screen1(input,output);
2
3      {--------------------------------------------------}
4      {Illustrates some screen handling facilities by   }
5      {drawing randomly sized and coloured windows      }
6      {--------------------------------------------------}
7
8      uses CRT;
9      var
10        x       :integer;
11        y       :integer;
12        i       :integer;
13
14     begin
15       textbackground(Black);{Clear screen            }
16       clrscr;
17
18       for i:= 1 to 100 do
19         begin
20         {Draw random windows                         }
21           x := Random(60);      {Random x position    }
22           y := Random(15);      {Random y position    }
23           window(x, y, x + Random(10), y + Random(8));
24           textbackground( Random(16) + 1);
25           clrscr;      {Set window to random colour   }
26                                 {in the range 1 to 16 }
27           delay(200); {Pause for 200 millisecs        }
28         end;
29
30     end.
```

KeyPressed and Readkey

Two other useful functions to be found in Turbo Pascal's CRT unit are KeyPressed and ReadKey. KeyPressed returns a boolean value of true if there is a character in the keyboard buffer and false if the buffer is empty. The keyboard buffer is simply an area of memory which is used to store, temporarily, characters entered through the keyboard. KeyPressed can therefore be used to detect any use of the keyboard. A common application of KeyPressed is as a means of terminating a loop, as illustrated by the following program fragment.

```
repeat
      {instructions to be repeated}
until keypressed;
```

Each time through the repeat loop `KeyPressed` tests the keyboard buffer: if a key has been pressed, the keyboard buffer will have at least one entry, `KeyPressed` returns `true` and the loop terminates, otherwise `KeyPressed` returns `false` and the loop repeats once more.

`Readkey` allows you to capture a keystroke by reading the first character in the keyboard buffer. If the keyboard buffer is empty, it waits until a character is available and then returns its value. The advantage of using `ReadKey` rather than `read` or `readln` is that it is not necessary to press ⏎.

Example program 2

The program shown in Listing 29.23 echoes only numeric characters to the screen, ignoring characters that are not in the range 0 to 9. The repeat loop terminates as soon as the space bar is pressed.

Listing 29.23. Using readkey.

```
1    program EchoNumbers(input,output);
2    {-------------------------------------------------------------}
3    {Program to display numeric digits entered at keyboard and to}
4    {ignore any other characters typed. The program terminates   }
5    {when the space bar is pressed.                              }
6    {-------------------------------------------------------------}
7
8    uses CRT;
9
10   var
11     key     :char;
12
13   begin
14     repeat
15       key:= readkey;
16       if (key = '0') and (key '9') then write(key);
17     until key = ' ';
18   end.
```

Sound and NoSound

Finally, these two procedures allow you to use your computer's built-in speaker. `Sound(Pitch)` causes the speaker to emit a tone whose pitch is determined by the integer parameter, `Pitch`. Thus, `Sound(500)` produces a tone with pitch 500Hz. `NoSound` terminates the tone produced by `Sound`. Thus to produce a tone of 300Hz for half a second within a program you could use:

```
sound(300);
delay(500);
nosound;
```

Example program 3

As a final example Listing 29.24 uses all of the screen handling functions and procedures discussed in a program which measures how quickly you are able to press a key after being given a signal.

Listing 29.24. Screen handling example.

```
1    program reflexes(input, output);
2
3    {----------------------------------------------------------------}
4    {A program to illustrate some screen handling facilities.        }
5    {The user is invited to test his/her reflexes by pressing a key  }
6    {as quickly as possible. The average of three attempts is        }
7    {calculated and displayed in millisecond units.                  }
8    {----------------------------------------------------------------}
9
10   uses crt;
11   const
12     ROW           =2; {The row base position for screen text        }
13     COLUMN        =5; {The column base position for screen text     }
14
15   var
16     i             :integer; {A for loop control variable            }
17     Total         :integer; {The total time for the three attempts  }
18   {.............................oOo................................}
19
20   procedure FlushKeyboardBuffer;
21
22   {----------------------------------------------------------------}
23   {This makes sure that there are no characters in the standard     }
24   {input buffer. The function readkey removes a single character    }
25   {from the keyboard buffer. Keypressed is true while there is at   }
26   {least one character in the buffer                                }
27   {----------------------------------------------------------------}
28
29   var
30     key :char;
31
32   begin
33     while keypressed do
34       key:= readkey;
35   end;
36   {.............................oOo................................}
37
38   procedure PressAnyKey;
39
40   {----------------------------------------------------------------}
41   {A procedure that waits until a key is pressed before            }
42   {continuing with the next instruction                            }
43   {----------------------------------------------------------------}
```

```
44
45  begin
46    FlushKeyboardBuffer;        {Ensure that the keyboard buffer is  }
47                                    {empty                              }
48    repeat until keypressed;  {Do nothing until a key is pressed   }
49  end;
50  {...........................oOo...............................}
51
52  procedure instructions;
53
54  {-----------------------------------------------------------------}
55  {Displays the instructions for using the program                  }
56  {-----------------------------------------------------------------}
57
58  begin
59    window(10,10,70,20);        {Define the text window            }
60    textcolor(yellow);          {Text colour set to yellow         }
61    textbackground(blue);       {Background text clour is blue     }
62    clrscr;
63    gotoxy(COLUMN, ROW);
64    writeln('Put your finger on any key and as soon as');
65    gotoxy(COLUMN, ROW+1);
66    writeln('this window changes colour, press it');
67    gotoxy(COLUMN, ROW+3);
68    writeln('You will get three tries and the program');
69    gotoxy(COLUMN, ROW+4);
70    writeln('will calculate your average response time');
71    gotoxy(COLUMN +5, ROW+6);
72    write('Press any key to begin');
73    PressAnyKey;
74  end;
75  {........................oOo...............................}
76
77  function Time(attempt:integer):integer;
78
79  {-----------------------------------------------------------------}
80  {Uses the delay() procedure to determine the response time in  }
81  {milliseconds required for hitting the space bar.              }
82  {-----------------------------------------------------------------}
83
84  var
85    Millisecs :integer;
86
87  begin
88    clrscr;
89    textcolor(yellow);
90    gotoxy(COLUMN, ROW);
91    case attempt of
92      1:write('First attempt starting..');
93      2:write('Second attempt starting..');
```

```pascal
 94       3:write('Third attempt starting..');
 95     end;
 96     randomize;                {Initialise the random number generator }
 97
 98     Millisecs:= 0;
 99     delay(1000);              {Pause for one second before timing   }
100       textcolor(red + blink);
101       write(' NOW!');
102       delay(random(5000));    {Random delay of up to 5 seconds      }
103       FlushKeyboardBuffer;    {Make sure that there are no           }
104                               {characters in the keyboard buffer    }
105       textbackground(Red);
106       clrscr;                 {The signal to press the space bar    }
107
108       repeat
109         delay(1);
110         Millisecs:= Millisecs + 1;{Count how many millisecs expire}
111       until keypressed; {Look for user hitting any key }
112       Time:= Millisecs; {Return time taken to respond }
113     end;
114 {...........................oOo...........................}
115
116 procedure Results(Average:real);
117
118 {-----------------------------------------------------------}
119 {Displays the average time taken over the three attempts     }
120 {-----------------------------------------------------------}
121
122 begin
123     textbackground(LightGray);
124     textcolor(Black);
125     clrscr;
126     gotoxy(COLUMN, ROW);
127     write('Your average response time was ', Average:5:0,
128             ' milliseconds');
129     gotoxy(COLUMN, ROW + 5);
130     write('Press any key to continue');
131     PressAnyKey;
132 end;
133
134 begin
135     Total:= 0; {Set the total time to 0 }
136     for i:= 1 to 3 do          {Repeat the trial three times       }
137     begin
138       Instructions; {Display the user instructions }
139       Total:= Total + Time(i);{Accumulate time for each trial     }
140     end;
141     Results(Total/3);          {Display result of the three trials}
142 end.
```

The main program starts on line *134*. The procedure Instructions explains that the user is to press a key as quickly as he/she can when a rectangular window changes colour. The function Time() times how long it took to do so in milliseconds. This time is added to a running total which accumulates the times for three attempts. Results() displays the average time the user took to respond. The program makes good use of user-defined functions and procedures, and the comments in the program Listing 29.24 explain their operation, but it is worth adding some further explanation regarding the procedure PressAnyKey and associated functions and procedures. As mentioned earlier, the buffer memory associated with the keyboard temporarily stores the values of key depressions made while the program is running, and these values can be accessed using the ReadKey function which extracts the first available character in the buffer. By repeatedly using this function to read single characters until there are no more left in the buffer, FlushKeyboard-Buffer empties the buffer in preparation for using the KeyPressed function. This is to ensure that KeyPressed will detect only the next key depression and not any that have been made previously.

Records and files

Many computer applications involve processing data which has already been stored as a *file* on a backing storage medium such as magnetic disk. A file is often organised as a sequential collection of *records*, each one containing information about the subject of the file. For example, a car file might contain details of a number of different cars, each record dealing with a single car and containing such information as make, model, engine capacity, number of doors, colour, insurance group, extras, and so on. *Sequentially* organised files contain records which can only be accessed in the order in which they were originally stored in the file, whereas *randomly* organised files contain records which can be accessed in any order. However, since standard Pascal provides facilities for processing sequential files only, the example programs in this section do not deal with Turbo Pascal's procedures and functions for processing randomly organised files.

Before we examine some file handling methods, however, it is necessary to discuss *user-defined data types*.

User-defined data types

As you know by now, every variable used in a program must be associated with a data type. Up to now the data types that we have used have been integer, real, char, boolean, string[] and array[]. However, Pascal allows us to create our own data types based on these. For example, suppose that within a program we wanted to use two similar arrays of integers, each containing ten elements. Then we could declare them as follows:

```
var
    List1 :array[1..10] of integer;
    List2 :array[1..10] of integer;
```

Another method of achieving exactly the same result is to use type to define a new data type called List, and then use it to declare the variables List1 and List2:

```
type
    List = array[1..10] of integer;
var
    List1, List2 :List;
```

The type declaration can also be used in conjunction with the reserved word record to define a more complicated data structure. For example, to define a Car type we could write

```
type
     Car = record
               Make  :string[15];
               Model :string[20];
               InsGp :integer;
               Cost  :real;
           end;
```

and now we can declare variables to be of type `Car`:

```
var
          SportsCar, FamilyCar, HatchBack :Car;
```

In order to identify a variable (or *field*) within the record we must use the *dot notation*. For instance, to store information in the record variable, `SportsCar`, we could use the following instructions:

```
write('Make of car? ');
readln(SportsCar.Make);
write('Model? ');
readln(SportsCar.Model);
write('Insurance Group? ');
readln(SportsCar.InsGp);
write('Cost? ');
readln(SpotrsCar.Cost);
```

The field within the record is specified after the dot; this allows a number of related items to be grouped together as a unit (that is, as a *record*), while still allowing each part (or *field*) to be accessed separately. Now, to define a collection, or *file*, of such records, we need to use the reserved word `file`:

```
type
     Car = record
               Make  :string[15];
               Model :string[20];
               InsGp :integer;
               Cost  :real;
             end;
     Cars = file of Car;
var
     Hondas :Cars;
     Fords  :Cars;
```

The type, `Cars`, is defined as a file of `Car` records and this allows us to assign this file type to our own identifiers `Hondas` and `Fords`. The programs in the following sections illustrate how files defined like this may be created, read and searched.

Creating a sequential file using `assign`, `rewrite` and `write`

The main program starting at line *59* in Listing 29.25 shows how a sequential file of car details can be created. The program shows that an `assign` statement is used to link the name of the file within the program (`CarFile`) with the name of the actual file stored on magnetic disk (`FileName`). The name of the disk file has been defined earlier in the program as the string constant 'a:\cars.dat'. This means that when write instructions are used later to store car records in the file, the data will be recorded using the filename 'a:\cars.dat'. Once this link between the internal and external files has been established in the program, it is then necessary to open the file for *output* using rewrite(CarFile). This tells the system that the file, CarFile, is to be created.

Listing 29.25 Creating a sequential Car file.

```
1    program CreateFile(input, output);
2    {------------------------------------------------------------}
3    {A program which creates a car file containing a number of car}
4    {records.                                                     }
5    {------------------------------------------------------------}
6    uses CRT;
7
8    const
9      FileName = 'a:\Cars.dat';          {The name of the file on disk}
10
11   type
12     Car =  record                        {The structure of each record}
13                 Make       :string[10];
14                 Model      :string[10];
15                 InsGp      :integer;
16               Cost :real;
17              end;
18     Cars = file of Car;
19
20   var
21     CarRec      :Car;
22     CarFile     :Cars;
23     Answer      :char;
24
25   procedure GetRec(var CarRec:Car);
26   {------------------------------------------------------------}
27   {Gets and returns the data for a single record.              }
28   {------------------------------------------------------------}
29
30   begin
31     clrscr;
32     writeln;
33     writeln('Please enter Car details as follows:');
34     writeln;
35     write('Make(eg Ford): ');
36     readln(CarRec.Make);
37     writeln;
28     write('Model(eg Escort): ');
```

```
39      readln(CarRec.Model);
40      writeln;
41      write('Insurance Group(eg 7): ');
42      readln(CarRec.InsGp);
43      writeln;
44      write('Cost(eg 8450.50): ');
45      readln(CarRec.Cost);
46      writeln;
47    end;
48
49    procedure WriteRec(var File1:Cars; Rec1:Car);
50    begin
51      writeln;
52      write('OK to save this record?(Y/N) ');
53      readln(Answer);
54      if upcase(Answer) = 'Y' then
55        write(File1, Rec1);        {Writes the record           }
56      writeln;
57    end;
58
59    begin
60      assign(CarFile, Filename); {Links CarFile with the actual}
61                                 {file held on backing storage.}
62      rewrite(CarFile);          {Opens the file for output     }
63      repeat
64        GetRec(CarRec);          {Gets the Car details          }
65        WriteRec(CarFile, CarRec);
66        write('Add another record to the file?(Y/N)');
67        readln(Answer);
68      until upcase(Answer)   'Y';
69
70      close(CarFile);            {Closes the file               }
71    end.
```

Most of the remainder of the program is within a loop which repeats the following sequence of operations:

1. Get the details for a car record, `CarRec` - this is accomplished using the procedure `GetRec` which asks the user to type in the appropriate information and returns the car record using a variable parameter.

2. Store the record obtained by the procedure `GetRec`. The procedure `WriteRec` first asks for confirmation before writing the record to the file. The whole record and the appropriate file are both passed as parameters; `Rec1` is defined as a value parameter of type `Car` record but the file *must* be passed as a *variable* parameter. The format for the instruction to write a record to a file is similar to the familiar `write` instruction we have used many times before; the difference is that the first item in the brackets must be the internal name of the file. Note that the function `upcase` has been used

to force the user's answer to be an uppercase letter because the `if` instruction on line *54* compares the answer typed in with the capital letter 'Y' only.

3. Ask the user if he/she wishes to add another record to the file. The program loop terminates when the user answers 'Y' to the question.

Finally, the `close(CarFile)` statement tells the system that no more records are to be added to the car file. It is important to note that if the file is now re-opened using `rewrite`, more records *can not be appended to the existing ones*; the file must be completely *recreated* since `rewrite` effectively causes the named file to be destroyed. Later in this chapter we describe a program which does allow you to add more records to a file.

The output from the program is shown below:

```
Please enter Car details as follows:

Make(eg Ford): Honda ⏎
Model(eg Escort): Civic ⏎
Insurance Group(eg 7): 5 ⏎
Cost(eg 8450.50): 8100 ⏎

OK to save this record?(Y/N) y ⏎
Add another record to the file?(Y/N) n ⏎
```

Reading a file using `assign`, `reset` and `read`

Whether a file is being created or read the same assign command must be used to link the internal and external file names. Thus before attempting to read the car file created by the previous program it is first necessary to use `assign(CarFile, Filename)` again. This appears on line *32* of Listing 29.26.

Listing 29.26. Reading the Car file.

```
1     program File2(input,output);
2     {----------------------------------------------------------}
3     {A program which reads a car file and displays and         }
4     {prints its contents.                                      }
5     {----------------------------------------------------------}
6
7     uses CRT,
8          PRINTER;                    {To allow output to be printed}
9
10    const
11       FileName = 'a:\cars.dat';
12
13    type
14       Car = record                       {The record structure    }
15                    Make    :string[10];
16                    Model   :string[10];
```

```
17                  InsGp    :integer;
18                   Cost    :real;
19              end;
20      Cars = file of Car;
21   var
22      CarFile       :Cars;
23      CarRec        :Car;
24
25   begin
26     clrscr;
27     writeln;
28     writeln('Reading ', FileName, ' ....' );
29     writeln;
30     assign(CarFile, FileName); {Links CarFile to the actual }
31                                {file held on floppy disk     }
32     reset(CarFile); {Open file for input }
33     while not eof(CarFile) do  {Keep reading until no        }
34                                {records are left             }
35       begin
36         read(CarFile, CarRec);
37         writeln(CarRec.Make:12,
38                   CarRec.Model:12,
39                   CarRec.InsGp:4,
40                   CarRec.Cost:10:2);{Display record on the screen}
41         writeln(LST, CarRec.Make:12,
42                   CarRec.Model:12,
43                   CarRec.InsGp:4,
44                   CarRec.Cost:10:2); {Print record           }
45       end;
46     writeln;
47     writeln('End of ', Filename);
48     close(CarFile);                {Close the file           }
49     writeln;
50     write('Press <Enter> to continue');
51     readln;
52   end.
```

The reset instruction is used to *open a file for input*, that is, to enable it to be read. The records within the file are accessed using a read instruction which contains the name of the file to be read and the name of the record which is to receive the data obtained from the backing storage device: read(CarFile, CarRec). Once the data has been read from the file it is displayed using a writeln instruction which uses the dot notation to separate the fields within the car record. The while loop uses the eof (end of file) function to determine whether there are any more records left to be read from the file; when the end of the file is detected, the eof function returns a boolean value of true, otherwise it returns false. Thus the logical expression not eof(CarFile) has a value of true while there are more records to be read, and it has a value of false when the end of the file is reached.

Here is a typical ouput from the program:

```
Reading a:\cars.dat ...

        Ford        Escort       7       8450.50
        Ford        Fiesta       5       7200.00
        Ford        Probe       10      11000.00
        Honda       Civic        5       8100.00
        Honda       Prelude      9       9900.00
         VW         Golf        11      10200.00
         Vw         Polo         8       8400.00
       Nissan       Micra        5       6500.00
      Vauxhall      Corsa        5       6400.00
      Vauxhall      Cavalier     8       9500.00
        Fiat        Uno          4       5900.45
      Ferrari       Dino        16      25000.00
      Ferrari       Daytona     16      35500.00

   End of a:\cars.dat
```

Another of Turbo Pascal's units, `Printer`, contains procedures to enable information to be printed. Line *41* in Listing 29.26 shows that by using `LST` at the beginning of the `writeln` instruction, the same results that are displayed on the screen can also be output to a printer connected to the computer.

Extending a file

There is no direct way in standard Pascal to extend a file that has already been created. However, there is a relatively easy way to overcome this shortcoming. The solution is to adopt the following scheme:

1. Make a copy of the file by reading each record and then copying them to a temporary file. The original file is therefore opened for input and the copy file is opened for output. After all of the records have been copied, the original file is closed but the temporary file is left open so that more records can be added to it.

2. The new records that are to be added to the original file are each read and then immediately written to the copy file. The copy file is closed when all of the new records have been stored.

3. The copy file is then opened for input and all of the records in it are written to the original file thus, in effect adding the new records to it.

The program shown in Listing 29.27 does exactly this. Understandably, the program makes use of a number of procedures that also appeared in Listing 29.25, a previous program to create the car file. The main additional procedure is called `DuplicateFile` which copies one file into another. It takes two variable parameters called `SourceFile` (the file to be copied) and `DestFile` (the file to which the records are to be copied). This means that the same procedure can be used to make a temporary copy of the original car file and also to transfer the new extended file in the copy back to the original file.

Listing 29.27.   Extending the Car file.

```
1      program File3(input,output);
2      {-------------------------------------------------------------}
3      {Appends a number of records to the end of a file.            }
4      {-------------------------------------------------------------}
5
6      uses CRT,
7
8      const
9        FileName = 'a:\cars.dat'; {The name of the file on disk   }
10       CopyName = 'a:\copy.dat'; {The copy file name             }
11
12     type
13       Car = record                {The structure of each record   }
14                     Make    :string[10];
15                     Model   :string[10];
16                     InsGp   :integer;
17                     Cost    :real;
18                  end;
19       Cars = file of Car;
20
21     var
22       CarFile     :Cars;
23       Copy        :Cars;
24       CarRec      :Car;
25       Count :integer;
26       Answer :char;
27
28     procedure DuplicateFile(var SourceFile, DestFile:Cars);
29     var
30       Count :integer;
31
32     begin
33       reset(SourceFile);          {Open source file for input   }
34       rewrite(DestFile);          {Open copy file for output    }
35       Count :=0;                  {Record count variable        }
36
37       while not eof(SourceFile) do {Keep reading until no more   }
38                                    {records left }
39         begin
40           read(SourceFile, CarRec);
41           write(DestFile, CarRec);
42           Count:= Count + 1;
43         end;
```

```
44
45      writeln;
46      write('Finished : ');
47      writeln(Count, ' records copied');
48
49    end;
50
51    procedure GetRec(var CarRec:Car);
52    {----------------------------------------------------------------}
53    {Gets and returns the data for a single record.                  }
54    {----------------------------------------------------------------}
55
56    begin
57      clrscr;
58      writeln;
59      writeln('Please enter Car details as follows:');
60      writeln;
61      write('Make(eg Ford): ');
62      readln(CarRec.Make);
63      writeln;
64      write('Model(eg Escort): ');
65      readln(CarRec.Model);
66      writeln;
67      write('Insurance Group(eg 7): ');
68      readln(CarRec.InsGp);
69      writeln;
70      write('Cost(eg 8450.50): ');
71      readln(CarRec.Cost);
72      writeln;
73    end;
74
75    procedure WriteRec(var File1:Cars; Rec1:Car);
76    begin
77      writeln;
78      write('OK to save this record?(Y/N) ');
79      readln(Answer);
80      if upcase(Answer) = 'Y' then
81        write(File1, Rec1);    {Writes the record              }
82      writeln;
83    end;
84
85    begin
86      assign(CarFile, FileName);
87      assign(Copy, CopyName);
88      clrscr;
```

```
89
90      writeln('Copying ',FileName, ' to ', CopyName,'...');
91      DuplicateFile(CarFile, Copy);
92      writeln;
93
94      repeat
95        GetRec(CarRec);          {Gets the Car details          }
96        WriteRec(Copy, CarRec); {Writes the record to the file  }
97        write('Add another record to the file?(Y/N)');
98        readln(Answer);
99      until upcase(Answer)  'Y';
100
101     writeln('Copying ',CopyName, ' to ', FileName,'...');
102    ' DuplicateFile(Copy, CarFile);
103     writeln;
104     writeln('Press <Enter> to continue');
105     readln;
106
107     close(CarFile);
108     close(Copy);
109   end.
```

Notice that in this program two files, the original and the temporary copy, are open at the same time, but when one of them is open for output, the other is always open for input. The output from the program is shown next.

```
Please enter Car details as follows:

Make(eg Ford) : Honda ⏎
Model(eg Escort) : Civic ⏎
Insurance Group(eg 7) : 5 ⏎
Cost(eg 8450.50) : 8100 ⏎

OK to save this record?(Y/N) y ⏎
Add another record to the file?(Y/N) n ⏎
Copying a:\copy.dat to a:\Cars.dat...
Finished : 14 records copied

Press <Enter> to continue
```

Searching a file

Searching a sequential file for certain records involves opening the file for input and then reading each record in turn and checking to see if it meets some criteria. For example, we might want to search the car file in order to extract all the cars made by Ford, or we might just want to find a particular car, such as a Fiat Uno. The program in Listing 29.28 allows the user to specify an approximate car price and then it searches the car file for all cars that cost within £1000 of the price entered. For example, if the user entered £8000, the program would print out all cars that cost between £7000 and £9000.

Listing 29.28.   Searching the Car file.

```
1     program File4(input,output);
2     {----------------------------------------------------------}
3     {A program which reads a car file and displays details of  }
4     {cars which are within £1000 of a specified price          }
5     {----------------------------------------------------------}
6
7     uses CRT;
8
9     const
10      FileName = 'a:\cars.dat';      {The name of the file on disk}
11
12    type
13      Car = record                   {The structure of each record}
14                 Make     :string[10];
15                 Model    :string[10];
16                 InsGp    :integer;
17                 Cost     :real;
18             end;
19      Cars = file of Car;
20
21    var
22      CarFile      :Cars;
23      CarRec       :Car;
24      Price        :real;
25
26    begin
27      clrscr;
28      writeln;
29      write('Enter the approximate price of cars to be listed: ');
30      readln(Price);
31      writeln;
32      writeln('Cars which are within £1000 of £', Price:0:0, ' :');
33      assign(CarFile, FileName);     {Links CarFile to actual file }
34                                     {held on floppy disk          }
35      reset(CarFile);                {Open file for input          }
36      while not eof(CarFile) do      {Read until no records left   }
37        begin
38           read(CarFile, CarRec);
39           if (CarRec.Cost >= Price - 1000) and
40                (CarRec.Cost <= Price + 1000) then
```

```
41                  writeln(                 {Display record on screen   }
42                      CarRec.Make:12,
43                      CarRec.Model:12,
44                      CarRec.InsGp:4,
45                      '£':3,CarRec.Cost:0:0);
46          end;
47      writeln;
48      writeln('End of ', Filename);
49      close(CarFile); {Close the file }
50      writeln;
51      write('Press <Enter> to continue');
52      readln;
53   end.
```

As you might expect, this program is very similar to the program which read and displayed the contents of the car file. The instruction which is used to identify and display the required records starts on line *39*:

```
if (CarRec.Cost >= Price - 1000) and
      (CarRec.Cost <= Price + 1000) then
      writeln(                 {Display record on screen }
              CarRec.Make:12,
              CarRec.Model:12,
              CarRec.InsGp:4,
              '£':3,CarRec.Cost:0:0);
```

The if statement contains two conditions connected by the and operator; if the cost of the car (Car-Rec.Cost) is both greater than Price - 1000 *and* less than Price + 1000, in other words within £1000 of Price, then the current record is displayed. The writeln instruction has been split over several lines for clarity. The output from the program is shown below:

```
Enter the approximate price of cars to be listed: £8000 ⏎
Cars which are within £1000 of £8000 :

        Ford Escort    7    £8451
        Ford Fiesta    5    £7200
        Honda Civic    5    £8100
        VW Polo        8    £8400

End of a:\cars.dat

Press <Enter> to continue
```

Reference section

This section describes a number of Pascal's standard functions and some of the additional functions provided by Turbo Pascal.

Standard Pascal functions

abs

Returns the absolute, that is unsigned, value of a real or integer value.

Examples

If x is a real variable then

    1.   x:= abs(-3.7)   gives   x = 3.7

    2.   x:= abs(24.3)   gives   x = 24.3

If i is an integer variable then

    3.   i:= abs(-6)   gives   i = 6

    4.   i:= abs(3.232)

        is not allowed since the type of the returned value (real) is not the same as the type of the argument (integer).

exp

Returns the exponential of the argument, that is e^a, where a is the value of the parameter supplied in brackets and e is a mathemetical constant approximately equal to 2.72.

Example

If x is a real variable then

    x:= exp(2)   gives   x = 7.39 (that is, $x=e^2$)

ln

Returns the natural logarithm of the argument, that is, the inverse of the exp function.

Example

If x is a real variable then

    x:= ln(7.39)   gives   x = 2

sqr

Returns the square of the argument, that is x^2, where x is the argument.

Examples

If x is a real variable then

 1. x := sqr(-3.1) gives x = 9.61

 2. x := sqr(3.1)   gives x = 9.61

If i is an integer variable then

 3. i := sqr(-6)   gives i = 36

 4. i := sqr(3.232

   is not allowed since the type of the returned value (real) is not the same as the type of the argument (integer).

Sqrt

Returns the square root of the operand, that is √x, where x is a positive valued argument.

Examples

If x is a real variable then

 1. x := sqrt(16.3) gives x = 4.04

 2. x := sqrt(-16.3) is not allowed since x is negative

If i is an integer variable then

 3. i := sqrt(16)   gives i = 4

 4. i := sqrt(-16) is not allowed since i is negative

sin

Returns the sine of the argument which must be in radians.

Example

Since 1 radian = $\dfrac{180}{\pi}$ degrees, to convert an angle from degrees to radians we must divide the angle by $\dfrac{180}{\pi}$ where $\pi \approx 3.1416$

Thus, if x is a real variable and we want the sine of 30^0, then

$$x := \sin(30/(180/3.1416)) \quad \text{gives} \quad x = \text{sine}(30^0) = 0.5$$

cos

Returns the cosine of the argument which must be in radians. See sin above for converting degrees to radians.

Example

If x is a real variable and we want the cosine of 30^0, then

$$x := \cos(30/(180/3.1416)) \quad \text{gives} \quad x = \text{cosine}(30^0) \approx 0.87$$

Note that the `sin` and the `cos` functions can be used together for finding the tangent of an angle, since $\tan \theta = \sin \theta / \cos \theta$

arctan

Returns the arc tangent of the argument in radians. This is the inverse of finding the tangent of an angle.

Example

If x is a real variable and we want to find the arc tangent of 1 then

$$x := \arctan(1)*(180/3.1416) \quad \text{gives} \quad x = \text{arctangent}(1) = 45^0$$

round

Returns the nearest integer type value to the real type value provided.

Examples

If i is an integer variable then

1. `i := round(34.3)`   gives $i = 34$

2. `i := round(34.8)`   gives $i = 35$

trunc

Converts a real type value to an integer type value by removing the fractional part of the real value.

Examples

If i is an integer variable then

1. `i := trunc(34.3)`   gives $i = 34$

2. `i := trunc(34.8)`   gives $i = 34$

3. `i := trunc(.975)`   gives $i = 0$

ord

This gives the ASCII numeric value for characters.

Examples

If c is an integer variable then

1.   `c:= ord('a')`   gives   c = 97

2.   `c:= ord('A')`   gives   c = 65

3.   `c:= ord('?')`   gives   c = 63

chr

Returns the character equivalent of a numeric code in the range 0 to 255

Examples

If c is an character variable then

1.   `c:= chr(97)`   gives   c = 'a'

2.   `c:= chr(65)`   gives   c = 'A'

3.   `c:= chr(230)`   gives   c = '?'

The following program prints the full character set:

```
program CharSet(input, output);
var
c :char;
i :integer;
begin
    for i:= 0 to 255 do
    writeln(i:10, chr(i):10);
end.
```

odd

Returns TRUE if the argument is an odd number and FALSE if it is an even number. The argument must be an integer. The sign of the argument is ignored.

Examples

If t is a boolean variable then

1.   `t:= odd(23)`   gives   t = TRUE

2.   `t:= odd(22)`   gives   t = FALSE

3.   `t:= odd(-23)`   gives   t = TRUE

4.   `t:= odd(0)`   gives   t = FALSE

3.   `t:= odd(7.5)`   is not allowed since the argument must be an integer.

Some Turbo Pascal functions

These functions are always available in Turbo Pascal and do not require a unit declaration.

Length

Returns the length of a string.

Example

If `s1:= '1234567'` and `len` is an integer variable then

　　　　`len:= length(s1)`   gives   len = 7;

Concat

Joins together a number of strings. The strings are provided as arguments to the function.

Examples

If string variables `s1`, `s2` and `s3` have the values

```
s1= 'One, two, three o clock '
s2= 'four o clock '
s3= 'rock'
```

and `s4` is another string variable then

　　　　`s4:= concat(s1, s2, s3)` gives s4= 'One, two, three o clock four o clock rock'

Copy

This allows a set of characters, or a *substring*, to be copied from a string. It has the form:

```
copy(Str, StartChar, NumOfChars)
```

where `Str` is the string from which the substring is to be copied,

`StartChar` is the position within `Str` from which to start copying and `NumOfChars` is how many characters are to be copied.

Examples

If s1 = 'Copy me please'

    1.   `s2:= copy(s1, 6, 2)`   gives   s2 = 'me'

    2.   `s3:= copy(s1, 1, length(s1))`   gives   s3 = 'Copy me please'

Pos

Returns the starting position of a substring within a string. Returns zero if the substring is not found.

Examples

    1.   `p:= pos('Koteikan, Windsor Tce' , ',')` gives   p=9

    2.   `p:= pos('abcde', 'z')`   gives   p=0

Upcase

Converts a letter to capitals, that is, upper case. Non letters are not affected.

Examples

    1.   `Capital:= upcase('x');`   gives   Capital='X'

    2.   `Capital:= upcase('X');`   gives   Capital='X'

    3.   `Capital:= upcase('3');`   gives   Capital='3'

    4.   `readln(Answer);`

    5.   `if upcase(Answer) = 'Y' then writeln('The Y key was pressed');`

(This is a good way to ensure that pressing both 'y' and 'Y' can be detected).

Random

Generates a random number in the range 0 to *n*-1 where *n* is the integer value supplied to the function.

Example

        `writeln(random(10) + 1)`

generates a random number between 1 and 10 inclusively.

Randomize

This is a procedure used in conjunction with random function described above. It initialises the random number generator using the system clock so that each time a program is run it does not generate exactly the same set of random numbers.

Chapter 30

C Programming

This chapter addresses the task of developing a piece of software using the programming language C. Here we look at C in enough depth for you to be able to develop your own simple programs, provided of course that you have access to a C compiler. Though the programs presented in this chapter were written and tested using Turbo C, they should work with any standard version of C. Turbo C was chosen because it provides an ideal, easy to use environment for developing programs since it combines in one package all the tools required for the task. For example, it has: (i) an *editor* for creating and editing source programs; (ii) a *compiler* to check the syntax of a program, to report and identify errors and to produce object code; (iii) a *linker* to produce executable code; (iv) a *debugger* to help with locating runtime errors; (v) a *file manager* to allow you to quickly save, retrieve and print source programs.

The structure of a C program

The C programming language allows a considerable amount of flexibility in the organization of a program but, as illustrated in Figure 30.1, we will use a form of organization that allows easy comparison with a Pascal program.

The #include files, which are defined at the beginning of a C program, allow you to include in the program C code which has been written previously. This means that useful or frequently required operations may be gathered together into a file and attached to another program before it is compiled. Almost invariably, at least one #include file will be defined here. The reason for this will be explained when we look at the first example program. Any global constants or variables are defined next. These are items of data which will be available to the main program and to every function defined in the program.

Figure 30.1. The general structure of a C program

```
                          #include files


                  Global identifier declarations


functionA()
{
    /*identifiers and code for functionA       */
}


functionB()
{
    /*identifiers and code for functionB       */
}
```

```
functionN()
{
    /*identifiers and code for functionN        */

void main()
{

    /*identifiers and code for main program     */

}
```

Subprograms, in the form of functions, are defined next. Unlike Pascal which allows the definition of procedures and functions, C allows only functions to be defined. However, a function need not return a value to the calling program, which means that such a function is, in effect, a procedure. The starting point for every C program is the function called main(). This is like the main program part of a Pascal program.

C is a very concise language compared to most high-level programming languages. It has only twelve keywords for programming statements, enough to allow programs to use the main types of control structures for loops, decisions and branching:

```
break    case    continue   default   do       else
for      goto    if         return    switch   while
```

However, C provides powerful facilities for extending the language by means of *function libraries*. These are files which contain pre-compiled subprograms, called *functions*, that may be used just like program statements. There are standard libraries for input/output, screen handling, graphics, mathematics and many other classes of operations. Programmers can also produce their own libraries tailored to their particular needs. Functions that are contained in libraries can be made available by declaring them in #include header files at the beginning of a program. Thus the line

```
#include <stdio.h>
```

placed at the beginning of a program makes a number of standard input/output functions available for use in the program. In the example programs that follow, you will frequently see the statements printf() and scanf() used; these are both examples of functions contained in the standard C library for input/output operations. This feature of being able to extend the language makes C very flexible and therefore ideal for the development of a wide range of different types of applications.

Program example1

As a simple example to illustrate these ideas, Listing 30.1 shows a program which calculates the total cost of a purchased item by calculating VAT and adding it to the price of the item. The algorithm on which the program is based is as follows:

1.   Ask the user to enter the price of the item

2.   Store the price

3. *Calculate the VAT at 17.5% (i.e. multiply the price by 0.175)*

4. *Calculate the total price by adding the VAT to the price*

5. *Display the total cost on the screen.*

Note that the line numbers preceding each line in the program are included in the example programs presented in this chapter only for ease of reference to specific lines when describing them. *Line numbers are not part of the C language and should not be included if you intend to compile and run the example programs.*

Listing 30.1.   Calculating the total cost of an item.

```
1    /* Program Example1 */
2    #include <stdio.h>
3    const float VAT=0.175;
4    void main()
5    {
6      float Price;
7      float Tax;
8      float TotalCost;
9
10       printf("Enter price of the item ");
11       scanf("%f", &Price);
12       Tax = Price * VAT;
13       TotalCost = Price + Tax;
14       printf("The Total cost is: %8.2f", TotalCost);
15   }
```

The operation of Example1 is as follows:

Line *1* is a comment line used to identify the program. It will be ignored by a C compiler.

Line *2* causes the compiler to include a file called stdio.h at the beginning of the program before it commences checking the program and converting it into object code.

Line *3* declares the variable VAT as being a real number constant with value 0.175.

Line *4* is the starting point of the program when it is executed. The significance of the word void will be discussed later. The executable instructions in main() are enclosed between { on line *5* and } on line *15*.

Lines *6* - *8* declare three *variables* Price, Tax and TotalCost each as being of type float. Variables are used to store data, which in this case are in the form of real numbers, that is, numbers which are not whole numbers. Every variable used in a C program must be declared in this way, with the type of the variable preceding its name.

Line *10* causes the message 'Enter price of the item' to be displayed on the screen.

Line *11* stores causes the computer to pause and accept numeric data typed in to be stored in the variable Price before continuing. The formatting string, `"%f"`, causes the data entered at the keyboard to be converted into a real number and stored in the variable Price.

Line *12* stores the result of Price multiplied by VAT in the variable Tax.

Line *13* stores the result of adding Price and Tax in TotalCost.

Line *14* then displays the text, 'The total cost is: ' followed by the value stored in TotalCost. The total cost is shown as a total of eight characters with two figures after the decimal point.

Some general remarks

Before going on to explore C in more depth, it is worth mentioning a few general points at this stage:

1. C is *case sensitive*, that is, it distinguishes between the use of capitals and lower-case letters. Thus it would regard Price, price and PRICE as being three different variables.

2. C uses the semicolon to indicate the end of an instruction, which is why you will see a semicolon at the end of most of the lines in a program. (You will quickly learn where a semicolon is not necessary). If you forget to terminate a complete instruction with a semicolon, the compiler will 'think' that the instruction is continued on the next line and, more often than not, it will say that there is an error in the next line.

3. It is a good idea to include comment lines (that is, text enclosed between '/*' and '*/') to describe the purpose of lines or sections of your program. Particularly for large, complex programs, this is very helpful if it is necessary to change the program at some later date.

4. Using spaces, blank lines and indentation can greatly improve the appearance and the clarity of a program, thus making the program easier to read and understand if it has to be modified later for any reason.

5. Programming involves meticulous attention to detail; omitting punctuation marks, including them in the wrong place or making spelling mistakes will usually lead to the compiler reporting syntax errors, but sometimes such slips might cause serious errors which are more difficult to detect, so be very careful to form instructions precisely.

Identifiers and data types

The term *identifier* is a general term used for *variables*, *constants* and other programmer-defined names such as *procedures* and *functions*. Variables and constants are always associated with a data *type*. C requires that variables are given a type such as int (integer) or float (real) so that the necessary amount of memory can be reserved for their use.

Variables

A variable, which represents an item of data such as a single number, has a name and a current value. Variables are given names such as Amount, Total or Numb3 and are assigned values by program instructions. These values are stored in the memory of the computer and they are accessed whenever a variable is referenced in a program instruction. So, for example, in the instruction `Total = Price + Tax;` the value associated with the variable `Price` is added to the value of the variable `Tax` and the sum is then assigned to the variable `Total`. If in a previous instruction `Total` had already been assigned a value, that value would be replaced by the new one.

Constants

Constants too are assigned values, but only once after the word `const`. The constant `VAT` in Listing 30.1 is an example. Constants are intended to retain their values throughout the execution of a program; C does not allow you to use a constant in an instruction which tries to change the value of the constant. Thus, if in Listing 30.1, you included in the main program an instruction such as `VAT = 0.2;` the C compiler would report an error.

Naming identifiers

C imposes a number of restrictions concerning the formation of names for identifiers:

1. The name must consist only of alphabetic and numeric characters and the underscore character, '_'. The name can not, however, consist only of the underscore character.

2. The name must start with an alphabetic character, or the underscore character.

3. The name must not be a *keyword*. Keywords are special words which are part of the language. A complete list of keywords is provided below:

```
auto       default   float   noalias    static    void
break      do        for     register   struct    volatile
case       double    goto    return     switch    while
char       else      if      short      typedef
const      enum      int     signed     union
continue   extern    long    sizeof     unsigned
```

Examples of valid identifiers:

```
first_Num    NUMBER1    abc31    Counter    x    MAX_
```

Examples of invalid identifiers

```
12abc              (starts with a numeric character)
first-number       (contains a hyphen)
var 1              (contains a space)
long               (a keyword)
```

Data types

As well as having names and values, variables are also given a *type*. Three commonly used types are `int`, `float` and `char` (character). The type must be shown before the name of the variable, as illustrated on lines *6 - 8* of Listing 30.1. More examples of type declarations are shown next:

```
float Amount;
char CodeLetter;
int NumberOfItems;
```

The type `float` means that these variables can be used for numbers such as 123.456, 0.22 or –9.93, that is, signed numbers that are not whole numbers. The computer holds `real` numbers in floating-point form so that very large, and very small numbers can be stored.

Signed whole numbers, that is, `int` values are stored as two's complement binary values in the computer. Some examples of integers are 23, 0, –1, 32767 and –559.

`char` means that the named variable (`CodeLetter` in the example above) stores a single character such as 'a', 'D', '6' or '?'.

Performing calculations

It is probable that every program that you will ever write will contain at least one calculation, and this is true of the majority of programs. It is not surprising therefore that C and other high-level languages make calculations easy to perform. Arithmetic instructions simply involve defining what arithmetic operations are to be performed on numeric identifiers and constants. The four common arithmetic operations - add, subtract, multiply and divide - use the symbols +, –, * and /, respectively. The examples of arithmetic operations provided in Table 30.1 assume that the following data declarations have been made:

```
const float PI = 3.142;
int Length, Width, Perimeter;
float Area, Radius, Gallons, Miles, Mpg;
float x;
```

expression	C statement
Area = Length × Width;	`Area = Length*Width;`
Area = πr^2	`Area = PI*Radius*Radius;`
Perimeter = 2 × (Length + Width)	`Perimeter = 2*(Length + Width);`
mpg = gallons ÷ miles	`Mpg = Gallons/Miles;`
x = 0	`x = 0;`

Table 30.1. *Examples of arithmetic operations with real variables*

All of the statements in Table 30.1 involve calculating a value using `float` or `int` variables or a combination of them. C determines automatically how to deal with expressions containing a mixture of data types, but it is advisable always to assign a `float` variable to the result of an arithmetic expression that may produce an answer which is not a whole number. In other words, the type of the left-hand side of an assignment statement should match the type of the right-hand side unless there is a reason to break this rule.

Another point to note is that C provides two operators that can be used for division operations. The '/' divide operator may be used with any values, `float` or `int`, but if both values are integers, the result is of type `float` and it can be assigned to either a `float` variable or to an `int` variable. If it is assigned to a variable of type `int`, the fractional part of the result will be discarded and only the integer part will remain. The second divide operator, `%`, is only allowed to be used with integers. The *remainder* when one integer is divided by another is produced by the % operator. Some examples, shown in Table 30.2, should help to clarify these points.

operands	example	answer	answer type
float/float	7.3/0.2	36.5	float
	0.5/0.25	2.0	float
float/int	13.9/5	2.78	float
int/float	1116/7.2	155.0	float
int/int	33/11	3	int
	33/10	3	int
	3/5	0	int
int % int	33/10	3	int
	10/33	10	int
int % float	Not allowed		
float % int	Not allowed		
float % float	Not allowed		

Table 30.2. *Examples of divide operations*

Listing 30.2 is an example of the use of mixed integer and real arithmetic. The program converts a number of grammes into pounds and ounces. The two constants, Gm_per_oz and Oz_per_lb, declared before main() give the number of grammes per ounce and the number of ounces per pound respectively.

Listing 30.2.   Mixed real and integer arithmetic

```
1    /* Program Example2 */
2    #include <stdio.h>
3    #include <conio.h>
4    const float Gm_per_oz = 28.4;
5    const int Oz_per_lb = 16;
6
7    void main()
8    {
9      int Grammes;
10     float Total_oz, Oz;
11     int Lbs;
12
13     clrscr();
14     printf("Type the weight in grammes and press Enter: ");
15     scanf("%d", &Grammes);
16     Total_oz = Grammes/Gm_per_oz;
17     Lbs = Total_oz/Oz_per_lb;
18     Oz = Total_oz - Lbs*Oz_per_lb;
19     printf("%d gm is equivalent to %d lb %4.1f oz", Grammes, Lbs, Oz);
20   }
```

The program operates as follows:

Line 2 includes the header file stdio.h required for the printf() and scanf() functions.

Line *3* includes the header file `conio.h` required for the `clrscr()` - clear screen - function used on line *13*.

Lines *4* **and** *5* declare the two constants used in the program.

Lines *9* - *11* declare the four variables used in the program. `Grammes` is an integer variable which is used to store the weight in grammes to be converted to pounds and ounces; `Total_oz` is used to store the ounce equivalent of the weight in grammes; `Oz` stores the number of ounces after the weight has been converted into pounds and ounces; `Lbs` stores the whole number of pounds after conversion.

Line *13* executes the predefined function `clrscr()` which clears the screen.

Line *14* displays the prompt to enter the weight to be converted into pounds and ounces.

Line *15* stores the number entered at the keyboard in the integer variable `Grammes`.

Line *16* converts the weight into ounces and stores the total number of ounces in the real variable `Total_oz`.

Line *17* divides the number of ounces by 16 to produce the number of pounds. This calculation produces a real value, that is, a value containing a fractional part but, because this value is assigned to the integer variable `Lbs`, the fractional part is ignored.

Line *18* subtracts the number of ounces calculated with `Lbs*Oz_per_lb`, from the total number of ounces, in order to calculate the number of remaining ounces.

Line *19* prints the results. The formatting string, `"%d gm is equivalent to %d lb %4.1f oz"`, specifies that `Grammes` is to be displayed as an integer (the first `%d`), `Lbs` is to be displayed as an integer (the second `%d`) and `Oz` is to be displayed as a real number having a minimum of four characters including a decimal point and one figure after the decimal point (`%4.1f`).

Here is an example of what the program does when it is run:

```
Enter the weight in grammes: 1000 ⏎

1000 gm is equivalent to 2 lbs 3.2 oz
```

Operator precedence

The term 'operator precedence' applies to the order in which the operators in an arithmetic expression are used. For example, to evaluate the expression

$$x = y + 3z$$

z is multiplied by 3 before the result is added to y; the multiply operator thus has precedence over the addition operator. If y had a value of 2 and z had a value of 4, x would be calculated as

$$x = 2 + 3 \times 4 = 2 + 12 = 14$$

The higher the precedence of an operator, the sooner it is used in the evaluation of an expression. The use of parentheses within an expression can alter the way a calculation is performed. So, in the above expression, to force the addition to be performed before the multiplication, we would write $x = (y + 3) \times z$. This would result in y being added to 3 before multiplying by z. Thus,

$$x = (2 + 3) \times 4 = 5 \times 4 = 20$$

In C, the operators $*$, $/$ and $\%$ have equal precedence; this means that in an expression involving two or more of them, they are simply used in the order that they appear in the expression. These four operators all have higher precedence than $+$ and $-$. Again, $+$ and $-$ have the same precedence. As a further example, consider the program in Listing 30.3.

Listing 30.3.   An example to illustrate operator precedence

```
1      /* Program Example3 */
2      #include <stdio.h>
3
4      void main()
5      {
6        float x1;
7        float y1;
8        int n;
9
10         n = 11;
11         y1 = 5;
12         x1 = 1.0/2.0*(y1 + n/y1);
13
14         printf("%8.2f", x1);
15
16     }
```

The order of evaluation of line *12* is as follows:

1.	`1.0/2.0`	i.e.	`0.5`	
2.	`n/y1`	i.e.	`11/5.0`	=2.2
3.	`y1 + n/y1`	i.e.	`5.0 + 2.2`	=7.2
4.	`1.0/2.0*(y1 + n/y1)`	i.e.	`0.5*7.2`	=3.6

Reading and displaying information

Practically every program requires that data are provided by some input device such as a keyboard and that results are produced on an output device such as a monitor. C provides a number of functions to simplify these operations, two of the most generally useful being `printf()` and `scanf()`. In this section we examine these functions in more detail. The `scanf()` function uses data provided by a standard input device such as a keyboard to assign values to variables. You use the `scanf()` function to read real numbers, integers, single characters or strings of characters into appropriately declared variables. For example, the statement

```
scanf("%f", &Price);
```

would cause the program to wait for the user to enter a number to be stored in the real variable Price. The user presses the ⏎ key to signify the end of data entry. It is good practice to include a printf() instruction to precede scanf() to inform the user what information is required. So, for example, the statements

```
printf("Please enter the price of the item: ");
scanf("%f", &Price);
```

would cause the computer to display

```
Please enter the price of the item:
```

on the display screen and then, with the text cursor remaining on the same line, wait for the user to type in a value and press the ⏎ key. Listing 30.4 illustrates the use of printf() and scanf().

Listing 30.4. Using the printf() and scanf() instructions

```
1    /* Program Example4            */
2    /* To convert inches to centimetres */
3    #include <stdio.h>
4    const float CENTIMETRES_PER_INCH=2.54;
5    void main()
6    {
7      float Centimetres;
8      float Inches;
9      printf("Enter length in inches: ");
10     scanf("%f", &Inches);
11     Centimetres = Inches*CENTIMETRES_PER_INCH;
12     printf("\n");
13     printf("A length of %5.2f inches", Inches);
14     printf(" is equivalent to ");
15     printf("%5.2f centimetres\n", Centimetres);
16   }
```

The program would produce the following output when run:

```
Enter the length in inches: 12 ⏎
```

```
A length of 12.00 inches is equivalent to 30.48 centimetres
```

The output shows that the user entered the number *12* followed by ⏎ when prompted to type in the length in inches.

printf()

The printf() function is used to display combinations of text and variables. In its simplest form it allows text to be output by including it within a control string enclosed between double quotes:

```
printf("Enter the length in inches: ")
```

If \n is included in the control string, a carriage return and line feed are generated when the program is run. This is useful for making your output clear and easy to read. For example, to generate two line feeds before the text is displayed you could write

```
printf("\n\nEnter the length in inches: ");
```

The \ character is used in C programs to indicate that the next character represents a special character. Thus \n means that n is to be interpreted as a line feed. Table 30.3 shows a list of control characters that can be used in control strings in the printf() function.

control char	effect
\a	bell
\b	backspace
\f	form feed
\n	new line
\r	carriage return
\\	backslash
\?	question mark
\'	single quote
\"	double quote
\ddd	ASCII code for a character, where ddd is an octal number in the range 000 to 377
\xdd	ASCII code for a character, where dd is a hexadecimal number in the range 00 to FF

Table 30.3. *Control characters for use with* printf() *function*

When the printf() function is required to display the values of variables, format specifications must be included within the control string. For example, consider line *13* of Listing 30.4:

```
printf("A length of %5.2f inches", Inches);
```

The % sign indicates that a variable is to be displayed at this position. Immediately following this symbol is a width specifier which indicates the minimum field size to be used to display the variable. In this example, a minimum of five character positions are to be used. The width includes a decimal point if decimal places are to be displayed.

field format	meaning
d,i	decimal integer
u	unsigned decimal integer
f	fixed point
c	single character
s	string
e,E	exponential
g,G	exponential or fixed point whichever is more compact

Table 30.4. *Field formats*

Next comes the number of decimal places to be presented. In our example two decimal places are to appear. Values are right justified by default, but by preceding the width specifier by a hyphen, the value will be left justified in the display field. If no width or precision are specified, the number will still be displayed. Finally, the letter f indicates that the number is to be shown as a fixed point real number. The possible field formats that can appear in this position are shown in Table 30.4

Table 30.5 contains a number of examples using various output formats.

value	format	output	remarks
15.234	%10.1f	ssssss15.2	Six leading spaces are added
6.6666	%10.1f	sssssss6.7	The figure after the decimal point is rounded up
6.6666	%0.2f	6.67	The minimum number of digits is displayed
-8.3124	%0.3f	-8.312	As above
234.5	%f	234.500000	The maximum number of decimal places is displayed
123	%5d	ss123	Two leading spaces included in the field
123	%2d	123	Minimum number of figures displayed and no leading spaces
25.23	%-10.2f	s25.23ssss	Left justified. Space for sign
25.23	%10.2e	ss2.52e+01	Exponential format. Two dec. places
25.23	%g	25.23	Most concise form

Table 30.5. *Examples of various output formats and their effects*

When several fields are to be output, the control string must contain one format specification for each of the fields. For example,

```
printf("%2d : %2d : %2d", hours, minutes, seconds);
```

would display a line of the form

```
10 : 23 : 5
```

The value contained in hours is displayed first, followed by minutes and seconds, that is, in the order that they are listed after the control string. Note that the colons (:) have no special meaning in the control string.

scanf()

The scanf() function is used to read characters typed in at the keyboard. As with the printf() function, a formatting string specifies how the data is to be interpreted. For instance, to read an integer into a variable called Quantity, you would write

```
scanf("%d", &Quantity);
```

Note the use of the ampersand (&) in front of the name of the variable. The scanf() function requires you to specify the *address* of the variable into which data from the keyboard is to be transferred, and not simply the name of the variable. The & sign preceding the name of a variable is interpreted as the starting address for the area of memory assigned to the variable. If you accidentally omit the &, the C compiler will not always report an errror, and the program will probably produce apparently spurious values. It is therefore very important to take great care when using scanf() to include the & signs where required.

When you want to read several values using a single scanf() function, each variable must be assigned its own format specification. The scanf() function regards a *white space* character, such as a space or line feed or tab character, as a separator. So, for example, to read in a single character into the char variable Status, followed by reading a real number into the float variable Salary, you might use

```
scanf("%c%d", &Status, &Salary);
```

As with printf(), the format specification allows you to specify the input of integers (using %d), reals (using %f, %e or %g), single characters (using %c), and strings of characters (using %s). We will deal with the input and output of strings later in the chapter.

Loops

A very frequent programming requirement is to perform a set of instructions several times. Rather than writing the set of instructions several times (which is impractical for all but a small number of repetitions), they are controlled by a special instruction which causes them to be repeated as many times as desired. Such program constructs are called *loops*, and each repetition of a set of statements is often called an *iteration*. For example, suppose a program is required to read 10 numbers, add each one to a running total and then display the final total. The program in Listing 30.5 accomplishes this task using a loop.

Listing 30.5.   Using a for loop to total numbers

```
1     /* Program Example5                        */
2     /* To add ten numbers               */
3     #include <stdio.h>
4     void main()
5     {
6       float Number;
7       float Total;
8       int Count;
9         Total = 0;
10          for(Count=1; Count 0; Count++)
11            {
12                printf("\nEnter number #%d ", Count);
13                scanf("%f", &Number);
14                Total = Total + Number;
15            }
16        printf("\nThe total is %10.2f ", Total);
17    }
```

The for loop starting on line *10* contains three parts within the brackets, each separated with a semi-colon. The first part, Count = 1, initialises a variable, Count, to a value of 1. Thereafter, each time the statements within the loop are repeated, the third part of the instruction, Count++, is performed. This adds 1 to the value of Count. The second part of the instruction, Count <=10 in this case, is the condition that determines how many times the loop is repeated - while the condition is true the loop continues but as as soon as it becomes false, the loop terminates and the program carries on with the next instruction following the loop, that is the instruction on line *16*. The statements to be repeated by the loop are enclosed between { and }. The instruction on line *15*,

```
Total:= Total + Number;
```

is a means of accumulating a total. It causes the value of Total to be replaced by its current value plus the value of the variable Number. On line *9*, Total is first set to zero, so that if Number was given a value of, say, 10, Total := 0 + 10 = 10. If on line *14*, Number was then given a value of 12, Total := 10 + 12 = 22, and so on. In this way Total accumulates the values assigned to Number after each scanf() instruction. *Notice that there is no semi-colon at the end of line 10*; putting a semi-colon at the end of the line will cause the loop to simply repeat the for instruction itself and not the instructions following the for statement. The program repeatedly reads a real value and adds it to a running total. When ten values have been processed in this way, the program exits the for loop and displays the final total. Here is an example of the program output:

```
Enter number #1 3 ⏎
Enter number #2 5 ⏎
Enter number #3 1 ⏎
Enter number #4 7.8 ⏎
Enter number #5 5.5 ⏎
Enter number #6 10 ⏎
Enter number #7 -3.4 ⏎
Enter number #8 16.9 ⏎
Enter number #9 -23 ⏎
Enter number #10 12.22 ⏎


The total is 35.02
```

Listing 30.6 is a further example of the use of the for loop.

Listing 30.6.   Using a for loop to display a conversion table

---

```
1     /* Program Example6              */
2     /* Conversion table              */
3
4     #include <stdio.h>
5     const float CONVERSION_FACTOR = 2.54;
6     const int   MAX_INCHES = 12;
7
8     void main()
9     {
10      int Inches;
11      float Centimetres;
12      printf("\n%20s%20s", "Inches", "Centimetres");
13      printf("\n%20s%20s", "------", "-----------");
14      for(Inches=1; Inches MAX_INCHES; Inches++)
15        {
16          Centimetres = Inches * CONVERSION_FACTOR;
17          printf("\n%17d%20.2f", Inches, Centimetres);
18        }
19    }
```

The output produced looks like this:

```
Inches          Centimetres
-------         ------------
1                 2.54
2                 5.08
etc               etc
12               30.48
```

A slight variation in the format of a `for` statement allows the count variable to go down from a high value to a low value. For example, you could write

```
for( i=12; i=1; i--) ....
```

which would cause the variable `i` to start at 12 and go down to 1 in steps of 1.

The `for` statement is a very useful means of implementing a loop, but certain programming problems require a different approach to repeating a set of instructions. For example, consider the following outline program description:

> *Read a set of real numbers representing the cost of a number of items. Accumulate the total cost of the items until a value of zero is entered, then display the number of items purchased and their total cost.*

Here it is not known how many times the loop is to be repeated: the user decides when to terminate the loop by entering a *rogue value*, (zero in this case). The rogue value is used in another type of loop instruction, the `while` instruction. Listing 30.7 shows how a `while` loop can be used in conjunction with a rogue value. The rogue value is defined as a constant on line *4*. Because the user may want to terminate the program immediately, without entering any values, the program asks for a purchase amount before entering the loop starting on line *14*. The `while` instruction requires that a true/false expression is included in brackets after the word 'while'. Thus the expression, `Amount > ROGUEVALUE`, will be true if `Amount` entered is greater than zero, and it will be false if `Amount` is not greater than zero, that is if it is equal to, or less than zero. When the expression is true, the statements between the immediately following { and }, that is lines *19* to *21*, will be executed; as soon as the expression becomes false, the loop terminates and the program goes on to line *23*.

Notice that the last instruction in the lines to be repeated is the `scanf()` instruction to read another value: this means that because the next instruction to be executed is the `while` instruction, the value typed in by the user is immediately compared with the rogue value. This ensures that the rogue value is not processed as a data item.

Listing 30.7.   Using a while loop and a rogue value

```
1       /* Program Example7                              */
2       /* To illustrate the use of a rogue value */
3       #include <stdio.h>
4       const int ROGUE_VALUE = 0
5
6       void main()
7       {
```

```
8        int Count;
9        float Amount;
10       float Total;
11
12       Total = 0;
13       Count = 0;
14       printf("Enter the cost of the first item, or 0 to end :");
15       scanf("%f", &Amount);
16       while(Amount > ROGUE_VALUE)
17          {
18          Count++;
19          Total = Total + Amount;
20          printf("Enter the cost of the next item, or 0 to end :");
21          scanf("%f", &Amount);
22          }
23       printf("\n\n%d items were purchased.", Count);
24       printf(\n"The total cost was: £%0.2f", Total);
25       }
```

Here is a typical output from the program:

```
Enter the cost of the first item, or 0 to end :23.45 ⏎
Enter the cost of the next item, or 0 to end:6.12 ⏎
Enter the cost of the next item, or 0 to end:5.99 ⏎
Enter the cost of the next item, or 0 to end:0 ⏎


3 items were purchased.
The total cost was: £35.56
```

Notice that the increment instruction on line *18*, Count++, is used as a means of counting the number of times the loop is executed. The instruction simply adds 1 to the variable, Count, each time the instructions within the loop are repeated.

The true/false expression on line *16* in the while statement uses the *relational operator*, >, meaning 'greater than', to compare Amount with ROGUEVALUE. There are in fact six different relational operators that can be used in such logical expressions, and these are shown in Table 30.6.

They are used according to the relationship between two values that is to be established. Whatever logical expression is used, the result of the comparison will either be true or false - if true,

relational operator	meaning
>	Greater than
> =	Greater than or equal to
<	Less than
< =	Less than or equal to
= =	Equal to
!=	Not equal to

Table 30.6.   *Relational operators used in logical expressions.*

the while loop will repeat; if false the loop will terminate. More examples of the use of these operators is provided in the next section which deals with the use of logical expressions in making program decisions.

Decisions

Suppose a program is required to display multiple-choice questions with one correct answer out of three possible choices. For example, one of the questions could be:

```
A BYTE is the name given to

    (a)  Four bits
    (b)  Eight bits
    (c)  Sixteen bits

Your answer is:
```

The program is also required to display the message

```
Correct - well done!
```

if the answer is correct, and display a message such as

```
Sorry, the correct answer is (b)
```

if the answer provided is incorrect.

The program must, therefore, be able to take two alternate courses of action depending on the answer supplied. An if statement is one possible way of achieving this requirement. The appropriate form of the if statement is illustrated in Listing 30.8 which shows the C code required to display the question above and provide the response appropriate to the letter 'a', 'b' or 'c', typed in.

Listing 30.8.   Using an if statement

```
1     /* Program Example8              */
2     /* A multiple choice question    */
3     #include <stdio.h>
4
5     void main()
6     {
7       char Answer;
8
9       printf( "Enter the letter corresponding to the ");
10      printf( "correct answer to the following question: ");
11      printf("\n");
12      printf("A BYTE is the name given to");
13      printf("\n(a) Four bits");
14      printf("\n(b) Eight bits");
15      printf("\n(c) Sixteen bits");
16
17      printf("\nYour answer is: ");
18      scanf("%c", &Answer);
```

```
19
20    if(Answer == 'b')
21       printf("Correct - well done!\n");
22    else
23       printf("Sorry, the correct answer is (b)\n");
24    }
```

The output from the program is shown below:

```
Enter the letter corresponding to the correct answer to the
following question:
A BYTE is the name given to
   (a)  Four bits
   (b)  Eight bits
   (c)  Sixteen bits
Your answer is: a ⏎
Sorry, the correct answer is (b)
```

The `if` statement extending over lines *20* to *23* shows how the program can take one of two possible courses of action depending on the value of a variable. We saw in the last section concerning the use of the `while` statement that logical expressions are either true or false. This is also the case with the logical expression `Answer == 'b'` in the `if` statement on line *20*. If the letter stored in the character variable `Answer` is the letter 'b', then the logical expression `Answer == 'b'` will be true, otherwise it will be false. If it is true, the statement following the word `then` is executed (that is, line *21*), otherwise the statement after `else` is executed (that is, line *23*).

The general form of the `if` statement is

```
if (logical_expression)
   statement1;
else
   statement 2;
```

`statement 1` is the instruction that is performed if `logical_expression` is true; `statement 2` is performed if `logical_expression` is false. Note that either `statement 1` or `statement 2` or both of them can be a block of instructions enclosed between { and } as illustrated below:

```
if (Answer == 'b' )
   printf("Correct - well done!\n");
else
   {
      printf("Sorry, the correct answer is (b)\n");
      printf("There are eight bits in a byte\n");
   }
```

Sometimes it is necessary to choose between more than just two courses of action in a program. For example, Listing 30.9 shows a program which converts a percentage mark to a pass, merit, distinction or fail grade. The program repeatedly accepts marks and converts them to grades until the mark entered is the rogue value –1 (or any negative integer value) signifying the end of the mark inputs. The rules that are used to determine the grade are as follow:

1.   *For a distinction the mark must be over 80.*

2.   *For a merit the mark must be greater than or equal to 60 and less than 80.*

3.   *For a pass the mark must be greater than or equal to 40 and less than 60.*

4.   *Below 40 is a fail.*

Listing 30.9.   The `if..else if` construction

```
1     /* Program Example9            */
2     /* Convert mark to a grade     */
3     #include <stdio.h>
4     const int Dist = 80;
5     const int Merit = 60;
6     const int Pass = 40;
7
8     void main()
9     {
10      int Mark;
11
12      printf( "Enter the first mark (-1 to end) :");
13      scanf("%d", &Mark);
14      while(Mark =0)
15        {
16           if (Mark = Dist) printf("Distinction\n");
17           else if (Mark >= Merit && Mark Dist) printf("Merit\n");
18           else if (Mark >= Pass && Mark Merit) printf("Pass\n");
19           else if (Mark < Pass) printf("Fail\n");
20
21           printf( "Enter the next mark (-1 to end) :");
22           scanf("%d", &Mark);
23        }
24   }
```

The `if` statement between lines *16* and *19* reflects this logic exactly. It is possible to chain `if` statements in this way to cope with quite complex lines of reasoning. Added flexibility is provided by the use of the logical and operator, `&&`, used for the the logical expressions on lines *17* and *18*. The `&&` operator requires that both of the minor logical expressions it connects are true for the complete logical expression to be true. If either or both are false, then the whole expression is false. Logical operators are discussed in more detail in the next section. Here is a typical output from the program:

```
Please enter the first mark(-1 to end): 46 ⏎
Pass
Please enter the next mark(-1 to end): 68 ⏎
Merit
Please enter the next mark(-1 to end):32 ⏎
Fail
```

```
Please enter the next mark(-1 to end):83
Distinction
Please enter the next mark(-1 to end):-1
```

Logical operators

Logical operators allow you to combine logical expressions. There are three logical operators in C : and (&&), or (||) and not (!). An example of the use of the && operator was provided in Listing 30.9. The && and the || operators are always placed between two logical expressions, and they each combine these logical expressions to produce a value of true or false. Table 30.7 shows the rules that are applied by C to determine whether a compound logical expression is true or false. This type of table is usually called a *truth table*.

(Expr 1)	(Expr 2)	(Expr 1) || (Expr 2)	(Expr 1) && (Expr 2)
true	true	true	true
true	false	true	false
false	true	true	false
false	false	false	false

Table 30.7. *Truth table for the* and *and* or *logical operators.*

Referring back to Listing 30.9 in the previous section, on line *21*, where the compound logical expression (Mark >= MERIT) && (Mark < DIST) is used to determine whether the mark is equivalent to a merit grade. Both logical expressions must be true for the complete expression to be true.

With the || operator, however, only one of the expressions needs to be true for the complete expression to be true. For example, consider the program in Listing 30.10 which reads some text and counts how many vowels it contains. The program uses a for loop to test each letter in turn in the text against each possible vowel. If the current letter is a vowel, that is 'a', 'e', 'i', 'o' or 'u', a count is incremented.

Listing 30.10. Illustrating the use of the || logical operator

```
1     /* Program Example10              */
2     /* Counting vowels in a string    */
3     #include <stdio.h>
4     #include <string.h>
5
6     void main()
7     {
8       int Vowel_count;
9       char Letters[80];
10      int Length_of_text;
11      int c;
12
13      Vowel_count = 0;
14      printf("Type text followed by ENTER: \n");
15      gets(Letters);
16      Length_of_text = strlen(Letters);
```

```
17
18      for(c=0; c Length_of_text; c++)
19        if (
20              (Letters[c] == 'a') ||
21              (Letters[c] == 'e') ||
22              (Letters[c] == 'i') ||
23              (Letters[c] == 'o') ||
24              (Letters[c] == 'u')
25            ) Vowel_count++;
26          printf("The text contained %d vowels\n" , Vowel_count);
27      }
```

The header file `string.h` included at the beginning of the program allows us to use functions which perform operations on strings. We will use some of these functions in later programs, but for the present example we use only the function that provides us with the length of a string, namely `strlen()`.

A string in C is declared as a set of characters. Thus line *9* in Listing 30.10 declares the string `Letters` as a set of 80 characters, each character stored in `Letters` being accessed by specifying its position within the text, with the first position starting at 0.. For example, if the text entered was the string 'hello there', then `Letters[0]` is the letter 'h', `Letters[1]` is the letter 'e', `Letters[2]` is the letter 'l', and so on. The `for` loop control variable, c, starts at 0 and goes up in steps of 1 to the length of the string minus 1(that is, 10 for the string 'hello there').

Note that a string is always terminated with a special character, \0, called the null character, which occupies a character position in the space allocated to the string. This means that in our example, the maximum number of characters that could be typed in is 79, not 80 as you might expect. The length of the string is determined by the pre-defined C function `strlen()`, on line *16*, which requires a string name as its single argument. The length of the string returned by `strlen()` does not include the terminating character, \0.

Notice also that `scanf()` has not been used to read the string on line *15*. This is because `scanf()` treats spaces as delimiters when fields are being entered, so that using `scanf()` rather than `gets()` - *get string* - would have prevented us from being able to have spaces in the text. Here is the output from the program when the string 'the cat sat on the mat' is typed in:

Type text followed by ENTER: **the cat sat on the mat** ⏎

The text contained 6 vowels

Note that the program will only work with lower-case text. The reason is that lower-case letters 'a', 'b', 'c', etc are represented in a computer using a different set of codes from the equivalent upper-case letters 'A', 'B', 'C', etc.

The third logical operator is the not operator, !, which simply reverses the logical value of a logical expression. Thus, the logical expression ! (x > 3) is true only when x is *not* greater than 3. Similarly, the logical expression ! (Balance <= 0) is true only when Balance has a value that is *not* less than or equal to zero.

More control statements

Listing 30.11 draws together two further C control statements, namely the do..while and the switch statements using a progam which allows you to convert Pounds sterling into one of three foreign currencies: American Dollars, German Marks or French Francs. The do..while statement provides a third method of constructing a loop. It is similar to the while statement in that it uses a logical condition to determine when to exit the loop, but the difference is that the condition appears at the end rather than at the beginning of the loop. This means that the loop will be executed at least once, which is appropriate for this example in which the loop repeatedly executes instructions which display a menu and ask the user to choose one of the menu options. In this example, the loop repeats the statements between lines *11* to *67* while the condition inside the round brackets on line *68* is true, that is, when the user enters the letter 'X' or 'x' to exit the program.

Listing 30.11.   Using the switch and do..while statements in a menu program

```
1      /* Program Example11                                     */
2      /* Currency conversion with menus, using switch statement */
3      #include <stdio.h>
4      #include <conio.h>
5      const float DOLLARS = 1.5;
6      const float MARKS = 3.4;
7      const float FRANCS = 11.0;
8
9      void main()
10     {
11       char Choice;
12       float Currency;
13       float Pounds;
14       char Keyboard_buffer[255];
15
16       do
17       {
18         clrscr();
19         printf("\nCurrency conversion program");
20         printf("\n(M)arks");
21         printf("\n(D)ollars");
22         printf("\n(F)rancs");
23         printf("\ne(X)it");
24         printf("\nWhich currency do you wish to convert to Pounds? ");
25         scanf("%c", &Choice);
26         printf("\n");
27
28         switch(Choice)
29         {
30           case 'D': case 'd':
31             printf("\nEnter the amount to convert to Dollars ");
32             scanf("%f", &Pounds);
33             Currency = Pounds*DOLLARS;
34             printf("\nYou would get %0.0f Dollars for %0.0f Pounds",
                        Currency, Pounds);
35             printf("\nPress any key to return to the menu");
```

```
36                  flushall(); getch();
37                  break;
38             case 'M': case 'm':
39                  printf("\nEnter the amount to convert to Marks ");
40                  scanf("%f", &Pounds);
41                  Currency = Pounds*MARKS;
42                  printf("\nYou would get %0.0f Marks for %0.0f Pounds",
                           Currency, Pounds);
43                  printf("\nPress any key to return to the menu");
44                  flushall(); getch();
45                  break;
46             case 'F': case 'f':
47                  printf("\nEnter the amount to convert to Francs ");
48                  scanf("%f", &Pounds);
49                  Currency = Pounds*FRANCS;
50                  printf("\nYou would get %0.0f Francs for %0.0f Pounds",
                           Currency, Pounds);
51                  printf("\nPress any key to return to the menu");
52                  flushall(); getch();
53                  break;
54             case 'X': case 'x':
55                  printf("\nExiting program..");
56                  break;
57             default:
58                  printf("\nInvalid option. Please try again");
59                  printf("\nPress ENTER to return to the menu");
60                  flushall(); getch();
61                  break;
62          } /* end switch */
63       }
64     while(!(Choice == 'X' || Choice == 'x'));
65  }
```

The switch statement is an alternative method to the if statement for choosing between alternative courses of action within a program.

The expression in brackets after the word switch must evaluate to an integer value. C matches the value of the expression against the case values specified on the subsequent lines; when a match is found, the corresponding statements are executed up to the first break statement, after which the switch statement is immediately exited without considering any remaining values. If there are no values that match the variable, the case statement does nothing unless the default option is used in which event the supplied statements are executed. In Listing 30.11, the switch statement is used to select the block of statements corresponding to the menu option chosen by the user. The user can choose one of four options using the letters 'D', 'M', 'F' or 'X'; to allow for the possibility of either upper or lower case letters being entered, both are included as case values. Note that separating case values only by a semi-colon allows a common set of statements to be performed for a number of different values. Thus, by writing

```
        case 'D': case 'd':
```

the same set of statements will be executed whether 'd' or 'D' is matched.

Note the use of

```
flushall(); getch();
```

on lines *36*, *44*, *52* and *60*. The flushall() function removes any unused characters in the keyboard input buffer. Remember that scanf() ignores white space characters when reading data to be stored in variables; it leaves them in the keyboard buffer. This means, for example, that after a number followed by ⏎ has been typed, a newline white space character will remain in the input buffer. (The keyboard input buffer is a temporary storage area used for storing characters entered at the keyboard. Input instructions retrieve characters from the buffer as if they have just been typed.) flushall() will remove newline and any other characters in the buffer so that the next input instruction does not use them. The getch() function allows you to capture a single key depression without the need to press ⏎. Although this method of waiting for a key to be pressed may appear to be a little complicated, it has the advantage of avoiding unexpected results when using the scanf() function for data input.

Returning to the switch() statement, here are some program fragments which should help to clarify its use:

Example 1

```
int Month, Days;
.......
.......
switch(Month)
{
  case 1:case 3:case 5:case 7:case 8:case 10:case 12:
    Days:= 31;
    break;
  case 4:case 6:case 9:case 11:
    Days:= 30;
    break;
  case 2 :
    Days:= 28;
    break;
}
```

Month contains a number corresponding to the month of the year, where January = 1, February = 2 ..... December = 12. The switch statement is used to store in the variable, Days, the number of days in the month whose number is stored in Month. Thus if Month contained the number 8 corresponding to August, Days would be assigned the value 31.

Example 2

```
const int TRUE = 1;
const int FALSE = 0;
int Smoker;
......
......
switch(Smoker)
{
```

```
    case TRUE:
      printf("Smoking seriously damages your health!");
      break;
    case FALSE:
      printf("Good for you!");
      break;
  }
```

If the integer variable, Smoker, has been assigned a value of TRUE (that is 1) prior to the switch statement, the health warning will be displayed, otherwise the complimentary message 'Good for you!' will be displayed.

This is equivalent to using the if statement

```
  if (Smoker)
    printf("Smoking seriously damages your health!");
  else
    printf("Good for you!");
```

Note that it is because Smoker is an integer variable having a value of TRUE or FALSE, that it can be used as a logical expression in an if statement as illustrated above.

Example 3

```
    char Letter;
    int Vowel_count;
    int Consonant_count;
    .....
    .....
    switch(Letter)
    {
      case 'a':case 'e':case 'i':case 'o':case 'u' :
        Vowel_count++;
      case 'A':case 'E':case 'I':case 'O':case 'U' :
        Vowel_count++;
      case ',':case '.':case ';':case ':':case'(':case ')':case ' ':
        /* No action required */
      default: Consonant_count++;
    }
```

Here the program adds one to a vowel count if Letter contains either an upper or lower case letter; otherwise it adds one to a consonant count. Punctuation marks, brackets and spaces are ignored. Note that using if statements to perform this task would be much more difficult.

Arrays

An *array* is a data structure which allows you to store a number of items of data without having to allocate separate variable names to them. Arrays, like all other identifiers, must be declared before they are used. For example, the following declaration is for an array of five integers:

```
int Array1[5];
```

This single declaration is in effect defining five variables called `Array[0]`, `Array[1]`, `Array[2]`, `Array[3]` and `Array[4]`, each of which can store a single integer value. The integer value inside the square brackets is called the array's *index*, and it is allowed only to take the range of values specified in the declaration (0 to 4 inclusive in this example). Each of these identifiers can be used just like any ordinary integer variable. For instance, to set each of them to zero could be accomplished as follows:

```
Array[1]  = 0;
Array[2]  = 0;
Array[3]  = 0;
Array[4]  = 0;
Array[5]  = 0;
```

However, we could accomplish the same operation by using an integer variable as an index and by putting a single assignment statement in a `for` loop:

```
for (i= 0; i 5; i++) Array[i]= 0;
```

Now the count variable `i` takes on the integer values 0 to 4 and again each element in the array is set to zero. The obvious advantage of using a variable for an index is that arrays can then be used very effectively within loops, and they allow the manipulation of as many or as few numbers as appropriate to the task in hand. Notice that the same `for` loop could initialize 5000 array elements as easily as 5 elements:

```
for (i= 0; i 5000; i++) Array[i]= 0;
```

This would be an exceedingly difficult task to accomplish without the use of an array. Listing 30.12 illustrates the use of an array of real numbers. The program reads five numbers into an array and then finds the position within the array of the smallest number. It then swaps this number with the first number in the list before displaying the re-ordered array.

Listing 30.12.   Using an array

```
1      /* Program Example 12   */
2      /* Using arrays          */
3      #include <stdio.h>
4      const int MAXNUMS = 5;
5
6      void main()
7      {
8        float List[MAXNUMS];
9        int i, position;
10       float temp;
```

```
11
12      /* Read in the numbers */
13      for(i=0; i<XNUMS; i++)
14        scanf("%f", &List[i]);
15
16      position = 0;
17      /* Find the position of the smallest value */
18      for(i=0; i<XNUMS; i++)
19        if(List[i]<List[position] ) position = i;
20
21      /* Swap the smallest value with the first value in the list */
22      temp = List[0];
23      List[0] = List[position];
24      List[position] = temp;
25
26      /* Display the new list */
27      printf("\n");
28      for(i=0; i<XNUMS; i++) printf("%10.2f", List[i]);
29    }
```

The program first defines a constant MAXNUMS to be the maximum size of the real array, Array1. Lines *12* to *14* are to read in the five numbers with appropriate user prompts. Thus the first number is read into Array1[0], the second into Array1[1], and so on up to the last number which is read into Array1[4]. The second for loop starting on line *18* compares each number in the array in turn with the first number; if one is found that is smaller than the first, its position within the array is stored in position. By the time the last number in the array has been compared with the first one, the smallest number has been located. It is then swapped with the first number in the array by the lines *22* to *24*.

A typical output from the program might be as follows:

```
Enter 5 numbers

     Enter number 1 :5.7
     Enter number 2 : 3.9
     Enter number 3 :9.1
     Enter number 4 :1.7
     Enter number 5 :98.4

The new list is as follows:

     1.7    3.9    9.1    5.7    98.4
```

As a final example in this section on arrays, Listing 30.13 shows a program which uses a random number generator to select five lottery numbers in the range 1 to 49.

Listing 30.13.   Using random numbers and an array to generate lottery numbers

```
1     /* Program Example 13                        */
2     /* Further example of the use of an array */
3     #include <stdio.h>
4     #include <conio.h>
5     #include <stdlib.h>
6
7     const int NUMOFNUMS = 5;
8     const int MAXNUM =49;
9     void main()
10    {
11       int LuckyNums[MAXNUM+1];
12       int Num;
13       int i;
14       int Count;
15
16       clrscr();
17       printf("Lottery number generator");
18       printf("\n");
19
20       randomize();
21       for(i=0; i MAXNUM; i++) LuckyNums[i] = 0;
22
23       for(Count=1; Count NUMOFNUMS; Count++)
24       {
25         Num = random(MAXNUM) + 1;
26         while(LuckyNums[Num] != 0)
27           Num = random(MAXNUM) +1;
28         LuckyNums[Num] = Num;
29         printf("%5d", Num);
30       }
31
32       printf("\n\nPress ENTER to exit program");
33       getchar();
34    }
```

The random numbers are generated using the pre-defined function random(N) which produces a random number in the range specified by its single integer argument, N, within the brackets. For example, random(11) would produce a random number between 1 and 10 inclusively. Thus, on line *25*, the statement

```
Num = random(MAXNUM + 1);
```

assigns a random number between 1 and 49 to the variable Num. The randomize instruction on line *20* simply initialises the random number generator so that it does not produce the same sequence of random numbers every time the program is run. Line *21* initialises each element to zero in the array LuckyNums [] which is to be used to store the five random numbers. The reason for the while loop on lines *26* and *27* is to ensure that the same random number is not used more than once. The loop keeps generating random numbers until it finds one that has not been generated previously. For instance, if the first random number generated on line *25* was the number 36, then this would be stored in Num. The while loop will only generate another random number if Luckynums [36] contains zero, showing that 36 has not previously been generated. As soon as the while loop finds an empty slot, the number is stored in the array and immediately displayed on the screen. The process repeats until five different numbers have been generated.

Pre-defined procedures and functions

High-level languages almost invariably provide libraries of useful pre-written programs that are available to the programmer. These programs, which are often termed *pre-defined procedures* and *functions*, have previously been written, compiled and thoroughly tested so that they can be used by programmers with confidence that they are error-free. In C such libraries of functions are declared in header files by lines such as

```
#include <stdio.h>
```

Some library programs require you to provide information in the form of *parameters* at the time they are called. An example of such a program is the delay(T) function which requires you to supply a delay, T, in milliseconds inside the brackets. In Turbo C this function requires the following header declaration:

```
#include <dos.h>
```

Functions always return an item of information when they are used. For example, in Listing 30.13 we saw that the function random(N) returned to the calling program a random number in the range 0 to N-1, where N is an integer value. It was noted earlier that printf, and scanf are library functions rather than instructions such as for and if which are integral parts of the C language. A number of C functions, together with the appropriate header files, are described at the end of this chapter.

Simple user-defined procedures

Functions are often called *subprograms* or *subroutines* because they form only part of a complete program. We saw in the previous section that C provides many pre-written functions that you can use in your own programs, but it is also possible for you to write your own. These are called *user-defined* functions.

A C function is very similar to a C program, the main difference being that a function cannot stand by itself - it must form part of another program. Like identifiers such as constants and variables, functions must also be declared at the beginning of the program before they are used. The structure of a program containing two functions called functionA() and functionB() is illustrated at the start of this chapter, in Figure 30.1

The two function definitions appear before void main(). The definitions of the functions look exactly like a main program, each having their own constants and variables declarations (if required) and their own code. The program shown in Listing 30.14. illustrates the use of simple functions to cycle through three rudimentary pictures of faces in order to give the appearance of a face winking alternate eyes. The program uses three functions, Face1, Face2 and Face3, each of which uses keyboard characters to display a face. The functions are executed in main() by simply naming them. Thus, on line *42*, Face1 causes the instructions in function Face1 to be executed. The program then continues with delay(500) on line *43*, a pre-defined function which causes a delay of 500 milliseconds - this function is declared in the header on line *6*.

Listing 30.14.   Using functions to make a face wink

```
1    /* Program Example 14                 */
2    /* Animates a face using simple functions */
3
4    #include <stdio.h>
5    #include <conio.h>
6    #include <dos.h>
7
8    void Face1()
9    {
10     clrscr();
11     puts("          ");
12     puts("   - -    ");
13     puts("< O O > ");
14     puts(" | ^ |   ");
15     puts("   ~-~    ");
16   }
17   void Face2()
18   {
19     clrscr();
20     puts("          ");
21     puts("   - -    ");
22     puts("< O o > ");
23     puts(" | ^ |   ");
24     puts("   ~V~    ");
25   }
26   void Face3()
27   {
28     clrscr();
29     puts("          ");
30     puts("   - -    ");
31     puts("< o O > ");
32     puts(" | ^ |   ");
33     puts("   ~V~    ");
34   }
35
36   void main()
37   {
38     int i;
39
40     for(i=1; i0; i++)
```

```
41      {
42        Face1();
43        delay(500);
44        Face2();
45        delay(500);
46        Face1();
47        delay(500);
48        Face3();
49        delay(500);
50      }
51    }
```

Each of the functions uses the pre-defined `clrscr()` function to clear the screen so that the face stays in the same place and appears to wink. Notice that the logic of the main program is easy to follow by the use of functions - this is one of their major advantages. Another feature of this program is that although the function `Face1` is used twice, the code required for it appears only once in its definition. This economical use of program code is another major advantage of using functions in C programs.

Global vs local variables

Earlier we said that a function is allowed to have its own variables declarations. When this is the case, the variables declared in the function are termed *local* variables. This means that these variables only have values while the function is being executed; once the function has been completed and control has returned to the main program, local variables cannot be accessed. On the other hand, *global* variables, which are defined before `main()`, are always available while the program is running, even to functions. Note, however, that if a variable declared in a function has the same name as a variable declared in the main program, the local variable only can be used in the function. These ideas are best illustrated with the aid of an example such as that shown in Listing 30.15.

Listing 30.15.   A program to illustrate the difference between global and local variables

```
1     /* Program Example15            */
2     /* Displays local and global strings */
3     #include <stdio.h>
4     #include <conio.h>
5
6     char Greeting[20] = "Hello"; /* Global variable */
7
8     void Func1()
9     {
10      char Greeting1[20]= "How do"; /* Local variable */
11
12      textcolor(RED);
13      cprintf("Func1    Greeting1    local %15s\r\n",   Greeting1);
14      getchar();
15      cprintf("Func1    Greeting    global %15s\r\n",   Greeting);
16      getchar();
17
```

```
18    }
19    void Func2()
20    {
21      char Greeting2[20] = "Howdy"; /* Local variable */
22
23      textcolor(BLUE);
24      cprintf("Func2     Greeting2   local %15s\r\n",  Greeting2);
25      getchar();
26      cprintf("Func2     Greeting    global %15s\r\n", Greeting);
27      getchar();
28    }
29
30    void main()
31    {
32      char Greeting[20] = "Hi"; /* Local variable */
33
34      clrscr();
35      cprintf("Source   Variable    Scope   Value\r\n");
36      cprintf("--------------------------------------------------- \r\n");
37      textcolor(YELLOW);
38      cprintf("Main     Greeting    local %15s\r\n",  Greeting);
39      getchar();
40      Func1();
41      Func2();
42    }
```

The program declares three string variables: Greeting which is a global variable defined on line *6*, Greeting1 a variable local to function Func1() and declared on line *10*, Greeting2 a variable local to function Func2() and defined on line *21* and finally Greeting a local variable declared in main() on line *32*. The main program assigns a value ("Hi") to Greeting on line *32* and displays it. Because this is a local variable it takes precedence over the global variable with the same name defined on line *6*. Then when Func1 is executed, the local variable Greeting1 is assigned a value ("How do") on line *10* and then displays that string. This function also displays global variable Greeting ("Hello") Finally, when Func2 is executed, it displays the contents of the local variable Greeting2 followed by the global variable Greeting again. Note that an attempt to include a line such as

```
cprintf("%s", Greeting2);
```

after line *31* in the main program would result in an error since, once Func2 has terminated, the local variable Greeting2 does not exist. Here is what the program produces as its output:

```
Source   Variable   Scope   Value
-------------------------------------
main     Greeting   local   Hi
Func1    Greeting1  local   How do
Func1    Greeting   global  Hello
Func2    Greeting2  local   Howdy
Func2    Greeting   global  Hello
```

Each line of the output indicates the source of the line, that is whether it is generated from the main program or from a function, the name of the variable whose value is being displayed, whether the variable is local or global, and the contents of the variable. The pre-defined screen output function `cprintf()` is almost the same as `printf()`, the difference being that it allows the colour of text, as set by `textcolor()`, to appear on the screen. Another difference is that it requires `\r` in the formatting string to produce a carriage return. (See the later section on screen handling for more information on text colour commands).

Using parameters in procedures

The 'wink' program shown in Listing 30.14 uses the simplest form of function which performs a task without any need to communicate with `main()`. However, there will be many instances when you will want to use information available in the main program. As we saw in the previous section, global variables provide one means of accomplishing this, but for sound reasons current programming practice discourages the use of global variables for this purpose. Usually a much better method is to use functions which have either *value parameters* or *variable parameters*.

Value parameters

Listing 30.16 is a modification of the program shown in Listing 30.14. Notice that another function, `Wink()`, has been included. This new function uses a *value parameter*, called `Eye`, which is defined within brackets after the function name on line *36*. A value parameter allows you to pass a value to a function from the main program or from another function. Thus, on line *51*, the value of the `for` loop variable `k` is passed to the function `Wink`. `k` takes the values 1, 2 and 3 which are used to decide which of the three functions, `Face1`, `Face2` or `Face3` to execute. In effect, this causes each of the latter three functions to be executed in turn. The outer `for` loop makes this cycle of three functions to repeat ten times. When one loop is controlled by an outer loop in this fashion, they are called *nested loops*.

Listing 30.16. A program to illustrate the use of value parameters

```
1     /* Program Example 16                  */
2     /* Using value parameters with a function */
3
4     #include <stdio.h>
5     #include <conio.h>
6     #include <dos.h>
7
8     void Face1()
9     {
10      clrscr();
11      puts("           ");
12      puts("   -  -    ");
13      puts("< O O >  ");
14      puts("  |  ^  |   ");
15      puts("    ~-~    ");
16    }
17    void Face2()
18    {
19      clrscr();
20      puts("           ");
21      puts("   -  -    ");
```

```
22        puts("< O o > ");
23        puts(" | ^ |   ");
24        puts("   ~V~    ");
25      }
26    void Face3()
27      {
28        clrscr();
29        puts("           ");
30        puts("   - -     ");
31        puts("< o O > ");
32        puts(" | ^ |   ");
33        puts("   ~V~    ");
34      }
35
36    void Wink(int Eye)
37      {
38        switch(Eye)
39        {
40          case 1: Face1();break;
41          case 2: Face2();break;
42          case 3: Face3();break;
43        }
44      }
45
46    void main()
47      {
48        int i, k;
49
50        for(i=1; i0; i++)
51          for(k=1; k; k++)
52          {
53            Wink(k);
54            delay(500);
55          }
56      }
```

The number of parameters that you can use in a function is not limited to one - you can use as many as you like as long as you declare them in the function definition and include them within the brackets when you call the function from the main program. For example, suppose that we wanted to include the pre-defined delay function on line *54* within the procedure Wink() as shown in the program fragment which follows.

```
void Wink(int Eye, int Time);
  {
  switch(Eye)
    {
    case 1:
```

```
             Face1();
             delay(Time);
             break;
         case 2:
             Face2;
             delay(Time);
             break;
         case 3:
             Face3;
             delay(Time);
             break;
     }
   }
```

Now `Wink()` has two value parameters and these would both be included in any call to the procedure, as shown in the example below.

```
     for (i=1; i0; i++)
       for(k=1; k; k++) Wink(k, 500);
```

An important point about value parameters is that they provide a *one-way transfer of information* from the main program to a function. Variables used as value parameters when a function is called are unaffected by any processing that has occurred within the function; this is not the case, however, with *reference parameters*.

Reference parameters

Listing 30.17 is an example of a program which incorporates a function that uses two reference parameters.

Listing 30.17.   A program to illustrate the use of reference parameters

```
1     /* Program Example17                                    */
2     /* Using reference parameters in a function to order two numbers */
3
4     #include <stdio.h>
5     /* Function defined below */
6     void Sort(float& a, float& b)
7     {
8       float Temp;
9       if(a > b)
10        {
11          Temp = a;
12          a = b;
13          b = Temp;
14        }
15    }
16
17    void main()
18    {
```

```
19      float Num1, Num2;
20      printf("\nEnter two numbers: ");
21      scanf("%f%f", &Num1, &Num2);
22      Sort(Num1, Num2);
23      printf("The ordered numbers are: %10.2f %10.2f", Num1, Num2);
24    }
```

The program simply sorts two numbers into ascending order of magnitude using a function. The function has two reference parameters, a and b, which it compares: if a is greater than b, the values in a and b are swapped over. The main program asks the user to enter two numbers, it calls the function using the two numbers stored in Num1 and Num2, and then displays them when the function has finished. Here is a typical run of the program:

```
Enter two numbers: 34.6 17.32 ⏎
The ordered numbers are: 17.32    34.6
```

Notice that the values contained in Num1 and Num2, which were exchanged in the function using the variables a and b, have been swapped over. Thus, *reference parameters allow a two-way exchange of data* between a program and a function. Just like a variable, a function can be given a type which defines the form of the return value it produces. Up to now, the type has been void, indicating that the functions we have been describing do not return values. The full format of a function definition is as follows: type FunctionName(parameter list). In addition, you must use the return keyword followed by the value to be returned within the function. For example, for a function called Triangle_type which accepts three positive real numbers, in ascending order of magnitude, representing the three sides of a triangle and which returns an integer value of 0, 2 or 3 indicating how many of its sides are equal, the function definition in Listing 30.18 might be appropriate.

Listing 30.18.   A function to determine the type of triangle represented by three numbers

```
1      int Triangle_type(float a, float b, float c)
2      {
3        int Count;
4        int Ttype;
5
6        Count = 0;
7        if(a == b) Count++;
8        if(b == c) Count++;
9        if(c == a) Count++;
10       switch(Count)
11       {
12         case 0:Ttype = 0; break; /* Scalene */
13         case 1:Ttype = 2; break; /* Isosceles */
14         case 2: break; /* Not possible */
15         case 3:Ttype = 3; break; /* Equilateral */
16       }
17       return Ttype;
18     }
```

The three sides are passed as value parameters to the variables a, b and c. The if statements on lines 7 to 9 increment Count if any two sides are the same. The values that Count can assume are 0 for no sides equal, 1 if two sides are equal and 3 if all three sides are equal; a value of 2 is not possible when the three sides are arranged in ascending order of magnitude. The number of equal sides is stored in Ttype by the switch statement and it is this value which is returned by the function to the calling program by line 17. Note that because this function returns a value it can be used like a variable in an arithmetic expression or in a logical expression or in a write statement. For example, it would be perfectly valid to write

```
if (Triangle_type(x, y, z) == 3) printf("Equilateral triangle");
```

Writing programs using procedures and functions

Listing 30.19 illustrates the use of user-defined functions in a program which allows two people to use the computer to play noughts and crosses. The program uses functions appropriate to a variety of situations. The main program alternately gets X and O moves, checking each time for a winning or drawn position. The program terminates when someone has won or after nine moves have been made.

Listing 30.19.   Noughts and crosses game

```
1      /* Program Example19                                        */
2      /*---------------------------------------------------------*/
3      /* A program which makes use of different forms of functions to */
4      /* allow two players to play noughts and crosses. The computer  */
5      /* checks for a win or draw automatically, and makes sure that  */
6      /* illegal moves are not made. The board is a grid numbered     */
7      /* 1 to 9. Each Player in turn selects a number and the grid is */
8      /* redrawn with the X or O in that position.                    */
9      /* X always starts first.                                       */
10     /*---------------------------------------------------------*/
11
12     #include <conio.h> /* Screen handling functions header file    */
13     #include <stdio.h> /* Standard i-o handling functions header file*/
14
15     char Grid[10]; /* Global data structure to store board position  */
16                    /* Grid[0] is not used                           */
17     enum {FALSE, TRUE}; /* Set up boolean values: FALSE=0, TRUE=1    */
18
19     void InitGrid()
20     /*---------------------------------------------------------*/
21     /* This sets up the board with the positions numbered from 1 to 9*/
22     /*---------------------------------------------------------*/
23     {
24       Grid[1]='1';
25       Grid[2]='2';
26       Grid[3]='3';
27       Grid[4]='4';
28       Grid[5]='5';
29       Grid[6]='6';
30       Grid[7]='7';
31       Grid[8]='8';
```

```
32      Grid[9]='9';
33    }
34
35    void DrawGrid()
36    /*----------------------------------------------------------------*/
37    /* This draws the current board after every move */
38    /*----------------------------------------------------------------*/
39
40    {
41      clrscr();
42      printf(" %c | %c | %c\n", Grid[1], Grid[2], Grid[3]);
43      printf("---|---|---\n");
44      printf(" %c | %c | %c\n", Grid[4], Grid[5], Grid[6]);
45      printf("---|---|---\n");
46      printf(" %c | %c | %c\n", Grid[7], Grid[8], Grid[9]);
47      printf("\n");
48    };
49
50    int CheckMove(int Move)
51    /*-----------------------------------------------------------------*/
52    /* Validates every move to make sure that a number from 1 to 9 is */
53    /* chosen and that the selected position is not already occupied  */
54    /*by an X or O.                                                   */
55    /* Parameters: Move - integer value parameter                     */
56    /* Return value: Boolean - TRUE if valid move, FALSE if invalid   */
57    /*------------------------- ----------------------------------------*/
58
59    {
60      int Check_Move = TRUE;
61
62      if (Move < 1 || Move > 9)
63        {
64           printf("Invalid position - enter a number between 1 and 9");
65           Check_Move= FALSE;
66        }
67      else if (Grid[Move] == 'X' || Grid[Move] == 'O')
68        {
69           printf("This position has already been used");
70           Check_Move= FALSE;
71        }
72      return Check_Move;
73    }
74
75    int GetXmove()
76    /*----------------------------------------------------------------*/
77    /* This accepts the X move from the player. If the move is        */
78    /* invalid, the player is required to enter the move again.       */
79    /* Parameters: None                                               */
80    /* Return value: Integer in the range 1 to 9                      */
81    /*----------------------------------------------------------------*/
```

```
82    {
83      int Xpos;
84      int ValidXMove;
85        do
86          {
87             printf("\n");
88             printf("Enter position( 1 to 9 ) for X move: ");
89             scanf("%d", &Xpos);
90             ValidXMove= CheckMove(Xpos);
91          }
92        while(!ValidXMove);
93        return Xpos;
94    }
95
96    int GetOmove()
97    /*------------------------------------------------------------------*/
98    /* This accepts the O move from the player. If the move is          */
99    /* invalid, the player is required to enter the move again.         */
100   /* Parameters: None                                                 */
101   /* Return value: Integer in the range 1 to 9                        */
102   /*------------------------------------------------------------------*/
103   {
104     int Opos;
105     int ValidOMove;
106
107       do
108         {
109            printf("\n");
110            printf("Enter position( 1 to 9 ) for O move: ");
111            scanf("%d", &Opos);
112            ValidOMove= CheckMove(Opos);
113         }
114       while(!ValidOMove);
115       return Opos;
116   }
117
118   int CheckForWinner()
119   /*------------------------------------------------------------------*/
120   /* This checks for a line of Xs or Os in one of the 7              */
121   /* possible ways. It determines whether a row, column or           */
122   /* diagonal contains the same character (ie an X or an O).         */
123   /* Parameters: None                                                 */
124   /* Return value: Boolean - TRUE if there is a winner, FALSE        */
125   /* otherwise                                                        */
126   /*------------------------------------------------------------------*/
127
128   {
129     int Check_For_Winner;
130
131     if((Grid[1]==Grid[2]) && (Grid[2]==Grid[3]) ||
```

```
132              (Grid[4]==Grid[5]) && (Grid[5]==Grid[6]) ||
133              (Grid[7]==Grid[8]) && (Grid[8]==Grid[9]) ||
134              (Grid[1]==Grid[4]) && (Grid[4]==Grid[7]) ||
135              (Grid[2]==Grid[5]) && (Grid[5]==Grid[8]) ||
136              (Grid[3]==Grid[6]) && (Grid[6]==Grid[9]) ||
137              (Grid[1]==Grid[5]) && (Grid[5]==Grid[9]) ||
138              (Grid[3]==Grid[5]) && (Grid[5]==Grid[7]))
139            Check_For_Winner= TRUE;
140      else Check_For_Winner= FALSE;
141      return Check_For_Winner;
142    };
143
144    void main()
145    {
146      int Count= 0;        /* Counts the number of valid moves made  */
147      int Move;            /* Board position for the next move       */
148      int Winner= FALSE;   /* Boolean variable which becomes true
149                                    when there is a winner           */
150      int XMove= TRUE;     /* Keeps track of whose move it is:
151                                    TRUE for X move
152                                    FALSE for Y move                 */
153      InitGrid();          /* Call function to initialise the board  */
154
155      DrawGrid();          /* Display the initial board position     */
156
157      /* Loop to repeat the playing sequence                         */
158      while (Count 9 && !Winner)
159      {
160        switch (XMove)
161          {
162            case TRUE:          /* Do this if it is X's move         */
163                Move = GetXmove(); /* Get the X move position        */
164                Grid[Move] ='X';   /* Store it in the data structure */
165                XMove = FALSE;     /* Make it O's move next          */
166                break;
167            case FALSE:         /* Do this if it is O's move         */
168                Move = GetOmove(); /* Get the O move position        */
169                Grid[Move]= 'O';   /* Store it in the data structure */
170                XMove = TRUE;      /* Make it X's move next          */
171                break;
172          }
173
174      Count++;                       /* Increment count after every move */
175
176      DrawGrid();                    /* Show the current board position   */
177
178      /* Check to see if the game is a win or draw                   */
179      Winner = CheckForWinner();
180      if(Winner)
181        printf("End of Game: %c has won", Grid[Move]);
```

```
182        else if(Count==9)
183          printf("A draw");
184
185      }
186    flushall();
187    getchar();
188  }
```

The six functions, `InitGrid`, `DrawGrid`, `CheckMove`, `GetXMove`, `GetYMove` and `CheckForWin-ner`, used in the program are described in the following sections.

InitGrid

This function initialises the character array, `Grid[]`, which is a global array used throughout the program by every function. The function is used only once and does not require any parameters.

DrawGrid

This function draws the current board position. Initially the board is displayed like this:

```
    1 | 2 | 3
   ---|---|---
    4 | 5 | 6
   ---|---|---
    7 | 8 | 9
```

The numbers are replaced by Xs and Os as the game progresses.

CheckMove

This function has a single integer value parameter called `Move` which represents the current player's choice of board position. The function first checks that the integer is in the range 1 to 9 before checking the contents of `Grid[Move]` to ensure that the position is not already occupied with an X or an O. If the move is valid, the function returns a boolean value of `TRUE`, otherwise it returns `FALSE`. `CheckMove` is used by the following two functions.

GetXMove

This function asks the X player to type in a number from 1 to 9 representing a board position. If the move is valid, the function terminates and the position entered by the player is returned as an integer value; if the move is invalid (see function `CheckMove`) the player is requested to try again.

GetOMove

This function asks the O player to type in a number from 1 to 9. Otherwise it is structurally identical to `GetXMove`.

CheckForWinner

This function checks individually the three rows, three columns and two diagonals that they contain the same character. If one of these lines does contain the same character, then one of the players has won. For example, if the diagonal represented by Grid[1], Grid[5] and Grid[9] all contain an X, then the X player has won.

Guidelines for using functions

Here are some guidelines for writing functions:

- Instead of using global variables, try to use functions with value or reference parameters wherever possible.

- Keep function sizes small (no more than about a page in length). This is to make them easier to understand and follow.

- Use a single function for a single task. Do not have a single function doing several jobs.

- Document the function as it is being written, for your benefit and for that of anyone else who has to understand your code.

- Test each function thoroughly before writing another function in the same program.

Advantages of using functions

All good programmers make full use of procedures and functions, and in fact their use is essential to the development of all but the most trivial programs. There are a number of good reasons for making this statement:

- They allow a large, complex program to be built up from a number of smaller or more manageable units. This facilitates a team approach to program development by allowing each unit to be written and tested independently of the rest of the program.

- They can reduce the amount of code required for a program. Once a subprogram has been developed, it can be used as many times as required within a program using the same code.

- They can reduce the amount of time required to write a program if libraries of re-usable functions and procedures are available. This is much the same as building electronic circuits using standard electronic components.

Screen handling

Turbo C provides a number of useful screen handling functions. We have already used two of these functions: clrscr() to clear the screen and delay() to make the computer pause while executing a program. You must include the following line in your program in order to use the screen handling functions described in this section:

```
#include <conio.h>
```

A number of other useful functions are described next.

window()

Defines a text window on the screen. The syntax of the procedure is

```
window(X1,Y1,X2,Y2)
```

where the four parameters are explained by the following diagram. To set a text window containing ten lines at the top of the screen use

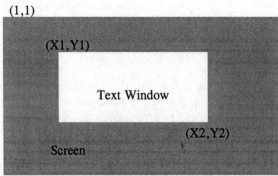

```
window(1,1,80,10)
```

To return the current window to the full screen size use

```
window(1,1,80,25)
```

clreol()

Clears all characters from the cursor position to the end of the line without moving the cursor. It uses the current text window.

delline()

Deletes the line containing the cursor in the current text window.

gotoxy()

Moves the cursor to X, Y, where X is the column and Y is the row relative to the top left corner of the current window which has the coordinates (1, 1). Thus to move the cursor to row 5, column 10, you would use GotoXY(10,5).

insline()

Inserts a line in the current text window above the line that the cursor is on.

textcolor()

This sets the colour for subsequently displayed text. There are sixteen colours and you can specify each one by name or by using the equivalent number as shown in Table 30.8. Thus, to set the text colour to red, you could use either textcolor(RED) or textcolor(4).

colour	value	colour	value	colour	value	colour	value
Black	0	Red	4	DarkGray	8	LightRed	12
Blue	1	Magenta	5	LightBlue	9	LightMagenta	13
Green	2	Brown	6	LightGreen	10	Yellow	14
Cyan	3	LightGray	7	LightCyan	11	White	15

Table 30.8.

By using the pre-defined constant, BLINK, you can make the text flash, for example, `textcolor(BLUE + BLINK)`.

`textbackground()`

This allows you to set one of eight different colours for the text background. The colours are shown in the first eight rows of the table. Thus to set the background colour to light grey you could use either `textbackground(LIGHTGRAY)` or `textbackground(7)`. Note that if you clear the screen using `clrscr()` after setting the background colour, the whole of the current text window will change to that colour.

Example program 1

The example shown in Listing 30.20 illustrates the use of text windows and text background colours by drawing random windows of different colours.

Listing 30.20.   Using text windows

```
1    /* Program Example20        */
2    /* Screen handling functions */
3
4    #include <conio.h>
5    #include <stdlib>
6    #include <dos.h>
7
8    void main()
9    {
10     int x, y, i;
11
12     for(i=1; i100; i++)
13       {
14          x = random(60);
15          y = random(15);
16          window(x, y, x + random(10), y + random(8));
17          textbackground(random(8));
18          clrscr();
19          delay(1000);
20       }
21   }
```

kbhit (), getche () and getch ()

Three other useful functions are kbhit(), getche() and getch(). Function kbhit() returns a nonzero value (equivalent to true) if there is a character in the keyboard buffer and zero if the buffer is empty (equivalent to false). The keyboard buffer is simply an area of memory which is used to store, temporarily, characters entered through the keyboard. Function kbhit() can therefore be used to detect any use of the keyboard. Characters can be retrieved with getche() and getch(). A common application of kbhit() is as a means of terminating a loop, as illustrated by the following program fragment:

```
while(!kbhit())
   {
      /* instructions to be repeated */
   }
```

Each time through the while loop kbhit() tests the keyboard buffer: if a key has been pressed, the keyboard buffer will have at least one entry, kbhit() returns true and the loop terminates, otherwise kbhit() returns false and the loop repeats once more.

getche() allows you to capture a keystroke by reading the first character in the keyboard buffer. If the keyboard buffer is empty, it waits until a character is available and then returns its value. Note that getch() behaves in the same way except that the character is not echoed to the screen.

Example program 2

The program shown in Listing 30.21 echoes only numeric characters to the screen, ignoring characters that are not in the range 0 to 9. The while loop terminates as soon as the space bar is pressed. The function putch() on line *17* is used to display the single character stored in key if it is in the range 0 to 9, that is, a numeric character.

Listing 30.21. Using getch() and putch()

```
1     /* Program Example21 */
2     /*-----------------------------------------------------------*/
3     /* Program to display numeric digits entered at the keyboard */
4     /* and to ignore any other characters typed. The program     */
5     /* terminates when the space bar is pressed.                  */
6     /*-----------------------------------------------------------*/
7
8     #include <conio.h>
9
10    void main()
11    {
12      char key;
13
14      do
15         {
16            key = getch();
17            if (key >= '0' && key <= '9') putch(key);
```

```
18          }
19      while(key != ' ');
20    }
```

Sound and NoSound

Finally, these two procedures allow you to use your computer's built-in speaker. Sound(Pitch) causes the speaker to emit a tone whose pitch is determined by the integer parameter, Pitch. Thus, Sound(500) produces a tone with pitch 500Hz. NoSound terminates the tone produced by Sound. Thus to produce a tone of 300Hz for half a second within a program you could use:

```
sound(300);
delay(500);
nosound;
```

Example program 3

As a final example Listing 30.22 uses all of the screen handling functions discussed in a program which measures how quickly you are able to press a key after being given a signal.

Listing 30.22.   Using various screen handling functions

```
1     /* Program Example22                                            */
2     /*------------------------------------------------------------*/
3     /* Program to illustrate some screen handling facilities. The  */
4     /* user is invited to test his/her reflexes by pressing a key  */
5     /* as quickly as possible. The average of three attempts is    */
6     /* calculated and displayed in millisecond units               */
7     /*------------------------------------------------------------*/
8
9     #include <conio.h>
10    #include <stdio.h>
11    #include <stdlib.h>
12    #include <dos.h>
13
14    const int ROW = 2;    /* The row base position for screen text */
15    const int COLUMN = 5; /* The coloumn base position             */
16
17    void FlushKeyboardBuffer()
18    /*------------------------------------------------------------*/
19    /* This makes sure that there are no characters available in   */
20    /* the keyboard buffer.                                        */
21    /*------------------------------------------------------------*/
22
23    {
24       while(kbhit()) getch();       /* Read and discard any previous */
25                                     /* keystrokes                    */
26    }
27    /*------------------------------oOo---------------------------*/
28
```

```
29    void Beep(int Tone)
30    /*---------------------------------------------- ------------*/
31    /* Makes a short warning sound                              */
32    /*----------------------------------------------------------*/
33    {
34      sound(Tone);
35      delay(10);
36      nosound();
37    }
38    /*-----------------------------oOo--------------------------------*/
39
40    void PressAnyKey()
41    /*----------------------------------------------------------*/
42    /* Waits for any key being depressed before continuing      */
43    /*----------------------------------------------------------*/
44    {
45      FlushKeyboardBuffer();
46      gotoxy(COLUMN, ROW+8);
47      cprintf("Press any key to continue");
48      while(!kbhit());
49    }
50    /*-----------------------------oOo--------------------------------*/
51
52    void Instructions()
53    /*----------------------------------------------------------*/
54    /* Displays the instructions for using the program          */
55    /*----------------------------------------------------------*/
56    {
57      clrscr();
58      window(10, 10, 70, 20); /* Define the text window */
59      textcolor(YELLOW);
60      textbackground(BLUE);
61      clrscr();
62      gotoxy(COLUMN, ROW);
63      cprintf("Put a finger any key and as soon as you hear a\r\n");
64      gotoxy(COLUMN, ROW+1);
65      cprintf(" signal and the screen changes colour, press it\r\n");
66      gotoxy(COLUMN, ROW+3);
67      cprintf("You will get three tries and the program\r\n");
68      gotoxy(COLUMN, ROW+4);
69      cprintf("will calculate your average response time\r\n");
70      gotoxy(COLUMN, ROW+6);
71      PressAnyKey();
72    }
73    /*-----------------------------oOo----------------------------------*/
74
75    int Time(int Attempt)
76    /*----------------------------------------------------------*/
77    /* Uses the delay() function to determine the response time in  */
78    /* milliseconds for hitting a key                           */
```

```
79      /*-------------------------------------------------------------*/
80      {
81         int Millisecs;
82
83         clrscr();
84         textcolor(YELLOW);
85         gotoxy(COLUMN, ROW);
86         switch(Attempt)
87            {
88               case 1: cprintf("First attempt starting..");break;
89               case 2: cprintf("Second attempt starting..");break;
90               case 3: cprintf("Third attempt starting.."); break;
91            }
92         randomize();            /* Init the random number function    */
93         Millisecs = 0;
94         delay(1000);            /* Pause for one second before timing */
95         textcolor(RED + BLINK);
96         cprintf(" NOW!");       /* random delay of up to 5 seconds    */
97         delay(random(5000));
98         FlushKeyboardBuffer();
99         textbackground(RED);
100        clrscr();               /* The signals to press a key as      */
101        Beep(1500);             /* quickly as possible                */
102        do
103           {
104              delay(1);
105              Millisecs++;       /* Count how much time elapses..      */
106           } while(!kbhit()); /* .. before any key is pressed         */
107        return Millisecs;
108     }
109     /*----------------------oOo--------------------------------*/
110
111     void Results(float Average)
112     /*-------------------------------------------------------------*/
113     /* Displays the average time taken over the three attempts */
114     /*-------------------------------------------------------------*/
115     {
116        textbackground(LIGHTGRAY);
117        textcolor(BLACK);
118        clrscr();
119        gotoxy(COLUMN, ROW);
120        cprintf("Your average response time was %5.0f milliseconds", Average);
121        gotoxy(COLUMN, ROW+5);
122        PressAnyKey();
123     }
124     /*----------------------oOo--------------------------------*/
125
126     void main()
127     {
128        int Total;
```

```
129     int i;
130
131     Total = 0;                  /* Init total time for attempts    */
132     for(i=1; i<=3; i++)         /* Repeat the trial 3 times         */
133       {
134         Instructions();         /* Display the user instructions    */
135         Total = Total + Time(i);
136       }
137
138     Results(Total/3); /* Display the average time taken */
139     }
140     /*-------------------------oOo--------------------------------*/
```

The main program starts on line *126*. The function `Instructions` explains that the user is to press a key as quickly as he/she can when a short sound signal is heard and a rectangular window changes colour. The function `Time()` times how long in milliseconds it took to react to the signal. This time is added to a running total which accumulates the times for three attempts. `Results()` displays the average time the user took to respond. The program makes good use of user-defined functions, and the comments in the program listing explain their operation, but it is worth adding some further explanation regarding the function `PressAnyKey()`. As mentioned earlier, the buffer memory associated with the keyboard temporarily stores the values of key depressions made while the program is running, and these values can be accessed using `getch()`. By repeatedly using this function to read single characters until there are no more left in the buffer, `FlushKeyboardBuffer()` empties the buffer in preparation for using the `kbhit()` function subsequently. This is to ensure that `kbhit()` will detect only the next key depression and not any that have been made previously.

Records and files

Many computer applications involve processing data which has already been stored as a *file* on a backing storage medium such as magnetic disk. A file is often organized as a sequential collection of *records*, each one containing information about the subject of the file. For example, a car file might contain details of a number of different cars, each record dealing with a single car and containing such information as make, model, engine capacity, number of doors, colour, insurance group, extras, and so on. *Sequentially* organized files contain records which can only be accessed in the order in which they were originally stored in the file, whereas *randomly* organized files contain records which can be accessed in any order. However, because of space limitations, the example programs in this section deal only with Turbo C's functions for processing sequentially organized files. Before we examine some file handling methods, however, it is necessary to discuss *user-defined data types*.

User-defined data types

As you know by now, every variable used in a program must be associated with a data type. Up to now the data types that we have used have been `int`, `float`, `char`, and `array[]`. However, C allows us to define our own data types based on combinations of these standard types by creating structures using the keyword `struct`. For example, to define a data structure for a `Car` type we could write:

```
struct Car
{
  char Make[15];
  char Model[20];
  int InsGp;
  float Cost;
}
```

and now we can declare variables to be of type Car:

```
Car  SportsCar, FamilyCar, HatchBack;
```

We have thus created a data structure that can be used to define a record within a file. In order to identify a variable (or *field*) within the record we must use the *dot notation*. For instance, to store information in the structure, SportsCar, we could use the following instructions:

```
printf("Make of car? ");
scanf("%s", &SportsCar.Make);
printf('Model? ");
scanf("%s", &SportsCar.Model);
printf("Insurance Group? ");
scanf("%d", &SportsCar.InsGp);
printf("Cost? ");
scanf("%f", &SportsCar.Cost);
```

The field within the record is specified after the dot; this allows a number of related items to be grouped together as a unit (that is, as a *record*), while still allowing each part (or *field*) to be accessed separately. Now, to define a collection, or *file*, of such records, we need to use a declaration such as

```
FILE *CarFile;
```

This, combined with an fopen() function such as that shown below, allows us to create and add to a file consisting of car records

```
CarFile = fopen("a:\cars.dat", "a");
```

This statement prepares the computer system to handle a sequentially organized file, stored on drive a: and called cars.dat, using fwrite() and fread() functions for writing and reading complete records. The programs in the following sections illustrate how files defined like this may be created, read and searched.

Creating a sequential file using `fopen` and `fwrite`

The main program starting at line 77 in Listing 30.23 shows how a sequential file of car details can be created. The program shows that the fopen() function is used to link the name of the file (CarFile) within the program with the name of the actual file (FileName) stored on magnetic disk. The name of the disk file has been #defined earlier in the program as "a:\\cars.dat". This means that when write instructions are used later to store car records in the file, the data will be recorded using the filename "a:\cars.dat". The double slash in the line

```
#define FileName "a:\\Cars.dat"
```

is required because C uses the \ symbol before special control characters (as in \n for newline) - the double slash is interpreted as a single slash when used this way. The #define instruction tells the C compiler to replace every incidence of FileName with "a:\\Cars.dat" before compiling the program. The fopen() function also requires a string to indicate the mode in which the file is to be used. Table 30.9 shows some of the different modes possible.

Mode	Description
r	Open for reading only
w	Create for writing. If a file by that name already exists, it will be overwritten.
a	Append. Open for writing at end of file or create for writing if a file by that name does not exist

Table 30.9. *File modes*

The function fopen() returns a 'handle' to be used to identify the file in subsequent operations. Line *80* in main() defines this handle with the declaration FILE *CarFile. Thus, whenever the car file is to be accessed, the file handle, CarFile, is used to associate it with the file "a:\Cars.dat".

The program uses a structure called rec which defines the format of car records used in the file to be created.

Listing 30.23.   Creating and extending a sequential Car file

```
1      /* Program Example23                                    */
2      /*----------------------------------------------------*/
3      /* A program which creates a car file containing a number of car */
4      /* records and allows further records to be added to the end of  */
5      /* the file.                                             */
6      /*----------------------------------------------------*/
7
8      #include <stdio.h>
9      #include <conio.h>
10     #include <ctype.h>
11
12     #define FileName "a:\\Cars.dat"    /*The name of the file on disk*/
13
14     struct rec
15       {                              /*The structure of each car record*/
16         char Make[10];
17         char Model[10];
18         int InsGp;
19         float Cost;
20       };
21
22     void FlushKeyboardBuffer()
23     /*----------------------------------------------------*/
24     /* This makes sure that there are no characters left in          */
25     /* the keyboard buffer.                                  */
26     /*----------------------------------------------------*/
27
28     {
```

```
29        while(kbhit()) getch();         /* Read and discard any previous */
30                                         /* keystrokes */
31    }
32    /*----------------------------oOo--------------------------------*/
33
34
35    rec GetRec()
36    /*--------------------------------------------------------------*/
37    /* Gets and returns the data for a single record.               */
38    /*--------------------------------------------------------------*/
39
40    {
41      rec Car;
42
43      clrscr();
44      printf("\nPlease enter Car details as follows:");
45      printf("\nMake(eg Ford): ");
46      scanf("%s", Car.Make);
47      printf("\nModel(eg Escort): ");
48      scanf("%s", Car.Model);
49      printf("\nInsurance Group(eg 7): ");
50      scanf("%d", &Car.InsGp);
51      printf("\nCost(eg 8450.50): ");
52      scanf("%f", &Car.Cost);
53      printf("\n");
54
55      return Car;
56    }
57    /*----------------------------oOo--------------------------------*/
58
59    void WriteRec(FILE *file_handle, rec Car)
60    /*--------------------------------------------------------------*/
61    /* Adds the new record to the file                              */
62    /* file_handle: a file pointer which identifies the file        */
63    /* Car : a car record                                           */
64    /*--------------------------------------------------------------*/
65    {
66      char Answer;
67
68      FlushKeyboardBuffer();
69      printf("\nOK to save this record?(Y/N) ");
70      Answer = getche();
71      if(toupper(Answer) == 'Y')               /* write car rec to file */
72        fwrite(&Car, sizeof(Car), 1, file_handle);
73      printf("\n");
74    }
75    /*----------------------------oOo--------------------------------*/
76
77    void main()
78    {
```

```
79      rec CarRec;
80      FILE *CarFile;
81      char Answer;
82
83      CarFile = fopen(FileName, "a"); /* Links CarFile with the    */
84                                      /* actual file held on disk. */
85                                      /* Opens file for append.    */
86      do
87        {
88          CarRec= GetRec();                  /* Gets the Car details    */
89          WriteRec(CarFile, CarRec);
90          FlushKeyboardBuffer();
91          printf("Add another record to the file?(Y/N)");
92          Answer = getche();
93        }
94      while(toupper(Answer) == 'Y');
95
96      fclose(CarFile);                       /* Closes the file         */
97    }
98    /*--------------------------oOo----------------------------------*/
```

Most of the remainder of the program is contained within a loop which repeats the following sequence of operations:

1. Get the details for a car record, `CarRec` - this is accomplished using the function `GetRec()` which asks the user to type in the appropriate information and returns the car record.

2. Store the record obtained by the function `GetRec`. The function `WriteRec()` first asks for confirmation before writing the record to the file. The whole record and the appropriate file are both passed as parameters. The format for the instruction to write a record to a file is as follows:

    `fwrite(pointer, size, number of items, file handle)`

    where

`pointer`	is the location in memory of the start of the car record
`size`	is the size of the record in bytes
`number of items`	is the number of records of the specified size to be written
`file handle`	specifies the file to be used

    Thus

    `fwrite(&Car, sizeof(Car), 1, file_handle)`

    specifies that a single `Car` record, starting at address `&Car`, of size returned by the function `sizeof(Car)` is to be written to the file specified by `file_handle`. Note that the function `toupper()` has been used to force the user's answer to be an uppercase letter because the `if` instruction on line *71* compares the answer typed in with the capital letter 'Y' only.

3.   Ask the user if he/she wishes to add another record to the file. The program loop terminates when the user answers anything other than 'Y' to the question.

Finally, the `fclose(CarFile)` statement tells the system that the channel to the disk file may be terminated. Below is an example of the output from the program:

```
Please enter Car details as follows:

Make(eg Ford): Honda ⏎
Model(eg Escort): Civic ⏎
Insurance Group(eg 7): 5 ⏎
Cost(eg 8450.50): 8100 ⏎

OK to save this record?(Y/N) y ⏎
Add another record to the file?(Y/N) n ⏎
```

Reading a file using `fopen` and `fread`

Whether a file is being created or read the same `fopen()` command must be used to link the internal and external file names. Thus, before attempting to read the car file created by the previous program, it is first necessary to use `fopen(FileName, mode)` again. This appears on line *37* of Listing 30.24. This time the mode is set to `"r"`, that is, read.

Listing 30.24.   Reading the Car file

```
1     /* Program Example24                                          */
2     /*----------------------------------------------------------*/
3     /* A program which reads and displays a car file containing a  */
4     /* number of car records.                                     */
5     /*----------------------------------------------------------*/
6     #include <stdio.h>
7     #include <conio.h>
8     #include <ctype.h>
9
10    #define FileName "a:\\Cars.dat" /*The name of the file on disk   */
11
12    struct rec
13      {                               /*The structure of each car record*/
14        char Make[10];
15        char Model[10];
16        int InsGp;
17        float Cost;
18      };
19
20    void FlushKeyboardBuffer()
21    /*----------------------------------------------------------*/
22    /* This makes sure that there are no characters available in  */
23    /* the keyboard buffer.                                       */
24    /*----------------------------------------------------------*/
```

```
25
26    {
27      while(kbhit()) getch();        /* Read and discard any previous */
28                                     /* keSstrokes                   */
29    }
30    /*------------------------------oOo------------------------------*/
31
32    void main()
33    {
34      rec CarRec;
35      FILE *CarFile;
36
37      CarFile = fopen(FileName, "r");
28                                     /* Links CarFile with the actual */
39                                     /* file held on backing storage. */
40      clrscr();
41      printf("\nReading %s...\n", FileName);
42
43      while(fread(&CarRec, sizeof(CarRec), 1, CarFile))
44         {
45            printf("\n%12s%12s%4d%10.2f", CarRec.Make, CarRec.Model,
46                   CarRec.InsGp, CarRec.Cost);
47         }
48      printf("\n\nEnd of %s. ", FileName);
49      fclose(CarFile);                        /* Closes the file */
50
51      FlushKeyboardBuffer();
52      printf(" Press any key to continue..");
53      getche();
54    }
```

The `fopen()` function is used to *open a file for input*, that is, to enable it to be read. The records within the file are accessed using the `fread()` function which contains the name of the file to be read and the name of the record which is to receive the data obtained from the backing storage device: `fread(&CarRec, sizeof(CarRec,1, CarFile,)`. Once the data has been read from the file it is displayed using a `printf()` function which uses the dot notation to separate the fields within the car record. The `while` loop uses the `fread` function to determine whether there are any more records left to be read from the file; when the end of the file is detected, the `fread()` function returns a boolean value of `true`, otherwise it returns `false`.

Below is an example of the output from the program:

```
    Reading a:\cars.dat ...


            Ford        Escort       7     8450.50
            Ford        Fiesta       5     7200.00
            Ford        Probe       10    11000.00
            Honda        Civic       5     8100.00
            Honda      Prelude       9     9900.00
              VW          Golf      11    10200.00
```

```
         VW          Polo       8      8400.00
      Nissan       Micra       5      6500.00
    Vauxhall       Corsa       5      6400.00
    Vauxhall    Cavalier       8      9500.00
        Fiat         Uno       4      5900.45
     Ferrari        Dino      16     25000.00
     Ferrari     Daytona      16     35500.00

   End of a:\cars.dat
```

In order to send output to an online printer you can use the `fprintf()` function. For example, by replacing line *45*

```
printf("\n%12s%12s%4d%10.2f", CarRec.Make, CarRec.Model,
       CarRec.InsGp, CarRec.Cost);
```

with

```
fprintf(stdprn,"\n%12s%12s%4d%10.2f", CarRec.Make, CarRec.Model,
        CarRec.InsGp, CarRec.Cost);
```

the car record would be printed instead of displayed on the screen. `stdprn` is Turbo C's standard printer output stream name, just as `stdin` and `stdout` are the names of the standard streams for keyboard input and monitor output respectively.

Searching a file

Searching a sequential file for certain records involves opening the file for input and then reading each record in turn and checking to see if it meets some criteria. For example, we might want to search the car file in order to extract all the cars made by Ford, or we might just want to find a particular car, such as a Fiat Uno. The program in Listing 30.25 allows the user to specify an approximate car price and then it searches the car file for all cars that cost within £1000 of the price entered. For example, if the user entered £8000, the program would print out all cars that cost between £7000 and £9000.

Listing 30.25. Searching the Car file

```
1    /* Program Example25                                          */
2    /*-----------------------------------------------------------*/
3    /* A program which reads a car file and displays details of   */
4    /* cars which are within £1000 of a specified price           */
5    /*-----------------------------------------------------------*/
6
7    #include <stdio.h>
8    #include <conio.h>
9    #include <ctype.h>
10
11   #define FileName "a:\\Cars.dat"     /*The name of the file on disk*/
12
13   struct rec
14     {                              /*The structure of each car record*/
```

```
15        char Make[10];
16        char Model[10];
17        int InsGp;
18        float Cost;
19      };
20
21    void FlushKeyboardBuffer()
22    /*-------------------------------------------------------------*/
23    /* This makes sure that there are no characters left in       */
24    /* the keyboard buffer.                                       */
25    /*-------------------------------------------------------------*/
26
27    {
28      while(kbhit()) getch();      /* Read and discard any previous */
29                                   /* keystrokes */
30    }
31    /*---------------------------oOo---------------------------------*/
32
33    void main()
34    {
35      rec Car;
36      FILE *CarFile;
37      float Price;
38
39      CarFile = fopen(FileName, "r");
40
41      clrscr();
42      printf("Enter the approximate price of cars to be listed: £");
43      scanf("%f", &Price);
44
45      printf("\nCars which are within £1000 of £%0.0f :", Price);
46
47      while(fread(&Car, sizeof(Car), 1, CarFile))
48
49        if( (Car.Cost >= Price - 1000) && (Car.Cost <= Price + 1000) )
50          {
51            printf("\n%12s%12s%4d%10.2f", Car.Make, Car.Model,
52                    Car.InsGp, Car.Cost);
53          }
54
55      printf("\n\nEnd of %s. ", FileName);
56      fclose(CarFile);                             /* Closes the file */
57
58      FlushKeyboardBuffer();
59      printf(" Press any key to continue..");
60      getche();
61    }
62    /*---------------------------oOo---------------------------------*/
```

As you might expect, this program is very similar to the program which read and displayed the contents of the car file. The instruction which is used to identify and display the required records starts on line *49*:

```
if( (Car.Cost >= Price - 1000) && (Car.Cost <= Price + 1000) )
  {
      printf("\n%12s%12s%4d%10.2f", Car.Make, Car.Model,
      Car.InsGp, Car.Cost);
  }
```

The `if` statement contains two conditions connected by the `&&` (and) operator; if the cost of the car (`CarRec.Cost`) is both greater than `Price - 1000` *and* less than `Price + 1000`, in other words within £1000 of `Price`, then the current record is displayed. The output from the program is shown below:

```
Enter the approximate price of cars to be listed: £8000 ⏎
Cars which are within £1000 of £8000 :


        Ford        Escort        7        £8451
        Ford        Fiesta        5        £7200
       Honda         Civic        5        £8100
          VW          Polo        8        £8400


End of a:\cars.dat


Press <Enter> to continue
```

Exercises

Program design, programming and program testing

For each of the following problems, design, implement and thoroughly test the program.

Decisions

1. Read a number and display a message which states whether the number is positive, negative or zero.

2. Read a number and print it only if it is between 10 and 20.

3. Read a number followed by a single letter code. The number represents the price of an item and the code indicates whether tax is to be added to the price. If the code is "V" then the tax is 20% of the item's cost. If the code is "X" then the item is not taxed. Print out the total cost of the item.

4. Read three positive, non-zero integers which may represent the sides of a triangle. The numbers are in ascending order of size. Determine whether or not the numbers do represent the sides of a triangle.

5. Extend the previous question to determine the type of triangle if one is possible with the values provided. Assume that the only types of triangles to consider are:

   - scalene- no equal sides;

   - isosceles - two equal sides;

   - equilateral - three equal sides.

6. Read in a single character and print a message indicating whether or not it is a vowel.

Loops

7. Write separate programs to produce conversion tables for:

   (i)   Inches to centimetres (1 to 20 inches, 1 inch = 2.54 centimetres);

   (ii)   Pounds to kilograms (1 to 10 pounds, 2.2 pounds per kilogram);

   (iii) Square yards to square metres (10, 20 ,30,..., 100 sq yds 1yd = .91 m)

8. The cost and discount code of a number of items are to be entered by a user. The program must print out each item's cost, discount and cost less discount. The discount codes are as follows:

Code	Discount
A	5%
B	10%
C	15%

The program will terminate when the user enters 0 for the cost of the item. The program must then print the total cost of all the items entered.

9. Write a program to repeatedly display a menu containing a number of options for converting between different units, plus one option to exit the program. The user must enter a number or letter corresponding to a menu item. Valid entries are to accept a numeric value from the user and apply and display the appropriate conversion, invalid entries are reported and the user is reminded about what choices are valid, and the exit option terminates the program. An example is given below.

```
                            Menu


              1      Inches to centimetres

              2      Centimetres to inches

              3      Pounds to Kilograms
                etc
              4      Exit


              Please enter option number :
```

10. A program reads an integer representing the number of gas bills to be processed, followed by that number of customer details. Each set of customer details consists of a customer number, a single character code representing the type of customer and the number of units used. Customers are of type 'D' (domestic) or 'B' (business). Domestic customers are charged 8p per unit and business customers are charged 10p per unit. For each customer print the customer number, the number of units used and the cost of the gas used. Print the total number of units used for this batch of customers and the total amount charged.

11. Repeat the previous question assuming that all the domestic users are first and that separate totals are required for domestic and business users.

Strings

12. Read two strings and compare them. Print a message to indicate whether or not they are identical.

13. Repeat the previous problem but ignore case. For example, your program should regard the strings "Hello There", "HELLO THERE", and "hello there" as being identical.

14. Read a string representing a sentence and print the number of words in the sentence. Assume that words are separated by no more than one space and that there are no punctuation marks in the text.

15. Write separate programs to enter and store a string of up to 80 characters and then:

    (i)   Count the number of leading spaces;

    (ii)   Count the number of trailing spaces;

    (iii)   Count the number of embedded spaces;

    (iv)   Count the number of leading, trailing and embedded spaces;

    (v)   Remove leading and trailing spaces from a string, and reduce multiple embedded spaces to single spaces.

16. Read a string containing a sentence and print the words in reverse order. For example, the sentence "the cat sat on the mat" would become, "mat the on sat cat the".

17. Read a string and determine whether it is purely alphabetic, purely numeric or a mixture of alphabetic and numeric characters.

Arrays

18. Read 15 values into a numeric array and then:

    (i)   print the contents the array;

    (ii)   find the average of the numbers stored in the array;

    (iii)   copy the array into a duplicate array, but in reverse order. Print the contents of both arrays.

19. Read a set of numbers and swap the first number with the largest in the set. Then, starting from the second value, find the largest number in the remaining list and swap it with the second value. Repeat this process until the list has been sorted into ascending order of magnitude.

Validation

20. Post codes have the following possible formats:

    (i)   *aa99 9aa*

    (ii)   *aa9 9aa*

    (iii)   *a9a 9aa*

    where *a* represents an alphabetic character and *9* represents a numeric character.

Write a program to validate a post code, assuming that only uppercase letters are used and there is a single space separating the two parts of the post code.

21. As for the previous problem but allow upper and lower case letters, leading spaces, trailing spaces and more than one space between the two parts of the code.

Encoding

22. Many names that sound the same are often spelled differently and this can cause problems in information systems. For example, Waites, Waits and Whaites all sound the same though they are all spelled differently and contain different numbers of letters. A coding system called Soundex can be used to solve this problem by converting a name into a code based on the following algorithm.

(i)   The first letter of the name is used as the first letter of the code.

(ii)   All subsequent vowels, and the letters H, W and Y are ignored.

(iii)   Double letters are replaced by single instances of the letter.

(iv)   Then this code, apart from the first character, is converted into a number by substituting the letters in the following table by numeric digits.

letter	substitute digit
BFPV	1
CGJKQSXZ	2
DT	3
L	4
MN	5
R	6

(v)   The code is restricted to four characters including the leading letter.

(vi)   If the code is less than four characters it is padded with zeros.

Write a program to convert a name into its equivalent Soundex code. Some examples are given below.

Morton becomes *M635*

Morten becomes *M635*

Waites becomes *W320*

Whaites becomes *W320*

Waits becomes *W320*

23. The following table illustrates the Morse code.

A	.-	N	-.
B	-...	O	---
C	-.-.	P	.--.
D	-..	Q	--.-
E	.	R	.-.
F	..-.	S	...
G	--.	T	-
H	....	U	..-
I	..	V	...-
J	.---	W	.--
K	-.-	X	-..-
L	.-..	Y	-.---
M	--	Z	--..

(i) Write a program to read in a word (or a sentence if you wish) and output it in Morse code.

(ii) Add sound so that when a letter is pressed on the keyboard the appropriate Morse code is heard.

24. A form of encoding used on the Internet is called "rot13" encoding. It involves taking each letter of the alphabet and replacing it by the letter 13 positions further on in the alphabet as shown in the following table.

letter	replacement letter	letter	replacement letter	letter	replacement letter
A	N	J	W	S	F
B	O	K	X	T	G
C	P	L	Y	U	H
D	Q	M	Z	V	I
E	R	N	A	W	J
F	S	O	B	X	K
G	T	P	C	Y	L
H	U	Q	D	Z	M
I	V	R	E		

(i) Write a program to read a block of text and encode it using rot13. Spaces and punctuation marks do not need to be encoded.

(ii) Enhance the above program by also encoding punctuation marks and spaces.

(iii) Write a program to decode text which has been encoded using rot13.

(iv) Invent and implement your own encoding and decoding scheme using a different form of substitution.

Files

25. Write a program to create a video file. Each record will have the fields shown in the following table.

field	description	type	size	decimal places
Code	unique video code	text	6	
Title		text	30	
Certificate	PG 12 18 etc	text	2	
Cost	purchase price	real	5	2
Date	purchase date	date	6	
Hire code	single letter	text	1	
Available for hire	in or out	boolean		
Hired by	membership number	text	6	
Date hired	when member hired it	date	6	
Number of times hired		integer	4	0

(i)   Add procedures for the following tasks.

- Displaying a table of all videos in the file.

- Locating and displaying the details of a particular video given the video code.

- Displaying all available videos.

- Locating and displaying videos which have been hired more than a certain number of times.

26. Design and write a program capable of performing simple statistical analyses. The program should be able to:

(i)   store up to 100 numbers in a file;

(ii)   read and display a file containing numbers to be analysed;

(iii) calculate and display the mean, mode, median, minimum value, maximum value, range and standard deviation of the numbers;

(iv)   calculate and display a frequency table for a given number of equal classes.

Write the program using procedures and functions where appropriate and provide a user-friendly interface.

Chapter 31

Assembly Language Programming

In this section we describe the instruction set and assembly language for a hypothetical 16-bit microprocessor, the BEP/16. The instruction set has been designed to allow us to present a representative sample of typical microprocessor instructions, and to illustrate some simple programming tasks.

The chapter concludes with a number of small assembly language programs to illustrate how some common programming tasks may be implemented, and a final program is used to illustrate the way that an assembler produces a machine code program.

A typical microprocessor: the BEP/16

The BEP/16 is a simple, hypothetical 16-bit microprocessor loosely based on the Intel 8086/88. The BEP/16 processor contains the following 16-bit registers:

- 11 general-purpose registers, R0-R10

- a 16-bit Program Counter, PC

- a 16-bit Stack Pointer, SP

- a 16-bit Flag Register, FR

- a 16-bit Overflow Register, VR

Addressable RAM is limited to 64K bytes, though an additional 16K bytes are used for the stack. Memory is accessed in 16-bit words. The *flag register* contains the following flags:

- the carry flag (C)-bit0

- the zero flag (Z)-bit1

- the sign flag (S)-bit2

- the overflow flag (V)-bit3

- the trap flag (T)-bit4

Carry flag: the C flag is set (C=1) if there is a carry out from the most significant bit (m.s.b.) as a result of an arithmetic operation. The C flag is *cleared* (C=0) if there is no carry out.

Zero flag: the Z flag is set if the result of an operation is zero. It is cleared if the result is non-zero.

Sign flag: the S flag reflects the state of the m.s.b. after an arithmetic operation. S = 0 represents a positive value and S = 1 represents a negative value.

Overflow flag: the V flag is set when an arithmetic overflow occurs, that is when, as a result of a signed arithmetic operation, the most significant bit of the result is lost.

Trap flag: when set, the T flag puts the processor into single-step mode. Each instruction generates an internal interrupt which executes a program to display the contents of all the internal registers. The interrupt routine waits for a key depression before returning to the next program instruction.

Instruction opcodes are all 16-bit words with the format shown in Table 31.1.

2	6	4	4	bits
Mode	Operation	Reg1	Reg2	field

Table 31.1. *Instruction format*

The *Operation field* is a numeric code which specifies the type of instruction: ADD, MOV, JGT etc.

Reg1 and *Reg2* are codes, as defined in Table 31.2, for instructions which use one or two registers.

register	R0	R1	R2	R3	R4	R5	R6	R7
code	0000	0001	0010	0011	0100	0101	0110	0111
register	R8	R9	R10	VR	PC	FR	SP	
code	1000	1001	1010	1011	1100	1101	1110	

Table 31.2.

Where two registers are not necessary in an instruction, for example in MOV R3, @10, the code 1111 (hexadecimal F) is inserted into the unused register slot or slots in the instruction.

Examples of instructions using two registers are

```
MOV R1,R2
ADD R2,R4                 ;Arithmetic operations
LDR R0,&8000+R1           ;Indexed addressing
```

The *Mode* field contains a 2-bit code indicating the addressing mode to be used. The codes in Table 31.3 are used. The last three modes are appropriate to the LDR and STR instructions only.

Immediate operands are restricted to signed integers in the range –32768 to +32767. Instructions containing immediate operands or memory addresses require an extra 16-bit word.

addressing mode	code
Immediate	00
Direct	01
Indexed	10
Indirect	11

Table 31.3.

The instruction set is first summarized and then described in more detail in the next sections. In the summary, the flags that are affected (if any) are indicated by a 1 (flag set), a 0 (flag reset) or * (depends on the result of the instruction).

Summary

The instruction set is summarized in Table 31.4 (which covers several pages).

reg refers to any one of the registers.

addr is an address which may be a number or a symbolic address.

immed is an immediate operand which may be a single character enclosed in single quotes, or a number, or an identifier preceded by the @ symbol. Immediate numeric constants may also be preceded by the & symbol for hexadecimal constants or the % symbol for binary constants.

offset is used in indexed addressing to indicate an offset from a base address.

mnemonic	operation	formats	words	flags
				T V S Z C
ADC:Add with carry	Adds reg2 to reg1 then adds carry to reg1	ADC reg1,reg2 ADC reg,immed	1 2	- * * * *
ADD: Add	Adds reg2 to reg1	ADD reg1,reg2 ADD reg,immed	1	- * * * *
AND: Logical AND	Ands reg1 with reg2	AND reg1,reg2 AND reg,immed	1	- - * * -
CLC: Clear carry flag	C = 0	CLC	1	- - - - **0**
CLT: Clear trap flag	T = 0	CLT	1	**0** - - - -
CMP: Compare	Compares reg1 and reg2 and sets flags	CMP reg1,reg2 CMP reg,immed	1 2	- - * * *
DEC: Decrement	Subtracts 1 from operand	DEC reg DEC addr	1	- * * * * - * * * *
DIV: Divide	Divides reg1 by reg2 Unsigned integer division	DIV reg1,reg2 DIV reg,immed	1 2	- - - - *
HLT: Halt	Halts execution of the program	HLT	1	- - - - -
INC: Increment	Adds 1 to operand	INC reg INC addr	1 2	- * * * *

mnemonic	operation	formats	words	flags
				T V S Z C
Jcondition	Conditional jump		2	- - - - -
	Jump if equal	JEQ label		
	Jump if not equal	JNE label		
	Jump if overflow set	JVS label		
	Jump if overflow clear	JVC label		
	Jump if higher	JHI label		
	Jump if lower or same	JLS label		
	Jump if plus	JPL label		
	Jump if minus	JMI label		
	Jump if carry set	JCS label		
	Jump if carry clear	JCC label		
	Jump if greater or equal	JGE label		
	Jump if less than	JLT label		
	Jump if greater than	JGT label		
	Jump if less or equal	JLE label		
JMP: Unconditional jump		JMP label	2	- - - - -
JSR: Jump to subroutine	Pushes the PC to stack then jumps to label	JSR label	2	- - - - -
LDR: Load register	Copies memory address contents to register	LDR reg,addr	2	- - * * -
		LDR reg,addr +offset	2	
		LDR reg,[addr]	2	
MOV: Move	Copies reg2 to reg1	MOV reg1,reg2	1	- - * * -
		MOV reg,immed	2	
MUL: Unsigned multiply	Multiplies reg1 by reg2	MUL reg1,reg2	1	- - - - *
		MUL reg,immed	2	
NOP: No operation		NOP	1	- - - - -
NOT: Logical NOT	Inverts operand	NOT reg	1	- - * * -
OR: Logical OR	Ors reg1 with reg2	OR reg1,reg2	1	- - * * -

mnemonic	operation	formats	words	flags
				T V S Z C
		OR reg,immed	2	
POP: Pop from stack	Top of stack is copied to operand and the stack pointer is decremented	POP reg	1	- - * * -
PUSH: Push on stack	Increments the stack and copies operand to top of stack	PUSH reg	1	- - * * -
ROL: Rotate left	Rotates operand specified number of places left	ROL reg1,reg2 ROL reg,immed	1 2	- - * * *
ROR: Rotate right	Rotates operand specified number of places right	ROR reg1,reg2 ROR reg,immed	1 2	- - * * *
RRX: Rotate right extend	Rotates operand through the carry flag	RRX reg1,reg2 RRX reg,immed	1 2	- - * * *
RTS: Return from subroutine	Copies the top of the stack to PC	RTS	1	- - - - -
SAR: Arithmetic shift	Shifts operand specified number of places right retaining sign of operand	SAR reg1,reg2 SAR reg,immed	1 2	- - * * *
SBB: Subtract with borrow	Subtracts reg2 from reg1 then subtracts carry from reg1	SBB reg1,reg2 SBB reg,immed	1 2	- * * * *
SEC: Set carry flag	C = 1	SEC	1	- - - - 1
SET: Set trap flag	T = 1	SET	1	1 - - - -
SHL: Shift left	Shifts operand specified number of places left	SHL reg1,reg2 SHL reg,immed	1 2	- - * * *
SHR: Shift right	Shifts operand specified number of places right	SHR reg1,reg2 SHR reg,immed	1 2	- - * * *
STR: Store register	Copies contents of register to memory	STR reg,addr STR reg,addr +offset STR reg,[addr]	2 2 2	- - * * -

mnemonic	operation	formats	words	flags
				T V S Z C
SUB: Subtract	Subtracts reg2 from reg1	SUB reg1,reg2	1	- * * * *
		SUB reg,immed	2	
SWI: Software interrupt	Invokes an operating system routine	SWI addr	2	- - - - -
XOR: Logical exclusive or	Exclusively ors reg1 with reg2	XOR reg1,reg2	1	- - * * -
		XOR reg,immed	2	

Table 31.4.

Data transfer instructions: MOV, LDR, STR

This set of instructions deals with transferring data to and from memory, and between internal registers.

MOV: Copies a word from from a source operand to a destination operand. The source operand may be an immediate constant or a register, but the destination must be a register.

LDR: Copies the contents of a memory location to a specified register. Three memory addressing modes are supported:

direct, as in LDR R1, &1234 or LDR R3, cost, where cost is a symbolic memory address;

indexed, as in LDR R4, table+R1, where table is a memory address and R1 contains a value to be added to table before the contents of the resulting address are loaded into R4;

indirect, as in LDR R2,[vector], where vector contains an address, the contents of which are loaded into R2.

STR: Copies the contents of a specified register to a memory location. Uses the same addressing modes as Load Register.

Arithmetic instructions: ADD, ADC, SUB, SBB, MUL, DIV, CMP, INC, DEC

This set of instructions allows simple arithmetic operations to be performed on the contents of registers. The multiply and divide instructions use the overflow register (VR) to hold part of the result of the operations.

ADD: Performs addition on two words, putting the sum in the first operand. For example, the instruction ADD R10, @3 would add 3 to the contents of R10. Note that, since any register is allowed to be used in this instruction, unconditional jumps may be performed using instructions of the form ADD PC, R2. This would add the contents of R2 to the contents of the PC, thus causing a relative jump to the resulting address. An absolute jump would result from MOV PC, R4, assuming that R4 contained a valid address to which to branch.

ADC: Similar to ADD, the difference being that the current contents of the carry flag are also added to the first operand. This facilitates multiple-precision addition.

SUB: Subtracts the second operand from the first operand, putting the difference in the first operand. For example, SUB R5, R3 subtracts the contents of R3 from R5 and stores the difference in R5. In a similar way to that described for ADD, this instruction could also be used to manipulate the PC.

SBB: Similar to SUB, but subtracts the carry flag, the equivalent of a borrow, from the first operand. Again, this is used for multiple precision arithmetic.

CMP: Performs the same operation as SUB, but does not store the difference in the first operand. It is used to compare two values and set appropriate flags (V, C and Z) according to the result so that a conditional branch instruction may follow it.

MUL: Multiplies two 16-bit unsigned numbers to produce a 32-bit product. The carry flag is set if the product exceeds the size of a 16-bit register; in this instance, the overflow (the most significant word) is stored in VR, the overflow register, which is reserved for this purpose, though it may also be used as a general-purpose register.

DIV: Divides the first unsigned operand by the second and stores the integer quotient in the first. The remainder after division is stored in VR.

INC: Adds 1 to the specified register or memory location.

DEC: Subtracts 1 from the specified register or memory location.

Transfer of control instructions: JMP, Jcond, JSR, RTS, SWI

This set of instructions allows the normal sequential flow of instructions to be modified. Normally, the PC is incremented after every fetch cycle so that each instruction is performed in the order in which it is stored in memory; this set of instructions allows the contents of the PC to be changed to any value in the memory space so that program instructions may be executed in orders other than sequential. This allows, for instance, sections of code to be repeated in a loop, and it facilitates decomposing a single complex program into smaller more manageable subprograms.

JMP: Causes an unconditional jump by adding a signed offset to the PC. That is, it performs a relative jump forwards or backwards. The assembler automatically converts label addresses to the appropriate offsets.

JEQ: Performs the transfer of control only if $Z=1$, that is, if the result of an arithmetic operation was zero.

JNE: Performs the transfer of control only if $Z=0$, that is, if the result of an arithmetic operation was not zero.

JVS: Performs the transfer of control only if $V=1$, that is, if the result of an arithmetic operation produces a value which cannot be represented in the 16-bit destination register.

JVC: Performs the transfer of control only if $V=0$.

JHI: Performs the transfer of control assuming that a previous comparison was between two unsigned numbers and that the first was greater than the second, that is $C=0$ and $Z=0$.

JLS: Performs the transfer of control assuming that a previous comparison was between two unsigned numbers and that the first was less than or equal to the second, that is C=1 or Z=1.

JPL: Performs the transfer of control only if S=0, that is, the last operation produced a positive number with a sign bit of 0.

JMI: Performs the transfer of control only if S=1, that is, the last operation produced a negative number with a sign bit of 1.

JCS: Performs the transfer of control only if C=1. If this occurs then it means that the result of an operation could not be represented in 16 bits, and the carry flag represents the 17th bit of the destination register.

JCC: Performs the transfer of control only if C=0.

JGE: This assumes that the previous operation used signed integers in two's complement representation. The branch is performed if the first operand was greater or equal to the second operand, that is, (S=1 and V=1) or (S=0 and V=0).

JLT: This assumes that the previous operation used signed integers in two's complement representation. The branch is performed if the first operand was less than the second operand, that is, (S=1 and V=0) or (S=0 and V=1).

JGT: This again assumes signed arithmetic with the first operand greater than the second, that is, Z=0 and ((S=1 and V=1) or (S=0 and V=0)).

JLE: Again assuming signed arithmetic with the first operand less than or equal to the second, that is, Z=1 or ((S=1 and V=0) or (S=0 and V=1)).

JSR: Jumps to a subroutine after pushing the PC to the stack.

RTS: Returns from a subroutine by popping the top of the stack (assuming it contains the required return address) to the PC.

SWI: This instruction performs an indirect call to an operating system subroutine. It allows access to pre-written routines for standard tasks such as keyboard input and displaying text on the screen. Some of the possible calls are described in a later section in this chapter.

Shift and rotate instructions: SHR, SHL, SAR, ROL, ROR, RRX

This set of instructions is used for manipulating the contents of registers by shifting them left or right. They are often used for performing multiplication or division by powers of two.

SHR: Shifts the contents of the first operand a number of places right. The number of places is specified by the second operand which is either a register or an immediate numeric operand. For example, SHR R5, @4 would shift the contents of R5 four places right. Zeroes are moved into the most significant bit positions and the bits that are shifted out go into the carry flag. This instruction divides the first operand by a power of two; in the example above, R5 would be divided by 16 $(=2^4)$

SHL: As above, but shifts left. This time the most significant bit is moved into the carry flag after each bit shift, and zeroes are introduced at the least significant end of the word.

SAR: As SHR, but the sign (in the most significant bit) is retained. Thus two's complement numbers retain the appropriate sign.

ROR: Rotates the first operand a specified number of bits right. The number of bits rotated is determined by the second operand. At each bit shift, the bits are moved right one position and the least significant bit is rotated to the most significant bit position.

ROL: As ROR but the rotation is to the left.

RRX: As ROR but the carry register is included in the rotation. That is, it is a 17-bit rotation.

Logical operations: AND, OR, NOT, XOR

Logical instructions perform bit operations on the contents of a register. They are frequently used for performing masking operations on a binary word, to change certain bits without affecting the other bits in the word.

AND: Performs a logical AND operation with the two operands, storing the result in the first operand. For example, the instruction AND R4, %0111111101111111 would set bits 7 and 15 of R4 to 0 whilst leaving the rest of the bits unchanged.

OR: Performs a logical OR operation between the two operands, storing the result in the first operand. For example, the instruction OR R3, %0000000011111111 would set bits 0–7 of R3 to 1 and leave the remaining bits unchanged.

NOT: Inverts the operand, changing 1s to 0s and 0s to 1s. Thus the instruction NOT R1 followed by INC R1 would take the two's complement of R1.

XOR: Performs a logical exclusive OR operation with the two operands, storing the result in the first operand. For example, the instruction XOR R2,R2 clears the R2 register. This is faster than MOV R2, @0 because it uses only one word.

Stack operations: PUSH, POP

Stack operations are frequently used to preserve the contents of registers when subroutines are called. For example, if a subroutine uses registers R0, R3 and R4, then the first three instructions of the subroutine might be

```
PUSH R0
PUSH R3
PUSH R4
```

and the last instructions might be

```
POP  R4
POP  R3
POP  R0
RTS
```

so that initially the three registers are copied to the stack, and at the end of the subroutine they are restored to their initial values ready for returning to the calling program. This ensures that subroutines do not corrupt the contents of registers required by the calling program.

PUSH: Copies the contents of the specified register to the top of the stack and increments the stack pointer.

POP: Decrements the stack pointer and transfers the top of the stack to the specified register.

Flag operations: CLC, CLT, SEC, SET

These instructions allow the carry and the trap flags to be set or cleared. When the trap flag is set the processor operates in single-step mode for debugging purposes. After each instruction is executed, an interrupt is generated which calls an operating system routine to display or allow the user to change the contents of all the registers. The routine also allows memory locations to be displayed or changed.

CLC: Clears the carry flag, that is, C=0.

SEC: Sets the carry flag, that is, C=1.

CLT: Clears the trap flag, that is, T=0 and returns the processor to normal execution mode.

SET: Sets the trap flag, that is, T=1 and puts the processor into single-step, trace mode.

Other instructions: HLT, NOP

HLT: Terminates program execution, returning control to the operating system.

NOP: This instruction does not perform any function. Possible uses are in setting up timed delays in which one or more NOPs are included in a loop, or for modifying an assembled program without the need to re-assemble it. For example, in single-step mode, memory locations containing the program being executed could be replaced by NOPs to prevent the execution of certain instructions, JSRs perhaps.

Table 31.5 shows the numeric equivalents of the instruction mnemonic codes recognized by the assembler. The assembler uses these when converting the source program into machine code.

Mnemonic	Opcode	Mnemonic	Opcode
ADC	08	JSR	21
ADD	09	LDR	22
AND	0A		
CLC	0B	MOV	24
CLT	0C	MUL	25
CMP	0D	NOP	26
DEC	0E	NOT	27
DIV	0F	OR	28
HLT	10	POP	29
INC	11	PUSH	2A
JCC	12	ROL	2B
JCS	13	ROR	2C
JLT	14		
JEQ	15	RRX	2D
JGE	16	RTS	2E
JGT	17	SAR	2F
JHI	18	SBB	30
JLE	19	SEC	31
JLS	1A	SET	32
JMI	1B	SHL	33
JNE	1C	SHR	34
JPL	1D	STR	35
JVC	1E	SUB	36
JVS	1F	SWI	37

Table 31.5.

The BEP/16 macro assembler

The BEP/16 assembler facilitates low-level programming by offering the following facilities:

- the use of mnemonics for operation codes;

- the use of labels for branching instructions;

- the use of comments for annotating programs;

- symbolic addresses;

- convenient notations for the various addressing modes available;

- a number of pseudo-ops (directives) for controlling various assembler functions;

- the use of macros.

BEP/16 assembly language instruction format

Assembly language instructions, or statements, are divided into a number of fields: (i) *Operation code field*. This contains the instruction mnemonic and therefore must always be present in the instruction. (ii) *Operand(s) field*. The composition of this field depends on the operation and the addressing mode. It may contain zero or more operands which may be registers, addresses or immediate operands. (iii) *Label field*. This optional field allows the programmer to establish a point of reference in the program. Certain other instructions, such as branch instructions, use these labels in their operand field. (iv) *Comment field*. This is another optional field, ignored by the assembler, to allow the programmer to annotate the program.

Assemblers provide varying degrees of flexibility in how these fields may be combined in program statements. Fields are separated from one another by means of *delimiters*, which are special characters (such as spaces, semi-colons or colons) recognised by the assembler as serving this function.

Listing 31.1 shows a short assembly language subroutine illustrating the concepts explained above. Internal registers are designated R0, R1, R2 etc. The subroutine adds the numbers 5 to 14 inclusive, that is, the 10 consecutive numbers starting with 5, by accumulating them in register R2.

Listing 31.1. Addition of ten consecutive numbers

label	Opcode	Operand(s)	comments
start:	MOV	R0, @10	; init loop counter
	MOV	R1, @5	; start value, R1=5
	MOV	R2, @0	; clear running total, R2=0
loop:	ADD	R2, R1	; accumulate total, R2=R2+R1
	INC	R1	; add 1 to R1
	DEC	R0	; decrement R0
	JGT	loop	; branch to label if R0>0
	RTS		; return from subroutine

The labels start and loop are identified by the use of the colon delimiter. MOV, ADD, INC, DEC, and JGT are opcode mnemonics as defined in Table 31.4. Opcodes are followed by a space delimiter. Where there are two operands, they are separated by the comma delimiter. Immediate operands are preceded by the @ sign. Comments always start with a semi-colon and continue to the end of the line. Labels and comments are usually allowed to be on separate lines:

```
;
; This is a comment on a separate line
;
; The label below is also on a separate line
;
start:
  MOV R0, @10  ; init loop counter
  MOV R1, @5   ; start value, R1=5
etc.
```

Semi-colons by themselves, as illustrated above, provide a convenient way of making the program easier to read.

Software interrupt routines (SWIs)

It is often possible to use operating system subroutines from within an assembly language. The BEP/16 provides the SWI instruction for this purpose. The opcode, SWI, is followed by either the address of a pointer to the operating system routine or an identifier representing the address of the pointer. Some of the identifiers recognised by the BEP/16 assembler and used in the example programs at the end of the chapter are as shown in Table 31.6.

OS routine	address	function
getInt	&F000	Read a 16-bit integer in denary form from the keyboard.
		Value returned in R0.
putInt	&F004	Display the contents of R0 on the VDU as a denary integer.
getChar	&F008	Read a character from the keyboard.
		ASCII value returned in R0. Character is echoed to VDU.
putChar	&F00C	Display ASCII character in R0 on VDU.

Table 31.6.

These addresses form a table of addresses of the actual routines. The SWI instruction uses the operand provided in the instruction as a pointer to the appropriate routine. This allows for the operating system routines to be located in different areas in different machines while still retaining the same SWI call. Other SWI calls allow graphics operations to be performed and input/output devices to be used.

Addressing modes

The BEP/16 offers seven addressing modes: *immediate*; *register*; *implied*; *direct*; *indexed*; *indirect*; *relative*.

Three of these modes, namely Direct, Indexed and Indirect are exclusively used in conjunction with STR and LDR for accessing memory. The functions of the addressing modes are explained next.

Immediate

In this mode, the operand is contained within the instruction itself, that is, the operand is a constant numeric value stored in a location immediately following the operation code. For example,

```
MOV R0, @100
```

contains the immediate value 100 which is stored immediately after the opcode MOV R0. The instruction, when executed, would transfer the immediate operand 100 from memory to the R0 register.

Examples

```
SAR R5, @3          ; Arithmetic shift right 3 places
DC R3, @&30         ; Add with carry hex 30 (ie 48)
SUB R1, @num        ; Subtract the value stored in num from R1
```

Register

Here, the operand is one of the internal registers.

Examples

```
MOV R2, R3          ; Transfer contents of R3 to R2
ADD R2, R2          ; Add contents of R2 to itself
MOV PC, R7          ; Transfer contents of R7 to PC
                    ; ie jump to address in R7
```

Implied

Sometimes termed *inherent* addressing, this is where the operand is implied in the operation code. For example, the instruction NOP requires no operand because the opcode itself specifies the action to be performed (which is nothing in this case).

Direct

Here the instruction refers to an address in memory which is to be accessed. Only the operation codes LDR and STR use this mode. For example,

```
LDR R5, &1E00
```

transfers the contents of location &1E00 to R5.

Examples

```
LDR R0, base        ; Load R0 with the contents of the address
                    ; stored in the label base
STR R1, value       ; Store the contents of R1 in address value
```

Indexed

In this mode an offset is added to a direct address to produce an effective address to be accessed. The offset may be an immediate operand or the contents of a register. Again, this addressing mode is restricted to the LDR and STR instructions. For example, the indexed instruction

```
        LDR R1, base + R0
```

loads R1 with the contents of address base plus the contents of register R0. So if the label base contained the address 5000, and R0 contained the number 6, R1 would be loaded with the contents of the word at location 5006.

Examples

```
        LDR R4, base + @2           ; Add 2 to base and load R4 with
                                    ; the contents of this address
        STR R1, &FF00 + R0          ; Add R0 to hex FF00 and load R1 with
                                    ; the contents of this address
```

Indirect

Here the second operand, in square brackets, contains the *address* of the value to be accessed; this is an indirect reference to a memory address. Square brackets are used to indicate indirection. For example, suppose that location &1000 contained the number 65 and location &3000 contained the number &1000, then the instruction

```
        LDR R4, [&3000]
```

would first access location &3000 to retrieve the actual address of the operand, that is location &1000, and then load the number in location &1000 into register R4. Thus R4 would contain the number 65 after execution of this instruction.

Examples

```
        LDR R6, [pointers]      ; Load R6 with contents of the address stored
                                ; in the location represented by pointers
        STR R7, [table]         ; Store the value in R7 in the word pointed to
                                ; by the contents ;of table
```

Relative

This mode is used in conjunction with transfer of control instructions such as JGT, JEQ etc. The label following the instruction is converted by the assembler into an offset (from the position of the current instruction) which is to be added to the program counter at runtime in order to effect a jump. Using an offset to the program counter (PC), rather than an absolute value to be transferred to the PC, allows programs to be made relocatable, since branch references are always relative to the current value of the PC. The offset may be positive for a forward branch, or negative to branch back to a previous instruction.

As an example, consider the short program described in Listing 31.1. It is assumed that the subprogram starts at location 1000, as shown in Listing 31.2, so that the numbers at the left-hand side represent the start locations of each instruction.

Listing 31.2.

```
1000    start:    MOV      R0, @10      ; init loop counter
1002              MOV      R1, @5       ; start value, R1=5
1006              MOV      R2, @0       ; clear running total, R2=0
1008    loop:     ADD      R2, R1       ; accumulate total, R2=R2+R1
```

```
1009            INC        R1           ; add 1 to R1
100A            DEC        R0           ; decrement R0
100B            JGT        loop         ; branch to label if R0>0
100D            RTS                     ; return from subroutine
```

The label in the instruction JGT loop is converted to a word offset of –5 by the assembler since the PC would be pointing to the next instruction following it at location 100E after the JGT instruction had been fetched and loop is at address 1008.

Assembler directives

Assembler directives, or pseudo-operations, are instructions to the assembler to perform functions which are not directly translatable into machine code. They perform such functions as reserving blocks of memory for use by the program, or for assigning values to identifiers. The BEP/16 supports the use of the following directives: DATA; EQU; ORG; RES; ON; OFF

The DATA directive

This directive allows data to be stored in memory and assignment of an optional symbolic address to the starting location of the data. For example, the directive

```
flag      DATA      0
```

stores the value 0 at the current address being allocated by the assembler and gives it the symbolic name flag. Thus, an instruction such as

```
LDR R6, flag
```

will load the value stored in address flag into register R6, that is, R6 will contain the value 0. Similarly,

```
STR R0, flag
```

will transfer the contents of register R0 to the location represented by flag.

A set of values can be stored using

```
list     DATA      1,2,4,8,16
```

such that the numbers are stored in consecutive words of memory starting at address list.

The DATA directive can also be used to allocate memory space for strings:

```
text     DATA      "This is a string"
```

This would store the ASCII values of the characters in the string in consecutive locations starting at address text. The string is terminated with a null value (0).

Long strings or lists of integers may be spread over several lines:

```
lines     DATA      "121 Hope Street"
          DATA      "Bilsworth"
          DATA      "Lancashire"

values    DATA      43,-15,35,0
          DATA      5,67,222,-9,1
          DATA      -1
```

The EQUate directive

The EQU directive merely assigns a value to an identifier and enters it into the assembler's symbol table.

Examples

```
end       EQU       -1        ; end = -1
CR        EQU       &0D       ; CR = 13. The & means hexadecimal
base      EQU       'A'       ; base = 65. The ASCII value of the
                              ; letter A is stored in the identifier base
```

The ORiGin directive

As the assembler is translating the program into machine-code, it maintains a location counter containing the address of the next instruction to be assembled. The ORG directive allows the programmer to determine the starting value of this counter, which determines where in memory the machine-code is to be loaded before it is executed. The ORG directive can be used more than once to cause different parts of the program to be loaded into different parts of memory. ORG directives are typically used for the following purposes: *interrupt routines*; *user stack allocation*; *subroutines*; *lookup tables*.

Examples

```
ORG    1000       ; Set location counter to 1000
ORG    &8000      ; Set location counter to hexadecimal 8000
ORG    INTRTNS    ; Set location counter to value stored in INTRTNS
```

The REServe directive

This directive allows memory space to be reserved, similarly to the DATA directive, but without assigning any values to the reserved locations. This allows the programmer to reserve RAM for such purposes as lookup tables, indirection addresses, temporary buffers, stacks etc.

Examples

```
table   RES    100       ; Reserve 100 locations starting at address table
heap    RES    &FF       ; Reserve hexadecimal FF (255) locations
buf     RES    maxlen    ;Reserve maxlen locations. maxlen could be a ;macro
                         name or ;have been defined by an EQU ;directive
```

The ON/OFF directives

These are used to put the program into single step, debug mode when it is executed. The ON directive has the effect of setting the Trap flag (T) and OFF resets the flag. This results in an operating system debug routine being invoked after the execution of every instruction, allowing the contents of registers and memory locations to be displayed.

Macros

The BEP/16 assembler supports the use of multi-line macros. A macro allows you to give a name to a sequence of instructions so that you can merely refer to this name whenever you want that particular sequence of instructions inserted into your source program. The assembler will take care of actually replacing the macro name with the appropriate sequence of instructions. The macro may also contain up to eight dummy operands. A macro is declared with #MACRO followed by the macro name with a list of (optional) dummy operand names, comma delimited, in parentheses. The actual macro is then listed using the dummy operands where necessary. The macro is terminated with #ENDM. Macros must be defined before they appear in the source program because the assembler first inserts macros into the source program before assembling it.

Example 1

Use meaningful names for registers:

```
#MACRO counter
R1
#ENDM
```

or equivalently,

```
#MACRO counter R1 #ENDM
```

This macro allows you to use the identifier counter instead of a register name. The assembler would replace every incidence of counter with R1. Thus, an instruction such as

```
INC counter
```

would become

```
INC R1
```

Example 2

Exchange the contents of any two registers (excluding R0):

```
#MACRO swap(a,b)
MOV R0, a
MOV a, b
MOV b, R0
#ENDM
```

The macro name is swap and it has two dummy operands, a and b.

Suppose that within the program a line contained the macro reference

```
. . . . . . .
  swap(R2,R6)
. . . . . . .
```

etc.

The assembler would replace the macro by

```
. . . . . . .
  MOV R0, R2
  MOV R2, R6
  MOV R6, R0
. . . . . . .
```

etc.

Macros have a number of advantages, including:

(i) reducing the size of the source program; (ii) the assembler automatically handles any changes to the macro definition, by making the corresponding changes to the source code wherever the macro appears; (iii) once a macro has been debugged, it can be used with confidence every time it is subsequently used; (iv) macros can be used to clarify and simplify the source code, as shown in Example 1 (Listing 31.3).

Programming examples

The following examples illustrate a number of commonly encountered programming tasks. We also take the opportunity to introduce appropriate assembler directives and macros as illustrations of their usefulness in aiding program writing and program clarity.

Arithmetic

Listing 31.3   Programming example 1

```
;Program to illustrate 16-bit integer arithmetic. There are no checks
;for overflow. The two numbers, a and b, are input from the keyboard and
;the program calculates a² - b², using (a+b)(a-b).
      ;
      ORG 0              ; Origin at 0
      ;
      SWI getInt         ; Operating system call to get a 16-bit integer
                         ; from the keyboard.
                         ; Value is returned in R0
      MOV R1, R0         ; Store the first value in R1
      SWI getInt         ; Get the second value
      MOV R2, R0         ; Store in R2
      MOV R3, R1         ; R3 = a
      ADD R3, R2         ; R3 = a+b
      MOV R4, R1         ; R4 = a
```

```
        SUB R4, R2          ; R4 = a-b
        MUL R3, R4          ; R3 = (a+b)(a-b)
        MOV R0, R3          ; Copy answer to R0
        SWI putInt          ; Operating system call to output a 16-bit
                            ; integer in R0 to the VDU.
        HLT                 ; Terminate program.
```

Memory transfer

Listing 31.4   Programming example 2

```
;This program reads a string of characters terminated by a carriage
;return character (ASCII value 13) and stores the string in
;consecutive words in memory using indexed addressing. Each word
;contains a single character.
        ;
        maxlen  EQU 100             ; Set max string length
        CR      EQU 13              ; ASCII value of carriage return
        ;
                ORG 0
        String  RES maxlen          ; Reserve space for string
        ;
                ORG 1000            ; Start of program
        Start:
                MOV R1, @0          ; R1=0
        Loop:
                SWI getChar         ; Read character
                STR R0, String + R1 ; R1 is offset from string base
                                    ;address
                CMP R0, @CR         ; Look for end of string
                JEQ End             ; Stop if CR
                INC R1              ; Add 1 to index
                JMP Loop            ; Repeat
        End:
                HLT
```

Listing 31.5   Programming example 3

```
;Program to transfer a block of data from one part of memory to
;another. The address of the block to be moved, its destination start
;address and the number of words in the block are supplied to the
;program. The two blocks are not allowed to overlap.
        ;
                ORG 100
        source  RES 1               ; Start address of block
        dest    RES 1               ; Start address of destination
        len     RES 1               ; No. of words in block
```

```
        ;
                    LDR R0, len          ; Get no. of words to be copied
        Loop:       CMP R0, @0           ; Check for all words copied
                    JLE Finish           ; If so finish
                    LDR R1, [source]     ; Get word
                    STR R1, [dest]       ; Store in destination
                    DEC R0               ; Decrement count
                    INC source           ; Point to next word for transfer
                    INC dest             ; Point to destination of next word
                    JMP Loop
        Finish:
                    HLT
```

Logical and shift operations

Listing 31.6   Programming example 4

```
;Program to separate and display 2 ASCII characters in a 16-bit word. The
;character in the most significant byte of the word is printed first.
        ;
        mask        EQU &00FF           ; Used to mask off most significant char
                    ORG 100
        char        RES 1               ; Reserve one word
        ;
                    LDR R2, char        ; Load word into R2
                    MOV R0, R2          ; Make copy in R0
                    SHR R0, @8          ; Shift right 8 places to move most
                                        ; significant byte to the right
                                        ; of the word.
                    SWI putChar         ; Display single character in R0 on VDU
                    MOV R0, R2          ; Copy original word into R0 again
                    AND R0, @mask       ; Mask off most significant byte
                    SWI putChar         ; Display single character in R0 on VDU
                    HLT
```

Listing 31.7.   Programming example 5

```
;Program to pack two characters held in separate words into a single
;word.
        ;
        mask        EQU &00FF           ; Used to mask of most significant char
                    ORG 100
        char1       RES 1               ; Reserve one word for first character
        char2       RES 1               ; Reserve one word for second character
        pack        RES 1               ; Reserve one word for packed characters
        ;
```

```
            LDR R1, char1      ; Load first character into R1
            SHL R1, @8         ; Shift left one byte
            LDR R2, char2      ; Load second character into R2
            OR R1, R2          ; Combine the two characters in R1
            STR R1, pack       ; Write packed word
            HLT
```

Bubble sort

Listing 31.8.   Programming example 6

```
;Program to perform a bubble sort on a list of 16-bit integers held in
;a table in memory. The first element of the table contains the
;number of values to be sorted (maximum 500). The stack is used for
;swapping two elements of the array. The two numbers to be swapped
;are held in R5 and R6.
            ;
            ;
#MACRO      SWAP(A,B)
            PUSH A
            PUSH B
            POP A
            POP B
#ENDM
            ORG 0
table       RES 500
            ;
            ORG 600
            MOV R1, @0         ; R1 = 0
            MOV R3, @1         ; R3 = 1
            LDR R9, table      ; Get number of values
L1:         CMP R3, @0         ; List is sorted when R3 = 0
            JEQ End            ; Finish
            MOV R3, @0         ; Set flag = 0
            MOV R1, @0         ; Index to table of values
L2:         LDR R5, table + R1 ; First of two numbers to be compared
            INC R1
            LDR R6, table + R1 ; Second of the two numbers
            CMP R5, R6         ; Compare numbers
            JLE L3             ; Skip if R5 <= R6
            SWAP(R5,R6)        ; Macro to swap R5 and R6
            MOV R3, @1         ; Set flag
L3:         CMP R1, R9         ; At end of table?
            JLT L2             ; No: get next pair of numbers
            JMP L1             ; Yes: repeat pass if necessary
End:        HLT
```

The assembly process

The BEP/16 assembler performs three passes of the source code:

- *Pass 1*: Comments are removed and macros are inserted where required.

- *Pass 2*: A symbol table is constructed, assembler directives are obeyed and instructions are converted into machine code where possible.

- *Pass 3*: Any forward referenced addresses are inserted with the aid of the symbol table.

These processes are illustrated by means of a program designed to display a box on the VDU using text characters. The original source program and the stages through which it goes in order to produce the object program are described in the following sections. The example program is shown in Listing 31.9.

Listing 31.9.

```
; ***********************************************
; *                                             *
; *         Program to draw a box like this      *
; *                                             *
; *         Width = 47    Ht = 7                *
; *                                             *
; ***********************************************


#MACRO     WIDTH     47      #ENDM
#MACRO     HT        7       #ENDM
#MACRO     CHAR1     '*'     #ENDM
#MACRO     CHAR2     ' '     #ENDM
;


cr         EQU       &0D
;          ORG       1000


;
;
Box:       MOV       R1, @WIDTH      ; Width of box
           MOV       R2, CHAR1       ; Solid line character, eg '*'
           MOV       R3, CHAR1       ; Box 'inside' character, eg space
           JSR       Line            ; Call subroutine to draw top line
           MOV       R3, CHAR2       ; Change middle of line character
           MOV       R4, @HT         ; Height of box
           SUB       R4, @2          ; Remove top and bottom lines
Middle:    JEQ       Bline           ; Test for any more middle lines
           JSR       Line            ; If yes draw a middle line
           DEC       R4              ; Decrement count
           JMP       Middle          ; Repeat if necessary
Bline:     MOV       R3, CHAR1       ; Restore middle of line character
           JSR       Line            ; Draw bottom line
```

```
        HLT

;
;-------------------------------
;Subroutine to display a line of the form:
;*************************              or,
;*                      *
;-------------------------------
;
Line:   PUSH    R1              ; Save R1



        PUSH    R0              ; Save R2
        MOV     R0, R2          ; First character of line
        SWI     putChar
        MOV     R0, R3          ; Middle character ready for displaying
        SUB     R1, @2          ; Remove first and last characters
Loop:   JEQ     Last            ; Check for more characters
        SWI     putChar         ; Draw middle character, eg space
        DEC     R1              ; Decrement count
        JMP     Loop            ; Repeat if necessary
Last:   MOV     R0, R2          ; Draw last character, eg '*'
        SWI     putChar
        MOV     R0, @cr         ; Carriage return control character
        SWI     putChar
        POP     R0              ; Restore registers
        POP     R1
        RTS                     ; Return from subroutine
```

The program displays a line consisting of a single character repeated a number of times determined by the value specified in the macro WIDTH. The character displayed is the macro CHAR1. The subroutine Line is called to display the line. The body of the box is displayed using two characters: one, the same as that for the first line, is used for the start and end of the line; the other character, CHAR2, is used for characters in between these two. This second type of line is repeated a number of times determined by the value specified by the macro HT. The program then completes the box by displaying another line identical to the first. This is illustrated next with CHAR1 a '*' and CHAR2 a space.

```
****************************************  } First line
*                                      *  } Repeated lines
*                                      *  }
*                                      *  }
*                                      *  }
*                                      *  }
****************************************  } Last line
```

The subroutine, Line, displays a line by printing CHAR1 once, a number of CHAR2 and terminated by CHAR1. The subroutine also prints a carriage return character (ASCII value 13) so that each line starts on a new line. By making the two characters the same, a line of a single character may be displayed.

The output from the first pass is shown in Listing 31.10.

Listing 31.10. First pass output

```
         ORG     1000
Box:     MOV     R1, @20
         MOV     R2, '*'
         MOV     R3, '*'
         JSR     Line
         MOV     R3, ' '
         MOV     R4, @10
         SUB     R4, @2
Middle:  JEQ     Bline
         JSR     Line
         DEC     R4
         JMP     Middle
Bline:   MOV     R3, '*'
         JSR     Line
         HLT
Line:    PUSH    R1
         PUSH    R0
         MOV     R0, R2
         SWI     putChar
         MOV     R0, R3
         SUB     R1, @2
Loop:    JEQ     Last
         SWI     putChar
         DEC     R1
         JMP     Loop
Last:    MOV     R0, R2
         SWI     putChar
         MOV     R0, @cr
         SWI     putChar
         POP     R0
         POP     R1
         RTS
```

The first pass substitutes all the macros defined at the beginning of the program wherever the macro names are encountered in the source program. In addition, comments and any blank lines are removed. This constitutes the assembler's pre-processing phase.

In the second pass shown in Listing 31.11, the assembler obeys any embedded directives, such as ORG and EQU, and as far as it is able, converts the instructions into machine code, storing the program in the area of memory specified in the ORG directive or starting at location 0 if no origin is given. The starting memory location of each instruction, occupying one or two 16-bit words, is shown in Listing 31.11.

Listing 31.11.   Second pass output

Loc	Word1	Word2			
1000	241F	0014	Box:	MOV	R1, @20
1002	242F	002A		MOV	R2, '*'
1004	243F	002A		MOV	R3, '*'
1006	21FF	****		JSR	Line
1008	243F	0020		MOV	R3, ' '
100A	244F	000A		MOV	R4, @10
100C	364F	0002		SUB	R4, @2
100E	15FF	****	Middle:	JEQ	Bline
1010	21FF	****		JSR	Line
1012	0E4F			DEC	R4
1013	20FF	FFF9		JMP	Middle
1015	243F	002A	Bline:	MOV	R3, '*'
1017	21FF	****		JSR	Line
1019	10FF			HLT	
101A	2A1F		Line	PUSH	R1
101B	2A0F			PUSH	R0
101C	2402			MOV	R0, R2
101D	37FF	F00C		SWI	putChar
101F	2403			MOV	R0, R3
1020	361F	0002		SUB	R1, @2
1022	15FF	****	Loop:	JEQ	Last
1024	37FF	F00C		SWI	putChar
1026	0E1F			DEC	R1
1027	20FF	FFF9		JMP	Loop
1029	2402			MOV	R0, R2
102A	37FF	F00C		SWI	putChar
102C	240F	000D	Last:	MOV	R0, @cr
102E	37FF	F00C		SWI	putChar
1031	290F			POP	R0
1032	291F			POP	R1
1033	2EFF			RTS	

As the program is scanned, any labels or other symbolic addresses are added to a symbol table which stores the name of the identifier and its address; where the assembler is unable to provide an address for a label, it puts a special marker (shown as asterisks in the listing above) and adds the identifier name to the symbol table. At the end of this pass, the assembler will have all the information it needs to complete the assembly process in the final pass.

At the end of the second pass, the symbol table would contain the information shown in Table 31.7.

identifier	type	location/value (hex)
cr	value	0D
Box	label	1000
Middle	label	100E
Bline	label	1015
Line	label	101A
Loop	label	1022

Table 31.7.

Notice in Listing 31.11 that transfer of control instructions (conditional and unconditional branches and jumps to subroutines) are converted into offsets relative to the position of the instruction. For example, at location `1013`, the instruction `JMP` middle specifies a jump address of `FFF9`, which is the two's complement representation of –7. Forward references translate to positive offsets. Remember that the offset is relative to the address of the instruction following the transfer of control, since this is the contents of the `PC` after the current instruction has been fetched. Relative offsets allow relocatable code to be written so that programs will be able to execute correctly wherever they are installed in memory.

Finally, in the third pass, shown in Listing 31.12, the missing jump offsets are inserted into the object program.

Listing 31.12.

Loc	Word1	Word2			
1000	241F	0014	Box:	MOV	R1, @20
1002	242F	002A		MOV	R2, '*'
1004	243F	002A		MOV	R3, '*'
1006	21FF	****		JSR	Line
1008	243F	0020		MOV	R3, ' '
100A	244F	000A		MOV	R4, @10
100C	364F	0002		SUB	R4, @2
100E	15FF	0005	Middle:	JEQ	Bline
1010	21FF	0008		JSR	Line
1012	0E4F			DEC	R4
1013	20FF	FFF9		JMP	Middle
1015	243F	002A	Bline:	MOV	R3, '*'
1017	21FF	0001		JSR	Line
1019	10FF			HLT	
101A	2A1F		Line:	PUSH	R1
101B	2A0F			PUSH	R0
101C	2402			MOV	R0, R2
101D	37FF	F00C		SWI	putChar
101F	2403			MOV	R0, R3
1020	361F	0002		SUB	R1, @2
1022	15FF	0005	Loop	JEQ	Last
1024	37FF	F00C		SWI	putChar
1026	0E1F			DEC	R1
1027	20FF	FFF9		JMP	Loop
1029	2402		Last	MOV	R0, R2
102A	37FF	F00C		SWI	putChar
102C	240F	000D		MOV	R0, @13
102E	37FF	F00C		SWI	putChar
1031	290F			POP	R0
1032	291F			POP	R1
1033	2EFF			RTS	

Exercises

1. Describe the operation of a three-pass macro assembler. Your description should include the following:

    - the purpose of each pass;

    - how macros are dealt with;

    - how assembler directives are dealt with;

    - construction of symbol tables;

    - dealing with forward and backward references.

2. With examples explain the following addressing modes:

    - direct;

    - indexed;

    - indirect.

3. Write a program to input two integers and output their sum, difference and product.

4. Read two integer values, *a* and *b*, and perform the following calculations.

    - $2a + 3b$

    - $a^2 - b^2$

    - $5a^2 + 3a - 1$

5. Write a program to sort two integers into ascending order of magnitude.

6. Repeat the previous exercise using stack operations.

7. Use a loop and indexed addressing to sum the contents of a set of contiguous memory locations. The end of the list is a memory location containing a negative value.

8. Explain the operation of the different shifting and rotating operations. Give examples in binary notation.

9.   Demonstrate the effect of each of the shifting and rotating operations:

- SHR

- SHL

- SAR

- ROR

- ROL

- RRX

by applying them to a given word and then outputting each result to the screen.

Chapter 32
Data Structures

A sound knowledge of basic data structures is essential for any computer programmer. A programming task will almost invariably involve the manipulation of a set of data which normally will be organized according to some coherent structure. It could be that the data is to be read in and processed, in which case a detailed knowledge of its structure is obviously essential. Furthermore, processing the data might involve organizing it in a way that facilitates its subsequent retrieval, as in information retrieval applications. Output from the program might require that the data is presented in yet another form. So a single program might be required to handle a number of data structures; only by having a thorough knowledge of basic data structures can the programmer choose, or design, the structures most appropriate to the problems being addressed.

From a programming viewpoint, the study of data structures involves two aspects, namely, the theoretical principles upon which the structures are founded, and the practicalities of implementing them using a computer. This chapter addresses both of these considerations by describing a number of important data structures and their applications to programming tasks. A data structure is essentially a number of data items, also called elements or nodes, with some relationship linking them together. Each item consists of one or more named parts called fields occupying one or more memory locations in the computer. In its simplest form, an element can be a single field located in a single word of memory. A list of numbers

memory location	contents
1000	56
1001	34
1002	123
1003	11
1004	77

Table 32.1. *Array data structure*

occupying consecutive memory locations in a computer is a simple data structure called an array and an example is shown in Table 32.1.

The relationship linking the individual elements is merely the order in which they are stored in memory. In order to access the next element in the list (that is, an element's successor) it is necessary only to increment the memory address; the previous element at any point in the list (that is an elements predecessor) is found by decrementing the current memory address. This simple structural relationship allows the list to be accessed in sequential order.

Data structures such as linked lists provide pointers linking elements together. So, for example, to access the above numeric list in ascending order of magnitude, an extra field could be added to each element to point to the next element in the sequence, as shown in Table 32.2.

memory location	link field	value
1000	1004	56
1001	1000	34
1002	0000	123
1003	1001	11
1004	1002	77

Figure 32.2. *Linked list*

Now, starting with location 1003 and following the links, the list can be accessed in ascending order: the link contained in location 1003 indicates that the number succeeding 11 is in location 1001; location 1001 contains the number 34 plus a pointer showing that the next number in the sequence is to be found at location 1000; the list terminates at location 1002 which contains the final number, 123, and a zero link indicating that there are no more elements in the list. Linked lists make it easier to insert or delete elements at any position in the sequence of items, at the cost of increased complexity and increased memory demands. Other data structures such as stacks and queues restrict access to elements to certain points of a sequential data structure, normally the start or end. With stacks, elements may only be added or deleted at one end of the list; queues allow items to be added at one end and deleted at the other.

The attraction of using a simple array data structure is that a data item may be accessed by means of a simple key which specifies its position within the array. So, for example, if we used an array to store details of a collection of 30 videos, and we assigned to each of them a different code number in the range 1 to 30, searching the array for the details of a particular video would merely entail entering the code number; the required details would be obtained in a fixed length of time by using the code number as an index value.

However, if for a video hire shop we also wanted to use an array to store its videos, so that any one could be accessed in the shortest possible time, the amount of storage space required would be prohibitive. For instance, using a six-digit key would require 1,000,000 digits to be stored for the keys alone, and then the video details would be in addition. If the key was to be used to encode information concerning the video - how many duplicates, children's or adult's for example - then we would expect that out of these 1,000,000 possible keys only a relatively small proportion of them would be used. Suppose that this proportion is 10%, that is, the system is only intended to cope with a maximum of 1,000 videos. Then 90% of the space allocated to the storage of video details would be wasted. What is required is a method of mapping the 1,000,000 keys to a table containing only 1,000 keys. Hashing allows us to do this by applying a *hash function* to the key to produce an integer, in a much smaller range, which is used as the actual index to the table containing the records. The chief disadvantage of this scheme is that the hashing function will most probably generate non-unique index values, that is, two different keys could easily produce exactly the same index. This is termed a *collision*, and any hashing process must allow for this occurrence and cope with it using a *collision resolution strategy*.

Where a data structure is to be searched using an alphabetic key such as a surname, which could be incorrectly spelled, a useful method of coping with this problem is to use *Soundex Coding*. This allows words which sound alike, though spelled differently, to be given an identical code. Because of its usefulness in many application areas, the chapter concludes with a description of soundex coding and a soundex algorithm.

Arrays

Storage of arrays

High-level procedural languages such as BASIC, COBOL and Pascal allow programmers to manipulate tabular data stored in *arrays*. The programmer merely declares the name, size and dimension of the array and the language processor takes care of allocating memory for it. The immediate access store (memory) of a computer consists of a large number of memory locations, each with its own unique address (see Chapter 4). Memory locations have addresses ranging from 0 to $n1$, where n represents the total number of memory locations available in the computer. For example, in a computer which has 640K bytes of user memory, byte addresses will range from 0 to $(640 \times 1024)1$, that is, 0 to 655359. If a programmer defines a one-dimensional array of, say, twenty integers each occupying a single word, then the language processor must assign sufficient storage space for the array in user RAM and be able to find any array element as quickly as possible. Locating an array element requires a small calculation involving the starting address of the array, which is termed the *base address*, and the number of bytes per array element. For example, suppose we have a one-dimensional array A_k of single byte words, where k is over the range 0 to 20, with base address b. Then element A_0 will have address $b + 0 = b$. Element A_1 will have address $b + 1$, and, in general, element A_k will have address $b + k$.

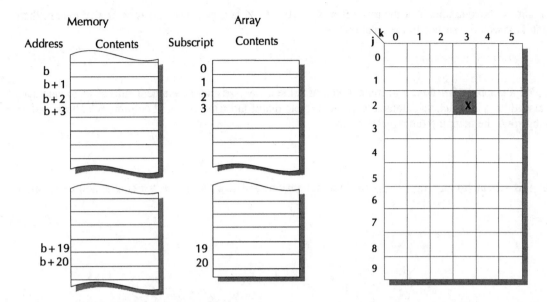

Figure 32.1. *Array-memory relationship* **Figure 32.2.** *Two-dimensional array $T_{j,k}$*

Figure 32.1 shows the relationship between array elements and memory locations.

Because the memory of a computer is essentially a one-dimensional array of memory locations, when it is required to represent a two-dimensional table, a slightly more complicated calculation is necessary: the language processor must convert the subscripts of two-dimensional array element into a one-dimensional physical memory address. Consider the storage requirements of a two-dimensional array, $T_{j,k}$ single word integers and size 10×6 that is, a table with 10 rows (j=0 to 9) and 6 columns (k=0 to 5) as shown in Figure 32.2. If the base address is at location b, and the array is stored row by row, then the elements of the array might be stored in memory as shown in Figure 32.3.

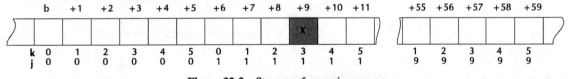

Figure 32.3. *Storage of array in memory*

The positions marked by an × in Figures 32.2 and 32.3 show the correspondence between a two-dimensional array element and the same elements memory address. The calculation required to convert the position of a two-dimensional array element $T_{j,k}$ to a memory location, M, is

$$M = b + j \times 6 + k$$

For example, element $T_{0,3}$ would occupy the location

$$M = b + 0 \times 6 + 3 = b + 3,$$

and element $T_{3,2}$ would be at location

$$M = b + 3 \times 6 + 2 = b + 20$$

The calculations above assume that the array is of size 10×6. In general, if the array is of size $m \times n$, then an element Tj,k would translate to the location

$$M = b + j \times n + k$$

This is called a *mapping function*, a formula which uses the array size and the element subscripts to calculate the memory address at which that element is located. Note that if the array is stored column by column rather than row by row, the mapping function becomes

$$M = b + k \times m + j$$

Extending this scheme to an array, $D_{i,j,k}$, of three dimensions and size $l \times m \times n$, the conversion calculation becomes,

$$M = b + i \times m \times n + j \times n + k$$

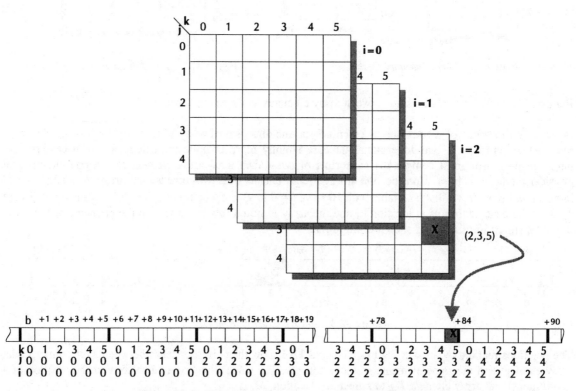

Figure 32.4. *Three-dimensional array and memory mappings*

Figure 32.4 illustrates the correspondence between array elements and memory locations for a three-dimensional table of size $3 \times 5 \times 6$.

Here, i can be considered to be the subscript which specifies a number of tables, each of size $j \times k$. Thus, $D_{2,3,5}$ references element $(3,5)$ of the third table (for which $i=2$). This corresponds to the location

$$M = b + 2 \times 5 \times 6 + 3 \times 6 + 5 = b + 83$$

Further application of the principles explained above allow arrays of any number of dimensions to be handled.

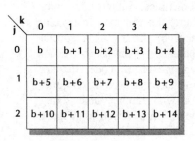

Figure 32.5. *Iliffe vector*

Iliffe vectors

When speed has a higher priority than memory requirements, a *table look-up* scheme is sometimes adopted for accessing array elements. The main drawback of using a mapping function is the time taken to perform the address calculation, which will generally involve one or more relatively slow multiplication operations. The number of calculations can be significantly reduced by pre-calculating row or column addresses and storing them in another table. For example, suppose that we have a 3 × 5 array as illustrated in Figure 32.5. We first calculate, and then store in three consecutive memory locations, the starting address for each of the three rows. This is called an Iliffe vector (see Figure 32.5).

So, given the row subscript for the array element to be accessed, the Iliffe vector is consulted for the starting address of that row, and the location of the required element is found by using the column subscript as an offset to be added to this row address. When implemented in assembly language or machine code using appropriate addressing modes, this scheme virtually eliminates the necessity for any address calculations.

Access tables

The principle of using a table containing the starting addresses of data items is particularly useful for accessing elements of string arrays. Figure 32.6 shows how an access table is used to point to the starting locations of string array elements stored in memory.

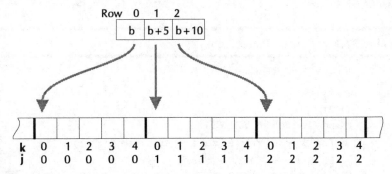

Figure 32.6. *Access table pointing to string array elements in memory*

The array S_k ($k = 0$ to 4) to be represented consists of a number of string elements of variable sizes, each terminated by a special character indicating the end of the string. In this instance, the strings, with their subscripts, are:

```
0 CPU
1 Disk Drive
2 Printer
3 Random Access Memory
4 Monitor
```

The access table contains entries which point to the starting locations of each of the strings in order. For example, if the element S_3 was to be accessed, the entry in the access table corresponding to this element (that is, the element with subscript 3) provides the starting address for S_3 which has a value Random Access Memory.

Sometimes, rather than indicating the end of a string element by means of a special character, such as an ASCII carriage return code, the access table is used in conjunction with another table giving the length of the string (Figure 32.7).

This scheme improves access speed but at the expense of additional storage requirements.

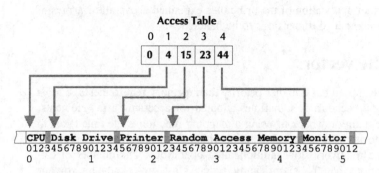

Figure 32.7. *Access table giving length of string in memory*

Search strategies

Having stored a number of data items in an array, it is more than likely that it will be necessary at some time to search the data structure for the occurrence of specific items of data. For example, suppose that an array A_k ($k=0$ to 9999) is being used to store stolen credit card numbers, and it is to be searched in order to ascertain whether a shop customer is using a stolen credit card. The search algorithm might be as shown in Listing 32.1.

Listing 32.1.   Sequential search

```
{search_array}
k:= 0
pos:= -1
card_found: = FALSE
while k < array_size and not card_found
  if S(k) = Card_number
    then card_found:= TRUE;
      pos:= k
  endif
k:= k+1
endwhile
if card_found
  then card number is located in S(pos)
      else card number is not in stolen cards list
endif
```

Each element in the list is compared with the number of the customer's card; if a match is found, the iteration is terminated by setting the boolean variable `card_found` to true, and the position of the value in the array is stored in the variable `pos`; if the loop ends and the variable `card_found` still has a value of false, then the customer's card is not in the list of stolen credit cards. This technique is called a *sequential search*. Though very straightforward, a sequential search can be very time consuming, since it could necessitate the complete list of 10,000 elements being searched. A faster method is possible if the list of card numbers is in ascending or descending numerical order. This alternative method is called *binary search*, or sometimes *binary chop*.

For example, suppose that the list of stolen card numbers is in ascending numerical order, then a binary search proceeds as follows:

1. Set the array subscript to `mid`, middle value. In this case `mid` is 9999/2, which is 5000 to the nearest integer.

2. Compare required `card_number` with `S(mid)`.

3. (a) If `card_number` < `S(mid)` then `card_number` can only be in the first half of the array.

    (b) If `card_number` > `S(mid)` then card_number can only be somewhere in the latter half of the array.

    (c) If `card_number` = `S(mid)` then the card number has been found.

4. If the card number has not yet been found, repeat from step 1 using mid as the size of the array.

The procedure successively reduces the size of the array to be searched by a factor of two. For an array of size 10,000, this means that only a maximum of 14 elements need to be examined in order to determine whether a particular element is a member of the list. Thus, for 10,000 elements, the search size reduces as shown in Table 32.2

Notice that 2^{14} is the smallest power of 2 which exceeds the maximum array size of 10,000:

$$2^{13} = 8,192 \text{ which is less than } 10,000;$$
$$2^{14} = 16,384 \text{ which is greater than } 10,000.$$

This is how the maximum figure of 14 comparisons has been derived.

A more formal version of the binary search algorithm can be stated as in Listing 32.2.

number of comparisons	array size to be searched
0	10,000
1	5,000
2	2,500
3	1,250
4	625
5	313
6	157
7	79
8	40
9	20
10	10
11	5
12	3
13	2
14	1

Table 32.2. *Array sizes and number of comparisons in binary chop*

Listing 32.2   Binary chop

```
{binary}
low:= 0
high:= array_size - 1
pos:= -1
card_found:= FALSE
while low < high and not card_found
  mid:= int((low + high))/2
  select
    when S(mid) = card_number
      card_found:= TRUE
      pos:= mid
```

```
            high:= mid - 1
      when S(mid) < card_number :
         low:= mid + 1
   endselect
endwhile
if card_found
   then stolen card number is located in S(pos)
         else card number is not in list
endif
```

In order to select the appropriate part of the array to be searched, the algorithm uses two variables, `low` and `high`, to store the lower and upper bounds of that part of the array. They are used to calculate the mid point, `mid`, (rounded to the nearest integer value using the `int` function), so that the value stored there can be compared with the value required (the card number, in this example). Each time the comparison fails, the lower or upper bound is adjusted and the procedure is repeated. The process continues until either the value is located or the lower and upper bounds coincide, in which case the value does not exist in the array. The variable `pos` is used to store the position of the value if it exists in the array; a negative value for `pos` indicates that the search was unsuccessful. The binary search method will usually be employed when the array size is large, otherwise the processing overheads caused by the algorithm's increased complexity make it unsuitable.

The stack

A *stack* is a data structure characterized by the expression Last In First Out (LIFO), meaning that the most recent item added to the stack is the first one which can be removed from the stack. A *stack pointer* is used to keep track of the last item added to the stack, that is, the current top of the stack. Suppose that we wish to implement a stack using a one-dimensional array, S_i where $i=1$ to 5. A special register, *sp*, must be reserved as the stack pointer, and this will have an initial value of 0 indicating that the stack is empty. To add, or *push*, an item to the stack, the following steps are required:

1. Check that there is room in the stack to add another item. In this case, the stack is full when *sp* has a value of 5, that is, when all of the elements in the array S_i have been used to store items. When the stack pointer is at its maximum value, and another item is required to be stored on the stack, a *stack overflow* condition has occurred, and it will not be possible to push the item onto the stack.

2. If an overflow condition does not exist, the stack pointer is incremented and the item is transferred to the array element pointed to by the stack pointer.

For example, suppose that the number 15 is to be pushed to the stack. After completing the operation the state of the stack will be as shown in Table 32.4.

i	S_i	
1	15	sp = 3
2	-	
3	-	
4	-	
5	-	

Table 32.4 *One item pushed to the stack*

After adding two more numbers the stack will contain three elements and the stack pointer will have a value of 3, as shown in Table 32.5. The algorithm for pushing a value to a stack can be summarized as follows:

i	S$_i$	
1	15	
2	6	
3	21	sp=3
4	-	
5	-	

Table 32.5. *Stack with three items*

```
algorithm push          {add item to top of stack}
if sp < maximum stack size {test for overflow}
   then sp := sp + 1;     {increment stack ptr}

      Ssp := item         {push item}

   else Stack overflow
endif
end
```

To remove an item from the stack, often called *pulling* or *popping* a value, requires the reverse procedure:

1. Check that the stack is not empty, that is, sp is greater than zero. If the stack is empty, an attempt to pull a non-existent value causes a *stack underflow* condition to arise.

2. If the stack is not empty, the item on the top of the stack, as shown by the stack pointer, is transferred to its destination and the stack pointer is decremented.

i	S$_i$	
1	15	
2	6	sp=2
3	21	
4	-	
5	-	

Thus, after pulling a value from the stack S_i, it would be in the state shown in Table 32.6. Notice that the value pulled from the stack, 21 in this instance, still exists in the stack; it is not necessary to actually remove a value from the stack since, by decrementing the stack pointer, this is effectively what has happened. Pulling a value from a stack is effected by copying the value to its destination before decrementing the stack pointer. The top of the stack is now the second element of the array which contains the value 6.

Table 32.6. *Pulling a value from the stack*

To summarize, the algorithm for pulling a value from a stack is:

```
algorithm pop {remove item from top of stack}
   if sp > 0 {that is, stack is not empty}
      then item := Ssp; {transfer item to destination}
         sp := sp - 1 {decrement stack pointer}
      else stack underflow
   endif
end
```

Application of stacks

The stack is used frequently in programming languages for control structures. In Acorn's BASIC, for example, GOSUB, FOR...NEXT, REPEAT...UNTIL and procedure/function calls all use stacks in their implementation.

The GOSUB instruction causes control to be transferred to the line specified in the instruction. Subroutine instructions are executed as normal until a RETURN instruction is encountered, whereupon control returns to the instruction following the last GOSUB instruction executed. Thus, with the fragments of BASIC code illustrated in Listing 32.3, the subroutine starting at line 1000 is called at line 100 by the GOSUB 1000 instruction. The BASIC interpreter must store its current position in the program so that after executing the subroutine it can return control to this same position when a RETURN instruction is encountered. This is accomplished by pushing the return address to a stack prior to jumping to the start of the subroutine.

Listing 32.3.

```
10 REM *** Mainline program ***
.............
.............
90 REM Call subroutine at line 1000
100 GOSUB 1000
105 REM Program contines here after completing subroutine
110 LET a = x + 1
120
990 STOP
999 REM *** End of Mainline program
REM *** Subroutine code goes here
1010
.............
etc
.............
1490 RETURN
```

When a RETURN instruction is executed, the top of the stack is pulled and the interpreter continues from that address. In this way the same subroutine can be called from different parts of the program and control will always return to the instruction following the GOSUB instruction. Another reason for using a stack is that it facilitates the use of nested control structures. In the example shown in Listing 32.3 it is possible to have another GOSUB instruction in the subroutine at line 1100. (See Listing 32.4).

Listing 32.4.

```
10 REM *** Mainline program ***
.............
.............
90 REM Call subroutine at line 1000
100 GOSUB 1000
105 REM Program contines here after completing subroutine
110 LET a = x + 1
120
.............
etc
.............
990 STOP
999 REM *** End of Mainline program ***
1000 REM *** Subroutine code goes here ***
1010
.............
1100 GOSUB 2000
```

```
1200
. . . . . . . . . . . .
1490 RETURN
2000 REM *** Code for second subroutine goes here ***
2010
. . . . . . . . . .
etc
2490 RETURN
```

In this instance the stack is used twice: the return address appropriate to the subroutine call at line 100 is pushed to the stack, then the return address for the second, nested, subroutine call is pushed to the stack during execution of the first subroutine at line 1100.

When the RETURN statement at line 2490 is executed, BASIC pulls the top of the GOSUB stack causing control to return to line 1200, the line following the most recent GOSUB instruction. The RETURN statement at line 1490 causes BASIC to pull the new top of the stack which provides the return address for the first GOSUB call at line 100. This technique allows subroutines to be nested to any depth, subject to the size of the GOSUB stack.

The same principle applies to the management of FOR..NEXT loops in BASIC. A separate stack is used to store information regarding the FOR..NEXT control variables. The BASIC interpreter stores on the stack five pieces of information when it encounters a FOR statement: (i) the address of the control variable; (ii) the type of the control variable; (iii) STEP size; (iv) TO limit; (v) the address of the next statement following FOR.

The stack pointer is incremented by the number of words occupied by this information, and then the statement following the FOR instruction is executed. A NEXT instruction will cause BASIC to use the information on the top of the stack to either repeat the statements between the FOR and F"Courier New"NEXT instructions, or to exit the loop if the control variable has exceeded its maximum value. If the latter is the case, the FOR..NEXT stack pointer will be decremented to remove the top of the stack thus terminating this loop. The use of a stack again allows nesting of FOR..NEXT loops, subject to a depth governed by the size of the FOR..NEXT stack.

A REPEAT..UNTIL stack is used in a similar way to that of the FOR..NEXT stack, though the procedures for managing REPEAT..UNTIL loops are simpler.

Procedures and functions in BASIC are handled in a similar manner to the GOSUB structure, but the BASIC interpreter has to cope with additional problems associated with passing parameters and saving the values of local variables so that they can subsequently be restored. These extra problems are once again overcome by the use of stacks.

The queue

The data structure known as a *queue* has the same characteristics as the queues we encounter in everyday life. For instance, a queue at the checkout counter of a supermarket increases at its rear as customers join the queue to have their purchases totalled, and only reduces in size when a customer is served at the head of the queue, the checkout counter. A queue of cars at traffic lights behaves in a similar manner, with cars exiting the queue only at its head and joining the queue only at its rear.

A *queue* is a data structure in which elements are added only at the rear of a linear list and removed only from the front, or head, of the list. A queue is often given the name FIFO list, from the initial letters of the words in the phrase First In First Out which describes the order of processing the elements of the list. Suppose that an array, Q_k ($k=0$ to 31), is to be used as a queue. Head will be used to keep track of the front of the queue and Rear, the end of the queue as shown in Figure 32.9.

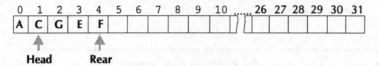

Figure 32.9. *A queue*

Initially, the queue is empty so that Head = Rear = 0. When an item is added to the queue, Rear is incremented; when an item is removed from the list, Head is incremented. Assuming that the queue is simply storing single alphabetic characters, Table 32.7 illustrates the operation of the queue for ten queue operations.

operation	item	Head	Rear	state of queue
		0	0	empty
1. Add item	A	0	1	A
2. Add item	C	0	2	AC
3. Add item	G	0	3	ACG
4. Add item	E	0	4	ACGE
5. Remove item	A	1	4	CGE
6. Add item	F	1	5	CGEF
7. Remove item	C	2	5	GEF
8. Remove item	G	3	5	EF
9. Remove item	E	4	5	F
10. Remove item	F	5	5	empty

Table 32.7. *Queue operations*

The following algorithms show how items are added to a queue and removed from a queue, assuming array_size is the maximum size of the array *Q* used for storing the queue.

```
algorithm queue {Add item to queue}
  if Rear <= array_size  1
    then Q(Rear):= item
      Rear := Rear 1
    else Queue is full
  endif
end

algorithm queue {Remove item from queue}
  if Rear <> Head
    then item := Q(Head)
      Head := Head + 1
    else Queue is empty
  endif
end
```

Notice that the queue is empty when the head pointer has the same value as the rear pointer. Notice also that, unlike a queue in real life, as items are added and removed, the queue moves through the array since both the head and rear pointers are incremented. This means that eventually the queue will run out of space, at which time an overflow condition will occur.One solution to this problem is to implement a circular queue which re-uses array elements that are empty.

Circular queues

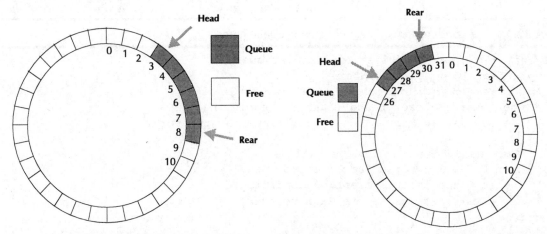

Figure 32.10. *Principles of circular queue*　　**Figure 32.11.** *Circular queue with Rear at upper bound*

Figure 32.10 illustrates the principles of a circular queue. The circular arrangement of the array elements is merely a means of illustrating the principles of operation of a circular queue; the data structure used to store the queue is physically the same as before, that is, a one-dimensional array. Head and Rear are again used, but this time when either of them reach a value equal to m, the upper bound of the array, they start again at the beginning, using up elements which previously have been removed from the queue. The diagram shows the queue in a state where ten items have been added to the queue and three items have been removed. Figure 32.11 shows that the queue has completely traversed the array such that Rear is equal to m, and there are five items in the queue. The next item to be added to the queue will be inserted at position 1, so that Rear has a value of 0 rather than m + 1. In other words, when Rear exceeds the upper bound reserved for the queue, it takes the value of the lower bound. The same thing applies to the Head of the queue. Figure 32.12 shows the queue, having traversed all the elements of the array, starting to re-use unoccupied positions at the beginning of the array.

A slight difficulty with a circular queue is being able to differentiate between an empty queue and a full queue; the condition for a non-empty queue can no longer be that Rear < Head since, depending how many items have been added and removed, it is possible for a non-empty queue to be such that Rear has larger value than Head. Figures 32.11 and 32.12 illustrate both queue states, the first where Head < Rear and the second where Head > Rear.

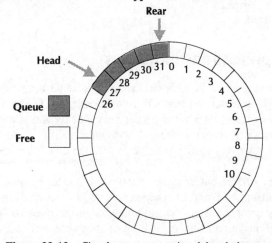

Figure 32.12. *Circular queue re-using deleted elements*

One solution to this problem is to adopt the convention that `Head` always points to the array element immediately preceding the first item in the queue rather pointing to the first item itself; since `Rear` points to the last item in the queue, the condition that `Head = Rear` indicates an empty queue. `Head` and `Rear` are initialized to be equal to the arrays upper bound rather than zero. Thus, initially, the queue is empty.

The queue becomes full only when the rear pointer catches up with the head pointer. The algorithms shown in Listing 32.5 define the processes of adding an item to a circular queue and removing an item from a circular queue.

Listing 32.5.   Algorithms for adding and deleting queue items

```
algorithm c_queue {Add item to circular queue}
temp:= Rear {Copy Rear Pointer}
  if Rear = Upper_bound {check for upper limit}
    then Rear := Lower_bound {start at beginning or..
      else Rear := Rear + 1  .. increment rear pointer}
  endif
  if Rear Head {check for queue full}
    then Q(Rear) := item {add item to queue}
      else Queue is full{overflow condition}
        Rear := temp{restore Rear pointer}
  endif
end

algorithm c_dequeue{Remove item from circular queue}
  if Head Rear{check for queue not empty}
    then
      if Head = Upper_bound   {check for upper limit}
        then Head := Lower_bound{start at beginning or..
          else Head := Head + 1.. increment head pointer}
      endif
      item := Q(Head){remove item from queue}
    else Queue is empty{underflow condition}
  endif
end
```

Applications of queues

Most printers in common use today contain a quantity of RAM for the purpose of temporarily storing (or *buffering*) data transmitted from a computer. The buffer allows the computer to transmit, for example, a few kilobytes of data to the printer very quickly and allows the printer to print it autonomously, (that is, without further intervention from the computer). This allows the computer to continue processing other tasks while the relatively slow printer deals with the data it has received.

The printer buffer must operate as a queue, because the data must be printed in the same order as it was transmitted from the computer. As data is received by the printer, it is added to the buffer queue until either the computer stops transmitting data or the queue is full. The printer then commences to process the data in the queue, starting at the head of the queue and ending when the queue is empty. This process of filling up the buffer quickly and then emptying it at the speed of the printer, continues until the computer ceases to transmit data. Buffers may range in size from a few kilobytes to several megabytes of RAM. A microprocessor in the printer itself deals with the way the data queue is processed.

Circular queues are frequently used by operating systems for spooling operations. For example, in a multi-user system in which a printer is shared between a number of users, print jobs may be spooled to a disk drive. The queue thus formed on the disk will be processed by the printer in the order the jobs were received (unless a priority system is in operation). As one job is printed, room will be available on the disk area allocated to the printer for another job; the circular queue principle applied to spooling will allow optimum use of the disk area allocated to print jobs. The operating system keeps track of the appropriate queue head and rear pointers required to operate the circular queue.

Linked lists

Suppose that we are using an array to store a number of alphabetic items in alphabetical order as shown in Table 32.7. Adding a new item such as Gregory, while maintaining the alphabetic ordering, is easy (Table 32.8. The item is merely added to the end of the list. However, to insert Crawford requires rather more effort: all of those entries after Craddock must be moved down the array so that Crawford may be inserted immediately after Craddock. The list is then as shown in Table 32.9. For a list containing hundreds or thousands of entries, this process could be considerably time-consuming.

element	data
0	Aaron
1	Abelson
2	Bateman
3	Craddock
4	Dunfy
5	Eastman
6	
7	
8	
9	

Table 32.7

element	data
0	Aaron
1	Abelson
2	Bateman
3	Craddock
4	Dunfy
5	Eastman
6	Gregory
7	
8	
9	

Table 32.8

element	data
0	Aaron
1	Abelson
2	Bateman
3	Craddock
4	Crawford
5	Dunfy
6	Eastman
7	Gregory
8	
9	

Table 32.9

An alternative approach is to introduce a second array containing pointers which link the elements together in the required order. Now an element, or *node*, contains a pointer in addition to the data. So, returning to the original list in Table 32.7, it would be represented as follows in Table 32.10 (on the next page).

The original list is now in *linked list* form. Given the start position of the list, stored in Start, the pointers link the items together in the correct alphabetical order. The end of the list is indicated by a *null pointer*, in this case –1. Another pointer, Free, keeps track of the next free location for storing new items, and it is incremented whenever a new item is inserted or added to the list. Adding Gregory to the list would entail changing the Eastman pointer from 1 to 6 (that is, the value currently given by Free) and putting Gregory at the position indicated by Free (Table 32.11).

	node	data	pointer
start	0	Aaron	1
	1	Abelson	2
	2	Bateman	3
	3	Craddock	4
	4	Dunfy	5
	5	Eastman	–1
free	6		
	7		
	8		
	9		

Table 32.10. *Linked list*

	node	data	pointer
start	0	Aaron	1
	1	Abelson	2
	2	Bateman	3
	3	Craddock	4
	4	Dunfy	5
	5	Eastman	6
	6	Gregory	–1
free	7		
	8		
	9		

Table 32.11. *Adding Gregory to the linked list*

Gregory is given a null pointer (–1) to indicate that it is the last item in the list, and Free is incremented.

In pseudocode form, the steps illustrated above to add an item to the end of a linked list are as shown in Listing 32.6.

Listing 32.6.   Adding a node to a linked list

```
algorithm add_node
  i := Start;{copy start pointer}
  while ptr(i)null{follow pointers until null pointer found}
    i := ptr(i)
  endwhile  ptr(i) := Free{link new item to current last node}
  data(Free) := item{store new data in next free node}
  ptr(Free) := null {store null pointer in next free node}
  Free := Free + 1 {increment next free ptr}
end
```

The notation ptr(i) is used for the pointer located at node i, and data(i) represents the data at node i. For example, in the alphabetical list above, ptr(2) = 3 and data(2) = Bateman.

Now, to add Crawford only one pointer is altered, rather than re-arranging the items in the array, and the new node is added to the end of the list (Table 32.12).

Thus, the order of accessing the array in alphabetical order is 0 - 1 - 2 - 3 - 7 - 4 - 5 - 6.

	node	data	pointer	
start	0	Aaron	1	
	1	Abelson	2	
	2	Bateman	3	
	3	Craddock	7	
	4	Dunfy	5	
	5	Eastman	6	
	6	Gregory	1	
	7	Crawford	4	inserted node
free	8			
	9			

Table 32.12. *Inserting a node into linked list*

In pseudocode, the algorithm for inserting a node to maintain the alphabetic ordering, is shown in Listing 32.7.

Listing 32.7. Algorithm for insertion of node into linked list

```
algorithm insert_node
  i := Start {copy start pointer}
  found := FALSE
    repeat
      if data(i) > item{ie alphabetically}
            or Start = null {allow for empty list}
          then found := TRUE{insertion position found}
          else p := i {save current node}
            i := ptr(p) {next node in list}
      endif
    until found {insertion position located}
            or i = null {reached end of list}
      if i = start
          then data(Free) := item {insert at head of list}
            ptr(Free) := Start
            Start := Free
          else ptr(p) = Free; {insert in body of list}
            data(Free) := item
            ptr(Free) := i
      endif
      Free := Free + 1 {increment next-free pointer}
  end
```

The increased complexity of this algorithm arises partially from the necessity to allow for the list being initially empty, this state being recognised by Start containing a null pointer. If the list is empty initially, then Start is set equal to Free which contains a pointer to the first available node, and the new data together with a null pointer are stored in this node. To delete a node merely entails ensuring that its predecessor's pointer links the node following it. For example, to delete Bateman, the pointers would be adjusted as shown in Table 32.13.

The pointer order is now 0 – 1 – 3 – 7 – 4 – 5 – 6, which misses out the third item in the array containing Bateman.

	node	data	pointer	
start	0	Aaron	1	
	1	Abelson	3	
	2	Bateman	3	deleted node
	3	Craddock	7	
	4	Dunfy	5	
	5	Eastman	6	
	6	Gregory	1	
	7	Crawford	4	
free	8			
	9			

Table 32.13. *Adjustment of pointers after deletion of node*

The pseudocode algorithm is shown in Listing 32.8.

Listing 32.8.   Algorithm for deleting node from list

```
algorithm delete_node
  i := Start                            {copy start pointer}
  found := FALSE
  repeat
    if data(i) = item or Start = null   {ie found node or empty
                                        list}
      then found := TRUE                {deletion position found}
      else p := i                       {save current node}
        i := ptr(p)                     {next node in list}
    endif
  until found or i = null               {deletion position located
                                        or reached end of list}

  if Start = null or i = null           {ie empty list or reached
                                        end of list without
                                        finding node}

    then node does not exist!           {not possible to delete
                                        node}

    else if i = start
            then Start := ptr(i)        {delete head of list}
            else ptr(p) := ptr(i)       {skip node in body of list}
          endif
  endif
end
```

The algorithm allows for three special cases: (i) the list is empty - this means that it is not possible to delete an element; (ii) the item to be deleted is not in the list - again, it is not possible to delete this item; (iii) the item to be deleted is the first one in the list - this requires that Start must be set to point to the second node in the linked list.

With a linked list it is possible to locate any element by following the pointers, irrespective of the physical location of the item. Rather than storing the list in consecutive elements of an array, confined to a certain range of memory locations, it is perfectly feasible to store the elements of the linked list

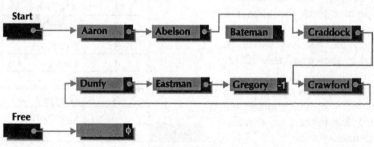

Figure 32.13.

anywhere in the memory space allocated to a user program. For this reason, an alternative, and more general, diagrammatic form is often used for linked lists, in which each node contains one or more pointers and one or more words of data. For example, the linked list immediately above might be represented as shown in Figure 32.13.

Arrowed lines are used to show the order in which nodes are linked together, and special nodes indicate the start point of the list and the next free node.

Linked lists have a number of advantages over arrays :

- Greater flexibility for the location of nodes in memory (it is even possible for nodes to be located on auxiliary storage, such as magnetic disks, rather than in main memory).

- The ease with which nodes may be added or deleted from the list.

- By adding more pointers, the list may be traversed in a number of different orders.

On the debit side for linked lists:

- Locating specific items necessitates searching the list from the start node, whereas arrays allow direct access to elements.

- Linked lists require more memory because of the need for pointers.

- Linked lists involve more housekeeping operations because of the necessity to change pointers when adding or deleting nodes.

Applications of linked lists

With an interpreted language such as BASIC, variables must be accessed as quickly as possible so that program processing speed is acceptably fast. One method of ensuring this is by the use of linked lists.

In one such scheme, used by Acorn BASIC, variables starting with the same character are given their own linked list, so that there is a linked list for each possible starting character. Though the lists are quite separate, each with its own start pointer, they occupy a common area of memory and link around each other. Each node in the linked lists con-

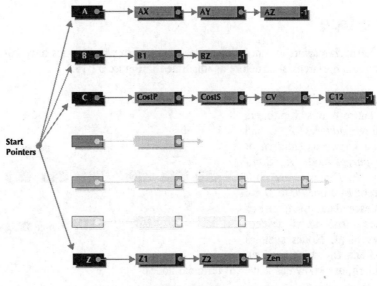

Figure 32.14.

tains the name and value of the variable, plus a pointer to the next variable with the same starting letter. Figure 32.14 illustrates this scheme at the stage where a number of variables with starting letters A, B or C have been created.

The start pointers for the linked lists are stored in a table in a specific area of memory. The first pointer in the table contains the address of the node for the first variable starting with the letter A to be created in the current program, in this case AX. This node contains a pointer to the second variable created, AY, and its node contains a pointer to AZ, the last variable created starting with the letter A. Similar lists occur for the variables starting with B (B1 and B2) and C *(CostP, CostS, CV* and *C12)*. Because the lists link around each other, there is a common free-space pointer for all the lists.

To find a particular variable's node, the starting letter of the variable is converted into an address giving the start pointer for its linked list, and the nodes of this list are traversed in pointer order until the variable is located. For example, suppose that the table of start pointers was at memory location 1000, and the variable *BZ* is to be accessed. The letter *B* is first converted into a number indicating its position in the alphabet, that is 2, and this is added to the start address of the table.

Thus, $1000 + 2 = 1002$ is the location of the start pointer for the linked list of variables beginning with B. The first node in the list is for variable B1, which is not the one required, so its pointer is used to access the next node in the list. This time the variable found is *BZ* as required.

For a program containing many variables, this scheme can dramatically reduce the time required to locate a certain variable, provided variable names are chosen with different starting letters. It is worth noting that in this instance, a knowledge of the internal organization of an interpreter can help the programmer to write more efficient programs.

Linked lists are also used for procedures and functions so that they can be located as quickly as possible no matter where in the program they are referenced. Otherwise, a program would have to be searched sequentially from the beginning every time a procedure or function was invoked.

The tree

The term *tree* refers to a non-linear data structure in which nodes have two or more pointers to other nodes, forming a hierarchical structure as illustrated in Figure 32.15.

Node A is the *root* node of the entire tree with pointers to three *subtrees*. *B*, *C* and *D* are known as *children* of the *parent* node *A*. Similarly, *E*, *F* and *G* are children of *B*. Nodes *B* to *N* are all descendants of *A*, just as nodes *L* to *N* are all descendants of *D*. Nodes such as *H*, *I* and *L*, which have no children, are known as leaves or terminal nodes.

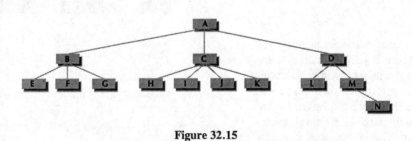

Figure 32.15

Trees are useful for representing hierarchical relationships between data items, such as those found in databases. For example, a record in an employee file might have the structure shown in Figure 32.16.

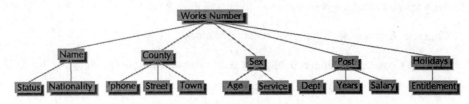

Figure 32.16.

Stored as a tree, the data can be accessed in a number of ways. For example, extracting the first level of the tree provides a summary of the employee, giving Name, Home county, Sex, Post and Holidays taken; accessing only the fourth subtree provides details of the employees current position; accessing the tree in order of the five subtrees provides all the employees details.

A binary tree is a particular type of tree which has more uses than a general tree as described above, and is also much easier to implement. Binary trees are described in the following two sections.

Binary trees

A binary tree is a special type of tree in which each parent has a maximum of two children which are linked to the parent node using a left pointer and a right pointer. The general form of a binary tree is shown in Figure 32.17.

Binary trees have many important applications, a number of which are described in the next section. This section explores the nature of binary trees, how they are created, modified and accessed.

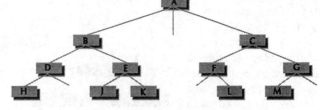

Figure 32.17.

In the previous section we saw that in order to locate a specific node in a linked list it is necessary to search the list from the beginning, following the pointers linking the nodes together in the appropriate order. For a list containing a large number of elements, this process could be very time consuming. The solution to the same problem with an array structure was to use the binary search technique (see section on Search Strategies); the same principle can be applied to a linked list if the list is in the form of a *binary tree*. Consider the alphabetically ordered linked list described earlier in the section on linked lists and shown in Figure 32.18.

Figure 32.18.

Now suppose that the same list is represented as a binary tree with two pointers in each node, one pointing to an element alphabetically less than the node data (a *left pointer*) and the other pointing to an element alphabetically greater than the node data (a *right pointer*). (See Figure 32.19).

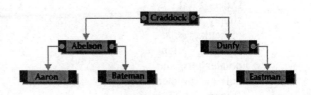

Figure 32.19.

If we were looking for *Eastman*, the procedure would be as follows:

(i)   Compare *Eastman* with the *root* node, *Craddock*.

(ii)   Because *Craddock* is alphabetically less than *Eastman*, follow the right pointer to *Dunfy*.

(iii)   Compare *Eastman* with *Dunfy*.

(iv)   *Dunfy* is alphabetically less than *Eastman* so again follow the right pointer to *Eastman*.

(v)   The next comparison shows that the required node has been located.

Each comparison confines the search to either the upper or lower part of the alphabetic list, thus significantly reducing the number of comparisons needed to locate the element required.

To add an element, *Crawford* for example, to the configuration shown above, whilst retaining the alphabetic ordering, is merely a matter of searching for the new item until a null pointer is encountered. In this example, a null pointer occurs when attempting to go left at *Dunfy*. *Crawford* is installed in the next free node and *Dunfy's* left pointer points to it. The new tree is shown in Figure 32.20.

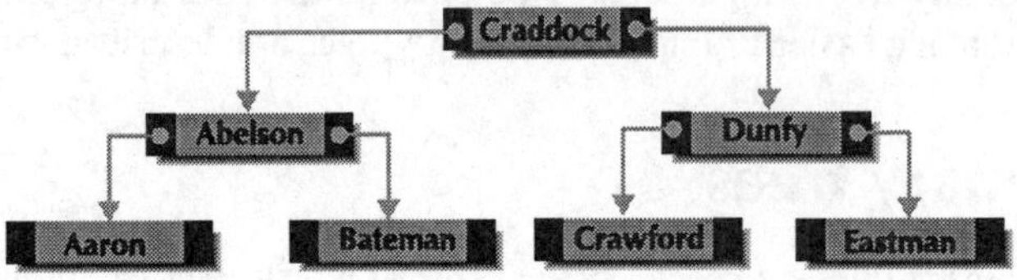

Figure 32.20.

Unfortunately, deleting a node is not quite so simple. Three cases can arise, and these are described with reference to Figure 32.21 which is an extended form of the binary tree shown above.

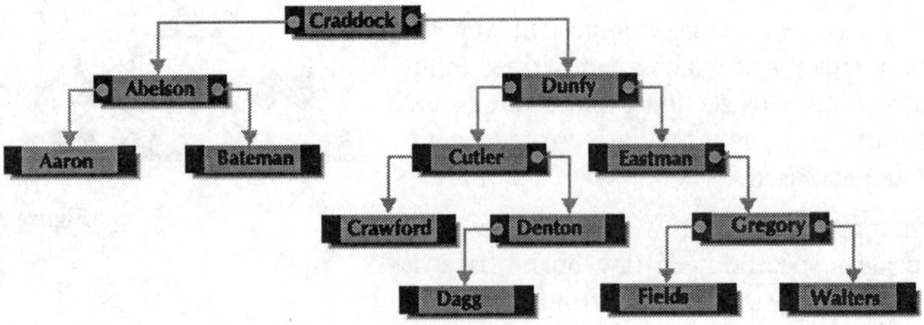

Figure 32.21.

(i)   The node to be deleted is a terminal node, or leaf, having null left and right pointers. *Bateman* is an example of such a node. Deleting it is simply a matter of setting *Abelson's* right pointer to the null pointer (Figure 32.22).

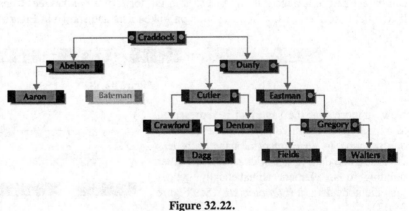

Figure 32.22.

(ii)   The node to be deleted contains one null pointer. *Eastman* is an example of this type of node. This case is handled in the same way as deleting a node from a linked list - *Dunfy's* right pointer is replaced by *Eastman's* right pointer (Figure 32.23).

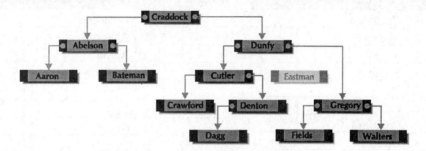

Figure 32.23.

(iii)   The node to be deleted contains no null pointers. There are two possibilities here: replace the deleted entry with an entry from its right subtree, or an entry from its left subtree. We will consider both of these using Dunfy as the item to be deleted from the original tree.

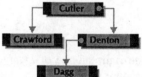

Taking the left subtree first, the procedure is to search the left subtree for the alphabetically largest entry by following the right pointers at each node until a null pointer is found. The left subtree of *Dunfy* is shown in Figure 32.24 and the largest value is *Denton*. In order that *Dunfy* can be deleted whilst still retaining the correct ordering, it is replaced by *Denton* and a number of pointers are adjusted as shown in Figure 32.25.

Figure 32.24.

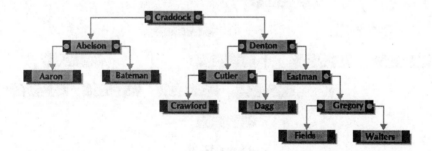

Figure 32.25.

Denton's pointers are replaced by *Dunfy's* pointers; *Craddock's* pointer now points to *Denton*; *Cutler's* right pointer now points to *Dagg*.

Note that for clarity the diagram above gives the impression that nodes have been moved around, but all that occurs in practice is that pointers are changed to alter the nodes that are to be linked together or deleted; the *Dunfy* node still exists in the tree but is effectively deleted because no node pointers reference it.

This is made clear when the tree is represented in tabular form. Table 32.14 shows the structure of the original tree. With the node *Dunfy* deleted, the result is as shown in Table 32.15.

node	left	data	right
0	1	Craddock	4
1	2	Abelson	3
2	1	Aaron	1
3	1	Bateman	1
4	5	Dunfy	9
5	6	Cutler	7
6	1	Crawford	1
7	8	Denton	1
8	1	Dagg	1
9	1	Eastman	10
10	11	Gregory	12
11	1	Fields	1
12	1	Walters	1

Table 32.14.

node	left	data	right	
0	1	Craddock	7	
1	2	Abelson	3	
2	1	Aaron	1	
3	1	Bateman	1	
4	5	Dunfy	9	deleted
5	6	Cutler	18	
6	1	Crawford	1	
7	5	Denton	9	
8	1	Dagg	1	
9	1	Eastman	10	
10	11	Gregory	12	
11	1	Fields	1	
12	1	Walters	1	

Table 32.15.

If the right subtree of *Dunfy* is selected rather than the left subtree to search for a replacement, then the procedure is very similar; this time the left pointers are followed in order to find the alphabetically smallest item, which then replaces *Dunfy*. In this case the smallest item is *Eastman* and the tree becomes as shown in Figure 32.26.

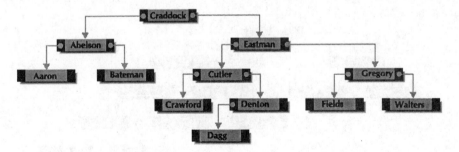

Figure 32.26.

Methods of tree traversal

Having created a binary tree, it is likely that it will need to be accessed in some particular order, alphabetically for example. The algorithm for visiting the data items of a binary tree in alphabetical order is an example of *in-order* traversal and can be stated quite simply:

```
In-order traversal:
   visit the left subtree in in-order then
   visit the root node then
   visit the right subtree in in-order.
```

Notice that the algorithm makes reference to itself. In other words, the algorithm for visiting a subtree is exactly the same as that for visiting a tree. The seemingly endless process of visiting trees within trees within trees etc. continues until a null pointer is encountered, allowing the process to terminate, or *bottom out*. The operation of the algorithm is best illustrated by means of an example. Consider the tree shown in Figure 32.27.

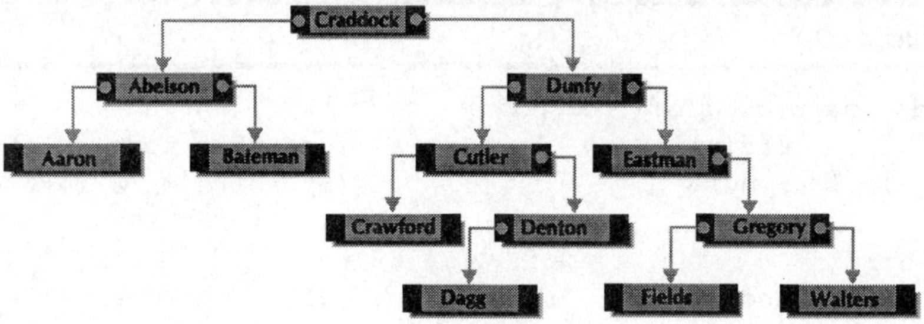

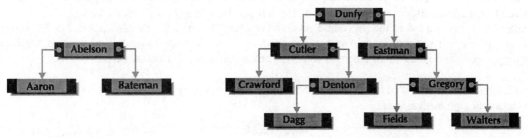

Figure 32.27.

Suppose that this tree is to be printed in alphabetical order, that is, an in-order traversal is to be performed. Then the procedure would be as follows. The left subtree of the *root node*, *Craddock* is shown in Figure 32.28.

To print this subtree, we must first print its left subtree, which is just the entry *Aaron* which has no descendants. We therefore print 'Aaron'. Now we can print the node data, 'Abelson' and turn to the right subtree of *Abelson*. This right subtree is simply *Bateman*, which is then printed.

This completes the printing of the left subtree of *Craddock*, so now 'Craddock' can be printed. Now the right subtree of *Craddock* is to be printed. The right subtree of *Craddock* has as its root node *Dunfy* (Figure 32.29).

Figure 32.28.   **Figure 32.29.**

We must first print *Dunfy's* left subtree, which is shown in Figure 32.30. *Cutler's* left subtree is *Crawford* which is a terminal node and is therefore printed. 'Cutler' is then printed, followed by 'Dagg' then 'Denton'. This completes the printing

Figure 32.30.   **Figure 32.31.**

of *Dunfy's* left subtree, so 'Dunfy' is printed followed by its right subtree (shown in Figure 32.31). In order, this subtree would be printed: 'Eastman' – 'Fields' – 'Gregory' – 'Walters', which completes the process.

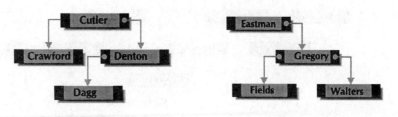

The simplicity of this method is also reflected in the pseudocode version of the algorithm. We begin by defining a procedure called Tree which prints a tree starting at a specified node (Listing 32.9).

Listing 32.9.

```
define procedure Tree(node)
  l := lptr(node)              {get this node's left pointer}
  if l <> null                 {if there is a left subtree, print it}
     then Tree(l)
  endif
  print(node)                  {print the data at this node}
  r := rptr(node)              {get this node's right pointer}
  if r <> null                 {if there is a right subtree, print it}
     then Tree(r)
  endif
endprocedure Tree
```

Notice that this procedure calls itself; this is termed *recursion*, a very useful programming device. The procedure Tree is invoked to print the left subtree at a particlar node by passing the left pointer as a procedure *parameter*, or to print the right subtree by passing the right pointer as a procedure parameter. A procedure parameter allows values to be transmitted to the procedure which are local to the procedure, having no existence outside the procedure.

In Listing 32.9, node is a parameter which initially points to the root node. By making the procedure call, Tree(root), the procedure is invoked with the value of root passed to the parameter node. In the procedure, node is used to get the value of the left pointer using l = lptr(node). If it is not a null pointer, l is now passed to the procedure recursively using Tree(l), and now node has the value of the pointer for the left subtree. In this way, the procedure Tree is used recursively to process subtrees, only printing a node and going on to the right subtree when a null pointer is encountered.

To illustrate the operation of the pseudocode, consider the binary tree shown in Figure 32.32 which is to be processed in alphabetical order.

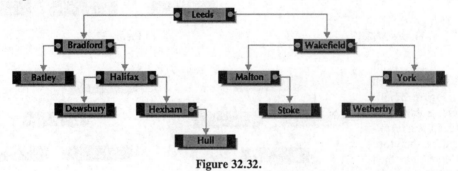

Figure 32.32.

The equivalent table is Table 32.16.

node	left	data	right
0	1	Leeds	6
1	4	Bradford	2
2	5	Halifax	3
3	1	Hexham	9
4	1	Batley	1
5	1	Dewsbury	1
6	10	Wakefield	7
7	8	York	1
8	1	Wetherby	1
9	1	Hull	1
10	1	Malton	11
11	1	Stoke	1

Table 32.16.

Table 32.17 traces the pseudocode in Listing 32.9, indicating the action taken at each invocation of `Tree`. Only the pointer currently relevant is indicated in the two pointer columns. The process is started by the call `Tree(0)`.

As each invocation of `Tree` is completed, control is returned to the point where the procedure was called. For example, if currently the root node of a subtree is node 7, *York*, then `exit Tree(7)` returns control to the instruction following `call Tree(7)` which happens to be the end of `Tree(6)`, *Wakefield*; similarly, `exit Tree(6)` returns control to the point where `Tree(6)` was called, the end of `Tree(0)`. Successively returning to parent nodes is the bottoming out process referred to above, and it relies heavily on the use of a stack (see the earlier section on applications of stacks).

Using the recursive procedure, `Tree`, hides the use of the stack because of the way that

node	left	data	right	action
0	1	Leeds		call Tree(1)
1	4	Bradford		call Tree(4)
4	1	Batley		print 'Batley'
4		Batley	1	exit Tree(4)
1		Bradford		print 'Bradford'
1		Bradford	2	call Tree(2)
2	5	Halifax		call Tree(5)
5	1	Dewsbury		print ''Dewsbury
5		Dewsbury	1	exit Tree(5)
2		Halifax		print 'Halifax'
2		Halifax	3	call Tree(3)
3	1	Hexham		print 'Hexham'
3		Hexham	9	call Tree(9)
9	1	Hull		print 'Hull'
9		Hull	1	exit Tree(9)
3		Hexham		exit Tree(3)
2		Halifax		exit Tree(2)
1		Bradford		exit Tree(1)
0		Leeds	6	call Tree(6)
6	10	Wakefield		call Tree(10)
10	1	Malton		call Tree(11)
10		Malton	11	print 'Stoke'
11	1	Stoke		exit Tree(11)
11		Stoke	1	exit Tree(10)
10		Malton		print 'Wakefield'
6		Wakefield		call Tree(7)
6		Wakefield	7	call Tree(8)
7		York		print 'Wetherby'
8		Wetherby		exit Tree(8)
8		Wetherby	1	print 'York'
7		York		exit Tree(7)
7		York	1	exit Tree(6)
6		Wakefield		exit Tree(0)
0		Leeds		

Table 32.17.

procedure parameters are handled. On entering a procedure, the current values of its parameters are pushed to a stack and are replaced by the values passed to the procedure; the original values of the parameters are restored only when the procedure is exited. For example, the procedure call `Tree(2)` passes the value 2 to the parameter `node`. At this point, `Tree(1)` is being processed with `node` having a value of 1. So before `node` takes the value 2, its current value, that is 1, is pushed onto the stack. Then `node` is given the value 2 and the procedure is executed. When control returns to the point following the call `Tree(2)`, the top of the stack, the value 1, is pulled and copied to `node` thus restoring it to its local value.

The tree traversal algorithm given above is called in-order tree traversal, one of three main methods of accessing trees. The other two methods are called *pre-order* and *post-order traversal*. These are defined as follow:

```
Pre-order traversal:
visit the root node, then
visit all the nodes in the left subtree in pre-order, then
visit all the nodes in the right subtree in pre-order
```

With reference to the tree above, pre-order traversal would produce the list:

> Leeds Bradford Batley Halifax Dewsbury Hexham Hull Wakefield Malton Stoke York Wetherby

```
Post-order traversal:
visit all the nodes of the left subtree in post-order, then
visit all the nodes in the right subtree in post-order, then
visit the root node
```

This would produce the list:

> Batley Dewsbury Hull Hexham Halifax Bradford Stoke Malton Wetherby York Wakefield Leeds

Notice that the definitions of pre-order and post-order traversals again are recursive, allowing them to be handled in the same way as the in-order traversal.

Applications of binary trees

Sorting

A binary tree can be used to order a set of integers using the algorithm given in Listing 32.10.

Listing 32.10.

```
algorithm tree_sort
  repeat
    read num                        {get next number}
    addnode(0)                      {call procedure}
  until no_more_numbers             {continue until all numbers
                                     read}

end

define procedure addnode(node)
  if data(node) > num
    then if lptr(node) = null
            then createnode(num)
            else addnode(lptr(node))     {recurse using lptr}
         endif
    else if rptr(node) = null
```

```
         then createnode(num)
         else addnode(rptr(node))      {recurse using rptr}
       endif
  endif
endprocedure addnode
```

Initially, the first number in the list is stored in the root node. Then, in turn, each of the remaining numbers is compared with the current root node (that is, `data(node)`) to determine whether the number should be in the left subtree or the right subtree. If the number is greater, then it must go somewhere in the right subtree, otherwise it must go somewhere in the left subtree. If the appropriate subtree pointer is null, a new node is created containing the number and the subtree pointer links it to the tree; when the subtree pointer is not null, the process calls itself (recurses) using the pointer as the new root node. The procedure `createnode(num)`, referred to in the algorithm merely allocates space for new nodes, stores the number in the new node and links it to the tree by adjusting the parents left or right pointer.

As an example, suppose the following list of numbers is to be used to created an ordered tree as described above: 57 10 26 13 85 2 30 63 120

The tree would assume the form shown in Figure 32.33

The numbers could be visited in ascending order using in-order traversal, as described in the previous section, to give the list

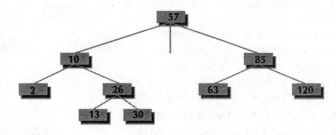

Figure 32.33.

        2 10 13 26 30 57 63 85 120

Representing arithmetic expressions

Compilers often transform arithmetic expressions into more manageable forms prior to generating object code. A binary tree representation of an arithmetic expression is one such transformation. Consider the expression

        B + C*D

The equivalent binary tree representation is shown in Figure 32.34.

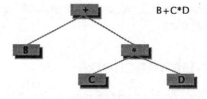

Figure 32.34.

An in-order traversal of the tree produces the original expression. This type of representation is relatively easy to handle by a compiler: if a node contains an operator, the left subtree is evaluated, the right subtree is evaluated and the two values obtained are the operands for the operator at that node. If a subtree also contains an operator node, the same procedure is used recursively to produce the intermediate result. In the example above, + at the root node causes the left subtree to be evaluated, resulting in the value assigned to *B*; however, the right subtree contains the operator node * (multiplication) causing a recursive call to its left and right subtrees before the multiplication, *C*D*, can be evaluated.

Figures 32.35 to 32.37 provide some further examples of expressions represented as binary trees:

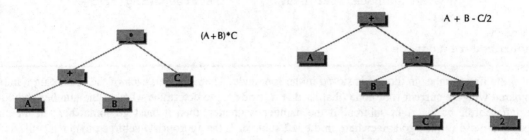

Figure 32.35.   Figure 32.36.

All of the expressions provided above are in *infix notation*, that is, with the arithmetic operators positioned between the operands. Thus, to add two numbers, A and B, using infix notation we would write $A + B$. There are two other standard notations for arithmetic expressions, namely, *postfix* and *prefix* notations. In postfix notation, $A + B$ is written $AB+$ and in prefix, $+AB$. By traversing the binary tree in in-order we saw that the infix expression resulted. Perhaps unsurprisingly, traversing the tree in post-order gives the postfix expression, and traversing the tree in pre-order gives the prefix expression. Table 32.18 shows the same expressions in the three different forms.

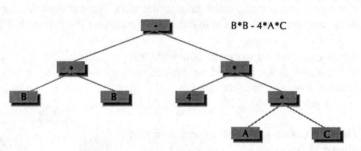

Figure 32.37.

Infix	Postfix	Prefix
B+C*D	BCD*+	+B*CD
(A+B)*C	AB+C*	*+ABC
A+BC/2	ABC2/+	+AB/C2
B*B4*A*C	BB*4AC**	*BB*4*AC

Table 32.18.

Postfix notation is also known by the name Reverse Polish notation, extensively used in the programming language Forth and of general importance in computing.

Hash functions

A hash function takes a numeric key lying within a certain range of values and transforms it into a table index which is within a smaller range of values. For example, if we have, say, under 200 data items with keys in the range 135246 to 791824 which are to be stored in a table of size 200, the mapping function will need to perform some mathematical operation on any given key to convert it to a number in the range 0 to 198. This number produced by the hash function is an index to the table. Furthermore, it is desirable to use a hash function which evenly maps key values to table index values in order to avoid two keys producing the same hash value.

A commonly used method of producing this even spread of hash values is to use the MOD function. This is simply a function which returns the integer remainder after one integer is divided by another. For instance, MOD(11,4) = 3, since 11/4 = 2 remainder 3.

In the example above we could use 199 (prime numbers give a more random spread than non-primes) as the modulus, that is the number used as the divisor, in order to generate an index value in the range 0 to 198. Table 32.19 shows some examples of keys and corresponding table index values.

key	index
123456	76
232345	112
232324	91
436170	161
660912	33
376888	181
234023	198
456000	91
345999	137

Table 32.19.

Having used a hash function to establish the position of a data item within a table, and having stored it there, it is simply a matter of applying the same hash function again to the items key in order to locate it at some future time. This allows almost direct access to items stored in this manner.

Notice that the third and the eighth keys both give an index value of 91. This is termed a *collision* and some method of coping with this eventuality must be devised; *collision resolution strategies* are discussed in the next section.

As another example of hash functions, suppose that this time the keys of the data items are alphanumeric, containing up to eight characters, and that there are no more than, say, 50 items to be stored in a table of size 60. The first step is to convert the key to an integer; an easy way to do this is to sum the ASCII values of the characters in the key. Table 32.20 illustrates this procedure:

key	ASCII values								sum	MOD59
williams	119	105	108	108	105	97	109	115	866	40
knott	107	110	111	116	116				679	30
smith	115	109	105	116	104				668	19
jones	106	111	110	101	115				662	13
waites	119	97	105	116	101	115			772	5
craven	99	114	97	118	101	110			758	50
gold	103	111	108	100					541	10
collins	99	111	108	108	105	110	115		875	49
bates	98	97	116	101	115				646	56

Table 32.20.

The ASCII values are then summed, and finally they are expressed as a MOD 59 number which is, as before, the index of the data item in the storage table.

Collision resolution strategies

When a hash function produces the same value from two different keys, a *collision* is said to have occurred. Two common methods of coping with collisions are:

- direct chaining;

- open addressing.

In *direct chaining* each data item is extended to include a pointer to another item. Initially this pointer is a null pointer, but if a collision occurs, it is used to record the location of a collision item in some overflow area. Thus each element in the storage table is either empty, or contains the first item of a linked list of items all having the same hash value. Where collisions have not occurred, these linked lists contain only one item. Figure 32.38 illustrates this data structure.

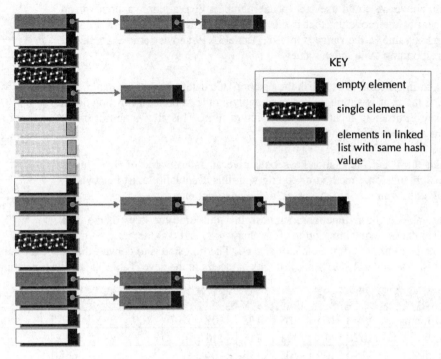

Figure 32.38.

With *open addressing*, collision items are stored in the next available location in the storage table. Thus, if the table element for a particular item is already occupied, the remaining table is searched sequentially until a vacant slot is found for it. The table is searched circularly. That is, if the end of the table is reached before a vacant slot is found, the search continues at the beginning of the table.

Applications of hash tables

Earlier in this chapter we saw that linked lists could be used for dynamic allocation of variables by an interpreter. In fact, this particular application of linked lists also incorporates an elementary form of hashing using direct chaining: the first letter of an identifier is used as an index to a table of pointers to linked lists of all identifiers starting wih the same letter.

Another application of hash functions is described in Chapter 15. In address generation a hash function is used to determine the disk block address for a record to allow the record to be accessed as quickly as possible.

A third application of hash functions is in the production of symbol tables by compilers. In this instance, as identifiers are encountered in the source code, a table containing details of their type and value must be consulted. If an identifier does not have an entry in the symbol table, one must be inserted; if it does have an entry already, further information may need to be added. Because of the frequency with which the symbol table needs to be consulted, and because of its central role in the compilation process, it is important that accessing it is made to be as efficient as possible; the use of hash functions is a possible solution.

Soundex coding

If the user of a personnel records system were to be asked to locate a record having the key 'Waites', then it is unlikely that the record would be retrieved if the user typed in 'Whaites' or 'Waits'. A possible solution is to convert the name to a *Soundex Code* defined as follows:

letter	code
B F P V	1
C G J K Q S X Z	2
D T	3
L	4
M N	5
R	6

Table 32.21.

- the first letter of the name is the first letter of the code

- all vowels and the letters H, W and Y are ignored

- double letters are replaced by a single instance of the letter

- the remaining letters are replaced by values according to Table 32.21.

- the code is restricted to four characters in length

- if the code contains less than four characters, it is padded with trailing zeros.

Table 32.22 provides some examples of names converted to soundex codes.

Soundex coding techniques are used extensively by the police force for searching criminal records. It is important to find all similar sounding names from their files because of the high probability of a name being reported incorrectly.

Soundex coding is also very useful for helping to make interactive information retrieval systems more user friendly. For example, rather than the computer saying, "There are no personnel records with the name JOHNSON", it reported,

name	Soundex Code
Waites	W320
Whaites	W320
Waits	W320
Williams	W452
Johnson	J525
Jonson	J525
Johnsen	J525
Morton	M635
Morten	M635
Summerville	S561

Table 32.22.

"There are no personnel records with the name JOHNSON, but here is a list of records closely matching this name: A. JONSON, B. JOHNSEN... etc", this would be much more useful to the user.

Exercises

1. Define the following terms using diagrams where appropriate:

    (i)   array;

    (ii)   Illiffe vector;

    (iii)   access table;

    (iv)   stack;

    (v)   queue;

    (vi)   linked list;

    (vii)   binary tree;

    (viii) hash function.

2. Give two applications of each of the following:

    (i)   stack;

    (ii)   queue;

    (iii)   linked list;

    (iv)   binary tree;

    (v)   hash function;

    (vi)   soundex coding.

3. What is meant by the term 'tree traversal'? Explain the difference between pre-order and post order tree traversal.

4. What are 'collision resolution strategies'?

Chapter 33
Sorting Techniques

For computing purposes, a distinction has to be made between internal and external sorting. Where large volumes of data have to be sorted, such as entire files held on magnetic tape or disk, an external sort is used; this involves repeated transfers of data between memory and backing storage media. The basis of all such external sorting is *merging*, a process of forming one single sorted sequence from two previously sorted sequences.

Merging

The pseudocode, Merge in Listing 33.1 describes the process of merging two files, `File1` and `File2`, into a new file, `File3`. If the files were held on magnetic tape, then three tape drives would be needed to effect the merge.

Listing 33.1.   Merging two files into a third

```
{Merge}
open File1, File2, File3                              {initialize}
read File1
read File2
while not eof(File1) and not eof(File2)               {start of main
                                                      processing loop}

  if RecordKey(File1) < RecordKey(File2) then
      write Record(File1) to File3, read File1
    else write Record(File2) to File3, read File2
  endif
endwhile                                              {one file is now
                                                      empty}

while not eof(FileN)
  write to File3, read FileN
endwhile
```

Merge sort

The merge algorithm assumes that the two files to be merged are already sorted, but the same process, used repeatedly, can be used to sort a completely unsorted file. The following example presupposes the use of three files, `File1`, `File2` and `File3`, and a set of record keys with no repeated values.

Stage 1

`File3` contains the sequence

        (18 26) (3 9 34) (5 21) (14)(6)

The brackets denote that there are already groups of values in ascending sequence, referred to as *runs*.

Place alternate runs into `File1` and `File2`, thus

```
File1: (18 26) (5 21)(6)
File2: (3 9 34) (14)
```

Stage 2

Using the following procedure, `File1` and `File2` onto `File3`. *Compare the leading values from* `File1` *and* `File2` *and write to* `File3` *the smallest of the two which is also greater than the immediately preceding value written to* `File3`. *If both are smaller than the latter, write the smaller of the two.*

Thus, proceeding with the values currently in `File1` and `File2`, the first pair for `File1` and `File2` are 18 and 3, respectively; 3 is the smaller value and since `File3` is, at present, empty, 3 is selected.

```
File1: (18 26) (5 21) (6)
File2: (9 34) (14)
File3: 3
```

Next, 18 and 9 are compared and 9 is selected because it is smallest and also greater than 3, the last value written to `File3`.

```
File1: (18 26) (5 21) (6)
File2: (34) (14)
File3: 3 9
```

Of the next pairs 18 and 34, 18 is smaller but greater than the trailing value, 9, in `File3`.

```
File1: (26) (5 21) (6)
File2: (34) (14)
File3: 3 9 18
```

Comparing the next pair, 26 and 34, the former is selected.

```
File1: (5 21) (6)
File2: (34) (14)
File3: 3 9 18 26
```

Comparison of 5 and 34 results in the selection of 34, because 5 is less than 26, the trailing value in `File3`.

```
File1: (5 21) (6)
File2: (14)
File3: 3 9 18 26 34
```

The next comparison reveals that 5 and 14 are both less than 34, so 5 is selected.

```
File1: (21) (6)
File2: (14)
File3: 3 9 18 26 34 5
```

14 is the next chosen value.

```
File1: (21) (6)
File2:
File3: 3 9 18 26 34 5 14
```

File2 is now empty and the remaining values in File1 are transferred to File3.

```
File3: (3 9 18 26 34) (5 14 21) (6)
```

Stage 1 is repeated.

The runs have increased in length and are directed alternately to File1 and File2

```
File1: (3 9 18 26 34) (6)
File2: (5 14 21)
```

Stage 2 is repeated, merging the runs in File1 and File2 back to File3, to produce

```
File3: (3 5 9 14 18 21 26 34) (6)
```

Stage 1 is repeated and runs are written alternately to File1 and File2

```
File1: (3 5 9 14 18 21 26 34)
File2: (6)
```

Stage 2 again merges File1 and File2 onto File3, this time as a completely sorted sequence.

```
File3: 3 5 6 9 14 18 21 26 34
```

The algorithm in Listing 33.2 describes the process. X denotes the most recent value written to File3, A is the smaller of the two leading values in File1 and File2 and B the larger.

Listing 33.2.   Merge sort

```
{mergesort}                                {open File1, File2, File3}
  repeat
    procedure split_and_merge              {split File3 into File1
                                           and File2, putting
                                           alternate runs into
                                           alternate files}

    while not eof(File1)and not eof(File2)
      if eof(File3) or (X < A) or (B < X) then
          write A to File3
        else write B to File3
      endif
    endwhile                               {one of files is now
                                           empty}

    while not eof(FileN)
      write to File3
    endwhile
  until File3                              {consists of only one run}
```

4-file merge sort

The efficiency of a merge sort can be increased with the use of four files as follows.

The following values are to be sorted

```
21 14 54 6 87 15 32 76 38 23 44 16 17
```

This time, single values are written alternately to `File1` and `File2`

```
File1: 21 54 87 32 38 44 17
File2: 14 6 15 76 23 16
```

The values are successively merged in pairs using `File3` and `File4` alternately.

```
File3: (14 21)(15 87)(23 38)(17)
File4: (6 54)(32 76)(16 44)
```

These runs are now merged alternately to `File1` and `File2`.

```
File1: (6 14 21 54) (16 23 38 44)
File2: (15 32 76 87) (17)
```

The extended runs are merged alternately to `File3` and `File4`.

```
File3: (6 14 15 21 32 54 76 87)
File4: (16 17 23 38 44)
```

A final merge back to `File1` only, produces the final sorted sequence.

```
File1: 6 14 15 16 17 21 23 32 38 44 54 76 87
```

Internal sorting, which is the subject of study in the following sections, involves the sorting of items entirely within memory into a strict ascending or descending order. For programming purposes, the items to be sorted are held in a one-dimensional array. The purpose of the data items will vary according to the application, but they may serve, for example, as keys to logical records. Direct access files frequently make use of indexes to identify the locations of individual records on a storage medium. Searching such an index for a particular record key value is often more efficient if the index is sorted into a particular sequence. The study of sorting algorithms is a long standing area of research in computer science and many highly efficient but complex methods have been developed. In order that the main principles of sorting can be understood, this text provides a detailed description of three relatively simple sorting techniques: *exchange* or 'bubble' sort; *selection* sort; *insertion* sort; and two more complex methods: *shell* sort; *quicksort*.

Each narrative description is followed by:

- an outline of the main programming requirements needed to implement the sort in a high level language;

- pseudocode with detailed annotation of the main processes;

- annotated sample programs implemented in Turbo Pascal.

Exchange or bubble sort

If it is assumed, for example, that items are to be sorted into ascending sequence, then the idea of the bubble sort is that, firstly the smallest value 'bubbles' to the top or beginning of the list, followed by the second smallest into the second position, the third smallest into third position and so on. The process can best be illustrated by a practical example as follows.

Consider a one-dimensional array of 5 elements, each containing an integer value. The array is known by the symbol M and each element in the array is identified by its subscript. The array elements and their contents are shown in Table 33.1.

array elements	M(1)	M(2)	M(3)	M(4)	M(5)
contents	3	6	2	1	5

Table 33.1.

The bubble sort requires that the array of values be scanned repeatedly and that with each scan, or more properly, *pass*, adjacent pairs of numbers are compared to see if they are in the required order; if necessary they exchange positions. In the above example, the first pair, 3 and 6, are compared and found to be in the correct order; no exchange is necessary. Then the second and third items, 6 and 2, are compared, found to be in the incorrect order and are exchanged. The array now appears as in Table 33.2. The first pass continues with the comparison of the third and fourth items, 6 and 1; these require exchanging and the list is as shown in Table 33.3. The first pass ends with a comparison of the fourth and fifth items, now 6 and 5 respectively; again, an exchange is required. At the end of this first pass, the sequence appears as in Table 33.4.

array elements	M(1)	M(2)	M(3)	M(4)	M(5)
contents	3	2	6	1	5

Table 33.2.

array elements	M(1)	M(2)	M(3)	M(4)	M(5)
contents	3	2	1	6	5

Table 33.3.

array elements	M(1)	M(2)	M(3)	M(4)	M(5)
contents	3	2	1	5	6

Table 33.4.

The sort is not yet complete and further passes are needed. The complete process is illustrated in Table 33.5, below (continues onto next page). Shading indicates those values currently being compared and, if necessary, exchanged.

array elements	exchange	M(1)	M(2)	M(3)	M(4)	M(5)
begin Pass 1	no	3	6	2	1	5
	yes	3	6	2	1	5
	yes	3	2	6	1	5
	yes	3	2	1	6	5
end Pass 1		3	2	1	5	6
begin Pass 2	yes	3	2	1	5	6
	yes	2	3	1	5	6
	no	2	1	3	5	6
	no	2	1	3	5	6
end Pass 2		2	1	3	5	6
begin Pass 3	yes	2	1	3	5	6

	exchange	M(1)	M(2)	M(3)	M(4)	M(5)
	no	1	2	3	5	6
	no	1	2	3	5	6
	no	1	2	3	5	6
end Pass 3		1	2	3	5	6
begin Pass 4	no	1	2	3	5	6
	no	1	2	3	5	6
	no	1	2	3	5	6
	no	1	2	3	5	6
end Pass 4		1	2	3	5	6

Table 33.5.

A number of features can be identified in the above process:

- with each pass, the smallest value moves one position towards the beginning (the left) of the array;

- after the first pass, the largest value is at the end of the array. At the end of each subsequent pass, the next largest number moves to its correct position;

- the sort has been completed before the final pass.

Referring to this last feature, the sort is complete by the end of Pass 3. Why then is a further pass necessary? The answer is that the first comparison in Pass 3 results in an exchange between the values 2 and 1. If it is assumed that the occurrence of an exchange indicates that the sort is not complete, then a further pass is needed to determine that the array is sorted; that is, there have been no exchanges. The maximum number of passes required is always N-1, N being the number of items in the array. Frequently, the sort is complete well before this maximum is reached and any further passes are wasted. Consider the sequence in Table 33.6

array elements	exchange	M(1)	M(2)	M(3)	M(4)	M(5)	M(6)
initial contents		3	1	2	6	7	9
begin Pass 1	yes	3	1	2	6	7	9
	yes	1	3	2	6	7	9
	no	1	2	3	6	7	9
	no	1	2	3	6	7	9
	no	1	2	3	6	7	9
end Pass 1		1	2	3	6	7	9
begin Pass 2	no	1	2	3	6	7	9
	no	1	2	3	6	7	9
	no	1	2	3	6	7	9
	no	1	2	3	6	7	9
	no	1	2	3	6	7	9
end Pass 2		1	2	3	6	7	9

Table 33.6.

The maximum number of passes necessary should be N-1, that is, 5. Instead, the sort is completed by the end of the first pass and confirmed by the lack of exchanges in the second pass.

Program requirements

Comparison of adjacent values in an array. Assuming that the values are held in a one-dimensional array, reference is made to elements within the array by subscript. For example, the 4th element in an array called List, is addressed by List(4). To carry out a pass of all the elements in an array requires the use of a program loop to increment the subscript from 1 to N, the variable N being the size of the array. This can reduce by 1 after each complete pass, because the largest number 'sinks' to the bottom of the list and therefore need not be considered in subsequent passes; the efficiency of the algorithm is thus improved. For the sake of simplicity, this particular feature is not used in the illustrative algorithm or programs.

Exchanging the positions of adjacent values. Assuming that the programming language in use does not provide an 'exchange' or 'swap' instruction, then a temporary store is required to allow the exchange to take place, For example, to exchange the contents of two variables, first and second, using a temporary store, hold, requires the following processes:

1. Copy contents of First into Hold;

2. Copy contents of Second into First;

3. Copy contents of Hold into Second.

location	First	Second	Hold
initial contents	6	3	
after process 1	6	3	6
after process 2	3	3	6
after process 3	3	6	6

Table 33.7.

This is illustrated in Table 33.7, with some example values.

Detecting completion of the sort. A flag or sentinel variable, initialized for example, to 0 at the beginning of each pass and set to 1 if any exchanges take place during a pass, can be used to detect the completion of the sort before the maximum number of passes has been completed. For simplicity, the pseudocode in Listing 33.3 does not include this feature, although it is used in the sample Pascal program.

Listing 33.3.   Bubble sort pseudocode

```
{Bubble sort}
Number:= N                      {number of values and subscript of
                                last item}
Passes:=1                       {initialize passes}
while Passes <= Number - 1 do   {control number of passes}
  Item := 1                     {set array subscript}
  while Item <= Number - 1 do   {loop for one pass}
    if M(Item) > M(Item + 1) then
        swap                    {swap if necessary}
    endif
    Item := Item + 1            {increment subscript}
  endwhile                      {end of single pass}
  Passes := Passes + 1          {increment passes}
endwhile                        {end of all passes}
```

Listing 33.4.   Bubble sort in Turbo Pascal

```pascal
program Bubble (input, output);
const
  number = 20;                                    {number of values} {to
                                                  sort}
var
  M :array[1..number] of integer;                 {declare array}
  Exchange :boolean;                              {flag for swap}
  Item, Passes, Spare :integer;
begin
  for Item := 1 to Number do                      {fill array M}
    begin
      writeln('number');
      readln(M[Item]);
    end;
  Passes := 1;                                    {initialize to} {first
                                                  pass}

  Exchange := true;
  while (Passes <= Number - 1) and (Exchange) do  {control passes}
    begin
      Item := 1;                                  {initialize element}
                                                  {pointer}

      Exchange := false;                          {initialize swap}
                                                  {flag before each}
                                                  {pass}

      while Item <= Number - 1 do                 {control number of}
                                                  {comparisons}

        begin
          if M[Item] > M[Item +1] then            {compare adjacent}
                                                  {values}
            begin                                 {swap elements}
              Spare := M[Item];
              M[Item] := M[Item + 1];
              M[Item + 1] := Spare;
              Exchange := true;                   {set flag to}
                                                  {indicate swap}

            end;
              Item := Item + 1;                   {move pointer to}
                                                  {next element}

        end;
          Passes := Passes + 1;                   {increment pass}
                                                  {counter}

    end;
      for Item := 1 to Number do                  {display sorted}
                                                  {array}

        begin
          writeln(M[Item]);
        end;
end.
```

Selection sort

This method also requires the comparison and exchange of elements in a list. It is based on the principal that the item with the lowest value is exchanged with the item at the beginning or head of the list and that the process is repeated with N-1 items, N-2 items and so on, until only the largest item is left. Table 33.8 shows array M containing six, unsorted, integer values.

M(1)	M(2)	M(3)	M(4)	M(5)	M(6)
15	8	-3	62	24	12

Table 33.8.

The list is to be sorted into strict ascending sequence, as shown in Table 33.9.

M(1)	M(2)	M(3)	M(4)	M(5)	M(6)
-3	8	12	15	24	62

Table 33.9.

Table 33.10 shows the scanning process, the shaded values indicating the length of the list to be examined in each scan.

M(1)	M(2)	M(3)	M(4)	M(5)	M(6)	action
15	8	-3	62	24	12	starting sequence
-3	8	15	62	24	12	3 exchanged with 15 at head of list
-3	8	15	62	24	12	no exchange needed
-3	8	12	62	24	15	12 exchanged with 15 at head of list
-3	8	12	15	24	62	15 exchanged with 62 at head of list
-3	8	12	15	24	62	no exchange needed

Table 33.10.

The first pass of N items returns the value of -3 as being the smallest value in the list; this value moves to the head of the list and the previous head, 15, is moved to the position formerly occupied by -3. The list to be scanned is now N-1 items and has the value 8 at its head. The next pass reveals 8 as the smallest value, but no exchange is made because it already heads the shortened list. The next pass examines N-2 items and returns 12 as the lowest value, which is exchanged with 15 at the head of the shortened list. The process continues until only two items remain, 24 at the head and 62 at the rear; no exchange is needed and the list is sorted.

Program requirements

Certain features are similar to those of the bubble sort described earlier.

- Comparison of values in different locations in an array.

- Exchange of values in different, although not necessarily adjacent, positions in the array.

- The use of a pointer to allow element positions to be stored and incremented and also to be used as a subscript to refer to the contents of an individual location.

- The use of a temporary store to enable an exchange of element positions.

Listing 33.5.   Selection sort pseudocode

```
{Selection}
Number:= N                                    {number of values to sort}
for Head := 1 to N - 1                        {increment head}
  PresentValue := M(Head)                     {value of current head}
  PresentPntr := Head                         {position of current head}
  for NextOne := PresentPntr + 1 to N         {increment search pointer}
    if M(NextOne) < PresentValue then
      PresentValue := M(NextOne)              {store smaller value and
      PresentPntr := NextOne                  its position in the list}
    endif
  endfor
  if PresentPntr <> Head then                 {check smallest value not
                                              already at head}
    Temp := M(Head)                           {temp is a temporary store
                                              for the swap}
    M(head) := M(PresentPntr)                 {exchange smallest/head
                                              values}
    M(PresentPntr) := Temp
  endif
endfor
```

The use of a temporary location `Temp` in the above algorithm is not strictly necessary, since the smallest value is assigned to `PresentValue` at the end of a pass and as the following program implementation illustrates, the swap could be implemented with:

```
M(PresentPntr) := M(Head);
M(Head) := PresentValue;
```

Listing 33.6.   Selection sort in Turbo Pascal

```
program Selection (input, output);
const
  Number = 20;
var
  M :array[1..Number] of integer;
  Head, NextOne, PresentValue,
  PresentPntr :integer;
begin
  for NextOne := 1 to Number do
    begin
      write ('number');
      readln (M[NextOne]);
    end;
  for Head := 1 to Number - 1 do
    begin
      PresentValue := M[Head];
      PresentPntr := Head;
```

```
        for NextOne := PresentPntr + 1 to Number do
          begin
              if M[NextOne] < PresentValue then
                begin
                    PresentValue := M[NextOne];
                    PresentPntr := NextOne;
                end;
          end;
          if PresentPntr <> Head then
              begin
                  M[PresentPntr] := M[Head];
                  M[Head] := PresentValue;
              end;
      end;
      for NextOne := 1 to Number do
        begin
            writeln(M[NextOne]);
        end;
end.
```

Insertion sort

This method can best be illustrated with the example of an unsorted pack of playing cards. Assuming that the cards are to be put into a row of ascending sequence (the least value on the left), the procedure may be as follows: (i) take the first card from the source pile and begin the destination row; (ii) continuing with the rest of the source pile, pick one card at a time and place it in the correct sequence in the destination row. The process of finding the correct point of insertion requires repeated comparisons and where an insertion requires it, movement of cards to make space in the sequence. Thus, the card to be inserted, x, is compared with successive cards in the destination row (beginning from the largest value at the right hand end of the destination row) and where x is less than the card under comparison, the latter is moved to the right; otherwise x is inserted in the next position to the right.

Program requirements

The procedures are fairly simple, although a practical exercise with a pack of cards should help to clarify them. As with previous sorts, reference to array subscripts is required to allow comparison with different elements in the array. Nested loops are needed; the outer one for selecting successive values to be inserted into a destination sequence and the inner for allowing the insertion value to be compared with those already in sequence. Control of the outer loop does not present a problem as it simply ensures that all values are inserted, starting with the second; the first obviously needs no comparison as it is the first to be inserted. The inner loop controls the movement of values through the destination list to allow insertion of new values at the appropriate points. This loop may be terminated under two distinct conditions:

(i)   a value in the destination sequence is less than the value to be inserted;

(ii)   there are no further items to the left in the destination sequence.

To ensure termination under these conditions, a *flag* or *sentinel* is used. In the pseudocode and program implementations, array element (0) is used to store the value to be inserted, thus ensuring that when the left hand end is reached, no further comparisons are made.

The pseudocode in Listing 33.7 illustrates the procedure; the analogy of a pack of cards is continued.

Listing 33.7   Insertion sort pseudocode

```
{Insertion sort}
for PickCard = 2 to NumInPack        {pick cards singly, starting with
                                      second}

  InHand := M(PickCard)              {store value of card to insert}
  M(0) := InHand                     {to prevent insertion beyond left end
                                      of destination sequence}

  J := PickCard - 1                  {ensures comparison with first card}
  while InHand < M(J) do             {card to insert < next card to the
                                      left in destination sequence}

    M(J + 1) := M(J)                 {move card > card to insert, to the
                                      right}

    J := J - 1                       {pointer to next card compared with
                                      card to insert}

  endwhile
  M(J + 1) := InHand                 {insert card into destination
                                      sequence}

endfor
```

Listing 33.8.   Insertion sort in Turbo Pascal

```
program insertion (input, output);
  const
      CardsInPack = 20;
  var
      M :array[0..NumInPack] of integer;
      Card, PickCard, InHand, J :integer;
begin
  for Card := 1 to NumInPack do
    begin
      write ('number');
      readln (M[Card]);
    end;
  for PickCard := 2 to NumInPack do
    begin
      InHand := M[PickCard];
      M[0] := InHand;
      J := PickCard - 1;
      while InHand < M[J] do
        begin
          M[J + 1] := M[J];
          J := J - 1;
        end;
      M[J + 1] := InHand;
    end;
  for Card := 1 to NumInPack do
    begin
```

```
        writeln (M[Card]);
     end;
  end.
```

Comparative efficiency of sorting methods

The sorts described so far are not the most sophisticated, and in many cases, are not very quick. They are, however, relatively simple to understand and they have been chosen for this reason. More efficient, and consequently more complex, sorting algorithms include the:

Shell sort

Named after its designer, D.L. Shell in 1959, it is a refinement of the insertion sort and divides the list into groups which are sorted separately. For example, with an array of eight items, those which are four positions apart are sorted first; the four groups will each contain two items. A second pass groups and sorts afresh the items which are two positions apart; this involves two groups, each with 4 items. Finally, all items (only one position apart) are sorted in a final pass. With each pass, the *distance* between the keys is halved, effectively changing the contents of each group. Successive passes continue until the distance between the elements in a group is one. The idea of the Shell sort is that the early passes compare items which are widely separated and thus remove the main disorders in the array. Later passes may then require fewer movements of items. The Turbo Pascal programs for the Shell sort (Listing 33.10) and the Quicksort (Listing 33.12) include routines for the generation of random numbers and the calculation of execution times. These routines can be used in all the Pascal sort programs in this chapter to test the effectiveness of each on various sets of random numbers. The performance of the Quicksort is particularly impressive, with the Shell sort taking a close second place.

Listing 33.9   Shell sort pseudocode

```
{Shell sort}
NumKeys := N
Gap := NumKeys                          {set gap to full list}
repeat
  Pntr1 := 1                            {set pointer to top of
                                         list}

  Gap := trunc(Gap/2)                   {calculate gap between
                                         keys}

  Pntr2 := Pntr1 + Gap                  {set pointer to 2nd
                                         key}

  repeat
    if M(Pntr1) > M(Pntr2) then         {compare keys}
      Exchange                          {call procedure
                                         Exchange}

    endif
    Pntr1 := Pntr1 + 1                  {move pointers down
                                         the list}

    Pntr2 := Pntr2 + 1
  until Pntr2 > NumKeys                 {test for bottom of
                                         list}

  until Gap =1                          {sort completed}
```

```
procedure Exchange
Temp := M(Pntr1)                                    {swap keys using
                                                    temporary location}

M(Pntr1) := M(Pntr2)
M(Pntr2) := Temp
Pntr4 := Pntr1                                      {set pointers for pass}
Pntr3 := Pntr1 - Gap
while (Pntr3 > 0) and (M(Pntr3) > M(Pntr4)) do      {not top of list and
                                                    swap needed}

  Temp := M(Pntr3)                                  {swap keys}
  M(Pntr3) := M(Pntr4)
  M(Pntr4) := Temp
  Pntr3 := Pntr3 - Gap                              {move pointers up the
                                                    list}

  Pntr4 := Pntr4 - Gap
endwhile
```

Listing 33.10   Shell sort in Turbo Pascal

```
program Shell (output);
uses dos;
const
  NumKeys = 1000;
var
  M :array[1..NumKeys] of integer;
  I, Item, Gap, Pntr1,
  Pntr2, Pntr3, Pntr4, Temp :integer;
  Hrs, Min, Sec, Sec100 :word;

procedure Exchange;
begin
  Temp := M[Pntr1];
  M[Pntr1] := M[Pntr2];
  M[Pntr2] :=Temp;
  Pntr4 :=Pntr1;
  Pntr3 :=Pntr1 - Gap;
  while (Pntr3 > 0) and (M[Pntr3] >M[Pntr4]) do
  begin
    Temp := M[Pntr3];
    M[Pntr3] :=M[Pntr4];
    M[Pntr4] :=Temp;
    Pntr3 :=Pntr3 - Gap;
    Pntr4 :=Pntr4 - Gap;
  end;
end;

procedure SortList
begin
  settime(0, 0, 0, 0);
  Gap :=NumKeys;
```

```
    repeat
      Pntr1 :=1;
      Gap :=trunc(Gap/2);
      Pntr2 := Pntr1 + Gap;
      repeat
        if M[Pntr1] > M[Pntr2] then
            Exchange;
        Pntr1 :=Pntr1 + 1;
        Pntr2 :=Pntr2 + 1;
      until Pntr2 > NumKeys;
    until Gap =1;
    gettime(Hrs, Min, Sec, Sec100);
end;

procedure ShowTime;
begin
  writeln(Hrs:10, Min:15, Sec:20, Sec100:25);
end;

begin
  write('Creating', NumKeys, 'random numbers');
  randomize;
  for I:=1 to NumKeys do
    begin
      M[I]:=random(30000);
    end;
  writeln;
  write('Sorting', NumKeys, 'random numbers');
  SortList
  writeln;
  for I:=1 to NumKeys do
    begin
      write(M[I]:8);
    end;
  ShowTime;
end.
```

Quicksort

This *partition* sort was invented by C.A.R Hoare, who called it 'Quicksort' because of its remarkable speed. It is based on the exchange principle used in the bubble sort described earlier and is one of the fastest array sorting techniques, for large numbers of items, currently available. Quicksort is based on the general principle that exchanges should preferably be made between items which are located a large distance apart in an array. Initially, the array is divided into two partitions, using the mid-point. Beginning at the left-most position in the array, the item in this position is compared with the item at the mid-point position. If the former is less than the latter, the next item in the partition is compared with the mid-point element. The comparisons with the mid-point item are repeated with successive items in the partition until one is found which is greater than or equal to the mid-point item. The same process is used on the right-hand partition until an item is found which is less than or equal to that at the mid-point position. Once items are found in both partitions which satisfy these respective conditions, they are swapped. Successive comparisons and swaps are carried out until each item in each partition has been compared with the mid-point item. The whole process continues *recursively* (it calls itself repeatedly), further sub-dividing the partitions, until each sub-partition contains only one item, when the array is sorted. The topic of recursion is dealt with the chapter on Data Structures.

Listing 33.11.   Quicksort pseudocode

```
{Quicksort}
NumKeys := N                        {number of keys to sort}
Lo := 1                             {store lower limit of array}
Hi := NumKeys                       {store upper limit of array}
Qsort(Lo, Hi)                       {call recursive sort} procedure
                                    passing initial parameters}

end


procedure Qsort(LowEnd, TopEnd)     {recursive sort procedure}
LeftPntr := LowEnd                  {set pointers to current}  left
                                    and right partition} limits}

RightPntr := TopEnd
MidValue := M((LowEnd + TopEnd)/2)  {store value at mid point
                                    between new left and right
                                    partitions}

repeat
  while M(LeftPntr) < MidValue do   {continue pass of left
                                    partition while mid value
                                    greater than each key examined}

    LeftPntr := LeftPntr + 1
  endwhile
  while MidValue < M(RightPntr) do  {continue pass of right
                                    partition while mid value less
                                    than each key examined}

    RightPntr := RightPntr - 1
  endwhile
  if LeftPntr <= RightPntr then     {provided the pointers have not
                                    yet crossed, swap the smaller
                                    key from the right partition
                                    with the larger key in the left}

    Temp := M(LeftPntr)
    M(LeftPntr) := M(RightPntr)
    M(RightPntr) := Temp
    LeftPntr := LeftPntr + 1        {move left pointer one right}
    RightPntr : = RightPntr - 1     {move right pointer one left}
  endif
until LeftPntr > RightPntr          {until pointers cross}
if LowEnd < RightPntr then          {if left partition still has
                                    more than one element}

  Qsort(Lowend, RightPntr)          {procedure calls itself to sort
                                    left partition with new
                                    parameters}

endif
```

```
  if LeftPntr < TopEnd then              {if right partition still has
                                          more than one element}
    Qsort(LeftPntr, TopEnd)              {procedure calls itself to sort
                                          right partition with new
                                          parameters}

  endif
```

Listing 33.12.   Quicksort in Turbo Pascal

```
program Quicksort(output);
uses dos;
const
  NumKeys = 1000;
var
  M :array[1..NumKeys] of integer;
  I, Lo, Hi :integer;
  Hrs, Min, Sec, Sec100 :word;

procedure Qsort(var LowEnd, TopEnd :integer);
var
  leftpntr, rightpntr, midvalue,
  temp :integer;
begin
  LeftPntr := LowEnd;
  RightPntr := TopEnd;
  MidValue := M[(LowEnd + TopEnd) div 2];
  repeat
    while M[LeftPntr] < MidValue do
      LeftPntr := LeftPntr + 1;
    while MidValue < M[RightPntr] do
      RightPntr := RightPntr - 1;
    if LeftPntr < RightPntr then
      begin
        Temp := M[LeftPntr];
        M[LeftPntr] := M[RightPntr];
        M[RightPntr] := Temp;
        LeftPntr := LeftPntr + 1;
        RightPntr := RightPntr - 1;
      end;
  until LeftPntr > RightPntr;
  if LowEnd < RightPntr then
    Qsort(LowEnd, RightPntr);
  if LeftPntr < TopEnd then
    Qsort(LeftPntr, TopEnd);
end;

procedure ShowTime;
begin
  writeln(Hrs:10, Min:15, Sec:20, Sec100:25);
end;
```

```
begin
  write('Creating', numkeys, 'random numbers...');
  randomize;
  for I:=1 to NumKeys do
    begin
      M[I]:=random(30000);
    end;
  writeln;
  write('Sorting', numkeys, 'random numbers...');
  settime(0,0,0,0);
  Lo := 1;
  Hi := NumKeys;
  Qsort(Lo, Hi);
  gettime(Hrs, Min, Sec, Sec100);
  writeln;
  for I:=1 to NumKeys do
    begin
      write(M[I]:8);
    end;
  ShowTime;
end.
```

Quicksort's speed stems from the fact that the early passes bring items close to their final sequence, leaving the last few passes to make only minor changes.

Tree sort

This is a selection sort and is described in the chapter on Data Structures. Like Quicksort, the binary tree sort uses the technique of recursion.

Comparison of sorting methods

Comparing the efficiency of various sorting algorithms with one another requires careful use of 'bench test' data to ensure that comparisons are fair and specialists in the subject of sorting have spent a great deal of time analysing the various methods. It is beyond the scope of this text to pursue such analysis in detail, but some broad comparisons can be made of the relative efficiency of the simple sorts described so far. It must be said that where only a few items are to be sorted, little tangible benefit will be gained from using a sophisticated sort, as opposed to a simple one. With a larger number of items, the limitations of simple sorting algorithms, such as the bubble sort, soon become apparent. Another factor which may affect a sort's performance is the degree to which items are out of order to begin with.

The bubble sort is probably the least efficient and is rarely used by experienced programmers. It is, however, a simple sort to understand and provides a good introduction to any programmer wishing to develop their skill in this area. The selection sort generally performs better than the insertion sort, except when the items are almost in order to begin with.

Chapter 34
Business Applications

Financial accounting is largely concerned with past events. *Cost and management* accounting aims to provide management with information to support their decisions on the planning of future business activity. Accounting systems should provide management with information to:

- establish and monitor the financial targets of the business. One target may be to increase sales of a particular product by 10 per cent over the next six months. A parallel target could be to cut, by 5 per cent, its unit production cost. Targets are usually fairly specific so that their achievement, or otherwise, can be determined;

- control income and expenditure within the business. Financial accounting is concerned with the whole of the business whereas cost accounting identifies cost centres (for different parts of the business). Analysing costs and revenues in this way allows a business to allocate financial budgets for various areas of the business and determine the contribution of each area to the profitability of the business.

Numerous commercial software packages are available for both financial and cost accounting applications, but this chapter concentrates on financial accounting systems and related applications.

Financial accounting systems

The following section describes the various financial accounting systems of a typical business and the main features of accounting software. To begin with some associated terminology is defined and some basic concepts are explained.

The ledgers

Business accounts are needed to record:

- *debtor* transactions; debtors are people or organizations who owe money to the business for goods or services provided (credit sales);

- *creditor* transactions; creditors are people or organizations to whom the business owes money, for the supply of goods (credit purchases).

These transactions are recorded in the *sales ledger* and the *purchases ledger* respectively. A third ledger, the *nominal* (or *general*) *ledger* is used to record the overall income and expenditure of the business, with each transaction classified according to its purpose.

Sales ledger

General description

The purpose of the sales ledger is to keep a record of amounts owed to a business by its trading customers or clients. It contains a record for each customer with a credit arrangement. Most businesses permit their customers to buy goods on credit. The goods are usually supplied on the understanding that, once payment has been requested, the debt will be paid for within a specified period of, for example, 14 or 30 days. Payment is requested with the use of a customer addressed *invoice*, which contains details of goods supplied, the amount owing and credit days given. Once a customer order has been accepted and processed, the total amount due for the order is recorded in the relevant customers account in the sales ledger and the balance owing is increased accordingly. When a payment is received from the customer, the amount is entered to the customer's account and the balance owing is decreased by the appropriate amount.

There are two main approaches to sales ledger maintenance, *balance forward* and *open item*.

- Balance forward. This method provides: an opening balance (the amount owing at the beginning of the month); the transactions for that month, giving the date, type (for example, goods sold or payment received); the amount of each transaction; a closing balance. The closing balance at the end of the month is carried forward as the opening balance for the next month. A *statement of account*, detailing all the transactions for the month will normally be sent to the customer and a copy filed away for business records. The customer's account in the sales ledger will not then contain details of the previous month's transactions so any query will require reference to the filed statements of account.

- Open item. The open item method is more complicated in that each invoice is identified by a code and requires payments from customers to be matched against the relevant invoices. All payments received and relating to a particular invoice are recorded against it until it is completely paid off. This method can make control difficult as some customers may make part payments, which cannot be tied to a particular invoice. If a customer does not specify to which invoice a particular payment relates it is normally assigned to the oldest invoice(s). Once an invoice has been completely settled it is cleared from the ledger and any subsequent statements of account.

Package requirements and facilities

Customer master file

When setting up the Sales Ledger system, one of the first tasks is to open an account for each customer. These accounts are maintained in a sales ledger *master file*, which is updated by sales and account settlement transactions. A typical package should provide as a minimum, the following data item types for each customer record:

- *account number* - used to identify uniquely a customer record;

- *name and address* - this will normally be the customers address to which statements of account and invoices are sent;

- *credit limit* - the maximum amount of credit to be allowed to the customer at any one time. This is checked by sales staff before an order is authorized for processing;

- *balance* - this is the balance of the customer's account at any one time.

A choice is usually provided to select the form of sales ledger required, either *open item* or *balance forward* (see previous section). Normally, when the file is first created, a zero balance is recorded and outstanding transactions are entered to produce a current balance. An open item system stores details of any unpaid invoices. Each invoice can be associated with a particular customer account through the account number.

Transaction entries

Transactions may be applied directly to customer accounts in the sales ledger (*transaction processing*) or they may be initially stored as a transaction file for a *batch* updating run. Whichever method the package uses, it should allow for the entry of the following transaction types:

- *invoice* - this is sent to the customer requesting payment concerning a particular order. The amount of the invoice is debited to the customer's account in the sales ledger, thus increasing the amount owing;

- *credit note.* If, for example, goods are returned by a customer or there is a dispute concerning the goods, a credit note is issued by the business to the customer. The amount of the credit note will be credited to the customer's account in the sales ledger, thus reducing the balance owing. Credit notes are often printed in red to distinguish them from invoices;

- *receipt* - this is any payment or remittance received from a customer in whole or partial settlement of an invoice. Such an entry will be credited to the customer's account and reduce the balance owing accordingly.

The following data may be entered with each type of transaction:

- *account number* - essential to identify the computer record. Although some packages allow for the entry of a shortened customer name (if the account number has been forgotten) the account number is still necessary to identify uniquely a record;

- *date of transaction*;

- *amount of transaction*;

- *transaction reference* - normally this is the invoice number to which the transaction relates.

Outputs

The following facilities may be expected:

- *single account enquiry* - details of an individual customer's account can be displayed on screen. Retrieval may be by account number or a search facility, using a shortened version of the customer name. If more than one record is retrieved by this method they may be scanned through on screen until the required record is found;

- *customer statement printing* - it is essential that the system can produce monthly statements for sending to customers;

- *debtors age analysis* - this provides a schedule of the total amounts owing by customers, categorized according to the time various portions of the total debt have been outstanding (unpaid). It is important for a business to make financial provision for the possibility of *bad debts*. These are debts which are unlikely to be settled and may have to be taken out of business profits. From their own experience of the trade, the proprietor of a business should be able to estimate the percentage of each debt that is likely to become bad. Generally, the longer the debt has been outstanding, the greater the likelihood that it will remain unpaid;

- *customers over credit limit* - this may form the basis of a black list of customers. Any new order from one of these customers has to be authorized by management. On the other hand, the appearance of certain customers on the list may suggest that some increased credit limits are needed. When a business is successful, it often needs more credit to expand further;

- *dormant account list* - if there has been no activity on an account for some time, it may warrant removal from the file. Alternatively, it may be useful to contact the customer to see if further business may be forthcoming.

Validation and control

The package should provide for careful validation of transactions and the protection of records from unauthorized access or amendment. Generally, for example, a customer record cannot be removed from the sales ledger while the account is still live (there is a balance outstanding). More details of validation and control are given in Chapter 17.

Purchase ledger

General description

The purchase ledger function mirrors that of the sales ledger, except that it contains an account for each *supplier*, from whom the business buys goods. When trading with a supplier, it is usually through credit arrangements, similar to those provided by the business for its own customers. Thus, the business receives an invoice requesting payment, within a certain period, for goods purchased. The amount of the invoice is credited to the supplier's account and the balance owing to the supplier is increased accordingly. When payment is made to a supplier, in full or part settlement of an invoice, the supplier's account is debited by the appropriate amount and the balance is decreased. Most purchase ledger systems operate on an open item basis. Each supplier invoice is given a reference number and when payment is made to a supplier, the reference number can be used to allocate the payment to a particular invoice.

Package requirements and facilities

Supplier master file

The supplier master file contains the suppliers' (*creditors'*) accounts. It is updated by supplier invoices and payments to suppliers. A typical package should provide, as a minimum, the following data item types for each supplier record:

- *account number*- used to identify uniquely a supplier record;

- *name and address* - the name and address of the supplier business;

- *credit limit* - the maximum amount of credit allowed to the business by the supplier at any one time. A check should be kept on this to avoid rejection of orders;

- *settlement discount* - this is the amount of discount given by a supplier if an invoice is settled within a specified discount period;

- *due date* - the system may issue a reminder when payment is due. A report may be printed, on request, listing all invoice amounts due for payment within, say, 7 days;

- *balance* - the current balance on the account.

A choice is usually provided to select the form of purchase ledger required (either open item or balance forward).

Transactions

Transactions may update the supplier accounts directly (transaction processing) or they may be initially stored as a transaction file for a later updating run. A purchase ledger package should allow for the following transactions:

- *supplier invoices* - before entry, each invoice must be checked against the appropriate order and then against the relevant delivery note, for actual receipt of goods. The balance on a supplier's account (the amount owed to the supplier) is increased by an invoice entry. Some packages allow unsatisfactory (there may be doubt about the delivery of the goods) invoices to be held in abeyance until cleared;

- *approved payments* - once an invoice has been cleared for payment, a voucher may be raised to ensure payment, on or before a due date, and discount for prompt payment. The entry of the payment value decreases the balance of a supplier's account and thus the amount owed by the business to the supplier. Cheques may be produced automatically on the due date, but there should be some checking procedure to ensure that payments are properly authorized;

- *adjustments* - to reverse entries made in error.

Outputs

The following output facilities may be expected:

- *single account enquiries* - details of an individual supplier's account can be displayed on screen; retrieval may be through a supplier code;

- *payment advice slip* - this may be produced to accompany a payment to a supplier. Each payment slip details the invoice reference, the amount due and the value of the payment remitted. Payment advice slips help the supplier, who may be using an open item sales ledger system;

- *automatic cheques* - the package may, with the use of pre-printed stationery, produce cheques for payment to suppliers, as and when invoices fall due. There must be a careful checking and authorization procedure to prevent incorrect payments being made;

- *unpaid invoices* - a list of all outstanding invoices, together with details of supplier, amount owing and due date;

- *creditors' age analysis* - this is the supplier equivalent of debtors' age analysis. The report provides a schedule of total balances owing to suppliers, analysed according to the time the debt has been outstanding. The report may be used to determine which payments should be given priority over others.

Nominal ledger

General description

The nominal ledger is used to record the income and expenditure of a business, classified according to purpose. Thus, for example, it contains an account for *sales*; sales totals are entered on a daily basis. The sales ledger analyses sales by customer, whereas the *sales account* provides a cumulative total for sales, as the accounting year progresses. The *purchases account* in the nominal ledger fulfils a similar purpose for purchases by the business. Other income and expenditure accounts recorded in the nominal ledger may include, for example, *rent*, *heating* and *wages*. If some items of income and expenditure are too small to warrant separate analysis, there may also be *sundry income* and *sundry expenditure* accounts. The information held in the nominal ledger accounts is used to draw up a *profit and loss account*. This account provides information on the trading performance of the business over the year. A *balance sheet* can then be produced to give a snapshot view of the assets and liabilities of a business, on a particular date.

Package requirements and facilities

Nominal accounts master file

When an account is opened in the nominal ledger, the following data item types should be available:

- *account code* - each account is given a code, to allow the allocation of transactions. For example, an entry for a gas bill payment may be directed to the Heating account by the code 012;

- *account name* - for example, Sales, Heating, Rent;

- *balance*.

Associated with each account are a number of transactions processed during the current accounting period.

Transactions

- *sales and purchases* - these may be entered periodically as accumulated totals or, in an integrated accounts system, values may be posted automatically, at the same time as they update customer and supplier accounts in the sales ledger and purchase ledger;

- *other income and expenditure* - entries concerning, for example, wages, rent, rates or heating.

Outputs

Typical output facilities include:

- *trial balance* - this is a list of debit and credit balances categorized by account. The balances are taken from the nominal ledger and the total of debit balances should agree with the total of credit balances;

- *transaction report* - a full list of transactions which may be used for error checking purposes, or as an audit trail, to allow the validity of transactions to be checked by an external auditor. The topic of auditing is described in more detail in Chapter 17;

- *trading and profit and loss account* - a statement of the trading performance of the business over a given period;

- *balance sheet* - a statement of the assets and liabilities of a business, at a particular date.

The major benefit of the computerized nominal ledger is that these reports can be produced easily and upon request. The manual production of a trial balance, trading and profit and loss statement and balance sheet can be a laborious and time consuming task. Many small businesses, operating manual systems, have difficulty in completing their annual accounts promptly for annual tax assessment.

Apart from the basic ledgers described in the previous section, there are other applications which can benefit from computerization. They include:

- stock control;

- sales order processing and invoicing.

Stock control

General description

Different businesses hold different kinds of stock. For example, a grocer holds some perishable and some non-perishable stocks of food and a clothing manufacturer holds stocks of materials and finished articles of clothing. Any trader's stock needs to be controlled, but the reasons for control may vary from one business to another. For example, a grocer wants to keep the full range of food items that customers expect, but does not want to be left with stocks of unsold items, especially if they are perishable. A clothing manufacturer's stocks will not perish if they are unsold, but space occupied by unwanted goods could be occupied by more popular items. On the other hand, if the manufacturer runs out of raw materials the production process can be slowed or even halted. Apart from such differences, there are some common reasons for wanting efficient stock control:

- excessive stock levels tie up valuable cash resources and increase business costs. The cash could be used to finance further business;

- inability to satisfy customer orders promptly because of insufficient stocks, can often lead to loss of custom.

It is possible to identify some typical objectives of a stock control system and these can be used to measure the usefulness of facilities commonly offered by computer packages:

- to maintain levels of stock which will be sufficient to meet customer demand promptly;

- to provide a mechanism which removes the need for excessively high safety margins of stock to cover customer demand. This is usually effected by setting minimum stock levels which the computer can use to report variations outside these levels;

- to provide automatic re-ordering of stock items which fall below minimum levels;

- to provide management with up-to-date information on stock levels and values of stock held. Stock valuation is also needed for accounting purposes.

Stock control requires that an individual record is maintained for each type of stock item held. Apart from details concerning the description and price of the stock item, each record should have a balance indicating the number of units held. A unit may be, for example, a box, 500 grammes or a tonne. The balance is adjusted whenever units of that particular stock item are sold or purchased. Manual or computerized records can only give recorded levels of stock. Physical stock checks need to be carried out to determine the actual levels. If there is a difference between the recorded stock level of an item and the actual stock of that item, it could be because of pilferage or damage. Alternatively, some transactions for the item may not have been applied to the stock file.

Package requirements and facilities

Stock master file

The stock master file contains records for each item of stock and each record may usefully contain the following data item types:

- *Stock code or reference* - each stock item type should have a unique reference, for example, A0035. The code should be designed so that it is useful to the user. For example, an initial alphabetic character may be used to differentiate between raw materials (R) and finished goods (F) and the remaining digits may have ranges which indicate particular product groupings. The stock file may also be used to record any consumable items used by a business, for example, stationery and printer ribbons. The initial character of the stock code could be used to identify such a grouping. The number and type of characters in a code, as well as its format, are usually limited by the package because the code will also be used by the software to determine a record's location within the file;

- *Description* - although users may become used to referring to individual products by their codes or references, a description is needed for the production of, for example, purchase orders or customer invoices;

- *Analysis code* - this may be used in conjunction with sales orders so that they can be analysed by product group. If, for example, a clothing manufacturer produces different types of ski jacket, it is important for production planning purposes to know the relative popularity of each type;

- *Unit size* - for example, box, metre, tonne, kilo;

- *Re-order level* - this is the stock level at which an item is to be re-ordered, for example, 30 boxes. Reaching this level may trigger an automatic re-order when the appropriate program option is run. Alternatively it may be necessary to request a summary report which highlights all items at or below their re-order level. The decision on what the re-order level should be for any particular item will depend on the *sales turnover* (the number of units sold per day or week) and the *lead time* (the time taken for delivery after a purchase order is placed with a supplier). Seasonal changes in sales figures will require that re-order levels for individual items are changed for time to time;

- *Re-order quantity* - this is the number of item units to be re-ordered from a supplier when new stock is required;

- *Bin reference* - this may be used to indicate the physical location of stock items within, for example, a warehouse;

- *Minimum stock level* - when an item falls to this level, a warning is given that the stock level of the item is dangerously low. As with the re-order level, the warning may be produced by a request for a special summary report which highlights such items. Even though the re-order level warning may have already been given, it is possible that no new stocks were ordered or that the supplier was unusually slow with deliveries;

- *Cost price* - the price paid by the business for the stock item;

- *Sale price* - the price charged to the customer. The package may allow the storage of more than one sale price to differentiate between, for example, retail and wholesale customers;

- *VAT code* - different items may attract different rates of Value Added Tax (VAT);

- *Supplier code* - if orders can be produced automatically, then the supplier code may be used to access a supplier file, for the address and other details needed to produce an order;

- *Quantity issued* - generally, several values may be entered, so that the turnover of an item can be viewed for different periods, for example, from 3 months ago to date, the preceding 3 month period and so on;

- *Stock allocated* - a quantity may not have been issued but may have been allocated to a customer order or factory requisition;

- *Quantity in stock* - the current recorded level of stock. This will change whenever an issue, receipt or adjustment transaction is entered.

Transactions

- *Goods received* - stock received from a supplier;

- *Goods returned* - for example, stock returned by a customer or unused raw materials returned from the factory;

- *Goods issued* - this may result from a customer order or from a factory requisition, if the business has a manufacturing process;

- *Stock allocated* - this will not reduce the quantity in stock figure but the amount allocated should be used to offset the quantity in stock when judging what is available;

- *Amendments* - for, example, there may be amendments to price, re-order level or supplier code.

The method used to update the stock master file will depend on how up-to-date the figures need to be (this will depend on how tight stock levels are) and how often the data entry operator can get at the computer. To keep the file up-to-date throughout the day, physical stock changes have to be notified immediately to stock control and the transactions have to be entered as they occur. Unfortunately, this means that a single-user system would be unavailable to any other users, such as sales staff, who needed to know quantities in stock. A networked system with central file storage, would allow continual updating and enquiry access. If the stock levels are sufficiently high to allow differences to arise between physical and book totals without risking shortages, then daily batch updating may be acceptable. In such a situation, an enquiry on a stock item may reveal, for example, a book stock of 200 units, when the physical stock is only 120 units (80 having been issued since the last update at the end of the preceding day).

Outputs

Typical outputs from a stock control package include:

- *Stock enquiry* - details concerning a stock item may be displayed on screen, or printed;

- *Stock out report* - a list of stock items which have reached a level of zero;

- *Re-order report* - a list of stock items which have fallen to their re-order level, together with supplier details and recommended re-order quantities;

- *Stock list* - a full or limited (for example, within a certain stock code range) list of stock items, giving details of quantities held and their value. The value may be calculated using the cost or sale price, depending on the costing method used by the business;

- *Outstanding order report* - a list of all purchase orders not yet fulfilled and the dates ordered. This may be used to chase up orders when stocks are falling dangerously low.

This is not an exhaustive list and some packages offer many other analytical reports which can help a business to maintain an efficient customer service and plan future production and purchasing more effectively.

A stock control case study

The Astex Homecare chain of DIY stores has branches all over the country and each branch maintains stocks of thousands of items used in the home. These items range from building materials such as sand and cement to bedroom furniture, fitted kitchens, bathroom suites, ceramic wall and floor tiles, lights and light fittings, garden materials such as plants, plant pots and garden furniture, nails, screws, paint, wallpaper and numerous other common household goods.

Each branch has its own small computer system dedicated to dealing with the *point of sale* (POS) terminals located at the customer tills. The POS terminals are used to record purchases and provide customer bills by scanning the bar code on each purchase using a hand-held scanner. The stock number contained in the bar code is fed by the POS terminal to the local computer which returns the description and price to be printed on the customers' receipts as well as the bill totals.

Each branch maintains its own stock file on the local computer but ordering stock is controlled by a mainframe computer at the Astex head office. Each Astex branch is laid out according to a *merchandise layout plan* (MLP) in which the store is organized into a large number of four foot sections, each having its own MLP code. Each item of stock is allocated to one MLP section and its computer record contains the MLP code together with the minimum and maximum stock level for that particular section of the store. When an item has been sold, the relevant information is transmitted automatically by the local computer to the mainframe at head office. The head office computer determines from the MLP data whether the item needs to be re-ordered from a supplier. It uses the MLP information regarding minimum and maximum stock levels in order to determine how many of a particular item to order.

Overnight, while the stores are closed, the head office computer transmits suggested ordering information back to the individual branches where order sheets are printed out on local laser printers, so that they can be checked manually by the appropriate personnel before stock is ordered. This manual monitoring of computer-generated information allows the information system to cope with unexpected situations and prevents the occurrence of gross errors. About ninety percent of all orders can be made electronically using communication links to the computers used by suppliers. Other suppliers not linked to the central Astex computer are contacted manually by telephone.

The security of the Astex information systems are ensured in two major ways. Firstly, because of the importance of the local computer system for producing customer bills, a backup processor is always available for use in the event of the primary processor failing. Secondly, access to the various users of the computer systems is provided on several different levels. Each person who uses the computer system has his or her own access code which provides access to only those areas he or she is authorized to use. These measures are essential to maintain the security and reliable operation of such large-scale systems.

Sales order processing and invoicing

Sales order processing

Sales order processing is concerned with the handling of customers' sales orders. It has three main functions:

- validation of orders. This means checking, for example, that the goods ordered are supplied by the business or that the customer's credit status warrants the order's completion;

- to identify quantities of individual items ordered. A customer may request several different items on the same order form. An item will probably appear on many different order forms and the quantities for each need to be totalled to provide lists (picking lists) for warehouse staff to retrieve the goods;

- to monitor back orders. If an order cannot be fulfilled it may be held in abeyance until new stocks arrive. The system should be able to report all outstanding back orders on request.

The efficient processing of customer orders is of obvious importance to the success of a business and in whatever form an order is received, the details should be immediately recorded. Preferably, the details should be recorded on a pre-designed order form which ensures that all relevant details are taken. The order details should include:

- the date the order is received;

- the customer's order number;

- a description of each item required including any necessary stock references or codes;

- the quantity of each item ordered;

- the price per item excluding VAT;

- the total order value excluding VAT;

- any discount which is offered to the customer;

- the VAT amount which is to be added to the total price;

- the total order value including VAT;

- the delivery date required.

Invoicing

The invoice is the bill to the customer, requesting payment for goods or services supplied by the business. The following section describes typical package facilities which allow the integration of the sales order processing and invoicing systems.

Package requirements and facilities

To be effective, the sales order processing system needs to have access to the customer file (sales ledger) for customer details and to the stock file, so that prices can be extracted according to stock item codes entered with the order. This latter facility means that the system may also be integrated with invoicing.

Files

- *Customer file*. When a customer account number or name is keyed in with an order, the package usually accesses the customer file and displays the address details, so that the operator can confirm the delivery address or type in an alternative address if this is required. The process also ensures that all orders are processed for registered customers;

- *Stock file*. As stock item codes are entered from an order form, the system accesses the price and displays it on the screen for confirmation by the operator. Access to the stock file also ensures that only valid stock codes are used;

- *Completed order file*. This is used for the generation of invoices after an order's completion;

- *Back order file*. This is needed to ensure that orders which cannot be fulfilled immediately are kept on file and processed as soon as goods become available.

Transactions

- *Sales order* - details concerning an individual order, including customer number, items required (by item code), quantity of each item, delivery date, discount allowed and the date of the order.

Outputs

- *Invoice* - an invoice can be generated by using the details of customer number, stock codes and quantities from the order, together with information retrieved from the customer and stock files;

- *Back order report* - a report can be requested detailing all unsatisfied orders. This is useful for planning production schedules or generating special purchase orders;

- *Picking list* - a summary of the quantities required of each item ordered. These are used by warehouse staff to extract the goods needed to make up orders for delivery;

- *Sales data* - details of each customer's order need to be extended to include the financial ledgers (sales, purchase and nominal ledger). Such integration should not usually be attempted all at once but full integration does reduce the number of inputs necessary and automates many of the updating procedures described in this chapter.

Payroll

The task of calculating wages for a large company having hundreds or even thousands of employees is an enormous task. It involves taking into account some or all of the following factors:

- number of hours worked;

- amount of overtime;

- bonus payment;

- sickness leave;

- type of employee (for example, waged or salaried, shop floor or management);

- deductions (for example, national insurance contributions and union fees);

- holidays;

- tax code;

- tax rate;

- cash analysis.

The gross pay is calculated from the hours worked and hourly pay rate, for weekly paid employees, and is a standard sum for salaried employees. Added to this gross payment are any allowances from overtime or bonuses, for example. Tax is calculated and subtracted from the total earnings and other deductions such as national insurance, union fees and pension contributions are also taken from it. Thus the total calculation is quite complicated, and it will probably be different for each employee.

Producing payslips manually is therefore very time consuming and prone to error, so computers are particularly well suited to the task. Most computerized payroll systems use batch processing in which long-term employee information held on a master file is used in conjunction with a transaction file containing recent information such as hours worked and overtime details. The transaction file changes from week to week or month to month but most of the information on the master file either does not change at all or changes only occasionally.

If employees are paid weekly, at the end of each week details of hours worked, bonus payments, overtime payments and deductions are recorded on a payroll transaction file which contains a record for every employee. This sequential transaction file is then sorted into employee number order so that it is in the same order as the payroll master file. The two files are then used by the computer to calculate and print the payslips, and to update the master file which must keep track of such things as tax paid to date, total national insurance contributions and holiday and sickness leave for each employee for the current tax year. A *systems flowchart*, as illustrated in Figure 34.1, is often used to describe business data processing systems such as this.

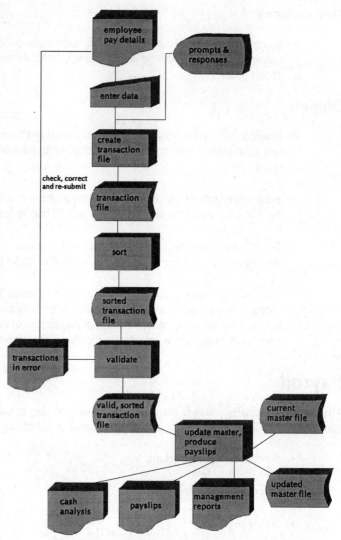

Figure 34.1. Systems flowchart for payroll system

The systems flowchart shows the computer operations involved in a payroll run. Payroll systems normally use batch processing when the majority of the employees need to be paid. This lends itself to the use of magnetic tape devices (the flowchart does not specify the medium) which are restricted to sequential access. The payroll data is first stored on the payroll transaction file using keyboards as the input devices. Each employee's pay information is stored in a separate record identified by employee number. Because the master file records are stored on tape in order of employee number, the transaction file must also be sorted into the same order. This is to avoid having to search for matching master file and transaction file records for each employee - because both files are in the same order, the next record in each file should be for the same employee. The sorted transaction file must be validated by the computer before processing the payroll data to produce payslips. This process performs various checks on the transaction file to ensure that only correct data will be processed. Any errors detected at this stage must be corrected before the payslips are generated.

Finally, the validated and sorted transaction file is processed against the payroll master file in order to produce the payslips. In addition to updating the master file, the payroll system might also produce summary reports for the management personnel of the company, and, if employees are paid by cash rather than by cheque or transfer to a bank account, a *cash analysis* might be produced. The cash analysis calculates exactly how many of each currency denomination will be required for all the pay packets, so that the correct money can be obtained from a bank. Each payslip would also have a corresponding breakdown for a single pay packet to make it easier for the cashiers to make up the pay packets.

A large company will probably use a mainframe computer for the task of processing the payroll information. Data entry will often be carried out using key-to-tape systems by a number of data entry clerks, and the output of the payslips will probably be by means of pre-printed stationery used on a line printer for speed. Backing storage will normally be in the form of magnetic tape or magnetic disk, but sequential *batch processing* will almost invariably be used. Of course, small companies having only a few employees might use a microcomputer system for the payroll, or even produce the payslips manually without the use of a computer at all.

Booking systems

Travel agents

If you go to a travel agent to book a seat on a major international airline, the travel agent will need to check the airline for the availability of the flight that you require. This normally involves communicating with the airlines computer to obtain up-to-date flight information. Remember that the same thing can be happening from all over the world: numerous travel agents could be accessing the same airlines computer at the same time, several of them even trying to book seats on the same flight that you want.

To cope with this type of demand, the airline will use a mainframe computer allowing on-line communication with each travel agent via the public telephone network. Each travel agency will have one or more terminals connected by modem to the airlines computer. Flight reservations will be performed in *real-time*, that is, the mainframe's flight and passenger information will be updated immediately to prevent the possibility of double-booking a seat on a particular flight. This ensures that the information that the travel agent obtains will be completely accurate and reliable. This form of processing, where a master file is updated immediately, is called *transaction processing* (see Chapter 16).

The process of reserving a seat on a flight is further complicated by the fact that several airlines might have scheduled flights to your destination, each offering different flight times, facilities and costs. Rather than contacting each one separately, a process that could take a considerable amount of time, the travel agent links into a wide area network(WAN) which connects the main computers of the different airlines. This allows the agent to choose the most appropriate flight for you and book it immediately. Though each airline in the system might have a different passenger reservation information system, the network software presents the same information format to the travel agents and takes care of transferring data in the correct format to the individual computer systems of the airlines.

When you have decided on your choice of airline and flight, your details are entered at the travel agent's terminal. While this is happening, other travel agents are prevented from accessing that particular flight record. On completion of the reservation, the flight record becomes available again. Booking cancellations and changes are handled in the same way. Your ticket, which will have been produced by the airline's computer, is usually sent out to you a few days prior to the departure date. Individual airline's computers also produce passenger lists automatically for use at the departure airports.

An airline's master passenger reservation and flight information file will be held on a high-capacity magnetic disk drive. For backup purposes, in case the master file is in some way lost or partly erased, or the disk drive fails, a separate disk drive will be used to hold an exact duplicate of the master file, and this duplicate file will be updated at the same time as the other master file. This duplication is necessary because the master file will be in constant use, night and day, and there will be no opportunity to stop updating it in order to make a backup on magnetic tape. For the same reasons of security, there will also be a duplicate main computer immediately ready to be used if the other one fails for some reason. Because of the importance of the fast response time required of the system, it will almost certainly be used exclusively for passenger booking purposes, and it will have been designed to operate without break, 24 hours a day, every day of the year.

Similar real-time systems are used by holiday firms, some of which are able to offer thousands of holidays all over the world. Travel agents must have access to accurate information regarding the availability of all the holidays on offer. Again it is important to ensure that exactly the same holiday is not sold to more than one customer, so the booking file held on the holiday company's main computer must be completely up-to-date.

Hotel booking

Hotels frequently use booking systems for keeping track of room reservations made by guests. These systems generally provide additional facilities relating to hotel management, typically keeping track of guests accounts and producing hotel room usage information.

When someone reserves a room in the hotel, a record is created in the guest file. The file contains three types of data:

- details of the guest, such as name, address, telephone number;

- room details, such as type (single, double etc.), number, period of occupancy;

- charges incurred by the guest during the stay at the hotel. For each charge, the item code, cost and date will be recorded.

The first two types of data are entered at the time the reservation is made; items and services bought by the guest during his or her stay, such as telephone calls, drinks, newspapers and extra meals, are recorded as and when they occur. When the guest leaves, the hotel system calculates the total bill and prints out an itemized list that the guest can check.

A hotel management system such as this can easily be implemented with a microcomputer system, though large hotel chains might also have a large central computer at their headquarters for general accounting purposes (such as producing financial reports covering the whole chain of hotels, and for payroll calculations).

Library systems

Dotherstaff College is a split site college of further and higher education. Each site has a large library which has recently been supplied with a microcomputer network for a library automation system called Alice, produced by a software company called Softlink. The software has a number of interlinked modules covering all aspects of typical library operation.

- Catalogue and Classification - managing the book database;

- Circulation - managing borrowers;

- Enquiries - information retrieval;

- Acquisition - ordering books;

- Reports and utilities- producing reports of publishers' details, author details and library usage figures;

- Periodicals- managing the ordering of magazines.

Catalogue and classification

This module is mainly used for the addition of new titles to the book database. Book details can be created, edited and deleted, as well as allowing the file to be browsed through, or searched.

Circulation

The circulation module is used for managing borrowers' details. To borrow a book from the library a borrower must produce his or her ticket on which there is a unique bar code. This bar code is scanned by a librarian and the borrower's record then appears on the screen. When the bar code of the book is scanned, the code is stored in the borrower's record. To return a book, the bar code of the book is scanned or typed in and the book is automatically removed from the borrower's record. The system also allows the display of all books currently borrowed by any person. Periodically, about every two weeks, the borrower file is searched for overdue items so that reminders can be generated automatically.

Enquiry

The enquiry module is used by staff and students to search the book database for books satisfying certain criteria. For example, a user can type in the name of an author and obtain a list of all books in the library written by that person. The title of a book, or part of the title can be entered and a list of books closely matching the title will be displayed. Alternatively, one or more keywords can be used to produce a list of books which contain the keywords in the title. The book information retrieved by an enquiry is summarized on the screen in several sections containing such things as the book titles, subjects covered and author(s). Any book selected from the list can have its full details displayed on screen or printed. This type of enquiry facility can save a great deal of time searching shelves or catalogues for specific information.

The network used for the library information system currently supports about 20 terminals, but it is also linked to the main college networks which provide access to other software such as word processors and spreadsheets.

Management applications

Management information systems (MIS)

Although computers can perform routine processing tasks very efficiently, it is generally recognized that limiting a compute'rs use to the processing of operational information constitutes a waste of computer power.

An MIS is designed to make use of the computer's power of selection and analysis to produce useful management information.

An MIS has a number of key features:

- it produces information beyond that required for routine data processing;

- timing of information production is critical;

- the information it produces is an aid to decision-making;

- it is usually based on the database concept (explained in Chapter 24).

The claims for MIS are sometimes excessive. It is rarely the complete answer to all a company's information needs, but when successfully implemented, it provides a valuable information advantage over competitors.

Decision support systems (DSS)

A DSS aims to provide a more flexible decision tool than that supplied by a MIS which tends to produce information in an anticipated, pre-defined form and as such, does not allow managers to make ad hoc requests for information. DSS tend to be narrower in scope than MIS, often making use of general-purpose software packages. Examples of DSS include electronic spreadsheets, such as Microsoft Excel and relational database management systems such as Access and Paradox. The main features of these and other packages are described in some detail in Chapter 12. Additionally, *financial modelling* (Chapter 36) and statistical packages are considered to be DSS tools. A major benefit is the independence they allow for information control by individual managers and executives. When, for example, a sales manager requires a report on sales figures for the last three months, a microcomputer with database package may provide the report more quickly than a centralized data processing department.

Application objectives

A number of general objectives can be identified as being of relevance to most applications, in most organizations:

- Improved *operational efficiency*. *Speed* and *accuracy* of operations should be radically improved. This is not automatic as the computer-based system may be badly designed and the staff may be ill-trained, but given proper design and implementation, administrative systems will normally be more efficient.

- Better *control of resources*. Administrative systems such as those for financial control and the control of resources such as staff and raw materials, benefit particularly from the rapid production of up-to-date information by computer.

- Improved *productivity*. Redundancy does not always follow computerization, particularly if the organization is an expanding business. Computer-based systems should permit large increases in the volumes of business which can be handled without the need for extra staff.

- Improved *security of information*. With proper physical security, clear operational procedures to restrict access to computer facilities to those properly authorized, and with sophisticated use of software control mechanisms such as passwords, information can be made more secure than equivalent manual systems.

- Opportunities to *share data*. This is most likely where database systems and networked computer systems are employed.

- Improved *quality of information* for *decision taking* at the operational, strategic and corporate levels in an organization. *Operational decisions* concern day-to-day operations, such as handling of customer orders or delivery of new stocks. At the *strategic level*, decisions may relate to issues such as production planning and the selection of suppliers. *Corporate decision* examples include the setting of prices, targeting of markets and the manufacture of new products. Most systems generate a range of management information reports, drawn from the routine processing of transactions and these are primarily of use at the strategic level, but may also help with corporate decisions. Accounts software, for example, produces reports on outstanding debts, potential bad debtors, dates when payments to suppliers are due and analysis of sales patterns.

- Improved *external image*. An organization can improve its external image by the improved presentation of correspondence and by an improved service to its customers or clients, but badly designed procedures can also make life more difficult for them.

- Improved *working conditions*. This is highly debatable in respect of an office environment, but computer-based manufacturing systems usually provide a less dirty and dangerous environment for employees, as much of the work is done by robots and other computer-controlled machinery.

Selecting an appropriate system

Whether batch processing, one of the on-line types, or distributed processing (Chapter 16) is appropriate depends on a number of factors:

- the type and size of organization. Large organizations generally have larger volumes of data to handle, than do small ones. Batch processing is efficient in the sense that it is a concentrated activity and if transactions can be accumulated and handled together, then it may be more efficient than dealing with each transaction as it arises. On the other hand, delay may prevent achievement of an important objective, such as the provision of up-to-date management information. Distributed processing, through computer networks, is an increasingly popular option for a medium or large organization, because it gives local control to branches and allows data to be shared and communicated across the whole organization;

- the activity (for example, financial accounts, hotel booking);

- the objectives of the activity (see previous section).

As explained in Chapters 16 and 17, a batch processing system provides numerous opportunities to ensure the accuracy of data, as it passes through the system. In this way, the type satisfies one of the main objectives of many systems and if this were the only criterion for selection, all systems would use batch processing. Of course, there are other criteria which must be applied to the selection process, including: system purpose(s);

size and type of organization; other objectives, such as security, speed, or the provision of extra management information. For example, an airline's passenger reservation system cannot be effective unless files are updated at the time each reservation is made and transaction processing is found to be appropriate. An organization's stock control system may need to reflect stock changes on the same basis as the airline reservation system, particularly if delivery has to be immediate. Discount stores, such as Argos, sell a huge range of consumer items and some are expensive; it is not desirable to hold high stock levels, because this ties up large amounts of cash, so the stock records need to be updated as goods are delivered and sold. In some organizations, stock movements (stock received and stock issued) do not have to be instantly reflected in stock records, because delivery times to customers can be longer, perhaps up to several weeks. If the goods are not of high value, then it may be convenient to hold larger stocks, which ensure the satisfaction of customer demand. For example, if the stock record for an item shows 1000 units and 50 units is the maximum customer requirement, then a physical stock level which is only 800 units, is not an immediate problem.

The size of the organization is also a significant factor in determining the most appropriate type of data handling system. A small plumbing firm, perhaps consisting of two partners and a couple of employees is unlikely to include anyone to keep the accounts; this will probably be the job of one of the partners, who will only have time to do the work at weekends. Thus, customer invoices and payments are dealt with in a batch, perhaps every week. As a small firm, a major objective will be to collect customer debts as quickly as possible and the computerized system can help to do this, in the limited time that the partner has to deal with such matters.

Chapter 35
Industrial and Control Applications

In recent years, computerization of industrial and control applications has become commonplace and essential to the success of a modern industrial economy. This chapter examines this increasingly important area of computing.

Computer-aided design (CAD)

With the use of a graphics terminal and mouse, or similar device, a designer can produce and modify designs more rapidly than is possible with a conventional drawing board. Ideas can be sketched on the screen, stored, recalled and modified. The computer can also be instructed to analyse a design for comparison with some specified criteria. Drawings can be rotated and tilted on the screen to reveal different three-dimensional views. CAD is used in the design of ships, cars, buildings, microprocessor circuits, clothing and many other products. With the use of CAD a manufacturer has a distinct advantage over non-computerized competitors, in terms of speed and flexibility of design.

Computer-aided manufacture (CAM)

A number of areas of computer use can be identified in the manufacturing process.

- Industrial robots and process control;
- Computer numerical control (CNC) of machine tools;
- Integrated CAD/CAM;
- Automated materials handling;
- Flexible manufacturing systems (FMS).

Industrial robots

Basically, a robot replaces the actions of a human arm and consists of 3 main elements, a mechanical arm with wrist joint, power unit and microprocessor or central controlling computer. To be called a robot, it must be able to react, albeit in a limited way, to external events and alter its course of action according to a stored program. Such sensitivity to the environment is provided by sensors, for example, to recognize stylized characters and differentiate between shapes. The main areas of use are in spot welding, paint spraying, die casting and to a lesser but increasing extent, assembly.

Use of robots can provide significant benefits for industry, its employees and the population in general:

- operation in environments unsuitable for the health of workers;

- performance of tasks, particularly those which are repetitive, at a consistent level of quality, which is generally high, and without fatigue;

- lack of human weaknesses generally allows robots to be many times more productive and, apart from small specialist companies, car manufacturers could not stay in business without the use of extensive automation;

- labour costs are drastically reduced and the capital costs of robots are recoverable through increased production and a consequent fall in the unit costs of production (the cost of producing a single unit of a particular product).

Clearly, there are potential drawbacks to the use of robots, although the degree of disadvantage depends largely on how much human control is retained. For example, an aircraft can be landed virtually without pilot intervention, but it would be placing rather too much faith in a system's reliability and ability to deal with exceptional circumstances, to fly without a pilot. Thus, the consequences of an automated systems failure need to be taken into account when determining the level of reliance to be placed on it and the fallback procedures which need to be employed. Social disadvantages of using robots are examined in Chapter 38.

Computer numerical control (CNC)

CNC operation of machine tools has been widespread for some years because the repetitive nature of machining tasks lends itself to simple programming. However, as is the case with robots, the use of microprocessors allows the machine tool to vary its actions according to external information. The actions of the machine can be compared with a design pattern held by the computer. Any significant variations from the pattern are signalled to the machine tool which, through the microprocessor, reacts appropriately (known as Computer Aided Quality Assessment - CAQ). Other information regarding tool wear or damage can be picked up by sensors and communicated to the human supervisor who takes remedial action.

Integrated CAD/CAM

In fully integrated CAD/CAM systems, the designs produced using CAD are fed straight through to the software which controls the CNC machine tools, which can then produce the design piece. The CAD software checks the compatibility of the design with a component specification already stored in the computer.

Automated materials handling

A fully automated materials handling system consists of a number of sub-systems:

- stock control;

- part or pallet co-ordination;

- storage and retrieval;

- conveyor control.

Installation generally proceeds one sub-system at a time, each being fully tested before proceeding with the next sub-system. A materials handling system, controlled by a central computer, allocates storage locations in the warehouse, automatically re-orders when a pre-determined minimum level is reached, retrieves parts as required by the factory and delivers them by conveyor belt to the waiting robots or CNC machines.

Flexible manufacturing systems (FMS)

Such systems are beneficial where production batches are small and necessitate frequent changes in the sequence and types of processes. The aim of FMS is to remove, as far as possible, the need for human intervention (other than a supervisor or machine minder) in the production process. The main elements of FMS are, CNC machine tools (with diagnostic facilities), robots, conveyor belt and central computer with controlling software. In simple terms, the computer has information on parts, machine tools and operations required. The robots serve the CNC machines by presenting them with parts to be machined and loading the correct machine tools from racks.

Control systems

As the name suggests, a *control system* controls the operation of some process. The human body, for example, contains a temperature control system which maintains it at a constant temperature. If your body becomes too hot, it produces perspiration which cools it down, and if you become too cold you warm yourself by shivering. A muscle control system operates whenever you try to catch a ball: your senses provide constant data regarding the position of the ball and the position of your body so that you can adjust the position of your hands to coincide with the trajectory of the ball. A domestic central heating system is a control system in which the temperature of the air in a house is regulated, for example, by means of a boiler pumping hot water through radiators. The output of the boiler is controlled by thermostats which sense the temperature of the air in their vicinities, switching the boiler on when the temperature drops below a required level, and switching it off when that level has been attained. In computer control systems, a computer is the component of the control system which uses data from sensors in order to maintain the outputs of the system at certain levels.

Many control systems involve the use of *measurement systems* to provide data concerning the current output of the system, so that the output can be increased or reduced to maintain it at a certain level. In engineering, measurement systems are used in many different ways and for many different purposes. Sometimes a measurement system is simply required to monitor some process by obtaining data about it. For example, a rotating vane anemometer might be used to provide wind speed data for an athletics meeting. Some measurement systems are used to ensure that a device is operating according to specification for safety or quality reasons. An example is a microwave leakage tester, which measures microwave emissions from commercial microwave appliances and displays the strength of the emissions on the integral meter. Other measurement systems provide data for control systems. For example, in a computer-controlled car engine management system, a measurement system provides information regarding the composition of exhaust gases for the microprocessor which automatically adjusts the engine settings to keep emissions within required limits.

Control systems are used to monitor and control physical systems automatically. Such systems almost invariably use devices called *transducers* to convert from one form of energy into another. Most transducers used in computer control systems convert some form of energy into electrical signals that can processed by a computer, or they convert signals from a computer into a form that can be displayed or converted into mechanical movement. Here are some examples of such transducers:

- *Thermistor* - the electrical resistance of the material used in a thermistor varies according to the temperature of the material.

- *Strain gauge* - the electrical resistance of the material used in a strain gauge varies according to the mechanical strain applied to the material.

- *Seven-segment display* - this converts digital information into characters that can be read.

- *Stepper-motor* - this converts electrical pulses into small, controlled angular movements of the shaft of an electric motor.

- *Loudspeaker* - this converts electrical energy into sound.

The first two are examples of input transducers, and the other three are output devices.

Another important feature of control systems is *feedback*. Feedback is the process of regulating the system by using output information to control the input, thereby keeping the output within certain limits. This usually involves using the computer to compare the input signal, or signals, with some critical values. If the input signals show that the quantities being measured need to be adjusted, output signals are used to activate devices which affect the quantities. For example, a control system for maintaining the temperature of a vat of liquid at a constant 20 degrees Centigrade will use a sensor to monitor the temperature of the vat and a heater to increase its temperature if it cools below the required value. A computer program could be used to compare the actual temperature of the vat, as supplied by the sensor, with the desired temperature; a temperature lower than that required will result in the computer issuing an output control signal to activate the heating element. Figure 35.1 illustrates the main features of a control system.

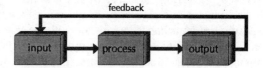

Figure 35.1. *Components of a control system*

A control system for heating water

An example of a control system which illustrates the concepts discussed above is the domestic water heater (see Figure 35.2). The insulated water tank contains a combined *heating element* and *thermostat*. The thermostat is simply a heat activated switch which is off when the temperature of the water reaches a certain level, and is on when the water temperature is below that level. The heating element is connected to the electricity supply via the thermostat so that while the temperature of the water is below a certain level, the heating element is on, otherwise it is off. The control box contains the connections between the heater, the thermostat and the power supply.

In this simple control system for regulating the temperature of the water in the tank, the thermostat is the transducer, heat generated by the heating element is

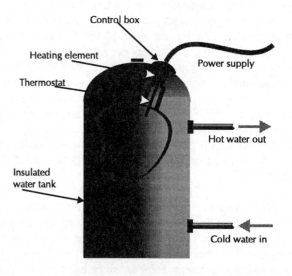

Figure 35.3. *Immersion heater control system*

the output and *feedback* is provided by the resulting temperature of the water. The thermostat switches the heater off when the water reaches the required temperature. When hot water is drawn from the tank, cold water enters and reduces the temperature of the water. This reduction in temperature is detected by the thermostat which activates the heater, thus heating the water until it again reaches the required temperature. Thus the output (heat) provides feedback to the transducer so that the water temperature can be regulated. Of course, this simple control system does not require a computer to control it but, if there were such a requirement, a computer could easily be used. The mechanical thermostat could be replaced by a different transducer providing a voltage proportional to the temperature of the water. This signal could be monitored by a computer and compared with the

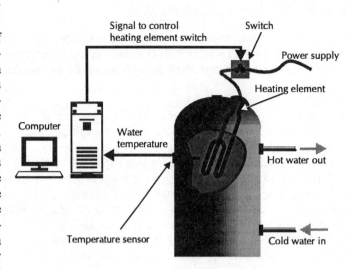

Figure 35.3. *Computer-controlled water heating system*

required temperature of the water. The computer could easily control a relay to switch the heater on when the temperature falls below a pre-determined minimum value and switch it off when the temperature exceeds a pre-determined maximum value. The computer controlled version is shown in Figure 35.3. In this version the water temperature is detected by a sensor immersed in the water. A voltage proportional to the water temperature is transmitted to the computer which determines whether it is necessary to turn on an electronic switch to activate the heating element.

Computer control system components

Because PCs are so popular and now provide powerful, cost-effective solutions to many processing problems, more PCs are being used in both process monitoring and control applications. Consequently, many plug-in devices have been developed to simplify these tasks, and software has also kept pace with development needs. The components of a typical PC-based control system are:

- Sensor(s) to monitor the process.

- Signal conditioning module to convert sensor signals to meet input/output specifications. As well as being the front end for a DAQ board, these also isolate the computer from the environment.

- Data acquisition board (DAQ) which plugs directly into the PC. Input and output transducers can be connected directly to them (depending on the type) or through signal conditioning modules. These boards often can perform a variety of functions, including analogue to digital conversion, digital to analogue conversion and digital input/output.

- Interface software which facilitates control and communication through the DAQ board.

The heat regulating system described in the next section illustrates how these components combine to form a computer control system.

A heat regulating system

Since the signal from any temperature sensing device, whatever the type of transducer employed, is a continuously varying (that is, *analogue*) signal, it must be amplified using a signal conditioning unit and then converted into a *binary* signal using an *analogue-to-digital converter* (ADC) before it can be used directly by a computer.

The analogue signal from the sensor unit is converted to binary signals by the ADC. ADCs take as input a voltage in a certain range and produce a number of parallel binary outputs which represent the current input voltage. A typical ADC will provide eight binary outputs corresponding to the input voltage. So, if the input range is –5V to +5V , a binary output of 0 corresponds to –5V, an output of binary 127 corresponds to 0V and +5V is represented by 255 in binary. Figure 35.4 illustrates an ADC producing a binary output of 240 corresponding approximately to an input of 4V.

Figure 35.5. *PC control system using a DAQ board*

Let us suppose, for example, that a certain microprocessor-controlled washing machine allows the selection of a large range of water temperature settings. Such an appliance might use a system similar to that just described to convert water temperatures between 0°C and 100°C to a binary signal. If the ADC produces an 8 bit binary output corresponding to an input voltage in the range 0V to 5V, the temperature range 0°C to 100°C will be represented by a binary signal in the range 0 to 255 (that is, 00000000 to 11111111 in binary) such that binary 0 represents 0°C and binary 255 represents 100°C. Since a temperature transducer is unlikely to generate the voltage range required by the ADC, namely 0V to 5V, it must first be conditioned. Thus after the transducer signal had been conditioned, a temperature of 25°C would produce about 1.25V and this would translate to binary 63 (00111111).

Figure 35.5 illustrates the use of an ADC contained within a PC data acquisition (DAQ) board in a simple system intended to maintain a tank of liquid at a certain temperature. The DAQ board also allows the PC to output a digital control signal to operate a power switch which activates the tank's heating element.

The figure shows a temperature sensor immersed in a tank of warm liquid. The sensor contains a thermal transducer and an electronic circuit that produces as output an analogue signal in the form of a voltage proportional to the temperature of the liquid in the tank. The output from the sensor unit is converted to binary by the ADC. A computer program then compares the temperature of the liquid, as represented by the binary signal, with the required temperature of the liquid and activates the heating element switch accordingly. Note that the temperature sensor unit, switch and ADC all require a power supply to function.

Control systems applications

Computer control systems are used in a wide variety of application areas, including:

- Process monitoring and control - see *Process Control Systems* later in this section;

- Data logging - gathering and recording data;

- Quality control - testing products to ensure that they fulfil specific standards of quality;

- Machine control - for example, controlling the machines used in manufacturing processes. Includes the use of robots (see later).

The following sections describe the application of computer control in motor vehicles, chemical processes and manufacturing. To simplify the illustrations, the signal conditioning and converting components of the systems are not shown.

Control systems used in cars

Some modern cars, particularly in the USA, have a cruise control that allows a driver to set the speed of the car to be maintained automatically by pressing a button. A microprocessor is used to monitor the speed of the car, from data provided by a sensor, and continuously compare it with the required speed. If the car starts to slow down while going up a hill or speeds up going down a hill, the microprocessor activates a control that changes the car's speed. Figure 35.6 illustrates this idea.

The microprocessor uses *feedback* provided by the speed sensor to determine whether the car is travelling at the required speed. Some systems have sensors which use the rotation rate of the wheel drive shafts to determine the speed of the car, while others use microwave technology to measure the Doppler shift of a signal bounced off the road. If the microprocessor detects

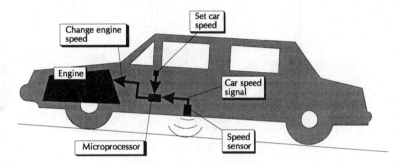

Figure 35.6. *Cruise control for a car*

that the car is travelling slower than the required speed, it increases the delivery of fuel to the engine. This speeds the car up so that the difference between the actual speed and the required speed is reduced. The microprocessor continuously reacts to speed changes as they occur and adjusts the fuel delivery to keep the car travelling at a nearly constant speed. The driver, by braking or accelerating, can override the cruise control and assume normal control of the car at any instant.

Early versions of this type of control were achieved using complicated electromechanical devices, but the advent of cheap microprocessors rapidly caused them to be replaced with computer-based machines. The great advantage of using a microprocessor in this type of application is that its function can be duplicated by a more powerful computer system used for the purpose of designing and evaluating the final system before putting it into production. This reduces the time taken to produce a workable system and allows its performance to be thoroughly investigated and modified easily before testing it in a car.

Another application of control systems in cars is the *anti-locking brake system,* usually known as *ABS*. These devices prevent locking of the wheels during braking so that:

- The vehicle does not tend to swerve during braking;

- The vehicle can still be steered during braking;

- Stopping distances are reduced;

- Tyre damage during emergency braking is eliminated;

- Less physical effort is required of the driver in emergency situations.

Cars with an ABS fitted are therefore considerably safer in hazardous conditions than those having ordinary braking systems. Figure 35.7 illustrates the components of one type of ABS system. The rotational speed of

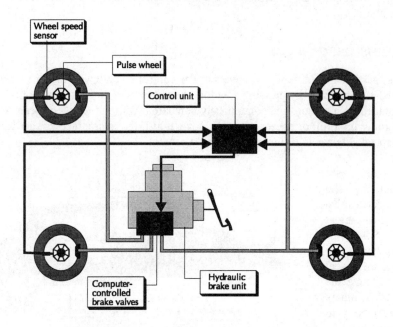

Figure 35.7. *Anti-locking brake system (ABS) on a car*

the wheels, continuously measured by the wheel speed sensors, are transmitted to the ABS control unit. The control unit processes the rotation data for each wheel separately and if a wheel is in danger of locking, it sends a signal to the brake valves to reduce the braking effect for that wheel. If the braking effect on a wheel is too weak, the control unit increases the braking effect, still ensuring that the wheel does not lock.

The wheel sensors measure the rotational speed of the wheels from the pulse-generating wheels which revolve at the same speed as the road wheels. The pulse-generating wheels generate a voltage in the sensor proportional to the speed at which they are revolving.

The ABS control unit contains two microprocessors which perform exactly the same functions of using the wheel rotation information to control braking. Two microprocessors are used for safety: they continuously monitor and test each other to ensure that the ABS system is operating correctly. If a fault in the ABS system is detected by one of the microprocessors, the system shuts itself down and normal manual braking is made available.

Engine management systems

Engine management systems use a microprocessor to monitor and control the operation of a car's engine. Though devices to control such things as exhaust emissions, fuel supply and ignition timing have been available for years, recent regulations regarding pollution control have resulted in new computer-controlled systems which integrate a number of functions and use feedback to continuously regulate the operation of the engine. These systems sample exhaust gases to provide feedback to the computer system which modifies the engine settings to keep emissions within required limits. A modern engine management system can provide system support for such things as:

- ignition timing;

- fuel injection;

- exhaust gas recirculation;

- engine idle speed.

Process control systems

The term *process control* is applied to systems which involve the automatic control of manufacturing, material handling, or treatment handling of processes. Such processes were controlled mechanically or manually in the past, but the advent of microprocessors allowed digital control systems to take over. Microprocessor-based control systems allowed process control to become more efficient and profitable by providing a means of responding to changes much more rapidly than was previously possible. Process control systems are typically found in industries that produce chemicals, steel, aluminium, food, beverages, petroleum products etc. For example, suppose that a certain chemical process requires that a concentration of a particular chemical is maintained in a tank from which fluid is being drained at the same time as other chemicals are being added. A sensor in the tank provides continuous information to a microprocessor regarding the concentration of the chemical concerned (see Figure 35.8). The output to be controlled here is the concentration of the chemical in the tank. The difference between the required concentration and the concentration as measured by the sensor is compared by the controller. If the difference between the two becomes too large, the controller opens the flow valve until the difference is reduced to an acceptable

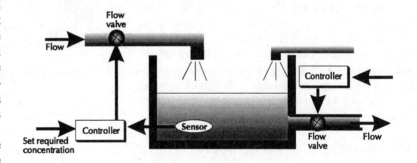

Figure 35.8. *Chemical process control*

level. The process has been controlled when the concentration of the chemical is maintained at the required level. Note that there may be several processes interacting with each other, with each separate controller keeping its particular process under control.

Robotics

Since 1962, when General Motors of the USA first used a robot commercially on one of its production lines, they have been used profitably for a wide range of tasks. The word robot was first coined by a Czechoslovakian playwright called Karel Capek who in 1921 used the Czech word robota, meaning worker, to describe a human-like machine which served humanity in one of his plays. Later, Isaac Asimov, a very popular science fiction writer, was the first person to use the word robotics to refer to the science of robots. Though as yet robots are not advanced enough to need them, Asimov's well-known Laws of Robotics may be required in the not too distant future. His three laws state that:

1.   *A robot must not harm a human being or, through inaction, allow one to come to harm.*

2.   *A robot must always obey human beings unless that is in conflict with the First Law.*

3.   *A robot must protect itself from harm unless that is in conflict with the first or second laws.*

Asimov's fictional robots had very advanced positronic brains which gave them the power to reason like humans, but the robots in use today are much more rudimentary machines usually used for fairly simple and repetitive tasks. It will be some time before intelligent, humanoid robots are more than just an interesting theme for novels.

According to the Robot Institute of America, a robot is a *reprogrammable, multifunctional manipulator designed to move material parts, tools or specialized devices through variable programmed motions for the performance of a variety of tasks*. However, there are many very different types of machines that are covered by this definition. Most robots have an arm with a number of joints linking the sections. Joints rotate or slide or combine the two movements, as illustrated in Figure 35.9. Until recently, nearly all robots were mounted on a stationary base and were therefore fixed in one position. However, with the availability of low-cost computers able to cope with the added problems caused by providing mobility, manufacturers now provide robots which can move in a number of different ways. Most mobile robots are restricted to moving on a track either on the ground or on an overhead gantry, but there are some robots with wheels used as household assistants. Some robots have been equipped with legs so that they are able to walk over uneven terrain, but there are many problems associated with making such machines, and they are still in the very early stages of development.

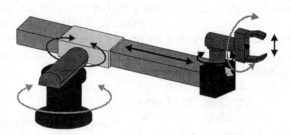

Figure 35.9. *Example of a robot arm*

The advantages of using robots

Some of the reasons for using robots in industry are:

*   Although robots are very expensive, when the cost is averaged over several years, the cost per hour of using a robot is much less than using human labour. One of the main reasons for this is that robots, unlike people, do not need such things as holidays, sick leave (except when they break down), medical benefits or pensions.

*   Robots work nearly 100% of the time at their tasks, whereas people have to be given tea breaks and lunch breaks and time off for other reasons.

*   Robots do not make mistakes resulting from tiredness or lack of attention because they repeat the same operations in exactly the same way every time almost without fail.

*   Robots can work much faster and with more accuracy at some tasks than human workers can. This results in the production of more and better quality articles.

- Certain manufacturing operations take place in conditions hazardous to humans but harmless to robots. For example, robots are not affected by red hot flying sparks in a steel forge, or by toxic fumes given off by certain types of paint.

Because robots can be programmed to perform many different sequences of movements, a single robot can be used to perform a wide variety of tasks, whereas a machine made to perform a specific task is limited to doing that one thing.

Uses of robots

Robots have been used for many years to do simple tasks in factories, such as picking up items at one location and feeding them to a machine at another fixed location. Another common use of robots is spray painting. Here, a spray paint nozzle is attached to the robot arm which is programmed to move through a sequence of movements to carry out the painting operation. Many robots are also used for spot welding in the automobile industry. These robots use welding guns to weld car chassis and body frames together at a number of programmed points.

More sophisticated robots, called *adaptive robots*, which are able to sense their environment and use this data to modify their behaviour, are used for more complex tasks such as: the assembly of small products; the inspection of automobile bodies travelling along an assembly line so that faulty assembly of components can be recorded and later corrected; and welding metal along seams which cannot be precisely aligned beforehand. These applications have resulted from the development of computer controlled vision systems which allow the robot to recognize simple shapes.

Measurement systems

In general, measurement systems have three component parts:

1. A sensor, or *transducer,* as it is frequently termed, responds in some measurable way to the quantity of interest. For example, in a hot wire anemometer, the transducer is a thermistor (see later) whose electrical resistance changes according to air movement.

Figure 35.10. *Input and output signals for a hot wire anenometer*

2. A *signal conditioning* device which converts the physical response of the transducer into a form suitable for operating a display device. In the hot wire anemometer example mentioned previously, the signal conditioner is an independently powered electrical circuit which converts the resistance changes of the thermistor into an electrical signal suitable for driving a digital or analogue wind-speed display. Some conditioning circuits are *amplifiers* which convert small electrical signals into signals which can drive a display. In computer control systems, the output from the measuring device must be converted into a form suitable for input to a computer. Since a computer processes binary data, an *analogue-to-digital converter* will often form an additional signal conditioning stage. Figure 35.11 illustrates these types of conditioning devices. Signal conditioning circuits are also called *signal converters* and *signal processors*.

3.   A *display* which takes the signal from the conditioning element and presents it in a form which can be interpreted by an observer. For example, the output from an amplifier could be used to deflect the needle of a meter or it could be converted into a digital signal to be displayed as figures on a computer screen or another type of digital display.

Figure 35.12 illustrates a complete measurement system consisting of a transducer, a signal conditioner and a display element.

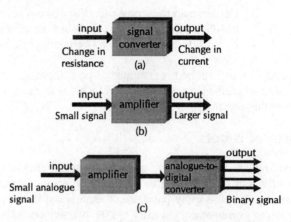

Figure 35.11. *Three types of sugnal conditioning devices (a) signal converter (c) amplifier (c) analogue to digital converter*

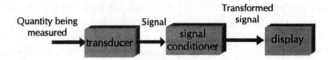

Figure 35.12. *The three components of a measurement system*

Chapter 36

Modelling and Simulation

The term *modelling* is used in information technology for computer applications which, for example, are used to investigate, analyse or plan a complex activity, or to *simulate* a complex process. Some models are concerned with investigating financial systems using a software tool such as a *spreadsheet* program. For example, a manufacturing company might use a spreadsheet-based model to determine the minimum number of items the company must produce in order to make a profit.

Other computer models are concerned with representing physical systems. For example, before a new chemical plant is built, its designers often will first model the complex arrangement of pipes and other equipment using a 3-D computer graphics program, and also simulate its operation with other types of software. In this way many potential problems can be identified and solved before construction work is started. This chapter begins by describing the nature and purpose of mathematical models and simulations. Some of the areas that have benefited from modelling and simulation are discussed in the next section. There are then some spreadsheet-based examples of simulations, followed by an investigation of the application of 3-D computer graphics programs to modelling.

Mathematical models

Physical models are usually simplified versions of actual objects or objects that may be constructed at some later date. Thus, a car manufacturer might produce a scaled-down model of a new car to investigate its wind-resistance characteristics. Though the model accurately represents the shape of the car, it is much easier to construct than a full-sized working version. Producing a model therefore provides a convenient and cheap method of investigating certain aspects of the final product. A *mathematical model* takes modelling a stage further: it provides a means of investigating something without the need to make a physical model. Mathematical models are symbolic representations of things that we want to know more about. For example, a mathematical model of the distance travelled by a body accelerating from rest is

$$s = \frac{1}{2}at^2$$

where s is the distance travelled, a is the acceleration of the body and t is the time period. This mathematical model now allows us to investigate the effects of different accelerations and different time periods on the distance travelled by the body, without having to build a working model. Using this model it can be predicted that a body uniformly accelerating at 5 metres/sec^2 for ten seconds will have travelled

$$\frac{1}{2} \times 5 \times 10^2 \text{ metres,}$$

that is, 250 metres. Of course not all mathematical models are as simple as this. Some mathematical models attempt to describe much more complex things such as human behaviour or weather patterns. Such complex models involve defining the relationships between the many variables of the system being modelled, and they almost invariably require the use of very powerful computers to investigate them.

Simulation

In computer science, *simulation* refers to the use of computers to model and investigate systems which involve some changing process. Thus a computer simulation will generally incorporate a mathematical model of the system of interest. The purpose of a computer simulation often is to enable experimental measurements to be made or to predict behaviour. Simulation can provide an experimental system for designers to investigate behaviour under a variety of different circumstances, or it may be used to provide a teaching aid for the system being simulated.

The prime reason for developing a simulation is that the cost of experimenting with the actual system is prohibitive, and since simulations are themselves expensive, there must be very sound economical reasons for justifying their use. For example, it is much cheaper and quicker to test a large number of design variations of a nuclear reactor by using a simulation rather than by building prototypes. More possible reasons for simulating a complex system are:

- *Testing* - it is necessary to test the system to destruction, that is, identify the factors that will cause it to fail and a complex device might be too expensive to use for the investigation.

- *Safety* - it is too dangerous or expensive to use the actual equipment. An example is teaching an aircraft pilot to respond to a range of emergency situations.

- *Prediction* - an accurate model is needed of an existing system so that its future behaviour can be predicted accurately. A good example of this is weather forecasting.

- *Speed and flexibility* - the system might require frequent modification and development. For example, in control systems electronically-based instruments can be simulated by a computer. These so-called virtual instruments allow devices, such as meters and indicators, and other electronic components, to be represented by software which is cheaper and easier to modify or replace than physical devices.

Simulation parameters

A mathematical model of a system usually consists of a linked set of formulae in which the result of one formula may affect others. These formulae will generally use one or more key factors, or *parameters*; altering the value of a parameter will generally alter the overall behaviour of the system. A number of different types of parameters can be identified:

- *Controllable inputs*. These are factors, or *variables*, which are under the direct control of the system designers. For example, in a stock control simulation where items of stock are continually being sold to customers and received from suppliers, two of the controllable inputs are likely to be the re-order quantity and re-order level. In a traffic lights simulation, the timing of the red/green cycle is also under the control of the system designers.

- *Non-controllable inputs*. These are factors which are not under the direct control of the system designers. For example, in a simulation of a supermarket checkout queue, the arrival rate of customers is an input variable which cannot be controlled, but there will be some statistical information regarding its characteristics. Similarly in a traffic lights simulation, the arrival and departure rates of vehicles at the junction are not directly under the control of the designers. These types of variables frequently have characteristics which can be described using probability.

- *Seasonal variations*. Some factors, again not under the control of the system designers, can vary significantly according to the time of day, the day of the week, or the season of the year. For instance, traffic density is usually heavier in the morning when people are travelling to work and in the evening when people are returning home, than at other times of the day. Supermarkets often attract more customers at the weekend and just before bank holidays, than on other days.

Monte Carlo simulation

One common technique used in simulation is called the *Monte Carlo* method which uses random numbers to solve problems. The method is particularly suitable for problems which involve statistical uncertainty. For example, when you throw a die, you are never certain which number is going to show: there is an equal probability of each of the number 1 to 6 appearing. A computer program could be used to generate a random number in the range 1 to 6 in order to simulate a die being thrown. This is a simple application of the Monte Carlo method.

Most high-level programming languages and spreadsheet programs provide random number generators. However, the random number function usually will return a fraction between 0 and 1, but this can be converted into the required range quite simply. For instance, if we multiply the random number by 6, add one and ignore the fractional part of the number, we will have a random number between 1 and 6. Thus if the random number was 0.3245 then when multiplied by 6 it gives 1.9470. Adding 1 gives 2.9470, and ignoring the fractional part gives us our random number 2. The queue simulation example later in this chapter uses random numbers produced by a spreadsheet to simulate traffic arriving at traffic lights.

Applications

Mathematical models and simulation are used in many areas including:

Marketing. This involves activities related to getting goods from the producer to the consumer. Marketing research involves the use of surveys, tests, and statistical studies to analyse consumer trends, to identify profitable markets for products or services and to produce sales predictions. Such research and forecasts require mathematical models of social behaviour and consumers' needs for various products. The cost implications of predicted demands for goods can also be modelled so that a company can be fully prepared to cope with the production, distribution and sale of the products.

Sociology is a social science that deals with the study of human social relations or group life. Quantitative sociology, which attempts to analyse sociological phenomena using mathematics, ranges from the presentation of large amounts of descriptive statistical data to the use of advanced mathematical models and computer simulations of social processes. One popular area of investigation is identification of the factors that are mainly responsible for people succeeding or failing in their chosen occupations.

Social psychology is a branch of psychology concerned with the scientific study of the behaviour of individuals as influenced, directly or indirectly, by social factors. Social psychologists are interested in the thinking, emotions, desires, and judgements of individuals, as well as in their outward behaviour. Numerous kinds of research methods and techniques are being used in social psychology. In recent years accurate mathematical models of social behaviour have been used increasingly in psychological studies. Such models allow predictions of social behaviour to be made, given a system of social relationships.

Educational psychology involves the application of scientific method to the study of the behaviour of people in instructional settings. Different theories of learning help educational psychologists understand, predict, and control human behaviour. For example, educational psychologists have worked out mathematical models of learning that predict the probability of a student making a correct response to a multiple-choice question. These mathematical theories are used to design computerized instruction in reading, mathematics, and second-language learning.

Weather forecasting involves reporting, predicting, and studying the weather, including temperature, moisture, barometric pressure, and wind speed and direction. In addition to their regular and special services to the public, weather services conduct research projects. In their meteorological investigations, primarily concerned with forecasting techniques and storm behaviour, these agencies make use of the findings from studies of mathematical modelling of the general circulation of the atmosphere, advances in radar meteorology, high-speed computer methods, and earth-orbiting artificial satellites.

Fluid mechanics is a physical science dealing with the action of fluids at rest or in motion, and with applications and devices in engineering using fluids. Fluid mechanics is basic to such diverse fields as aeronautics, chemical, civil, and mechanical engineering, meteorology, naval architecture, and oceanography. Turbulent flows cannot be analysed solely from computed predictions and depend on a mixture of experimental data and mathematical models for their analysis, with much of modern fluid-mechanics research still being devoted to better models of turbulence. The nature and complexity of turbulent flow can be observed as cigarette smoke rises into very still air. At first it rises in a stable streamline motion but after some distance it becomes unstable and breaks up into an intertwining eddy pattern.

Population biology is the study of populations of animals and plants. A population is a group of interbreeding organisms in a specific region - for example, the members of a species of fish in a lake. Populations are analysed in terms of their variability, density, and stability, and of the environmental and other processes and circumstances that affect these characteristics. Among such key features of a given population are birth and death rates; the distribution of ages and sexes; behavioural patterns of competition and co-operation; predator-prey, host-parasite, and other relationships with different species; food supplies and other environmental considerations; and migration patterns. To analyse populations biologists try to develop mathematical models of the group under study that incorporate as many of these variables as possible. Such models enable scientists to predict what effect a change in any one factor may have on a population as a whole.

Catastrophe theory is the term for an attempt to develop a mathematical modelling system for dealing with abruptly changing natural events. One such physical 'catastrophe', for example, could be an avalanche resulting from a gradual build-up of snow. In the area of human relations, a 'catastrophe' could be someone suddenly losing his or her temper after being patient for a long period. Catastrophe theory was primarily intended to be useful for describing events in the biological and social sciences.

Science education. Laboratory experiments to determine the characteristics of falling bodies, colliding balls, pendulums and projectiles can all be simulated quite easily by a computer. Students can investigate the effects of changing various parameters such as the weight of the pendulum, or the speed of colliding objects, or the angle at which an object is projected, or any one of a number of other factors that affect the experiment of interest.

Medical education. Medical diagnosis is a very complex activity and very difficult to learn. Though the typical symptoms of most ailments are well-known, the manner in which a given illness manifests itself varies from patient to patient. This means that physicians must acquire the ability to assign the correct level of importance to each recognisable symptom in order to make a correct diagnosis.

Computers can help with this task by simulating illnesses and associated symptoms. The computer model of the illness can be set up so that the symptoms vary each time the same illness is simulated. The computer might present a case study of a patient, supplying the student with the type of information gained from tests and by questioning the patient. The student is then required to arrive at a diagnosis of the ailment and suggest appropriate treatment. The student's diagnosis and suggested treatment can then be compared with the correct ones stored in the computer in order to provide feedback concerning the accuracy of the student's analysis. In this way, students can very quickly 'experience' many different manifestations of a particular illness, a situation which could be very difficult to organize using actual patients.

Computers can also be used to show the effects of drugs on the human body. How long a drug remains active in the bloodstream and the concentration of the drug after repeated doses are very important factors. However, because of the complexity of the human body and the great number of factors which contribute to the effects of a particular drug, predicting the effects of a drug is very difficult. Computer simulations which use complex theoretical models of the human body can allow students to experiment with typical drug dosages and observe the resulting effects. A common approach is to present the student with a number of screens of text and/or graphical information. After this information has been assimilated, the student is then in a position to understand the purpose of the simulation and what information must be supplied. By providing typical drug characteristics and dosages, the student can observe the predicted affect of the drug as simulated by the computer. Finally, the student completes a multiple-choice test which is marked by the computer. Any weaknesses in the student's understanding of the material can thus be identified and remedied by suggesting that the student repeats certain parts of the simulation program.

With the enormous increase in desk top computing power over recent years, it is now feasible to produce computer programs which use graphics to allow students to explore the human body in great detail. Software simulates the structure and function of the nervous, circulatory, immune and other systems of the body using multimedia. Though they are not used as replacements for actually dissecting cadavers, these products can give students a useful grounding in physiology and anatomy.

Queuing theory. This deals with the analysis of the waiting lines that occur in many areas of modern life. Whenever something is in demand, there is the possibility of a queue of some description forming, resulting in restricted access to resources, or losses in time, money and patience. Efforts to avoid and control congestion are therefore of great interest to providers of services which can cause queues, and this has led to the study of waiting lines using mathematical models and simulation. An area which has benefited greatly from queuing theory is that of time-shared computer systems in which each user is given a small amount of processing time and users waiting their turn are put in a queue; the computer decides which job will be serviced next and for how long using a scheduling algorithm based on queuing theory.

Instrumentation. Computer measurement systems frequently involve monitoring a physical system, analysing the data gathered and displaying the results. Traditionally, many such systems have used hardware components, such as filters, frequency analysers, meters and LED displays, but computers can be used to replace many of these devices. *Virtual instruments* allow many physical devices to be simulated using a computer. A virtual instrument uses software components to process the data measured externally to the computer, and to present results of processing using realistic representations of instrument panels containing meters, switches, digital and other types of displays. (See Figure 36.1). Graphically based programming languages allow complex processing tasks to be programmed by connecting together symbols which represent electronic devices.

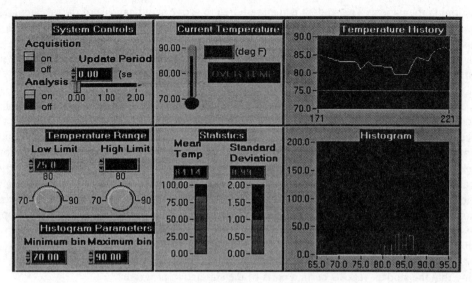

Figure 36.1. *An example of a virtual instrument*

The advantage of this approach is that new devices can be constructed, tested and modified without the need to produce costly, purpose-built hardware devices.

Three-dimensional models. Many software products are available for simulating the structure of solid objects. These programs allow designers to create three-dimensional drawings of objects which can be viewed from any angle, rotated, and modified using a wide variety of software tools. Many 3D drawing programs also allow objects to be animated. For example, detailed computer models of buildings are used as the basis of *fly-throughs* in which a simulated camera navigates through the building, going from

Figure 36.2. *An example of a 3D model of a building*

room to room, zooming in and out. Simulations such as this, animated or otherwise, allow complex objects to be visualised prior to production, thus speeding up and reducing the design process.

Modelling and simulation using spreadsheets

In this section we look at the use of spreadsheet for performing a break-even analysis to investigate a manufacturing business, to simulate a stock control system and to simulate traffic arriving at traffic lights. The skills part of this book explains in detail the operation and use of spreadsheet programs. Here we limit explanations to special functions that are required for simulation purposes and to the formulas that are required for the various calculations involved.

Financial planning - break-even analysis

The prime objective of most organizations is the achievement of profit. In order to make a profit the organization must earn sufficient revenue from the sale of its products to exceed the costs that it has incurred in operating and producing. It is usually a relatively simple task to calculate revenue: simply determine the number of goods which have been sold and multiply this quantity by the price per item. The calculation of cost is slightly more complicated owing to the fact that the organization incurs a variety of different costs in producing its products. *Fixed costs* remain constant irrespective of the number of items produced. Examples include rent on the premises or local council rates. Therefore, as production rises the fixed cost per item reduces. Other costs, however, increase with production. These are called *variable costs*. Raw materials are an example of variable costs since as more items are produced, more raw materials are required. Combining fixed and variable costs gives the organization its total costs and it is these which must exceed its total revenue before it can make a profit. Clearly then, an organization may make a loss if its output is low, but as it produces and sells more it will eventually move through a *break-even point* into profit. As the name suggests, the break-even point is where the organization neither makes a loss nor a profit – it simply breaks even. Management are obviously very interested to know the level of production required to exceed the break-even point and make a profit. Combining the revenue and cost figures in order to determine the break-even point is called *break-even analysis*, and a graphical representation of the figures is termed a *break-even chart*. An example of a break-even analysis and equivalent chart are shown in Figure 36.3.

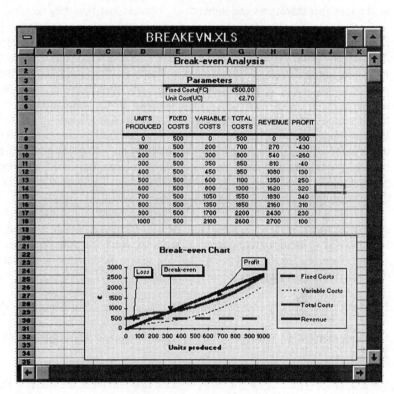

Figure 36.3. *Break-even analysis*

The UNITS PRODUCED and VARIABLE COSTS columns of the spreadsheet are constant values. FIXED COSTS are copied from the Fixed Costs(FC) parameter cell. The TOTAL COSTS column is the sum of FIXED COSTS and VARIABLE COSTS. The REVENUE is calculated by multiplying the units produced by the Unit Cost(UC) parameter. Finally, the profit is found by subtracting the TOTAL COSTS from the REVENUE.

The break-even chart, shown beneath the spreadsheet, graphs the three costs and the revenue figures; the break-even point is where the TOTAL COSTS curve crosses the REVENUE line. Profit occurs to the right of the break-even point, and you can see that in this case, when the fixed costs are at £500 and the selling price is £2.70, the break-even point occurs when just over 300 items are produced. Interestingly, the graph also shows that maximum profit occurs when between 600 and 700 items are produced and that at about 1000 items the company again breaks even.

Stock control simulation

Suppose that Agros is a large retail outlet which sells a wide range of household materials. It has a computerised stock control, or *inventory*, system which deals with obtaining, storing and supplying the goods it offers to the general public. Agros provides free catalogues containing descriptions of items which customers can obtain by visiting one of their outlets. The items shown in the catalogue are kept in a warehouse attached to the outlet. It is of vital importance to Agros to ensure that it has a full range of items in stock so that customers can immediately obtain those that they require.

If an item is out of stock, the potential customer might decide to shop elsewhere thus causing Agros to lose the sale, and possibly future sales too. Agros attempts to prevent this situation by ordering quantities of those items that are in danger of being sold out. However, the time taken for the items to arrive from the suppliers may be several days, by which time the goods still could have sold out. Moreover, if the demand for an item is overestimated, and there are a large number of the item in the warehouse, Agros again loses money because each item incurs a warehouse storage cost. Agros must try to achieve a balance between over-ordering and under-ordering goods. This would be an easy problem to solve if Agros knew exactly what the demand for a particular item is likely to be at any one time, but unfortunately this is never the case. Possibly the best prediction of demand will still involve a large amount of uncertainty. For example, past experience might provide an estimate of the average demand per day for an item, but the actual demand on a particular day will probably fluctuate fairly randomly.

A possible means of investigating this type of system is therefore a Monte Carlo simulation in which demand is simulated using a random number generator such as that described in the previous example. Before showing how a spreadsheet can be used for such a simulation, a number of terms commonly used in stock control systems, are described.

Demand – the quantity of a product that customers are willing to purchase.

Opening stock – the number of items of stock immediately available for purchase at the start of trading on any day.

Closing stock – the number of items of stock that remain in the outlet at the close of trading on any particular day.

Re-order quantity – the number of items of stock ordered from a supplier at any one time.

Re-order level – the minimum number of items held in stock before the item is re-ordered. As soon as the level of stock reaches this level, or drops below it, the re-order quantity is ordered from the supplier.

Carrying costs – the cost of storing an item waiting to be sold.

Stock out costs – the financial loss incurred when the demand for an item exceeds the stock level. In other words, a company loses money when it cannot supply an item to a customer because that item is out of stock. The term *Loss of Goodwill* also applies to this type of loss, because the disappointed customer might not use the outlet in the future.

Order costs – the cost to the company of making an order or a re-order quantity of a product; this in addition to the actual cost of buying the items from the supplier. Each time an order is generated, there is an order cost.

Lead time – this is the time it takes to receive an item from the supplier once the order has been generated.

The simulation shown in Figure 36.4 illustrates the effects of the stock control parameters, shown at the top of the spreadsheet, over a period of fourteen days.

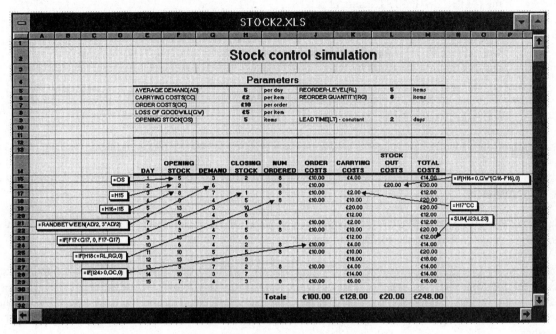

Figure 36.4. *A stock control simulation*

The columns in the table have been calculated as follows:

- OPENING STOCK - On the first day of the simulation period this is the value OS which appears in the parameter table. On the second day it is the closing stock value for the first day, that is, the number of stock items left after close of business the previous day. On the third and subsequent days it is the closing value for the previous day plus any stock that was ordered two days previously. Thus, for day four, the opening stock (10) is the sum of the third day's closing stock (2) and the quantity ordered on the second day (8).

- DEMAND - This is produced using a random number generator which produces a random number between half the average demand and one and a half times the average demand. For example, if the average demand is 6 items per day, a random number between 3 and 9 is generated. This represents the actual demand for the item on a particular day, and this is where the uncertainty factor is introduced.

- CLOSING STOCK - the number of items remaining in the warehouse/storeroom at close of trading on that day.

- NUM ORDERED - the number of items ordered that day. This will be either the re-order quantity, if the closing stock level is equal to or below the re-order level, or zero if the CLOSING STOCK level is greater than the re-order level.

- ORDER COSTS - each time the item is re-ordered, there is an order cost incurred.

- CARRYING COSTS - there is a charge for each item in stock at the close of trading on each day. Thus, on day 5, CLOSING STOCK was 9 and the order costs at £2 per item means that the CARRYING COSTS amount to £18.

- STOCK OUT COSTS - a fixed cost is incurred for each item out of stock that a customer was willing to buy. This is calculated by subtracting OPENING STOCK from DEMAND and multiplying the result by the LOSS OF GOODWILL cost shown in the parameter table.

- TOTAL COSTS - calculated by summing ORDER COSTS, CARRYING COSTS and STOCK OUT COSTS.

The column totals for the four costs calculated are shown below the appropriate columns.

Examples of the spreadsheet formulas used for these calculations are shown in the shadowed formula boxes on the spreadsheet.

Note that the OPENING STOCK parameter is a constant value that can be changed in this particular simulation only by changing the formulas in the OPEN STOCK column.

Each time the spreadsheet is recalculated (by pressing F9 in Excel) new DEMAND random numbers are generated for each day, and the resulting costs are displayed. This allows investigation of the effects of changing the various parameters, for example, the investigation of the effect on the total costs of increasing the re-order level, or of reducing the re-order quantity, or the effect of changing both of these parameters together.

Simulating vehicles arriving at traffic lights

At a road junction controlled by traffic lights, vehicles arriving at the junction form a queue when the lights are on red. The size of the queue depends on two factors: the length of time the lights remain on red and the rate at which vehicles arrive at the junction. When the lights turn to green, the queue reduces as vehicles pass through the junction. At the same time, however, vehicles are still arriving at the junction while the lights are on green.

In this simple simulation (Figure 36.5), we use four *parameters*, that is factors which affect the size of the queue:

1.   The average rate of arrival of vehicles at the lights. We assume that if the average rate is say, A, then during any stop period the actual rate is modelled by generating a random number between A/2 and 3A/2. For example, if the average arrival rate is 4 vehicles per minute, then we generate a random number between 2 and 6 and use this as the actual arrival rate for one instance of the lights being on red. We generate a new value for the actual arrival rate the next time the (simulated) lights turn to red.

2.   The average rate of departure from the lights. We use the same scheme as for the arrival rate: if the average departure rate is L vehicles per minute, then we generate a

random number between L/2 and 3L/2 to represent the actual departure rate for one instance of the lights being on green. We generate a new value for the actual departure rate the next time the lights turn to green.

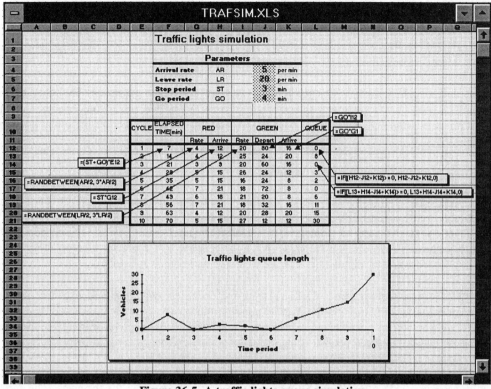

Figure 36.5. A traffic lights queue simulation

3. The length of time (in minutes) the lights are on red. This affects the build-up of the vehicle queue, since the longer the lights are on red, the greater is the number of vehicles that will arrive at the junction and join the end of the queue.

4. The length of time (in minutes) the lights are on green. This controls how many vehicles can leave the queue.

A complete cycle of the lights is one stop (i.e. red) period followed by one go (i.e. green) period. The simulation calculates the size of the queue after each of these cycles. As an example, suppose that the average arrival rate at the lights (called *AR* on the spreadsheet) is 5 vehicles per minute, the average departure rate (*LR*) is 20 vehicles per minute, the lights are on red for 3 minutes (*ST*) and green for 4 minutes (*GO*), then for the first cycle, assuming that there were no vehicles waiting, the calculation might go as follows:

1. Vehicles arriving when lights are on red : 3×R1 = 3×2 = **6** to the nearest whole number (assuming R1 was 2), where R1 represents a random number between 1.5 and 4.5

2. Vehicles leaving the junction when lights are on green : 4×R2= 4×5 = **20** to the nearest whole number (assuming R2 was 5), where R2 represents a random number between 2 and 6.

3.   Vehicles arriving at the junction while the lights are on green : 4×R1 = 4×2 = **8** to the nearest whole number.

Therefore, the queue length after one cycle of the lights is given by

4.   Vehicles arriving(red) – Vehicles departing(green) + Vehicles arriving(green)

=   6 – 20 + 8 = -6.

The negative number indicates that it was possible for six more vehicles to go through the lights than actually arrived at the junction. This would give a queue length of zero. A positive value would mean that a queue of vehicles still remained after the lights turned back to red, and this would be used as the initial queue size for the next cycle.

The Excel spreadsheet uses two important functions:

- RANDBETWEEN(bottom, top) produces a random integer greater than or equal to *bottom* and less than or equal to *top*. If this function is not available, the standard RAND() function can be used as follows: INT(RAND()*(top-bottom+1) + bottom). The INT function rounds down the value inside the brackets to the nearest integer; the complete expression again produces an integer between *top* and *bottom* inclusively.

- IF(condition, true, false) tests the specified *condition* and executes the *true* expression if it is true and the *false* expression otherwise. The IF function is required to check whether the queue length is negative, indicating that no vehicles were left in the queue at the end of the green period. If the queue length is negative, it is set to zero.

All of the different types of formulas used are shown on the spreadsheet. Note that the simulation parameters have been given names (AR, LR, ST and GO) in order to clarify their use in the formulas. The spreadsheet recalculation facility has been set to manual so that function key F9 must be pressed in order to generate a new set of random numbers and for their effects to be shown. The graph automatically reflects the change in the queue after each recalculation.

Once the simulation spreadsheet has been created, the effects of changing the parameters can be investigated. This allows the parameters to be set to values which reduce the probability of a large queue of vehicles forming. The parameter that is least likely to change frequently is the departure rate of vehicles, and the arrival rate is not under the direct control of the system designer; however, the timing of the signals is under the control of the designer and this type of simulation provides the opportunity of doing detailed analysis of how crucial the timing is likely to be in the reduction of large traffic jams. The principles used in this study could equally be used to investigate other types of queues, for example, supermarket checkouts or entrances and exits to football stadiums. Finally, note that this simulation could be improved in a number of ways. For instance, more accurate models could be devised for the arrival and departure rates, or perhaps another parameter representing the number of available lanes could be introduced, or the time of day could be taken into account, since this would affect the volume of traffic.

Chapter 37
The Internet

The Internet is a world-wide network composed of thousands of smaller regional networks scattered throughout the globe. A common set of communication protocols enables every computer connected to the Internet to interchange information with every other computer so connected. On any given day it connects roughly 20 million users in over 50 countries. Over the last 25 years, the Internet has grown to include government and educational institutions, and, more recently, commercial organizations.

Figure 37.1 shows the estimated coverage of the Internet in 1995. The countries in black have facilities to connect to the Internet, though the number of people with Internet access in these countries varies widely. Countries in white may have access to e-mail, local isolated networks, or no facilities for connection to networks at all.

No single person or organization owns the Internet. There are companies that help manage different parts of the networks that tie everything together, but there is no single governing body that controls what happens on the Internet. The networks within different countries are funded and managed locally according to local policies.

The Internet began in early 1969 under the experimental project ARPAnet. ARPA (Advanced Research Projects Agency, later known as the Defense Advanced Research Projects

Figure 37.1. *Internet world coverage*

Agency) wanted to demonstrate the feasibility of building computer networks over a wide area such that the loss of a number of hosts on that network did not disrupt it. So ARPA initially interconnected four computers and linked them with Internet Protocol (IP), and the Internet grew from there. In the 70s and 80s US universities began to link with DARPAnet so that it could be used for academic research, and in 1991 the U.S. government lifted its ban on commercial use of the Internet. The considerable business opportunities provided by the Internet ensures that it will continue to grow.

Today the Internet is a huge collection of different, intercommunicating networks funded by commercial, government and educational organizations. It has developed to handle larger volumes of data, software has become more powerful and user-friendly, and the types of services available have grown. The Internet now links more than 150 countries.

All types of computers make up the hardware connected on the Internet. They vary from PCs, Macintoshes and UNIX workstations to minicomputers, mainframes and supercomputers. Anyone who wants to have access to the enormous amount of information available regionally or around the world can use the Internet.

They can access electronic libraries, receive periodicals, exchange ideas, read the news, post questions with newsgroups, examine the weather (from reports or satellite photos), obtain the latest stock market prices and currency exchange rates, and access public government information on trade, laws, research and other subjects.

It is likely that in the very near future, every school will be connected to the Internet, an Internet connection in your house will be no more unusual than a telephone line and, if you run a business, the Internet will be a vital tool.

Here are some interesting facts concerning the Internet:

- It is estimated that the Internet now connects over 3.5 million computers;

- On average, more than 1000 computers are added to the Internet daily;

- The amount of data crossing the Internet grows by 10% each month;

- Each day world-wide over 10 million people directly (and 25 million indirectly) use the Internet to send and receive electronic mail.

Connecting to the Internet

Figure 37.2 shows a PC connected to the Internet via a remote service provider which is itself a LAN (Local Area Network).

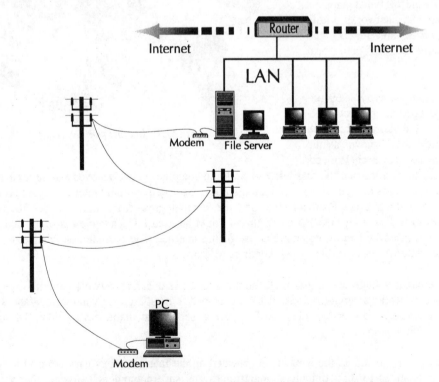

Figure 37.2. *A PC linked to a service provider for connecting to the Internet*

The PC connects to the service provider using a modem and the telephone system. The service provider is directly connected to the Internet by means of a *router,* a computer that provides the link to special data transmission lines required to access the Internet. A large organization might have its own direct link to the Internet, but many private users rely on commercial service providers for the connection, for which they must pay a subscription.

Uses of the Internet

The Internet is essentially a tool for transferring information between computers. This can be achieved in numerous ways and for various purposes. For example, *E-mail* is a convenient, quick and cheap alternative to the postal system for business and personal correspondence; *File Transfer Protocol (FTP)* allows large amounts of information to be transferred between two computers very conveniently; *Usenet,* the world-wide collection of interest groups, or *Newsgroups*, allows groups of people with similar interests to exchange views and information. Another important use of the Internet is the remote control of computer systems via *Telnet*. The *World-Wide Web* provides a uniform means of accessing and transferring information in the form of hypermedia documents. Accessing these documents does not require any particular machine or operating system. These and other Internet services are discussed in the following sections.

Note that programs used on the Internet can be classified as being either *server* or *client*. Server programs operate at Internet sites where the particular Internet service being used is provided; the program which is used to access a site, on a home PC for example, is the client program. For instance, a Web server at a Web site processes requests made by client programs called Web *browsers*.

The World-wide Web

Abbreviated to the Web and WWW, this is the fastest growing Internet service. Though the World-Wide Web is mostly used on the Internet, the two terms do not mean the same thing. The Web refers to a world wide collection of knowledge, while the Internet refers to the physical side of the global network, an enormous collection of cables and computers. The World-Wide Web uses the Internet for the transmission of hypermedia documents between computer users connected to the Internet. As with the Internet, nobody actually owns the World-Wide Web. People are responsible for the documents they author and make available publicly on the Web. Via the Internet, hundreds of thousands of people around the world are making information available from their homes, schools, colleges and workplaces. The aim of WWW is to make all on-line knowledge part of one interconnected web of documents and services.

The World-Wide Web began in March 1989, when Tim Berners-Lee of the European Particle Physics Laboratory (known as CERN, a collective of European high-energy physics researchers) proposed the project as a means of distributing research results and ideas effectively throughout the organization. The initial project proposal outlined a simple system of using networked hypertext to transmit to members of the high-energy physics community. By the end of 1990, the first piece of Web software was introduced on a NeXT machine. It had the capability to view and transmit hypertext documents to other people on the Internet, and came with the capability to edit hypertext documents on the screen. Since then hundreds of people throughout the world have contributed their time writing Web software and documents, or telling others about the Web. Given that many sites are private (hidden behind corporate firewalls or not connected to the public Internet), it can be safely stated that there are at least 4,500 hypertext Web servers in use throughout the world and in excess of a quarter of a million active Web users.

The World-Wide Web is officially described as a wide-area hypermedia information retrieval initiative aiming to give universal access to a large universe of documents. What the World-Wide Web (WWW, W3) project has done is provide users on computer networks with a consistent means to access a variety of media in a simplified fashion. With the aid of a popular software interface to the Web called a *browser* (described later), the WWW has changed the way people view and create information. The first true global hypermedia network, it is revolutionizing many elements of society, including commerce, politics, and literature.

Hypertext and hypermedia

The operation of the Web relies mainly on *hypertext* as its means of interacting with users. Hypertext is basically the same as ordinary text - it can be stored, read, searched, or edited -with an important exception: hypertext contains links to other places within the same document or to other documents. A Web browser indicates text links by the use of colour or by underlining. For example, Figure 37.3 shows part of a document called Writing Java Programs which contains three underlying links to other documents, the second one being The Anatomy of a Java Application.

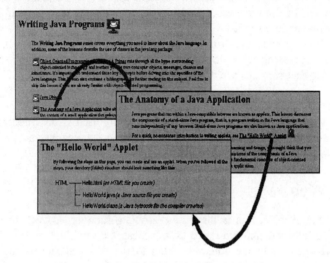

Figure 37.3. *Three linked hypertext documents*

This latter document in turn contains a link to a third document called The Hello World Applet. The first document would be retrieved from the WWW using a browser and the user, by pointing and clicking with a mouse on a link, will cause the browser to retrieve the appropriate document automatically, no matter where it is located.

Hypermedia is hypertext with a difference - hypermedia documents contain links not only to other pieces of text, but also to other forms o +1Xf media, namely sounds, images, and movies. Images themselves can be selected to link to sounds or documents. Hypermedia simply combines hypertext and multimedia. Figure 37.4 shows a browser displaying a hypermedia document with three buttons that, when clicked with a mouse, would demonstrate sound, graphics and video files.

The appearance of a hypermedia document when it is displayed by a browser is determined partly by the browser which provides a certain amount of control over such things as -1Xtext fonts and colours, mainly by the language used to encode the document. This language is *HyperText Mark-up Language* (HTML). HTML is described in more detail in a later section of this chapter.

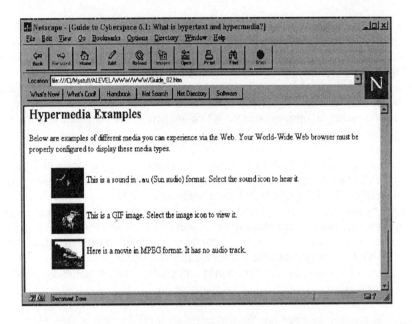

Figure 37.4. *A Hypermedia document being displayed by a Netscape browser*

Web browsers

These are graphical interface client programs to help users to navigate through the Web, to transmit and to receive information from other users or information providers. By using a browser, the user does not have to know the format and location of the information: he or she simply jumps from site to site by clicking on hypertext links. Examples of commercially available browsers are Netscape's *Navigator*, NCSA's *Mosaic*, Microsoft's *Explorer* and *Hot Java* produced by Sun Systems. Figure 37.5 shows Microsoft's Explorer displaying a page which describes the Mosaic browser.

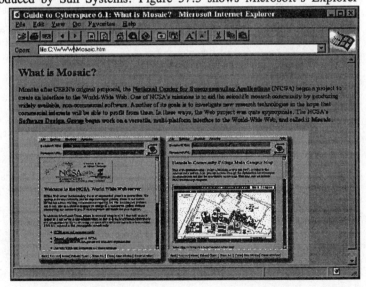

The browser has a menu bar on top, where the user can quit, get help on using the program, and change certain display characteristics such as the screen font size, the background colour, etc. A scroll bar allows the user to scroll the document page up and down. Because there is no limit to how wide or small a hypermedia document can be, scroll bars are often needed in case the document is larger than the viewing window.

Although there are many different ways to represent a document on the screen, it is often called a page. Usually, those responsible for creating a given collection of interrelated documents also create a special document which is intended to be viewed first - one that contains introductory

Figure 37.5. *A typical Web browser for a graphic user interface*

information and/or a master menu of documents within that collection. This type of document is called a home page and is generally associated with a particular site, person, or named collection. The example document has a picture of NCSA's Mosaic browser and hypertext in which two phrases are underlined. These phrases are hyperlinks (or links) - typically, clicking on one of them with a mouse will cause another document to appear on the screen, which may hold more images and hyperlinks to other places. There is no one way to represent text that is linked to other things - some browsers underline, others use special colours, and many give the user a variety of options. Images which are part of the document and are displayed within the page are called *inline images*.

There is usually a toolbar at the top or bottom of the screen. This contains buttons which perform frequently used operations. For example, a set of navigation buttons is provided because a user might go to many different pages by selecting links in hypertext and there needs to be some method of retracing one's steps and reviewing the documents that have been explored. The back button shows the previously viewed document. The forward button shows the pages in the order the user previously viewed them. An open button allows the user to connect to other documents and networked resources by specifying the address of the document or resource to connect to. The user might be able to connect to a document stored locally on the same machine being used or one stored somewhere in another country. Typically, such a document would be transferred over the Internet in its entirety.

The print button allows the user to print out the document seen on the screen. The user may be given the choice of printing the document with images and formatting as seen on the screen or as a text-only document.

How the Web works

Web software is designed around a distributed client-server architecture. A Web client (called a Web browser if it is intended for interactive use) is a program which can send requests for documents to any Web server. A Web server is a program that, upon receipt of a request, sends the document requested (or an error message if appropriate) back to the requesting client. Using a distributed architecture means that a client program may be running on a completely separate machine from that of the server, possibly in another room or even in another country. Because the task of document storage is left to the server and the task of document presentation is left to the client, each program can concentrate on those duties and progress independently of each other. Because servers usually operate only when documents are requested, they put a minimal amount of workload on the computers they run on.

Here is an example of how the process works:

1.   Running a Web client program, such as a browser, the user selects a hyperlink in a piece of hypertext connecting to another document - Java Programming for example.

2.   The Web client uses the address associated with that hyperlink to connect to the Web server at a specified network address and asks for the document associated with Java Programming.

3.   The server responds by sending the text and any other media within that text (pictures, sounds, or video clips) to the client, which the client then renders for presentation on the user's screen.

The World-Wide Web is composed of thousands of these virtual transactions taking place per hour throughout the world, creating a web of information flow. Web servers are now beginning to include encryption and client authentication abilities, allowing them to send and receive secure data and be more selective as to which clients receive information. This allows freer communications among Web users and ensures that sensitive data is kept private. In the near future, it will be harder to compromise the security of commercial servers and educational servers which want to keep information local.

The language that Web clients and servers use to communicate with each other is called the *HyperText Transfer Protocol* (HTTP). All Web clients and servers must be able to speak HTTP in order to send and receive hypermedia documents. For this reason, Web servers are often called HTTP servers.

HTML - The Hypertext Markup Language

The standard language the Web uses for creating and recognizing hypermedia documents is the Hypertext Markup Language (HTML).

An important characteristic of HTML is its ease of use. Web documents are typically written in HTML and are usually named with the suffix .html. HTML documents are nothing more than standard 7-bit ASCII files with formatting codes that contain information about layout (text styles, document titles, paragraphs, lists) and hyperlinks. Figure 37.6 shows the HTML document that is being displayed by the browser shown in Figure 37.5.

```
<html>
<head>
<title> Guide to Cyberspace 6.1: What is Mosaic? </title>
</head>
<body>
<h1> <font SIZE= +3>What is Mosaic? </font> </h1>
<p>Months after CERN's original proposal, the <b>
<a href= "http://www.ncsa.uiuc.edu/">
National Center for Supercomputing Applications</a> </b>(<b>NCSA</b>) began
a project to create an interface to the World-Wide Web. One of NCSA's missions is
to aid the scientific research community by producing widely available,
non-commercial software. Another of its goals is to investigate new research
technologies in the hope that commercial interests will be able to profit
from them. In these ways, the Web project was quite appropriate. The NCSA's
<b> <a href= "http://www.ncsa.uiuc.edu/SDG/SDGIntro.html">Software Design
Group</a> </b> began work on a versatile, multi-platform interface to the
World-Wide Web, and called it <b>Mosaic</b>.</p>
<p> <img src= "mosaics.gif" alt= "" border=0 height=275 width=547> </p>
</body>
</html>
```

Figure 37.6. *An HTML document*

Note the *tags* indicated by keywords enclosed between < and >. Most tags are of the form <tagname> ..... <tagname>, with the text being controlled by the tag appearing between the two parts. For example, text enclosed between <h1> and </h1> is shown as a major heading by the browser, and text between

<b> and </b> is shown as bold type. Hypertext links are indicated by <a....> and </a>. An example of a hypertext link is:

<a href "http://www.ncsa.uiuc.edu/"> National Center for Supercomputing Applications </a>

This tag causes the browser to show National Center for Supercomputing Applications as a hypertext link by displaying it underlined and in a different colour from ordinary text, and the location of the page is indicated by the Internet address:

"http://www.ncsa.uiuc.edu/SDG/SDGIntro.html"

Images, such as the picture of the Mosaic browser, use the <img.....> tag. The tag

<img src="mosaics.gif" alt="" border=0 height=275 width=547>

indicates, among other things, that the source of the image to be displayed is to be found in the same directory as the parent document under the filename, "mosaics.gif". The file extension .gif is the standard format for Web page inline graphics.

One of the major attractions of using HTML is that every WWW browser can understand it, no matter what machine the browser is being run on. This means that Web page developers do not need to worry about producing different versions for different computer platforms.

Uniform Resource Locators

The World-Wide Web uses what are called Uniform Resource Locators (URLs) to represent hypermedia links and links to network services within HTML documents. It is possible to represent nearly any file or service on the Internet with a URL. The first part of the URL (before the two slashes) specifies the method of access. The second is typically the address of the computer which the data or service is located on. Further parts may specify the names of files, the port to connect to, or the text to search for in a database. A URL is always a single unbroken line with no spaces.

Sites that run World-Wide Web servers are typically named with a www at the beginning of the network address.

Here are some examples of URLs:

- http://www.nc.edu/nw/book.html - Connects to an HTTP server and retrieves an HTML document called 'book.html' in a directory called 'nw'

- file://www.nc.edu/sound.au -Retrieves a sound file called 'sound.au' and plays it.

- file://www.abc.com/picture.gif -Retrieves a picture and displays it, either in a separate program or within a hypermedia document.

- file://www.bcd.org/dd/ - Displays the contents of directory 'dd'.

- ftp://www.wer.uk.co/pub/file.txt - Opens an FTP connection to www.uk.co and retrieves a text file.

- gopher://www.hcc.hawaii.edu - Connects to the Gopher at www.hcc.hawaii.edu.

- telnet://www.nc.edu:1234 - Telnets to www.nc.edu at port 1234.

- news:alt.hypertext - Reads the latest Usenet news by connecting to a news host and returns the articles in the alt.hypertext newsgroup in hypermedia format.

Most Web browsers allow the user to specify a URL and connect to that document or service. When selecting hypertext in an HTML document, the user is actually sending a request to open a URL. In this way, hyperlinks can be made not only to other texts and media, but also to other network services. Web browsers are not simply Web clients, but are also full-featured FTP, Gopher, and telnet clients (see later for a discussion of these Internet services).

WWW Search Engines

The WWW is a vast, distributed repository of information, and more is being added to the Web each day. However, the only consistent characteristics of the information available are the manner in which it is coded, that is, in HTML, and the way in which it can be located, that is, by using URLs. To access this huge bank of information, dispersed over the entire world, and locate specific information on a certain subject, there are numerous information retrieval utilities which provide access to databases of Web page details. These *search engines* allow Web users to enter search criteria in the form of keywords or phrases and they retrieve summaries of all database entries satisfying the search criteria. Of the many information retrieval services available, some of the most well known include *InfoSeek*, *Magellan*, *Lycos* and *Yahoo*.

Figure 37.7 shows the Magellan search engine being used to find information on shiatsu.

Figure 37.7. *A keyword entered in the Magellan WWW search engine*

The search produced short summaries of over 100 Web pages containing the keyword shiatsu, the first few of which are shown in Figure 37.8. Clicking on any of the links shown as underlined headings would cause the browser to retrieve the appropriate page which might also have links to further pages containing related information.

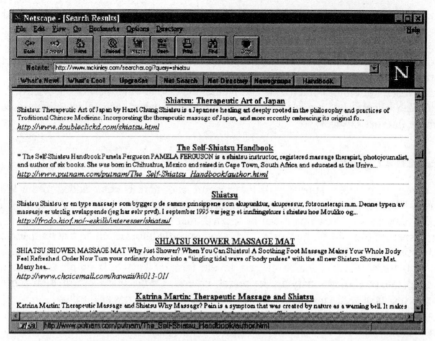

Figure 37.8. *A partial list of the result of searching for the keyword shiatsu using the Magellan search engine*

Gopher

Gopher is an Internet-wide tool used to search for and retrieve text-based information stored at Gopher sites throughout the world. One way to picture Gopherspace is to think of each Gopher site as a page in an extremely large index of information. Gopher resources include research results (both governmental and commercial), special-interest groups and databases of almost any kind of documented information.

A Gopher *client* is a software package that allows you to search this master index for information that meets your criteria. There are Gopher clients available for most computers.

With its user-friendly menu-based interface, Gopher spares the user the need to learn many computer commands. In effect, Gopher presents the Internet as if it were all part of a single directory system. There are numerous programs specifically designed to access Gopher sites, but general purpose Web browsers, such as Netscape, will also handle Gopher. Figure 37.9 shows Netscape displaying a Gopher menu at the University of Minnesota in the USA where Gopher was created. As can be seen, the menu contains a mixture of different types of files, including text documents (for example, 'About Gopher'), further directories of files (for example, 'Gopher News Archive'), video clips (for example, 'Gopher T shirt on MTV movie') and pictures (for example, 'Gopher t shirt on MTV #1').

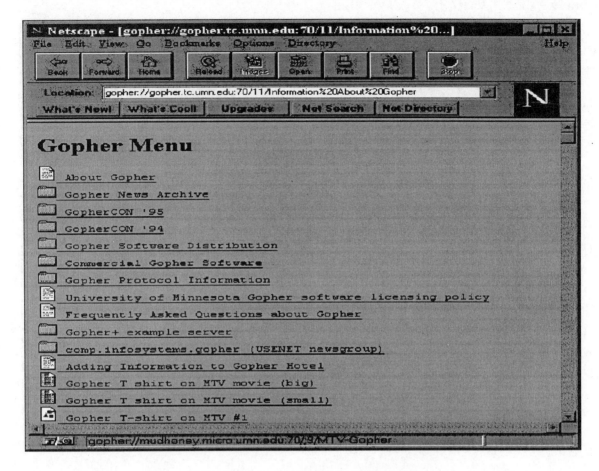

Figure 37.9. *A Gopher menu displayed by a Netscape browser*

Figure 37.10 (next page)shows the information received by the browser when the link to the first document, About Gopher, was selected.

Because information held on Gopher servers is accessed through menu hierarchies, which is time consuming if many levels of menus have to be negotiated, a widely available tool called *Veronica* is used to search Gopherspace for keywords. Veronica uses a database which has been compiled from Gopher servers - almost every item offered by a Gopher server is indexed by Veronica. Veronica uses Gopher client programs to act as user interfaces, allowing searches to be performed and presenting the results of searches, in much the same way as search engines available through Web browsers function.

WAIS (Wide Area Information Servers)

WAIS is a networked information retrieval system. Client applications are able to retrieve text or multimedia documents stored on the servers. and request documents using keywords. Servers search a full text index for the documents and return a list of documents containing the keyword. The client may then request the server to send a copy of any of the documents found. Although the name Wide Area implies the use of the large networks such as the Internet to connect clients to servers distributed around the network, WAIS can be used between a client and server on the same machine or a client and server on the same LAN.

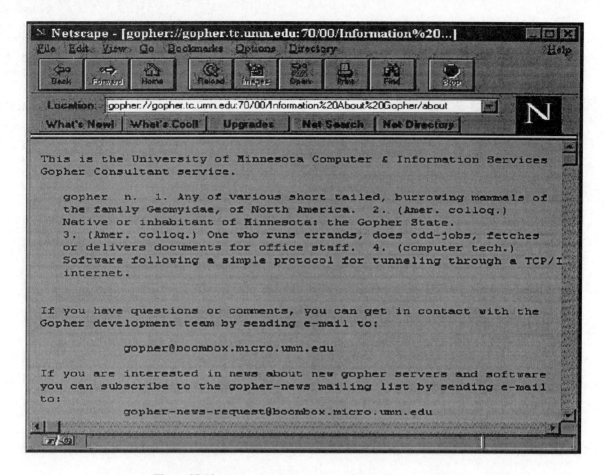

Figure 37.10. *A text document retrieved from a Gopher menu*

Currently, there are a large number of servers running and topics range from recipes and movies to bibliographies, technical documents, and newsgroup archives.

The information that is provided by WAIS is not limited to ASCII text only. With WAIS you can also get multimedia information like pictures, graphics, sounds and even video. WAIS uses natural language queries to find relevant documents. The result of the query is a set of documents which contain the words of the query. The documents that provided the most hits with the given query are placed at the top of the list of documents. WAIS databases can be accessed using specific WAIS client programs, or alternatively Gopher, Telnet and Web browser client programs.

E-mail

The most used application of the Internet is electronic mail, or *e-mail* as it is widely known. E-mail is primarily used to send and receive text-based messages such as personal or business letters, orders, reports and statements.

To use Internet e-mail, access to a computer that is connected to the Internet and has e-mail software is required. Most commercial Internet service providers include e-mail facilities in their subscriber services. Subscribers are given an identifying code called an e-mail *address*. The service provider collects and forwards mail sent from that address and holds mail to be received by that address until able to deliver it. The service provider thus acts like a post office, and in fact there is a close analogy between the way that e-mail is implemented and the traditional manual postal system (which is disparagingly termed snail mail by e-mail devotees). The same principles apply to e-mail users who do not rely on commercial service providers - messages are automatically forwarded from users to their destinations and incoming mail is stored on their service provider's computer until the user is able to accept it.

The process of composing and sending an e-mail message is as follows:

1. The message to be sent is composed (usually off-line) using some form of text editor.

2. A *mailer* program is used to connect to the Internet and transmit the message to its destination computer. The mailer examines the code containing the address to which the message is to be sent and makes a decision regarding how the message should be routed to the destination before sending it on its way.

3. The message is automatically passed from computer to computer until it arrives at the recipient's *mailbox*, which is generally a special directory used for storing messages that are waiting to be read.

4. The recipient accesses his/her mailbox and removes any messages that have arrived.

Because e-mail is delivered by electronic means, it is much faster than the manual system, taking minutes or seconds rather than days to arrive at practically any destination in the world. Though the technology that makes e-mail possible is complex, from a user's viewpoint e-mail is simple to use and extremely useful.

FTP

File Transfer Protocol (FTP) provides the facility to transfer files between two computers on the Internet. There are thousands of FTP sites all over the Internet with data files, software, and information for almost any interest. Figure 37.11 shows an FTP program being used to provide a link between a PC and a remote computer.

The file directory structures of both machines are being displayed in adjacent windows, allowing files to be selected and transferred between the two machines.

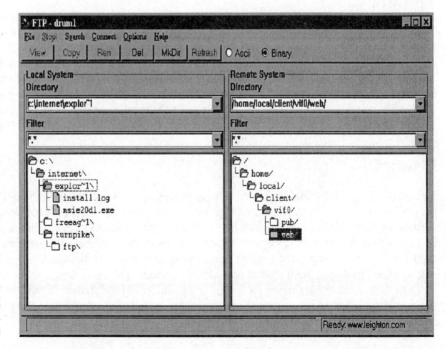

Figure 37.11. *An FTP program being used to link two computers*

Some FTP programs require typed commands to accomplish file-handling operations, but modern programs usually provide convenient graphical user interfaces such as the one illustrated.

Though there are other methods of transferring files between computers on the Internet, FTP allows such tasks to be performed quickly and easily. It is worth noting, however, that in order to access a remote host computer in this way, you need to have:

- The host name, that is, the Internet name of the computer system to which you hope to connect. This will be used by your FTP software to establish a link to the host. A typical host name might be of the form *www.layton.com*.

- A valid login name and a password that will allow you to access the host. These are obviously for security purposes - many computer systems on the Internet contain confidential information that only authorized personnel should be able to access. However, unrestricted files that are available on host computers can often be accessed by using the special visitor password *anonymous*.

In Figure 37.11, the user, through the FTP software, has already provided an acceptable login name and a password and consequently has been given access to the host system.

Closely associated with FTP, *Archie* is a program that periodically searches all FTP sites on its master list, and stores the filenames it finds in a central database. This information is then made available to users to retrieve via FTP. This, in common with other types of search engines found on the Internet, provides a convenient method of locating items of information that could be in an FTP site anywhere in the world.

Telnet

Telnet allows you to use a remote computer system from your local system. For example, an employee of an organisation which is on the Internet and supports Telnet working, could use the firm's computer system from home. The employee would simply Telnet the employer's computer system using his/her home PC and, once connected, could run programs available on the remote system. The Telnet software provides an interface window through which commands can be issued and results displayed. This *virtual terminal* allows the remote computer to be controlled as if it were the local computer. Any task that can be performed on a workstation connected directly to the remote computer can also be done using a Telnet connection.

Usenet

Usenet is a large collection of newsgroups (in excess of 13,000 at this time of writing) . Newsgroups allow people with common interests to exchange views, ask questions and provide information using the Internet. Almost anything you care to find can be found as a newsgroup, which acts like a community bulletin board spread across millions of computer systems worldwide. Anyone can participate in these groups, and moderation ranges from strict to none. Everything imaginable is discussed, from selling and trading goods and services, to discussing the latest episode of a popular TV show. Subscribers can read news articles, and reply to them - either by posting their own news articles, or by sending E-mail to the authors. Since Usenet news is not limited to any political or geographic boundaries, it provides the possibility of being able to interact with an enormous number of individuals.

A program called a *newsreader* allows access to a newsgroup and the articles available for reading, retrieval of articles of interest and the posting of articles for others to read. Each article has a header which summarizes the contents of the article, and the newsreader can be configured either to read all available article headers or those that meet certain criteria.

Figure 37.12 shows a Microsoft Windows newsreader displaying a selection of headers for a newsgroup devoted to the Internet language Java. The shaded item with the document symbol to the left has been retrieved so that the full article (See Figure 37.5) could be read.

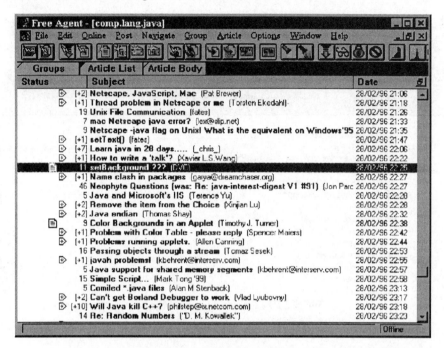

Figure 37.12. *A Newsreader program showing a selection of article headers for the newsgroup* **comp.lang.java**

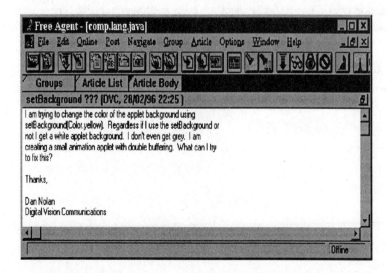

Figure 37.13. *The body of the article corresponding to the shaded header in Figure 37.12*

The author of the article posing the question 'setBackground???' hopes that someone with a similar interest in Java will know the answer and post it to the newsgroup.

As mentioned earlier, there are now well over 13,000 different newsgroups with many new ones adding to the list every day. To give you an idea of the range of interests represented, Figure 37.14 shows a number of recent additions.

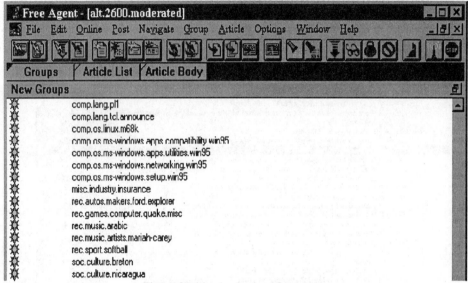

Figure 37.14. *A selection of newsgroups*

IRC

IRC, or *Internet Relay Chat*, is a multi-user talk program. IRC allows several people to simultaneously participate in a discussion over a particular channel, or even multiple channels. There is no restriction to the number of people that can participate in a given discussion, or the number of channels that can be formed over IRC.

All conversations take place in real time and IRC has been used extensively for live coverage of such things as world events, news and sports commentary. It is also an extremely inexpensive substitute for long distance calling.

Chapter 38
Organizational and Social Issues

The introduction of a computer to an organization cannot be effective if computerization simply means the transfer of manual files to computer storage and the automation of some of the existing clerical procedures. To achieve the full potential of computerization, an organization needs to implement certain changes which will affect its staff and its form of management. This chapter examines the functions of Management Information Services and the roles of its staff, the possible effects of computerization on staff in other functional areas and the implications of distributing computing power. In many organizations, a separate department has overall responsibility for computer system provision and operation.

Management Information Services

Some organizations still use the title Data Processing Department, but because of its changing role in producing management information as well as in carrying out the routine data processing tasks, the title Management Information Services is used in this text.

As its title implies, this department fulfils a servicing function and in large organizations, generally has some centralized computer facility which carries out most of the computerized data processing. Smaller organizations may not have a central facility but instead have microcomputer systems in each department, or a small network. In this context however, it is proposed to concentrate on the provision in larger organisations.

Functions

Management Information Services provides two principal forms of information: *operational*; *management*.

Operational information

Each *functional area* has its own operational information needs. For example, payroll details and payslips are produced for Wages and Salaries and customer invoices for Sales Order Processing. Here is a typical list of such routine operations:

- Keeping stock records;

- Payment of suppliers;

- General ledger, sales and purchase accounting;

- Payroll;

- Invoicing;

- Production of delivery notes;

- Routine costing;

- Filing of customer orders.

This routine data processing work forms the bulk of the activity within Management Information Services, but there is an increasing demand for *management information*.

Management information

Such information is designed to assist with operations which require management involvement and may support decision making in respect of, for example:

- Production planning;

- Short term and long term forecasting;

- The setting of budgets;

- Decision making on financial policies;

- Marketing decisions;

- Sales management;

- Factory maintenance and management;

- Price determination;

- The selection of suppliers.

Although Management Information Services plays a central role, the widespread use of networks and the remote access which they provide means that some of the above operations can be carried out by staff, with or without the use of the centralized facility.

Example

Consider the situation of a Sales Manager who is planning a sales strategy in terms of which geographical locations to increase sales representatives visits. With the use of a microcomputer and database software package, records could be kept of sales staff. To obtain the required results, the SalesManager may also need information stored with Management Information Services and using a telecommunications link, the information could be downloaded from the central computer, combined with the information on sales staff and the database query facilities used to extract an appropriate report. With the use of a notebook and modem, access can be continued even when the manager is away from the office.

Figure 38.1 illustrates the staffing structure of a typical Management Information Services department.

The department is normally headed by a Management Information Services Manager or Data Processing (DP) Manager whose major responsibility is for the efficient running of the department in satisfying the organizations information needs.

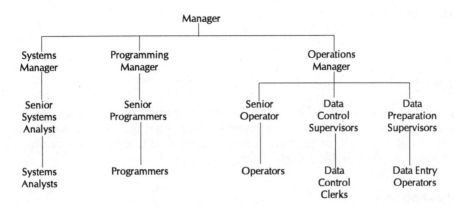

Figure 38.1. *Staffing structure of Management Information Services*

Beneath the control of the manager are staff involved in two specialist areas of work within the department:

- Systems development and maintenance;

- Operations.

Systems development and maintenance

The development of new computerized systems and the maintenance of existing systems involves specialist staff trained in *systems analysis* and *programming*.

Systems analysis is concerned with the design of new computerized systems according to requirements laid down by corporate management. Prior to the design stage there is an investigative stage which necessitates close consultation with potential users in the various functional areas of the organization, to discover their information needs.

The result of the design stage is a System Specification which, rather like an architects plans for a house, details all necessary materials and procedures to fulfil the specification. The specification will detail the clerical procedures necessary, the hardware required and most importantly, what the computer has to produce for the users. Once a system has been implemented it will require continual monitoring and modification as the information needs of the users change. These tasks are also part of the systems analysts job.

Programming is a task which perhaps lacks the creative element present in systems analysis and design. The programmers job is concerned with coding the necessary computer instructions in a *programming language* such as COBOL or DbaseIV, in order to implement the requirements laid down by the systems analysts, in the Program Specification (this forms part of the System Specification). Programmers involved in writing computer programs for user applications such as invoicing or payroll are known as *applications programmers*.

Operations

The Operations section is usually led by an Operations Manager who is responsible for three sub-sections:

- Data Control;

- Data Preparation;

- Computer Operations.

Data control

The staff in this section are responsible for the co-ordination and control of data flowing through the Operations section. The data received from, for example, Wages and Salaries to enable the payroll master file to be updated and payslips to be produced, has to be controlled to ensure its accuracy at all stages of processing. Chapter 17 describes the methods of control in detail.

Data preparation

The work in this section involves the encoding of data from source documents such as customers orders onto a machine-sensible medium. Currently, this is usually magnetic tape or disk. *Key-to-tape* systems are dedicated, off-line devices, which allow data to be encoded directly onto cassette tape, without the use of a central computer. Prior to processing by computer, the cassettes from the magnetic tape encoders (it is likely that many will be in use) are gathered together and the data is merged onto a large reel for input to the computer. This form of encoding is rather outmoded and *key-to-disk* systems are generally more popular for large volume encoding, making use of a minicomputer and a number of on-line keying stations. The processing power of the minicomputer allows much greater control, both in terms of *verification* and *validation* of the data, than is possible with key-to-tape systems. The data entered via the keying stations is stored on magnetic disk and can be input to the main computer directly from there, or after transfer to magnetic tape.

Computer operations

The staff in this section are essentially computer operators and responsible for the day-to-day running of the hardware, including the loading and unloading of input and output media, such as disk and tape. The computer hardware is controlled by the *operating system* with which the operator communicates regarding the processing of jobs and the resolution of any error conditions which may arise. This communication is effected through a terminal dedicated to that purpose.

Storage of magnetic tapes and disks

Depending on the size of the organization, the tape or disk library (the cataloguing and storage area for computer file media) may be staffed by a librarian or by the operators. In any event it is vital that information files are properly indexed and kept in a secure environment, protected from physical hazards and unauthorized access.

Implications of decentralizing computing power

The combined technologies of computing and telecommunications have facilitated the decentralization of computer power through wide and local area networks and stand-alone microcomputer systems. The main benefits for an organization may be as follow:

- The delegation of some information processing control to branch level management, hopefully results in systems which respond to local requirements. The control of information processing systems are thereby the responsibility of those who use them;

- More rapid, up-to-date information at the local level, because it is processed locally;

- The rapid distribution of centrally produced information via network systems;

- Provided that the local systems are linked to a central facility, then information which is locally produced can be transmitted and stored so as to be available at a corporate level. Overall control is not lost, but enhanced.

The above benefits are not automatic and may have certain implications for an organization:

- New hardware and software needs to be purchased, which is compatible with any existing centralized facility;

- Local management and workers need to be trained in the operation of any new system introduced, if the maximum benefit is to be obtained. The use of microcomputers with, for example, database and spreadsheet packages requires extensive training and this can be expensive;

- A complete re-appraisal of specialist staffing may be necessary, including, for example, the recruitment of systems analysts already familiar with the design and implementation of distributed systems;

- Specialist personnel, including programmers and operators, may be required at the local level;

- Decentralized systems present new problems in terms of controlling the security of information and the additional risks must be considered and covered.

Computers and employment

The rapid advances in computer and micro-electronic technologies have occurred during periods of considerable change in the Western economies and although many different factors have conspired towards the generally higher levels of unemployment, computerization has undoubtedly played a major role. No attempt is made in this text to relate particular numbers of employed or unemployed to computerization and discussion will centre on the identifiable effects of computerization on employment patterns and prospects. Computerization requires consideration of a number of possible effects/implications:

- re-training;

- re-deployment;

- de-skilling;

- changes in working practices;

- re-grading and changes in career prospects;

- redundancy;

- changes in working conditions (health and safety).

Each of the above can be identified in different types of job.

Office work

Computerization is common in most areas of office work, for example, word processing, electronic messaging, and accounting systems. Additionally in some specialized areas such as banking, automatic tellers are replacing humans for routine banking transactions and staffing requirements are likely to reduce quite drastically as new automated services such as telephone banking expand.

Re-training

Generally, an organization will choose to make full use of its existing staff, rather than search for new staff who already have the skills required. Depending on the nature of the job, the retraining needed may be radical or quite minor. For example, a typist has keyboard skills which are quite readily transferrable to the task of word processing and re-training needs centre on the concept of text editing, mailing lists and the use of floppy disks and printers. The aim is to give the operator the knowledge, skill and understanding to make maximum use of the facilities provided by a word processor. Word processing is a general skill which can be applied in different ways in different organizations. Similarly, the use of a software package for sales accounting or stock control needs knowledge and skills, some of which are transferable to other packages. Familiarity with computers in general and expertise in the use of some packages, provides an individual with the confidence to quickly pick up skills for new applications as they arise.

Re-deployment

Computerization generally reduces manpower requirements but increases the opportunities for business expansion. Re-deployment means moving staff from one area of work or responsibility to another, generally with retraining and is a common consequence of computerization in any area of work.

De-skilling

The judgement as to whether or not a job is de-skilled by computerization is a rather subjective one. For example, does a wages clerk using manual methods require a higher level of skill than a data entry operator? The answer is probably yes, although a trade union may argue otherwise in the interests of improved job re-grading. On the other hand it is generally accepted that higher level skills are required to use a word processor than a typewriter.

Changes in working practices

Staff may be required to carry out a wider range of tasks as a result of computerization. For example, in smaller offices a clerk may be required to answer customer enquiries and carry out data entry at a terminal.

Flexibility rather than specialization is often the key to the introduction of new technology. The lines of demarcation in the newspaper industry had to disappear before computerization could take place.

Re-grading and career prospects

Sometimes, improvements in job gradings are introduced in order to encourage staff to accept computerization. At the same time, career prospects in office work are generally diminished. In the banking industry, the prospects for managerial jobs have diminished drastically in the last two decades and currently, few clerical staff who did not enter the job with a degree have prospects for managerial posts.

Redundancy

Computerization of office work inevitably reduces the manpower requirements for an existing level of work, but redundancy does not always result, usually because computers are introduced in response to an expansion in the business of an organization.

Health and safety

Anxiety and stress frequently result from subjection to frequent and rapid change. Many staff, particularly older members, may feel anxious about the security of their jobs or possible redeployment and may become unhappy about personal contact being replaced by a computer screen. As they get older, many people prefer continuity rather than constant change and computerization usually means radical and frequent change. Anxiety can also result from a fear of falling behind, a common malady amongst people working with computers, because the changes and advances are so rapid.

Ergonomics

Certain health and safety problems can result from computer usage and ergonomically designed equipment and working environments can help minimize the hazards. A number of health and safety concerns are recognized in relation to VDU screens: exposure to radiation; induction of epileptic fits; mental and physical fatigue; eyestrain, eye damage and visual fatigue; muscular strain. Suitable working practices and well-designed equipment can largely avoid such dangers, for example, gentle lighting, lack of screen flicker and hourly breaks for VDU operators. Other concerns relate to the design of office furniture and the general office environment, including temperature and noise levels.

Manufacturing industry

Most of the factors described in relation to office work apply equally to factory work, but the following additional points are worth mentioning.

- *Job satisfaction.* Shop floor workers who supervise and service the machines have a cleaner, less dangerous job than traditionally skilled machinists. It may be surmised that young people, without the experience of the old skills, will look more favourably on such supervisory jobs than the older workers.

- *New job opportunities.* If automated systems such as Flexible Manufacturing Systems (FMS) are to be successful, then the number of jobs in factories using FMS must inevitably decrease. Opportunities lie in the creation of a new range of jobs, many of which are in software engineering and in the design of automated systems. The Japanese experience is that new, highly-skilled jobs are created in the development and design fields in companies manufacturing automated equipment and commercial machinery, whereas both skilled and unskilled jobs are lost in the companies using this equipment. The Japanese experience is being mirrored in the UK.

- *Increased unemployment*. Many older, skilled workers have been made redundant because of the loss or de-skilling of their jobs through automation. On the other hand, the redundancies may have occurred without automation because of loss of competitiveness.

Computers and society

There is general agreement that computers and related technologies will bring great social changes, but there are wide differences of opinion about what they will be, the rate at which they will occur and the extent to which they are beneficial. It must be emphasized that many of the following points are highly subjective and open to debate.

The *benefits* include:

- increased productivity;

- higher standard of living;

- cleaner and safer working conditions;

- shorter working hours;

- more leisure time.

The *costs* include:

- polarization of people into two groups - the technologically advantaged and disadvantaged;

- increasing crime and delinquency rates;

- the threat of a totalitarian state;

- invasion of privacy.

The remainder of this section looks at an important area of concern regarding the future impact of computers on society, namely tele-working. Some of the effects are already apparent.

Tele-working - the office at home

At present, millions of office workers travel by car or public transport to their respective places of work. Nearly all organizations carry out their business from centralized offices because information needs to be exchanged, usually on paper documents and decisions need to be made, which requires consultation between individuals. Through the use of telecommunications (most importantly, the Internet) and centrally available computer databases, some forward-looking organizations allow their staff to work from home, using a computer terminal. There are a number of advantages to be gained from home-based work.

Advantages of tele-working:

- savings in travel costs;

- no necessity to live within travelling distance;

- flexible hours of work;

- equality between men and women. Bringing up children can be a shared activity;

- savings for the organization in terms of expensive city-centre offices.

Disadvantages of tele-working:

- loss of social contact;

- need for quiet workroom at home. This can be difficult in a small flat;

- the difficulty of office accommodation is compounded when two or three members of a family all work from home;

- loss of visible status for senior staff in terms of a plush office and other staff to command.

Privacy, computer fraud and copyright

Personal privacy

Since the 1960s, there has been growing public concern about the threat that computers pose to personal privacy. Most countries, including the UK, have introduced legislation to safeguard the privacy of the individual. The Younger Report of 1972 identified ten principles which were intended as guidelines to computer users in the private sector. A Government White Paper was published in 1975 in response to the Younger Report, but no legislation followed. The Lindop Report of 1978 was followed by a White Paper in 1982 and this resulted in the 1984 Data Protection Act. Apart from public pressure concerning the protection of personal privacy, a major incentive for the Government to introduce the Act stemmed from the need to ratify the Council of Europe Data Protection Convention. In the absence of this ratification, firms within the UK could have been considerably disadvantaged in trading terms through the Conventions provision to allow participating countries to refuse the transfer of personal information to non-participating countries. The principles detailed in the Younger Report formed the foundation for future reports and the Data Protection Act. They are listed below.

- Information should be regarded as being held for a specific purpose and should not be used, without appropriate authorization, for other purposes.

- Access to information should be confined to those authorized to have it for the purpose for which it was supplied.

- The amount of information collected and held should be the minimum necessary for the achievement of a specified purpose.

- In computerized systems which handle information for statistical purposes, adequate provision should be made in their design for separating identities from the rest of the data.

- There should be arrangements whereby a subject could be told about the information held concerning him or her.

- The level of security to be achieved by a system should be specified in advance by the user and should include precautions against the deliberate abuse or misuse of information.

- A monitoring system should be provided to facilitate the detection of any violation of the security system.

- In the design of information systems, periods should be specified beyond which information should not be retained.

- Data held should be accurate. There should be machinery for the correction of inaccuracy and updating of information.

- Care should be taken in coding value judgements.

The White Paper which followed the Younger Report identified certain features of computerized information systems which could be a threat to personal privacy:

- The facility for storing vast quantities of data.

- The speed and power of computers make it possible for data to be retrieved quickly and easily from many access points;

- Data can be rapidly transferred between interconnected systems.

- Computers make it possible for data to be combined in ways which might otherwise not be practicable.

- Data is often transferred in a form not directly intelligible.

The 1984 Data Protection Act sets boundaries for the gathering and use of personal data. It requires all holders of computerized personal files to register with a Registrar appointed by the Home Secretary. The holder of personal data is required to keep to both the general terms of the Act, and to the specific purposes declared in the application for registration.

Terminology

The Act uses a number of terms which require some explanation:

- Data. Information held in a form which can be processed automatically. By this definition, manual information systems are not covered by the Act.

- Personal data. That which relates to a living individual who is identifiable from the information, including any which is based on fact or opinion.

- Data subject. The living individual who is the subject of the data.

- Data user. A person who processes or intends to process the data concerning a data subject.

Implications

The requirements of the Act may result in an organization having to pay more attention to the question of security against unauthorized access than would otherwise be the case; appropriate education and training of employees are also needed to ensure that they are aware of their responsibilities and are fully conversant with their roles in the security systems. The Act also provides the right of a data subject (with some exceptions) to obtain access to information concerning him or her. Normally, a data user must provide such information free of charge or for a nominal charge of around £10.

From the individuals point of view, the Act can be said to have a number of weaknesses:

- Penalties for infringement of the rules are thought to be weak and ineffective.

- There are a number of exemptions from the Act. Some holders do not need to register and there are exceptions to the right of access to ones own file. There are also limits to confidentiality.

- The Registrar is appointed by the Home Secretary and cannot therefore, be wholly independent.

Computer fraud

Computer fraud is invariably committed for financial gain, but unlike some forms of fraud, the perpetrator(s) will make considerable efforts to prevent discovery of any loss by the victim. The rewards for such efforts may be complete freedom from prosecution, or at least a delay in discovery of the fraud and a consequent chance of escape. Unless proper controls and checks are implemented, computer systems are particularly vulnerable to fraudulent activity, because much of the time processing and its results are hidden. The following section examines some methods for committing fraud and the measures which can be taken to foil them.

To extract money from a financial accounting system requires its diversion into fictitious, but accessible accounts. To avoid detection, appropriate adjustments must be made to ensure that the accounts still balance. Sometimes, fraudulent activity may involve the misappropriation of goods rather than cash. Frequently, the collusion of several people is necessary to effect a fraud, because responsibility for different stages of the processing cycle is likely to be shared. Some common methods of fraud are given below.

- Bogus data entry. This may involve entering additional, unauthorized data, modifying valid data or preventing its entry altogether. Such activity may take place during the data preparation or data entry stages.

- Bogus output. Output may be destroyed or altered to prevent discovery of fraudulent data entry or processing.

- Alteration of files. For example, an employee may alter his salary grading in the payroll file or adjust the amount owing in a colluding customers account.

- Program patching. This method requires access to program coding and a detailed knowledge of the functioning of the program in question, as well as the necessary programming skill. By introducing additional code, in the form of a conditional subroutine, certain circumstances determined by the perpetrator can trigger entry to the subroutine, which may, for example, channel funds to a fictitious account.

- Suspense accounts. Rejected and unreconciled transactions tend to be allocated to suspense accounts until they can be dealt with; fraud may be effected by directing such transactions to the account of someone colluding in the crime. Transactions can be tampered with at the input stage to ensure their rejection and allocation to the suspense/personal account.

Fraud prevention and detection

An organization can minimize the risk of computer fraud by:

- controlling access to computer hardware; in centralized systems with a limited number of specialist staff access can be readily controlled. On the other hand, if power is concentrated in the hands of few staff, then the opportunities for undetected fraud are increased. Distributed systems or centralized systems with remote access may increase the number of locations where fraud can be perpetrated;

- auditing of data and procedures; until hard copy is produced the contents of files remain invisible and a number of auditing techniques can be used to detect fraudulent entries or changes. The topic of auditing is dealt with in Chapter 17;

- careful monitoring of the programming function; program patching can be controlled by division of the programming task, so that an individual programmer does not have complete responsibility for one application program. Unauthorized alterations to existing software can be detected by auditing utilities which compare the object code of an operational program with an original and authorized copy.

Computer copyright

A computer program can now obtain the status of literary work and as such, retains protection for 50 years from the first publishing date. Computer software is now covered by the Copyright Designs and Patents Act 1988 and infringements include:

- the pirating of copyright protected software;

- the running of pirated software, in that a copy is created in memory;

- transmitting software over telecommunications links, thereby producing a copy.

The major software producers have funded an organization called FAST (Federation Against Software Theft) which successfully lobbied for the inclusion of computer software into the above-mentioned Act.

Examination Questions

Fundamental Concepts

JMB (May 1989) Paper 2

Q1. An arithmetic processor handles floating point numbers in 12 bit registers consisting of a 4 bit exponent in bits 0-3 (bit 0 is the least significant bit) and an 8 bit normalized mantissa in bits 4–11. The binary point of the mantissa is between bits 10 and 11. Both exponent and mantissa are in two's complement notation. The calculation (9·2) + (–0·375) is to be performed by this arithmetic processor.

    (a)   Show how the two numbers, 9·2 and –0·375, are held by the above processor. Explain any rounding used.   (10)

    (b)   Show how the processor would add together the representation of the two numbers, arrived at in part (a). What is the decimal equivalent of your answer?   (6)

    (c)   The calculation (9·2) + (–0·375) has the exact arithmetical result 8·825. Explain any difference between this and your answer obtained in b.   (2)

    (d)   Explain the precautions that should be taken to avoid errors when using conditional statements that involve testing floating point numbers.   (2)

ULSEB (June 1990) Paper 1

Q2. A twelve-bit register in a certain computer is split up such that 8 bits are used in fractional two's complement representation to represent the mantissa and the remaining 4 bits are used as an integer two's complement representation for the exponent. Using this register, write down the bit pattern which represents the following numbers in normalized form.

    (i) +1
    (ii) –3
    (ii) +0·125(iv) –0·25

    You should state any assumptions which you make.   (4)

ULSEB (June 1991) Paper 2

Q3. Biologists surveying a plot of land to assess its agricultural value are using the distribution of earthworms as one possible indicator. The region being surveyed is subdivided into a large number of squares. The land within each square is sampled systematically to provide an estimate of the earthworm population. In order to produce a schematic map of the whole area the estimated population figures are converted into one of four categories: abundant (or *a*), common (or *c*), relatively few (or *f*) and rare (or *r*). The nature of the land suggests that the earthworm population is likely to be concentrated mainly in a few squares. The data from the first few squares can be summarized by the string ffcfrrrfrrfcacfrr ... One technique of encoding the categories is as follows: *a* as 111 ; *c* as 110 ; *f* as 10 ; *r* as 0

    (a)   What sequence of categories would the binary string 1000111110 represent?   (1)

    (b)   Could the code for c be replaced by 101? Explain your answer.   (2)

    (c)   Discuss the effectiveness of the given encoding technique in this application.   (2)

ULSEB (June 1991) Paper 2

Q4. The continuous output of a scanning sensor is encoded prior to being displayed as a flat monochrome image. Examples of such sensors include a scanning electron microscope, a T.V. camera or a satellite radiometer. A corresponding digital image capable of being stored on a computer system can be considered as a two-dimensional array of integers in the range 0 to 255.

(i)   What tasks need to be performed in transforming the analogue representation into a digital representation? What might the numbers 0 to 255 represent when the digital image is displayed?   (2)

(ii)   What are the advantages of storing images in digital form?   (2)

(iii)   Provide a specification for a computer system (including architecture, peripherals and software) that would be capable of taking full advantage of the stored digital images. Give reasons for your choices.   (5)

(iv)   By stating any assumptions that you make, estimate the amount of storage required for a single displayed digital image on this system.   (2)

(v)   One application of image processing is in the field of medical radiology. Some hospitals store X-ray pictures in digital form. When a mass screening is conducted each stored digital image is scanned automatically for patterns that need to be drawn to the attention of experienced medical staff. Outline some of the issues that hospitals will need to consider before installing such a system.   (4)

JMB (June 1988) Paper 2

Q5. The adjacent figure shows the structure of a 16-bit central processing unit (CPU) and memory system. The register IN is an input buffer for data from the memory. The register OUT is an output buffer for the arithmetic and logic unit (ALU). An instruction comprises an 8-bit function code (F) and an 8-bit operand field (O).

(a)   Explain the use of the following registers: (i) IR - Instruction Register; (ii) ACC - Accumulator; (iii) PC - Program Counter; (iv) MBR - Memory Buffer Register; (v) MAR - Memory Address Register. (5)

(b)   What signals will be required on the memory control bus?   (2)

(c)   From the diagram construct the sequence of register transfers and memory control signals that carry out the following instructions: (i) Jump Relative- the program counter is to be incremented by the value in the operand field; (ii) Add Direct - the address of the value to be added is contained in the operand field; (iii) Load ACC Indexed - the value to be loaded has the base address of the table initially stored in the accumulator and the offset stored in the operand field. Explain your notation.   (13)

ULSEB (June 1990) Paper 2

Q6.

(a) A bus can be viewed as the circuitry used to carry data between the components of a system. The adjacent figure is a simplified representation of a single bus computer. No control signals are shown and the arrows indicate the possible flow of data. The following abbreviations have been

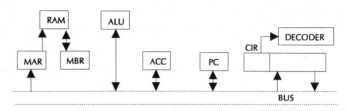

used: ACC - accumulator; MBR - memory buffer register; MAR - memory address register ALU - arithmetic logic unit; PC - program counter; CIR - current instruction register RAM - random access memory.

The processor handles single address instructions of the form: LOAD ACC, 2001, where 2001 is a memory location. An instruction comprises an operation-code followed by an address.

   (i)   Describe the sequence of events involved in the fetch process of the fetch-execute cycle. (2)

   (ii)   Describe carefully the sequence of events involved in the execution phase of each of the instructions LOAD ACC, 2001 ; transfer the contents of location 2001 to the accumulator JUMP 3000 ; jump to location 3000 (3)

   (iii)   What is the major disadvantage of having a single bus for the transfer of data? Suggest an alternative approach. (2)

Cambridge (May 1990) Paper 2

Q7.

   (a)   Write down an algorithm, using pseudocode or otherwise, which will store in LARGE and SMALL the largest and smallest values among a set of positive integer values stored in elements zero to MAX of an array named PLACE. (4)

   (b)   Your algorithm will eventually be translated into a machine-code program which uses indexed addressing. Explain why indexed addressing is used. (4)

   (c)   Use an example to illustrate the steps within the fetch, decode, execute cycle which perform the address calculations required for an instruction which uses indexed addressing. (4)

JMB (May 1989) Paper 1

Q8. A display device has two inputs, X and Y. The four possible combinations of inputs cause the indicated characters to be displayed:

INPUT		OUTPUT
X	Y	
0	0	E
0	1	1
1	0	2
1	1	3

The adjacent figure shows a railway terminus having three platforms numbered 1, 2 and 3. The points labelled A, B and C route the train entering the station into one of these platforms according to their setting. The points A and

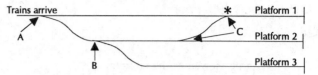

B have sensors indicating their orientation: 0 = direction set straight; 1 = direction set switched to the right.

The 'crossover' pair of points, C, always operate together and have a sensor detecting their mutual setting: 0 = both set straight; 1 = both set switched.

Note that it is dangerous for a train to be routed over the point labelled * when it is set against the direction of travel. The settings of the points are relayed to a logic circuit having the three sensor values, A, B and C, as inputs and producing two outputs X and Y. These outputs are fed to the display device described above. The display shows the platform number to which the next train entering the station is routed and if the points are dangerously set it shows the character 'E'.

(i)   Construct a truth table with column headings A, B, C, X and Y.   (5)

(ii) Derive minimized Boolean expressions for X and Y in terms of A, B and C.   (5)

(iii) Rather than using a logic circuit, a microcomputer is employed to perform the same task. Give one advantage of implementing a hardware only solution and two advantages of implementing a software solution to this problem.   (3)

(iv) Write an algorithm which will convert the decimal value corresponding to the 3-bit input value from the sensors into the decimal value of the two bits representing X and Y.   (3)

JMB (May 1990) Paper 1

Q9. In a certain type of central heating system a single boiler is used both to heat the hot water tank and to heat the radiators. The system is controlled by the signals received from three thermostats. These thermostats are: B - connected to the boiler. If the water in the boiler is at or above a critical temperature a 1 is output, otherwise a 0 is output; W - connected to the hot water tank. If the temperature of the water in the tank is below a predetermined setting a 1 is output, otherwise a 0 is output; H - in the hall of the house. If the temperature in the hall falls below a predetermined setting a 1 is output, otherwise a 0 is output. The flow of water round the system is controlled by two pumps: WP - controls the flow of water to the hot water tank and is activated if $W = 1$; RP - controls the flow of water around the radiators throughout the house and is activated if $H = 1$. The boiler will be switched on if the required temperature of the hot water tank or the hall has not been reached. However, the boiler must not be switched on if the temperature of the water in the boiler is at or above its critical value. The boiler cannot be switched on if both pumps off.

(a) As one solution to the method of control of the heating system a dedicated circuit has been suggested.

(i)   Draw up a truth table for the circuit which would use the three inputs from the thermostats and would control the boiler and each of the pumps.   (4)

(ii) Derive a simplified Boolean expression for the circuit required to control the boiler. Hence design a single logic circuit using only NOR or only NAND gates to control the boiler.   (6)

(b) An alternative solution using a microcomputer would involve the thermostats B, W and H, the water pumps WP and RP and the boiler being connected to the microcomputer. Develop an algorithm which could be used to produce a program to control the heating system. Within your algorithm you should assume a procedure GETVALUE (thermostat, state) which returns the value of the output (in the   parameter   state) from the appropriate thermostat.
(6)

JMB (June 1988) Paper 2
Q10.

(a) What is meant by BCD and why is it used? What is the BCD code for 149?   (4)

(b) A code convertor is required to convert BCD into the code given in the adjacent table.

The BCD codes for ten to fifteen can never be generated on the input side of the convertor, therefore the corresponding output bits can take either a 1 or 0 in the complete truth table. Using appropriate values in the output column for the input codes ten to fifteen, derive a simplified Boolean expression for the convertor circuit for each of the four code bits (b0 to b3) to be output.   (16)

Decimal value	Code b3	b2	b1	b0
0	0	0	0	0
1	0	0	0	1
2	0	0	1	1
3	0	0	1	0
4	0	1	1	0
5	0	1	1	1
6	0	1	0	1
7	0	1	0	0
8	1	1	0	0
9	1	0	0	0

ULSEB (June 1990) Paper 1

Q11. A mail order firm employs a number of agents who collect orders from customers and prepare the orders for input to a central computer. Each agent is provided with a portable device for encoding data on a suitable medium.

(a)   Briefly describe a possible hardware configuration of such a portable device.   (4)

(b)   How might errors be minimised: (i) as the agent inputs data; (ii) as the program accepts the data at the central computer?   (4)

(c)   Considering cost, convenience and accuracy, compare the use of a portable device with the use of an on-line terminal for this application.   (4)

(d)   The customers' accounts file is updated in batch mode at Head Office. Describe how the data collected by the agents might be processed for this purpose.   (3)

Computer Hardware

Welsh Joint Education Committee (May 1990) Paper 1

Q12. A large supermarket has thirty check-out stations, each with a point-of-sale terminal linked to a computer in the stock room in the basement. The supermarket is one of a chain of similar supermarkets, all supplied from a large warehouse through a centralized distribution system. Once each day the supermarket's computer is connected to the computer in the warehouse to communicate requirements for the supply of stock. A different basis is used for the supply of fresh food; the supermarket orders this direct from local suppliers each day, according to demand.

(a)   Discuss the functions carried out by this system and the advantages it offers:

(i)   to the manager of the supermarket;

(ii)   to the manager of the warehouse and the distribution system.   (10)

(b)   Occasional failures of equipment inevitably occur, affecting point-of-sale terminals, the supermarket computer, the communication links, or the warehouse computer. Discuss how the whole system can be designed to cope with such failures without causing serious loss of data or making it impossible for the supermarket to continue to function. (10)

JMB (June 1988) Paper 2

Q13.

(a)

(i)   Briefly explain why modems are needed in data transmission and why they will become obsolete when digital telephone systems are fully implemented.   (3)

(ii)   When fully implemented, such digital telephone systems will require A-D and D-A converters in the home. Why will these be needed and where will they be located?   (2)

(b) The adjacent figure represents a wide area network packet switched system consisting of seven intelligent terminals T(1) to T(7) and five nodes N(a) to N(e). Such a system sends packets of digital information between the geographically remote intelligent terminals.

(i)   Explain the transmission facilities of the nodes.   (3)

(ii)   Explain in general terms how data is routed through the network from terminal T(3) to T(5).   (3)

(iii)   Explain how the system can tell which terminal a packet is being sent to and how a terminal can tell where a packet has come from.   (2)

(iv)   Explain how packets sent from one terminal to another can arrive out of sequence.   (3)

(v)   What would be the effect to users of this system if node N(a) failed? What would be the effect of node N(e) failing?   (4)

ULSEB (June 1990) Paper 2

Q14. A financial institution has a large number of offices scattered throughout Britain. The company has invested in a substantial network of computers to monitor and control its trading activities.

(a)   What is meant by distributed data processing in this context and what facilities would you expect to be offered? What are the possible advantages of such a system over a centralized system?   (4)

(b)   Several offices in a small town need to send information to, and receive information from, a remote mainframe which houses a copy of the company's main database. The mainframe is heavily used by a number of sites. The only transmission medium currently accessible in the town is the standard voice grade telephone network. Briefly describe the problems of transmitting data over such a network and indicate how they can be overcome. Suggest, with reasons, an alternative transmission medium that could be considered.   (6)

(c)   The elements a[i,j] of a two-dimensional array are assigned the values 0 or 1. The maximum number of rows and columns is 8. The elements of the 8th column are chosen to make the number of ones in a row an even number. Similarly, the elements of the 8th row are chosen to make the number of ones in a column an even number.

(i)   If the elements a[1,1] to a[7,7] are as given in the following table, then write down the contents of the 8th row and 8th column.   (1)

	1	2	3	4	5	6	7	8
1	0	1	0	1	1	1	1	
2	1	1	1	0	0	0	0	
3	0	1	1	1	0	0	0	
4	1	0	1	0	1	0	1	
5	0	0	0	0	0	1	1	
6	1	1	1	0	0	0	1	
7	1	0	1	0	0	0	1	
8								

(ii)   If the contents of a[4,3] are changed from 1 to 0 how does this affect the 8th row and 8th column?   (1)

(iii)   Explain how the results of c(i) and c(ii) could be used to detect and correct an error in the transmission of data from a terminal to a computer. What are the drawbacks of this approach?   (3)

Computer Software

ULSEB (June 1990) Paper 2

Q15. Most database management packages allow the user to associate conditions with the fields of a record. These conditions are then activated during the data entry stage. Data entry is via the keyboard and the fields are displayed on a monitor.

Three conditions that can be placed on data entry to fields are:

- the data entered must be unique,
- the data must be verified,
- data entry is prohibited.

(a)   An application using such a package has records with fields: ORDER_NUMBER, PART_NUMBER, UNIT_COST, QUANTITY_ORDERED, VALUE_OF_ORDER. In this context, (i) give an example showing why the application would require data entry to a particular field to be unique; (ii) what is meant by verification? How might verification be achieved in this case? (iii) indicate why entry to a particular field might be prohibited? (iv) give an example of a command line a user might enter to obtain information via a query language.   (6)

(b)   One of the objectives of a database management system is to offer *program-data independence*. What is meant by this term?   (2)

Q16. A company specializing in the maintenance and repair of an extensive range of industrial and office equipment has administrative centres scattered throughout Britain. Each centre offers a 24-hour call out service. The local manager is responsible for scheduling and supervising the tasks allocated to each engineer attached to the centre. Each engineer can be qualified in one or more skills and for each skill is allocated a proficiency rating of 1 to 5 depending on experience and qualifications. One of the functions of the centralized administration system is to monitor the workforce to ensure an equitable distribution of skill across all centres. The attributes of interest in this application are: ENGINEER_CODE, ENGINEER_NAME, SKILL_CODE, SKILL_DESCRIPTION, PROFICIENCY_RATING, CENTRE, MANAGER. This information is subdivided and stored in two distinct files. The first file contains records with fields (ENGINEER_CODE, ENGINEER_NAME, CENTRE, MANAGER), whilst the second file contains records with the fields ENGINEER_CODE, SKILL_CODE, SKILL_DESCRIPTION, PROFICIENCY_RATING).

(a) Assume that a package supporting these files has been produced in-house using a general purpose high level language.

    (i)   Identify suitable primary keys for both records and justify why splitting the attributes over two files is useful in this case. (3)

    (ii)   Discuss the possible problems that still remain with keeping the data in the two files described above. Your answer should make reference to: the deletion of information about an engineer who has just retired after 30 years service; the addition of information about a skill before the necessary staff have been retrained or employed; amending the description of a skill with code 123. (4)

    (iii)   Explain how the use of subsidiary files, or extra fields, could help in answering queries of the form: "Find the names of all engineers with a proficiency rating of 5 in the skill with code 107". Explain any assumptions that you make about the file organizations involved. (3)

    (iv)   How might the two files be subdivided to alleviate the problems highlighted in part (ii)? (2)

(b) To what extent would the use of a database management system, together with a built-in non-procedural query language have affected the issues raised in part (a)? (3)

Q17. A European research project is concerned with the problem of developing software to translate text from one language to another. Studies have shown that a simple word for word translation produces hopeless results and that progress can only be made by analysing the syntactic structure of each sentence before attempting to translate it. A program development team is given the task of writing software which will accept sentences in English and will analyse and display their syntactic structure. Another team of language experts is already at work defining the rules of syntax for English sentences. There are several hundred of these rules, of which a few simplified ones are given in BNF below.

```
<sentence> :: = <noun phrase>  <verb phrase>|
                <noun phrase>  <verb phrase>  <noun phrase>|...
<noun phrase> :: = <noun>|<adjective>  <noun phrase>|
                <article>  <noun phrase>|<pronoun>|...
<verb phrase> :: = <verb>|  <adverb>  <verb>|...
```

The language experts are also creating a dictionary of words with their associated parts of speech - noun, verb, adjective and so on. A few entries in the dictionary are as follows.

a	<article>	hungry	<adjective>
bit	<verb>	the	<article>
dog	<noun>	unkindly	<adverb>
examiner	<noun>	weary	<adjective>
horrible	<adjective>		

(a)   Use the example rules and dictionary entries to show in detail the syntactic structure of the following sentence: 'a horrible hungry dog unkindly bit the weary examiner'.   (7)

(b)   Explain in general terms how you would set about designing the required software. Comment on any particular programming techniques which will be needed.   (13)

Numerous problems are likely to occur in practice. For example, some words can have different parts of speech depending on their context (such as bit), and due to the size and flexibility of the English language, the language experts will be unable to define the dictionary or the rules of syntax completely and unambiguously.

(c)   Discuss how the software could be designed to recognize such problems and to interact with a language expert so as to establish the correct syntax and then be able to cope with similar problems in the future.   (13)

JMB (May 1989) Paper 2

Q18. When developing large computer programs, it is very difficult to ensure that the procedure and variable names used are unique and are not being used elsewhere in the program.

(a)   Explain the features and mechanisms required in a high-level programming language to help programmers avoid the problem of conflicting variable or procedure names. Include in your answer an explanation of how conflict is avoided when passing parameters to and from procedures.   (6)

(b)   When a team is working together on a project with different programmers working on different program units, what additional features and precautions are required to avoid problems of conflicting variable and procedure names when the units are linked together?   (2)

(c)   In the program segment given below assume the procedure print generates a new line.

```
global integer n
n := 10
reduce (n - 5)
print (n)
STOP
```

The procedure reduce is given below.

```
procedure reduce (n : local integer)
begin
  if n < >1 then
    reduce (n - 1)
  endif
```

```
        print (n)
    end
```

(i) Using a trace table demonstrate the effect of executing the program segment clearly showing the printout. (8)

(ii) How many versions of the procedure `reduce` are stored by the computer when executing this program segment? (2)

(iii) What changes would make the program segment more readable? (2)

JMB (May 1989) Paper 1

Q19. A subprogram is otherwise known as a subroutine, procedure or function.

(a) Give three reasons why previously compiled subprograms are a useful software development aid. (6)

(b) A high-level language program comprises an uncompiled main program and two previously compiled subroutines, A and B.

    (i) Explain how a compiler, when compiling the main program, would treat the references to the subroutines. Name two other types of subprogram that may be referenced as a result of the compilation. (6)

    (ii) Describe the role of a linkage editor in consolidating the main program and the subprograms into an executable program. (4)

ULSEB (June 1991) Paper 1

Q20. Many high level programming languages support both WHILE..DO and REPEAT..UNTIL loops.

(a) Give an example of the use of each type of loop and explain why the stage at which the test is performed in the loop is relevant to your examples. (4)

(b) What are the problems of using real variables to control loop termination? Describe how the problems can be overcome. (3)

JMB (June 1988) Paper 2

Q21.

(a) A microcomputer has a 40 character by 25 line monitor display. Each character on the screen is represented by a character code stored in an area of memory called the 'screen memory'. The first 40 locations in the screen memory represent the first line of characters, the next 40 the second line and so on. Screen memory commences at location 5000. There is a location, 'CURSOR', which holds the address of the current cursor position within screen memory. Any changes in the contents of locations within screen memory, or CURSOR, are instantly and automatically reflected in the screen display. Construct algorithms to explain how the following fundamental screen handling procedures can be effected.

    (i) Move the cursor to the home position (top left hand corner of the screen). (1)

    (ii) Clear the screen. (2)

    (iii) Move the cursor to the beginning of the current line. (2)

    (iv) Delete the previous character but only if it is on the current line. (3)

(v)   Scroll the display up one line, losing the top line of text and producing a blank line at the bottom. (4)

(vi)   Move the cursor to the beginning of the next line. (4)

(b) Describe how a screen could be scrolled up and down without any loss of text. Discuss the limitations of this facility. (4)

AEB (June 1991) Paper 2

Q22.

(a)   Describe two of the main objectives of an operating system. (4)

(b)   A mainframe computer appears to communicate with a number of users and execute their programs simultaneously. Describe how the operating system can handle the requirements of each of these functions. Include in your answer an explanation of: (i) how it protects one program from another; (ii) how it shares resources amongst the programs; (iii) how it selects the next process to be executed. (12)

(c)   Explain the steps needed for a user to log on to the mainframe computer. Why are these steps needed? (4)

ULSEB (June 1991) Paper 1

Q23.

(a)   A computer software company is using a computer system with a number of terminals to develop software for its customers. During the working day a time slice system is used; at other times batch processing is employed. What priorities might the computer manager assign: (i) during the working day; (ii) at other times? (5)

(b)   Describe, by giving an example, how deadlock might occur in a multi-programming system. Explain (i) how deadlock can be avoided; (ii) if deadlock does occur how recovery may be effected; (iii) why peripheral devices are usually controlled by the operating system rather than by users' programs. (10)

JMB (May 1990) Paper 1

Q24.

(a)   Explain how a computer system is designed to handle an interrupt condition, describing both the hardware and the software provision. (4)

(b)   For four of the following interrupt conditions, explain what the condition is, why the condition might have arisen and how the operating system might handle it: (i) arithmetic overflow; (ii) clock; (iii) instruction error; (iv) memory parity error; (v) peripheral transfer complete; (vi) peripheral transfer error. (12)

Systems Analysis

ULSEB (June 1989) Paper 1

Q25. A small book-lending library has decided to install a computer system for the administration of loans. Each borrower is given a unique identification number. Each title is given a unique reference number and each copy of a book is given a unique accession number. The system keeps track of current loans and reservation requests. It immediately advises the librarian when borrowers attempt to borrow more books than they are allowed, and when reserved books have been returned. At the end of each day the system generates a recall list for newly overdue books. The system caters for the addition, removal and amendment of records of books and borrowers.

(a)   Describe briefly the processing of a transaction when a book is returned.   (3)

(b)   List three other input transactions which the system must support, and describe the data items to be entered.   (6)

(c)   Design a suitable menu-driven interface for the system, providing sketches of individual menus and indicating their inter-relationship. The size of the screen limits the number of choices on an individual menu to a maximum of 6.   (6)

ULSEB (June 1991) Paper 1

Q26. A large city railway station, which has sixteen platforms, has trains arriving and departing every few minutes during the day. To keep the travelling public informed of train movements a total of forty large visual display units (VDUs) are placed in prominent places throughout the station complex. Twenty of the VDUs display the information about the next ten arrivals and the other twenty display the information about the next ten departures. All the VDUs are connected to a central computer system which is controlled by an operator. For each train, the system stores information on its origin and destination, intermediate stations at which it stops, its time-tabled arrival/departure time, its expected arrival/departure and the number of the platform it uses.

(a)   What data structure could be used to store the information about the trains? Justify your answer.   (3)

(b)   How might data be captured: (i) about incoming trains; (ii) as trains depart from the station?   (4)

(c)   A suite of programs has been written for this application. (i) Design a testing strategy to be employed before such a system is fully implemented; (ii) Describe a suitable method of implementing the system and explain your answer.   (8)

ULSEB (June 1990) Paper 2

Q27. The information centre of a large organization has a computerized loan and return system for its books, manuals, journals, tapes etc. However, the catalogue for each category still exists as a number of separate card index files. It has been decided to computerize these catalogues to provide users with a single centralized catalogue which can be queried simultaneously by a number of users. The current computer system is not powerful enough to cope with this additional task. A firm of analysts is called in to recommend the steps to be taken and to supervise the transition process.

(a)   What are the likely problems involved in transferring these manual files onto disk? Suggest how these problems could be overcome.   (5)

(b)   Why is it important for the analysts to provide documentation for the new system even though it is running satisfactorily? Why are professional bodies within the computing industry keen to support documentation standards? Outline the content of the documentation that should be given to the staff who use the system at the information centre.   (7)

(c)   What change-over method do you think is appropriate in this case? Justify your choice.   (3)

ULSEB (June 1989) Paper 1

Q28. A company manufactures and markets screws. The company is considering computerizing some of its activities. The departments listed below, with their functions, could benefit from computerization.

Department	Functions
Ordering	Maintain stock of raw materials.
Production	Arrange production of screws according to known requirements and forecasts; ensure labour and machinery are available.
Sales	Receive orders; make forecasts and market screws.
Despatch	Make up and send out orders received.
Accounts	Process company's financial transactions.
Planning	Devise possible future developments.

(a) Describe, with the aid of a diagram, the data flow in to and out of the departments, being careful to indicate the direction of the flow. (7)

(b) Describe four tasks within the departments of the company in which a computer system could usefully be involved. (8)

Data Processing

JMB (May 1989) Paper 1

Q29. Many financial institutions now issue plastic cards which can be used at cash dispensers to withdraw money and, if requested, give details of the holder's account. These cash dispensers are available 24 hours a day, 7 days a week. When issued with a card the holder is given a PIN (Personal Identification Number). On the back of this card there is a thin strip containing magnetically encoded information relating to the holder's account. This strip has three rows on which information can be stored. The financial institutions have adopted two main ways of using the information on these strips.

Method 1. Stores the holder's account number on row 2, and on row 3 a coded version of the PIN, together with that holder's weekly cash withdrawal limit and the money removed so far that week. The system is normally on-line during the day and off-line at night.

Method 2. Stores only the holder's account number on row 2 and leaves row 3 empty. This method requires the system to be on-line at all times. The cash dispensers hold no information of the transactions which have been carried out.

To use the card it has to be inserted into the machine and the PIN entered when requested.

(a) (i) Why must method 2 be an on-line system? (ii) Why must the PIN on the card in method 1 be held in coded form? (2)

(b) Give an example of a potential invasion of privacy in this application. (1)

(c) Give an example of a potential breach of security in this application. (1)

(d) Describe how the security of each of these systems could be broken by the following people and in each case indicate what measures could be taken to prevent that breach of security: (i) members of the general public; (ii) the bank's computer staff. (5)

(e) Describe two checks which could be held in the rows of the magnetic strip to ensure that the data has been read correctly. (4)

(f)   Using method 2, when the card holder enters the PIN, what is it checked against?   (1)

(g)   Suggest what information could be held in row 1 of the card in both methods.   (2)

ULSEB (June 1990) Paper 2

Q30. A particular microcomputer has a built-in 130Mb sealed hard-disk drive. The operating system used has a file management module that views a disk as a collection of 1Kb blocks. The disk address of each block is 32 bits long. *Three tasks* performed by the file management system are: maintaining a directory of files on the disk; maintaining a list of 'free' blocks that can be allocated to a new file; keeping track of the blocks allocated to each file.

(a)   An entry in the directory contains the name of a file and a pointer to the first block allocated to that file. What other information might be found in this entry? An entry in a directory can also point to another (sub)directory of files. The user is thus offered a tree-structured file system. Indicate one advantage of such a system.   (4)

(b)   A collection of blocks has been set aside for a structure to keep track of the unallocated blocks. Confirm that each block can store up to 256 block addresses. Show by using a diagram how a linked list of blocks can be used to keep track of the unallocated blocks. Show also that when the disk is almost empty this structure occupies approximately 0.5 Mb of the disk.   (5)

(c)   Associated with each file is a table containing twelve entries. The first ten of these are the disk addresses of the first ten blocks of the file. The remaining two are only used if the size of the file becomes larger than 10 Kb. If needed, the eleventh entry is the address of a second level block which contains up to 256 block addresses and the twelfth entry is the address of a third level block which contains the address of 256 second level blocks. (i) Draw a diagram to show how blocks could be allocated to a 600Kb file. (ii) Show that by using this technique the size of a single file could exceed 64 Mb.   (6)

JMB (May 1989) Paper 2

Q31. A company intends storing details of its products on computer. At any time the company has a maximum of 1000 products. Each product has a unique four digit code associated with it. The systems analyst has decided that the file will require 500 blocks and will be organized randomly with each block in the file capable of holding two records. The location of the record on disk is obtained by a hashing algorithm which involves the following processes: (i) take the last three digits of the product code; (ii) divide this number by two; (iii) take the integer value of the result of this division. Using this algorithm the record for the product with code number 1427 will generate a block address of 213. However, products with code numbers 4426 and 2427 will also generate 213 as the block address even though each block is only capable of holding 2 records. When a block is full and the algorithm generates that block address again for the record being added, the next block is tested, and so on, until a free area is found into which the record is written.

(a)   Records with the following product numbers are submitted in the sequence indicated. Into which blocks will they be written, assuming the file is initially empty? 0462 3464 1465 1463 4462.   (3)

(b)   Write an algorithm for locating a record in the file.   (4)

(c)   If product 1465 is discontinued how would the record be deleted without re-organizing the file?   (2)

(d)   Write an algorithm for adding a record to the file.   (7)

(e)   Every six months the company performs a stock check and this requires the file to be printed out in product number order. Describe an efficient method of producing a tape file which could be used for this print-out.   (4)

ULSEB (1989 Specimen for 1991 Syllabus)

Q32.

(a)   Describe what is meant by an indexed sequential file organization. Why may it be necessary to maintain a multi-level index and overflow areas in the maintenance of this file structure.   (6)

(b)   A microcomputer system has been installed in a busy video hire shop. The backing storage for this system comprises a floppy disk drive, a 40 megabyte sealed hard disk drive (Winchester drive) and a high capacity magnetic tape unit. Two of the many tasks performed by this system are: to monitor the loan and return of the videos; there are, on average, 400 transactions per day; to provide a weekly listing of the popularity of all the films in stock over the previous 7 days. To perform these routine stock handling tasks a simple file is created with the fields - CODE-NUMBER, TITLE, COUNT, DATE-FOR-RETURN. The CODE-NUMBER is a unique field given to the video when it is added to stock and the COUNT field is used to sum the number of loans. (i) Justify why an indexed sequential file organization might be a suitable choice for the stock file and discuss the access methods available for each task. (ii) Outline briefly what extra processing will be carried out on the file during the weekly listing. (iii) Devise appropriate backup procedures to ensure that the shop is protected from a failure of the Winchester drive.   (9)

ULSEB (June 1991) Paper 1

Q33. A water company uses computer controlled equipment to monitor and control the quality of drinking water. Sensors are placed in various positions on the equipment to take digital measurements every minute. The computer has been programmed to respond to feedback from the sensors and input from the operator.

(a)   What data is likely to be captured by the sensors?   (2)

(b)   Describe situations in which the computer will respond to: (i) feedback; (ii) input from the operator.   (4)

Program Design and Implementation

JMB (May 1990) Paper 2

Q34. The contents of a block of Immediate Access Store for a byte orientated computer is shown below in hexadecimal (hex), starting at 1700 hex:

location								contents								
1700	54	68	65	20	63	6F	6D	6D	6F	6E	20	43	6F	72	6D	6F
1710	72	61	6E	74	20	6F	72	20	53	68	61	67	2C	20	6C	61
1720	79	73	20	65	67	67	73	20	69	6E	73	69	64	65	20	61
1730	20	70	61	70	65	72	20	62	61	67	2E	20	54	68	65	20
1740	72	65	61	73	6F	6E	20	66	6F	72	20	74	69	73	20	74
1750	68	65	72	65	20	69	73	20	6E	6F	20	64	6F	75	62	74

In the following subroutine, AX, BX and CX are all 16 bit registers. Each register can be used as a pair of 8 bit registers referenced as the H(High) 8 bits and the L(low) 8 bits (e.g. BL means the 8 low-order bits of BX).

```
;Subroutine - retrieve pixel colour for video display.
START:
LD      BX,   (X-COORD)    ;load BL with contents of location X-COORD, set BH to zero
SRL     BX,   2            ;shift right logical BX, 2 bit positions
LD      CX,   (Y-COORD)
MUL     CX,   50           ;multiply CX by 50 hex, result in CX
ADD     BX,   CX           ;add CX to BX, result in BX
ADD     BX,   1600         ;add 1600 hex to BX, result in BX
LD      AL,   [BX]         ;load AL with contents of memory byte whose address is in BX
LD      BX,   (X-COORD)
AND     BX,   3            ;logically AND BX with 3
INC     BX                 ;add 1 to BX
SLL     BX,   1            ;shift left logical BX, 1 bit position
ROL     AL,   BX           ;rotate left AL by n bit positions where n is the value stored in BX,
                           ;result in AL
AND     AL,   3
RET                        ;return to calling routine
```

(a)   If X-COORD contains the value 8E hex, Y-COORD contains the value 3 and the subroutine is called and executed once, what value is returned in AL? Use a trace table for AL, BX and CX to show clearly the working by which you obtained your answer.   (10)

(b)   If X-COORD is now set to the value 55 hex, Y-COORD set to the value 4 and the subroutine again called and executed once, what value is returned now in AL?   (6)

(c)   In this subroutine, X-COORD is the x coordinate and Y-COORD is the y coordinate of a pixel used by the video display of the computer. The value returned in AL represents the current colour setting of the pixel. How many possible colours are there for each pixel? Explain how you obtained your answer.   (4)

USLEB (June 1989) Paper 2

Q35.

(a)   Explain briefly why the process of sorting a file into key order is a common activity in data processing. Why is there a diversity of sorting algorithms available?   (4)

(b)   A one dimensional array has been initialised to: a[1] = 2; a[2] = 9; a[3] = 8; a[4] = 7; a[5] = 4; a[6] = 5; a[7] = 6. The procedure sort given below has been designed to sort integer arrays into ascending order. The procedure includes calls to two other pre-defined procedures display and swap and to a pre-defined function integer.part.of. The procedure display is called by a command of the form display(a) and it outputs the contents of the complete array starting on a new line. The procedure swap, called by swap(x,y), exchanges the contents of locations x and y. The function integer.part.of returns the largest integer smaller than, or equal to, its argument. After a call sort(a,1,7) using the above data the first two lines of output are 2 6 5 4 7 8 9 and 2 4 5 6 7 8 9. Work through the procedure carefully to confirm this result and show clearly how you arrive at your conclusion.   (7)

```
procedure sort(a,left,right);
(*comment: a is an array, left and right are integers*)
  i := left; j := right;
  mid := integer.part.of(left + right)/2);
  key := a[mid];

  repeat
    while a[i] < key do i := i + 1 endwhile;
    while a[j] > key do j := j - 1 endwhile;
    if i <= j then swap(a[i],a[j]);
              i := i + 1;
              j := j - 1;
    endif;
  until i > j;
  display(a);
  if left < j then sort(a,left,j);
  if i < right then sort(a,i,right);
endprocedure;
```

(b) Although the data has been sorted after two calls to the procedure sort explain why further calls will take place. (2)

(c) What parameter passing mechanism has been used in the procedure swap? (2)

Welsh Joint Education Committee (May 1990) Paper 1

Q36.

(a) An application requires a large number of names held in an array in main store to be sorted. The current sorting algorithm used is an insertion sort, but it has been found to be too slow. Describe a sorting algorithm which would be suitable for carrying out this task much more quickly. Illustrate the operation of your algorithm by showing how it sorts into alphabetical order the following list of names (you may use the initial letters only if you wish): Jones; Hammond; Burrows; David; Farthing; Lee; Monson; Gledhill; Arch; Coulson; Khan; Evans. (10)

(b) Describe an algorithm which determines the position of a key value in an ordered list by means of a binary search. Assuming that the twelve names above are A level examination candidates sitting, in alphabetical order, in seats 1 to 12 of the examination room, illustrate the operation of your algorithm to find the seat number of Hammond. (10)

ULSEB (June 1990) Paper 1

Q37.

(a) In the context of data structures, explain what is meant by a queue. (1)

(b) Briefly describe two distinct applications for which a queue is a suitable data structure. (4)

(c) Why are queues in computer systems usually implemented as circular queues? (2)

(d) Describe how a circular queue may be implemented using a one dimensional array. Give algorithms for inserting and removing items from this queue. (5)

(e) If these algorithms were written as procedures, what parameters would need to be passed between each of the procedures and the calling program? (3)

Cambridge (May 1989) Paper 1

Q38.

(a) Describe, with the aid of diagrams, how names may be stored in alphabetical order in a linked list structure by using arrays. Use the names Rachel, Majid, Sian, Mary, Jonathan as example data. (4)

(b) Show how the free space can be managed so that items can be easily added to or deleted from the linked list. Use as examples (i) adding the name Henry to the list; (ii) deleting the name Majid from the list. (4)

ULSEB (June 1991) Paper 2

Q39.

(a) Describe, with the aid of a suitable diagram, how a queue can be maintained using a linked list. Outline an algorithm for removing an item from this queue including the manipulation of the free list. You may assume that the queue is not empty. What are the advantages and disadvantages of linked storage to manipulate a queue? (6)

(b) The following tree structure is used to provide indexed access to a file. Each node of this tree can store 3 pointers and two sets of data in the order: (pointer, data, pointer, data, pointer), where the data comprises a key value and the corresponding disc address. In the diagram below only the key values of the records are shown and pointers are drawn as arrows. An entry of –1 for a key implies that there is no data and an entry of nil for a pointer implies that there is no corresponding link. If a node has the logical structure (p1, k1, p2, k2, p3) then, unless that pointers are nil, p1 points to a node containing keys with values <k1, p3 points to a node containing keys with values >k2, p2 points to a node containing values between k1 and k2 unless k2 = –1 when it points to a node with keys with values >k1. The software always arranges the contents of a node so that k1 < k2 (unless k2 = -1). Data has been added to the tree in the order of key values 20, 40, 10, 15, 30, 25, 14, 50 to give:

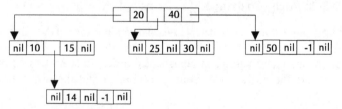

Draw diagrams of the tree after records with keys 38 and 12 have been added to the file. (3)

How might the software reorganize the original tree if the record with key 30 has to be deleted? (1)

How does the structure in the diagram above compare with the use of an ordered binary tree to perform the same task? By making appropriate assumptions compare the storage used and the average search time to locate an item. What happens if the record with key 12 is added? What might happen in the case of a very large file? (5)

Q40. A document file has been processed to produce a special text file consisting of words, each followed by a space, and with all punctuation removed. The following list is the specification of user requirements for a word counting program.

- Read the text file and produce a list, in alphabetical order, of all the different words found with the number of occurrences of each word.

- A 'word' consists of a sequence of characters followed by a space.

- The text file is terminated by an end-of-file marker.

- The list of different words produced is stored in an array called word-data which is kept in order while it is being built up rather than being sorted at the end. A linked list is NOT used.

Assume there is a function find-word that takes a word as its single argument and returns the position of this word in word-data, if found. If the word is not found, it returns the position where it should be inserted in word-data to maintain alphabetical order. Ignore any problems concerning the size of the text file or the size of word-data.

   (i)   Carefully describe the structure of word-data.   (2)

   (ii)   Derive a top down program design for these requirements by expanding `ProcessWord` in the following top level:

```
initialization
WHILE NOT eof DO
  ProcessWord
ENDWHILE
output word-data
```

No further refinement of `initialization` or `output word-data` is required. Stop your refinement when you consider your design is ready for coding.   (14)

Index